Social Psychology
Issues and Insights

The Lippincott College Psychology Series
under the editorship of
Dr. Carl P. Duncan
Northwestern University
and
Dr. Julius Wishner
University of Pennsylvania

second edition

Social Psychology

Issues and Insights

Goodwin Watson
Columbia University

David Johnson
University of Minnesota

J. B. Lippincott Company

Philadelphia New York Toronto

SECOND PRINTING

ISBN-0-397-47221-8
Library of Congress Catalog Card Number: 71-155875

Contents

Preface

Many years of experience in teaching social psychology to college undergraduates, to graduate students, and to doctoral candidates experimenting with theses have developed the viewpoints underlying this text.

Foremost is our conviction that social psychology, in the years ahead, should contribute far more than it has in the past to the enrichment of personal understanding and to a constructive attack on major social problems. Too many academic disciplines are taught only to prepare students to follow the methodological traditions of their mentors. Techniques, in the saddle, ride both teachers and students. "Scholarship" becomes a game in which the achievement of merit badges has no clear connection with any other concerns of humanity. Knowledge for its own sake has value, but, for most students of any subject, information is more valuable if it speaks to their existential concerns. From among the hundreds of thousands of published research studies which might have some bearing on social psychology, this book includes the selected hundreds which help to form fundamental concepts or which illuminate important issues. A basic text in social psychology should not attempt to cultivate the methodological sophistication required for doctoral and post-doctoral research. Only a few of the students taking this course will make their careers in laboratories of social psychology. Those few need far more understanding of experimental design and of the statistical operations than is suitable for the great majority who are to use what they learn of social psychology in their careers as homemakers, businessmen, professional practitioners, or citizens, and in their interpersonal relationships every day.

The emphasis on applying social psychology to vital activities in which most people are engaged does not diminish our concern about maintaining high standards of scientific method. Social psychology is here defined as the *scientific* study of human interaction and thus is differentiated from the contributions which come from ordinary observation, literary creations, historical or philosophical study. In almost every chapter some "Abstracts" are presented; each abstract states a problem, describes briefly the method of investigation, and summarizes some of the findings. On every topic scores of other studies are cited, with the expectation that interested students will want to look up some of these other investigations to see how the research was actually done. Some teachers may ask students to look up, report on, and make critical evaluations of some of the research here mentioned only in a sentence with the name of the experimenter and the date serving as keys to the full reference in the bibliography. The authors have found it useful, further, to ask students to replicate—perhaps on a small scale and with a few subjects—some of the studies which interest them. Students, in this way, come to realize that the findings of social psychology are not simply the prejudices of social scientists with which one may disagree at will.

This book has been written with a purpose and endeavor to avoid a narrow specialization and to encompass other areas of psychological research. While social psychology remains central, its relationships to educational psychology, clinical psychology, personality, developmental psychology, counseling psychology, psychotherapy, industrial psychology, and engineering psychology are kept in view. The perspective is even broader than that of psychology, for sociology, anthropology, psychiatry, and political science are also engaged in the scientific study of human interaction. More than most other texts in the field, this presentation recognizes and includes contributions from the related behavioral sciences.

Another feature of this text is that the research is viewed in historic depth. Some younger colleagues may have become too exclusively preoccupied with the most recent journals. For their own research this may be appropriate, although even here it might be true that there were insights and seminal beginnings more than a generation ago. Some of these may have been forgotten and lost. Sometimes they are rediscovered generations later. The student of this text is likely to find, on any topic, some references which reach back to the turn of the century and some from subsequent decades. Most references come from the last ten years because the volume of research has been mounting so rapidly, but the earlier, pioneer work is not ignored.

Distinguishing this text from any other known to the authors is the central notion of the Structure-Process-Attitude (S-P-A) sequence, as set forth in Chapter 6. Later chapters apply the approach to the understanding of social class, race relations, business organizations, new roles for women, and the effort to harmonize international relations.

The authors are aware of having explored further than many of their colleagues in earlier texts the implications of social psychological truths for the evaluation of personal and social values. Whenever one ventures beyond facts to seek their meaning for life, his thinking becomes controversial. The viewpoints here expressed are not intended as propaganda. They are intended to stimulate thoughtful inquiry. Disagreement, for good reasons, with the authors' conclusions may often represent a higher level of achievement than would docile acceptance of them. We all share a common quest for truth; each of us needs corrective encounters with those who see things differently. In the grand dialectic, theses must be stated if there are to be antitheses and emerging syntheses. In this sense, the text offers many springboards to thought, rather than final conclusions.

The first task for authors preparing a second edition of a text in a rapidly growing science is to present the more recently discovered facts and the more current theories around which research is taking place. This we have tried to do in every chapter. At the same time, some of the material in the first edition now seems less vital and cogent than it did in 1965, thus much has been deleted. Chapters on the media of mass communication and the social psychology of business and industry represent largely applications rather than new issues or insights and have been omitted from this edition. The emphasis on humanism has been expanded in this edition and integrated into the new material.

In this book the authors emphasize the application of social psychological knowledge to the solution of current social problems. To do this we have often stated our conclusions concerning the implications of research results to some of the major social problems our society now faces. We have expanded our treatment of certain areas within social psychology which are especially relevant to current social problems. In addition, we have emphasized the critical evaluation of the research results by including more material on scientific methodology. The first two chapters have considerably more emphasis upon scientific methodology, and methodological notes are presented in other chapters to help the reader critically evaluate the theory and research being presented. The authors believe that it is through the critical evaluation of current social psychological knowledge that further research will be generated which may provide more effective solutions to the problems our society faces.

Debts to our instructors, colleagues, and students are innumerable and immeasurable. To them we extend our thanks.

November, 1971

G.W.

D.W.J.

CHAPTER 1

What is social psychology?

DEFINITION

Social psychology is the scientific study of human interaction. It is a relatively new branch of science concerned with the experience and behavior of persons in social situations in which each responds in some way to the behavior of others.

Social stimuli

Human beings respond, of course, to many impersonal stimuli: to a rain drop, a flash of lightning, a clap of thunder, a glass of milk, a book. The rain drop does not seek to hit or to avoid our upturned face; the lightning takes no account of our closed eyes; the thunder rolls and echoes in total disregard of our covered ears or quaking fears; the milk does not protest if spilled rather than drunk; the book cannot alter its contents to suit the wandering thoughts of the reader. Social psychology focuses upon the more fascinating and complex situations in which people adapt their responses to one another: each person in achieving his own purposes needs to take into consideration the activities and presumed purposes of the other persons involved. A good social conversation, for example, is a flow in which one speaker proceeds from the ideas expressed by another person, adding his bit, and listening as later speakers react to his contribution.

Social psychology differs from the other areas of psychological study because of the special qualities of persons as we perceive them. Persons differ from the other objects in our environment, in being more mobile, more capricious and therefore unpredictable, more truly a locus of causation and power, and, above all, responsive. We must pay special attention to other "persons"—in contrast to "things"—because they are livelier, harder to understand or control, and more likely to initiate welcome or unwelcome events.

Interaction at a distance

Social interaction can be clearly recognized in all immediate face-to-face relationships, but human beings also respond continually to persons who are
more remote in place and time. For example, when we watch television, or
read what someone has written in a magazine, or vote for our candidate in
an election, or cash a check, or salute the flag, we are still responding to
what other human beings have done. Some people, however far away from
us, have written, edited, printed, and distributed the magazine we are reading. In voting, we interact not only with our candidate, but also with the
opposition and the innumerable others who have contributed in some way to
the campaign and to the underlying issues and policies. Cashing a check is
one small act in a long chain of social interaction which includes our earning
the money, depositing it, the bank accounting systems, and anything we do
with the money that may directly or indirectly affect other people. Even the
existence of private property, a money system, banks, and stores, is due to
the behavior, past and present, of other human beings. The salute to the flag
is a response, not just to that piece of colored cloth, but to our country—its
heroes, history, institutions, traditions, culture, ideals, and all that our fellow
citizens have done or are doing to sustain a national state.

In each of these examples, we respond to what others have done in the
past, but our action also becomes a stimulus to many future activities of
other persons. Television programs and magazine features survive or perish,
depending on how many of us watch or read them. Depending upon our
votes, in a democracy, candidates and policies come or go. We are the mak-
ers as well as the inheritors of history. We have become the kinds of persons
we are, largely in response to the setting left to us by our forefathers. We
speak the language, eat the food, work at jobs, play at games, live, love, and
worship in accord with the culture formed by our predecessors, but we do
not transmit that culture unchanged. Future generations will be a little different because of the way we have lived, our interests, our choices, our
words, and our work. The story of mankind describes an immense flow of
social interaction across the ages.

IMPORTANCE

Everything that people care very deeply about can profitably be studied as a
form of social interaction. Love is certainly an interacting response to others;
so are money, power, truth, beauty, and goodness. The most desperate failures in life can be seen as inappropriate social interaction. Failure on the job
has been found in several studies to arise many times as often from poor
interpersonal relations as from lack of technical skills.

Not infrequently a person who is a failure in one situation is successful in a different one. One love affair may not work out happily, but the same two persons may each achieve happiness with someone else. The difficulty, then, was not *in* each personality; it was in their particular kind of *interaction*. A man may fail on one job, but become highly successful at exactly the same kind of work in another setting where he is interacting with a different group of coworkers. The success or failure lies more in the interaction than in the individual.

The traditional, individualistic patterns of our thought have left many people unaware of the extent to which their lives are mingled with groups. Breakfast with a family, travel to work in a car pool, conferences and committees, luncheon clubs, factory teams, sales contacts, classrooms, court sessions, hospital wards, after-work cocktails or golf or community activities or social visits or family life—from morning to night the individual moves from group to group. A science which can improve social interaction will contribute to almost every hour of everyone's day.

Social problems

The problems of our broader society arise from complexes of interaction in which institutional structure (itself an accretion of past interactions which constrain present behavior), shared opinions and feelings (social norms), and activities of cooperation or conflict play a major part. The gravest and deepest concerns of our age lead us directly to problems of social interaction. The threat of a war of mass destruction is one immense, involved pattern of interactions. The recurring cycles of economic inflation and deflation, prosperity and depression, are forms of interaction among large numbers of people. Prejudice and discrimination, segregation and desegregation, are names for interaction patterns. Juvenile delinquency, political corruption, factional struggles, and totalitarian governments are better understood when analyzed as forms of interaction. It requires at least two persons, different in behavior but interacting, to make a criminal, a bribe, a fight or a tyranny. The aesthetic limitations of our society—the level of taste in popular entertainers; the prevailing ugliness of many large and small communities; the garish offensiveness of much expensive advertising; the neglect of the creative artist and poet—these, too, can profitably be translated into processes of social interaction. It appears that our "American way of life," justly extolled for its virtues, also sustains rates of ulcers, alcoholism, insanity, murder, and suicide that are among the highest in the world. Something often goes wrong in human interaction. It is the task of social psychology to shed some light on all these problems. In illuminating problems in human interaction, social psychology may be significantly advanced as a science. Dubos (1970) notes that the interplay between theoretical science and practical applications has been one of the most influential factors in the development of science. He states that the history of science proves that any effort to deal with practical problems inevitably points to new theoretical problems. Just as the study of infection enriched cellular and molecular biology and the search for better strains of corn opened new fields of genetics, the study of prejudice and conflict may open new fields of social psychology.

It would be unreasonable to expect any science, particularly one so young as social psychology, to have the complete answer to all the problems of human society. If the problems are ever solved, the solutions will come from contributions in history, economics, sociology, political science, anthropology, physiology, engineering, the arts, philosophy, and plain common sense, as well as from social psychology.

METHODS

The Value of the Scientific Method

To many students there is no subject more boring and tedious than the study of the scientific method and research methodology. Yet it is the scientific method which distinguishes psychology from creative arts such as drama and poetry, and everyday folklore such as proverbs, all of which deal with the study of human behavior. Taking proverbs as "self-evident" generalizations of common sense wisdom, we find them notorious for their contradictions. Two common examples are "Birds of a feather flock together" vs. "Opposites attract" and "Absence makes the heart grow fonder" vs. "Out of sight, out of mind." Countless "self-evident" truths have been proved false after centuries of practice. According to recent research, punishment is effective under only a limited set of conditions, yet for thousands of years people have used punishment to raise children because "everyone knows it works." For centuries it was "self-evident" that all sorts of illnesses could be cured by blood letting; no one knows how many thousands of people were killed by this medical practice.

When faced with contradictory theories about human behavior, how does one decide which one to follow? When faced with common sense knowledge, how does one assess its validity? Although the behavioral sciences have been accumulating systematic knowledge for over a hundred years, psychology is still a young science, and far too little is known about why individuals behave as they do. In many instances we must rely on common sense knowledge and personal experience in attempting to understand and predict our own behavior, and the behavior of others with whom we interact. The tenuousness and fallibility of common sense is all too evident. Increased understanding of human behavior rests upon systematic study by scientific procedures. The scientific method allows us to examine various areas of human behavior objectively, and to determine which theories are true, for which types of individuals, and under what circumstances.

Assumptions of the Scientific Method

Three major assumptions are made in applying the scientific method to the study of human behavior. First, we assume that what has been found to be true many times in the past will continue to hold true for the future. Without some permanence of natural phenomena, science cannot accurately predict the occurrence of an event. Since the sun has always come up in the morning, we predict that it will rise tomorrow morning. Since people are attracted to similar individuals, we assume that in the future the relationship between similarity and attraction will also hold. It is not necessary to assume that nature is absolutely uniform but science is possible only to the extent that nature is assumed to be consistent.

Second, science assumes that one can group together experiences, events, objects, and facts that are similar. These classification systems help identify, explain, and evaluate new phenomena. All individuals, for example, who have a certain income, educational, and occupational level can be classified as middle class. By classifying an individual as "middle class" we can predict with a reasonable degree of accuracy how he will react to a variety of cultural, political or social situations.

The third assumption is that all natural phenomena are determined by a cause or a set of causes. All events are preceded by some set of essential conditions and do not occur spontaneously. When a person engages in certain behavior, we assume that the behavior is not accidental or capricious but is caused by an interaction between the situation and the characteristics of the individual involved.

The Goals of Science

The goals of science are the prediction, understanding, and control of the relationship between two or more variables. To understand what a variable is, one must begin with properties. A *property* is a quality which is characteristic of some things but not of others—red is a property characteristic of fire and stop lights but not of water or bluebirds. A *variable* is a set of mutually exclusive properties; the variable of hair-color can have different properties, such as blonde and brunette, the variable of sex can have different properties, such as male or female, and the variable of age can have such different properties as old or young. Different properties on the same variable are commonly referred to as *values* of that variable.

When the knowledge of an object's value on one variable enables one to predict its value on another variable more accurately than one could without such knowledge, a *relationship* exists between the two variables. For example, there is a relationship between education and income, since you can predict an individual's income more accurately if you know his educational background than if you do not.

A *causal relationship* exists between two variables when a change in one produces a change in the other. If when you induce an individual to perceive another person as more similar to himself, his liking for that person increases, you can conclude that the increase in perceived similarity "caused" the rise in attraction, other things being equal. Three conditions must be met to infer a causal relationship. First, there must be evidence of covariation (changes in one variable must be accompanied by changes in another). Second, there must be evidence that the "cause" variable changes before the "effect" variable. Finally, there must be evidence that the results were not caused by some extraneous variable, that is, alternative explanations for the findings must be ruled out.

Prediction as a goal of science is based upon a correlational relationship between variables. If one knows a student's high school grade average, for example, one can predict his college grade average. When one is interested in prediction, both causal and noncausal relationships are helpful. Being able to predict an event does not mean, however, that one will understand it. Men were able to predict the effects of eating poisonous plants long before they were able to understand their precise chemical basis.

Understanding is based upon knowing the critical antecedent conditions which cause an event to take place. If one is interested in understanding why some individuals like each other and why others do not, one must know about such antecedent conditions as proximity, perceived similarity, and mutual goal facilitation. The greater the understanding of a relationship between two variables, the more precisely one may predict, and the greater the possibility for controlling the relationship between them.

Control is present when one can create a particular cause-effect sequence; that is, when one can provide the critical antecedent conditions to cause a desired event to take place. For example, in order to increase interpersonal attraction, an individual might increase the perceived similarity and the mutual goal facilitation of two individuals.

Methods of Science

The scientific method is above all a process of deliberate and controlled observation. The distinctive criterion of scientific observations is objectivity. Observations are arranged so that any observer would see the same results; no variation is allowed among subjects. This *intersubjectivity* testifies that the observation is uncontaminated by any factors except those common to all observers.

Most sciences begin with simple observation of the phenomena they wish to study. Men watched the behavior of ants and bees before any systematic zoology was developed. The simple observation of phenomena without any systematic techniques for insuring objectivity is called a *natural history* approach. A natural history approach has many advantages in social psychology. It is a relatively easy method for observing the social interaction taking place all around us. It interferes very little with the process being observed. If a social group is brought into the laboratory, given special tests, and subjected to strange conditions, the behavior of members will be affected by the setting and may be unlike their normal interaction. The natural history method can often be applied so that the subjects are not aware that they are being observed. J. Watson and her associates (1948) made an interesting contribution to social psychology simply by listening to conversations that could be easily overheard on the street, in parks, and in buses. They summarized 1001 conversations, reporting that most of what they overheard was about day-to-day affairs, with little reference to what historians might regard as the great public events of the time. The most common category was something about "myself and another." Men talked to other men most often about vocation, sports, and politics. Women talked to other women more about friends, clothes, shopping, love, and marriage. Simple observation of social acts in natural settings may also be written up as a social case history. Some of the classic social case histories, such as William F. Whyte's observation of gangs in "Street Corner Society" and Bruno Bettelheim's account of life in Nazi concentration camps, will be discussed in later chapters of this text. Individuals using the natural history method by observing social interaction in natural settings may either observe from the outside (an anthropologist observing a strange culture) or from the inside (a member of a group observing the behavior of other members).

Most sciences progress from natural history accounts of phenomena to controlled observation with instruments developed to objectify and systematize their observations or to laboratory experimentation. Observation of social behavior in natural settings is usually correlational research, while observation in the laboratory is usually experimental. The correlation study examines the covariation of two or more variables. If the presence or intensity of one variable tends to correspond with the presence or intensity of another, there is a correlation between them. For example, if one found that students with positive self-attitudes achieved higher grades than do students with negative self-attitudes, one could conclude that student's self-attitudes and their academic performance are correlated.

The fact that there is a correlation between two variables may allow the researcher to make statements about prediction, but not about causation. In a correlational relationship, it is not clear which variable "causes" the other. Does positive self-attitude "cause" a student to achieve, or does achievement "cause" positive self-attitude? It is also possible that the correlation between two variables may be caused by a third variable; any correlation between self-attitude and academic achievement, for example, may be "caused" by other variables such as IQ, early childhood experiences, or teacher attitudes toward the students.

In experimental research one distinguishes between the independent and dependent variables. An *experiment* may be defined as a situation in which one observes the relationship between two variables by deliberately producing a change in one and observing whether this produces a change in the other. The *independent variable* is the one the experimenter changes directly. The *dependent variable* is the one whose value is affected by the change in the independent variable; its value is dependent on the value of the independent variable. A researcher, for example, could conduct an experiment in which he deliberately changed his students' self-attitudes to see if an increase in positive academic self-attitude results in increased achievement in the classroom. The independent variable in this experiment is the students' self-attitudes, the dependent variable is their achievement.

The elimination of errors in observing relationships between variables is an important element in the scientific method. In some cases it is possible to measure the direction and extent of error in an observation and make a subsequent *correction* in the analysis and interpretation of the results. Measures of the extent to which respondents filling out a questionnaire lie or distort their responses in a socially desirable way are examples of measuring the extent and direction of error. In order to *eliminate* observational errors due to individual bias a researcher can use several observers or replicate the observation with a different observer. Finally, in setting up an experiment to study a limited number of independent variables, the researcher *insulates* the observation from other variables which might confound the results. In some experiments, an extraneous variable may affect the dependent variable, producing a change which is erroneously attributed to the independent variable. This can be prevented by such measures as carefully matching the subjects assigned to different conditions, or assigning subjects randomly.

In the research conducted in the behavioral sciences many subtle sources of error can distort the results of studies. One series of studies conducted by Rosenthal (1966), for example, demonstrated that research assistants familiar with the purpose of the experiment they are conducting are more likely to obtain the desired results than assistants who are not. This is not due to conscious dishonesty, but rather to subtle, not fully identified cues in the experimenter's behavior which convey the experimenter's hypotheses to the subjects. Orne (1962) conducted an informal experiment which demonstrated the remarkable compliance of college students in our culture in experimental situations. As one of a series of experiments he asked several acquaintances and strangers to do five pushups as a favor to him. The response was typically, "Why," or "What are you, some kind of nut?" He next asked several comparable individuals if they would like to participate in an experiment consisting of their doing five pushups. The typical response he received was, "Where do I do them?" Factors such as these greatly complicate the problems of causal inference and generalization in research in the behavioral sciences.

Box 1: Mathematical Aids in Research

Rigorous application of theory and critical examination of data, are facilitated by the use of mathematics. Standard statistical procedures enable social psychologists to test whether differences revealed by two procedures are so small that they could easily be obtained by chance, or are large enough to be "significant." In experimental studies, the size of the differences is related to statistical symbols, its standard deviation (S. D. or Sigma), and the ratio expressed in other statistical symbols such as "z" or "t." Another symbol often used in this connection is "p"— the probability that a difference of this size would be obtained by chance variation alone, in a series of similar comparisons. The symbols $p < .05$ or $p < .01$ or $p < .001$ mean that the probability of a difference as large as that found in the study, being due to the random or chance factors which affect any measure, is, respectively less than 5 in 100; or less than 1 in 100, or less than 1 in 1,000.

Another symbol frequently found in our summaries is "r," the coefficient of correlation. In general, an r shows the extent to which two measures are closely related. An r of 1.00 would mean perfect correspondence between the two; e.g., two competent persons measuring the height of 20 children, no two of whom are very much alike in stature. There is no reason why there should not be perfect agreement in such a task. On the other hand, if all 20 were close to 4'6" tall, slight variations in the reading of the yardstick might bring discrepancies between the measures noted by Observer A and Observer B. The correlation (r) might drop to .90 or .70 or even to .50. A purely chance relationship is expressed by an r of .00. The half-way point of agreement between .00 and 1.00 is an r of about .70. A negative r means that one measure rises as the other falls. Thus we might expect a negative coefficient of correlation between a good test of racial prejudice, and the number of friends of other races which a student can name. Those high in prejudice will be low in friends of other races; those low in prejudice will more probably have a number of such friends. But this would not lead to a perfect negative correlation (-1.00) since many other factors would influence participation in cross-racial friendships. A higher negative r might be found between the intelligence of high school students and the number of mistakes they would make on tests of reading or arithmetic. The lower the I.Q. the more the mistakes, and vice versa. In general, an r of .80 to 1.00 is regarded as high and showing a close correspondence of two measures. One of .50 to .80 is substantial and indicates a relationship with some significance. One of .20 to .50 is fairly low, but still above chance. If r is below .20 the two measures can be regarded as largely independent.

THE ROLE OF CONCEPTUALIZATION IN THEORY AND RESEARCH

In order to discuss the role of conceptualization in theory and research in social psychology it is necessary to introduce a few notions concerning perception. The way humans perceive determines the way observations concerning human behavior are made, and the way those observations are analyzed and placed in a theory. Perception begins as an act of *categorization;* perception employs categorization to determine meaning and to interpret what one perceives. Individuals define "reality" in terms of the categories into which they place experience. When a person touches a hot pan and burns himself, he places a series of sensations (heat, pain) in a series of categories (hot, hurt, burn) in order to interpret the reality of his experience. Thus the person thinks *"you stupid idiot,* you just touched a hot pan and burned yourself and it hurts."

As well as categorization, all perception includes *interpretation.* The interpretative aspects of perception can be clearly seen when one differentiates sensation from perception. Perception depends upon sensation. Essentially, sensation is the awareness of a stimulus while perception is the interpretation of that stimulus. The same sensation can have vastly different interpretations depending upon the situation. Thus hearing a loud noise could be ignored as unimportant, interpreted as an annoying distractor, or interpreted as a dangerous explosion, depending upon the situation and the state of the person.

Perception relies heavily upon *past experience.* From one's experience and learning he forms numerous categories into which he places new sensations. When one is confronted with a situation in which present categories do not seem adequate, one either develops new categories to handle the information or tries to twist the information until it fits an existing category. Thus when members of an isolated primitive culture see an airplane in flight for the first time, they may classify it as a "big bird."

Finally, when individuals observe the world they live in, they are bombarded with thousands of sensations and stimuli. It is not possible for the human nervous system to attend to everything and, therefore, perception has to be *selective.* Depending upon the motives currently acting upon the perceiver and the goals he is attempting to accomplish, his perception will selectively attend to the stimuli and sensations available. In a classroom, for example, the teacher's voice may be attended to during a lecture but blocked out as irrelevant after class has ended.

The categories into which individuals place their sensations and which they use to interpret stimuli from the environment are called *concepts.* The specification and clarification of concepts is an indispensable phase of theoretical work. Concepts provide the vocabulary by which the scientist can talk about the world. Some features of the world such as mountains, houses, trees, and tables are so prominent that they seem to demand names. Everyday language provides names for these phenomena. Other features are much more subtle, and can only be defined through a more rigorous examination of nature, man, and society than is made in ordinary life. These more covert aspects of experience, such as motivation, IQ, group cohesion, role, etc. are named by the concepts of science. Concepts must always be defined and scientific concepts must ultimately be defined in terms of observable characteristics. There are two criteria for an adequate definition of a concept. It must be identifiable. That is, it must be defined by observable characteristics so that we can readily determine whether we actually have an instance of the particular concept we are studying. Second, it must have significance and usefulness. A concept is significant only when it enters into laws; that is, when it is correlated with other concepts, events, facts. The more laws into which a concept enters, the more significant it is.

Scientific concepts are the distillations of everything that has been observed in research. They are the variables among which empirical relationships are sought. But definition of concepts is only a necessary first step to the main business of science, the discovery of truths about the world. An array of concepts does not constitute theory; a theory emerges only when concepts are interrelated in the form of a scheme. Because isolated concepts are of no theoretical value, the language of science also includes relational words such as: "greater than," "less than," "equal to," and "if . . . then." These are the terms of logic which give form to both ordinary and scientific statements.

Each science is distinguished by a unique language of terms and concepts, a unique view of the world, and a unique way of dividing reality into parts among which describable and consistent relationships are sought. The value of any science depends on how much its concepts and theories increase our ability to describe, predict and control portions of the world. Not surprisingly, the most significant advances in science are usually not discoveries of relationships among previously defined concepts, but are new conceptualizations of the empirical world. These "re-cuttings" of reality advance science when they provide a clearer or more consistent explanation of what we already know about the relationships among variables.

One of the purposes of this book is to give the student of social psychology a new vocabulary of social psychological concepts, which is the point at which learning a new scientific discipline begins. Hopefully, the chapters which follow will prepare the student to conceptualize as a particular type of scientist, the social psychologist.

The significance of research and theory

The world today is faced with a variety of serious social problems needing solutions. The development of sound social psychological theory has no intrinsic value; theory is of value only to the extent that it leads to the effective solution of problems. The greater the problem the more significant the theory which leads to its solution.

Research promotes theoretical advances in the important problem areas in three ways. First, a research study can destroy an old theory. By testing the theory in the real world, it may be found to be inadequate as a guide for understanding, predicting, and controlling the phenomena involved. Second, the study can lead to the creation of a new theory. Data gathered by the study may lead to a new conceptualization which clarifies many of the little understood aspects of the problem. Finally, the study can verify a new theory. The new theory can be tested and proven effective in predicting, controlling and understanding the relevant phenomena. The relationship between theory and research is complementary; theory is not useful unless it is verified by research and research findings which have no relation to a theory are trivial.

The science of social psychology

One essential characteristic of a science may be that it is profound, that is, it is a body of theoretical knowledge that is not trivial (Mazur, 1968). The scientist must have better theories than the layman, or he is not really a scientist at all. According to this criterion an empirical, theoretically connected body of knowledge is a science only when the individuals who know the theories know more about the real world than do the individuals who don't know the theories. It is an open question whether a trained social psychologist can solve social problems more effectively than someone who does not know any social psychology. Perhaps you, the reader, can answer that question by finding out if knowing the material in this book helps you to more effectively handle interpersonal situations.

In addition to being profound, four common criteria for evaluating a science are that it should be based upon observation (i.e., it should be empirical), it should attempt to summarize complex observations in abstract, logically related propositions which explain causal relationships in the subject matter (i.e., it should be theoretical), its theories should build upon one another in that new theories correct, extent, and refine the older ones (i.e., it should be cumulative), and it should be nonethical (i.e., it should not make ethical judgments about actions, it should merely explain them).

Although social psychology is empirical and theoretical, it may not be cumulative and nonethical. Koch (1969) states that theory in social psychology has not been refined and clarified but rather has been replaced by new theory. For several years one theory will be in "style" and generate considerable research, then another theory which is unrelated will come into vogue and generate considerable research. Many of these theories are held with highly emotional and almost religious fervor by many social psychologists for long periods of time, but so far they have faded away while new theories which do not, by and large, build upon past knowledge become current and dominant. In addition, social psychological theory and research is increasingly becoming used to establish social policy and guide the actions of practitioners involved in government, education, and industry. In such cases the values of the social psychologist and the practitioner may instill a strong ethical bias in the theory and how it is used.

Social psychology is currently one of the most exciting and promising sciences. Yet if it is going to be increasingly valuable to help our society deal with current social issues and problems it probably should become more cumulative in order to establish a broader, more valid body of theory.

Psychological models of man

There are a variety of research orientations, which for the sake of convenience make assumptions about the nature of man. Man has been conceptualized in psychological research as a telephone exchange, stimulation-maximizer, status-seeker, mutual ego-titillator, tension reducer, and congruence demander. Historically, the two views of man most widely used in psychology are the biological view represented by behaviorism and the Freudian view.

BIOLOGICAL VIEW OF MAN

The biological view of man accepts Darwin's belief that the social and psychological characteristics of man are the product of natural selection. All social and psychological characteristics, such as consciousness and reason, are adaptations to the environment which have proven to be significant weapons in the struggle for existence. As lions have developed sharp teeth and claws, humans have developed social relations and brain power. But what does man have to have to survive in his environment? What are the needs man has organized his resources to satisfy? Behaviorism states that in order to survive man must fulfill his primary drives for water, food, and a sexual mate. All psychological energy is seen to be aimed at obtaining the water and food to sustain life and a sexual mate to perpetuate the species. Through his power to reason and learn man has developed complex ways of satisfying his primary drives.

Many behaviorists hold that all social motives and acts are responses learned because they bring the individual direct or indirect gratification of his primary needs. They describe such complex behaviors as the development of love for another human being as the learning that certain persons and certain types of relationships are associated with less hunger, less thirst, more sexual gratification and less pain and fatigue. From this point of view individuals learn to love others because the others satisfy their basic needs. They conclude that all social concerns and values, being secondary drives, represent elaborations of certain biological needs. Other individuals are seen as simply sources of stimulation which facilitate or hinder the gratification of primary needs. Under the pressure of these drives humans utilize each other as they utilize objects; this is the content and significance of social relations. From this point of view the existence of society, the course of human history, the growth of human powers of reason have introduced no new objectives. For all of man's achievements his goals remain the same as those of other animals—to survive in the environment through meeting the basic biological needs.

FREUDIAN VIEW OF MAN

The conception of man presented by Freudian theory is that man has basic instinctual needs, primarily sexual, which need other humans to be satisfied. These needs have a blindly craving character; they know no limits, and their lack of restraint meets opposition from other individuals, primarily the person's parents. The child reacts to the restrictions that society imposes by a complex repression and transformation of his instincts. The principal thesis of Freud is that society suppresses human impulses and that the social order is built on instinctual repression. Fearful of the punishments that others can inflict, the child is forced to curb his impulses by taking account of reality. Freud insisted that a proper appreciation of reality was a necessary condition of sanity, and his therapeutic procedure aimed to extend the region of awareness and to strengthen the control of impulses. In his system reason was the harassed mediator between instinctive tendencies and the limitations of a harsh reality; the intellectual operations of judging and thinking are defense reactions which protect the individual from the overwhelming demands of instinct. The social character of man is then thought of as the individual submitting to external prohibitions and demands by "internalizing" them. Human society is maintained, and individuals are kept in line through force and fear.

FUNCTIONS AND DISFUNCTIONS OF VIEWS OF MAN

The function of such models is that by making a limited conceptualization of the nature of man, it is possible to conduct research and to build theories which explain, predict and potentially control man's behavior. It is much easier to take an individual apart and conceptualize aspects of his behavior, than it is to synthesize the "whole" of an individual and discuss the full complex nature of being human. The above models of man have proven helpful in generating theories and research on human behavior, but they can have undesirable consequences if taken too seriously. To overemphasize such aspects of human behavior as ego-centeredness, the presence of irrational emotions and actions, the use of thinking to rationalize one's actions, the influence of childhood experience on adult attitudes and behavior, and the role of arbitrary association and conditioning on the formation of personality and habits is to present a narrow and incomplete view of what a person is.

In the behavioral sciences, as contrasted with the physical sciences, the theories verified by research may actually affect the population they describe. The more powerful the theory, the greater the likelihood that it will influence the individuals whose behavior it explains. The danger of taking a conceptualization of the nature of man too seriously is that such conceptualizations not only summarize a research orientation but also influence future behavior of humans. In other words, the view of man upon which theory and research is based can become self-fulfilling prophecies. If a culture believes that it is human nature to be selfish and ego-centered, they may legitimize such behavior and socialize their children into being self-centered. If a society believes that the "basic" nature of man is to obtain pleasure and avoid pain, other aspects of human motivation and experience may be ignored and children may be socialized into expending a great deal of energy maximizing their pleasures and minimizing pain. At this point the theory stops being a conceptual tool to facilitate the discovery of "truth" about human behavior and becomes a guiding ideology which creates humans in its image. One of the major values of comparing different cultures or studying subcultures within a society is to clarify that alternative conceptualizations of the nature of man are available and workable.

HUMANISTIC VIEW OF MAN

Psychologists have often focused upon aspects of human behavior, such as learning, which can also be studied in other animals. In doing so they have often divided and segmented human behavior into a compartmentalized lowest common denominator. What is left out of such an orientation is the study of man as a whole person adjusting to a natural environment, and the study of aspects of behavior which are uniquely human, such as the role of understanding, the function of values, the creativeness of man reflected in the arts. These may be much more important in understanding human behavior than the principles of learning which are similar across several different species.

The ultimate goal of humanistic psychology is a complete description of what it means to be alive as a human being. The humanistic psychologist concerns himself with those aspects of human experience which have importance in daily living. He typically is concerned not only with describing human behavior, but also with asking how human experience may be extended, enriched, and made more meaningful. In addition to the study of man, humanistic psychologists have often been involved in developing methods for enlarging and enriching human experience.

The model of man on which humanistic psychology is based views the individual as living with purpose and intent, as a subject in the midst of his own living, acting on the world, changing himself and others with whom he interacts. While man's reactiveness is recognized, it is regarded as less distinctive of human experience than those ways in which humans distinguish themselves from objects, other species, and each other (e.g., conceptual thinking, imagination, mystical concern and inquiry, artistic creation, invention and discovery). Man is seen as striving to develop his abilities to accomplish his goals and to experience a sense of fulfillment in his life. From the humanistic point of view, man is believed to be at an early stage in the evolution of his own possibilities.

WHITHER MAN?

Asch (1952) noted that the basis of all the social disciplines must be a comprehensive conception of human nature. When psychology looks at its conceptualizations of the nature of man it may find that they limit the possibilities of visualizing what humans as a species may become. Is the basic nature of humans that of an animal governed by instinctual impulses from the past or that of an animal whose major motivation is to obtain pleasure and avoid pain, whose learning is simply association and conditioning to meet his physiological needs? If so the future of the human race is not very exciting; humans may learn new ways to express their instincts or they may make new associations for the satisfaction of basic needs. But is it possible that man is an animal who has just begun to realize his potential? Is man the finished product of an evolutionary process, or is he the beginning of another evolutionary process, the results of which cannot be visualized at this time? Is it possible that man has just begun to create a new world for himself in which his present potential will be expanded ten or one-hundred fold? It would be an exaggeration to believe that the psychological conceptualizations of man will actually determine what he becomes, yet they will certainly have some effect. It may be important whether these conceptions limit the future development of man, or help to realize the full potential of being human.

PARTICIPATION

The student beginning work in social psychology is urged to supplement his reading by first-hand observation, testing, and experiment. Natural-history methods can be applied to group processes on the campus or back in the student's home town. Participant-observer techniques can be utilized in classes, committees, fraternities, and other social groups. Attitudes on vital current issues can be explored through polls of a carefully chosen sample of students or other citizens. Relationships between attitude scores and sex, social class or other basic variables can be explored with a test constructed by a small group of students working together. Other students may organize groups to discuss the lectures, text or supplementary readings, and they may study their own processes as well as the subject matter. Still other groups may act out human-relations situations in which the members wish to develop more skill. These are sometimes called role-playing groups or psychodrama projects. If a student group tries to carry out, on a small scale and perhaps with some modifications, experiments like those reported in the textbook, they will learn far more about the scientific study of social interaction than reading alone could contribute. As later chapters turn attention to race relations, sex roles, propaganda, public opinion, international tensions, and processes of social change, students should be able to review their own experiences in relation to the topic, reexamine prejudices, propose some theories of their own, and work out ways of collecting evidence which would test their theories. A course in social psychology—or any other science—which is limited to memorizing what previous investigators have found omits the most stimulating and exciting aspect of the work of the investigator. A student's first observations, hunches, explorations, tests, and experiments may lack the technical finesse of the experienced research worker, but this is not too serious a limitation. What is vitally important at the beginning is the excitement of venturing a little out into the frontier of the unknown, using one's own mind, asking a real question in such a way that observation, tests or experiment can discover an answer. Every student of this text can share, intellectually and emotionally, in the great adventure of scientific research in human interaction.

Students are also urged to use a critical approach in thinking about the research reports and the conclusions presented in subsequent chapters. In each chapter, a few important studies have been summarized to illustrate research characteristics of the topic or area. Each summary presents: the purpose; the subjects; the procedures; and some of the findings. The summary does not make explicit the recurring pertinent scientific questions: "How valid are these findings? How far can they be generalized? What refinements would purify the variables? How do the underlying concepts and generalizations fit into the structure of our developing science?" It is hoped that students and instructors will continually raise and explore thoughtfully the questions which move knowledge from simple facts to meaningful laws and principles.

It is recognized, of course, that most students of this book do not intend to make a career of research. Only a few will dedicate their lives to scientific investigation. Hence, attention is also given to the bearing of social psychological facts and theories on the practical concerns and puzzling issues of life. Each chapter will include suggestions about ways in which students relate to practical decisions at home or school, in work or community life.

SUMMARY

Social psychology is the scientific study of human interaction. Man's ability to survive in his environment depends on his interaction with other human beings, sometimes individually, sometimes in institutions and organizations. One purpose of social psychology is to help us improve our social interactions, on both the large and small scale.

One of the major tools of social psychology is the scientific method that makes three major assumptions: (1) that there is a permanence of natural phenomena; (2) that experiences, events, objects and facts can be categorized; and (3) that natural phenomena are determined by a cause or set of causes. Granted these three assumptions, the goal of science is prediction, understanding and control of the cause-effect relationship between two or more variables. Science usually begins with simple observation with no insurance of objectivity. The laboratory method is controlled observation with a greater insurance of objectivity. Much of the scientific method deals with the elimination of errors in observing relationships between variables.

To understand conceptualization in research, it is necessary to understand perception. In order to find meaning in what he perceives, man must first categorize his experiences. Next he must interpret his experiences. The same experience under different circumstances has different meanings. Past experience determines the categories man uses and the interpretations he gives his present experiences. Sometimes new categories must be created. Man cannot react to all the stimuli of his environment and thus he must be selective.

The categories into which we divide our experience are called concepts. Concepts must be defined in terms of observable characteristics, and must be useful and meaningful. When concepts are interrelated, a theory starts to emerge. One science is distinguished from others by its unique concepts. The most significant advances in science are not so much made by interrelating old concepts as by forming new ones. In the following chapters we shall become familiar with some of the concepts unique to the science of social psychology.

It is doubtful, at present, if any of the social sciences is truly a science, because it is doubtful whether the theories of social science have lead to a better grasp of reality. So far, most theories have easily been replaced by others.

Two of the most dominant views of man are represented by the behaviorist and the Freudian view. According to the biological view of man, all psychological energy is aimed at meeting primary drives for water, food and a sexual mate. Social concerns, being secondary drives, are merely elaborations of certain biological needs. According to Freud, man has basic instinctual needs, primarily sexual, which need other humans to be satisfied. Society represses these human impulses and social order is based on instinctual repression. The trouble with both theories is that they present a narrow and incomplete view of man. Theories can influence and limit as well as explain the behavior of humans.

The humanistic approach to behavior is broader. The model of man on which humanistic psychology is based views individuals as living with purpose and intent, as subjects in the midst of their own living, acting in the world, changing themselves and others with whom they interact. This is a more optimistic, creative view which enables man to grow and develop.

Students are invited to observe and ask their own questions about human interaction.

CHAPTER 2

Dyads, interpersonal relations, and the analysis of social interaction

THE TRANSFORMATION OF MAN IN SOCIETY

We are all deeply dependent upon others for many things, and our survival depends upon the interrelationships we have formed with other human beings. It is within the interdependent relationships we have with others that we acquire our modes of behaving and our outlook on the world. Other individuals, the groups to which we belong, the society within which we are born determine to a great extent what it means to be human and what we, as individuals, develop into. How we behave at the dinner table, what we value as food, the attitudes we have about eating, all are formed from the interdependent relationships we have growing up in our culture. Would you be the same person if you have been born into a New Guinea village rather than a highly industrialized society? Would you still be motivated by the same desires, emotionally moved by the same situations, attracted to the same type of individuals?

Social psychology begins with the assumption that individual humans possess authentic properties characteristic of our species, which are modified in distinctive ways through our actions in society. A baby does not interact with other humans as a completely blank page; he has structural characteristics which respond to social conditions and which give him the potential for speech, work, and friendship. The individual without social experience is not fully a human being; he must undergo great changes in the environment of his society and family. He learns to laugh or cry, feel anguish or joy, as a result of certain actions of others. The relationships within which he finds himself can create mental illness or mental health. It is within interpersonal relations that a child is transformed into a human being, a functioning part of a family, group and society.

Within this chapter we shall first define what we mean by social interaction and dyad, discuss the need for social approval which binds us together, and explain how perception and communication influence how we understand one another. We shall then discuss what is considered to be the "heart" of dyadic relationships, interpersonal attraction and influence. Two classical dyadic relationships will be discussed, the mother-child and the teacher-student dyads. Finally we shall discuss the nature of "health-producing," constructive interpersonal relationships.

Traditionally social psychology has segmented aspects of interpersonal relationships in order to do controlled research. The structure of this chapter reflects this practice. For the sake of simplicity and our crude methodology, we must segment human relationships to some extent in order to verify hypotheses about how individuals related to one another. But the reader must be aware that such segmentation is to some extent dehumanizing and it misrepresents the complexity and beauty of relationships among "whole" persons.

DYAD INTERACTION

The simplest unit in which social interaction is possible consists of two members. Any two persons interacting constitute a dyad—a husband and wife, a mother and baby, a couple dancing, two competing tennis players, a teacher and pupil, a policeman and a criminal, a foreign ambassador and the president. The range of dyads extends across the whole human race.

Dyadic interaction requires that the actions of one partner serve as stimuli to which the other is responding; ordinarily both are adapting to each other. George Herbert Mead (1934), one of America's first writers on social psychology, describes a dog fight as a model of one kind of dyadic interaction. Each dog continually adjusts his position to the other; each shifts, sways, lowers or raises his head, advances or retreats, even before any fighting actually begins.

From past experience and from a knowledge of one's society and membership groups, individuals involved in social interaction develop mutual expectancies concerning how the other will behave. Thus when one is confiding in a friend, he has definite expectations concerning how the friend will respond based upon past experience with him and upon societal and group prescriptions on how friends should behave. Based upon one's expectations, we implicitly evaluate the behavior of others with whom we interact in terms of the appropriateness of their behavior, the value attached to others, their actions and motives, and the satisfactions they provide.

Through social interaction children learn how to behave appropriately to the rules, regulations, and expectations of one's society. Through interpersonal interaction a person develops a distinctive personality (e.g., Sears, 1951; Secord and Backman, 1961). The self-attitudes of an individual depend, to a large extent, upon how other individuals treat him. Finally, there is evidence that under certain conditions social interaction reduces the effect of stress. Schachter (1959), for example, demonstrated that under stressful conditions of fear or hunger, college students show an increasing desire to have contact with others.

At the heart of dyadic interaction is some awareness by each person of the experience of the other. Social interaction involves predicting the outlook and behavior of the individuals with whom one is involved. George Kelly (1963, p. 95) gives a compelling example of anticipating others behavior while driving. He says:

. . . we stake our lives hundreds of times a day on our accuracy in predicting what the drivers of the oncoming cars will do. The orderly, extremely complex, and precise weaving of traffic is really an amazing example of people predicting each other's behavior through subsuming each other's perception of a situation. Yet actually each of us knows very little about the higher motives and the complex aspirations of the oncoming drivers, upon whose behavior our own lives depend. It is enough, for the purpose of avoiding collisions, that we understand or subsume only certain specific aspects of their construction systems.

The study of social interaction in dyads provides the opportunity to investigate many fundamental and elementary processes of social psychology. We will discuss the problem of communication first in relation to the dyad and later in relation to groups and networks extending to millions. How one person influences another is at the heart of more complex processes of teaching, child rearing and propaganda. The cohesive and disruptive forces discussed in dyads will later be seen in ingroup unity and outgroup hostility on a worldwide scale. We can study what happens when two persons try to solve problems together, and as we do so we shall become aware of elements which enter into the work of all committees and conferences. One vital social phenomenon—love—reaches its highest development in the dyad.

HOW WE UNDERSTAND
ONE ANOTHER

Communication

Scientists are often intrigued by what more naive observers take for granted. The child is certain that he can be aware of the feelings and thoughts of others and that he can communicate to others his own thoughts and feelings. Yet, upon more mature reflection, we know that we can never be *inside* the consciousness of another person. All we can see or hear of him is his behavior. He can never enter into the stream of our consciousness; he must comprehend us as best he can from the sounds we make and the movements of our face, hands, and body. We seem permanently barred from visiting the mind of another person, except by the inferences we might draw from his actions. How then can we feel so confident that two persons really communicate?

Consider a simple dyadic interaction. John, crossing the campus, calls "Hi!" to his friend Jeanne, who waves back. This little incident contains eleven stages:

John's greeting
1. recognizes Jeanne
2. wants to greet her
3. calls out, "Hi!"

Transmission
4. sound waves with possible interference from other noise

Jeanne's experience
5. the greeting
6. from voice or a look, recognizes John
7. decides how cordial she wants to be
8. waves her hand

Transmission
9. light waves, with possible interference

John's experience
10. sees the gesture
11. interprets Jeanne's response to him

Jeanne surmised something about John's feelings from his tone of voice; he surmised something about hers from her gesture. Besides the linguistic content of communication, individuals respond to a wide variety of nonverbal cues. Despite the wealth of verbal and nonverbal cues, it may be difficult to determine what another is actually communicating. Part of the problem in communication is that verbal messages include distortions and ambiguities due to unobservable motives. Does the person really mean what he is saying? Does he feel the way he says he feels? Words can be used to communicate the truth or lies, to confuse as well as clarify, to mislead as well as to guide. This is less true of nonverbal communication.

A great many forms of nonverbal behavior can communicate feelings (Mehrabian, 1968): (1) tone of voice, (2) touching, (3) facial expression, (4) spatial distance from the addressee, (5) relaxation of posture, (6) rate of speech, and (7) number of errors in speech. Some of these are generally recognized as informative, others, such as posture, have a more subtle effect. Tone of voice, for example, conveys emotions. Davitz and Davitz (1959) demonstrated that an actress reciting the alphabet was able to convey a series of emotions that could be correctly interpreted by listeners 53 percent of the time (chance probability was 10 percent). Anger, nervousness, and happiness were the emotions most often correctly identified. Kramer (1964) replicated Davitz's findings, demonstrating that even when a person spoke Japanese, judges who did not know the language were able to label correctly the emotions portrayed. Mehrabian (1968) has concluded, furthermore, from a variety of research studies that the total impact of a communication is 7 percent verbal, 38 percent tone of voice, and 55 percent facial expression.

Other nonverbal cues also are important in communication. Untrained adults and children can easily infer that they are liked or disliked from whether (and how) someone touches them (Mehrabian, 1968). Helen Keller, completely blind and deaf, by holding her mother's hand could sense at once when something in the street excited or frightened her mother. There is an interesting example of contagion by muscular communication in Helen Keller's story of her life. She was walking with her mother when a boy threw a Fourth-of-July firecracker which startled her mother. Helen, unable to hear or to see at once asked, "what are we afraid of?" Holding her mother's hand, the child responded with appropriate smiles and turns of her head to noises and the speech of others; if her hands were put on a table she gave no sign of response to similar stimuli (Keller, 1903).

Correct judgments of the feelings of others are especially difficult when different degrees of emotion, or contradictory emotions, are expressed simultaneously through different aspects of behavior. How does one respond to a person who smiles while he says he is angry? What does one infer from the behavior of a person who says he feels fine but whose facial expression indicates that he is in deep pain? Shapiro (1968) has demonstrated that when individuals are confronted with a contradiction between a person's facial expression and his words, some will choose to believe the words and disregard the facial epression and others will believe the facial expression and disregard the words. His data indicate considerable consistency in whether a person chooses to believe facial or verbal messages.

The perception of persons

Without a stable environment, behavior would become random. If a person never knew how physical objects and other humans were going to behave, he could make no plans, engage in no goal seeking behavior, and have no control over the rewards and satisfactions he could achieve. Long experience with the physical environment and with friends makes us aware of the regularities in our environment; knowledge of these regularities enables us to predict and to some extent control the rewards we receive and the costs we incur in our daily lives. We know that dark clouds mean it may rain, that certain expressions mean we should be friendly or distant in relating to an individual.

Interpersonal perception refers to the ways in which individuals perceive the behavior of other individuals, the inferences they make about the "causes" of such behavior, and the resulting understanding and impression of the persons engaging in the behavior. Interpersonal perception is critical to the establishment of stable human relationships. In order to respond to other individuals, a person has to perceive their actions accurately, make correct inferences about their "causes" and evaluate them in some consistent and meaningful scheme. He can then respond in a way which will maximize the rewards possible for himself in the relationships.

In the following section on interpersonal perception, we shall examine the characteristics which apply to the accurate perception of both physical and interpersonal stimuli. We shall also study the factors which affect the way we perceive stimuli and develop organized impressions of other individuals to stabilize our interpersonal environment.

Structural factors

There are certain structural features of perception which arise from the nature of physical stimuli as they relate to the human neurological system. Much of the research and theory related to the structural factors in perception originated in Gestalt Psychology. The Gestalt psychologists studied the way in which perception is affected by patterned relationships; indeed, the German word "Gestalt" means a pattern or configuration. Gestalt psychology came up with two key notions concerning perception. The first is that perception is organized into a "whole" which is more than just the sum of its separate parts, and the second is that the organization of the "whole" tends to be as good as the prevailing conditions allow. Deutsch and Krauss (1965) note that there are three implications of the notion that perception is organized:

1. If perceptions are organized, then even if all the elements in the situation being perceived are changed, some aspects of perception will remain constant so long as the interrelations among the elements do not change. Thus if all the notes in a song are raised half an octave the melody will not be changed and, therefore, the song will still be quite recognizable. If all the personnel in an organization are replaced, the structure of the organization will still appear the same to an observer.

2. If perceptions are organized, the perception of any element will be affected by the total field of which it is a part. Thus the perception of a person's behavior will be influenced by the perceived social context of the behavior—a man disrobing in the locker room of a gym, for example, will be perceived quite differently than someone doing the same thing in downtown Chicago. The terrible poverty in many large metropolitan areas will be per-

ceived quite differently if one has just come from a wealthy suburb or if one has just returned from India.

3. If perceptions are organized, the interrelationships among the elements are perceived rather than the elements themselves. A musical melody is the interrelation among notes. Social phenomena such as cooperation, love, conflict, leadership all involve relationships among individuals.

The second notion of Gestalt psychology states that perceptual organization is neither arbitrary nor haphazard but is directed toward achieving a certain ideal state of simplicity and order. Although the properties of good perceptual organization have not been clearly specified, some principles of Gestalt perceptual organization have implications for social psychology.

Assimilation and contrast. One of the most vague and general principles of Gestalt psychology is that perceptual organization is, in a sense, bipolar. Perceptual organization will either be directed toward minimizing stimulus differences so that the perceptual field becomes homogeneous, or toward accentuating the differences if the stimulus differences exceed a certain level or if there is an abrupt discontinuity between parts of the visual field. Thus we tend to perceive a person either as assimilated to his group (all whites look alike) or contrasted (John does not look like a Johnson). For an example of assimilation and contrast see figure 2-1.

Figure 2-1. Assimilation and contrast
The ring is seen as a uniform gray in spite of the fact that contrast should be operating. That is because the ring is seen as a whole and each half is assimilated to the other half. Divide the ring by placing a pencil along the boundary between the black and the white fields. Assimilation then breaks down, since the ring no longer appears continuous and contrast is free to operate. Thus, the left half of the ring on the black ground appears brighter than the right half on the white ground. (Adapted from Deutsch and Krauss, 1965.)

Perceptual Grouping. Deutsch and Krauss (1965) list a number of principles for determining what will be perceived as being grouped together or unified in a visual field. Homogeneity is thought to be based on such factors as the common fate of the elements perceived, their similarity, their proximity, a common boundary, past experience, expectations, and the need to create a cause and effect relationship among elements. Examples of these factors can be seen in figure 2-2.

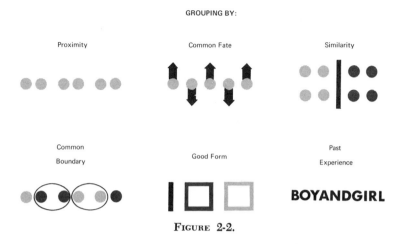

FIGURE 2-2.

Of the various ways in which perceptions are grouped, one of the most interesting for person perception is the imputation of causality. When stimuli are encountered in certain proximal or sequential relationships, one is perceived to be the cause of the other. If a given event is followed by an observed outcome, that event takes on the quality of a "causal factor." This is the basis for the notion of luck and many other magical beliefs seen in the use of such charms as a rabbit's foot.

Structural properties of perception are by no means separable from the functional features arising from past experience and present motivational states. Patterns of perception may be learned. Hence, motivational-perceptual processes depend to a considerable degree on learning.

Functional factors

The specific content of our perceptions (that is, the categories we are using to define our experience, the frame of references we are operating under, and the motives currently influencing our perceptions) are referred to as the "functional" features of perception. These functional features are more important in person perception than are the structural features which dominate object perception. Perhaps the most important difference is that persons, as social objects, are centers of action and intention. From the perceiver's point of view, other persons have relative autonomy, freedom of motion and response, and the capacity for capriciousness and impulsiveness that do not characterize rocks or flowers. We assume that individuals have motives and intentions directing their behavior; how we perceive their behavior is influenced by the motives and intentions we impute to them. Rocks and flowers are not assumed to have motives or intentions and our perceptions of them are based solely on their physical characteristics. Second, other individuals are aware of the perceiver and can take attitudes toward him that may affect his behavior. If his boss comes into the room a person will act differently than if his peer enters. When a teacher wants to evaluate a student's performance, the student may engage in quite different behavior than when his little brother wants to evaluate him. For many people, "impression management" is a major activity; that is, they spend time and effort in trying to create what they feel is a favorable impression on other individuals. The fact that individuals strive to influence the perceiver's impression of them is a unique aspect of person perception.

A primary example of the effect of functional factors on social perception is the fact that the perception of any act is determined by both the actual physical perception and by the perception of the context in which it occurs. A person's experiences with objects, events, and people become organized into a frame of reference, an enduring cognitive system of percepts, ideas, and beliefs which influences his perceptions. Thus Bartlett (1932) demonstrated that if English school children were asked to repeat a story which originated in another culture, they simplified, elaborated, and accentuated specific elements of the story to make it more consistent with their own culture. One major source of misunderstanding in interpersonal relationships arises when two individuals with different frames of reference argue about the interpretation of the same action.

A person's perceptions are influenced by his expectations and preconceptions. Due to his expectations a person may have a mental set which is conducive to perceiving some events but not others. Postman and Brown (1952) demonstrated that subjects who had just succeeded on a task recognized success words exposed briefly in a tachistoscope, while subjects who had just failed recognized failure words. Dearborn and Simon (1958) found that industrial executives looking at exactly the same information select for emphasis those aspects of a complex problem which relate to the activities and goals of their particular department. Thus, a person's background creates expectations which influence the way in which he interprets certain stimuli.

Besides the factors within a person which affect his perceptions, one makes assumptions about inner factors of the persons being perceived. This is most systematically treated in attribution theory, which is discussed in the next section.

Attribution theory: From act to disposition

According to Heider (1958), individuals seek to understand the structures which cause events in their environment in order to predict and control the events with which they are faced. In person perception this tendency leads to attempts to understand why others behave as they do. If one understands the reasons for the behavior of others, he can stabilize his environment by being able to predict and possibly to control their behavior. For the most part, understanding the behavior of others involves the attributions of intentions, motives, values, and personality traits.

In dyadic relationships a great deal is assumed about the motives, intentions and values of the other, and this strongly influences subsequent behavior. For example, individuals relate differently to those they think are trying to manipulate them, and those they believe are sincerely concerned about them as individuals. They relate differently to people they think are being sarcastic as compared to those they view as supportive. Such inferences are constantly being made about the "inner states" of others.

What is the process by which individuals make assumptions about the inner states of others? The person attempting to understand another individual first observes the other's actions, and then attempts to find a sufficient reason for those actions, which often involves attributing intentions and values to the actor. In order to know whether Mary likes him or not, Jim observes how she treats him, attempts to find reasons for her actions (that is, attributes intentions and motives) and comes to a conclusion about her attraction to him.

To understand how a person analyzes the actions of another, an act may be defined as a choice among alternatives designed to secure maximum outcome at minimum cost. If Mary accepts a date with John, her act is perceived as the result of a decision process in which she had a series of alternatives (accept, refuse, postpone the decision) and she chose the one most desirable to her. Thus the perceiver, John, assumes that the actor, Mary, is attempting to secure certain outcomes which give maximum rewards at minimum costs. Acts have effects, and because individuals act in order to achieve these effects, there are direct links of inference between effects and intentions. One assumes another's intentions (Mary wants to date John) on the basis of the effects of their actions (since she accepted, they will go on a date).

In attempting to attribute intentions to the actor the perceiver has to know two things. (Jones and Davis, 1965) First, did the actor know that these particular effects would follow his actions? Unforeseen consequences cannot reflect intentions and, therefore, only the effects the actor knew would follow from his actions can qualify as reflecting intentions. Second, did the actor have the ability to bring about the consequences in response to his intentions? An actor cannot achieve his objectives simply by desiring to do so; he must have the capacities and skills needed for their attainment. When a person's actions have certain consequences, therefore, it is important for the perceiver to determine whether the person was capable of producing these consequences in response to his intentions. Especially when the person *fails* to achieve certain consequences, there may be ambiguity concerning whether he ever actually intended to achieve them, or whether he was unable to do so. Whatever the consequences of an act, intention cannot be attributed unless the person had the ability to achieve deliberately the consequence. A person who has never played basketball but makes a difficult shot, for example, will not be perceived as skillful; rather the consequences of his action will be attributed to luck.

Knowledge of the consequences of one's actions and the ability to bring about the consequences are preconditions for the attribution of intentions. Establishing the intentions of the actor, however, is only the waystation to determining his more stable dispositions, his attitudes, beliefs, and values. Only through knowledge of another's dispositions can one predict and control the other's behavior dependably. If you know that a friend values his practical jokes, you can predict that in certain situations he will attempt to pull a practical joke or that he can be influenced to behave in certain ways if you can convince him that the situation is ripe for a good joke. The more important the actor's behavior in the perceiver's frame of reference, the more likely the perceiver is to treat intentions, once inferred, as cues or indices or more stable dispositions such as attitudes, beliefs, and values.

Once the perceiver has assumed that at least some of the consequences of an action were intended, he has to decide which effects were the primary goals of the actor, and what this reveals about the actor's dispositions (Jones and Gerard, 1967). The perceiver assumes that the actor engaged in a rational decision process where he estimated the number of alternative actions open to him and considered the efficacy of each in obtaining his objectives. By his decision to engage in a certain action, the actor reveals certain information about his dispositions. Decisions are, of course, not always rational or deliberate. The more information the perceiver can obtain about the decision process of the actor, the more accurate the inferences he can make about his dispositions.

In making inferences about the decision process the actor engaged in before acting, the perceiver is influenced by the actor's frame of reference, the context in which he thinks the behavior occurred. The perceiver, therefore, seeks information not only about the decision processes of the actor, but also about the situational context as seen by the actor. The same objective situation may be subjectively different for the actor and the observer.

Thus in an attempt to understand other individuals with whom he interacts, a person observes their behavior and its consequences. He then infers the intentions of the actor by deciding whether the decision was conscious and rational, whether the actor had the ability to achieve the consequences deliberately and whether he knew that those specific consequences would result from his action. Once intention has been established, the perceiver infers more stable dispositions such as attitudes, beliefs, and values, in the actor. Finally, the inferred dispositions enables the perceiver to make predictions concerning the actor's behavior in future situations and also to influence the actor by appealing to his values, beliefs, or attitudes. This process is represented in figure 2-3.

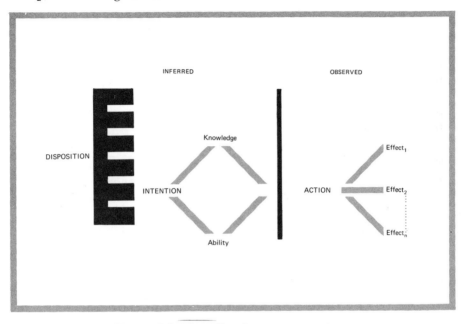

FIGURE 2-3. The Effect-disposition paradigm.
(Taken from Jones and Davis, 1965.)

Organization of impressions

The attribution of intentions and dispositions is only the beginning of forming an impression of another person, and the discussion of the process has been highly simplified. Once the perceiver has inferred to his satisfaction that the actor has a certain disposition he can make further inferences about associated dispositions. One of the characteristics of person perception is that the perceiver often infers one disposition from another. Thus if we see a person mistreating an animal we form a coherent impression of his total personality by assuming that various other dispositions are highly correlated with "meanness." Or if we see a person being unusually concerned about what his classmates think about him, we make inferences concerning his total "insecure" personality. Or if a person seems rather shy and aloof when we meet him, we may infer a total personality structure which is associated with shyness and aloofness. Where do these inferences come from? How is it that we can make such judgments concerning other's personalities from just a few samples of their behavior? The answer may be that we learn to operate on

31

implicit theories of personality based upon our experience with other individuals and the cultural stereotypes imbedded in everyday language.

Asch (1952) was convinced that impressions of other individuals are organized into a unitary whole around central traits which dominate the other traits they are associated with. The meanings of the individual traits did not merely summate, according to Asch, but rather resulted in an emergent synthesis of organized meaning. According to Asch, the Gestalt assumption that the whole is more than the sum of its separate parts also applies to person perception. He conducted a series of experiments in which he demonstrated that if a perceiver has reason to believe that the actor is "warm" rather than "cold" it will affect the way in which he interprets other related attributes such as generosity and intelligence. In each series of combination of traits, some will be central and dominate the impression, and others will be peripheral. Thus when paired with attributes such as intelligent, skillful, industrious, and determined the attribute of warmth dominated the impression but when paired with such attributes as weak, obedient, and unambitious, warmth was not central. Asch thus argues that one has to know how various traits affect one another in combination in order to understand person impression. Studies by Bruner and his associates (1958) and Wishner (1960), however, show that relatively accurate predictions of how traits will combine in impressions can be made simply by summing the implications of the individual traits.

One function of having an organized impression of other individuals is that it gives constancy to one's views (Heider, 1958). A certain psychological economy results from constant impressions as one is then not obliged to alter his view of other individuals after every encounter. If a friend engages in certain acts, these are placed within the larger categories which make up one's impression of this friend. If the behaviors do not seem to fit one's perception of the friend, one is apt to overlook the discrepancy. If the discrepancy becomes too large or too frequent, one has to change his impression of the friend. A constant view of other people facilitates anticipating their behavior, and ensures that one will receive the interpersonal rewards, such as warmth and support, that he desires.

Once an impression is formed, psychological forces seem to keep the impressions balanced (Heider, 1958). One's friends are seen as liking the same things one likes and disliking the same things one dislikes, thus keeping a cognitive balance between elements in one's perceptual field. Such tendencies toward psychological balance enable one to predict that if a person likes one's best friend, he will also like oneself. If you experience a certain professor as obnoxious you expect that your friends will also find the professor obnoxious. This is not always confirmed. Such tendencies toward psychological balance are discussed in more detail later.

Research on impression formation and the verbal aspects of person impression indicates that if one wishes to predict how one person perceives another, the most crucial information to obtain is how much the first person likes the second. The attraction one has towards another individual affects considerably the type of attributions one will make about the other's dispositions.

Checking

Assuming that communication is often based upon both verbal content and nonverbal cues, and that one's perception of others is based upon inferences made about their dispositions, how does one insure accurate communication and accurate impression formation of other individuals? The primary way to insure accurate communication is through further communication aimed at verifying whether two individuals understand one another correctly. We form quick impressions of what others mean by what they say and do. These impressions are the starting point of our next operations. Usually the impressions are correct, but occasionally we become aware that something is wrong; some misunderstanding or incorrect impression has arisen. Then a process of investigation and correction takes place.

How much we rely on feedback from the other person becomes apparent in a distressing telephone conversation in which we speak our piece but against so much noise that we cannot quite comprehend the replies. One social psychologist experimented with limiting the feedback during problem solving (Bavelas, 1957). The psychologist gave one partner a diagram for the arrangement of dominoes; the other, connected by telephone, had the dominoes and tried to follow directions. With one-way communication only, and no feedback, no dyad succceeded. The person receiving instructions soon found himself bewildered and frustrated. When the second man could react, even when limited to a push-button signal for "Yes" or "No," the task could be accomplished. Restriction on the communication brought about rejection of each partner by the other. Each viewed his coworker as stupid and lacking in understanding. Later, we shall see also that some hierarchical structures in social institutions have a similarly restricting effect upon communication and similarly generate hostility within the organization.

Telepathy

In this chapter, we have assumed that all the various dyads communicate only by speech, gestures, expressions, and contact. There is another hypothesis: that underlying all of these and in some instances operating without them, there is some kind of direct communication between mind and mind. Telepathy is one form of extrasensory perception. Does it exist? Under what conditions can it be demonstrated?

The largest body of evidence is summarized by Rhine (1937, 1940, 1947). He used an experimental setup which carefully screened out possible cues from sight or sound. One partner in a dyad looked at a card while the other tried to guess which of five symbols his partner was viewing. Most participants could do little better than they would by chance. Yet, one psychologist reported that in 74 runs of a series of 25 guesses, where the average, by chance, would be only 5 correct, one subject averaged 18.24 correct, and scored over 20 right in 9 successive runs. (Riess, 1937, 1939). The odds against such a performance by chance alone are staggeringly large. In 2,100 trials, the critical ratio was 53.57, while a critical ratio as large as 3.00 would occur only once in a thousand times by chance. Rhine has reported data from more than 900,000 properly controlled trials, with a critical ratio of 39.9.

Critics have been understandably reluctant to accept a phenomenon which seems so contrary to most of our assumptions about matter and mind. The experimental controls have been carefully scrutinized and the mathematics of probability re-examined. It would probably be correct to say that today most psychologists are uncomfortable because they cannot wholly accept nor clearly disprove the results.

The other kind of evidence comes from several hundred incidents which have been investigated by the Society for Psychical Research. Gardner Murphy recently reported a few of these (1961). A woman awoke with a start and the impression of a sharp blow on her mouth. Later she learned that her husband, out for an early sail, had been hit on the mouth at that moment by the tiller of the boat. Several teeth were knocked out. In another case, a businessman was on a trip to Rochester, New York. He felt an urgent message that he must go on to Buffalo. He went, against all his better judgment, and at a hotel in Buffalo where he had never stayed before, found a message from his wife, desperate because their small daughter was dying. In his book, *Mental Radio* (1930), Upton Sinclair reported his wife Craig's extraordinary success in hundreds of instances receiving and drawing an image approximately correctly from the mind of Mr. Sinclair or other relatives or friends. The "radio" analogy breaks down because distance does not seem to have any clear effect.

Rhine (1940) reports from informants he trusts incidents involving: a woman wakened by a nightmare about her brother shooting himself in the haymow and later discovering that the event had occurred as portrayed in the dream; two professors writing to each other the same day because each had dreamed of the other the preceding night; a mother impelled to leave a bridge game and call home at the moment her daughter met with an accident; a banker moved to unaccustomed tears while reading about a man's death in a novel associated the experience with his father, then in another continent, and later found the unexpected death confirmed. Most of the accounts could be supported by independent witnesses. Will coincidence suffice to explain them? Whenever a discussion of such events arises in a class or an informal gathering, one or two persons present are likely to contribute similar incidents from their own personal experience. It is conceivable that laws governing this special kind of non-physical communication will some day be discovered, and man may bring under deliberate control a process the evidence for which is still fragile and sporadic.

Need for social approval

Earlier in this chapter we noted that individuals become socialized into what their society defines as human within interpersonal relationships. It is through the ability of individuals to appeal to the motives of other individuals that much of socialization and interpersonal influence takes place. Persons are quite commonly motivated by a need for social approval. The *need for social approval* is simply the need to have other individuals esteem, value, and approve of oneself.

Before we discuss the motive of social approval, it may be helpful to explore just what a motive is. The concept of motive was not invented by psychologists; like most concepts used in psychology, it was taken from ordinary language. Before psychology aspired to be a science, individuals were analyzing the motivations of their companions, friends, and fellow group members. Today a husband may assess the motives of his wife, a salesman may assess the motives of his client, and a student may assess the motives of his teacher. It is from such everyday experience and common language concepts that psychology begins its study of human behavior.

A motive has a goal object or a goal condition. Individuals are motivated to accomplish a goal or to reach certain conditions which they feel will be rewarding. Motivation may be of high or low intensity. Persons may be thought of as possessing motivation of a given strength either for the moment (such as hunger before meal-time) or for long periods of time (such as striving for social approval).

Motives are not directly available to the senses. One does not "see" or "feel" a motive in another person; motives can only be inferred from a person's behavior. The basic behavioral pattern from which we infer motivation is "directionality." A person manifests directionality when he behaves like a guided missile. He not only aims at a given goal; he manifests perseverance and adaptability in getting there. As circumstances change and impediments are encountered, he shifts course to stay on target. The notion that the same motive exists in a number of persons with varying intensity depends primarily upon the observation that one person will maintain directionality in circumstances that deter another.

A person's motives may or may not be fully apparent to himself. There are clinical data which indicate that often the motives of an individual as he interacts with his family, friends, and fellow workers may be quite different from what he believes them to be. Clinical psychologists study samples of behavior to discover the "real" motivation of individuals they are treating. The research psychologist must either depend upon his subjects to provide him with accurate information concerning their motives, or find a measure that takes little time but which reveals more concerning a person's motives than the person can report himself.

Very little of the social interaction in which people are involved seems to be motivated directly by biological necessity. Humans seem to be motivated much of the time by learned needs derived from their socialization into their culture and society. One of these learned needs is the desire for social approval, to have others value one as a person and respond warmly to one's actions. Often these social needs are more powerful than biological needs, such as when a person risks his life for the social values of his group. The need for positive approval is so strong that the inability to obtain acceptance is basic to many forms of mental illness. A child who is not loved or accepted or approved of by his parents, peers, or teachers may develop serious incapacities in relating to others which lead him to behave in ways that are defined as "mentally ill" in his society.

One of the more common explanations for the development of the need for social approval comes from learning theory. It seems that individuals learn to seek others' regard at an early age and have always done so. A classical conditioning model of learning explains this motive by arguing that the warm acceptance of the child's mother may often accompany the satisfaction received in eating or tactile pleasure. Thus the need to receive warm acceptance from others is developed through associating it with the fulfillment of physiological needs. From the viewpoint of an operant learning model, the need for social approval may be developed through learning that the acceptance and approval of one's parents and peers enables one to receive more basic rewards from them.

However the need for social approval is developed, there is considerable evidence that very subtle indicators of social approval can modify behavior. The research on the effects of operant conditioning on human subjects illustrates this point. Verplanck (1955) demonstrated that rewarding the occurrence of personal opinions through such expressions as "you're right," or "I agree" increase significantly the number of opinions a person states in a conversation. Bachrach, Candland, and Gibson (1961) have demonstrated that such indications of positive group approval as "Yes," "Good," or "Mum," and such negative ones as "No," or shaking the head affect the frequency of opinions expressed in conversations. In a study by Matarazzo and his associates (1964), Civil Service applicants were tested under various conditions to see what effect indications of social approval would have on their behavior. A 45-minute interview consisting of three stages of 15 minutes each was conducted with each subject. In the first time period the interviewer talked as little as possible while encouraging the interviewee to talk about anything that came to mind. During the second 15-minute period the interviewer nodded his head slightly but affirmatively whenever the applicant began to say something until he stopped. During this time period the interviewer might nod his head anywhere from 500 to 1000 times. In the third period, the interviewer terminated the head-nodding. Throughout the entire interview the psychologist took special care not to introduce other reinforcing stimuli, such as smiling or talking excessively with the interviewee. From figure 2-4 one can see that the head nodding had a strong effect on the duration of the applicant's speech. For the first interviewer, the effect of nodding his head during periods when the applicants were talking, was to increase periods of talking by 48 percent; for the second interviewer the increase was 67 percent. Both increases were highly reliable on a statistical basis. In the third period when the interviewers ceased to nod their heads, the duration of talking also began to decrease. Finally, it may be seen that the verbal output of the two interviewers showed remarkably similar verbal patterns during all three periods.

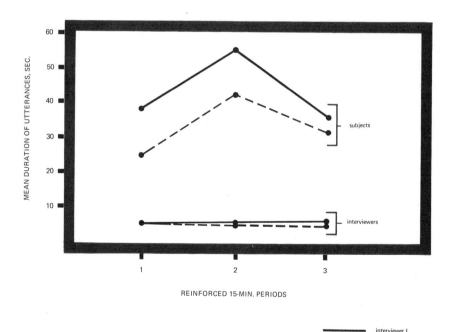

FIGURE 2-4. The effects of affirmative head nodding on the duration of utterances in an interview.

(Adapted from Matarazzo, Saslow, Wiens, Weitman, and Allen, 1964.)

The evidence accumulated in the past fifteen years indicates that the behavior of others can be subtly manipulated by approving or disapproving selected types of remarks in a conversation. The greater the person's awareness of the things for which he is being approved, furthermore, the more likely he is to respond with the desired type of behavior. But not all subjects respond in the same way to the reinforcing properties of minimal approval. Some are more responsive than others, some extinguish very quickly, others very slowly; one person may be very responsive one day but unresponsive another. Individuals are complex beings with different past histories and experiences, so there is no reason to expect that a given reinforcer will have an equal effect on all persons at all times. By careful manipulation of two new concepts, deprivation and satiation, the effects of a reinforcer can be normalized to a large extent, even over a diversity of subjects.

The concepts of deprivation and satiation were derived in animal experimentation with physiological drives. An unfed or food-deprived animal will be more reactive to food as a reinforcement than will an animal that has just eaten or is food-satiated. The question is whether learned drives in humans operate in a similar fashion. Will a person who has been deprived of or satiated with social approval be more or less responsive to the approval of others?

The relative degree of deprivation or satiation of learned needs is determined by chronic and situational factors. Chronic factors can be traced to the long-term history of the person while situational factors are dependent upon the immediate situation in which the person finds himself.

The state of chronic need for social approval has been discussed by such psychotherapists as Alfred Adler, Karen Horney, Erich Fromm, and Carl Rogers and has been studied systematically by two social psychologists named Crowne and Marlowe. On the basis of their clinical experience, the psychotherapists feel that individuals who have a long-term deficiency in social acceptance or social approval seem to be depressed, anxious, and inclined to have defective interpersonal relationships. They state that the desirable state, from the mental health point of view, is one in which a person has a sufficient level of self-regard that he does not require the continued approval of others. While this seems to be a reasonable argument, more systematic, empirical, controlled research has to be conducted on the chronic need for social approval, since clinical evidence alone is not sufficient verification for a hypothesis.

Crowne and Marlowe (1964) developed a scale to measure the need for social approval. Half of its statements are culturally acceptable, but probably untrue and half are true, but probably undesirable. For example, if a person answered "true" to the question, "I am always careful about my manner of dress," and "false" to "I like to gossip at times," he would be answering in the socially desirable way. The socially desirable response typically en-

snares the person in a "little white lie" about himself. After all, is there anyone who is always careful about his manner of dress, or never indulges in
gossip? On the basis of a series of studies, the researchers found that those
who score high on their scale are significantly more likely to conform to the
judgments of others than are those who score low.

One of the experiments which validated the Crowne and Marlowe scale
was conducted by Crowne and Strickland (1961). In this study they manipulated the reinforcement given to subjects who scored high or low on the
Crowne and Marlowe scale of need for social approval. The subjects received either positive, negative, or neutral reinforcement. Subjects were reinforced each time they uttered a plural noun with either a subtle "mm-hmm"
and an affirmative but slight nod of the head or with a negatively toned "uh-
uh" or with no reaction from the experimenter. When no reinforcement was
given, there were no differences between the subjects high and low in the
need for social approval. When positive reinforcement was given, the subjects high in need for approval reacted much more positively than did subjects low on need for approval. When negative reinforcement was given,
high need for approval subjects were much more affected by minimal disapproval than were low need for approval subjects. Thus it seems that a chronic
high need for approval predisposes one not only to engage in behavior that
elicits even minimum approval from others, but also to avoid doing that which
yields even the slightest disapproval.

The reinforcement value of social approval may depend not only on the
needs of the person developed over time, but also on what he has received in
the immediate situation. One of the clearest demonstrations of the dependency of learned need states on the immediate situation stems from the work
on the social behavior of children. Gewirtz and Baer (1958) selected roughly
equal numbers of middle-class boys and girls from the first and second
grades of a school. Subjects were randomly assigned to one of three conditions: a deprivation condition in which they were systematically deprived of
social approval, a saturation condition in which they received an abundance
of approval, and a nondeprivation condition in which they were neither deprived nor saturated. In the deprivation condition a female experimenter
came in to the classroom to bring the child to the experiment. As they
walked the several hundred feet down the corridor to the experimental
room, the experimenter said as little as possible. After they had reached their
destination she told the child that the game he was to play was temporarily
in use and that he would have to wait a short time. The child was then left
alone for 20 minutes. In the saturation condition the experimenter maintained a pleasant and interested attitude toward the child during the walk,
and praised and admired him as much as possible. During the 20-minute
wait the child was given pictures or cut-out designs with which to play. For
the entire period the experimenter steadily administered praise and admira-

tion at whatever the child did or said about himself. During the 20-minute period each child received approximately 30 such reactions. In the nondeprivation condition, subjects were treated much as they were in the deprivation condition during their walk to the experimental room, but they were not exposed to the 20 minutes of isolation; instead they were immediately allowed to play the game.

The amount of social approval received prior to the marble game had a marked influence on children's responsiveness to reinforcement in the game itself. Those children who had been deprived of social approval were most affected by approval as a reinforcer. Subjects who had been satiated were even less responsive than the control or nondeprivation subjects. Children in the deprivation condition, furthermore, initiated more attempts at gaining the experimenter's attention during the first four minutes of the game situation than did the subjects in the nondeprivation condition. Although subject to criticism, these results led support to the general proposition that the value of a given reinforcer may be altered within a situation.

One of the learned needs which acts as a powerful motive in human interactions, therefore, is the need for social approval. The degree to which a person can be influenced by the approval of others depends upon his chronic or situational deprivation of social approval. Such motives as the need for social approval represents the basis for enduring interpersonal relationships. The heart of such relationships, interpersonal attraction, is examined in the next section.

Interpersonal attraction

Falling in love, making friends, experiencing the warmth, comradeship, and intimacy of close personal relationships is one of the most exciting aspects of being alive. Much of human society and action seems based upon the attraction individuals have for each other. The words in common language describing aspects of interpersonal attraction, such as "like" and "love," "dislike" and "hate" are among the most frequently used in the English language. To a social psychologist it becomes interesting to ask how do individuals become friends, why did John fall in love with Mary and not Jane? What causes the deep pain often experienced when two close friends move to different communities?

Almost all researchers who are interested in interpersonal attraction investigate variables which may affect the positive and negative attitudes one individual may have toward another. Thus "liking" or "disliking" may be conceptualized as expressions of attitudes toward a particular person. An *attitude* simply represents a person's predisposition to respond toward a particular person or group of persons, a particular object or group of objects in a favorable or unfavorable manner. The concept attitude originated from attempts to predict the behavior of individuals. When we say we know what a person's attitude is, we mean that we have some bits of evidence from the person's past behavior which make us confident that we can predict his future behavior in related situations. Since an attitude is a predisposition, it is carried around inside an individual, perhaps as a particular pattern of neural connections in the brain and nervous system. Since it is internal, it cannot be observed or measured directly and, therefore, it is assumed to exist on the basis of overt behavior. For this reason, the concept of attitude as generally defined by most psychologists falls under the category of *hypothetical construct*. A hypothetical construct is an entity or process which is presumed to exist even though it is not directly observable or measurable.

In the following pages we shall discuss several sources of interpersonal attraction. After the research and theory on interpersonal attraction has been presented, we shall discuss what many consider the most interesting areas of human relationships, friendship, romantic love and marriage.

PROPINQUITY

What happens when individuals live in close proximity to each other? Does propinquity commonly increase attraction between individuals or does it increase hostility? Propinquity refers to the physical closeness or contact between individuals. There are a large number of studies which demonstrate that, other things being equal, the closer two individuals are located geographically, the more likely it is that they will be attracted to each other. Thus, it is a commonly accepted notion that propinquity has a strong influence on one's friendship choices. A repeated finding concerning marital choices, for example, is that individuals find spouses who live close by. Factors affecting choice of friends and mates will be reported on more fully, later in the chapter.

There is, however, also evidence that the less physical distance there is between two individuals, the more likely it is that they will dislike each other. Police records provide evidence that close proximity to another individual may produce interpersonal hostility as well as interpersonal attraction. The Detroit Police Department's 1967 Annual Report indicates that in the majority of robberies the perpetrator was either related to, or acquainted with, the victim. Thieves seem to be more likely to rob an acquaintance than a stranger, at least in Detroit. Aggravated assault, like thievery, appears to be directed toward intimates, according to J. Edgar Hoover (1966) and most murders are committed by spouses. While proximity may be a necessary condition for attraction, it appears that it also may be a necessary condition for hatred.

It is obvious that any strong feeling or perception about another person, positive or negative, would have to be based upon some information about the person's characteristics. From this point of view both attraction and dislike will be related to proximity, since we cannot have feelings for another person unless we interact with him, and the closer we are physically, the higher the probability that we will interact. What proximity appears to allow and what distance prevents is an opportunity to obtain information and to accumulate experience regarding the rewards or punishments we are likely to receive from the other person. The function of propinquity quite obviously is to allow other factors which can increase attraction or decrease attraction to operate. Thus, the question, "Under what conditions will proximity increase attraction and under what conditions will it increase dislike?", would be answered by specifying the other factors in the situation once interaction between two individuals actually took place.

Newcomb (1956) states that propinquity is the most effective primary influence on positive attraction. In an extensive study of interpersonal attraction, he invited 34 students (17 in each of two years) transferring to the University of Michigan to live together in a house near campus (Newcomb, 1961). None of the 17 men in each of the groups had known one another before. All agreed to take part in the program of research. Over the course of a semester of living together, each of these two separate groups filled out attitude scales and value measures, and also estimated the attitudes of the others in the house. Newcomb wanted to determine the bases for attraction. Initial attraction was found to be highly related to propinquity, as measured by the proximity of the students' room assignments. Later attraction grew out of greater similarity in perceived attitudes. Regardless of whether the students were attracted to each other or not, their accuracy in perceiving the attitudes of the others increased over the semester. Thus once proximity has brought two individuals into interaction, other factors such as the perceived similarity of attitudes and values influence their attraction toward each other.

The "exposure-attitude" hypothesis has a long history in psychology. Fechner (1876) was the first to recognize that the familiar seems more likable. Recently Zajonc (1970) reviewed evidence leading him to the conclusion: "Repeated exposure makes words more positive, food more appetizing, strangers more acceptable. Repeated exposure will increase the attraction between two people or two animals." In another report (1968) Zajonc demonstrated that Turkish words, almost meaningless to his student subjects, were judged to have good rather than bad meanings after more frequent exposure. Long ago Meyer (1903) demonstrated that bits of strange Oriental music became more acceptable as they were heard more often. Zajonc also cites the amusing instance of an Oregon State University student who came regularly to class covered (except for his bare feet) by a large black bag. Although he did not speak or respond, the bizarre and unknown character grew more and more acceptable to his fellow students. The village idiot may be more loved by his neighbors than is a handsome, talented stranger. Cairns

(1966) has shown that lambs raised with a dog preferred him to a ewe. The almost universal biological phenomena of pair-bonding is largely a consequence of propinquity (Morris, 1967).

People who are in close proximity often perceive themselves to be in the same social unit. Individuals living in a dormitory for example perceive themselves to be roommates, part of a certain floor, in a certain wing, in a certain dorm. All of these social units are determined by proximity. Heider (1958) argues that people who perceive themselves as belonging together in the same social unit will tend to be attracted to each other. Darley and Berscheid (1967) demonstrated that subjects expressed more liking for a person they expected to be their discussion partner than for another they did not expect to communicate with. Potential interaction can be a powerful determinant of attraction. Berscheid, Boye and Darley (1968) found that when subjects anticipated interacting with an objectively undesirable person, they would actually *choose* voluntarily to interact with this negative person more readily than did other subjects who did anticipate any association with him. These studies support Heider's theory.

An interesting account of how the attraction toward a person in close proximity can change due to situational variables is given by a French anthropologist, Poincins (1943) who writes about his attitude toward Paddy Gibson, a trader with whom he spent most of an arctic winter.

I liked Gibson as soon as I saw him, and from the moment of my arrival we got on exceedingly well. He was a man of poise and order; he took life calmly and philosophically; he had an endless budget of stories. In the beginning we would sit for hours . . . discussing with warmth and friendliness every topic that suggested itself, and I soon felt a real affection for him.

Now as winter closed in round us, and week after week our world narrowed until it was reduced—in mind, at any rate—to the dimensions of a trap, I went from impatience to restlessness, and from restlessness finally to monomania. I began to rage inwardly and the very traits in my friend . . . which had struck me at the beginning as admirable, ultimately seemed to me detestable.

The time came when I could no longer bear the sight of this man who was unfailingly kind to me.

A simple class experiment may serve to test the hypothesis that interaction will increase liking for one another, and to demonstrate how such a hypothesis may be crudely investigated. At the first session of a course, each student receives, when class begins, a copy of the following rating scale:

RATING SCALE FOR LIKING OF PARTNER

10 Like more than most others I know
9 Like much
8 Like some
7 Like a little
6 Like slightly more than average
5 Dislike slightly more than average
4 Dislike a little
3 Dislike some
2 Dislike much
1 Dislike more than most others I know

First Rating: Before speaking   _____

Second Rating: After introductory conversation   _____

Third Rating: After nonverbal communication   _____

Fourth Rating: After sharing first impressions: (Positive)   _____

Fifth Rating: After sharing first impressions: (Negative)   _____

First, students are asked to pair nonverbally with a partner who is almost or quite a stranger. No words are to be spoken, and after two silent minutes together the first rating is made privately by each person. A period of five minutes follows during which each student introduces himself to his partner. The second rating is then made by each person privately. During the next five minutes, each pair communicates *nonverbally*—looking at each other, touching the other's face, exchanging hand clasps, walking arm-in-arm, shoving, dancing, all spontaneously and without words. The third rating is then made. The fourth period consists of five minutes during which each person tells his partner some of his *favorable* first impressions ("The things I like most about you are . . .") after which they make their fourth rating. Finally, the pair have five minutes to tell each other some of the things they didn't like at first, some negative feeling ("At first, I thought I might not like you because . . ."). The final rating is then made.

This experiment takes only about half an hour. The Reaction Forms are stapled together by pairs, tabulated and averaged by a small committee of student volunteers. They report the average liking at each of the five stages and also check to see whether any pairs deviated markedly from the class trend. In most trials of the experiment, the liking increases with interaction; it increases markedly between the first and second ratings and between the third and fourth. It continues to increase, although less markedly, from fourth to fifth. In one variant we asked students at the fifth rating to report whether or not they felt their partner was being wholly open and frank in telling about possible negative feelings. A special tally of those rating their partner as very open and frank showed that liking rose significantly more in this subgroup than in the pairs who saw their partner as courteous or diplomatic, but not quite frank. These results indicate that honest feedback may increase rapport more than does the usual effort to avoid possible hurt to the other's feelings.

SIMILARITY AND COMPLEMENTARITY

One of the most interesting issues in interpersonal attraction can be summarized by the two sayings, "Birds of a feather flock together" and "Opposites attract." Folk psychology frequently sums up a wealth of human experience and wisdom, but it is often frustrating because of its contradictions. It can also be frustrating because it is indiscriminate. Newcomb (1956), for example, has noted that according to folk psychology, people who are similar may be attracted to each other (being birds of a feather), but it seems quite unlikely that such similarities such as shape of the head or size of the foot lead to attraction. The appropriate question concerning such contradictions and indiscriminateness of folk psychology is, "under what conditions will similarity lead to attraction and under what conditions will complementarity lead to attraction?"

According to Heider's (1958) balance theory, entities which are perceived to belong together are perceived to be attracted to each other. Entities which are perceived to be different are imagined not to find each other attractive. Thus separate entities which are perceived as similar tend to be perceived as belonging together. From this theory one can derive the hypothesis that persons who are perceived to be similar to oneself will be liked and conversely persons who are liked will be perceived as being similar to oneself; this assumes that one likes oneself.

The proposition that individuals who like one another perceive themselves as being more similar than they really are is supported by a variety of research studies. Byrne and Blaylock (1963) and Levinger and Breedlove (1966) found that husbands and wives perceive a greater degree of attitude similarity between themselves than actually exists. Byrne and Wong (1962) asked subjects with varying degrees of prejudice against Negroes to estimate how similar the attitudes of a Negro and a white stranger were to their own. Prejudiced subjects estimated that they would agree with the Negro less often than they would agree with the white stranger. Unprejudiced subjects assumed that the Negro stranger and the white stranger were equally likely to share their attitudes. Newcomb (1961), in his study of interpersonal attraction at the University of Michigan, found that the more a man liked another resident, the more he tended to assume that the other would agree with him on important and relevant matters.

Attitude similarity does produce interpersonal attraction. Newcomb (1961) demonstrated that given the opportunity for individuals to become acquainted with each other's attitudes, attraction is predictable from measured attitudinal agreement. By determining beforehand how similar individuals were before moving into a dormitory, one could predict which would be attracted after a long acquaintance, but not who would be friends initially. It evidently took the students a certain amount of time to become familiar with the attitudes and values of everyone living in the house. Byrne (1969) and his associates have conducted several experiments which confirm the hypothesis that attitude similarity is a determinant of interpersonal attraction; the higher the proportion of similar attitudes, the greater the liking for the other person.

The more important to oneself the attitudes of the other are, the greater the attraction. Individuals who expressed similar attitudes were judged to be more intelligent, better informed, more moral, and better adjusted than the persons with dissimilar attitudes. These favorable judgments were even more positive if the other agreed with the individual on important issues than if they agreed only on unimportant ones.

Finally, on the basis of physical characteristics, intelligence and education, and social characteristics such as family background and social class, individuals seem to be more attracted to, and to marry, similar individuals (Berscheid & Walster, 1969). In addition, Dymond (1954) and Cattell and Nesselroade (1967) found that happily married spouses were more similar to each other than were unhappily married spouses.

Once a relationship between attitude similarity and attraction for another individual has been established, many social psychologists begin to wonder why people behave that way. What attracts persons to those who are similar to them? A reason may be a preference for balance such as was discussed at the beginning of this section. Byrne (1969) holds a different point of view and explains the findings of his research with a reinforcement model involving the concept of consensual validation. He states that an individual receives positive reinforcement if a stranger has similar attitudes since this indicates that his interpretation of the environment has some validity. Positive affect is elicited as a result, and through simple conditioning, becomes associated with the other individual. Thus, one will tend to be attracted to individuals with similar attitudes to the extent that the reinforcement from consensual validation elicits positive affect and becomes associated with the other. Through a series of studies he presents evidence that consensual validation is in fact reinforcing to subjects (Byrne, 1969). Berscheid and Walster (1969) argue that attitude similarity may produce attraction because attitudes can be used to predict another's future behavior and, therefore, when we know a stranger's attitudes, we know what to expect in interaction with him. When his attitudes are similar to ours, his behavior is highly predictable. Johnson and Johnson (1970), finally, argue that the relationship between attitude similarity and attraction is based largely upon the expectation that in interaction with the other he will facilitate the accomplishment of one's goals. They provide evidence that attitude similarity is highly related to expected cooperative behavior from the other.

There are then, a variety of explanations as to what accounts for the relationship between attitude similarity and attraction. There is research evidence to support all the different theories. Until some social psychologist can specify the conditions under which each possible theory holds and does not hold, there will be little advancement in the theory.

Turning now to the complementarity hypothesis that "opposites attract," there have been a variety of investigations of the hypothesis that individuals with complementary needs will be attracted to each other, primarily in the areas of marriage and friendship. Robert Winch (1952) proposed a theory of complementary needs in which he hypothesized that each individual chooses to mate with that person who is most likely to provide him or her with maximum need-gratification. He felt that need-gratification would occur between two individuals of complementary personalities in two different ways. The first type is when the needs gratified in one person are of a different kind than those gratified in the other person, such as when a domineering person interacts with a submissive person. The second type is when the needs of the two individuals are similar, but of different intensities, such as when a person high in need to dominate interacts with a person low in need to dominate. A number of studies have been conducted on the Winch theory and most of them have not supported it. One of the better studies in the area was conducted by Kerckhoff and Davis (1962) who found that early in a male-female relationship, social status variables such as socioeconomic class, religion, and so on appear to have the major influence on whether or not a couple will continue to date. After the couple has been dating for a while, consensus on values becomes an important determinant of whether or not the relationship will continue. Finally, after a long relationship, the complementarity of their needs becomes important.

A more specific statement was made of Winch's hypothesis by Schutz (1960) who theorized that individuals with a high need for control will be attracted to individuals with a high need to be controlled, while individuals with a high need for affection or with a high need to be included by others will be attracted to others with similar needs.

A hypothesis somewhat similar to the need-completion theory was investigated by Cattell and Nesselroade (1967). They proposed that a desire to possess characteristics (by sharing them with the possessed partner) which the individual felt to be necessary to his self-concept or to his or her social and general life adjustment would be a major motivation for marriage. This is called the *need-completion principle*, an example of which is a socially awkward person being attracted to a socially adroit and poised partner. The researchers did find support for their hypothesis that need-completion is a factor in interpersonal attraction. Berscheid and Walster (1969), furthermore, state that there is considerable evidence that when individuals perceive that their friends are different from themselves, the dissimilar friend is perceived to possess traits the individual lacks, but admires and wishes he possessed.

The bulk of the evidence, however, indicates that friends perceive each other as being more similar in personality than do nonfriends (Berscheid and Walster, 1969). This evidence supports the similarity theories and does not support the need-complementarity and need-completion theories. While the research demonstrates a relationship (or correlation) between similarity and friendship, it does not clarify whether friends become similar due to their association with each other or whether individuals select as friends individuals similar to themselves, or whether some other variable, such as proximity, influences the ways in which individuals form relationships and causes the relationship between similarity and attraction.

Most of the research conducted upon friendship, marriage and interpersonal attraction is correlational. The researchers measure the similarity of attitudes and the attraction between two individuals, for example, and then calculate the correlation between the two variables. Such a correlation is a simple number that tells to what extent the two things are related, that is, to what extent variations in one variable correspond to variations in the other. Without the knowledge of how one thing varies with another, psychologists would find it impossible to make predictions about human behavior. And whenever causal relationships are involved, without knowledge of covariation, psychologists would be unable to control one thing by manipulating another. As was discussed in Chapter 1, the coefficient of correlation is a summarizing number which tells a story concerning the relationship between two variables. It can vary from a value of $+1.00$ (which means perfect positive correlation) through zero (which means complete independence or no relationship whatsoever) on down to -1.00 (which means perfect negative correlation). Any coefficient of correlation that is not zero and that is also statistically significant denotes some degree of relationship between the two variables. Figure 2-5 shows a correlation plotted between two variables.

The size of the coefficient of correlation, however, is always relative to the situation under which it is obtained, and does not represent any absolute natural or cosmic fact. To speak of a relationship between similarity and attraction is in many ways absurd; one needs to specify which type of similarity measured under what circumstances in what type of people, and to specify what kind of attraction measured by what instruments or judged by what standards. In other words, the future research on attraction and similarity or complementarity should focus on the conditions under which opposites at-

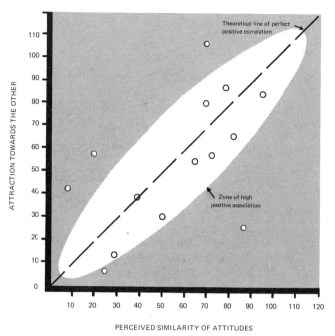

FIGURE 2-5. Correlation plot showing association of perceived similarity of attitudes and attraction toward the other individual. The coefficient of correlation is .54, significant at the .05 level. (Hypothetical data)

tract and the conditions under which similarity attracts, not upon measuring some general relationship in a certain population. Determining the conditions under which certain relationships hold is often the most useful way to advance knowledge in a theoretical area.

REDUCTION OF ANXIETY AND STRESS

The psychological principle which is most frequently used to predict interpersonal attraction is the principle of reinforcement: we like those who reward us, and we dislike those who punish us. While this statement is generally accepted, it is of limited value in trying to predict the extent to which two individuals will like each other. Many things may be rewarding or punishing to any individual at any given time, and it is difficult to predict in advance what effect a given act will have upon another. What is rewarding for one person may be punishing for another and what is rewarding for one person at one time may be punishing at another time. For this reason, researchers in interpersonal attraction have studied which behaviors and events most people, most of the time, will find rewarding.

There is considerable evidence that when individuals feel anxious, afraid, lonely, or unsure of themselves, the sheer presence of others is particularly rewarding. Schachter (1959), for example, tested the hypothesis that anxiety will lead to an increased desire to be with other individuals. He recruited college women to participate in an experiment which was represented to involve an electric shock. The description of the shock experiment was designed to make some of the women highly anxious, while leaving the remainder of the women calm. After the description was presented, he asked the subjects whether they preferred to wait for the experiment to begin with other girls or by themselves, or if they had no preference. His results support the hypothesis that highly anxious people, compared with minimally anxious individuals, will seek the company of others. Sixty-three percent of the subjects in the high-anxiety condition wanted to wait with other subjects, while only 33 percent of the subjects in the low-anxiety condition wished to wait with others (See figure 2-6). These findings have been replicated by several different investigations. Schachter (1959) presents further evidence that anxious people do not wish to be in the company of just any other person. Instead, they seem to prefer to associate with others who are in a similar situation. It seems that misery does not love just any kind of company, it loves only miserable company.

	Number Choosing			Overall intensity
	Together	Don't care	Alone	
High Anxiety	20	9	3	$+.88$
Low Anxiety	10	18	2	$+.35$
	X^2 Tog. $vs.$ Dc $+$ A $= 5.27$			$t = 2.83$
	$.02 < p < .05$			$p < .01$

FIGURE 2-6. Relationship of anxiety to the affiliative tendency. (Taken from Schachter, S. *The Psychology of Affiliation.* Stanford, Calif.: Stanford University Press, 1959.)

There is some evidence that individuals who are placed in a stressful situation show less severe physiological disturbance if other individuals are present than if they are not. Bovard (1959) developed an interesting theory that the presence of a familiar person in a stressful situation calls forth a competing response in the individual which inhibits, masks, or screens the stress stimulus so that it has a minimal effect. Several studies with animals indicate that they experience less stress to the identical stimulus when a familiar animal of the same species is present. Research on humans involving small groups suggest that such groups provide a great deal of support to its members when they are under stress. Combat studies, for example, suggest that a small group such as a bomber crew is very effective in sustaining members under severe battle stress (Mandlebaum, 1952).

Even when individuals are not under stress, social isolation for any prolonged period of time seems to be a painful experience. Schachter's (1959) examination of the autobiographical reports of religious hermits, prisoners of war, and castaways makes it clear that isolation is devastating.

Thus, anxiety, stress, and social isolation all seem to be conditions under which individuals will be attracted to others who are present or in similar circumstances.

RECIPROCATION OF LIKING

An observer from another planet would notice immediately that the desire for the esteem of others is a very strong and pervasive motivation of human beings. Advertising spends a great deal of money associating various products with interpersonal esteem from others. Countless everyday observations provide a great deal of evidence that we value highly the esteem of others and will work hard to obtain this reward. If esteem is indeed a reward, and if it is true that we tend to like those who reward us, it follows that we should like people who like us. Newcomb (1961) has demonstrated that individuals tend to believe that the people they like reciprocate their liking. Backman and Secord (1959) provide some evidence that we tend to like those who like us. Ossorio and Davis (1966) state that the tendency to like people who like us is sufficiently commonplace that the reciprocity-of-liking rule is a necessary and "nonempirical" principle of human behavior.

There are exceptions to the rule that we like those who like us. According to balance theory, for example, we should like those who like us only if we like ourselves; if we dislike ourselves, we should like those who dislike us, and dislike those who like us as their feelings are incongruent with our own. Deutsch and Solomon (1959), Dickoff (1961), and Berscheid, Walster, and Walster (in press) provide evidence that although people like those who give them positive evaluations more than they like those who give them negative evaluations, the degree to which the other's evaluation of oneself is congruent with one's own self-evaluations affects how we respond to the other. Thus it may be concluded that the other's esteem does act as a positive reinforcer and produces reciprocal liking, but it is much more effective in producing liking when it is congruent with the subject's own evaluation of himself.

COOPERATION AND COMPETITION

In real-life situations, other people are normally instrumental in helping us obtain our goals, or in hindering us from their achievement, rather than directly rewarding or punishing our behavior. There is considerable evidence that we like those who facilitate our goal accomplishment (Deutsch, 1969; Berkowitz and Daniels, 1963; Goranson and Berkowitz, 1966) and that we dislike those who frustrate us (Deutsch, 1969; Burnstein and Worchel, 1962). Thus, to be in a cooperative relationship with another produces liking, while to be in a competitive relationship with another tends to produce dislike. Even when two individuals dislike each other intensely, cooperation in achieving several mutually desired goals seems to produce liking (Sherif, 1966; Johnson and Lewicki, 1969). Thus it may be that one of the most effective ways to increase attraction among individuals is repeatedly to place them in situations where they have to cooperate to obtain their desired goals.

ACCIDENTAL CONSEQUENCES AND HARMING ANOTHER

There are two potent determinants of one's liking for another which have no relation to the other's characteristics (Berscheid and Walster, 1969). The first is the effect of chance consequences upon liking, and the second is the effect of our treatment of others upon attraction. Many things that happen to individuals are beyond their control. Yet these incidents can be potent determiners of others' attitudes toward the individual, since we often assume automatically that other people get what they deserve. Since we know that individuals often do influence the things that happen to them, the best guess in an ambiguous situation is that the person is probably at least partially responsible for his fate. People who are involved in serious accidents, for example, may be perceived as being at least partially responsible. If nothing else, such beliefs help a bystander believe that such calamities will never happen to him. Walster (1966) conducted a study in which she demonstrated that the more serious an accident was, the more the person's behavior was blamed as the cause.

Harm-doers may react in three quite different ways to harming another (Berscheid and Walster, 1969); they may justify their harmful action, they may attempt to compensate the victim for the harm he has suffered, or they may punish themselves in some way for injuring the other (this latter reaction seems to be less obvious, as it is reported only in the clinical literature). It is important to know when a harm-doer is likely to react to his harmdoing by compensating the victim or by justifying the victim's suffering. In the first case he accepts responsibility for his harm-doing, tries to make up for his unacceptable behavior, and presumably will be less inclined to do the same thing again. In the latter case he denies responsibility for his behavior, convinces himself that his behavior is acceptable, and presumably will be willing to repeat his behavior. There are several situational variables which seem to determine whether or not a harm-doer responds to his victim with justice or with justification.

The first situational variable is the adequacy of available restitution, that is, the extent to which the compensation will benefit the victim, relative to the harm done him. The more adequate a harm-doer perceives an available compensation to be, the greater is the probability that he will choose to restore equity by compensating the victim (Berscheid and Walster, 1967; Berscheid, Walster, and Barclay, in preparation). Although the victim may prefer an inadequate compensation to no compensation at all, the harm-doer seems to feel that a partial compensation is an unsatisfactory way to restore equity, as the victim is still left in a deprived state. An excessive compensation only replaces one kind of inequity with another. Berscheid and Walster (1968) demonstrated that individuals will be less likely to compensate their victims (and presumably more likely to justify the victims suffering instead) when available compensations are inadequate or excessive, than when they are adequate. If these findings are fully accepted they lead to the interesting notion that if one feels that he has been unduly harmed by another, he should portray his suffering as equal to whatever compensation is available. If he seems to suffer too much or too little, then he will encourage the harm-doer to justify his actions and not compensate the victim at all!

For the victim who is still vulnerable to the harm-doer, the harm-doer's justification of his harmful act is potentially dangerous. Not only does the harm-doer have a distorted assessment of his actions, but he may commit further acts based on his distorted perceptions (Berscheid, Boye, and Darley, 1968). For his self-protection, the victim may wish to restore equity to the relationship before the harm-doer justifies his actions and repeats them. If a suitable compensation is not available, equity can be restored through the victim's retaliation. Fear of future retaliation may deter the harm-doer from repeating his action. Berscheid, Boye, and Walster (in press) conducted an experiment which demonstrated that harm-doers who experienced retaliation from the victim did not derogate the victim, while harm-doers who did not experience retaliation did. It should be noted, however, that such a cycle of harm-doing and retaliation is easy to escalate and could end up in the destruction of both parties, not their peaceful coexistence.

Public commitment has been shown to be an important determinant of whether or not a person will be willing to admit error and to change his mind in studies of attitude change. Walster and Prestholdt (1969) extended this finding to the area of harm-doing by demonstrating that commitment is a crucial variable in determining whether a person will change his mind in the face of new information or will attempt to justify his unjust treatment and continue to treat the other unjustly.

It is probably true that one is more likely to justify the suffering of a victim he never expects to see again than the suffering of a victim with whom he anticipates future contact. Davis and Jones (1960) found that subjects who expected to see their victim after delivering a cruel evaluation to him did not derogate him, while subjects who did not anticipate any subsequent interaction did derogate the victim. Walster, Berscheid, and Barclay (1967) demonstrated that one is less likely to distort the victim's characteristics to justify the harm-doing when the distortions are likely to be challenged by future objective evidence than when they are not. Because familiarity leads to increased probability of accurate perception of the victim's characteristics, harm-doing is more likely to be justified when the victim is segregated from the harm-doer than when he is not. When black Americans are segregated from white racists, for example, it is easy for individuals who exploit Negroes to reduce whatever distress they feel by derogating the exploited. It is easy for them to maintain that Negroes deserve being exploited (e.g., "they are shiftless and lazy and don't want to work") or that they are not really suffering (e.g., "A Negro can live better on $1 than a white man can on $5").

Looking at the other side of the coin, we can ask how an individual will respond after conferring an undeserved benefit on someone. Gerard (1966) points out that Aristotle and Aquinas both believed that a benefactor comes to love the recipient of his favors. When one reviews the research in the area, the data supporting the hypothesis that doing a favor for someone produces liking for the recipient are consistent but weak. Perhaps the strongest study is one by Jecker and Landy (in press) which demonstrated that if subjects were led to help someone they disliked, they would try to justify doing the undeserved favor by increasing their esteem for the other. The reason hypothesized to account for such an effect is that when one does not like a person he has no reason to expect that the person will reciprocate a kindness, and therefore has little justification for performing a favor. In order to resolve the dissonance produced by knowing that one has performed a favor with no apparent justification, he will come to like the benefited.

Friendship

One of the most common forms of dyad is that of preferred friends. No one questions the value of friendship in human life—for many persons the bond with a friend gives meaning and worth to all other experience. Yet friendship is difficult to study scientifically, partly because it is hard to define. There are all degrees of friendship; the word may be applied to a casual acquaintance or to a deep, long-standing, confidential relationship which means more than most love affairs. Friendships are as complex and varied as the personalities of various friends.

Dozens of psychologists have explored the best-friend choices of children. Moreno (1934) has invented a technique called *sociometry* for investigating the extent to which members of a group are chosen by one another. Pupils in a class may be asked to choose a partner to share a desk, to help out on a project, or to be invited to a party. Choices differ, depending on the proposed activity, but the technique brings out some important patterns. About one child in five turns out—in a typical class—to be an *isolate*. None of his classmates choose him. Personality problems usually accompany such isolation, both as cause and as effect of the rejection. At the other extreme, most groups have a few "stars," chosen by many of their classmates. In the next chapter, sociometric analysis will be discussed further. In the present connection, our interest is mainly in *pairs*, each member of which chooses the other.

Earlier we stated that frequency of interaction is highly correlated with liking. It follows that friendships are most often formed where circumstances have facilitated interaction. Among children and adolescents, friendship dyads have been found to depend heavily upon residential propinquity, closeness in age, socioeconomic class, and interests. Best friends in the lower grades of elementary school commonly live very near one another. Choices are seldom made outside the same school class. Similarity in size and intelligence is less important than similarity of age, school grade, and special hobbies. From age 5 to 12, most best friends are of the same sex.

It would be unwise to extrapolate from these studies of children to adult friendships. Strong and genuine friendships frequently arise between men and women, contradicting a popular adolescent view that any cross-sex tie must involve romantic or sexual love. Friendships may endure over years of separation with wide variation in interests. Friendships between the young and old are not unknown.

One of the best empirical studies of friendship was made in Puerto Rico by Sanchez-Hidalgo (1951), who interviewed each member of 40 same-sex pairs of college-age friends. Responses to the question, "What does a best friend do for me?" emphasized ego-support through such activities as: "I am important to him," "Recognizes my abilities," "Seeks my advice," "Thinks my ideas important," "Praises me," and "Remembers me." Almost equal in frequency of mention were activities that protected the friend's ego: "Keeps me from loneliness," "Defends me if someone gossips or critizes," "Calms me when I'm excited or worried," "Shares my depressions," "Does not criticize me," "Does not brag," "Keeps up my courage," "Makes me feel secure." Activities of helpfulness, such as: "Does me a good turn," "Lends a hand," "Cooperates," "Assists," and so forth, came third and were more important for dyads of men than for women. Sanchez-Hidalgo characterized friendship dyads in general as *symbiotic*, meaning that each friend found some of his important life needs met by the other. One friend may obtain a sense of relaxation and peace of mind from his friend, while the other member of the pair values more the stimulation of new ideas and broader experience he finds in the relationship. The wider the range of needs met by one friend for the other, and the deeper and more essential these satisfactions, the stronger the bonds of the friendship. It is doubtful whether a one-sided contribution that meets needs for one friend but not for the other, will prove viable. In symbiosis, there is value for both partners.

A study (Watson, Riesman, 1964) of grouping and conversation at 26 parties showed that dyads differed significantly from larger social systems. Conversation was more intimate, especially between comparative strangers who frequently began their relationship by more thoughtful, self-revelatory, and appreciative expressions than were used by those already well acquainted. In dyads, *achievement* (meaning appreciation of individual effort as valuable and productive) was a more common theme than it was in larger groups; larger groups tended more toward *nihilism* (cynical derogation of conventional institutions or values). The authors present as a tentative hypothesis that the more optimistic themes of the dyad are related to the fact that each member has more power to influence what goes on in a small group of two.

There is a marked difference in self-confidence and feeling of adequacy between a person alone and a person accompanied by his friend. In a study of responses of young children to frustration occasioned by separating them from new toys they have just begun to enjoy, it was found that if the dyad were composed of two children who were close friends, they were more aggressive in their attacks upon the adult experimenter than was true of dyads composed of more casual acquaintances (Wright, 1943). At times of emergency, danger, and bereavement, when we are particularly vulnerable to the human predicament, nothing else helps so much as the quiet, sustaining presence of a friend.

Can one make a friend of another person whom he has previously disliked? In accordance with the principle of consonance, most people do not engage in this experiment. Yet it can be done. Thompson (reported by Sorokin, 1950) found that when college students deliberately tried to treat companions they had disliked as if they were friends, it usually brought an unexpectedly friendly response, making the next act of friendliness much easier than the first one. As a counterbalance to this benign approach, we may refer to another study, (also reported by Sorokin) in which relationships between a nurse and a patient improved following a flare-up—an aggressive interchange. What happened, apparently, was that the mutual dislike had been carefully concealed beneath polite formalities. The breakthrough of an honest, spontaneous personal response was welcomed, and laid the foundation for more genuine interaction and hence for better liking of each other.

Most commentators on friendship, whether amateur or professional psychologists, stress the importance of sincerity and straightforwardness. It is implicitly recognized that there is much that is false in most human relationships. We exert ourselves to obtain certain ends—striving to get the task done or to be a good employer or to please the customer. In school we want to be liked by other students and approved by the teachers. Thus we are constantly putting our best foot forward, concealing negative or hostile feelings, and wearing whatever mask seems appropriate. Some people, constantly living for the approval of others, become as superficial as the various masks they wear. One feels that there is no real identity behind the endless succession of masks. One of the virtues of good friendship is that masks can be laid aside. A person feels secure with his friend: His friend knows and accepts his real self, with all its limitations and weaknesses. Therefore he need not pretend or cover up. The assurance that the friend will understand and accept adds to his own self-acceptance and confidence. One may be even freer to be oneself in the presence of an accepting friend than one is when alone.

Rifts in friendship often occur when it has been assumed that the friend understands, but he does not; or that he accepts what it turns out he is unable to accept. It takes a long period of acquaintance, with many testings, to build a solid friendship. The intuitive feeling that someone we have recently met is a perfect friend is usually an illusion. To quote Emerson:

"Our friendships hurry to short and poor conclusions, because we have made them a texture of wine and dreams, instead of the tough fibre of the human heart. The laws of friendship are austere and eternal, of one web with the laws of nature and of morals. But we have aimed at a swift and petty benefit, to suck a sudden sweetness. We snatch at the slowest fruit in the whole garden of God, which many summers and many winters must ripen.

Sex, love, and marriage

Despite the evident human concern with the dyadic relationships of sex, love, and marriage, social psychologists have done relatively little research in these areas. Alfred Kinsey (1948) aptly refers to "man's absorbing interest in sex and his astounding ignorance of it; his desire to know and his unwillingness to face the facts."

The usual criteria for defining an instinct: (1) having a physiological, biochemical basis in the organism; (2) appearing in all human cultures; (3) being difficult to suppress; and (4) being found also in other mammals—all apply clearly to mating. Yet anthropologists report that social norms in differing cultures lead to very different sex attitudes and behaviors. (More on this in Chapter 8. Children in some societies freely play at sexual intercourse; in other cultures any evidence of sex interest by children is taboo.

Neither sex interest nor love appears suddenly and fully developed at adolescence. Both form during childhood years. We noted earlier that imprinting of certain animals during the first days or weeks of life can affect their sexual behavior at maturity. Freud's observations on the Oedipus complex in human males (and its parallel, the Electra complex in females) postulates a connection between the unconscious attachment of a child about four years old to the parent of opposite sex, and the love objects in the child's later life. Hamilton (1929) found a considerable correlation between the terms men used to describe the personality of their mothers and those they used to describe the personality of their wives. Psychoanalytic observations are often unconvincing to those who have not had the special and unusual opportunity of the analyst to study intensively the fantasies and recollections of patients during hundreds of hours and under conditions fostering frankness and intimacy. But no psychoanalytic sophistication is required to make it seem plausible that small children, when they think of growing up and living with someone of the opposite sex, should first choose the person they have already learned to live with and to love.

In our society, initiative in a male-female sexual relationship is expected from the male. Kinsey's data indicate that boys and men at every age level are sexually more active than girls and women. The social psychologist asks whether such differences are innate or the product of social norms. The evidence supports both factors. Generally, in animals (Ford, Beach, 1951) and in men, the male is more quickly aroused to sexual excitement and is more easily conditioned to respond to a variety of associated stimuli: sights, sounds, odors, portions of the anatomy (genital and other). Most "perversions" and "fetishisms" have been observed among males. Yet there are times in most dyadic sexual relationships when the female is more aroused and demanding than is the male, and, as we shall report in Chapter 8, there are cultures in which the initiative is customarily assigned to the female.

Although sex drive and love are associated, there are important differences between them (Reik, 1954). Sex is stimulated quite directly by glandular secretions; love is integral to the whole personality. Sex goes through a cycle of tension and satisfaction; love remains constant. Erotic drives may be rather indiscriminate and are stimulated by novelty; love is highly discriminating and cherishes exclusiveness and continuity. There has been some controversy among psychologists about whether sex and love motivations have the same roots. Freud saw affection as derived from erotic pleasure. Fromm (1956) argues that desire for intercourse is only one manifestation of the larger and more inclusive impulse toward human brotherhood. We have seen that in the child the two kinds of experience are usually kept separate. The child's playmates in sex exploration are not the human beings he most loves (Bühler, 1935). One of the functions of adolescent caresses, kisses, and petting is to weld together these two strands of development as they unite in a good marriage.

Both sex and love may sometimes find expression in dyads of the same sex. Adolescents segregated in boarding schools or penal institutions frequently develop homosexual attachments, mostly temporary, but often involving strong affection (Kosofsky, Ellis, 1958; Halleck, Hersko, 1962). In American culture homosexual attachments have commonly been regarded as "queer" or perverse. There are many indications today of more general acceptance. Love between two persons of the same sex can enrich life as truly as love of the opposite sex.

A social psychological model for marriage would include: (1) the unity of love and sex; (2) frequent, close interaction with increasing and almost continuous liking for each other; (3) joint responsibility, deliberately undertaken, to carry out the social role of building and nurturing a family. The first two can exist in love affairs outside marriage; the unique factor in marriage is the public and private commitment to the family project. All societies recognize this important step with some kinds of ceremony and legal and status differentials.

The motivation for sex relations and for marriage includes more than the sexual impulses. Mating behavior, whether in or outside marriage, may satisfy needs for economic security, for "proving" one's masculinity or femininity, to dominate and control the other person, to revenge oneself upon another (the jilted lover rebounds), to win acceptance in a certain circle, or to achieve status in the society. These supplementary or secondary gains often become the primary factors in a decision to marry. The stability of a marriage based on love is likely to be greater than if it rests on the secondary gains.

Abstract 1

TITLE	Mate Selection
AUTHOR	Robert F. Winch
PROBLEM	Do we marry persons similar or opposite in personality traits?
SUBJECTS	25 married couples, all undergraduates at Northwestern University; white, non-Jewish.
PROCEDURE	Interviews designed to bring out the kind of needs defined by H. A. Murray (1938). The interview included case history, early memories, developmental stages, and was supplemented by Thematic Apperception Test (stories made up about ambiguous pictures). Each person was rated on the basis of all available information.
SOME FINDINGS	One relationship accounted for most of the positive results: Whenever one spouse was high in dominance the other was more deferential and self-effacing.

Case studies illustrate four types of complementariness: mother-son; "Ibsenian" (in which the husband dominates but provides protection nurturance to a dependent wife); master-servant girl in which the husband dominates and the wife serves his needs; and the "Thurberian" in which the wife is dominant but expects to be cared for; the man is submissive but nurturant.

SOURCE: New York: Harper and Brothers, 1958.

Selection

Contemporary American culture places great stress on finding the one right partner. Other cultures in which marriages are arranged by parents or elders recognize that a "suitable" mate is desirable, but foster no illusion of the "one and only."

Historically, we know that the glorification of romantic love is characteristic of only a few cultures and of our own only since the twelfth century. In ancient Greece and Rome, amorous attachment was not the foundation for marriage; men experienced it more often with courtesans or with attractive boys. The anthropologist Linton (1936) implies that even in modern man, the passionate spouse is usually consciously or unconsciously acting a prescribed role and trying to feel something which may not be genuinely moving. The hero of the modern American movie is always a romantic lover just as the hero of the old Arab epic is commonly an epileptic. A cynic might suspect that in any ordinary population the percentage of people capable of romantic love of the Hollywood type is about as large as that of persons able to throw genuine epileptic fits. However, given a little social encouragement, either situation can be adequately simulated without the performer's admitting even to himself that the performance is not genuine.

An essayist, under the title: *The Romantic Route to Divorce* (de-Rougemont, 1948) criticizes the prevailing emphasis on trying to find the one, ordained-by-Heaven ideal lover:

> The type of love on which a great majority of Western marriages is founded is a fever, generally light and considered infinitely interesting to contract. . . .
>
> . . . We are in the act of trying out—and failing miserably at it—one of the most pathological experiments that a civilized society has ever imagined, namely, the basing of marriage, which is lasting, upon romance, which is a passing fancy. . . .

Successful marriages are carefully built, not found by happy chance. Love is a vital ingredient and certain similarities, as shown in the study summarized in Abstract 2, are likely to be helpful. While some of the data are more sociological than psychological, they often point to psychological correlates. For example "number of same-sex friends before marriage" can be regarded as an index to general amiability and that capacity for brotherly love which Fromm finds fundamental. Age at time of marriage is a census item, but it has implications for the amount of previous experience and the readiness to be "tied down" to child-care.

The marriages studied by Burgess and Cottrell were more likely to be happy if the couple were well educated, mature (the younger at marriage the greater the probability of distress), acquainted for years, warmly attached to the family of origin and to other friends. Although a big point is often made of difficulties caused by difference in age, education, or formal religious affiliation, these differences had no effect upon chances for happiness among the 526 couples in the study. Other investigators have found confirmation of some of these conclusions. A Gallup poll showed 83 percent

---

Abstract 2

TITLE   Predicting Success Or Failure in Marriage

AUTHORS   E. W. Burgess and L. S. Cottrell, Jr.

PROBLEM   What factors are related to successful marriage?

SUBJECTS   526 couples (of 7,000 queried), in Illinois, all married from one to 6 years. Over 90 percent had finished high school; 60 percent had had some college. Husbands averaged 27 years of age; wives, twenty-three.

PROCEDURES   Questionnaire responses related to self-rating on happiness, and a 26 item index of marital adjustment. Reliability, .88.

SOME FINDINGS   1. Most were happy in their marriage (21 percent "happy," 43 percent "very happy."

2. Happier couples were better educated; had known one another five years or more; were over 28 at time of marriage; came from homes with good cultural background; felt closely attached to their parents; had numerous friends of their sex before marriage.

3. Unhappy couples were more apt to live in cities than in the country; had more financial difficulties; and entered marriages despite parental disapproval.

4. Differences in age, education, and religion did not prevent normal happiness.

SOURCE: New York: Prentice-Hall, 1939.

---

of marriages between college graduates rated as successful, but only 71 percent for those whose education stopped at high school graduation, and 62 percent for the couples who never went to high school. A sociologist reported that if either partner were under 20, chances for an unhappy marriage were five times as great as if both were 25 or older (Hart, 1939). A psychiatrist reported that the happiness of a marriage showed a fair measure of correlation ($r = .40$) with happiness of the parents' marriage (Hamilton, 1929). Among 200 successful adults, the best indication of probable marital happiness was that each thought his spouse had a personality like the parent of opposite sex whom the individual had loved in childhood. He found, although cases were few, that if the wife were a little older than her husband, the chances of happiness were improved. Among Terman's (1938) 792 couples, difference in age or schooling or religious training was not a variable related to happiness. Happiness seemed to relate more to the harmony of the parents' marriage and good relations in the family of origin. Each of these is a statistical comparison; it deals with proportions and probabilities. For the couple deciding on marriage, their relationship is unique. Despite any of the factors which seem statistically to be a handicap, the particular marriage may work out very well.

Two psychological facts about sex seem difficult to assimilate within our standard marriage pattern. One is that teen-age boys have a powerful sex drive years before they are ready to assume the mature responsibilities of marriage. Masturbation, prostitution, and premarital liaisons afford some outlets but each raises other problems. A second is that most men and some women are polyerotic and, after a period of marital fidelity, are likely to be attracted by a novel partner. Kinsey reports that about half of all married men in America have had extramarital adventures. This indulgence is likely if the concept of marriage overemphasizes sexual attraction and underemphasizes responsible commitment and the cultivation of a unique dyad with abundant sources of satisfaction in shared living.

In one of the most carefully done studies of selection of romantic partners, Walster and her associates (1966) conducted a field study on romantic liking. They recruited 752 college freshmen to attend a dance in which partners were to be matched by computer. When the freshmen arrived to purchase their tickets, the physical attractiveness was secretly rated by a group of college sophomores. Considerable information was obtained on each subject from a series of questionnaires they filled out and from the University's records. Two days after the freshmen completed the questionnaires, they were randomly assigned to a date. At the dance, during the intermission, the students assessments of their dates were obtained. How often the couples actually dated was determined six months after the dance.

In trying to determine what the determinants of romantic liking are in our society the researchers investigated the compatibility of the randomly matched individuals on personality, physical and social characteristics. The evidence they obtained indicates that only physical attractiveness affected the number of times the freshmen dated each other. The correlation between a date's estimation of the partner's physical attractiveness and the expression of liking for the partner ranged from .69 to .78. It is clear that physical attractiveness was by far the most important determinant of how much a date would be liked by his or her partner. Physical attractiveness was found to be just as important for the men as for the women in influencing their date's liking for them.

Mutuality

Counselors report that one of the factors which commonly wreck a marriage is that the couple have virtually ceased to communicate. They sit opposite one another at meals, beside one another in the car; they may sleep contentedly together, but they have almost ceased to communicate. Each carries on his own monologue, and neither quite hears the other. They may exchange enough signals to keep their engagement calendar, get the shopping done and the bills paid, but they do not experience the other as a living, aspiring person. A study of complaints of married persons about their mate showed that, for both sexes alike, the three most frequent ones were something like:

1. Is careless, thoughtless
2. Selfish. Thinks only of self
3. Takes me for granted

Two who are deeply in love transcend self, loving the other as themselves. What hurts the beloved or brings joy to the beloved, affects the lover as if it were really he that is hurt or gladdened. In Martin Buber's words, "They experience (the beloved's) particular life in simple presence—not as a thing seen and touched, but from the innervations of his movements, from the 'inner' to his 'outer'." In contrast, Buber describes the varied "Eros of monologue" in which a partner is aware mainly of his own delightful sensations:

There a lover stamps around and is in love only with his passion. There one is wearing his differentiated feelings like medal-ribbons. There one is enjoying the adventures of his own fascinating effect. There one is gazing enraptured at the spectacle of his own supposed surrender. There one is collecting excitement. There one is displaying his "power." There one is preening himself with borrowed vitality. There one is delighting to exist simultaneously as himself and as an idol very unlike himself. . . . There one is experimenting. And so on and on—all the manifold monologists with their mirrors. (1947)

In contrast to this self-absorption is what Cyril Connolly (1945) has aptly called "The Eternal Duologue" in which a couple, genuinely married for many years, continue to share so much of their experience together that mere mention of a name, a time or a place, is sufficient to arouse a whole bubbling spring of the memories in which both always actively participate. Each becomes so accustomed to interaction with the other, in relation to countless daily details, that the death of either leaves the other as handicapped in mental life as he would be in locomotion if he lost one leg.

Power and influence in a dyad

Two individuals interacting adjust in many ways to each other. They speed up or slow down their rate of walking to keep pace together. One or both may put aside his own interests to talk about something of mutual interest. People adjust their expressions of attitudes to the person to whom they are talking, and sometimes the attitude itself is modified. Such can be labeled convergence of behavior or mutual influence. Two individuals in interaction are constantly influencing and being influenced by each other. They exercise social power over each other through their personal characteristics, the nature of their relationship, and the interdependencies between them.

To discuss the nature of power and influence in interpersonal relationships it is necessary to review why individuals enter relationships with others. In most dyads the two individuals are motivated to accomplish certain goals (for example, friendship, financial profit, learning) or to receive certain rewards (for example, social approval, prestige, money) from the relationship. A girl and a boy who are dating often are both goal oriented towards obtaining a depth of relationship which fulfills their needs to love and to be loved. The two individuals involved in a dyadic relationship can have the same goal, similar goals, mutually exclusive goals, or incompatible goals. Interaction between persons takes place in order to accomplish goals, and mutual power exists to the extent to which one can affect the goal accomplishment of the other.

In a dyadic relationship the two individuals are usually dependent upon each other for a variety of rewards and for information concerning how to achieve these rewards. Many of the important outcomes toward which people strive rest in the hands of other people; because this is so, people try to behave in ways that will influence others to reward them (provide these outcomes or information) rather than punish them (deny these outcomes or information). Reciprocally, the other will also be trying to achieve rewards rather than punishments. It is important to recognize that power is the inverse of dependence, for the crucial implication is that the person who has other relationships to which he can turn for support or assistance, is least susceptible to influence in the present one. Most contemporary theories of power recognize, either implicitly or explicitly, that the power of person A over person B requires the dependence of B upon A for his need satisfaction and upon the alternatives for need satisfaction open to B. Emerson (1962), for example, states that the dependency of B upon A is (1) directly proportional to B's motivational investment in goals mediated by A and (2) inversely proportional to the availability of those goals to B outside the A-B relationship. Thus the child's dependence upon his mother for social approval is directly proportional to his motivation to obtain social approval from his mother, and inversely proportional to his ability to obtain social approval from others, such as his friends, outside the relationship. The greater the desire to obtain social approval specifically from his mother and the smaller the number of others from whom he can obtain social approval, the greater his dependence upon the social approval of his mother. Secord and Backman (1964) in a slightly different formulation state that there are three variables which determine the power one individual has over another: resources, dependencies and alternatives.* A resource is a property of an individual such as a possession or an aspect of his behavior which enables him to

---

* In a relationship each person can achieve certain consequences, such as rewards (social approval) or punishments (social rejection), at certain costs (such as conforming to the other's expectations).

affect the rewards and costs experienced by another person. The value of such a resource is determined by the dependency of the other person on the individual for the resource. The degree to which B depends upon A for the resource is determined by the availability of alternate sources of rewards and means for reducing costs; in other words, upon the availability of the resource in other relationships.

There are two major ways in which one person may exert power over another in a dyadic relationship. The first is managing the rewards or punishments a person may receive in the relationship, and the second is controlling information which would facilitate the accomplishment of the other's goals.

OUTCOME CONTROL

Thibaut and Kelley (1959) assume that when two people interact, each action has certain costs (expenditure of energy, feelings of anxiety or guilt, risk of displeasing a third party) and certain consequences (rewards or punishments) received from the other. Thus when a young man proposes marriage to a girl, the action has certain costs such as anxiety concerning her answer or anger over a nonapproving mother. The action results in an outcome which is either rewarding (she accepts) or punishing (she rejects). The total "goodness" of outcome for the person is the sum of the costs incurred for taking the action and the rewards and punishments received from the other. It is usually assumed that an individual will attempt to maximize his goodness of outcome by trying to obtain the greatest rewarding behavior possible from the other, while minimizing his own costs.

A person "A" can exert outcome control over a person "B" when A's responses to B at least partly determine the goodness of outcome B can obtain. *Outcome control*, in other words, is the power to affect the rewards or punishments another may receive as a consequence of how he behaves in a situation.

Thibaut and Kelley (1959) make the assumption that the reward-punishment value of an outcome must always be calculated with reference to the actor's expectations. That is, whether A's response to B's action is rewarding or punishing to B depends upon what B expects A to do. If a young man proposing marriage to his girl expects the girl to laugh in his face, a polite but sincere refusal may be rewarding; if the boy expects the girl to faint with joy, a qualified yes may be punishing. In analyzing whether a response will be rewarding or punishing to another, Thibaut and Kelley propose two concepts dealing with expectations: comparison level and comparison level for alternatives. A person's *comparison level* is the average value of all the outcomes known to the person, each outcome weighted by its salience. It is defined as the level of reward, or positive outcome, that a person expects based on his experience in previous relationships and interactions. Outcomes more positive than the comparison level are gratifying; those below comparison level are disappointing or frustrating. If, then, B's previous interactions with A have led to highly gratifying consequences, or if B's previous interactions with individuals similar to A have led to highly gratifying consequences, B's comparison level for evaluating A's present behavior is high. If B's previous experience with A and similar people has not been very gratifying, B will not expect A's present behavior to be very gratifying. How B responds to A's behavior depends upon how A's behavior compares to B's comparison level.

The person's *comparison level for alternatives* is the best currently available alternative to the present relationship. It can be defined as the level of reward, or positive outcomes, that a person could realize in the best currently available alternative relationship. If a person's outcomes in a relationship fall below his comparison level for alternative relationships, he will tend to leave the current relationship in favor of the more attractive alternative. Thus, if a boy who has been refused in his proposal of marriage knows that another girl he likes as well will accept, he will leave the first relationship in favor of the second.

The level of outcomes received relative to one's comparison level defines the actor's degree of attraction to the relationship, whereas the level of outcomes received relative to one's comparison level for alternatives defines his dependence upon the relationship.

INFORMATION CONTROL

Action in a situation proceeds from some form of decision among alternatives, and in order to make a decision, the person uses whatever information he has about the consequences of the various alternatives, their costs to him, his ability to carry out the required behaviors, and so on. An individual needs all the relevant information he can get in order to deal competently with his environment. The notion of information dependence implies an explicit desire for facts that will give the environment more meaning and greater structure. Information is sought primarily for its potential for improving the person's outcomes. *Information dependence* can be defined, therefore, as the situation in which one person relies upon another for information about the nature of the environment, its meaning, and the possibilities of action within it (Jones and Gerard, 1967).

While the theory of the relationship between power and dependence is the most useful currently available in social psychology, there are many types of influence which are more subtle than such a theory would suggest. In the next two sections two further types of interpersonal influence are discussed, suggestion and hypnosis.

Suggestion

In a dyad, each member responds to the behavior of the other. He does things he would not do otherwise, or in ways he would not otherwise do them. Suggestion is continuous. A satiated hen, if placed with a hungry hen busily pecking at grain, starts eating again (Katz, 1937). A bored child who sees his partner quit work and start playing is likely to follow suit (Grosser, Polansky, Lippitt, 1951). A man with eyes closed, informed that he is leaning more and more forward, usually does so, although in some cases he reacts against the suggestion by leaning backward (Hull, 1933). Told that his outstretched arm is getting lighter and rising, a blindfolded subject usually lifts the arm slightly; in a small minority of cases he responds by a counteraction and lowers it (Aveling, Hargreaves, 1921). This pattern of general conformity, with a minority in protest reaction, will be confronted again on a larger scale when we study responses to advertising and other public propaganda. The term "suggestion" can denote all degrees of influence, from the slightest to full surrender to direction by another. It is common for individuals to underestimate the extent to which they are influenced by their associates. We cherish the illusion that our attitudes are self-generated. There is probably a sound psychological basis for the concern which most parents feel when their child begins to associate closely with a friend of whom they do not approve. Each child will surely have some influence on the values, standards, and behavior of his friend. The stronger, more confident, more settled, more prestigious partner will probably be imitated more extensively.

Hypnosis

The influence of one personality over another is most marked in the fascinating phenomenon of hypnosis. Aided by special conditions, such as bodily relaxation of the subject and concentrated attention, one person may achieve an extraordinary degree of influence over another. The submissive member of the hypnotic dyad may, in some cases, be led to believe himself asleep or awake, happy or depressed, fed or hungry (hunger contractions in the stomach have sometimes been observed to stop at the suggestion, under hypnosis, that a meal has been eaten); in pain or free from pain (hypnotic anesthesia sometimes works), or induced to act the part of a young child, an old man, or even a dog or cat. The influence of suggestion made during trance may persist after the hypnotized subject has returned to an apparently normal condition of self-direction. He may carry out a silly instruction hours later, and offer some rationalization when asked to account for his behavior (Hull, 1933). Erickson (1941) reports one case of a suggestion offered under hypnosis and carried out five years later. In another case (Erickson, 1943) a person who had acquired a strong aversion to orange flavors (as a result of taking castor oil in orange juice) and who had been unable to free himself from his complex, relived the experience under hypnosis and emerged free once again to enjoy orange juice.

Can a hypnotized person be made to commit crimes revolting to his conscience? Usually there are limits, even in the deepest hypnosis, beyond which the subject refuses to follow the suggestion of his hypnotist. Evidence of conflict and disturbance appears instead of compliance and the trance may terminate. On the other hand, subjects in hypnosis have been induced to regard a rattlesnake as a coiled hose, or to throw acid (Rowland, 1939), and in an exceptional case have been known to do something repugnant to their waking self. Watkins (1947) reported a soldier who attacked his superior officer with a knife, acting under the hypnotic delusion that the victim was a Japanese soldier.

Dyads of early life

Babies find security in the sensations of contact with the warm, soft, smooth skin of the mother. Harlow (1958) has studied the reactions of baby chimpanzees to two types of surrogate mother. One, of cold hard wire, held the bottle and so was associated with all the satisfactions of food. The other, of smooth cloth-covered foam rubber, provided a resilient surface to which the baby chimp could and did cling. When threatened and anxious, the little animal would consistently retreat to the safety and comfort of the cloth mother. The wire mother was not found reassuring, despite her provision of food. If the chimpanzee could not get to the soft pneumatic surface of the cloth mother, he gave easily recognized signs of deprivation and distress. Disturbance in the maternal-infant pattern of these apes was reflected in later behavior. Their socialization was defective, as compared with animals brought up under normal conditions, and their sexual adjustment was impaired (Seay *et al.*, 1964). Dr. Escalona (see Abstract 3) reports a relationship between a mother's feeling about her baby and the baby's behavior in eating. A human mother holding a baby, provides surface contact and also other forms of reassurance in the way she holds it. While the mother holds her baby, a social interaction can be observed. If the mother is too timid or rejecting, the baby often senses the awkwardness and rigidity and responds by crying. This makes the mother more frightened, tense or hostile and creates a vicious circle. A warm, loving, tender, accepting mother as she talks to and holds her baby creates a sense of security which operates in a "virtuous circle" to make both happier.

Evidence on the interaction between mother and infant has been reported by a psychologist in a penal institution for women. The study is summarized in Abstract 3 in a form which we shall follow throughout the text as we describe other examples of psychological research. Dr. Escalona brings out a relationship between a mother's feelings about her baby's behavior in eating.

Margaret Mead (1946) has reported an interesting observation of a baby in Bali who had usually been quite happy in the arms of an adolescent girl responsible for its care, but who on this day seemed to cry from fear. In the arms of another nurse the infant seemed contented again. The significant fact is that the first girl had just quarreled with her guardian and been expelled from the Temple Society of unmarried girls. Apparently the tension of the nurse was communicated kinesthetically, or at least, without depending on words.

An important factor in the mother-child dyad is the set of unconscious expectations which the mother holds for the child. These determine many of her reactions of pleasure or annoyance with the baby's behavior. Richter, a German psychiatrist (1963), has proposed, on the basis of longitudinal study of many disturbed children, that the parental fantasies, wishes, anxieties, and expectancies furnish the background for neurotic behavior in the offspring. He views children as caught in a kind of trap or maze or spider-web of these implicit demands which are not easy to understand. Explicit parental de-

---

Abstract 3

TITLE	Feeding Disturbances in Very Young Children
AUTHOR	Sibylle K. Escalona
PROBLEM	Why are some babies feeding problems although no physiological cause can be found? Is it related to the behavior of the adult taking care of the baby?
SUBJECTS AND PROCEDURE	At a reformatory for women some 50-60 babies under two years of age were observed.
SOME FINDINGS	1. During 20 months of observations, there were ten instances where infants refused the breast although no physical cause could be found. Eight of the ten mothers were exceptionally high strung, nervous, and irritable.
	2. In 15 instances babies rejected either orange juice or tomato juice; the baby's preference, in each case, agreed with the preferences of the student feeding that child.

SOURCE: *Amer. J. Orthopsychiat.*, 1945, XV, 76-80.

---

mands, on the other hand, can be coped with by the child. His emotional disturbance, therefore, is more apt to be related to pressures which are not so obvious and rational. Richter supports his thesis with numerous case histories focusing on the continuous "dialogue" between unconscious needs of the parent and the responses of the child.

We have been speaking of the child's response to the mother-figure, but it should be remembered that interaction is continuous and moves in both directions. When the Bali baby fussed, the adolescent girl doubtless grew more tense and this response increased the infant's discomfort. As a famous psychiatrist has expressed it (Sullivan, 1947):

It is biological for the infant when nursing to show certain expressive movements which are called the satisfaction response, and it is probably biological for
the parent concerned to see these things. Due to the empathic linkage, this, the
reaction of the parent to the satisfaction-response of the infant, communicates good
feeling to the infant and thus he learns that this response has power.

The importance of this first dyad for love experiences throughout life is
underlined by some striking observations of animals. Lorenz (1952) reports
that a Muscovy duck egg was hatched by a Greylag goose. For six weeks the
baby drake lived with the goose mother; then was reared with other little
ducklings by a mother duck. Ten months later, at sexual maturation, the
young drake pursued only Greylag geese. Lorenz calls this early conditioning "imprinting." Another report tells of doves reared by human care in isolation from other doves; at maturity their ideal of a mate was the hand of their
keeper.

Clinical studies of humans have not shown such definite "imprinting," but
agree on the importance of the early mother-child relationship as a foundation for personality. "The first demonstration of social trust in the baby is the
ease of his feeding, the depth of his sleep, the relaxation of his bowels,"
writes Erikson (1950). Whether a child enters later life experiences with a
basic trust and confidence which makes it easy to learn cooperation, or with
a basic mistrust and expectation of trouble, depends on the quality of this
earliest dyadic interaction.

Further evidence of the importance of a secure and satisfying social relationship to the growth of the infant is found in studies of maternal deprivation. Physical care is not all that babies need. At the turn of the century, the
mortality rate among foundlings brought to New York City's Municipal Infant's Hospital on Randall's Island was over 90 percent; similar data were
reported from other cities. The basic difficulty was not lack of food or sanita-
tion but lack of what hospitals have since come to call "TLC" (tender, loving
care). Spitz (1945) studied babies in an institution that gave adequate physical care but, for lack of help, left babies all day (except for feedings) to lie
in cubicles which screened them from all surrounding activity, with nothing
to do but look at the ceiling. Each nurse cared for eight children. Mortality
was much higher than in control studies; physical, intellectual, and emotional development, although normal at the beginning, became increasingly
retarded. Among 26 two-year-olds, at which age most children can walk and
say words, only two were able to speak a few words and the same two were
the only ones who walked.

During the latter half of the first year of life, babies in a good hospital
were observed by Spitz (1946) to suffer from a certain emotional disorder.
They wept, became irritable, lost interest in food, and in extreme cases, deteriorated in mind and body. Such a "disease" has been named "marasmus."
One remedy restored each of them to health and happiness: return to care

by their own mother. This specific social interaction experience had become so important for them that deprivation seemed to mean loss of interest in living.

The pioneer observations by Spitz led to a spate of studies, some in agreement with him and others finding no such effects. Bowlby (1951, 1961) has concluded, after reviewing the literature on maternal deprivation and separation anxiety, that mental health is gravely injured by disruption of the infant's normal interaction with the mother. A summary by the World Health Organization (1962) is in full agreement. Stone (1954), in another critical review, urges more careful delineation of what specific kinds of stimulation are given or missing, with what specific consequences. Dennis (1960) in some studies of institutionalized children in other countries, agrees. A report from Australia (Lyle, 1964) shows that adverse experiences of children with their mothers prior to institutionalization continued to depress verbal intelligence. Even institution children who had relatively adequate mothers prior to entry were retarded as compared with similar children who lived at home. Maternal deprivation has been found (Worling, 1966) to hamper later development of deep interpersonal relationships, to retard intellectual growth and to interfere with control of present impulses in the interest of long-range goals. If the deprivation begins early in the first year of life and continues for as long as three years, the damage appears irremediable.

Observations on children brought up in institutions like hospitals and orphanages, also show retardation after the first few months (Fischer, 1953; Bowlby, Cantab, 1953). Schaffer (1958) studied 76 infants hospitalized during the first year of life. Before seven months, they developed a blank, bewildered facial expression like that described by Spitz; if older, they showed excessive dependence on the mother, manifested by clinging, crying, and aversion to strangers. Rheingold (1956, 1959) demonstrated rather clearly that eight hours a day of "mothering" did improve personality development in institutional babies as compared with controls in the same environment. "Multiple mothering" by several adults was as good as the single mother, except that speech was developed sooner and better in relation to one mother figure.

Provence and Lipton (1962) followed 75 infants in an institution and compared their experiences and development with those of a control group living at home. Institutional babies became cumulatively more and more deficient in imaginative play, coordinated movement, pleasure and zest in activity. Baldwin (1956) summarizes the general conclusion: "By now, we can be reasonably sure that something about institutionalization has a deleterious effect upon personality development" (p. 263).

Stendler (1952) hypothesizes that there are two periods in early childhood in which relations to the mother are of critical importance: one, around 8 months of age, vital for good ego-development and a later one, around 30 months of age, which greatly affects the development of conscience and character (super-ego). The most serious effects of deprivation of the normal dyadic relationship of mother and infant have usually been reported when babies were between the ages of six months and two years. Earlier, a baby can accept various kinds of substitute mothering, but after a strong attachment has been formed to a particular person—her face, voice, and ways of handling—replacements seem unacceptable. Later, children become less dependent on *the one* mother figure. If deprived at home, they can seek a substitute elsewhere. Sears (1963) has found that children of nursery school age, if frustrated in their dependent demands at home, will show increased dependence on the teacher.

Some studies of animals indicate that impaired relations with others of all ages may be as significant as depriving them of mothers. Seay (1964) working with Harlow, found that two rhesus monkeys who were separated at birth from their mothers, but who had normal peer interaction, became adequate mothers; seven others deprived of both peer and mother relationships became grossly inadequate mothers.

In the next chapter we shall be concerned further with the effects of social isolation vs. normal participation.

SELF AND OTHERS

The first dyad is especially important for the life of the child because out of it emerges the child's primary feelings about himself and others. In the early days of infancy the baby has not yet discovered himself. He experiences the pleasant or the unpleasant, but there are no characters in this drama—things just occur. He has no clear notion of his mother or of himself. "Self" and "other" are combined in an undifferentiated blur. The first sorting out comes with awareness of activities the baby can control. He can change the view by moving his eyes, or he can move a hand or foot. This feels different from changes of experience he does not control. Touching his own skin gives a (double) sensation unlike touching mother's breast. He can't by himself make that nice mother-face appear. Gradually, then, he finds that part of his little world belongs to himself.

He separates "self" from "other"—usually mother. Yet each of the two has come from the same matrix of experience, previously recognized as satisfying or unsatisfying. If experiences prior to self-awareness were on the whole "good," so are both self and other when distinguished. Each part carries the tone of the former vague unity. If the earlier experience was frustrating and annoying, this, too, carries over to feelings about mother and about self. Consequently, acceptance of others goes with acceptance of self, and self-rejection accompanies hostility or disparaging attitudes toward others.

James M. Baldwin (1897), one of America's first social psychologists, saw and expressed clearly the close interdependence of "self" and "other." "See . . . how inextricably interwoven the ego and the alter really are! The development of the child's personality could not go on at all without the constant modification of his sense of himself by suggestions from others. So he himself, at every stage, is really in part someone else, even in his own thought of himself."

It was Charles H. Cooley (1902), a sociologist contemporary with Baldwin, who developed an idea from William James and formulated the famous theory of the "looking-glass self." Our feeling about ourselves is much influenced by what we imagine certain other people to see in us. "A self-idea of this sort (the looking-glass self) seems to have three principal elements: the imagination of our appearance to the other person; the imagination of his judgment of that appearance; and some sort of self-feeling, such as pride or mortification. The comparison with a looking-glass hardly suggests the second element, the imagined judgment, which is quite essential. . . . The character and weight of that other, in whose mind we see ourselves, makes all the difference with our feeling. . . . A man will boast to one person of an action—say some sharp transaction in trade—which he would be ashamed to own to another."

A careful statistical analysis of all statements made by ten patients in psychotherapy indicating their feeling about themselves and all statements indicating feeling about other persons, showed that as treatment succeeded, there was a reliable increase in self-acceptance and self-respect and also, along with this, an increase in acceptance of, and respect for, others (Sheerer, 1949). We cannot identify which is cause and which is effect, because the two are so intimately related. Whatever makes it easier for a person to accept certain limitations in himself, and unnecessary for him to be defensive about these characteristics, at the same time reduces his hostility toward other persons with similar characteristics. Or the sequence can be equally well followed in the other direction. Whatever reduces the sense of threat which an individual experiences in his interaction with other persons at the same time relaxes his need to condemn himself. As Rogers (1951) puts it: "When there is no need to defend, there is no need to attack." More positively, we love our neighbors *as* we love ourselves.

TRANSFERENCE—PARATAXIS

The parent-child dyad not only molds a general attitude of acceptance or rejection toward others, but also leaves the child with a predisposition to respond in certain specific ways to people whom he perceives as resembling one or the other parent. This is the phenomenon which Freud called *trans-*

ference. A boy who has usually felt that his father was remote, cold, and dominating is likely to expect the same kind of behavior from other men who have authority over him, for example his professor, his commanding officer, or his boss. The girl who, when four, easily "twists her father around her little finger" is likely at the age of 24 to prefer a man for a boss; she feels she knows how to get him to do what she wants.

Case 1, that of Albert, illustrates a common form of transference.

Case 1: Albert—The Silver Cord

Albert, a stocky man of 37, with quick intelligence and bright brown eyes, sought a woman psychoanalyst. His second marriage was on the rocks. His first marriage, to a woman ten years his senior, ended because Albert quickly lost interest in sex relations with her, but wanted to play around with several girl friends as he had done before marriage. The wife objected and, after Albert had tried several times in vain to reform, she got a divorce. Albert was lonesome, hated having to get his own meals, to care for his own laundry, and come home at night to an empty apartment. When he remarried after some months, he did not choose one of the younger girls he had been dating, but again turned to a woman more than five years his senior. Albert gave up his business, which was not going well, and went back to graduate study. His wife worked to support them. When she was ill, or indisposed by pregnancy, Albert found himself vaguely angry, resentful, and even hating the sight of her. When children came, Albert's wife gave up her job but bought a boarding house and still provided the family support. Albert dabbled vocationally in this and that, but couldn't settle into the husband role of being family provider. His wife was getting "fed up" with his "irresponsibility" and he was getting angry at his wife's "nagging." Analysis opened Albert's eyes to the fact—astonishing to him, although not so surprising to his friends—that his feeling for both wives had been more like that which, as a boy, he had felt toward his mother. He wanted to be cared for, and yet free to live his own life. He was not really seeing the actual qualities and needs of the woman he married; he was mentally fitting over them his mother's house dress. He saw them as bringing him reliable loving care. His was a "transference" neurosis.

Freud discovered the transference when he observed that patients during treatment were reenacting with him their earlier dyadic relationships. Some were acting as though he were a loving mother; others as though he were a stern and authoritarian father, although he had actually done nothing to justify either view. Gradually it became apparent that these colored expectations were not limited to the doctor-patient dyad but were active all through life. Harry Stack Sullivan, an American psychiatrist, suggested that a better name for the phenomenon would be *parataxis,* denoting a tendency to see another form or order or meaning alongside (or inside) that which is objectively present to the senses.

Each member of a dyad, on first meeting the other, gets some impression. This first reaction is largely parataxic. It grows out of previous experience with persons who have seemed in some way like the new acquaintance. Some people are inclined to take this first impression of others too seriously. They think of it as "intuition" and imagine that they have the gift of almost magical insight into the character of one they have just met for the first time. This is an untrustworthy impression. Any reader can verify this for himself by writing down and filing away the first impression of several persons when he first meets them; then comparing this with his feeling about them after months of friendship or working together. He must be careful, however, not to let his first impression prejudice his later contacts. If we have a hunch that someone is untrustworthy, we are likely to act toward him in a way which makes him suspicious of us and far from frank. If, on the other hand, we start with a feeling that the other is a warm, friendly person, and act in accord with this impression, he is very likely to respond to us with warmth. Hence we tend to make our first impressions come true. Wisdom in human relations counsels that we discount our first impressions and let our estimate of another person emerge slowly from his actual behavior in many situations over a period of time. Even "love at first sight," as we shall note later, is not to be trusted.

An unusually good opportunity to study parataxis is provided by groups meeting for psychotherapy. Each is encouraged to express frankly his reactions to the other members. At a first meeting of several strangers, even before anyone has spoken, each member has an impression of the way he is likely to feel about each of the others. Sometimes this impression is very clear and sharp. Usually it can be connected with some previous interpersonal relationship charged with feeling. One man in the group, for example, may feel that another, older man is going to antagonize him by being dictatorial, as the subject's father was (or seemed). He may feel also that he is going to like a certain girl whose brown eyes recall to him an adolescent sweetheart. Toward another man about his own age he may feel a budding envy and rivalry, recalling competition with his brother. A woman in the group he dislikes at once; she talks too fast, very much as his grandmother used to. Often, the same group member is seen at first by one neighbor as kind and indulgent, by another as stern and forbidding, and by a third as secretly seductive and lustful.

The danger of trusting first, intuitive impressions is well illustrated in a true story reported by a young professor. He had been invited to sit in as a member of the committee on the final oral examination of a candidate for the doctoral degree. He was new to the university faculty and had not met the candidate. As soon as the professor entered the room he experienced a sudden wave of distrust of the candidate, who was seated at the end of the table. He felt he would have no confidence in what the man would say. Fortunately, the professor had been through enough psychoanalysis to have learned to recognize and to mistrust such quick "intuition." Persistent effort to recall association enabled him to recognize that the candidate had disappointed him, years before, in an experience he had forgotten. A more naive man might have taken his feeling as evidence of keen insight into character—an ability to judge others on sight. That naive expectation might easily have seemed "confirmed" because the tone and nature of the examiner's questions could easily have brought out some shortcoming in the candidate.

A PRODUCT OF DYADIC RELATIONS

Interpersonal competence

Traditionally, all human motivation has been explained as resulting from primary drives such as hunger, thirst, and sex. White (1959), however, makes a strong case for the fact that there seems to be a great deal of human behavior directed toward producing effects upon the environment without immediate service to any aroused organic need. Such behaviors as exploring novel objects and places, grasping, crawling and walking, attending and perceiving, speaking and thinking, manipulating the surroundings, and altering the environment have been documented in research studies on animals and humans, but cannot be successfully conceptualized in terms of primary drives. White proposes that all these behaviors have a common biological significance: they are all part of the process whereby the animal or child learns to interact effectively with the environment.

As man is primarily a social animal, much of his environment is social, that is, other people. In order to deal competently with his environment, therefore, the person must learn to deal with other individuals effectively. White (1963) states that every interaction with another person can be said to have an aspect of competence. Acts directed toward another person are intended, consciously or unconsciously, to have an effect of some kind, and the extent to which they produce this effect can be taken as the measure of competence. White defines *competence* as the fitness or ability of a living organism to carry on those transactions with the environment which result in its maintaining itself, growing, and flourishing. In the human case, effectiveness in dealing with the environment is achieved largely through learning. White theorizes that since in the beginning a person cannot effectively carry on transactions with its environment, that is, it is highly dependent upon its parents for survival, all the behaviors relating to effectively dealing with the environment are learned. Both the successful and unsuccessful past actions of the person have taught him the ranges of his effectiveness. A person's sense of competence is the result of cumulative learning and develops through the effort and the efficacy of one's interaction with others. Although one would expect a high correlation between one's actual competence and one's feelings of being competent, the correlation is not perfect. Many times individuals feel less competent then they are, and some individuals may habitually feel incompetent when actually they are quite able to deal effectively with their environment.

White's notions of competence motivation provide an interesting beginning in looking at much of interpersonal behavior and at how one can develop skills in creating effective interpersonal relationships. Argyris (1962, 1964, 1968) has developed the conception of interpersonal competence to a more specific and useful theory of interpersonal behaviors. He defines *interpersonal competence* as the ability to cope effectively with interpersonal relationships. He states that three criteria of effective interpersonal competence are:

> 1. The individual perceives the interpersonal situation accurately. He is able to identify the relevant variables plus their interrelationships.
>
> 2. The individual is able to solve interpersonal problems in such a way that they remain solved. If, for example, interpersonal trust is low between two individuals, they may not have said to have solved the problem competently until they no longer distrust one another.
>
> 3. The solution is achieved in such a way that both individuals are still able to work with each other at least as effectively as when they began to solve their problems.

According to Argyris, therefore, a person's interpersonal competence is a function of his ability (and the ability of the others involved) to solve interpersonal problems. In many ways this ability is a quality of a relationship, not of individuals. In a marriage, for example, one person may be unable to establish a high level of trust in the relationship due to the inability of his spouse to trust others. The same person may be able to solve these interpersonal problems quite easily with other individuals who do not have such deep psychological problems.

As interpersonal competence is the ability to understand the effects of one's behavior and personality upon others with whom one is interacting, some degree of self-awareness is a precondition for competence. One way to increase self-awareness is to receive information from others as to how they perceive you, and how your behavior affects them. Thus Argyris states that to behave competently in interpersonal situations, the individual must be able to provide and receive information about his relationships with minimal distortion. If a person has a high need to control others, for example, he must be aware of this tendency, and be able to evaluate honestly how it affects his relationships. Argyris states that to provide even minimally distorted information, the individual needs a relatively high degree of self-awareness and self-acceptance. The more aware and accepting an individual is of those aspects of his self which are operating in a given situation, (1) the higher the probability that he will discuss them with minimal distortion and (2) the higher the probability that he will listen with minimal distortion. Thus if an individual is aware and accepting of his need to receive affection from others, he will tend to listen to reactions to his attempts to elicit affection and can provide reactions to others attempting to elicit affection which are minimally distorted.

Whether or not an individual becomes threatened by and distorts information about his interpersonal behavior may be related to a person's self-esteem (Argyris, 1964). Argyris hypothesizes that self-esteem is developed through dealing with problems in such a way that the person can attribute the solution of the problem to himself, to his abilities, to his efforts, to his work. A person develops self-esteem through experiencing psychological success in his interactions with the environment. Psychological success is experienced as one (Lewin, Dembo, Festinger, and Sears, 1944):

1. defines his own goals,
2. develops his own strategies to accomplish his goals,
3. relates the goals and the strategies to his central needs,
4. experiences a challenge in achieving the goal that stretches his present level of abilities.

An individual seeking psychological success will need a world in which he can experience a significant degree of (1) self-responsibility and self-control (to define his own goals and the strategies for their accomplishment), (2) commitment (to persevere to achieve his goals), (3) productiveness and work (to achieve his goals at a realistic level of aspiration), and (4) utilization of his more important abilities (in order that the accomplishment seems due to effort on his part). Self-esteem is increased by experiencing psychological success; competence is enhanced as psychological success increases.

In summary, according to Argyris's theory a person's interpersonal competence is a function of his ability to help solve interpersonal problems. Interpersonal problem solving ability is based upon the (1) self-awareness and self-acceptance of the individual and (2) his self-esteem. Self-awareness is increased by receiving information from others about how they perceive you and how your behavior affects them. Self-esteem is increased through experiencing psychological success in dealing with the environment.

Conclusion

In looking at the different aspects of dyadic relationship reviewed in this chapter, one is struck with the disparity between what social psychological research can tell us about human behavior, and the complexity and beauty of human behavior in actual relationships. The research on interpersonal attraction does not catch the depth of feeling and the increased sense of value, worth, and wonderment that comes from being in love and being loved. Attribution theory does not capture the sense of discovery involved in getting to know other individuals. The theory of power and dependence does not convey the feelings of satisfaction from being involved in meaningful partnerships. While scientific knowledge is steadily advancing toward understanding human behavior more completely, controlled research which must segment and isolate aspects of human experience may lose the "essense" of what the social psychologist is trying to study. Let us continually remind ourselves that the segmented knowledge we now have concerning human behavior is the birth, not the maturity, of understanding what it is to be a human.

SUMMARY

Man is a dependent being. He is born with certain structural characteristics, but it is only through interaction with other men that he becomes a fully realized human being. The most basic unit of such interaction is the dyad. The dyad is constituted of any two persons interacting. The actions of each individual serve as stimuli to which the other responds. Man learns the expectations of his society and develops his own personality through interaction with others.

In order to communicate with anyone we judge, from his behavior, what is inside his consciousness. Perception of another individual depends on both verbal and nonverbal signals. One study shows that the total impact of communication is 7 percent verbal, 38 percent tone of voice, and 55 percent facial expression. Nonverbal signals include tone of voice, touching, facial expression, spatial distance from the addressee, relaxation of posture, rate of speech, and number of errors in speech. Emotions most often correctly identified through nonverbal signals are anger, nervousness and happiness. Correct judgments about the feelings of others are especially difficult when different degrees of feelings or contradictory kinds of feelings are expressed simultaneously through different aspects of behavior.

The perception of one person by another is a complex procedure. First, we assume that another person's behavior is not random, but that it is influenced by certain motives and intentions. Our goal is to try to understand these motives, values and intentions. This is called "attribution theory." Second, the person being perceived, aware of his perceiver, may take certain attitudes toward him that will affect his, the actor's, behavior. This can be called "impression management." Third, the perception of an act is determined both by the individual's perception of the act itself, and by his perception of the content in which the act occurs, that is, his frame of reference. Once primary impressions are formed, they are checked for accuracy through further interaction of the two persons.

It was stated above that man becomes a full human being only through social interaction. Much of our behavior is motivated by a basic need for social approval. The need for social approval seems to be a learned need which varies from individual to individual. Some people chronically lack confidence and are more dependent on acceptance from others. Also, studies have shown that an individual's need for approval may vary with the situation. If he has recently met approval, his level of need may be lower.

Much of human society and action seems based upon the attraction individuals have for each other. There are, however, two potent determinants of one's liking for another which have nothing to do with the other's characteristics. The first is the effect of chance consequences upon liking. We tend to assume that individuals get what they deserve. This being true we tend to perceive the victim of misfortune somewhat negatively. Second, our liking for another is influenced by the effect of our treatment of others upon attraction. Depending on the situation, a harm-doer may justify his action, he may attempt to compensate his victim, or he may punish himself. On the other hand, studies show that a benefactor may come to love the recipient of his favors.

The antithetic proverbs "absence makes the heart grow fonder" and "out of sight, out of mind" confuse the issue of propinquity. Studies indicate that the closer two individuals are geographically, the more likely it is that they will be attracted to each other. On the other hand, the less distance there is between two individuals, the more likely it is that they will dislike each other. What proximity appears to allow and what distance prevents is an opportunity to obtain information and to accumulate experience regarding the rewards and punishments we are likely to receive from the other person. Thus attraction or repulsion depend on other factors in the situation (such as similarity of attitude and values) once interaction between two individuals actually takes place. Generally, we tend to favor the familiar, but we tend to react against overexposure.

Concerning the issues of similarity and complementarity, two more proverbs state opposing folk wisdoms: "Birds of a feather flock together" and "Opposites attract." Evidence supports the theory that persons perceived to be similar to oneself will be liked and, conversely, persons who are liked will be perceived as being similar. The notion that "opposites attract" seems to be valid if we interpret it to mean people with opposite or complementary needs will be attracted. For example, a person with a need to dominate may be attracted to a person with a need to be dominated. This may be called the "need completion theory." The bulk of evidence supports the similarity theories more than the need completion theories.

Anxiety, stress and social isolation are conditions under which individuals will be attracted to others who are present or in similar circumstances. Also, we tend to like those who are like us (more so if we like ourselves). Furthermore, there is considerable evidence that we like those who facilitate our goal accomplishment, and that we dislike those who frustrate it.

One of the most common forms of dyad is friendship. It exists between males and females, young and old. It endures over years of separation and wide varieties of interest. The wider the range of needs met by one friend for the other, the stronger the bonds of friendship.

Sex, love, and marriage are not necessarily related. For example, with the small child, playmates in sexual exploration are not the human beings he most loves. The American culture puts stress on romantic love, whereas cultures in which marriages are arranged by parents recognize that a "suitable mate" is desirable but foster no illusion about the "one and only." Ideally, however, sex, love and marriage are related. Studies show how this is most likely to occur if the characteristics of the spouse are similar to the characteristics of the parent of that sex. Also, a good marriage is more likely to result if the parents of the partners had a good marriage.

In a dyad, interaction between people takes place in order to accomplish goals, and mutual power exists to the extent to which one can affect the goal accomplishment of the other. There are two major ways in which one person may exert power over another in a dyadic relationship. The first is through being able to affect the rewards or punishments a person may receive as the result of a relationship, and the second is through control of information which would facilitate the accomplishment of the other's goals. Two other types of influence in a dyad are suggestion and hypnosis. The power of suggestion exists because, in a dyad, each member responds to the behavior of the other. Hypnosis is an example of the power of suggestion in its extreme form.

The mother-child relationship is perhaps the most important dyad. A critical factor in the mother-child dyad is the set of unconscious expectations which the mother holds for her child. These determine many of her reactions of pleasure or annoyance with the baby's behavior and thus, eventually, the child's self-concept. Studies have shown that a child depends on a warm secure relationship for his physical, emotional and intellectual development.

Finally, as an individual grows, his ability to have a good dyadic relationship depends on his interpersonal competence. This is dependent on his ability to solve interpersonal problems, which is dependent on (1) self-awareness and self-acceptance of the individual and (2) self-esteem.

CHAPTER 3

Belonging
in a Group

DEFINITION

What is a group?

Several people are sitting in the boarding area of an airport waiting to get on a plane. Are they a "group?" Although all intend to board the same plane, and they may all be bound for the same destination, and they can see and hear one another, three features essential to a group are lacking. One is *interaction*. Each is concerned only with his own thoughts. They are not stimulating one another or responding to one another. A second is *satisfaction*. The existence of a group satisfies some needs in each member. The need met may be different for different members. No one in that waiting room would mind if one or several other persons left. If they were a group, the absence of any member would be felt as something of a change. A group is sometimes defined by the fact that any member is missed. The third factor not present in the aggregation is intellectual recognition of their group unity by the members. *Self-awareness* of the group as a group, and of who belongs and who is outside the membership, is another feature of a genuine group. All members must exist as a group in the psychological field of each member.

We would therefore define a group as an aggregate of persons in face-to-face interaction, each aware of his own membership in the group, each aware of the others who belong in the group, and each obtaining some satisfactions from his participation with the others. Sociologists distinguish primary groups like the family from secondary groups like the political party to which one belongs. In this chapter we shall be concerned with the psychological experience of belonging to and participating in primary groups.

Charles H. Cooley, a pioneer sociologist, described "primary groups" and their psychological impact as follows:

> By primary groups I mean those characterized by intimate face-to-face association and cooperation. They are primary in several senses, but chiefly in that they are fundamental in forming the social nature and ideals of the individual. The

result of intimate association, psychologically, is a certain fusion of individualities in a common whole, so that one's very self, for many purposes at least, is the common life and purpose of the group. Perhaps the simplest way of describing this wholeness is by saying that it is a "we"; it involves the sort of sympathy and mutual identification for which "we" is the natural expression (1912).

SIZE OF GROUP

As a group increases in size, changes occur in the relationship among members. A *dyad*, which can meet our definition of a group, is a group in which feelings may reach unusual intensity; feelings of affection may be strong, yet Bales and Borgatta (1955) note that dyads show higher ratings on disagreement and antagonism than other size groups, perhaps because they can obtain a majority only if both parties agree. Three-person groups, or *triads*, are considered to be unstable because of the tendency toward coalition-formation (Caplow, 1956; Vinacke and Arkoff, 1957). Mills (1953) found that in triads there is a distinct tendency for two members to join together against the other member. In bargaining games in which there is one "powerful" member, the two "weaker" members tend to ally against the stronger (Caplow, 1956; Vinacke, 1959). One experienced group therapist has reported: "Our triad groups in general did not do well. Problems of rivalry and jealousy consumed a great deal of time and actively interfered with the therapeutic process" (Loeser, 1957). Simmel (1902) back at the turn of the century, pointed out that "there is no relationship so complete between three that each individual may not, under certain circumstances, be regarded by the other two as an intruder." He recognized, however, that when two disagree, the third member can mediate and reconcile.

There is no community of threes, from the conversation for an hour up to family life, in which there does not presently occur dissension, now between this pair, now between that, harmless or acute, momentary or permanent, of theoretical or practical nature, and in which the third does not exercise a mediatorial function. . . . Such mediations need not occur in words: a gesture, a way of listening, the quality of feeling which proceeds from a person, suffices to give to this dissent between two others a direction toward consensus.

Finally, when two members of a triad are hostile toward one another, the third holds the balance of power. Here is the simplest case of the political maxim: "Divide and rule."

When one moves to larger groups, much of the research has focused upon units within large organizations, such as work groups, departments, or factories. In a review of the research, Porter and Lawler (1965) state that the results are remarkably consistent in demonstrating that as the size of these units increases there is a decrease in job satisfaction and a concomitant increase in absenteeism, turnover of personnel, and labor disputes.

As groups increase in size, a smaller and smaller number of individuals become central to its organization, make decisions for it, and communicate to the total membership. In a discussion group, for example, as the group becomes larger, a smaller percentage of its members can speak to the group in a certain time period. The chairman tends to exercise stronger control, and remarks are made more often to the group as a whole. Second, as the group becomes larger, many members may not know one another, and there may be too many members for complete communication to occur among them. The increased difficulty of complete communication often affects the type of decision making procedures used and the overall cohesion of the group (splits may occur between factions). Third, larger agencies seem to depend upon impersonal means for communicating rules and policies, such as memos and policy statements. Finally, larger groups may be less cohesive than smaller ones, which may decrease the conformity of members to the group's norms.

Thus, the overall conclusions of the research seem to be that members find participation more satisfying and that group processes are more effective in smaller groups than in larger ones. There are, however, two major reservations which should be attached to these conclusions. First, research has not specified the conditions under which each of the variables studied will be affected by group size; it is clear that smaller groups, for example, will not *always*, under all circumstances, be more satisfying than large groups. Secondly, there may be variables not yet included in the research on which large groups will be superior to smaller ones. Certainly the increasing number of larger organizations in our society suggest that there may be advantages to larger size which behavioral science research has not yet been able to describe.

Gregariousness

NEED TO BELONG

It is within groups that the life of an individual is most often touched by the behavior of other individuals. The importance of group memberships upon the life of the average individual cannot be exaggerated. We are raised in a family; we are educated in groups; most individuals work in collaboration with fellow group members and with other groups; people worship in groups; even antisocial behavior often occurs in gangs. Being a member of groups is one of the most characteristic aspects of the human species; it is interesting to speculate on why this is so.

As was discussed in Chapter 2, man was not made to live alone; he is a social animal. The need to belong to groups is so evident in human behavior that when psychologists thought of "instincts" as a useful category, the "gregarious instinct" was always prominent. When humans are very young or very old they are highly dependent upon others for survival. Separation from the mother can threaten a baby's development and result in death; separation from society can accelerate the process of aging and result in the early death of an elderly person. At all stages of life the need to belong to groups seems very strong in most persons.

Social needs are characteristic of many other species of animals besides man. Most other animals are social beings. Allee (1938), reviewing the habits of living creatures from simple one-celled animals to the higher apes, finds that "the growing weight of evidence indicates that animals are rarely solitary, that they are almost necessarily members of loosely integrated ... communities." One-celled animals which would be unable, alone, to tolerate certain unfavorable environmental conditions like a dilute poison in the water or freezing cold, are able to survive by cohering in clusters. An amoeba separated from the group moves back toward the others. Köhler (1922), who spent the years of World War I on the island of Teneriffe observing a colony of chimpanzees, noted that if one were removed from the colony, the others would miss the absent member for a short time but would then forget him and go about their business. Not so for the one removed, however. He would press along the barrier to try to rejoin the others and would mourn and languish in apparent loneliness.

Individuals seem to get many different rewards or gratifications from affiliating with others. Schachter (1959), for example, found that the desire to be with a group is stronger when anxiety has been aroused. Variations in experimental conditions led him to conclude that subjects wished social confirmation that their behavior in a threatening situation was appropriate. They were assured by finding that others shared their feelings. Rabbie (1964), however, demonstrated that affiliation with others in a similar situation reduces anxiety only when the other is not perceived to be highly frightened. Apparently individuals want to affiliate in anxiety-provoking situations not so much to share experiences as to find a model that would reassure them. Further work has shown that people seek affiliation in order to assimilate not only anxiety, but also differences of opinion and a variety of other emotions (Wrightsman, 1960; Radloff, 1961; Schachter and Singer, 1962).

Man's inherent social nature and the obtaining of rewards such as the reduction of anxiety are but two of a variety of reasons why individuals affiliate with others in groups. A third reason is that there are many goals which can be accomplished only with the assistance of others. One cannot move a large piece of furniture, build complex machines, play a symphony, or run a government without the cooperation and coordination of others. The pooling of individual resources within a group, whether it is a teenage gang or a large industrial organization, makes possible for each contributor advantages he could never have gained through individual action. This will be discussed at length in Chapter 4 which deals with group productivity. Other reasons why individuals seek out groups has to do with the need for comparative information from others and the therapeutic aspects of group membership. These are discussed in the following sections.

SOCIAL COMPARISON THEORY

As discussed in Chapter 2, individuals are dependent upon others for information. One type of information-dependence is the need on the part of a person to (1) establish the correctness of his beliefs, attitudes, and values, and (2) find some standards for self-evaluation. In regard to self-evaluation, how can one know whether he is tall or short, fat or thin, pretty or homely, witty or dull except by some comparison with others? In regard to substantiating one's beliefs, is a pessimistic feeling that the world is blindly tumbling down a chute to hell a mere personal idiosyncracy, or is it supported and confirmed by what others are also feeling? It is in comparison with the abilities and characteristics of others that we evaluate ourselves. In comparison with the beliefs and opinions of others, we formulate and verify our own beliefs and opinions.

Festinger (1950, 1954) theorized that there is a continuum reflecting the physical evidential basis for any belief or attitude. At one end of the continuum are beliefs and attitudes based on hard facts of incontrovertible physical reality, such as the ability to cut glass with a diamond. At the other end of the continuum are beliefs and attitudes which cannot be easily checked against physical reality. Beliefs about the nature of God, attitudes toward other national, racial, and ethnic groups, and beliefs about events one did not observe directly are all beliefs for which a physical check does not exist. We may, for example, hold a very strong belief about what would have happened if the Vietnam War had been avoided, but there is obviously no way to check the correctness of such a belief; we can only speculate.

How does one establish confidence in attitudes and beliefs that are not supported by hard facts? Where does one go to substantiate opinions which have no factual basis? There are two general ways. First, one's attitudes, beliefs, and values must form some sort of coherent whole; new attitudes and beliefs must be checked against one's present values to ensure that there are no large discrepancies. Second, to the extent that others around him share his beliefs, one will attach validity to them. An individual's beliefs, values, and attitudes are greatly influenced by those of other individuals he feels are knowledgeable or desirable to emulate. Festinger (1950) states that when the dependence upon physical reality is low, the dependence upon social reality is correspondingly high. An opinion, belief or value is "correct" to the extent that it is anchored in a group of people with similar beliefs, attitudes, and values. It is, of course, not necessary that all people one associates with agree with one's attitudes, but it is important that some relevant "reference group" share one's opinions.

Although this discussion has separated the different bases for supporting one's attitudes, beliefs, and values, it should be noted that for the most part attitudes are based upon support from a combination of physical, social, and personal sources. Bits and pieces of physical evidence may be put together in such a way that one's personal values are substantiated and the resulting beliefs are congruent with the dictates of social reality. Physical and social evidence may be interpreted so as to give support to beliefs to which the person and his reference groups are strongly committed. A well-known example is taking the fact that one sees a black man sitting on a park bench as support for the belief that all black men are lazy and unwilling to work. This particular black may be on vacation or working on a night shift. Many strongly held beliefs can be substantiated in this way with poorly chosen or irrelevant instances of physical evidence.

Festinger's theory of social comparison assumes that individuals are driven to find out whether their opinions are correct. This same drive produces behavior directed toward obtaining an accurate appraisal of their own abilities. When "objective, nonsocial" means are not available, individuals evaluate their opinions and abilities by comparisons with the opinions and abilities of others. This drive to evaluate has been studied by several investigators. Gordon (1966) and Hakmiller (1966b) found that the wish to associate with others for social comparison purposes increased as opinion discrepancy decreased, and that the desire was greater when the others had been shown to be correct in their opinions than when they had been incorrect. When subjects were threatened with electric shock, they preferred to be with person who reported being slightly more nervous than themselves (Darley and Aronson, 1966). There is evidence, therefore, to support the assumption of a drive toward self-evaluation.

Festinger (1954) further postulated that since individuals want an accurate evaluation of their opinions and abilities, they will be more likely to compare themselves with others whose opinions or abilities are similar to their own, rather than widely discrepant. A person who is just learning how to play tennis, for example, will compare himself to other novices rather than to professional tennis players. The implication of this postulate for group formation is that individuals will tend to join groups whose members hold similar opinions or have similar abilities. The research evidence supporting this postulate is, however, only partially supportive. While there is evidence that social comparison can yield accurate and stable self-evaluation only when a person compares himself with a similar other (Radloff, 1966), this other will only be chosen for comparison when the characteristic to be judged is positively valued (Wheeler, 1966), and when the subject is unsure of his ability (Gordon, 1966; Hakmiller, 1966b). Similar others tend not to be chosen more frequently than dissimilar others when negative characteristics are being evaluated (Hakmiller, 1966a) or when relatively unfamiliar characteristics are being judged (Thornton & Arrowood, 1966).

Schachter (1959) extended the theory of social comparison to apply to the evaluation of emotions as well as to the evaluation of opinions and abilities. As was discussed in Chapter 2, he demonstrated that the tendency to affiliate with others undergoing a similar experience increased when subjects were made anxious. These findings can be explained through inferring that the subjects were unclear about the appropriateness of their anxiety and desired to be with others undergoing a similar experience in order to compare their reactions. In subsequent studies Schachter (1962) demonstrated that physical arousal produced in a subject by an injection of adrenalin could be interpreted as either euphoria or anger. How it was interpreted depended on social cues derived from the behavior of others. If other individuals in the same situation are euphoric, then the subject became euphoric, if the others were angry, then the subject became angry. Thus subjects may interpret a given physiological state to make it compatible with the emotions being expressed by others in the same situation.

Finally, Gordon (1966) has pointed out that individuals may join groups not only to verify their opinions but also to influence the opinions of others. He points out that many people like to advise and influence others. They may want to be in a group, not because they are uncertain but, on the contrary, because they feel confident of their own opinions and are eager to enlighten others. In Gordon's experiment, subjects who had been led to believe that their opinions (on how people would probably behave under circumstances only partly understood) were correct and those of their group were quite wrong, were most eager to exert influence.

THERAPEUTIC VALUES IN BELONGING

During the past dozen years there has been an enormous increase in the number of young people and adults participating in groups which focus mainly on the "here-and-now" feelings of members for one another. The movement began in 1947 when the first laboratory for training members in group dynamics was held at Bethel, Maine, under the leadership of Leland Bradford, Kenneth Benne, and Ronald Lippitt. Their groups were called "t-groups" (T for Training) and the name persists. Many other names have also been used; "sensitivity training" and "encounter groups" are common designations.

In the following chapter the value of such groups for learning will be discussed; in later chapters encounter groups will be mentioned as ways of reducing race or religious prejudice. In this chapter we are concerned with the direct emotional pay-off from such group experiences. There are now more than a hundred "Growth Centers" in this country which offer attractive opportunities to join a group for a week-end, a week, or longer. Special laboratories have been designed to help improve understanding of each other by couples, married or unmarried; to bridge the generation gap between parents and teenage children; to aid members of a class or a department in getting to know one another; and to strengthen some of the communion and unity which have, in the past, characterized many religious organizations. Numerous participants return to such groups again and again for renewal of the uplift they generate.

It is interesting to speculate on what aspects of our modern life have led to this huge upsurge in the demand for group encounter experiences. Has there been a reaction against technology and the impersonal character of most interaction in city life, which has led to the craving for more genuine intimacy, even under artificial and temporary conditions? Has there been disillusionment with bigness in nations, business and institutions, with a compensatory endeavor to create small groups where life goes better and yields deeper satisfactions? Whatever the explanation, the fact is that many persons who are reasonably successful in their work, family life and civic participation, experience a need from time to time for the added acceptance, warmth, intimacy and mutual support which characterize a good encounter group.

In t-groups one of the processes by which people learn is by receiving feedback from others. Self-awareness is a prerequisite for increasing one's interpersonal competence (see Chapter 2) and the effectiveness of our behavior depends in large measure on the feedback we receive from other people. This does not mean just verbal feedback, but also nonverbal feedback given through tone of voice, facial expression, body posture and so on. These nonverbal clues may tell us more about the impact of our behavior upon others than verbal clues, particularly in situations where social mores dictate that we must be polite or where we have learned it is not safe to communicate. Getting feedback from others gives us the opportunity to (1) increase our *awareness* of how other individuals perceive our behavior, (2) determine the *consequences* of our behavior, and (3) change our behavior if we wish to do so. All behavior is intended to result in certain consequences; all interpersonal behavior has some impact on others, and whether the consequences of our behavior are those we intend is an indication of our interpersonal competence. Through accurate feedback we can assess the consequences of our behavior by experimenting with different ways of handling interpersonal situations and receiving constant feedback on what we are doing, we can determine which of the available strategies is most effective in giving our behavior the impact we intend.

A simple model for looking at the relation between self-awareness and feedback often presented in t-groups is the Johari Window:

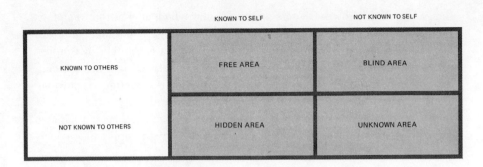

The Johari Window (named after its two originators, Joe Luft and Harry Ingham) illustrates that there are certain things each person knows about himself and certain things that he does not know. Correspondingly, there are certain things others know about a person and certain things that others do not know. Based upon the assumption that it takes energy to hide information from oneself and others, and that the more information known the clearer communication will be, participation in a t-group often results in enlarging the free area while decreasing the blind and hidden areas. As the group develops, a trusting atmosphere is established, individuals become more open in their communication about themselves, and the hidden area is reduced. Correspondingly, the group members give each other feedback which reduces the blind area. The increased self-awareness facilitates the development of interpersonal skills and personal development.

As the purpose of feedback is to provide constructive information to facilitate another's development, it is important to give feedback in a way which will not increase the defensiveness of the receiver. The more defensive an individual is, the less likely feedback will be accurately heard. Some characteristics of helpful, nonthreatening feedback are as follows:

1. Feedback should be focused on behavior rather than on the person. In giving feedback it is important to refer to what a person does rather than comment on what we imagine he is. Thus we might say that a person "talked considerably in this meeting" rather than that he "is a loud-mouth."

2. Feedback should be focused on description rather than judgment. Describing is a process of reporting what occurred, while judgment is an evaluation in terms of good or bad, right or wrong, nice or not nice. By avoiding evaluative language, the need for the receiver to react defensively is reduced.

3. Feedback should be focused on observations rather than inferences. Observations refer to what we can see or hear in the behavior of another person, while inferences refer to interpretations and conclusions which we make from what we see or hear.

Other aspects of constructive feedback are that it is solicited rather than imposed, it is specific rather than general, it is checked to ensure clear communication, it is directed towards behavior the receiver can do something about, and it is appropriately timed (usually as close in time to the observed behavior as possible).

The sense of being accepted as a unique person, the sense of belonging to a group, the sense of being valued and respected by others, are found not only in t-groups conducted by qualified psychologists but also in a variety of other groups, such as religious groups, clubs, therapy groups, classrooms, families, and so on. Whenever individuals interact in a group in which they enjoy themselves, feel support from their fellow members, obtain some release by talking out their problems, obtain a more objective view of themselves, increase their understanding of others, or feel that they have clarified some of the things which have been causing them difficulty, they have experienced the therapeutic value of belonging to a group.

GROUP FORMATION

Genetic development

Social feeling, the *we* experience, begins, for better or for worse, in the mother-child dyad. "The *We-collapse*, or, in other words, the phenomenon of unkindness between parents and children really provides the starting point of almost all the faulty developments and the countless sufferings in the history of man," wrote one experienced psychotherapist (Künkel). As the child learns to walk and to talk his social world expands. He may have brothers and sisters; if so, he early learns to balance the fun of playing with another against the cost of not always having his own way. Unhappy the child for whom the game is not worth this candle! In most pre-industrial societies, as in this country a century or two ago, the child's immediate environment includes a large family of relatives. He grows up in association with numerous cousins, uncles, and aunts as well as with his siblings and parents. He early acquires a sense of belonging in the larger kinship group. In typical communities of the United States today, families live apart from their close relatives. The sense of belonging in the larger family is weak. This is one of several social changes which underlie the rootless feeling of many moderns. Observation of young children in nursery schools (Ames, 1952) has shown that at 18 months of age most of the toddler's remarks are comments to himself on his own activities. At two years of age more remarks are directed to the teacher or are concerned with getting and keeping toys he wants. By three, he has begun to talk more with other children and to use the pronoun "we." His play relationships are still largely dyadic, with one other child at a time.

There is a simple rule of thumb which says that the number of children at a birthday party during early childhood should be about the same as the child's years of age. Not until age four or five or six do most children enjoy playing in groups that large.

First playmates are selected largely by closeness in age and residence. Indeed, friendship studies throughout the elementary school age show "best friends" usually living only a few doors away. In crowded city areas, whole gangs may be made up entirely of children living within one block of one street. Attendance at the same school and church makes for closer ties.

Gangs

At around ten years of age, boys and girls form clubs or gangs which are usually ephemeral. For a week or two there is great excitement—a name, a secret hide-away, a password—and much ado over who is admitted and who is excluded. Then the enterprise usually dies. A few months later, with some changes in membership, another club takes form. The children may elect officers—commonly as many officers as there are members. A badge may be worn; if an interested father is a lawyer, there may be some bylaws. This, too, passes.

In the underprivileged areas of large cities, gang life becomes the center of interest for most boys. Thrasher (1927) studying 1,313 gangs in Chicago in the 1920s found that most of them had begun as spontaneous play groups in a limited neighborhood. The setting was usually a deteriorated residential area in between a business or manufacturing center and the good residential sections. Size of gang varied from less than six to more than 100 members. Age varied from six to adult, with most in the age group 11 to 17. About half engaged definitely in delinquent or criminal activities while most of the others sometimes carried on projects which were morally questionable. Thrasher believes that a key factor is the first expression of outside social disapproval which then unites the in-group members in conspiratorial solidarity. He reports:

It does not become a gang . . . until it begins to excite disapproval and opposition. . . . It discovers a rival or an enemy in the gang in the next block; . . . parents and neighbors look upon it with suspicion or hostility; 'the old man around the corner,' the storekeepers, or the 'cops,' begin to give it 'shags' (chase it): or some representative of the community steps in and tries to break it up. This is the real beginning of the gang, for now it starts to draw itself more closely together. Gangs represent the spontaneous effort of boys to create a society for themselves where none adequate to their needs exists.

Abstract 4 summarizes some of the observations made by William F. Whyte during his several years as a participant-observer of street-corner organizations in "Eastern City." The gangs in Street Corner Society served only the purpose of making life more satisfying by giving a structure which ensured the gratifications of reliable companionship.

Abstract 4

TITLE   Street Corner Society

AUTHOR   William Foote Whyte

PROBLEM   To present the natural history of one or two gangs of boys in a city slum.

SUBJECTS   The Nortons, a dozen young fellows, led by Doc; the Italian Community Club, made up of college boys, led by Chick; all living in "Cornerville," a deteriorated area of "Eastern City."

PROCEDURE   Bill Whyte took a room in the area, struck up a street-corner acquaintance with the boys, won the confidence of the leaders, posed as a writer of a history of the old customs of the area, learned Italian, was a participant observer for 3½ years.

SOME FINDINGS   Gang association began in early boyhood, based on living in close proximity. The boys continued to meet in their particular area until their late twenties, continuing even after marriage. Activities fall into accepted routines; certain nights for bowling; certain seats in a certain restaurant; appearance at a certain corner at an expected time. "Fellows around here don't know what to do except within a radius of about three hundred yards."

Although outsiders might regard the social life of Cornerville as "disorganized" it has a sharply defined structure. Gang members recognize a hierarchy of leadership and systems of mutual rights and obligations. Doc, who fought his way to the top, is obligated to spend or lend whatever he had for his boys. Each member is required to help others whenever possible; the higher the status of the member the more obligated he is. Activity in the gang usually awaits the leader's appearance. The leader is supposed to have the best ideas, to be fair to all, to be pretty good at skills valued by the group, and to represent group members in dealing with the "outside." The leader works through his lieutenants; when his power is challenged it will probably be by one of his lieutenants. A follower may initiate action when he and the leader are the only ones involved (a dyad or "pair event"); when others are also concerned (a "set event"), the leader initiates. Decisions are usually made by simple consensus; as Doc put it: "As soon as you begin deciding questions by taking a vote, you'll see that some fellows are for you and some are against you, and in that way factions develop. It's best to get everybody to agree first and then you don't have to vote." Chick's gang, more middle class in outlook, fitted into the local Settlement House; Doc's boys gave it a try but moved out: "They consider us scum!" Limited experience and rigid patterns of interaction make any change and readjustment difficult for these boys. The gang was tied in, by personal friendship of its leaders, to a larger hierarchy of racketeers leading up to really "big shots," who sometimes included police officials.

SOURCE: Chicago: University of Chicago Press, 1943.

At one time social workers tried to lure promising individuals away from the gang to join in substitute activities at a settlement house or church. Then, since this usually failed, group workers capitalized on the solidarity of the gang and tried to bring the whole "natural group" into the neighborhood recreational center. This was more successful, but many gangs found middle-class respectability (as represented by Scouts, YMCAs, etc.) dull and alien. The next step was to send trained workers out into the neighborhood to be a friend to the gang. Most gangs want some sort of meeting place. Old basements were rented, renovated, and became "cellar clubs." Many gangs prefer this kind of headquarters to either a street corner or a well equipped recreational center. A skillful adult can become sufficiently accepted by the gang to be able to help the members achieve some of their more constructive goals without impairing the social fabric in which the boys are most comfortable.

Type of gang varies with social class, a variable to which we later devote a whole chapter. Upper-class cliques form junior sets at the country club. Middle-class cliques go to high school dances and the social affairs of young people's societies in churches. Lower-class youngsters lead more of their social life at roller skating rinks, dance halls, and pool room or candy store hangouts.

Most gang studies report on boys. A few gangs of girls are found, but there are often imitative and short-lived. Occasionally one or more girls associate with a gang of boys. Later the dances run by the boys include a fairly well recognized clique of neighborhood girls. The European tradition of a sheltered life for adolescent girls plays a part in keeping many of them off the streets in neighborhoods of foreign-born parents. In middle-class areas, girls congregate in pairs and often in larger groups, form cliques, share common hero-ideals, imitate certain heroines, and develop rituals. Boys and girls also join in coed groups, planning dances, hikes, staging plays or discussions, with or without formal organization.

Within any community, teen-age groups create small subcultures. In "Eastern City" Doc's gang differed from the college-bound boys. Even on a college campus a variety of subcultures can be found. There are well-dressed boys with neat haircuts, already thinking like corporation junior executives. There are carelessly dressed boys, taking study seriously and striving to excel in scholarship. There are campus politicians and members of athletic teams. There are the "radicals"—at one time called "hippies" or "yippies" or worse names—who have rejected the norms of the Establishment. Most interaction takes place within each such subculture, relatively little across the lines which separate them.

Joining by adults

Studies of social participation by adults commonly show only a limited amount of membership in formal organizations, but beneath the surface an extensive, pervasive, informal organization of social life. Among 2,223 adults in New York City in 1934, 52 percent belonged to no organization except a church (Komarovsky, 1946). In Springfield, Mass., in 1939, a sample of 100,000 adults showed 61 percent with no organizational affiliation (Kaplan, 1943). In Erie County, Ohio, in 1940, about half the voters did not belong to any club or institution or association (Lazersfeld *et al.*, 1944). In Boulder, Colorado, 29 percent belonged to no organization and 48 percent to none except a church (Bushee, 1954). A study of farm families in rural New York showed that in 11 percent, no member of the family belonged to any organization, while in 41 percent of the families at least one grown member claimed no membership. In 25 percent of the families, no member had attended any meeting of any organization during the past year (Anderson, Plambeck, 1943). A survey in Cincinnati reported 41 percent in some group or organization; 59 percent in none.

If we look more closely at the social life of the community, we discover that most of these unorganized individuals are not isolates. They have their friends, their patterns of meeting and talking together. Lundberg's study of a New England village (1938) provides typical examples of the informal social pattern which lies beneath the formal organization of the community. He inquired about friendship ties and frequency of visiting among the 1,500 residents. One "constellation" of 25 to 30 people related often to a single matriarch—a widow from an old established upper-class family. Another 40 persons, mainly factory workers, shared a connection with a worker's wife who was also a dressmaker. Almost all residents were linked in one or another of eight cliques.

Preferred groups

SOCIOMETRY

The term sociometry was introduced earlier in our discussion of friendship. Sociometric techniques record the attraction or repulsion which persons feel for one another.

The questions used in sociometric investigations vary. Moreno, who was then employed on the staff of an institution for delinquent girls, asked each member which other girls she would choose to have as cottage mates. Sometimes the question is: "Which pupils would you like to sit next to in the classroom?," or "Whom would you choose to work on a committee with you?" or "What children would you like to invite to your party?"

When each member of a social aggregate has registered sociometrically his degree of liking or his dislike for the others, the results can be studied in many ways. A sociogram is a graphic record of these interpersonal feelings. Each individual, as in figure 3-1, is represented by a circle. A choice for an-

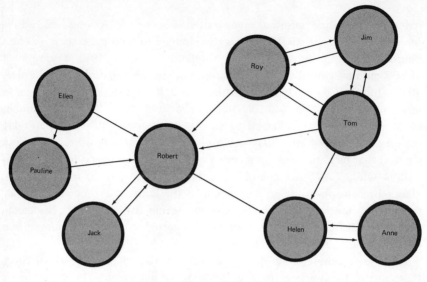

FIGURE 3-1.

other is represented by an arrow from the chooser to the chosen. Mutual choices are connected by a double arrow—one in each direction. In the simple sociogram of a group of nine junior high school pupils in figure 3-1, Robert and Jack form a mutual pair; so do Helen and Anne. Jim, Tom, and Roy form a sociometric triangle, each member choosing the other two. Robert is a "star"—he receives five choices from the eight other members of the group. Yet even a star is sometimes disappointed—Robert chooses Helen, but she chooses only her girl friend Anne. Ellen is the unhappy isolate. No one chooses her. Experience indicates that an isolate may have—both as a cause and as a result of the isolation—extraordinary problems of emotional adjustment. A sociogram of a club, a class, an office, a factory unit, a group of nurses or a neighborhood will usually show some stars, some pairs, perhaps a few triangles or chains, and almost always some isolates who are or will become personnel problems. If the group measured is fairly large, several cliques may be observed, as in Lundberg's study of the New England village, with relatively few ties to outsiders.

If persons indicate not only their choices but also their most pronounced rejections, it is possible to note additional forces in the group. Aversions may also be paired or organized by cliques. A "black star" is a target for many rejections.

Moreno found that choice of companions in a given group remained fairly stable; after three months 92 percent of the choices were the same. Mutual choices—pairs—increase from less than 10 percent at kindergarten age to over 25 percent by fifth grade.

Sociometric studies serve many purposes. They may sensitize a leader or supervisor to the interpersonal ties and tensions in his group. They may indicate real leaders. In one study of an institutional population, the girls more often chosen as preferred companions were (in 90 percent of the cases) the same as the girls receiving the highest votes for membership on the House Council (Jennings, 1947).

Moreno reported that the spread of rumors could be predicted from knowledge of the sociometric network. One day after a certain girl had been caught stealing, only the others in her clique knew about it; after a week the information was more widely known. An epidemic of runaway's (14 within 14 days) was found located within one network of close sociometric ties.

Sociometric techniques may be used to explore barriers such as those created in certain cultures by differences in sex, race, or age. Moreno found cross-sex choices by kindergarten children composing 25 percent of all selections. As boys and girls grew older they rejected one another's company. This reached its peak, in fourth grade, with only 3 percent of the choices across the gulf of sex difference. Then there was a gradual increase up to 8 percent in eighth grade, but even in high school cross-sex choices (to sit near, to serve on a committee with, to lunch with, to have as companion on a hike, to invite to a party) fell well below 50 percent.

It is sometimes charged that certain ethnic groups are too clannish. In a study (Watson, Harris, 1946) of fifth- and sixth-grade children in a school where one-third of the pupils were Jewish and two-thirds gentile, sociometric instruments checked the friendship choices. In-group choices made within the class were 78 percent for the gentiles and 24 percent for the Jews; among friends outside, gentiles chose 94 percent gentiles and Jews 72 percent Jews. By both indices the Jewish children were less clannish than their classmates.

Personality problems can often be identified by means of sociometric measures. A study (Kuhlen, Bretsh, 1947) of 700 high school pupils was accompanied by a check list of personality problems. Adolescents less well accepted (bottom 25 percent) by their peers showed more frequent problems such as: "being unhappy," "feeling that nobody understands me," "bashfulness," "feelings easily hurt," "getting tired very easily," "losing temper," and "headaches."

Leadership has been studied sociometrically. One study asked men to choose which of nine other colleagues in a ten-man group they would choose to work with, which they would choose to spend leisure time with, and which person's removal from the group would most change the group. The first two questions correlated about .40 with observer-rating on "leadership," but the third showed a correlation with observed leadership as high as .80 (Gibb, 1950).

In another study, using members of an Officer Candidate School, a variety of measures was tried: ratings by staff, personality test scores, achievement test scores, as well as choice by fellow platoon members for leadership. Tested against a criterion of "all-around ability as a combat officer," the sociometric measure proved better than any of the others (Williams, Leavitt, 1947). Another study, also on officer candidates, showed that "buddy ratings" were better measures of leadership than were intelligence tests, academic grades, or ratings by tactical officers (Wherry, Fryer, 1949).

Moreno and Jennings found that when girls were actually regrouped to correspond as closely as possible with their choices, morale and discipline improved. When pupils in school were regrouped according to their sociometric choices to maximize mutual acceptance, the morale of the classes rose (Zeleny, 1939). Thrasher (1947) refers to this as "assignment therapy." In another project (Kerstetter and Sargent, 1940), assignment therapy was used to separate members of a clique which had grown troublesome. Another application was made in youth work camps, and again it appeared that assigning congenial team mates made for better spirit all around (Faunce, Beigle, 1948).

Sociometric study of relationships among people who have just met one another for the first time has special value for understanding social perception. The transference—or parataxis—discussed earlier, appears distinctly. Later, these first impressions may be considerably revised on the basis of real experience. Sociometric ratings in a group in which the members have shared considerable experience and know one another quite well remain highly constant. In group psychotherapy, the feeling each member has about his fellow members is of major importance. Changes in these feelings are especially significant. The writer has found it helpful from time to time to ask patients in a psychotherapy group to make their own diagram of the group. In this experiment patients place themselves as a small circle in the center of the page, and place the circle for each other member of the group close to themselves if they feel strongly drawn to that person, but far away if they feel inclined to reject any association with that person. In one group, one patient drew a large circle for himself at the center, a small one in a far corner for the leader, and announced that so far as he was concerned the other members did not exist at all in his life space.

A refinement of the sociometric method asks members not only to rate or choose among the others, but also to report which others they expect will choose or reject them. This *relational analysis,* as it is sometimes termed, provides a basis for studying insight into the feelings of others. It is usually true that members with good insight are the overchosen and those who are not well liked by their fellows are not very clearly aware of this rejection. Perhaps, in emotional self-defense they need to believe that others do accept them. It is important also to distinguish between acceptance in a particular group and general acceptability. An individual may be quite congenial in one group but find himself out of place in a different one. Later we shall return to a discussion of factors which make some members more popular than others.

Interaction and liking

In the preceding chapter we presented briefly the generalization that *frequency of interaction is closely related to degree of liking for one another.* The relationship between interaction and attraction under conditions of free social mobility is circular. The more A, B, and C associate, the better they like one another; conversely, the better they like each other, the more they will associate.

If the correlation depended wholly upon free choice of companions, the principle would seem obvious and banal. The important fact is that if strangers are brought into some kind of cooperative activity, and are not free to withdraw, they usually become friendly.

The evidence supporting this conclusion comes both from everyday observations and from psychological research. We often see the familiar become the favored. Children who are frequently served a certain kind of food grow up to like it; the old home town for most people has a quality of warmth and charm unlike that of any strange city; the stories and music we heard repeatedly in childhood have a special appeal; old acquaintances have a special place in our lives. A typical research finding is that intimacy among college students can well be predicted from extent of contact (Fischer, 1953).

The writer once encountered the force of liking engendered by interaction in a way which almost upset a projected experiment. A large class was divided into small discussion groups. An observer in each group noted the frequency with which each member spoke. Our plan was, after five sessions, to re-constitute the groups, so that students who were quite articulate would be put in a group with others who talked fluently, while the silent members would join a group made up of others as reticent as they were. Our hypothesis followed Charles Beard's famous generalization of one thing he had learned from history: "When the sun goes down the stars come out!" We wanted to give the stars a chance. We did not want to bias the results by telling the students this; we explained that we were reshuffling groups in order to give everyone a chance to become acquainted with a different group of associates who would contribute different experiences and viewpoints. This seemed reasonable, since the purpose of the small groups was mainly to broaden the experience of the student by sharing and comparing views. What surprised us and almost wrecked the experiment was the protest of the students against being shifted away from their accustomed associates. Although they had met as strangers and had had only five 50-minute sessions together, already interaction had created bonds not lightly severed. We insisted on the change and after another month, bonds were just as strong in the new groups. Incidentally, the level of participation of the quiet members did rise, and strong competition reduced the excessive loquacity of the talkers, but there remained an important difference in activity level between the two types.

A corollary of the general relationship between interaction and liking is that those members within a group who interact more will like one another better. In a study of three small discussion groups made up of British students, the most talkative member proved to be also the most popular member in two groups and ranked second in popularity in the third group. Those who talked least were least popular (Klein, 1956). Again the relationship is probably circular; a sense of being well accepted by the group makes it easy to speak; a sense of rejection curbs participation.

High *activity* by a member does not always mean maximum *interaction* with others. One who talks too much in a group may be regarded as a nuisance and other members may cease to listen to him. Sometimes the member who makes most suggestions, particularly if the group task or situation is somewhat frustrating, becomes a target for resentment. Other members restrict their contact with him as much as possible. This relationship may also become circular; the over-talkative or rejected individual, feeling the barrier, talks louder, longer, and faster to try to break through.

If school classes are teacher-dominated, there is relatively less interaction among the students and correspondingly less friendship develops. Bovard (1951) showed that a group-centered method developed more liking for one another among the students than did a formal lecture method.

A study (Cogan, Shapiro, 1959) of sociometric reactions of group members at 10 intervals during a series of 47 meetings showed relatively high agreement within the group on which persons were most admired and most influential; much less agreement on the persons toward which members felt most warm and whom they liked best. Agreement on which members were disliked or made others angry, decreased as the sessions progressed. Agreement on the person one would most wish to be like (the ego-ideal) increased over time, as did agreement on whose contributions to the group most deserved attention. A general summary of the study would be that, as interaction continued, members came to considerable agreement on the achievement characteristics of their fellows; moderate agreement on the persons toward whom they felt warmth and liking; and very little agreement on the infrequent negative reactions.

The Army provides an unusually good setting in which to study the effect of interaction during enforced association among men of widely different characteristics. One investigator (Maisel, 1960) reported that of 1,156 men named as among the "three best friends" of each soldier after his first few days of training, 54 percent came from the same squad. (Only 25 percent would have been from the same squad if chance selection had operated.) After seven weeks of training, 61 percent of best friends came from the same squad. Men asked (by secret ballot) to name the fellow they would want to have *least* contact with, named someone in their own squad in only 16 percent of the cases.

A study during World War II (Stouffer *et al.*, 1949) showed that "pride in one's outfit" was about twice as strong among veterans who had seen combat as it was among troops who had trained together but had not yet shared the intense emotions of battle. Interaction during stress seemed to affect feelings about one another more than did more peripheral and superficial relationships.

One of the classics of social psychology is the series of experiments at the Hawthorne plant of Western Electric Company. In one of these investigations, a group of about a dozen men, engaged in wiring and soldering a complicated telephone bank, was removed from the larger factory work room to a special observation room. They were instructed to work as usual, but their behavior at work and leisure was unobtrusively recorded. Homans (1950), under the heading "Mutual Dependence of Interaction and Sentiment" reports one of the findings:

Just as all the members of the group, thrown together in the room, were to some extent friendly, with the exception of Mazmanian, so individuals within the group, thrown together by the geography of the room, the nature of their work, and common membership is soldering and inspection units, were friendly to an even greater extent. Winkowski, Taylor, Donovan, Steinhardt, and Allen, all working at the front of the room and in the same inspection unit, were all linked by friendships, and the same was true of soldering unit 3, but only one strong friendship, that of Hasulak for Steinhardt linked members of two different cliques.

Homans sums up the relationship between interaction and sentiment by reiterating that the more frequently and freely persons interact with one another, the stronger their sentiments of friendship for one another are apt to become.

Another impressive study was carried out in a new student housing project in Cambridge. Most people liked their new neighbors; satisfaction was probably unusually high because of the homogeneity in a community of graduate students. Yet it is striking that none was dissatisfied, and three out of four felt no need for friends outside their immediate neighbors. The most impressive fact is the concentration of choice on the people who happen to live next door, or those whose apartment door one frequently passes. Propinquity brought increased interactions and interaction facilitated friendship (Festinger, Schachter, Back, 1950).

In stating the general principle and in summarizing the evidence, we have consistently left room for exceptions. "Closely related," "usually," "probably," "often," "for most people," has been our form of statement. In a minority of cases, frequent interaction intensifies the antagonism and rejection. Some people hate their families, some despise their home town, some are glad to be rid of old neighbors and old co-workers. This is particularly likely to be true if the circumstances of association were annoying and frustrating—a quarrelsome family, a neighborhood of poverty and filth, an unpleasant job. Yet even in the most distressing circumstance, human association usually creates positive ties. Boys sent to a model institution or good foster homes because of the impossibly bad situation at home will sometimes run away to get back to the familiar filth. People who have worked together in great emergencies—floods, fires, wartime bombing, concentration camps—frequently feel a bond which comes from their shared suffering. A married couple may feel closer when they have to meet the challenge of poverty or the tragedy of disaster and bereavement, than they ever did in conditions of ease and comfort.

Association and interaction with other persons has both gratifying and annoying consequences. Interpersonal attraction is inevitably somewhat ambivalent. Learning theory indicates that satisfying experiences with another person or a group will reinforce tendencies to be with them and to do more things with them. Unpleasant and hurtful experiences with others reinforce avoidance tendencies. Even in the warm intimacy of a happy family, some experiences are frustrating and there are some impulses to resent, to hate, and to escape. When one is ill or lonely he may welcome association with another person whom he would not ordinarily want as a friend. Yet generally, and as a rule, most of our gratifications come from other persons—those who love us, feed us, clothe us, play with us, enlighten us, compliment us, or challenge us. Despite occasional irritation, the great majority of inter-personal encounters bring some satisfaction to our basic human needs for security, acceptance, mastery, intimate response, and new experience. No toy or plaything has the satisfaction potential of other persons; even the arts are more likely to pall.

Freud interprets the cohesive power of a group as another of the many manifestations of love. Customarily we use the word "love" to describe ties ranging from those that bind us in the most intimate and intense sexual union to the vague and diffuse feelings represented by love of country or of all our fellow men. Freud's observations led him to approve this inclusive usage. "A group is clearly held together by a power of some kind: and to what power could this feat better be ascribed than to Eros, who holds together everything in the world? . . . If an individual gives up his distinctiveness in a group and lets its other members influence him by suggestion, it gives one the feeling that he does it because he feels the need of being in harmony with them rather than in opposition to them, so that perhaps after all he does it 'for love of them'" (1951).

COHESION

In some groups members are strongly motivated to contribute to the group's well-being, to participate in its activities, and to help obtain the group objectives, while in other groups members are indifferent and apathetic. The attractiveness of group membership for the individual, the desire to remain a member of the group, refers to the cohesion of the group. *Group cohesion* is defined as "the resultant of all forces acting on members to remain in the group" (Festinger, 1950).

In a review of the literature on group cohesiveness, Cartwright (1968) states that all the forces acting upon members to remain in a group are determined jointly by certain properties of the group and by certain characteristics of the members. These forces have various effects which constitute the consequences of group cohesiveness. He presents a scheme for analyzing group cohesiveness, which is shown in figure 3-2.

A SCHEME FOR ANALYZING GROUP COHESIVENESS

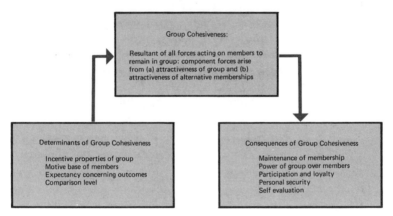

Group Cohesiveness:

Resultant of all forces acting on members to remain in group: component forces arise from (a) attractiveness of group and (b) attractiveness of alternative memberships

Determinants of Group Cohesiveness	Consequences of Group Cohesiveness
Incentive properties of group Motive base of members Expectancy concerning outcomes Comparison level	Maintenance of membership Power of group over members Participation and loyalty Personal security Self evaluation

FIGURE 3-2. A scheme for analyzing group cohesiveness.
(Taken from Cartwright and Zander, page 92.)

According to Cartwright, a person's attraction to a group is determined by his assessment of the desirable and undesirable consequences attendant upon membership in the group. The more favorable the outcomes he can expect from membership, the more an individual will be attracted to a group. The outcomes one expects to derive from memberships in a group depend upon such variables as the nature of the group and its goals, programs, characteristics of its members and prestige. Four of the major factors which may motivate individuals to feel attracted to a group are as follows. The first one is the attractiveness of other members; the more the individual likes other members of the group, the higher his attraction to the group is assumed to be. There are, however, other sources of attraction for a group than personal liking for the other members. Attraction to a classroom group, for example, may be based more upon learning than upon liking for classmates. The second factor involves the perceived similarity between oneself and the other members. Balance theory (Heider, 1958) holds that two individuals will be more attracted to each other the more similar their evaluations of objects in their common environment; this contention has been substantiated by a variety of research studies. Festingers' theory of social comparison, as

---

BOX 3:1–MEASURING COHESION

There are a variety of ways to measure group cohesiveness which have been used in research studies. One is to measure the number of close personal friends within a group. The assumption here is that the greater the interpersonal attraction among group members, the higher will be the cohesiveness. Other researchers have asked group members to rate their liking for the group as a whole. Questions designed to reveal how strongly members identify with a group or feel personally involved in it have been used by some researchers. Finally, researchers have asked group members to rate the strength of their desire to remain in the group. Each of these methods has produced indicators identifying something the investigators have termed group cohesiveness. These indicators have been found to be highly correlated in some studies, but not highly correlated in others. A standard, all-purpose procedure for measuring group cohesiveness does not exist.

To have a variety of operational definitions of cohesiveness which do not always correlate with one another indicates that either (1) the concept cohesiveness has not been clearly defined or (2) the concept cohesiveness is inadequate and should be replaced by other more specific concepts. A brief reference to the discussion on concepts in Chapter 1 is appropriate here. By the fairly rigorous definition of a concept given here (i.e., that it must be identifiable by observable characteristics and be meaningful and significant), it is evident that many of the concepts used in social psychological research and theory are not adequately defined. As social psychology develops as a field this situation will change, perhaps by refining many of the concepts now in use or perhaps by finding new concepts which "cut up" reality in more adequate ways.

---

was discussed previously in this chapter, holds that for comparison purposes an individual will be more attracted to situations in which others are similar to him in abilities and opinions than to ones in which others are divergent. Several studies have shown, however, that similarity does not always generate attraction (Seashore, 1954).

The goals of a group constitute another possible source of attraction; having distinctive purposes serves to attract to the group individuals with a particular motive base. A bird-watching club, for example, will attract individuals interested in bird-watching. The incentive value of a particular group goal for a particular person, however, will depend not only upon its content, but also upon how explicitly the goal is formulated, how clear the paths for goal attainment are, and how likely successful achievement is for the group (Raven and Rietsema, 1957). Finally, when the members of a group come together to accomplish a common goal and agree upon the strategies required to reach it, they become cooperatively interdependent within a group and consequently, more cohesive.

The various properties of groups, such as the attractiveness of other members, the similarity of other members, the nature of the group's goals, and the cooperative interdependence will all have motivational significance for potential members. A given property of a group, however, will have incentive value for a particular person only if it is appropriate to his motive base. A person's attraction to a group, therefore, is determined by his view of how the characteristics of the group relate to his needs and values. A person's motive base for attraction to the group consists of his needs for affiliation, inclusion, affection, power, security, money or other needs which can be met by membership.

Although a group may have an attractive program which will satisfy a person's needs, his attraction to the group is still influenced by two further factors. One is his expectancy that the apparent benefits will actually be given to him if he joins the group; the other is his comparison level, his conception of the level of outcomes that group membership will provide. If the person expects that although the group could potentially meet his needs, it actually will not, due to various circumstances, or if the level of outcomes is below that which he normally receives, his attraction to the group will be low.

Cartwright's (1968) review of certain research studies indicates that group cohesiveness has several definite consequences upon a group. He states that other things being equal, as cohesiveness increases there is an increase in the capacity of a group to retain members and in the degree of participation by members in group activities. The greater the group's cohesiveness, the greater the power it has to bring about conformity to its norms and to obtain acceptance of its goals and acceptance of its assignment to tasks and roles. Finally, highly cohesive groups provide a source of security for members which serves to reduce anxiety and to heighten self-esteem. From these consequences it is apparent that it is advantageous to practically any group to have a high degree of cohesiveness.

EQUAL STATUS

Differences in freedom of expression among members are related to their satisfaction in the group. In a classic study in group dynamics, reported in

Abstract 5, Leavitt (1951) showed that the "central" members of a group, who sent and received more messages than others, most enjoyed their job. The peripheral members, who could communicate back and forth with only one other person in the network, were most dissatisfied. The network of communication which was most efficient (the wheel) was least satisfying to the average worker.

Abstract 5

TITLE   Some Effects of Certain Communication Patterns on Group Performance

AUTHOR   Harold J. Leavitt

PROBLEM How does the structure of a network of communication in a task-centered group affect the performance and feelings of members?

SUBJECTS 100 male undergraduates at M.I.T. working in 20 groups of five men each.

PROCEDURE Subjects sat around a circular table, with partitions separating each member from every other. Communication was written messages passed through slots. Groups tried to solve the problem of finding which of a number of symbols was common to the different cards held by all members of the group. Four communication patterns were set up as follows:

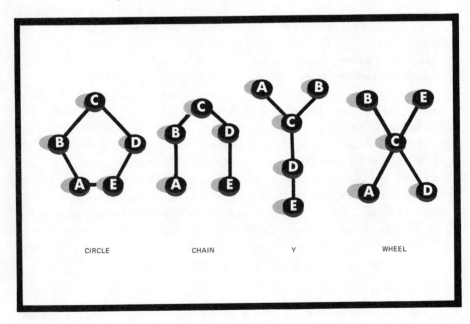

CIRCLE   CHAIN   Y   WHEEL

FIGURE 3-3.

SOME FINDINGS   Persons in the most *central* positions, such as C in the Y or Wheel, most enjoyed their group experience. Persons in the most peripheral positions, such as A and E on the Chain or A, B, and E on the Y, were more frustrated and dissatisfied. On the whole, the circle, with freest interaction was the most enjoyed by its members; the wheel, while quite as efficient in solving the problem, was disliked by four of its five members.

The time required, on the average, to solve the problems, did not differ significantly among patterns, although the wheel had a slight advantage.

SOURCE: *J. abnorm. soc. Psychol.*, 1951, XLV, 38-50.

In Leavitt's experiment, the highest level of member satisfaction was achieved by the circle, in which every member had the same freedom of interaction which every other member was given. Spontaneous communication is most readily achieved in peer groups, where members feel that they are all on the same level. The presence of a lower-status participant is less inhibiting than would be the presence of some higher-status authority figure. One study (Harvey, 1953) has shown that the abilities of persons in high-status positions are overestimated by subordinates who look up to them. This overestimation is gradually internalized by the important personage and he comes to think of himself as more superior than he really is. This is an occupational hazard of prestige positions, affecting teachers whose pupils often (but not always) are less knowledgeable, clergymen who preach, judges who pass sentence, managers who direct the work of others, and other officials, in or out of government, who are vested with authority. The wiser among them learn to deprecate their own powers and talents, giving subordinates genuine respect and appreciation.

A study (Foshay, 1951) of the frequency with which children showed considerate behavior toward classmates demonstrated that those children who rated *low* on the classroom Social Distance Scale because few children wanted to associate with them were inconsiderately treated both by the high-acceptance pupils and by other low-acceptance youngsters. Those who had high social status were usually given considerate treatment by fellow pupils at all social levels.

Status differences within any group tend to restrict communication. People commonly feel obliged to watch what they say to their superiors. When committees or discussion groups bring together people of different rank—military officers, for example, or doctors and nurses, or supervisors and workers—a deliberate effort is sometimes made to minimize the status differentials. "Whatever you may be outside the group, here you are to be plain Tom, Dick or Harry—no rank, no degrees, no prestige beyond that of every other member!" A similar rule—unspoken—often prevails at informal, off-duty, social gatherings.

A strong pressure toward equality arises from the need to make everyone feel at ease. When students are asked to grade one another, almost everyone is awarded an A; when asked to grade themselves the requirements of modesty may lead to a B, but a B for everyone. In one college department where democratic policies allowed every member to vote on promotion, all members not yet full professors were recommended each year for advancement. To promote good feeling and reduce rivalry, in many establishments waiters pool their tips and divide them evenly; and during hard times salesmen have been known voluntarily to pool and divide commissions. In factories where piecework pay would permit great variation in earnings, it often turns out that all remain close to an acceptable group norm. Helen, a new employee in a plant where 50 units was the usual day's output, soon passed that level. She was subjected to hints and direct warnings which led her to ease her pace. Separated from her fellow workers, she demonstrated that she could easily produce 70, 80, then 90 units. Back in the group, however, she felt she had better be content with an undistinguished 55.

Children, in one laboratory experiment, worked in groups of four, each child building one wall with toy bricks. Under highly competitive motivation, the fastest worker received all the candy, the others none. Under semicompetitive motivation, the child who laid the most bricks got the most candy; the second got less; the third still less; and the slowest only a little, but everyone got something. Under equalitarian rewards, each child received the same amount however fast or slow his work. The highly competitive motivation resulted in rapid but slipshod work by the fastest workers with poor coordination at corners where the walls joined. Those who knew they were losing ceased to make an effort. Equalitarian motivation led all the children to do a better quality of work, especially at the points at which cooperation was necessary. It was especially interesting that every child— even the ones who had won the top prizes—when given a choice, preferred the situation with equal rewards (Tseng, 1952).

The Zuni Indian culture is one that has fostered solidarity by disparaging any effort on the part of individuals to try to rise higher in status. A man who aspires to be a leader is criticized, laughed to scorn, and perhaps accused of sorcery. A young man who consistently outruns his competitors in foot-races, is debarred from further competition. The ideal Zuni citizen is seen as one who has his own dignity but has never endeavored to be better than his fellows. This culture, while highly cohesive, has some difficulty in filling necessary executive offices. During elections, the door of the hall is barred so that no one may escape, while pressure is exerted on one reluctant candidate after another until eventually someone yields and accepts the unwelcome responsibility.

Convergence

The accomplishment of any systematic activity depends upon coordinated behavior and attitudes of the individual's involved. Societies cannot be sustained, social systems cannot achieve their goals, groups cannot function, without the coordination of behavior and attitudes. Groups are a central fact of human life; they are the tools by which individuals organize to deal more effectively with their environment than they could as isolated individuals. They are the natural result of the social needs of individuals and the dependence upon others for the satisfaction of one's needs, including the need for survival and the perpetuation of the species. As humans organize into groups, their behavior and attitudes must converge in order to coordinate their behavior and to optimize their cooperation.

The next section of this chapter deals with convergence. We shall first discuss group norms as a major cause of coordinated activity, then conformity as a result of group norms, and mass hysteria as an unusual but powerful source of convergence in crises. Group decision making will be briefly discussed, and finally, the issues of which groups one identifies with and conforms to their norms. The issue of individuality will also be discussed.

Norms

Norms refer to the common evaluative beliefs which specify the forms of behavior appropriate for members of the group. They are the prescribed modes of conduct and belief that guide behavior and facilitate interaction by specifying the kinds of responses expected and acceptable in a particular situation. All groups have norms, either set formally or informally; a group of students who frequently party together for example, will have common ideas about what is acceptable and unacceptable behavior at a party, and what is expected of the participants. More formally organized groups such as classrooms will have norms concerning absence, when it is permissible to speak, arriving late, and accomplishing assigned work. In any group some norms specify the behavior expected of all group members, and other norms apply only to individuals in specific roles. In the classroom, for example, there are norms which govern both the teacher's and the students' behavior, but other norms may apply only to the teacher or only to the students. Since norms refer to the expected behavior sanctioned (rewarded or punished) by a group, they have a specific "ought" or "must" quality; group members should not disrupt the group's work, group members ought to participate, and so on.

The norms of any group vary in importance. Those that are less important to the objectives and values of the group usually allow for a greater range of behavior, and bring less severe pressures for individuals to conform than do norms which are highly relevant for group functioning.

In order for a group norm to influence an individual's behavior, the individual must recognize the existence of the regulation for behavior, perceive that other group members accept and follow the regulation, and accept and follow the regulation himself. At first, an individual may conform to a group norm because the group typically rewards conforming behavior and punishes nonconforming behavior. Later, the individual may internalize the norm and conform to it even when there are no other group members present. A regulation that all members should be on time for group meetings, for example, becomes a norm only to the extent that the individual group member accepts the regulation, perceives other group members as accepting the regulation, and the members of the group enforce the regulation among themselves.

Now that norms are defined, a person may wonder why they exist in the first place? Why do groups have norms? What are the functions of group norms in group life? There are several reasons. First, norms have the general function of tying individuals into the group so that they remain in the group and carry out specific assignments which help the group accomplish its goals. Without norms coordinating and integrating the behavior of different group members, systematic work on accomplishing the group goals could not take place. Second, norms form a common framework for interactions among group members, by specifying desirable and undesirable behaviors (Sherif, 1936; Festinger, 1950). This common frame of reference produces homogeneity of values among members of a group. Third, norms serve as substitutes for informal or short-term influence (Thibaut and Kelley, 1959). A leader, by using his power, can force group members to conform to his plan of work. This moment-to-moment exercise of power can be obviated by establishing relevant norms to influence the behavior of other group members. Both the weaker and the stronger parties tend to gain from the introduction of mutually acceptable norms which introduce regularity and control into the relationship without necessitating direct interpersonal application of power. The leader avoids the resistances and lack of wholehearted cooperation which often results from applying power in coercive ways; the group members gain increased ability to influence the leader through the norms which specify the leader's expected behavior and the limits of the leader's authority. Norms, in other words, protect group members from having leaders use their power in capricious ways and liberate the leader from constantly monitoring the behavior of low power individuals to insure that they are conforming.

Norms acquire power, therefore, because the individuals involved have given up some of their personal power to the norms. People allow themselves to be influenced by norms in ways which they would never allow themselves to be influenced by others, as norms often assume the characteristics of moral obligations. At the very least, conformity to the group's norms is a requirement for continued membership in the group.

Group norms have powerful influences upon the behavior of group members. In a classical experiment Sherif (1936) demonstrated that group standards exist and influence behavior in ambiguous situations, even when the group is not present. Asch's (1956) experiments demonstrated that even on matters of unambiguous fact many people will conform to an erroneous group judgment. Group norms may be so strong that new leaders, coming into the group, need to accommodate themselves to the well established customs and traditions. A man who is transferred in to manage a department in a business will become very unpopular and may fail if he tries to institute procedures which violate the group norms. Abstract 4 shows that even among kindergarten children a new leader—despite evidence of previous successful domination—usually cannot override the group norms. The power of group norms has been put to effective use in Alcoholics Anonymous. Thousands of men and women who were apparently unable to overcome self-destructive drinking have found it possible to change their individual conduct with the support of this organization. Regular attendance at testimonial meetings helps to reemphasize adherence to the new code. The member recognizes that his fellows have been through experiences like his own, and they speak his language. He is loyal to them and can count on their support. This program, while sometimes successful, has not appealed to many others who could not identify with its norms. The use of similar group methods has been used to control, change, and influence the behavior of delinquents and students (Johnson, 1970).

We must guard against letting the concept of norms lead us to expect too much agreement. While the norms of our society include respect for law and private property, we live among thieves who do not conform to this expectation. Some sociologists regard delinquent behavior as expression of the norm of a subgroup such as a gang or what Sutherland (1937) calls a "profession" of thieves. Merton (1949) proposed that when a society sets up goals and aspirations in its norms, but fails to provide the legitimate means for its members to realize these aims, some members will turn to illegitimate channels. Cohen (1955) has carried this argument forward. When lower-class boys find themselves sharing the same plight, with no realistic hope of achieving by respectable means high status and wealth to buy the widely-advertised material goods, they set up, not a subculture but a "counterculture" with norms which give substitute status and sanction a kind of revenge upon middle-class respectability (Cohen, 1955, Cloward, Oberlin, 1960). In any group there are individuals who do not conform to the group's norms at any one time; most individuals feel moved once in a while to stand up for a principle that is not popular in the groups to which they belong; others often make systematic attempts to change the nature of the group norms when disagreement arises.

CONFORMITY

In interpersonal relationships and in groups, there is a tendency for social relationships to move toward stability. The apparent resemblance among individuals who see one another and who talk together was among the first phenomena to attract the attention of social psychologists. Walter Bagehot, writing in 1873, noted "the necessity which rules all but the strongest men to imitate what is before their eyes." *Imitation*, one of the first concepts widely used in social psychology, was used to explain the mimicry of children, the acquisition of language and customs, the relative uniformity within each cultural group. Tarde (1890), a French political scientist, developed "laws" of imitation. One, for example, which he called the "law of descent" was based on observation that people lower in social status tried to imitate those whom they saw as their superiors. Subject nations imitate their conquerors. He noted that innovations begin in cities and are imitated by people in rural regions. Tarde did not distinguish the several different processes which he grouped under the one term. They ranged from unconscious, compulsive, irrational repetition of the responses others are making, to deliberate copying with ulterior motives.

In our society conformity has acquired a general negative connotation. Conformity to group norms is frequently thought of as violating one's principles in order to obtain group acceptance, or as selling out one's individuality in order to get ahead. Much of the research on conformity is based upon behaviors such as lying about one's perceptions or beliefs. Conforming to group norms, however, frequently improves the functioning of a group at no expense to the individual's principles or beliefs. Conforming to a classroom norm that one should not disturb others who are trying to study, for example, is beneficial for the classroom group and the individuals involved. There are, in other words, conditions under which conformity to group norms may violate important values and principles of an individual and other conditions under which conformity will support them.

Perhaps the most frequently researched area in conformity is conformity to group pressure. The studies by Sherif (1936) and Asch (1956) (see Abstract 6) both focus upon the effects of group pressure on individual judgments. Recent formulations of conformity, however, have defined it as a change in behavior or belief toward a group as a result of real or imagined group pressure (Kiesler and Kiesler, 1969) and have stated that in discussing conformity it is necessary to posit at least two dimensions: conformity—anticonformity and independence—dependence. (Willis, 1963; Allen, 1965; Hollander and Willis, 1967). The conformers and anticonformers both react to the group norm and base their behavior upon it, the conformers to agree with the norm and the anti-conformers to disagree with the norm. An independent person, on the other hand, does not give undue importance to the group norm in making his judgment.

As was mentioned earlier, not all behavior is covered by group norms. Not many groups care what foods their members eat or whether they prefer one brand of soft drinks to another. Group norms deal primarily with the behaviors affecting the accomplishment of the group's task and the ability of the

---

Abstract 6

TITLE   Effects of Group Pressure upon the Modification and Distortion of Judgments

AUTHOR   S. E. Asch

PROBLEM   Will people trust their own judgment when a majority of others disagree?

SUBJECTS   Fifty male college students

PROCEDURE   Subjects tried to choose which of several lines came closest in length to a line they had just seen. Each naïve subject found himself in a group (3 to 15 members) most or all of whom agreed on an answer different from his own. The student thus faced a conflict between accepting the evidence of his own eyes and going along with the group.

SOME FINDINGS   Sixty-eight percent of the individual estimates remained independent despite difference from the unanimous confederates; 32 percent were deflected part or all of the way to the unanimous judgment of their associates. One-fourth of the subjects made no concessions to the unanimous majority; one-third conformed in half or more of the trials. Whether the majority consisted, in absolute size, of 3 or 15 members made little difference, so long as it was unanimous. If one other member agreed with the naïve subject, the tendency to err in the direction of the majority estimate dropped from 32 percent to 10 percent.

If the subject reported his results secretly, the promajority errors were fewer.

SOURCE: H. Guetzkow (ed.), *Groups, Leadership, and Men.* Pittsburgh: Carnegie Press, 1951.

Abstract 7

TITLE   Interpersonal Communication in Small Groups

AUTHORS   Leon Festinger and John Thibaut

PROBLEM   How much pressure does a group exert on those who oppose the prevailing opinion?

SUBJECTS   41 groups of college students; 6-14 members in each group

PROCEDURES   Group members using a 7-point scale, reported their opinion on a controversial issue: one was in football strategy, another concerned the best type of foster home for a delinquent boy. Groups varied in range of opinion and in instruction: some were told to try to reach a unanimous opinion; others that "experts" had unanimously agreed on a correct solution and the group score would depend on the proportions of members selecting the correct answer; others to try to have a plurality for the best answer; still others only to discuss the question. All communication took place by written messages, which enabled identification of sender and addressee. This written discussion continued for 20 minutes.

SOME FINDINGS In all groups the person whose opinion deviated furthest from the rest of the group received the most communication. The stronger the pressure toward uniformity, the greater the proportion directed to extremes. If minority reports were permitted by the instructions, there was less tendency to concentrate communication on extreme deviates. Instead, subgroups formed. On the foster home problem, students originally had stronger feelings and fewer changed to agree with the majority. The higher the pressure toward uniformity, the greater the agreement reached in the group.

SOURCE: *J. abnorm. soc. Psychol.*, 1951, XLVI, 92-99.

---

group to maintain itself over time. In general, the more relevant the individual's behavior is to the accomplishment of the group's task and the maintenance of the group, the more the pressures toward conformity. Schachter (1951), Emerson (1954), and Schachter and his associates (1954), for example, have all found in their studies of deviation from group norms that the more the deviation was relevant to the purposes of the group, the greater was the rejection of the deviant by the group. Festinger (1950) and Allen (1965) state that there will be greater pressures to conform to task-related norms where goal attainment depends on the coordinated behavior of the group members. Raven and Rietsema (1957) found that the clearer the group goal and the path to the goal are to the group members, the stronger will be the pressures toward uniformity in task behavior.

Not everyone in the group is expected to conform to group norms to the same degree. According to Hollander and Willis (1967), there is more acceptance of nonconformity for the high-status members in some directions and greater restrictions in others. They say that this is due to the fact that leaders are often "keepers of the group's traditions" while at the same time expected to innovate and initiate change within the group. In general, nonconforming behaviors which are perceived by the group's members as potentially improving the group's ability to accomplish its task and maintain itself are accepted; nonconforming behaviors which interfere with group maintenance and task accomplishment are not accepted.

Reference groups

In a simple preindustrial society, individuals are strongly enmeshed in a given kinship group or tribe. They need not choose; birth places each person. In our complex civilization individuals do choose among many possible group affiliations. The groups in which a person feels that he belongs, or to which he aspires to belong, become his "reference groups." Merton's study, summarized in Abstract 8, illustrates the application of a theory of reference

Abstract 8

TITLE   Contributions to the Theory of Reference Group Behavior

AUTHOR   R. K. Merton

PROBLEM   How the concept of "reference group" can help to interpret various puzzling findings obtained in the study of attitudes of soldiers.

SUBJECTS   Many thousands of enlisted men and officers were tested during World War II under the auspices of the Research Branch, Information and Education Division of the War Department.

PROCEDURES   Merton picks out, from the large mass of data, four pertinent observations which need interpretation.

1. In the Air Force, where promotions were frequent, more men indicated dissatisfaction with the opportunity that "a soldier with ability" has for promotion than in the Military Police, where promotions were very infrequent. Fewer M.P.'s indicated dissatisfaction with chances for promotion. In general, the *less* the opportunity a branch of the service had for promotion, the more favorable its members were toward promotion opportunity.

2. Although most men overseas in wartime felt that those stationed in the United States "had it better," opinion polls did not indicate much lower morale abroad. Thus 32 percent of men overseas reported that they were "usually in good spirits;" the comparable figure for troops stationed in the United States was 41 percent.

3. Married men over 20 years of age were much more likely (41 percent) to say they should have been deferred, single men under 20 were less apt (10 percent) to feel that their induction was unfair.

4. An attitude of "ready to get into an actual battle-zone" was found among 45 percent of new troops abroad; 28 percent of equally inexperienced men who had been shifted as replacements into outfits which had been in combat; and 15 percent of veterans who had been in combat.

SOME FINDINGS   Each of the above observations can be explained with the aid of the concept of reference groups.

1. Air Force men, comparing their fate with comrades who had moved up rapidly, were more dissatisfied on promotion policies. Their reference group was their own, not another branch of the service.

2. Men overseas compared their fate with others, also overseas; the troops back home were not their reference group.

3. The married men were more dissatisfied because many of them knew of exceptions which draft boards had made; others "in their shoes" got a better break than they did.

4. Replacements identified with the veterans in the experienced combat units to which they were assigned; their attitudes shifted from what raw troops usually felt, to come closer to the prevailing view in the group in which they wanted to be accepted.

SOURCE: R. K. Merton, and P. F. Lazarsfeld, ed., *Continuities in Social Research: Studies in the Scope and Method of the American Soldier.* Glencoe, Ill.: The Free Press, 1950, pp. 40-105.

groups to interpreting attitudes in the Army.

Whether you consider yourself rich or poor depends upon your reference group. Compared with certain wealthy cliques, most of us would be "poor relations." Compared with villagers in India who are paid only a few cents for a day's work, we are grandly prosperous. To answer other questions about ourselves—are we intelligent? good looking? well adjusted? hard working? happy? right-thinking?—we need to define our reference group. In some circles we would rank at the top, in others, quite low.

Circumstances at any moment may determine which reference group is uppermost in an individual's mind. In one experiment (Charters, Newcomb, 1952) some psychology students were asked to answer a written attitude questionnaire in a classroom group where no reference had been made to their religious affiliation; other students were brought together in homogeneous groups of Catholics, Jews or Protestants, with their common faith emphasized, and given the same questionnaire. The Catholic students especially showed more deviation from Catholic norms when they thought of themselves as psychology students than they did when they came together as Catholics.

Conflict between reference groups

One of the most famous studies in the still young science of social psychology is Newcomb's exploration of political attitudes of Bennington College students during the depression years. The study is summarized in Abstract 9. Those girls whose reference groups, either by actual membership or by aspiration, were composed of campus leaders became more and more "progressive," in accordance with the college atmosphere prevailing at that time. Those girls who felt a little out of their element on the college campus, but who felt at ease in, or wanted particularly to be accepted by, the back-home circles remained conservative. In some cases the conflict between the expectations of the two kinds of reference groups became acute.

The mobility in contemporary American life confronts the individual with many conflicts. Group norms of the home give way to other norms as the

---

Abstract 9

TITLE   Personality and Social Change

AUTHOR   Theodore Newcomb

PROBLEM   How do student attitudes change as they go through a residential college with well established norms of attitude?

SUBJECTS   Students (women) at Bennington College, 1935-1939.

PROCEDURES   Tests of political-economic progressivism (PEP) were given to faculty and student body each year. A "Guess Who" technique secured nominations of girls regarded as outstanding in one or another aspect of personality or campus activity.

SOME FINDINGS   Scores decreased (i.e., became less conservative and more progressive) from an average of 44 for the freshmen, to 41 for the sophomores, 39 for juniors, 38 for seniors and the faculty scored still lower. In 1936, about 66 percent of the parents of students favored Landon for President; he was supported by 62 percent of the freshmen, 43 percent of sophomores and only 15 percent of juniors and seniors.

Freshmen estimated the average attitudes in the college as more conservative than they really were; seniors were more accurate and were keenly aware of the big difference between freshmen and themselves.

A sociometric test, based on nomination by each student of five girls "most worthy to represent Bennington College in a national convention," led to the finding that the students never named averaged 72 in their P.E.P. scores; those most often named averaged 54.

Students identified as "most absorbed in social life and weekends" included none from the lowest sixth (most progressive) on P.E.P. scores and more than half (59 percent) of those from the highest sixth. Students identified as "most absorbed in college community affairs" came often (36 percent) from the lowest sixth; none came from the top sixth. Students whose reference group was the campus leaders were progressive as freshmen and became more so; those whose reference group was their family and social life off-campus were more conservative. "Those individuals who become most fully assimilated into a community most completely adopt the behavior approved by it." Some, anxious for status but lacking certain essential abilities, adopted the prevailing attitudes as a way of identifying with the leaders. Those who participated least in the campus community were unaware of their exceptional conservatism.

SOURCE: New York Dryden Press, 1943.

---

child moves out to his play group, to high school, to college, to the Army, to work, to a home of his own, to a higher job in another community, and so on to retirement. Reference groups are shifted and sometimes their demands seem incompatible. The carefully brought up adolescent finds himself in a peer group where necking is *de rigeur*. The student proctor has been cited in one article (Stouffer, 1949) as a paradigm of conflict; his loyalty to friends pulls him one way; his responsibilities as a representative of the college administration draw him in an opposite direction. Many juvenile delinquents experience some conflict between what important reference groups seem to be demanding of them.

In one study of Jewish adolescents, Rosen (1955) found that if parents and peer group both observed dietary laws, 83 percent of the subjects also observed them and planned to comply with the laws in their own homes after marriage. If both were nonobservant, 88 percent of the youth followed this pattern. When attitudes of these two major reference groups were in conflict, 74 percent went with the peer group; only 26 percent with the parents. But for those cases which reported closer ties and more time spent with parents than with peers, 81 percent followed the parental norms.

Another type of conflict may be found in some chaplains with the armed forces; Jesus and the saints say "Love your enemy;" the Army does not. Conflicts which appear to exist within the individual personality can often be better understood as resulting from incompatible norms of reference groups.

Mass hysteria

A special kind of conformity is evident in the behavior of a mob rioting in anger or surging in panic to escape from a building on fire. The French sociologist, Gustave Le Bon, in his influential book *The Crowd* (1895), described the member of a crowd as in a state like hypnosis: "Having lost all his conscious personality, he obeys all the suggestions of the operator (leader) . . . and commits acts in utter contradiction with his character and habits." Another factor is that "the individual forming part of a crowd acquires, solely from numerical considerations, a feeling of invincible power which allows him to yield to instincts which, had he been alone, he would perforce have kept under restraint. He will be the less disposed to restrain himself from the consideration that, a crowd being anonymous, and in consequence irresponsible, the sentiment of responsibility which always controls individuals disappears entirely." Then "contagion" controls. Le Bon says, "In a crowd, every sentiment and act is contagious, and contagious to such a degree that an individual readily sacrifices his personal interest to the collective interest."

Freud (1921) observed that Le Bon's view of the crowd corresponded to the psychoanalytic concept of the *Id.* "The mass mind, as it has been outlined by Le Bon, shows not a single feature which a psychoanalyst would find any difficulty in placing. . . . A mass is impulsive, changeable and irritable. It is led almost exclusively by the unconscious. . . . It cannot tolerate any delay between its desire and the fulfillment of what it desires. It has a sense of omnipotence. . . . (It) is extraordinarily credulous . . . it has no critical faculty . . . It thinks in images . . . It wants to be ruled and oppressed and to fear its masters . . . Masses demand illusions and cannot do without them. They constantly give what is unreal precedence over what is real. . . ."

Almost everyone has at some time been caught up in the passions and activities of an irrational crowd. After a football victory, a stampede of college students in one Midwestern town tore down goalposts, then fences around the field, paraded down Main Street, and finally broke into the local movie theatre. Evangelists in some communities have almost hypnotized audiences in tents with oratory, singing, rhythmic chanting, clapping, and sometimes dancing. The sect called Holy Rollers is one of many in which spiritual ecstasy has been associated with involuntary physical spasms. Political leaders have stirred mobs into frantic activity; primitive war dances worked up to frenzied attack; lynch mobs have transformed normally friendly, law-abiding citizens into screaming, bloodthirsty maniacs.

Using a broad range of incidents from history, Smelser (1963) has sorted "collective behavior" into five categories: (1) panics; (2) crazes; (3) hostile outbursts; (4) norm-oriented movements; and (5) value-oriented movements. One of the conditions common to all of these is the absence of institutionalized means for reorganizing the social situation as desired.

One emotional effect of the group is likely to be reduction in an individual's sense of responsibility and caution. Contrary to what some would have predicted, group decisions frequently involve more readiness to take a risk than would have been true of the same persons acting individually. In an experiment in which prudence might lead to small financial gains with little risk, but recklessness might bring large gains or large losses, individuals were more apt to be prudent, groups more willing to venture rashly or daringly (Wallach, Kogan, Bem, 1962; also 1964). There was more risk taking by group consensus than when individuals decided for themselves or for the group. In the next chapter, this factor will be examined further.

Anyone in panic may act irrationally, but in a maddened crowd, the control of reason may be still further reduced. An ill-considered act by one person may stimulate or sanction something even more extreme in others. Orson Welles, in a radio broadcast, "Invasion from Mars," created so realistic a drama that hundreds of people took it seriously and started to flee (Cantril, 1940).

Race riots have taken place in recent years in a number of American communities, large and small, in the North as well as in the South. Lynch mobs appeared, especially but not exclusively in the Southern states, with peak fervor in the late nineteenth century. The modal pattern contained the following elements:

1. A ground of frustration and insecurity. Correlation of number of lynchings (1882-1930) with price of cotton was −.67. Participants were most apt to come from "poor white" sections.

2. An exciting rumor as the catalyst, frequently exploiting the sexual theme: Negro attacks white girl. Rape, in fact, was alleged in only about 25 percent of the recorded attempts at lynching. The race riots in Detroit, on a hot Sunday afternoon in June, 1943, were touched off by a rumor in Negro circles that white hoodlums had thrown a Negro baby off the bridge over the Detroit river; among whites the rumor was that Negroes had thrown a white baby off the bridge.

3. Action initiated by some less-inhibited "leaders." Intolerance of calmer counsel.

4. Unthinking participation by the mob, with individuals swept off their feet and carried along in blind conformity.

5. An outbreak of general violence—window-smashing, looting, arson. Persons with criminal records are unusually active at this stage.

6. Closing of ranks afterward; solidarity; no tattling. Punishment has been very rare.

Attacks on alleged pro-Germans in the Midwest during World War I; on Jews in Eastern Europe and in Hitler Germany; and on alleged "Reds" or "subversives" in the United States have shown many similarities. Deprivation, contagious excitement, inhibition of self-criticism, and blind conformity have led to outrageous acts.

An instance in which newspapers fanned the flames of mass hysteria has been reported by Johnson (1945) under the striking title: "The 'Phantom Anaesthetist' of Mattoon." A woman in an Illinois city of 16,000 reported to the police that someone had opened her bedroom window and sprayed her with a sickening, sweet-smelling gas which partially paralyzed her. The paper headlined next day: "Anaesthetic Prowler on Loose." The account led two other families to report that they had recently become mysteriously ill or upset during the night. During the next week 22 new cases reported attacks; only four of them were seen by physicians and all were diagnosed as hysteria. Just before the peak of the attacks the following story was carried in the Chicago Herald American:

Groggy as Londoners, under protracted aerial blitzing, this town's bewildered citizens reeled today under the repeated attacks of a mad anaesthetist who has sprayed a deadly nerve gas into 13 homes and has knocked out 27 victims. Seventy others dashing to the area in response to the alarm, fell under the influence of the gas last night. All skepticism has vanished and Mattoon grimly concedes it must fight haphazardly against a demented phantom adversary who has been seen only fleetingly and so far has evaded traps laid by city and state police and posses of townsmen.

(Page 1, Sept. 8, 1944)

A comparison of the "yielders," who thought they suffered attacks, with the total population of the city, showed that the suggestible were: more often women than men; over 20 years of age; had less education and came from lower economic levels.

Still another kind of hysterical conformity can be seen in meetings of such religious sects as have acquired names like Holy Rollers and Holy Jumpers. A sociologist (Hoult, 1958) reports that he once attended a religious celebration of the Church of Self-Realization of All Religions, where, after repeating the Hindu syllable Om over and over again for five minutes or more, he found himself making a weaving motion with the other participants and losing sense of time, place and distinctive self.

A dramatic account of "The Funeral of 'Sister President' " has been given by Douglass (1939). So many tried to attend the services in the little church that the building cracked and the crowd rushed over to the school. In excitement during the preaching and chanting, the audience stamped, shouted, screamed, and several fell prostrate. During the fifteenth century in Europe, whole communities joined in enthralling manias of religious dancing (Haecker).

In any mob or crowd, members show uniform behavior because they are moved by a common impulse. The distinctive features of individual personalities are submerged in the surge of emotional action. These are highly dramatic but exceptional circumstances. We return to the kind of convergence which characterizes all groups under more usual or normal conditions.

Obedience to Authority

From the first time that a child hears the word "no" to the time that a dying individual automatically takes various medicines, obedience for human beings is a life-long lesson in social interaction. In a world of fast moving traffic, overcrowded buildings, specified hunting seasons, we owe our continued existence to the obedience to authority of most of our citizens. Without obedience to the laws and norms of society, social life would be impossible; legal codes of some level of sophistication have been present in every society in recorded history. Yet obedience is submission, and in a democracy the conditions under which obedience to authority facilitates the development of our society, and the conditions under which obedience to authority undermines the democratic nature of our society are not always clear. In almost every society, persistent deviation from codes of behavior brings rejection and punishment.

If obedience to authority allows society to function, it is often fraught with harsh consequences as well. The leaders of one's groups or of one's country are never always right nor do they always have the good of any specific individual in mind when they take action. War, for example, is as old as nations themselves, yet this century has seen the achievement of scientific progress that has escalated military slaughter to massive scale. The horrors of world War II are still well within our range of memory, from the Nazi death camps with their daily quotas to the instant carnage of nuclear attack. Regardless of where, and under what circumstances, such policies and actions originated, only through the obedience of large numbers of individuals was enactment possible. Nor should we be amazed at the responses at the Nuremberg trials where the refrain was heard *ad nauseum*, "Those were my orders; I had no choice but to obey." The assassination of civilians in the Viet Nam village of My Lai demonstrated that American men in the armed forces also may yield to murderous impulses.

Most of the laboratory research dealing with how far a person will deviate from his own convictions in response to social pressure has dealt with actions and issues which were trivial in content. In the early 1960s, however, a program of research was initiated by Stanley Milgram to see just how far subjects would proceed before they refused to comply with the instructions of an experimenter. The purpose of his experiments was to isolate factors controlling the degree of obedience to experimental demands, and in manipulating those conditions to analyze the psychological process of obedience. The basic experimental format consisted of attempting to induce normal male adults to give another person, known to have a mild heart condition, electric shocks so severe as to be painful, agonizing, and dangerous. The situation was supposed to be a learning experiment; whenever the "learner" made an error he was to be punished. The degree of shock punishment could vary in 30 stages from 15 to 450 volts and from "slight shock," "very strong," "intense," "extreme intensity," "dangerous," to "XXX." Through a rigged drawing, the "learner" was a confederate to the experimenter who made random errors while the experimenter commanded the subject to administer increasingly severe shock. (In actuality, no shock was administered.) If the subject had not refused to administer the shock before the 300-volt level, the confederate (who was in an adjacent room) would kick against the wall and refuse to answer further questions. All behavior up to the point where the subject refused to follow the experimenter's instructions to administer an increasingly severe shock was considered to be obedience. In such a situation, at what point would you stop? How severe would a shock have to be in order for you to refuse to administer it? Fourteen Yale psychology majors predicted that less than 3 percent of the subjects would continue to the most potent shock level. In the actual results of the initial experiment (Milgram, 1963), of the forty subjects only five refused to go beyond the 300 volt level. Twenty-six of the subjects (65 percent) obeyed the orders of the experimenter to the end, proceeding to punish the learner until the most potent shock available was reached. Although a few subjects were calm throughout with only minimal signs of tension, many showed intense emotional and nervous tension with profuse sweating, trembling, stuttering, even weeping; when the experiment was over most showed signs of relief. In spite of these levels of tension, the significant majority completely conformed to the instructions of the authority (i.e., the experimenter). An observer of this initial experiment commented:

I observed a mature and initially poised businessman enter the laboratory smiling and confident. Within 20 minutes he was reduced to a twitching, stuttering, wreck, who was rapidly approaching a point of nervous collapse. He constantly pulled on his earlobe, and twisted his hands. At one point he pushed his fist into his forehand and muttered, "Oh god, let's stop it." And yet he continued to respond to every word of the experimenter and obeyed to the end. (p. 377)

Shortly after the early experiments were published, Baumrind (1964) among others raised a critical voice, expressing concern not only over the well-being of subjects, but the effect of such work on the image of social psychology. After the initial experiment was completed, Milgram (1964b) sent a written report of the experiment and its results to all participating subjects and requested them to respond to a questionnaire indicating their attitudes about the experiment. Ninety-two percent of the subjects responded and 83.7 percent indicated that the experiment was personally meaningful and valuable, even though the experience was far from pleasant. One of the most pointed comments was, "If this experiment serves to jar people out of complacency, it will have served its end."

In a subsequent study Milgram (1964a) studied the effects of group pressure on the obedience level of a naive subject. In a control condition subjects were allowed to set their own limits on the intensity of shock given the learner. In the experimental conditions, there were supposedly three subjects deciding on how much shock the "learner" should receive; two of the supposed subjects, however, were confederates of the experimenter and had been programmed to call for a one step increase in the amount of shock after each error. Although in the control condition only 15 percent of the subjects went above a moderate shock, 85 percent of the experimental subjects went above this level in conforming to their two partners. Twenty-five percent went all the way to the 375-volt "danger" level or above. Even though the subjects were not bound to the decisions of the confederates, and in spite of screams of agony from the suffering "learner," subjects without exception responded to group influence by proving willing to apply a shock at levels far above that reached in the control condition, or otherwise sanctioned in their own judgment.

In later experiments Milgram (1965a, 1965b) turned to the conditions under which disobedience to authority could be maximized. In one experiment he studied the proximity between the subject and the person receiving the shock. Proximity was varied from having the victim in an adjacent room, to hearing his voice, to having him in the same room, to having him refuse to place his hand upon a shockplate and the subject being instructed by the experimenter to force the victim's hand upon it. The data revealed that obedience was significantly reduced as the victim was rendered more immediate to the subject: 34 percent defied the experiment in the first condition, 37.5 percent in the voice feedback condition, 60 percent in the proximity condition, and 70 percent in the touch-proximity condition. Thus, the concrete, visible, and proximal presence of the victim acts in an important way to counteract the power of an authority.

In another series of experiments, Milgram (1965b) studied the effects of physical closeness and degree of surveillance of the experimenter upon the obedience of the subjects. Obedience was found to drop sharply as the experimenter was physically removed from the setting; thus obedience to destructive commands is highly dependent on the proximal relations between the authority and the subject.

Finally, Milgram (1965a) studied the effects of group pressure to disobey upon levels of subject obedience to authority. He arranged to have subjects participate in a group of three of which two were confederates who at a pre-arranged time rebelled against the experimenter's orders and refused to administer the shock. This had dramatic effects upon the level of subject obedience; 36 of the 40 subjects rebelled against the instructions of the experimenter after seeing the confederates do so. These findings are similar to the findings of Asch (1956) who found that when one other person deviated from a group judgment other members felt much more free to deviate also. The implications of these studies are interesting. It may be that when one disobeys in a group situation where there is strong pressure to conform, his disobedience may free others to also disobey.

The overall findings of Milgram's experiments perhaps surprised no one more than they surprised Milgram. As the findings of the Asch studies in the 1950s surprised social psychologists concerning the amount of conformity group pressure could induce, Milgram's findings are astounding in the amount of obedience to authority he induced. He notes (1965b):

With numbing regularity good people were seen to knuckle under to the demands of authority and perform actions that were callous and severe. Men who are in everyday life responsible and decent were seduced by the trappings of authority, by the control of their perceptions, and by the uncritical acceptance of the experimenter's definition of the situation, into performing harsh acts.

What is the limit to such obedience? At many points we attempted to establish a boundary. Cries from the victim were inserted; they were not effective enough. The victim claimed heart trouble; subjects still shock him on command. The victime pleaded that he be let free and his answers no longer registered on the signal box; subjects continued to shock him. At the outset, we had not conceived that such drastic procedures would be needed to generate disobedience, and each step was added only as the ineffectiveness of the earlier techniques became clear.

The results of the Milgram experiments are proundly disturbing. They raise the possibility that even in a democratic society such as the United States individuals are socialized in such a way that they cannot be counted upon to refuse to perform brutal and inhumane acts at the direction of a malevolent authority. A substantial proportion of people seem to do what they are told to do, irrespective of the content of the act and without limitations of conscience, so long as they perceive that the command comes from a legitimate authority. As Milgram (1965b) states, if an anonymous experimenter could successfully command adults to subdue a 50 year old man and force on him painful electric shocks against his protests, one can only wonder what government, with its vastly greater authority and prestige, can command of its citizens.

As has been repeatedly mentioned in this chapter, society cannot exist, groups cannot function unless there is coordinated behavior on the part of members to accomplish goals. In our society, with the current types of organizations we now have, obedience to authority is necessary to achieve such coordinated actions. But in a democracy, it is imperative that one's obedience to authority is not the blind obedience of Abraham who was willing to sacrifice his own son on demand, or of Eichmann who was willing to engineer the deaths of six million Jews on command, but a more considered obedience which differentiates beneficial from malevolent directives. As Harold J. Laski (1929) stated:

> . . . civilization means, above all, an unwillingness to inflict unnecessary pain. Within the ambit of that definition, those of us who heedlessly accept the commands of authority cannot yet claim to be civilized men. . . . Our business, if we desire to live a life not utterly devoid of meaning and significance, is to accept nothing which contradicts our basic experience merely because it comes to us from tradition or convention or authority.

Individuality

The attraction of group-belonging is only one side of a dynamic equilibrium; individuals also resist becoming involved in groups. Their resistance takes many forms. The obvious one is withdrawal. Every organization has its turnover and its absentee problems. Some people take pride in not being joiners—they like to accentuate their distinctiveness. A few become hermits. But resistance may also continue although the individual remains on the membership rolls and attends meetings. A member, seeking unconsciously or consciously to keep his individuality intact, avoiding concessions to fellow members, may sit quietly through the meeting, concealing his aloofness through apparent acquiescence. Or he may attempt to dominate the group; in this case he seems to be saying: "If the group becomes completely subordinate to my will, than I can be a member with no threat to my distinctive individuality." In other cases a pair or a clique may unite to oppose the generally accepted pattern of group purpose and action. The individual thus finds it possible to sustain both a feeling of belonging and at the same time his sense of separation.

The inner forces which oppose submergence in the group are like those which make it difficult for some people to make friends or to let themselves fall in love. They seem to be compounded of distrust of, or hostility to, the other, and a narcissistic love for the self with a need to affirm it. Distrust of others probably begins for everyone in the mother-infant dyad. No mother can always and in every way fulfill the demands of a baby. Inevitably, every parent in one way or another disappoints and frustrates the child. If such experiences are the exception, the need to defend oneself against groups is likely to be considerably weaker than the need to belong. Early experiences are, of course, intensified or modified by later social interactions which prove satisfying and dependable or which leave the individual feeling let down; his confidence betrayed.

A feeling about the self develops also from infancy. Some persons grow up with a need to preserve an exaggerated evaluation of their own perfection— their beauty, brains, personality, or saintliness. In moderation, self-approval is healthy. Most neurotics suffer from an inability to feel worth and value in themselves. Even the exaggerated, narcissistic self-love which makes egotists such unpleasant companions may originate as compensation for a lack of genuine self-acceptance.

It is not always easy to disentangle the mixed motives of conformity and self-assertion. Independent critical judgment may, in some cases, lead to the decision to go along with the prevailing view. A thoughtless counter-dependence may lead to negative conformity in which the decision to be different leaves the person still at the mercy of the crowd—he cannot conform even when that would be the right and best course. At present, numerous critics in America are attacking conformity and stressing the distinctive individual. A writer in a popular magazine comments: "Individuality is all the rage now." This kind of expression seems another evidence of acceptance of a prevailing norm.

Primitive societies are commonly believed to be more conforming because they are quite homogeneous. Yet Margaret Mead found among the Manus, three personality types (Mead, 1937). She could identify leaders, dependents, and independents. The leaders were aggressive in initiating lines of action; the dependents followed. The independents went off on their own; one with a tool in his hand; another talking geneology. They paid little attention to others and ignored cooperative plans. Similar types can no doubt be found on any college campus.

There are important values for the individual in group participation, but there are also important values in retaining proudly a distinctive self. Suspicion of certain others is sometimes a life-saver. It would be perilously naïve to assume that everyone we meet has our own best interest at heart, just as it is perilously cynical to assume that no one cares anything for anyone but himself. The person who asserts himself and resists group seduction, or pressure to conform, may be the one to whom future ages erect their monuments. History's innovators, heroes, saints, and martyrs have usually had to be nonconformists.

Some groups have norms which sanction individuality. They approve critical thinking, dissent, and resistance to conformity. They give what Hollander has called "idiosyncratic credit" (1958). They may do this only for high-status members who are admired for their unique behavior, or the privilege may extend to all members. In the following chapter we shall consider some differences in productivity between groups which follow their leader and those which encourage diversity.

Another kind of solution for the dilemma of conformity or deviation is for the individual to discover or to imagine a reference group which would support his views and in which he would not be a deviate. In a heterogeneous society like a large city today, one can find supporters and coworkers for almost any viewpoint. Newcomb (1963) advocates selection of the like-minded as "an adaptation to a world that includes both persons and issues." Then, one need not sacrifice either "belonging" or "principle"—they can be united.

Indeed, one may appeal, not to any living group of supporters, but to the verdict of history or the communion of the saints. William James (1890) said that one might gather strength to brave the condemnation of one's present associates "by the thought of other and better *possible* social judges than those whose verdict goes against me now" (p. 315).

SUMMARY

A group is defined by three criteria: interaction among members, satisfaction of member's needs: and self-awareness. The smallest group unit is the dyad or the two member group. The triad, or three member group is considered unstable because of the tendency toward coalition-formation. Members of a group generally seem to find small groups more satisfying than large groups.

Being a member of groups is one of the most characteristic aspects of the human species. Many goals can only be accomplished with the assistance of others. People seek affiliation in order to assimilate differences of opinion, anxiety and other emotions. Many goals can only be accomplished with the assistance of others. Individuals need the opinions of others to establish the correctness of their beliefs, values and attitudes, and to find some standards for self-evaluation. This is called the social comparison theory and it helps explain man's propensity to form groups.

During the past dozen years there has been an enormous increase in the participation of young people and adults in groups which focus mainly on the "here-and-now" feelings of members for one-another. The main function of most of these groups is to increase self-awareness and thereby facilitate the development of interpersonal skills and personal developments. This is accomplished when feedback for the group gives a person the opportunity to (1) increase his self-awareness of how others perceive his behavior, (2) determine the consequences of his behavior, and (3) change his behavior if he wishes to do so. Feedback should be given in a way that will not increase the defensiveness of the receiver.

Sociometry is a technique used to study groups. Sociometric techniques record the attraction or repulsion which persons feel for one another. This technique is useful in helping to identify both leaders and isolates.

127

The more frequently people interact with each other, the stronger their friendship is likely to become. Group cohesion is defined as "the resultant of all forces acting on members to remain in the group." Four factors which motivate individuals to feel attached to a group are: The attractiveness of other members; perceived similarity between oneself and others; nature of group goals; how characteristics of the group relate to individuals needs and values.

Norms are common beliefs of an evaluative type held by members of a group. All groups have norms, set formally or informally. One function of norms is tying individuals into groups so that they remain in them and carry out assignments which help the group accomplish its goals. Second, norms provide a common frame of reference for reacting to one another by specifying what behavior is desirable and undesirable. Third, norms serve as substitutes for informal or short term influence. That is to say, they stabilize behavior, and consequently reduce the necessity of high power individuals constantly monitoring the behavior of low power individuals to insure conformity. Conformity to the group's norms is a requirement for continued membership in the group. Group norms exert a strong influence on members, and a new leader must be careful not to violate established norms.

Imitation of the behavior of people we admire is called conformity. Some individuals conform to group norms, and some resist them. Both are influenced by group norms and are dependent; the independent person makes his own decision without being influenced by group norms. Groups tend to put pressure on individuals to follow their norms. The more the norm helps the group accomplish its goals, the more pressure is exerted. Some nonconformity is accepted if the group feels it may help in accomplishing its goals.

Conformity in its extreme is mass hysteria. In mass hysteria, the distinctive features of individual personalities are submerged in a surge of emotional action. Smelser (1963) has sorted collective behavior into five categories: (1) Panic; (2) Crazes; (3) Hostile outbursts; (4) Norm-oriented movements; and (5) Value-oriented movement.

The groups to which an individual belongs or aspires to belong are called reference groups. An individual generally belongs to more than one reference group. Conflict between norms of different reference groups frequently occurs.

Obedience to authority is necessary for groups to function. However it is often fraught with harsh consequences. Stanley Milgram (1965) ran experiments to determine how far subjects would proceed before they refused to comply with the instructions of an experimenter. He found that 65 percent of the subjects would carry out orders to the end of the procedure, no matter how contradictory the orders were to their values and sensitivity. When group pressure demanded. conformity to the dictates of authority, the individual was even more likely to follow commands. When the subject was made more aware of his activity, he was less likely to conform.

Individuals are attracted to group belonging but they also resist becoming involved in groups. It is not always easy to untangle the mixed motives of self-assertion. Margaret Mead (1937) identifies three types of individuals: the leaders, the dependents who tend to conform, and the independents who go their own way.

Group Productivity

IMPORTANCE OF
WORK BY GROUPS

An increasingly important part of the world's work is carried on by groups. Corporations today are seldom run by a "strong man;" more reliance is placed on boards, conferences, and committees. An executive in government, business, education or social welfare may spend as much as 90 percent of his working day in cooperative planning with small groups of staff or public. Our laws are written by legislative committees, enforced by operating commissions, and violations are judged by groups ranging from local juries to the Supreme Court. Education, which at one time was often dyadic—a tutor and one pupil—now proceeds largely in classes, large or small. Psychotherapy, once limited to a doctor-patient dyad, may be carried on in groups. Research, once the province of the single investigator, is increasingly done by teams. The Manhattan Project of World War II, leading to the first atomic bombs, involved hundreds of distinguished scientists and thousands of assistants. Since the Rand Corporation began to render important service to the government a generation ago, the so called "think-tank" has led to planning groups focused on future developments in communities, industries, and even universities. Group operations have two kinds of potential advantage over action by a single individual. One is in the caliber of thinking, the range of resources, and the critical scrutiny which enter the problem solving. The other is in the willingness with which people carry out decisions they have helped to make.

Yet, group sessions often prove quite ineffective. They turn out to be time-consuming, dull, and frustrating. Personalities clash; a few feel driven to dominate in order "to get something done;" others may then resign themselves to accepting whatever the leader wants. Although some students find stimulation in discussion groups, others shun them. "We never get anywhere!" is a common complaint.

Another common objection to work in groups is the fear that individuality may be submerged. In the preceding chapter we commented on the way in which persons may be carried along in the mass emotion of crowds and mobs. Feelings in committees and discussion groups are seldom so extreme, but individuals still may be swayed toward conformity. One of the conditions for good group work is expression of different opinions; this is often difficult because of pressure to get a working agreement.

Actually, as we shall see, groups may sometimes be more sane, moderate, well balanced and wise than their average member. There are some groups in which passions are inflamed and individuals do, as Freud and Le Bon observed, surrender their individual minds and morals, submerging their own selves in a kind of social torrent. There are other groups, however, in which each individual is helped to be more fully himself. A thoughtful group may make its members more rational, more self-critical, and more ready to revise personal prejudices in the light of objective evidence, than these members would be if they were studying alone.

Man has mastered control of steampower, internal combustion engines, electric motors and is beginning to use power from atomic fission and fusion. Our skill in exploiting the immense potentialities of the power of human cooperation has advanced very little from prehistoric times until rather recently. Now, scientific study of group dynamics is opening the way to better utilization of the creative energy of human personalities. We shall review first the evidence on how well groups can solve problems; then we shall go on to study factors which may increase the intellectual productivity of working groups.

A CLASS EXPERIMENT

The evidence which follows may be understood better if readers have first tried one or two experiments comparing the problem-solving ability of individuals and groups. One procedure is to develop a sheet of test problems on which everyone may have some limited knowledge, but no student is likely to know all the right answers. The problems may be chosen from any area where people have diverse opinions but where research has established firm answers not commonly known. One task frequently used calls for deciding the relative importance of certain items of equipment for a moon-exploration team. Another might make use of recent findings on environmental pollution and its remedies. Still another might cover racial or sex difference studies.

Each student answers the test, working in the usual individual isolation. Then the class is divided into small groups (5-7 members) to compare individual answers, to discuss differences, and to try to achieve consensus on the best answer to each question. A key giving the correct answers as determined by authoritative research is distributed. Each individual scores his own test and the first to finish in each group scores the group decisions. The group answers are compared with the poorest, the average, and the best individual in the group. How does the group result compare with the individual performances? Finally the class analyzes cases in which some individuals in a group had the right answer but the group decided on an inferior response.

Productivity of individuals and groups

A variety of studies have compared the productivity of individuals working alone or in groups. Abstract 10 reports a study conducted by one of the authors which demonstrated that group work was relatively more successful than individual performance especially for those questions in which the right answer, once hit upon, was readily apparent. Thorndike (1938) corroborated the findings of this study. In addition he found that although groups consistently surpassed the average performance both when the range of responses was definitely limited (as in multiple-choice tests), and when the range was unlimited (as in open-end completion tasks), the superiority was a little greater in the free-completion situation, where a larger range of responses could be used.

Shaw (1932) conducted a study comparing individual and group performance on a series of puzzle problems. One was how to ferry three "missionaries" and three "cannibals" across a river, with a boat which could carry only two at a time, with one cannibal and all missionaries able to row, and the condition imposed that cannibals must never outnumber missionaries on either side of the river. Twenty-one students, working alone, spent from 2½ to 29 minutes on this problem; none of them solved it correctly. Of five groups (4 students in each), three reached correct solutions in times varying from 12 to 34 minutes. Shaw found that groups averaged better than individuals on four of her six problems; on two there were no clear differences. Fox and Lorge (Fox, 1955) compared solutions to a practical military problem (getting a group of men across a mined road with certain available ropes, sticks, trees, and so on). They found the quality of solution by 70 groups of five officers each, averaged distinctly higher than the average of proposals by 70 officers working as individuals. In a comparison of the ability of individuals and groups to draw logical conclusions, Barnlund (1959) found the results after group discussion were better than those achieved by majority vote or by the average group member. Studies by Taylor, Berry and Block (1958) and by Dunnette, Campbell and Jaastad (1963), however, indicate that in brainstorming, group performance is not superior to the pooled output of the individuals.

In most comparisons, group performance in problem-solving is superior to the average individual performance, and is sometimes even superior to the best individual in the group. In our next section we will consider which facets of the problem-solving process might produce the relative superiority of group versus individual effort.

Abstract 10

TITLE   Do Groups Think More Effectively Than Individuals?

AUTHOR   Goodwin Watson

PROBLEM   Will students working in small groups solve intelligence tests better than they would if working alone?

SUBJECTS   68 graduate students

PROCEDURES   Three equivalent forms of an intelligence test were devised, each consisting of nine tasks suited to bright adults.

     Each student took one test alone; then he joined with other students in a group of four or five members to solve the second test cooperatively. The third form was again taken by each individual alone. The two individual performances were averaged to offset practice improvement and show about how well each individual would have done at the time he joined the group performance. Groups had had no previous practice in working together and were allowed only ten minutes per task.

SOME FINDINGS   In total score, 11 of the 15 groups excelled their *average* member; 6 of the 15 excelled their *best* individual performer. Tasks were found to vary in suitability for individual or group solution. In decoding a cipher or in drawing the rigidly correct logical conclusion from certain given facts, or in hitting upon the right word to meet certain specifications, 90 percent of groups reach a conclusion superior to their average member and 50 percent excelled their best member. A difficult reading-comprehension test, on the other hand, was better suited to individual performance; only 53 percent of the group surpassed their average member and 30 percent their best member. On a creative task—composing the wittiest possible limerick with a prescribed first line—80 percent of groups did better than their average individual performance, and 30 percent excelled the best individual creation. A rough overall estimate would lead to the expectation that a typical group, under conditions of limited time and no previous practice, might be expected to attain a level of effective intellectual performance of about the seventieth percentile of its members.

SOURCE: G. Murphy and L. B. Murphy, *Experimental Social Psychology*. New York: Harper and Brothers, 1931, pp. 539-543.

FACTORS IN GROUP SUPERIORITY

There are a variety of factors which may contribute to the superiority of group performance over individual, and which may hamper group problem solving. In this section we shall discuss the facilitating factors; in the following section the factors which may hamper group performance will be discussed. The main facilitating factors are: (1) stimulation from the presence of others, (2) pooling of resources, (3) probability of being able to use the insight of an unusually able individual, (4) canceling of chance errors, (5) correcting individual blind spots, (6) cumulative interaction, and (7) security in risk taking.

Presence of others

One of the first facts to impress investigators in social psychology is that the individual working in the presence of others performs somewhat differently than he would if working at the same task in isolation. Many years ago Floyd Allport (1920) published some data showing that students writing a chain of free word-associations in the presence of several others also doing the same task (they were told not to compete) scored slightly more replies than they did when working at the same task alone. When the task was to write down arguments for or against an idea, more arguments occurred to students writing in the presence of others, but the quality was not as good. In a series of routine clerical tasks (crossing out vowels, simple multiplication tasks) six subjects did better working in isolation; 13 did better working alongside others. An experiment on routine tasks with British school children (age 11-13) showed more than 80 percent making higher scores when working alone (Mukerji, 1940). A similar experiment with a group of 40 Ukrainian children trying to recall a series of seven words and seven associated numbers, showed a slightly better performance in the presence of the group (Elkin, 1926). Another psychologist (Travis, 1925) tested the eye-hand coordination of college men alone, and later in the presence of an audience of four to eight older students who were strangers to the one being tested. Scores with observers present were a little higher.

The best known research on this problem was done by Dashiell (1930) who varied the experiment, comparing subjects: (a) working entirely alone; (b) working alongside others around two large tables but told not to compete, that their performance would not be compared with others; (c) same situation as (b) but instructed to compete; and (d) working under the close scrutiny of two fellow students who served as "observers." Speed of work at three different tasks was consistently highest under "observation" (d), but accuracy under scrutiny was lowest. Competitive motivation increased speed but not accuracy. Work done in the presence of others also working (non-competitively) was neither as rapid nor as accurate as work when subjects were in a room alone. Putting all the evidence together we can conclude that group members will usually be stimulated by the presence of others to put forth more effort, but that attention to the others is somewhat disconcerting and likely to reduce accuracy.

There has been little interest recently in the effect of working in the presence of others until Zajonc (1965, 1966) published two reviews of the experimental results of both human and animal studies. He proposed that the presence of others, either a passive audience or others working on similar tasks, impairs the learning of new responses, but facilitates the performance of those that have already been learned. Presumably animals have generally motivating or arousing effects on other animals; people generally motivate or arouse other people. Human learning studies have frequently demonstrated that drive increases the probability of occurrence of those responses dominant in the subject's repertory. If the subject has previously learned or almost learned a solution, the correct response will be dominant and the presence of others will facilitate performance. If the task is complex and the correct response is not yet dominant in the hierarchy of possible responses, incorrect responses will be promoted by the presence of others. Zajonc (1965) concludes with some advice which is perhaps only half serious:

> If one were to draw one practical suggestion from (this) review . . . he would advise the student to study all alone, preferably in an isolated cubicle, and to arrange to take his examinations in the company of many other students, on stage, and in the presence of a large audience. The results of his examination would be beyond his wildest expectations, provided, of course, he had learned his material quite thoroughly. (p. 274)

Why does the presence of others have these effects, what is it about the presence of others that improves or degrades performance? Jones and Gerard (1967) state that the effects of an audience are mediated primarily through self-consciousness on the part of the subject, his concern with how he appears in the eyes of others. This has been termed *evaluation apprehension;* the concern that one is making a positive impression upon observers. This same process may also account for the abundant evidence that individuals show greater conformity when their responses are monitored by others than when they are permitted to respond privately or anonymously. Jones and Gerard state that there are two consequences of evaluation apprehension. The first is that the person's normal desire to perform well, to acquit himself with distinction or at least to avoid failure, is strengthened by the presence of others. Observers sit in judgment, and through his perception of the audience's reactions, the performer judges his own worth and capacities. The increased desire to do well motivates the individual to increase his speed of movement or reaction, and, therefore, the quantity of work per unit of time is typically increased. Second, the presence of observers may make the individual so self-conscious about how well he is performing (stage fright) that his attention is distracted from the task itself. A person who is giving a speech, and whose evaluation apprehension reaches too high a level will be likely to forget what he is trying to say.

Several things should be emphasized about the effects of the presence of others upon a person's performance. One is that the Zajonc proposition can be expected to hold only when others are observing or performing at the same level. Through vicarious learning and imitation one's performance will be *increased* if others are performing at a more advanced level. In addition, before research in this area can be generalized to many situations, our theoretical understanding of audience effects will need testing with a diversity of tasks, performers, audiences and observation settings. It appears that much depends on the personal significance of the audience for the performer, and this depends on his personality, the nature of the audience, and the type of task involved.

Pooled resources

Without any doubt the members of a group can pool their physical strengths (as in a tug of war) to accomplish physical feats that are beyond the capacity of individual members. Moede (1914), as reported in Chapter 1, measured the increased strength of pull on a rope when additional team members were added. Each new member increased the total pull, but by an amount less than he was able to pull when tested alone. This investigation fits in with the data just reported from experiments on group word-construction and making suggestions for maintaining morale. The performance of five persons is better than that of any one, but each of the five does not contribute as much in the group as he might if he had been working alone. If the task permits each contribution to be made individually and the contributions to be simply added together, the total achievement will be higher than the group achievement. In most group work, the full potential of each member is not utilized.

The real point of working in a group is that members have different contributions to make. The intellectual work that went into the construction of the first atomic bomb, for example, was the product of complementary skills brought into harmony and coordination. In most situations, the information needed to solve a problem is distributed among several different individuals, and only by pooling their resources can the group see all the pertinent difficulties and possible solutions. The complementary talents or knowledge must be properly coordinated through discussion or administrative decision; otherwise there is little reason to expect individuals to be outperformed by groups. The more accurately the resources of each member are judged, and the more the members are assigned to their areas of expertise, the more likely it is that a problem will yield to group effort.

Probability of the appearance of an able individual

Another kind of superiority for group thinking arises from the simple statistical probability that since people vary in ability in each group, there are likely to be some members well above the average group level. Assume that we design a problem so difficult that 80 percent of the students in a class are unable to solve it. Suppose, then, we divide the students into groups of five to work on this problem. If one of that top 20 percent is in each group, every group may come out with a correct solution, even though most of the group members were unable to figure out the solution by themselves. A considerable superiority of group performance over the average individual member could result simply by using as the group score the performance of the best individual members.

The several members of a group differ not only in intelligence but also in motivation. Some are more willing than others to do hard work. Practical problems may often require someone to do a time-consuming, pains-taking chore. If the problem is left to a single person, he may or may not be ready to put forth the necessary effort. If the problem is the joint responsibility of half-a-dozen committee members, the chance of having at least one of them willing to take on the difficult chore is increased. Indeed, a common complaint from class committees developing a group project is that some members shirk and leave most of the necessary work to one or two "eager beavers." This may not be good education—we shall discuss classroom groups later—but organizations are often more concerned about being sure that a certain job does get done. If a task is necessary and important, and if we cannot know whether any given individual will put forth the required effort, assignment to a group is likely to mean that at least one conscientious member does see that the work is properly accomplished.

Chance errors cancel out

Some errors are due to chance or random influences which operate differently on the various members of a group. Suppose some members happen to overestimate while others underestimate. If these are averaged, the result will be more accurate than the typical individual.

In one experiment of this kind (Gordon, 1924), 200 university students estimated the weight of ten similar looking cubes and tried to arrange them correctly from lightest to heaviest. The average individual success was indicated by a correlation of .41. If the answers of five students were averaged, the correlation of this average with the true order rose to .68. If ten individual judgments were combined, the accuracy rose to a correlation of .79; averaging in lots of 20 each gave a correlation of .86 and combining 50 estimates gave a correlation of .94. This takes place without any discussion or interaction, simply because chance errors tend to cancel out other chance errors.

Some decades ago a German psychologist made a composite photograph of the faces of school children, taking pictures of identical size so that the negatives could be superimposed to give a single print. The composite face of a number of boys turned out to be more regular, and hence more handsome, than any one of the individuals. The composite girl was prettier, but less distinctive, than any of the separate pictures. Even an artificial combination like this minimizes deviations from the norm.

In a roomful of students, where the actual temperature was 72°, each was asked to estimate the room temperature (Knight, 1921). The range was from 60° to 89°, with an average at 72.4°, very close to the truth. In the same study, fifteen advertisements, the returns from which were known, were rated by forty judges. Correlations of ratings with the actual pulling power of the ad ranged from −.71 to +.87 with an average at .18. Combined individual ranks into a single group ranking produced a correlation of .63. Ten of the forty judges surpassed the combined estimate.

A study of judgments of the number of dots on a card (there were 3,159) made by individual Air Force officers showed an average error of 3,330; in dyads the error fell to 1,081; in triads to 850 and for a group of six members to 773 (Ziller, 1957). On a judgment task (which facts were relevant to a given problem) scores rose steadily from 3.2 for individuals and 4.2 for dyads to 5.8 for groups of six.

If the individual judgments are all worthless or are consistently wrong, then nothing is gained by combining them. The guess of ten judges on where a roulette wheel will stop has no validity because none of the judges can do better than a zero correlation. When students were asked, for example in Knight's study, to estimate intelligence from photographs, and the average individual was more wrong than right (correlation of −.21) the group judgment was no better (correlation of −.18).

There is no wisdom gained from pooling ignorance, and if each member is wrong, the group does not set things right. Composite judgments are better than those of single individuals only when most individuals are partly right.

Blind spots corrected

It is easier for us to see other people's mistakes than it is to perceive our own. Some people prefer to work alone rather than in groups because, working alone, they are unchecked. In a group, however, someone may say "Wait a minute! Aren't you overlooking this point?" This can be annoying, but correction is useful. In a series of experiments in the Soviet Union, Bekhterev (1924) and his associates demonstrated the utility of social criticism. Pictures were shown for a brief period to groups; each individual then wrote down all the details he could remember. A discussion period followed in which the group tried to reach consensus about each item. The group decision corrected many of the mistaken ideas of deviate individuals.

In laboratory experiments, psychologists have usually used some kind of problem with a single identifiable "correct" solution. Such questions make for easy, valid scoring. There are important differences, however, between questions with one known right answer and the usual tasks of work groups in our society. We do not often assemble committees to solve puzzles in which all parts fall neatly into place after the correct idea is proposed. Their task is usually to forge some kind of workable compromise among conflicting interests, values, and considerations. With real problems it is not so easy to be sure which proposals are "wrong." Yet even in group work on creative tasks, members often contribute by rejecting leads which would only waste time.

In Lorge's studies, reported earlier, of the ability of individuals and groups to devise solutions for typical military problems (getting a patrol group across a mined road; raising morale at an isolated Arctic air base), group discussion frequently disposed of inadequate ideas which individuals, working alone, would have been content to recommend. While most of the best ideas could be traced to ingenious, creative individuals, the group rejected numerous plausible fallacies. Fewer "zany" and unworkable notions were able to get past the screen of group criticism.

If group thinking did nothing more than to correct or eliminate the answers which are much worse than average, that would be an important service to the world. Perhaps we suffer as much from crassly stupid and inept individual acts, which group consideration would surely have rejected, as we do from inability to reach the highest and most creative levels of thought.

Stimulation from cumulative interaction

Participation in group discussion can do more than filter out silly or harmful notions; it may also stimulate ideas which would not have occurred to individuals working alone. A model may be the musical "jam session" which is continuously creative. Each member responds to all the others.

Evidence that discussion adds something to the compilation of individual answers appears in the study of Barnlund (1959), reported earlier. After group discussion, decisions surpassed both the average vote and the best individual answers.

In another experiment (Timmons, 1939) subjects working alone and in groups rated five proposals for changing Ohio's system of paroling convicts. Results after group discussion were found better (closer to what experts believed) than the results achieved by any kind of pooling of individual ratings in "statisticized groups," (Lorge's term) whether based on averages or majority opinion.

The stimulating power of discussion appears particularly in meetings which succeed in devising a better solution than any single member had in mind when he came. Usually it has been found productive to encourage considerable "free wheeling" in a creative discussion. Fantastic ideas are tossed about for a while because they may help the thinking to take a new and productive turn.

A test of brain-storming techniques on one division of General Motors brought out over 100 ways in which a rough casting might be burred. Not all were really practical, but the objective in a brain-storming session is to prevent premature discard of an idea merely because it would be difficult, costly, disapproved by certain influential persons, or resisted because it upsets traditional concepts or ways of working.

It is not easy, in a practical situation, to adhere to the rule of listing even those suggestions which appear, at first glance, ridiculous. In one instance, reported to the writer, a comptroller refused a department head's request for added personnel to cope with a temporary emergency. He proposed, instead, that all concerned should brain-storm on ways of doing the work with the existing company personnel. One proposal, which the comptroller wanted to reject out of hand was that certain people in his office might be used. The rules previously agreed on forced him to listen, and this solution was later approved by all as the best.

A widely noted study by Taylor et al. (1958), compared the production by college men brain-storming alone with the output from groups of four. The production by individuals working alone were artificially collated in aggregates of four and these statisticized groups produced more ideas and better ideas than were recorded in the actual groups.

Meadow et al. (1959), found, in contrast to Taylor, that when students had been trained—rather than merely instructed—in the use of brain-storming methods, they produced more, and more creative, solutions.

A project in which groups tried to bring out in discussion all the similarities they could find in two pictures, showed "waves" of stimulation. Proposals would occur along one line until that vein was nearly exhausted. Someone would then suggest another type of similarity. This set off a round of other contributions following the new line. When this flagged, another approach was offered, stimulating a further flow of ideas using a different concept. Shaw (1961) calls the process by which one member of a group takes off from the ideas of a previous speaker "hitch-hiking."

We may now summarize the factors which often contribute to a high level of group performances: social stimulation; range of resources; probability of including some person(s) of high ability or strong motivation or both; canceling out of chance errors; correction of individual blind spots; and cumulative interaction.

Risk-taking

In Chapter 3 we mentioned that people in groups may be willing to venture further than they would on their own. A series of experiments (Stoner, 1961; Wallach et al., 1962 and 1964; Marquis, 1962) has confirmed this finding. The problems studied included a change to a job with less security but more chance of financial success; a high return but risky investment; a college where one could be fairly sure of being graduated as against one with more prestige but less certainty of success, and other problems. One study used actual winnings on quiz questions rather than hypothetical situations. The results fairly consistently support the probability of greater risk taking by a group than by the average individual judgments of the group members. One of Marquis' experiments focused on how a group would modify a decision made by its designated leader. Leaders reached their decisions after conducting a group discussion, but on a basis of personal responsibility. Then they had an opportunity for further free discussions with group members. Of 48 possible shifts in the leader's own decision after the second group session, 22 showed no change; two became more cautious; and 24 moved in the direction of taking greater risk. The leader designated was one whose own initial reaction was at the median for his group; hence group members were in equal numbers more cautious and more adventurous than he. Still both group decisions and leader decision involved more risk taking than either the members or the leader would have ventured on their own responsibility. In an experiment summarized in Chapter 5, Ziller (1957) reported that air crews after group discussion chose more risky decisions than their officers would have made.

This area of group production has not yet been studied fully enough to answer all important questions. Experience suggests that frequently boards and committees put a damper on individual initiative. Yet, apparently, at other times and perhaps more often, they give support to someone whose ideas are a little more creative and more advanced than those of the average member of the group.

COOPERATIVE ACTION
TOWARD GROUP GOALS

One of the most interesting phenomena characterizing group membership and participation is the relative balance achieved between the satisfaction of individual motives and the attainment of group goals. Group productivity is based primarily upon the commitment and motivation of members to accomplish the group's goals. Defining a group goal is a difficult task. For one thing, a person's perception of the group goal depends upon his reasons for joining the club originally, and his reasons for remaining a member. A member's commitment and motivation to accomplishing goals depends upon both the attractiveness of the goal for him and the perceived probability of the group's being able to accomplish the goal. Unless there is a reasonable chance of success, there will be little motivation to work toward it. It is assumed, furthermore, that a person may join because a group is instrumental in achieving some particular goal for him, but over a period of time may find other attractive and rewarding aspects of group membership. When this happens, group membership becomes functionally autonomous, that is, an end in itself rather than a means to an end (Allport, 1937). Finally, the members of the group can influence each other's desire to reach objectives that are highly valued by a significant number of group members and serve their collective interests.

In addition to the commitment and motivation to goal accomplishment of the membership of a group, there must be coordinated action toward the achievement of those desired goals. Group members pool their resources and talents to increase the likelihood of accomplishing shared objectives. In such a situation the level of cooperation among group members affects their productivity. A theory of cooperative action has been developed by Deutsch (1949, 1962).

Deutsch defines a cooperative social situation as one where the goals of the separate individuals are so linked together that there is a positive correlation between their goal attainments. Under pure cooperative conditions, an individual can obtain his goal only if the others with whom he is linked can obtain their goals. An example of a cooperative relationship is a baseball team. Their goal is to win the baseball game, and in such a team sport if one person accomplishes the goal of winning, every member of the team also accomplishes the goal.

From the definition of cooperation it follows that when any individual behaves in such a way as to increase his chances of goal attainment, he increases the chances that the other members with whom he is linked will also achieve their goals. Deutsch states that the psychological consequences of such a state of affairs are: (1) substitutability—the actions of members in a cooperative relationship are interchangeable. If one member has engaged in a certain behavior there is no need for others within the relationship to repeat the behavior; (2) positive cathexis—if the actions of one member in a cooperative relationship move the individuals towards their goal, his actions (and he as a person) will be favorably evaluated by the others; and (3) inducibility—if the actions of a person in a cooperative relationship move the others toward their goal, the others will be receptive to his attempts to induce them to engage in behavior which will facilitate his actions.

In a competitive social situation, the individual's goals are so linked that there is a negative correlation between their goal attainments (Deutsch, 1949, 1962). Under pure competition an individual can obtain his goal only if the others with whom he is linked cannot obtain their goals. An example of a competitive situation is an atheletic contest between two teams; both their goals are to win and if one team wins the other team has failed to accomplish its goal. In a competitive relationship, when any individual behaves in such a way as to increase his chances of goal attainment, he decreases the chances that the others with whom he is linked will achieve their goals. One may expect just the opposite of substitutability, positive cathexis, and positive inducibility if a person perceives another's actions are decreasing rather than increasing his chances of goal attainment. That is, he will hinder rather than facilitate, be negatively rather than positively influenced, dislike rather than like, correct rather than be satisfied with the other's actions.

Deutsch (1949) compared the effects of cooperative and competitive grading systems in experimental sections of an introductory college psychology course. In half of the sections the students were graded cooperatively; that is, all students in the same group received the same grade on the basis of how well the group's discussion and analysis of a human relations problem compared with other similar groups. In the other half of the sections, the students were graded competitively. They were told that the student who was judged to have contributed the most to their section's discussion and analysis of a human relations problem would get the highest grade, the next most productive student the next highest grade, and so on. Thus, in the competitive sections individuals competed against fellow group members for grades (a situation similar to most classrooms); in the cooperative sections individuals cooperated with their fellow group members to enable the group to do as well as possible in its competition with other groups. The results of the experiment indicated that the two different grading procedures had definite and predictable effects upon behavior in the classroom. Groups that were cooperatively interdependent with respect to grades were characterized by much friendlier discussion; they learned each other's names more rapidly, were more satisfied with their discussions, were more attentive to, and more influenced by what their fellow group members said, and they felt more secure personally. In the groups that were competitively interdependent with respect to grades, students behaved in more aggressive, obstructive, oppositional and self-defensive ways. There was less sense of being listened to and of being understood, and there were more misunderstandings and more frequent need for repetition of what had just been said. In both types of situations the students seemed equally and strongly motivated to do well in the course and no significant differences in individual learning were obtained.

A large number of studies have replicated Deutsch's findings and supported his theory. The theory has great relevance to discussions of group productivity, since conflicts of interest arise within any group, competitiveness around leadership and power, conflicting perceptions of what the group should do next, and attempts to influence. Many work groups become immobilized as the internal competitiveness obstructs the group's progress toward its overall goals. Effective coordination of member behavior toward the accomplishment of the overall group goals depends upon the development of cooperation among group members.

FACTORS HAMPERING
GROUP PERFORMANCE

What, now, are some of the ways in which groups are less efficient than their members would be if working alone? Six factors can be identified: (1) leaving one's share of the work to others; (2) conflicting goals; (3) failure to communicate; (4) interference of suggestions from various viewpoints; (5) frustration from interference and criticism; and (6) lack of the unity which characterizes the best aesthetic creativity. Most of these are readily apparent and require little explanation.

Leaving work to others

The "let George do it" attitude illustrates the tendency in groups to assume that someone else will take the necessary responsibility. Experience in panel presentations is that some members, if they do not have a specified responsibility, may skimp on preparation and rely on the inspiration of the moment. We have cited several studies supporting the conclusion that added members do not contribute to the group as much as they are capable of doing alone.

Conflicting goals

Members bring into a group project a variety of motives. Some may even want, consciously or unconsciously, to sabotage the group effort. Others have self-oriented needs (Fouriezos, *et al.*, 1950) e.g.: to get the better of certain rivals, to win affection from a pair member, to obtain emotional release for some feelings, to show off, to be a clown, or to withdraw. These all interfere with attention to the group enterprise. Self-oriented needs may interfere with production when working alone, also, but they are likely to be more vivid and demanding in the actual face-to-face relations with others. Member competition, discussed above, often hampers group effectiveness.

Even when members are genuinely work-oriented and anxious to achieve results, they may have different ideas about how to proceed. Each proposes steps toward the goal he has in mind; yet to others, these proposals may seem irrelevant or tangential or ill-timed. The "hidden agenda" is a concept which has proved useful in analyzing the work of a group. All groups proceed on two levels. One is the explicit, avowed rational purpose. The other level is often ignored as if members could really lay aside their private, covert purposes and feelings. Personal ties and resentments "should not" influence certain personnel decisions and may be covered over with calm, objective statistical approaches, but the discerning observer may note that the figures have been marshaled to boost one man and to defeat another.

Failure to communicate

Communication is essential for group thinking, but it may be restricted for many reasons. Some members may feel shy and reluctant to talk. Status differences may inhibit subordinates from appearing to criticize those of higher rank. Some people are apprehensive and defensive, and they take an excessive amount of talk and time to get around to any expression of their ideas. Sometimes it is hard to explain to others a distinction one sees quite clearly oneself. Many discussions founder for semantic reasons; words are being used with quite different connotations.

As a rule, the most talkative members are rated as contributing the best ideas in the group (Slater, 1955). However, the deviate and silent member is sometimes the one who, if he had spoken out, would have had a better idea than any the group has heard (Maier, Solem, 1952).

Full, free communication in group decision-making is desirable both for quality of the conclusion and also for its implementation. Sometimes the silent, inarticulate, or vaguely expressive member is concealing his reluctance to support the group decision.

Interference

In the experiment on making up words out of a set of letters, we earlier observed that if it had been possible to add together all the different words thought of by individual members (in a ten-minute period) the total would have been larger than that achieved by any group. Trying to funnel words in quickly through one secretary slowed down the rate of production. Occasionally, too, a word was driven out of the mind by conflicting suggestions from others. Often the contribution of a fellow member is distracting.

Because only one person can talk (and be heard by all others) at any one time, members in a discussion often have to wait to make their point. Sometimes the delay is so long that the whole course of the discussion has changed before the would-be speaker gets his chance to be heard. He may then drop the idea entirely, which deprives the group, or he may bring up his idea belatedly, but this causes the others to back-track when they have already moved on to other issues.

A good illustration of the interference among proposals was seen in the confused group effort to construct a crossword puzzle (Thorndike, 1938).

Frustration

All the difficulties listed above—the laziness of some members, the self-oriented behavior of others, the confusion of goals, the rambling talk of some speakers, the interference of lines of thought which do not run parallel—produce irritation and annoyance. Members who started out with good intent may give up in disgust, or may explode emotionally, ostensibly over some minor point. The course of group thinking never runs as smoothly as a computer.

One of the virtues of group consideration is also an irritant. We noted that group members often catch one another up on errors. This is wholesome for the end product, but a little hard on feelings. It is pleasanter for the individual to write along, developing his own ideas, than it is to offer them for group criticism and have them challenged (rightly or wrongly) at several points.

Insufficient unity for aesthetic creation

Group difficulty in designing a crossword puzzle is an evident case of the problem of endeavor to produce an artistic product by group effort. A work of art must have unity and coherence. A group of musicians can have fun improvising in a jam session but this is unlikely to produce a unified symphonic work. A school of painters can collaborate on a Rubens canvas, but only under the eventual direction of one mind. There have been instances of profitable collaboration—one thinks of Gilbert and Sullivan or Rodgers and Hammerstein—but no great dramas, poems or operas have been group products.

PROCESS IN WORKING GROUPS

Three different kinds of analysis mark three different historic periods in the study of group thinking.

"Group thinking" in the 1920s

Pioneer work in the 1920s followed John Dewey's famous analysis (1910) of the steps of individual problem solving. We engage in an on-going activity; an obstacle impedes our progress; we examine it for clues to the situation; we propose to ourselves some hypothesis; we test these, choose the one which best fits the facts, and resume the activity. Manuals for leaders of group thinking such as Harrison Elliott's *The Process of Group Thinking* (1928) suggest that the place to begin work in a group is with an exploration of the situation in which some difficulty has been felt. Members are urged to tell how the issue has come up in their own experience. People start talking more readily about incidents from their experience than about theories and abstractions. The reports serve an emotional as well as an intellectual purpose. They increase involvement while developing better awareness of the difficulty.

The second step is definition of the problem. Later investigations (Maier, Solem, 1962; Maier, 1963) have supported the observation that groups that are too "solution-minded" attempt prematurely to offer remedies. Then it is found that these solutions have missed the real point of the difficulty and the process must start over.

One of the differences between the novice and the expert in any field is the questions each asks. Getting the right question may be more than half of the process of effective problem solving. A common error (Maier, 1963) is the attribution of causes to personality rather than to situational factors. Another is to perceive some similarity to previous problems, and to assume too quickly that the formerly successful solutions will fit the present situation.

At the third stage, solutions are proposed and examined. Dewey described this process in the individual as dramatic imagination. The thinker constructs a scene showing how the contemplated action would probably develop and work out. At its best, this stage of group thinking represents search and examination rather than attack and defense. Personal feelings are a legitimate factor in solutions to most social problems, but are out of place in testing purely intellectual or scientific or technical answers.

Maier (1963) proposes as screening principles: (1) that solutions taken over from previous problem situations should be regarded skeptically and (2) that when members agree on a solution although disagreeing on their diagnosis of the problem, these answers are also likely to prove unsatisfactory. When generally acceptable proposals have been formulated, it is still important (if often uncongenial in impatient groups) to examine the exceptions.

As the original proposals are examined, amendments and qualifications arise. One advantage of the process of freely moving group thinking over traditional parliamentary procedure is that the best answer is not presumed to be available at the start. Parliamentary procedure starts, officially, with a motion which is seconded. The motion represents a crystallized statement of conclusion before the discussion takes place. Almost inevitably, it discourages revision and reformulation. If discussion brings out needed changes there may be amendments, amendments to the amendment, and substitute motions. The complications are due to the basic error of trying to formulate the answer, in the original motion, before the problem has been examined or the various alternatives scrutinized and modified. Good group procedure requires that the making of motions be deferred until the period of discussion is concluded; then the motion is likely to be merely a formal statement of the consensus which has been achieved.

Examination and comparison of the various alternative proposals usually reveals a need for additional facts. Apparent disagreement on the value of a line of action may rest upon quite different expectations of what outcomes would follow. At this point the group needs to consult experts, to search the relevant literature, or to design experiments. The importance of the issue under discussion governs the time and resources which can be invested in fact finding.

Eventually the group rejects alternatives which seem less desirable and concentrates on the best available solution. Ideally, the outcome of group thinking is an integration of the ideas, viewpoints, facts, and values contributed by every member. An integrative solution differs from a dominated or a compromise outcome. In power struggles one party—perhaps a single individual or a minority clique or a majority—imposes its view upon the others. Even if the majority triumphs in a perfectly fair vote, the decision is still not an integration. One side dominates and the other has to submit. A compromise is one step better. Each side gives up part of what it wants and gets something in return. The outcome is not wholly satisfactory to anyone. When a genuine integration is achieved, everyone is satisfied. Everyone's wants have been fully taken into account. The aim of group thinking is integration. Often this seems an ideal impossible of achievement. The Society of Friends has long relied upon a persistent quest for consensus in official decisions. A story is told of one congregation which had long been divided over whether to build a new meeting house. A visitor said to the clerk of the meeting after one prolonged session which adjourned with the question still unsettled: "How long do you think it will take to work this out?" "I don't know," replied the Quaker, "but when it is settled it will be right" (Chase, 1951).

The time required to achieve integration is not always wasted. A quick decision may not really be economical if it leaves tensions and the seeds of future conflicts. If people are to continue to work together or to live together as neighbors, a hasty decision which leaves some persons feeling resentful may be costly in the long run.

The final step in the process is putting the decision into action so that the movement of affairs which was interrupted by the initial difficulty can be resumed. If the agreed-upon solution does not "work," i.e., if the process does not move ahead smoothly, thought again tackles the problem of identifying the obstacle and examining new proposals. Living is continuous overcoming.

Interaction process analysis

Two decades later, another form of analysis of group procedure emerged. Bales (1950) in the Laboratory of Social Relations at Harvard, developed a set of categories designed to give a systematic classification of each act of participation in a group. As shown in Figure 4-1, the categories represent polarized dimensions; 1 is the opposite of 12; 2 of 11, etc. The first three are positive emotions; the last three express negative feelings. Categories 7, 8, and 9 request aid; 4, 5, and 6 offer it.

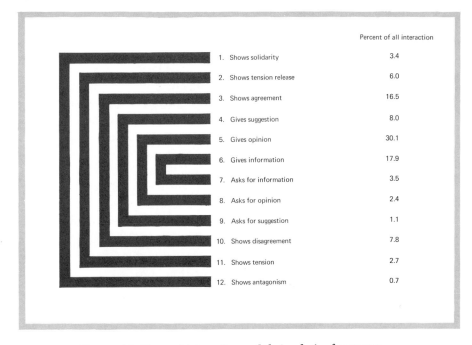

		Percent of all interaction
1.	Shows solidarity	3.4
2.	Shows tension release	6.0
3.	Shows agreement	16.5
4.	Gives suggestion	8.0
5.	Gives opinion	30.1
6.	Gives information	17.9
7.	Asks for information	3.5
8.	Asks for opinion	2.4
9.	Asks for suggestion	1.1
10.	Shows disagreement	7.8
11.	Shows tension	2.7
12.	Shows antagonism	0.7

FIGURE 4-1. Types of interaction and their relative frequency
(in 96 sessions of 24 different groups) (Bales, 1955).

Positive emotional expressions (items 1, 2, 3) are usually more than twice as frequent as negative emotional expressions (items 10, 11, 12). Opinions and information are much more often volunteered (46 percent) than requested (7 percent).

Bales (1952) was able to analyze the steps through which a working committee usually moves. A study of 22 committee work sessions, each divided into a first, second, and third phase, showed that the normal process began with *orientation* ("What is it?"); moved to relatively more concern with *evaluation* ("How do we feel about it?") and in the closing phase gave more attention to *control* ("What shall we do about it?"). As the discussion moved from the intellectual examination of the difficulty in the first phase, to evaluation and decision (control) the frequency of emotional expression increased.

A study (Borgatta, Bales, 1953) of the consistency with which an individual behaves as a group member was made for 126 subjects. Rescoring by the same judge gave satisfactory reliabilities (.65-.98). When the same fellow members were working at the same task, behavior categories "show tension release," "shows agreement," and "gives opinion" remained fairly stable characteristics of the individual. When members worked with other associates, no categories showed a consistency as high as r = .70. This means that the observed behavior is really interaction and dependent on the relationships with particular others.

The effect of the "others" was particularly studied by Stephan and Mishler (1952). They found that a member placed with others who are highly active in talking and initiating procedure will have a low rate; the same member, associated with quiet members who are slow to take part, will have a relatively high rate of initiation. The behavior of a member is an inverse function of the average interaction rate of his coparticipants.

As a rule, the member in the group who is most active in initiating verbal or other acts is also the one who receives most contributions directed toward him by others (Bales et al., 1951). The rank order is consistent from the highest initiation to the most passive. The member who seldom contributes is seldom addressed by others.

In another study (Bales, Borgatta, 1955) changes in categories of participation were studied as groups increased in size from two to seven members. All groups were composed of male college students discussing a human relations case study. Four groups of each size were used, and ratings on the twelve Bales categories averaged. The biggest difference related to group size was in category 11, "shows tension." Tension was greatest in groups of two and decreased quite consistently being only half as frequent in groups of six or seven members as in dyads. Correspondingly, joking, laughing, and other indications of a more relaxed attitude appeared more often in the larger group. Perhaps because of the greater interpersonal intimacy, the smaller groups seemed more threatening. Expressions of agreement, understanding and compliance were more frequent in the smaller groups, a finding consistent with the concept of greater tension. Suggestions and direction for others were more commonly offered in the larger group; this too fits with a feeling of less anxiety. Asking for information and for the opinion or feeling of others—a deferential behavior—was observed most often in dyads and triads. Disagreement and rejection of the ideas of others took place more freely in the larger groups.

The Bales categories do not represent the only ways of characterizing observed participation in groups. Heyns (1948), for example, designated some members as "idea men" and others as "reality testers." The "expert" is different from the highly goal-oriented member. Some, in their interpersonal relationships, tend to be supportive, others critical and rejecting. Some smooth over differences ("social harmonizer"); others try to explore and define the contrasting views.

CONTEMPORARY GROUP DYNAMICS

We have seen how, in the 1920s, Dewey's analysis of the act of thought was used as a guide to good group discussion. A later stage involved the use of categories for objective observation of ways in which members contribute. More recently, attention has been given to the dynamic factors underlying what goes on in the group. Laboratory studies of groups differing in size, composition, training, in mutual trust, and in cohesion, have led to a new profession of training persons to work more effectively within organizations.

Selection of members

In Chapter 3 we noted that as groups increase in size beyond eight or nine participants, a few members are likely to dominate and others to remain passive. Whether a group will be optimally productive depends also on how fully the necessary information, skills, and viewpoints are represented. The more homogeneous the participants, the less each member adds to the resources present in the others.

Gerard (1953) found that heterogeneous groups reached decisions which were not the average of individual choices, but were closer to the judgment of experts on the ideal problem-solution. Even diversity of temperament may be an asset. One comparison (Hoffman, 1959) of solutions to the problem of getting a squad across a mined road, devised by groups homogeneous in ten traits (measured by the Guilford Zimmerman Temperament Survey) with those devised by more heterogeneous groups showed more originality and constructive quality in the products of groups diverse in personality.

Freedom of communication

Observation of strangers as they begin to interact under laboratory conditions, with no predetermined leader or assigned task, has led one author (Bennis, 1964) to designate the phases of group development as follows:

I. Dependence
   a. Dependence; flight
   b. Counterdependence; fight
   c. Resolution
II. Interdependence
   a. Enchantment; flight
   b. Disenchantment; fight
   c. Consensual validation

In the first phase members are concerned mainly with the authority problem, supporting or resisting various claims to leadership. In the second they are concerned with the problem of intimacy and mutual trust. In the second phase, they create a false atmosphere of pseudo-harmony; disenchanted, they reject or attack one another. All this precedes the achievement of an atmosphere in which members freely express their views, receive genuine reactions, and are able to be highly productive.

A major obstacle to communication and trust arises from status differences. Those in higher positions can talk freely and be listened to, but often this is a one-way affair. One laboratory experiment (Heise, Miller, 1951) connected three-main groups by earphones in which noise might interfere. When communication was limited to one-way (A could talk only to B; B only to C; C only to A) a task took twice as long as with free back-and-forth talk. Introduction of noise on the line reduced efficiency to less than 20 percent of normal.

Many groups have an explicit or hidden power structure which impedes free communication. A study (Torrance, 1954) of problem solving by three-man B-26 combat crews (pilot, navigator, gunner) in which the pilot is in command, the navigator is a commissioned officer, and the gunner an enlisted man inferior in status to the two officers, showed that when one of the men had the right answer and the other two were mistaken, the pilots were almost always successful in persuading the other two to accept their view (94 percent). Under similar circumstances the navigators were not quite so successful (80 percent) and the gunners much less persuasive (63 percent) even when the low man on that totem pole had the answer the whole group needed.

Adequate time

The superiority of group achievement over individual work is dependent in part on having enough time. A short work period favors the individual response; it takes time for group members to become adjusted to one another, to express ideas, to assimilate one another's contributions, to interact, to criticize, and to integrate proposals. The larger the group the larger the time required.

One study (South, 1927) compared groups of three members and groups of six working at four different tasks: solving a bridge problem, solving a mechanical puzzle, matching emotions to photographs, and giving qualitative grades to English compositions. In the latter two tasks, in which it was difficult for the group to check which rating was most nearly correct, the larger groups took longer. On the first two tasks, which have an "Aha!" quality so that once the right answer is found it can be immediately recognized, the larger group with its greater resources of talent to draw upon, usually found the correct solution more quickly.

In another study (Hare, 1952) groups of Boy Scouts were given 20 minutes to discuss the relative importance of 10 pieces of camping equipment for a certain trip. Some groups contained five boys; others 12 boys each. In the smaller group, only 3 percent complained of too little time; but 22 percent made that criticism in the larger groups. Given the limited time, the small groups achieved more consensus than did the boys in the 12-member groups.

Fox and Lorge (1962) reported that in a 50-minute period individual written proposals were generally better than group products; with more time and training, group products surpassed individual solutions.

Anderson (1961) repeated our earlier study of group performance in making up words out of certain letters. Whereas we found, in a 10-minute period, that groups did not record as many different words as the total of individual papers would have provided, Anderson's groups, given 20 minutes, did achieve as many as the total of all individual responses. He also showed three-person-groups scoring about 17 percent more than did dyads.

Cohesion

Is a close, warm friendly group more or less efficient than one in which a more impersonal, matter-of-fact, businesslike attitude prevails?

Friendliness among the group members may work either way. On the one hand, when members are friendly they may waste a lot of time talking and joking about matters not closely related to the task. On the other, general good feeling in a group usually makes it easier for members to express themselves and to exchange views. A study of performance of military squads (Abstract 11), showed that groups in which members liked one another were actually more efficient in solving combat problems. Of course the correlation might equally well mean that more efficient groups develop more affection among members.

It is characteristic of the cohesive group that members cooperate readily with each other. One study (Haythorn, 1953) showed that groups which rated high in cohesion also rated high in productivity. In contrast, groups in which members made themselves disliked by dominating, eccentric or suspicious behavior were less productive. Again, the correlations could be interpreted either way.

A group which has been organized for some time and is accustomed to

---

Abstract 11

TITLE   The Use of a Sociometric Test as a Predictor of Combat Unit Effectiveness

AUTHOR   Daniel M. Goodacre, III

PROBLEM   Can a sociometric scale measuring group cohesion effectively predict group performance?

SUBJECTS   72 men in 12 reconnaissance platoon squads.

PROCEDURE   Each man was asked to indicate the men in his squad whom he would *want* and those he would *not want* to be with in a variety of situations, i.e., at a dance, during an attack, etc. The total number of men who were listed as wanted by the members of the group, minus the number of men who would not be wanted in any of these situations, was considered as the measure of group cohesion.

A field problem for scout squads from reconnaissance platoons was developed as a criterion of the effectiveness of the squads' performance. Twelve tactical situations, such as air attacks, outposting of road junctions, etc., were simulated.

SOME FINDINGS   The score that each squad obtained on the sociometric scale was correlated with the ease with which they solved the field problems. This correlation was .77. The probability of this relationship's being a chance one is less than one in one hundred.

SOURCE: *Sociometry*, 1951, XIV:148-152.

---

working as a team can withstand considerable internal conflict. French (1941) gave groups tasks which apparently could be done but were actually much more difficult than they seemed. *Ad hoc* groups—arbitrarily set up at the time of the experiment were soon disrupted by the frustration. "Traditioned" groups—basketball or football teams which had played together—expressed more interpersonal aggression but still did not break down or give up. There was more sense of freedom, more we-feeling and more equality of participation in the traditioned groups. If the tasks assigned were of a kind which a highly motivated and persistent group might be able to solve, indications were that more of the cohesive, traditioned groups would have succeeded.

Not all studies find that cohesion increases efficiency. A strong sense of belonging makes the individual want to conform to the group norm but the group norm may favor either better work or less careful work. In one experiment (Schachter, Ellertson, *et al.*, 1951) twelve groups of three girls each were led to feel very congenial; twelve more groups were led to feel disappointed in their associates. Some groups of each type received suggestions (believed to come from fellow group members) to speed up; other groups received notes which read something like: "Let's take it easy; I'm tired." Members in more cohesive groups were more inclined to follow the suggestion, whether for increased or for decreased production. Experience in industry has shown similar influences; organized workers may decide to speed up or to slow down production; if group loyalty is strong, these shared understandings are very potent.

A group climate which values only harmony and cordiality leads to repression of differences and criticisms, thus facilitating acceptance of defective or inferior products.

TRAINING AND EXPERIENCE

Most laboratory experiments on group thinking have been carried out with *ad hoc* groups, usually made up of students arbitrarily assigned to do certain tasks together. The real work of the world is seldom done this way. Committees work together for some time; boards may operate with much the same membership over years. These become traditioned groups; they are accustomed to certain ways of working together.

When individuals are first brought together to work as a group, they go through a necessary period of adjustment to one another. They need to test and evaluate each other and are likewise concerned about making a favorable impression on their fellow members. All of this interferes a little with efforts to concentrate on the task before them. They have to resolve any conflicts of power and mutual acceptance before the atmosphere for work is established. Traditioned groups can usually coordinate their contributions more easily. Sometimes, however, previous work together has led to rivalry, antagonisms, and other negative attitudes which impede communication.

Training in how to work as an effective group member is usually helpful. Fox (1955) in one set of experiments found no difference in the quality of solutions to the problem between the average individual and an average group brought together for the first time in an arbitrarily assembled group. Later, after men had had six months of training, group performance was substantially better than achievement by the average member working alone. Lorge (1953) also found that groups could improve their skill in cooperative planning.

Education has been slow to recognize its obligation—even the possibility—for training people to work effectively in groups. The tradition of the school room has been that each pupil does his own work and is graded on individual performance. Cooperation with the teacher is looked upon as an admirable character trait, but cooperation with fellow pupils without permission is still often regarded as cheating.

Since so much of the work of modern society is assigned to committees, commissions, boards, and other organized groups, and since the high ability of an individual working by himself does not guarantee a high contribution from him as a group member, an education that is only individualistic proves inadequate. Skill in working as a group member can be taught, just as skill in reading, mathematics, typing or swimming can be taught. The following list of objectives can be used as a check list for observing behavior of group members before and after training.

Some goals in training for group participation

The following qualities characterize an effective group member:

1. Aspires to become more effective; realizes he has much to learn.

2. Discounts his first impressions of others; keeps open and receptive.

3. Observes and listens carefully.

4. Expresses himself as frankly and openly as possible.

5. Confronts disagreements; examines differences rather than evades or smooths over.

6. Is not defensive; accepts his limitations; recognizes that it is easier for others to accept his human failings than his claim to superiority.

7. Reexamines problems before proposing remedies. Is problem-minded rather than solution-minded at the beginning. (Maier, Solem, 1962).

8. Checks his perceptions and understandings, seeking consensual validation. (Do others agree?)

9. Builds on the contributions of others; uses their resources where they supplement his own.

10. Defends the opportunity of minorities and deviates to be heard and understood.

11. Avoids lengthy statements, or dialogues which interest only the two members involved.

12. Is comfortable with periods of thoughtful silence.

13. Keeps alert to the need for better evidence and proposes ways to obtain it.

14. Shares in watching the continuing processes in the group, summarizing at appropriate turning points.

15. Tests proposed decisions to discover how extensively and genuinely these are supported.

16. Recognizes the value, in a continuing group, of maintaining morale; does not neglect the emotional aspects which make it satisfying for members to work together.

Practice: role-playing

Reading and approving a description of the good group member does not enable a person to act the part. The skills of group participation, like other skills, require practice and can be improved by coaching. The coach in this activity is usually an observer who records behavior of members during a group session and reports on what he has seen. Self-perception is often at variance with the facts. Highly active members may be more aware of the times they held themselves in check and waited for others to speak than of the fact that they talked more than any others in the group. Members may play one role monotonously in the group—may speak, for example, only to challenge some remark made by another member—without being aware of the stereotyped quality of this participation. They may show themselves as very defensive and yet be quite unaware of the impression they give. In accord with the consonance hypothesis they may interpret anything said by members whom they like as agreement and anything said by disliked associates as disagreement, although an objective observer would find both judgments erroneous or exaggerated.

One device used in training is role-playing which means spontaneous, unrehearsed acting out of a group situation. The training may begin with expression by some member that he has difficulty in preventing others from dominating the discussion or that he wishes he could more easily "show solidarity." After a bit of discussion to arouse interest, a typical situation is devised. The member may wish first to watch someone else play the part he finds difficult; eventually he tries it out. Now it is no longer a matter of theory; he has to perform. In the examples chosen, he would have to restrain the aggressive talker or express solidarity in an acceptable way. Role-playing scenes are best quickly cut after the main act has been finished. They can be repeated with other actors or with agreed on variations to make the task easier or harder. Frequently, audience discussion follows each role-playing, bringing out suggestions for improving future performances.

Training in a T-Group

For a group to be productive there are two additional requirements besides the ones previously discussed. They are that the individual members of the group are interpersonally competent (See Chapter 2) and that the group climate is such that the members can work together cooperatively. Both are necessary for productive work; if the group has a cooperative climate but interpersonally unskilled members, the work will deteriorate, and if the members are competent but the climate is not conducive to cooperative relationships, their skills will not be of much use. A group climate which facilitates the development of cooperative relationships is characterized by such factors as a high level of trust, openness of communication, and high concern and support for fellow members.

An education method which is used to develop interpersonal competence and to increase the cooperativeness of the climate of work groups is the sensitivity-training group, called "t-group" for short. The t-group is a highly flexible educational method which can be used to accomplish various goals. First, the t-group provides an opportunity for participants to learn how others see and interpret their behavior, and to gain insight into why they act in certain ways in certain situations. This goal can be labelled increased self-understanding. Both by helping others increase their self-awareness, and by increasing one's own understanding of why one reacts to others in certain ways, t-groups promote sensitivity to the behavior of others. A third possible goal is increased awareness and understanding of the types of processes which facilitate or inhibit the functioning of a group and the interactions between groups. Fourth, the participant obtains a set of exploratory concepts with which to diagnose social, interpersonal and intergroup situations, potentially increasing the participants' diagnostic skills. Fifth, individuals have an opportunity to experiment with behavioral styles which are not ordinarily a part of their repertoire, and may be able to find more effective ways of handling interpersonal problems. Sixth, participating in a t-group involved learning a set of inquiry skills concerning increasing one's awareness of the consequences of one's behavior, thus providing practice in a method of learning which can be applied in the future in non-t-group situations. Finally, participation in a t-group by a group of individuals who work together can change the group climate from nonproductive distrust, closed communication and hostility among the members to a climate emphasizing trust, open communication and concern and support for fellow members. In addition, specific interpersonal relationships which affect the quality of group work can be improved. The t-group experience is designed to maximize opportunities for the individual to expose his behavior, give and receive feedback, experiment with new behavior, develop an awareness and acceptance of self and others, and learn the nature of effective group functioning (Argyris, 1964b).

To achieve the goals of t-groups, the training takes place in self-directing, self-observing groups usually containing 8 to 12 members. Participants typically meet in a group that has no set agenda other than a general plan to study itself and its members. An inductive learning approach is emphasized where participants learn mainly from their own observation and experience, rather than from lectures and reading. The participant's learning results from his analysis of the way the group is functioning, from his own behavior and from his reactions to the behavior of other members and to what is happening with the group. The analysis of group members is facilitated by a professional trainer who helps participants clarify their feelings and experiences. The group strives for frank, free, open communication on a basis of mutual trust. This climate, when achieved, permits the group to use more fully the potential resources of all members, to reach decisions based upon true consensus, and to engage creatively, flexibly, and adaptively in cooperative action toward shared goals.

There are many factors affecting the quality of a t-group experience. The motivation of the participants, the skills of the trainer, the heterogeneity of group members, the length of the experience, and the setting in which it takes place all affect the quality of the learning. Perhaps the greatest advantage of t-groups lies in the flexibility to meet members' learning goals. Within the same group, for example, one member may experiment with different ways to express anger, another may learn how to accept warmth from others, another may be working on diagnostic skills, another on leadership style, and so on. Within any one group a variety of learning goals may be worked on at any given time. This intense personal learning experience, emphasizing emotional expression, often creates such a sense of closeness, mutual liking and intimacy that these emotional correlates to intense learning often seem beneficial and worthwhile in themselves.

More research has been conducted on the effects of t-groups than perhaps on any other change method with the exception of psychotherapy. At least four major reviews of the research have appeared (Buchanan, 1965; Stock, 1964; House, 1967; Campbell and Dunnette, 1968). On the basis of the research now conducted several conclusions may be reached. First, the evidence is reasonably convincing that coworkers of individuals who have participated in t-groups see them as being more skillful interpersonally than do coworkers of similar others who did not participate in t-groups. Abstract 12 illustrates this finding. Second, several studies indicate that individuals who have participated in t-groups can diagnose interpersonal situations better. Third, there is conflicting evidence concerning the effects of participating in a t-group upon self-perceptions. Many studies indicate that accuracy of self-perception is increased as a result of a t-group experience; other studies show no changes. The probable conclusion is that given individuals who are motivated to understand themselves better, the presence of "insightful" group members, a skilled trainer, and a t-group experience of adequate length, accuracy of self-perception will be increased.

Abstract 12

TITLE	The Effect of Laboratory Education upon Individual Behavior
AUTHOR	Douglas R. Bunker
PROBLEM	How do adults change as a result of t-group and laboratory experiences?
SUBJECTS	346 persons who had attended three-week (in 1960) or two-week (in 1961) training laboratories; compared with an equal number of matched controls.
PROCEDURE	Each participant rated himself eight to ten months after he had returned to his job. In addition, each was rated by from five to seven work associates: supervisors, peers, and subordinates. The questionnaire asked an open-ended question about changes in behavior in working with people. Responses were coded by a procedure giving better than 90 percent agreement among coders and also more than 90 percent on a recoded sample.

SOME FINDINGS   1. Ratings placed three times as many men who had experienced laboratory training, as compared with controls, in the top third in amount of changed observed.

2. Five times as many of the laboratory-trained group reported one or more changes verified independently by an associate.

3. The areas in which change among the laboratory-trained most exceeded change among controls were:
   a. increased sensitivity to others (35 percent *vs.* 10 percent)
   b. greater acceptance of others (49 percent *vs.* 29 percent)
   c. more openness to new information (42 percent *vs.* 23 percent)
   d. more receptive listening (34 percent *vs.* 16 percent)
   e. greater awareness of behavior (34 percent *vs.* 16 percent)
   f. heightened sensitivity to group processes (24 percent *vs.* 9 percent)
   g. better ability to relate to others (36 percent *vs.* 21 percent)
   h. more comfortable and at ease in social interaction (36 percent *vs.* 23 percent)
   i. more insight into self and role (36 percent *vs.* 24 percent)
   j. increased interdependent cooperation (38 percent *vs.* 27 percent)

SOURCE: *J. app. behav. sci.*, 1965, I: pp. 131-148

Out of the numerous studies conducted on t-groups, very few have provided unambiguous data about the effectiveness of t-groups as an educational method. The traditional way to obtain unambiguous knowledge seems simple. First, individuals who want to participate in a t-group are assigned to an experimental or a control group. Measures of the participants' behavior, attitudes, self-perceptions and so on are obtained before and after the training experience. Next, measured changes shown by the trainees between pre- and post-training periods are compared with changes, if any, occurring in the control group of similar, but untrained, persons. Using a control group has been seen as the only way to assure that changes observed in the experimental groups are actually the result of training procedures instead of possible artifactual effects resulting from the mere passage of time, poor reliability of measures, or events other than the training. Finally, it must be demonstrated that there is no interaction between the evaluation measures and the behavior of the participants during their training. If, for example, the participants are asked about the extent to which they trust others, they may be alerted to look for the answer during training which is most in line with the desires of the trainer when they are asked again after the training. A simple way to demonstrate such interaction effects involves the use of a control group which receives training but does not receive the pre-measure. Thus, the simplest design to seek unambiguous answers about the effects of t-groups would be:

	Before Measure	After Measure
Experimental Group 1	X	X
Experimental Group 2		X
Control Group	X	X

Actually, these seemingly simple standards for determining the effects of t-groups are very difficult to meet practically, and they have been applied only rarely in studies. As Argyris (1968) notes, the real research question is, do t-groups work (1) in nonexperimental situations, (2) with people who are performing nonexperimental roles, (3) at a cost (material or human) that is manageable by the client system, and (4) at an expenditure of time that is reasonable. An experimental design to answer this research question would be no small problem. Another obstacle is the fact that most t-groups are conducted by practitioners who have been employed to perform certain services for clients; it is difficult to limit what one does or who participates in order to satisfy the rules of scientific methodology. Further, it is difficult to demonstrate that control groups actually do not receive a similar experience during the research period. Bergin (1966) has indicated that individuals who were refused psychotherapy in order to create control groups for research projects sought out and received similar experiences from ministers, friends, bartenders, and so on. Thus, one's control groups may be, in fact, receiving similar experiences to the experimental groups. Another problem with research on t-groups is that there is no operational definition of what a t-group is; many different experiences may be lumped together under the title of t-group with no clear differentiation of what elements are essential to participant learning. As t-groups are used for many different purposes, furthermore, it is unclear what kinds of learning outcomes one should expect from any specific t-group effect. There is a lack of an explicit theory of learning for use in specifying the relationship between learning experiences and learning outcomes in t-groups, which further complicates the issue. Finally, since different participants in the same group may be working on diverse and perhaps unrelated learning goals, it may be difficult to specify a general outcome for all the participants in any one group. With such complexity, clear answers as to the conditions under which t-groups may be used effectively may have to wait until more sophisticated research methods are available.

A major problem with the use of t-groups as a method to increase interpersonal competence and the productivity of work groups is that a strongly positive reaction to participating in a t-group has led some participants to seek to conduct t-groups on their own. It appears relatively easy and the apparent power and emotional gratifications of the trainer seem very attractive. What has resulted is an increasing number of inadequately prepared trainers who practice their newly discovered insights and techniques on others in the naive conviction that their limited experience has resulted in their mastery of the skills and knowledge involved in group processes, interpersonal relations and individual change.

If one chooses to participate in a t-group, one should be concerned with the qualifications of the trainer. Four questions to ask about any trainer are: (1) does he have adequate training in a behavioral science? (2) what is his personal level of sensitivity, self-awareness, and self-understanding? (3) how much experience has he had as a participant and trainer in t-groups? and (4) is he certified by a professional organization such as the National Training Laboratory for Applied Behavioral Sciences? Unless one is satisfied that the trainer is fully qualified to be conducting a t-group, one may not wish to participate.

GROUP WORK
IN THE CLASSROOM

Education in the United States is a group process. Classrooms are groups, and within the classroom different groupings are frequently used to promote learning. In recent years a great deal of emphasis has been placed on individual needs and differences; this aspect of learning is a vital concern. From a practical point of view, it is apparent that teachers have neither the time nor the resources to attend to each child extensively. It is necessary for teachers to be aware of the functions of groups and to use the conditions under which they produce maximum learning. Education, although focusing upon the individual, must realize that the person is a member of a variety of groups and must operate within the context of the classroom as a group.

American culture, through its educational system, has idealized the concept of group cooperation, but has stressed individual competition in the classroom. Students may perceive themselves as being cooperatively interdependent with respect to the vague goal of learning but are usually forced to compete with each other in order to attain that goal. In this section, we shall review some of the major studies conducted on the facilitation of learning through the use of groups. For a more detailed discussion of the use of groups to facilitate learning see Johnson (1970).

Earlier in the chapter we discussed a variety of studies demonstrating the superiority of group performance over individual performances in learning tasks. This research is directly applicable to the question of how to maximize learning in the classroom. Perhaps the most consistent line of research on classroom learning and group variables has been upon the effect of group cooperation and individual competition upon classroom performance. Deutsch's (1949) original study has been discussed earlier in this chapter. Haines and McKeachie (1967) attempted to extend Deutsch's findings and specify the conditions under which cooperation will yield more student achievement than competition. They theorized that the amount of tension generated by the task was the primary variable affecting classroom performance. The actions of the other classmates could either reduce or increase tension. Since in the cooperatively interdependent classrooms there is high substitutability, there is much greater probability that cooperative group members will have tensions associated with the task reduced by the actions of other group members, and this reduced tension will result in higher performance in the classroom. In the competitively oriented classrooms, the actions of the other members will increase the tension associated with the task, resulting in decreased performance in the classroom. They found that cooperative groups did perform better than competitive groups in daily recitation, but upon examination of material covered over several weeks, there were no differences among the groups. Students in the cooperative groups, however, felt more satisfied and secure with the discussions and were friendlier and more congenial with each other.

In both the Deutsch and the Haines and McKeachie experiments, as well as in many of the studies which have corroborated their findings, the cooperative conditions studied were actually a combination of cooperation within the group and competitive between groups; thus in-group cooperation; outgroup competition. In other countries (Bronfenbrenner, 1962) similar combinations of ingroup cooperation and competition among groups have been used to facilitate classroom control and maximize individual learning in the classroom. Similar group structures have been used to resocialize delinquents in the United States and other countries (see Johnson, 1970). Thus it may be that schools could obtain more harmonious student-student relationships, increase the students' commitment and involvement to learning, and decrease the negative aspects of individual competition by restructuring classroom reward systems to promote cooperation among students and competition among groups.

SUMMARY

More and more of the world's work is carried on by groups. We have just begun to exploit this resource. Most studies show group performance to be superior to the average individual, and sometimes superior to even the best individual in the group.

A variety of factors may contribute to making group performance superior to individual performance. First, the mere presence of others seems to facilitate performance. This is because of evaluation apprehension, the concern that one is making a positive impression on observers. Second, by pooling resources, the performance of five persons is better than that of any one. The full potential of the individual may not be utilized, but each member has different contributions to make. A task is the product of complementary skills brought into harmony and coordination. Third, with several members in a group, there is a greater chance that someone will have the necessary intelligence and motivation to carry out the task. Fourth, chance errors cancel out. Some errors are due to chance or random influences which operate differently on the various members. However, composite judgments are better than those of individuals only when most individuals are partly right. Fifth, blind spots are corrected. It is easier to see other people's mistakes than it is to perceive our own. Participation in group discussion can do more than filter out silly notions; it may also stimulate ideas which would not occur to individuals working·alone. Finally there is more risk taking in a group. People in groups may be willing to venture further than they would on their own.

An important factor is the accord achieved between the satisfaction of individual motives and the attainment of group goals. Under pure cooperative conditions, an individual can obtain his goal only if the others with whom he is linked also achieve their goals. The psychological consequences of a pure cooperative situation are (1) substitutability—the actions of members in a cooperative situation are interchangeable, (2) positive cathexis—if the actions of one member move the group towards their goal, he will be evaluated favorably, and (3) inducibility—if the actions of an individual move the group towards the accomplishment of its goal, other members can be induced to engage in behavior which will facilitate his actions. Of course in a competitive situation the above factors are not present.

Factors which hamper group performance are (1) leaving one's share of the work to others; (2) conflicting goals; (3) failure to communicate; (4) interference of suggestions from various viewpoints; (5) frustration from interference and criticism, and (6) lack of the unity which characterizes the best aesthetic creativity.

There are six main stages to effective group thinking. The group begins with an exploration of the situation in which some difficulty has been felt. The second step is definition of the problem. At the third stage, solutions are proposed and examined. Examination and comparison of the various alternative proposals usually reveals a need for additional facts. Eventually the group rejects alternatives which seem less desirable and concentrates on the best available solution. The final step in the process is putting the decision into action so that the movement of affairs which was interrupted by the initial difficulty can be resumed.

Bales devised systematic studies to explore group behavior. He felt that group activities moved through three stages: (1) orientation (what is it?) (2) evaluation (How do we feel about it?) and (3) control (what shall we do about it?). Individual behavior varies with the behavior of other individuals and the size of the group. The activity of a member is hypothesized to be an inverse function of the average interaction rate of coparticipants.

Tension was found to be greater in small groups. When groups increase beyond 8-9 members, a few members are likely to dominate and the others remain passive. A heterogeneous group has more resources and is likely to come to better conclusions than a homogeneous group. To come to appropriate conclusions it is important to give the group enough time. Large groups need more time to exchange ideas than do small groups. Group cohesion can either increase or diminish productivity.

Training in how to work as an effective group member is usually helpful. To learn to be a good group member takes practice. This can be accomplished with the aid of an objective observer or, possibly, by role playing and follow-up discussions.

For a group to be productive, members of the group must be interpersonally competent and the group climate must be such that members can work together cooperatively. An educational method helpful in developing these factors is the sensitivity training group or the "t-group." To achieve the goals of t-groups, the training takes place in self-directing, self-observing groups usually containing 8 to 12 members. Participants typically meet in a group that has no agenda other than a general plan to study itself and the members within it. An inductive learning approach is emphasized by which participants learn mainly from their own observation and experience rather than from lectures and reading. The participant learns from both his own behavior and his reactions to the behavior of other members and what is taking place with the group. The analysis of group members is facilitated by a professional trainer who helps participants clarify their feelings and experiences. The group strives for frank, free, open communication on a basis of mutual trust. This climate, when achieved, permits the group to use the potential resources of all members more fully, to reach decisions based upon true consensus, and to engage creatively, flexibly, and adaptively in cooperative action toward shared goals. The function of the t-group is so complex, that clear answers to the conditions under which the t-group may be used effectively may have to wait until more sophisticated research methods are available. Before one participates in a t-group, he should be sure the leader is qualified.

It may be that schools could obtain more harmonious student-student relationships, increase the student's commitment and involvement to learning, and decrease the negative aspects of individual competition through restructuring classroom reward systems to promote cooperation among students and competiton among groups.

CHAPTER 5

Leaders, Teachers, Therapists

DEFINITION

Any time two or more individuals join together to attain a mutually desired goal, a group structure develops. In one sense leadership is a role which becomes part of the group's structure, and may be defined as influence directed toward the attainment of group goals. More specifically, *leadership constitutes an influence relationship between two or more persons who depend upon one another for the attainment of mutual goals within a group situation* (Hollander and Julian, 1969). The group situation involves such variables as the group's task, size, structure, resources, and history.

Hollander (1967) notes that the process of leadership can be considered as an influence relationship that occurs between mutually dependent group members and involves three factors: the leader with his attributes which include his motivations, perceptions, and resources relevant to the attainment of the group's goal; the followers, with their attributes which include motivations, perceptions, and relevant resources; and the situation within which they function. He goes on to distinguish between the concepts "leadership" and "leader." Leadership implies the existence of a particular influence relationship between two or more persons. A leader is a person with characteristics, including a given status, which allow him to exercise influence in line with the attainment of group goals.

Leadership, therefore, is a relationship concept implying two types of individuals, the leader and the followers. Without followers there can be no leader. The relationship between leaders and followers is usually built over time, and involves an exchange or transaction between the leader and the led in which they both give something and receive something. The leader receives status, recognition, esteem, and other reinforcements for contributing his resources toward the accomplishment of the group's goals. The followers obtain the leader's resources and his ability to structure the group's activities toward goal attainment in return for deferring to his influence and reinforcing him for successful leadership. Since both the leader and the led control resources the other desires, they both can influence the other's behavior. While leadership is defined in terms of successfully influencing other group members, the followers also influence the leader. As Homans (1961) states, "Influence over others is purchased at the price of allowing oneself to be influenced by others" (p. 286). Homans feels that to be influential, authority depends upon esteem; thus one's followers can partially control one's behavior by giving or denying esteem. There are a series of studies which demonstrate that symbolic manifestations of esteem activate a person to take a leader role. Pepinsky and his associates (1958) demonstrated that persons who were low on leadership behavior were led to behave far more actively in leadership behaviors by the group's evident support for their assertions. Other individuals known to be high on leadership behaviors in earlier situations were affected in precisely the opposite way by the group's evident disagreement with their statements. Other investigators have shown that the use of lights as reinforcers of leadership behavior exerts a significant effect on the target person's proportion of talking time as well as his perceived leadership status; the lights not only produced a heightening of leadership acts, but also created the impression of greater influence with the implication of legitimacy as well (Bavelas, Hastorf, Gross, and Kite, 1965; Zdep and Oakes, 1967).

Throughout history there has been a continuing popular belief that leaders are born. Aristotle, for example, once remarked, "From the hour of their birth some are marked out for subjugation, and others for command." There are men, such as John Kennedy or Malcolm X, who seem to dominate others through their force of personality and what they stand for. Thus one approach to the study of leadership is to examine the personality traits which may differentiate leaders from nonleaders. The next section reviews the theory and research generated by such an approach. Contemporary views of leadership in social psychology, however, emphasize the learned skills of leadership and stress the leadership functions to be fulfilled in the situation rather than the characteristics of the leader alone. Thus the theory and research dealing with the functional and contingency approaches to the study of leadership will also be discussed. We shall then look at leadership within organizations. Finally, we shall be concerned with two particular kinds of leaders, the teacher and the therapist.

TRAIT APPROACH TO LEADERSHIP

Far back in philosophical thought, the leader was conceptualized as someone possessing unique traits. Some individuals, for example, seem to rise to leadership in a range of settings. Before Benjamin Franklin reached 30 years of age, he had been chosen Public Printer for the colony of Pennsylvania, had founded the famous and influential Junto Club, had brought out the most widely read publication in America (*Poor Richard's Almanac*), had founded the first circulating library, and had been elected Grand Master of the Freemasons Lodge of Pennsylvania. The next year he inaugurated the first fire-fighting company in Pennsylvania and was chosen clerk of the Pennsylvania Assembly. He was one of the most successful business men in the colonies, but had enough interest in scholarship and research to be the founder (he was then 37 years old) of the American Philosophical Society. He continued to serve in a variety of leadership posts in politics, the Army, science, diplomacy and education, founding the Academy which became the University of Pennsylvania. He climaxed this brilliant career at 80 by leading in the group enterprise of writing the Constitution. A biographer (Fay, 1929) writes, "Nobody could approach him without being charmed by his conversation, his humor, wisdom, and kindness."

With individuals such as Ben Franklin in mind, research on leadership in the early part of this century focused upon individual traits, such as height, weight, appearance, intelligence, self-confidence, and so on, in an attempt to determine once and for all the factor or factors which *made* a person a leader. Numerous studies contrasted the characteristics of people who held leadership positions with those of people who did not. It was reported that leaders tend to be somewhat bigger and brighter than the rest of the members of a group, and they seemed to show better adjustment on various personality tests. Mann (1959) reviewed 125 studies of leadership and personality chacteristics representing over 700 findings (see Table 5-1). In his review, intelligence and personal adjustment seem to be correlated with leadership. It seems evident that intelligence may be a prerequisite for Franklin's kind of leadership, but it is doubtful whether Franklin or John Adams or George Washington possessed the highest I.Q.'s of their period

TABLE 5-1

Percentage of Significant Relationships Reported in a Positive or Negative Direction for 125 Studies, Representing 751 Findings on the Relationship of Various Personality Characteristics and Leadership. (After Mann, 1959.)

Personality Factors and Number of Studies of Each	Number of Findings	Percent Yielding Sig. Positive Relationship	Percent Yielding Sig. Negative Relationship	% Yielding Neither
Intelligence—28	(196)	46% (91)	1%° (1)	53% (104)
Adjustment—22	(164)	30% (50)	2%° (2)	68% (112)
Extroversion—22	(119)	31% (37)	5% (6)	64% (76)
Dominance—12	(39)	38% (15)	15% (6)	46% (18)
Masculinity—9	(70)	16% (11)	1%° (1)	83% (58)
Conservatism—17	(62)	5% (3)	27% (17)	68% (42)
Sensitivity—15	(101)	15% (15)	1% (1)	84% (85)

° Rounded upward.

(Cox, 1926). A follow-up of the careers of 1,000 highly intelligent children from California showed that relatively few of them had reached the roster of famous leaders (Terman, 1947). Twenty-five years after their childhood selection, none had attained high political office or the presidencies of corporations or colleges. Only 5 percent were in *Who's Who* and 13 percent in *American Men of Science.* There is evidence (Hollingworth, 1924) that when individuals have remarkably high intelligence they are too far beyond the rank-and-file to communicate readily and to arouse trust and confidence. The highly intelligent may lead in scholarship, but are unlikely to win out in the competitive struggles of business, the military, politics, or statesmanship. Leaders undoubtedly average above the median intellectual level of their followers, but mental ability by itself is no guarantee of influence, prominence, or power. Bass (1960) estimates an average correlation (based on 24 studies) of about .30 between verbal intelligence and leadership behavior.

Although personal adjustment is correlated with leadership in many groups, some leaders, like Adolf Hitler, have shown signs of emotional maladjustment. Perhaps more important than personal adjustment are the findings that leaders seem superior to their followers in energy, drive, determination to succeed, and in self-confidence. They lead because they want to; they work at it; they do not easily give up. Leadership usually implies success in some kind of struggle. Apathy and opposition must be overcome. This requires stamina. Several studies show that successful executives are high in need to achieve and desire for excellence in their performance (Cox, 1926; Gardner, 1948; American Management Association, 1948; McClelland *et al.,* 1953).

Charismatic leaders

Charismatic leaders are fascinating. Biographers try in vain to account for the magnetic attraction which centers in certain outstanding personalities. The term "charisma" implies some sort of divine grace, miraculously bestowed. Garibaldi won the loyalty of his Roman soldiers with an unusual appeal: "What I have to offer you is fatigue, danger, struggle and death; the chill of the cold night in the fall air, and heat under the burning sun; no lodgings, no provisions, but forced marches, dangerous watchposts, and the continual struggle with the bayonet against batteries—those who love freedom and their country may follow me!" Winston Churchill offered "blood, sweat, and tears" but sustained the faith and courage of millions. One thinks of Alexander, Julius Caesar, Washington, Robespierre, Bolívar, Lenin, Sun Yat-sen, and Gandhi—so widely different in personality and yet all able to inspire confidence and to demand sacrifice of even life itself from their followers. The attempt of most biographers and historians has been to discover the secret somehow in the character, personality, mind, or invisible aura of the charismatic leader himself. While most famous leaders do have considerable ability and strength, the differences between them and other human beings of their time is not of the same order as the differences in reputation.

A long line of faith healers from primitive medicine men to the evangelist Aimee Semple McPherson and contemporary miracle workers, testifies to the powerful effect which one man's faith in another may exert, even upon bodily processes. Franz Mesmer started his career in Vienna in 1777 with his apparent cure of a case of blindness by the use of magnets. Soon he discovered that stroking by his hands alone could produce similar therapeutic effects upon patients. Crowds besieged him in Paris despite reports by distinguished scholars accusing him of being a charlatan. It is not necessary to assume that Mesmer was dishonest. The results he achieved no doubt led him to conclude that he did possess mysterious powers. But 50 years later hypnosis was identified and provided the explanation for Mesmer's accomplishments.

In charismatic leadership we see the effects of something like hypnotic suggestion reinforced and magnified by social support. Often the leader's reputation for greatness reaches the followers in advance of their actual contact with him. They come to hear him, prepared to be awed. Stories of his achievements may run far beyond the facts—including such tributes as belief in his miraculous birth and precocious childhood. Even those who have come prepared to scoff find themsleves powerfully influenced by the enthusiastic responses of their neighbors in the audience. It is told of one man that when Wendell Phillips had finished a stirring oration against slavery, and the audience arose with wild applause, one skeptic was seen struggling against the counter currents of the crowd. He was observed stamping his feet and beating his hands together as enthusiastically as anyone in the hall, but shouting as he applauded: "The confounded liar! The confounded liar!"

The great charismatic religious leaders provide impressive evidence of the cumulative growth of a following. Moses, Buddha, Confucius, Jesus, and Mohammed each came in actual contact with only a few followers and were seldom widely acclaimed. Yet each in time became a figure who seemed to meet the spiritual needs of millions of adherents. It is no disparagement of the historic leaders themselves to recognize that their followers have created around the actual personality a somewhat different symbolic pattern which remains at the heart of the continuing religious movement.

Charismatic leaders are sometimes invented. Most peoples have tales of gigantic heroic figures. It is hard to disentangle the historic acts of a Perseus or Theseus or Sampson or Sir Lancelot from the accumulated legends. Was there ever a Paul Bunyan? It does not really matter. Surely the need that is met today by a figure like Santa Claus or Superman is independent of any historic figure. Each culture forms the heroes it unconsciously needs. Some of the psychological patterns or "archetypes" underlying the creation of folk-heroes have been reported by Campbell (1956).

There is no doubt that some leaders have a quality we call "charisma." But the concept "charisma" is not well defined and is difficult to apply in practice. Recently Tucker (1968) made an attempt to clarify what is meant by a charismatic leader. He notes that charismatic leaders inspire followers to accept their leadership out of love and passionate devotion to him. He stresses that the first determinant of charismatic response is situational; a state of acute distress predisposes individuals to perceive a leader offering salvation from distress as extraordinarily qualified and to follow him with enthusiastic loyalty. Weber (1947) stated that charismatic figures have been the natural leaders in time of psychic, physical, economic, ethical, religious, or political distress, and that charisma inspires its followers with a devotion born of distress and enthusiasm. Tucker (1968) also recognizes that the key to the charismatic response to the leader lies in the distress that his followers experience. The charismatic leader is one in whom, by virtue of unusual personal qualities, the promise or hope of salvation—deliverance from distress—appears to be embodied. He is a leader who convincingly offers himself to a group of persons in distress as one uniquely qualified to lead them out of their predicament. He is in essence a savior; charismatic leadership is specifically salvationist or messianic in nature.

Charisma is alien to the everyday, routine world. It demands new ways of life and thought. It rejects old rules and calls for change. It repudiates the past and is in this sense a specifically revolutionary force. It appears in the setting of a social movement for change. As an exponent of change, the charismatic leader evokes a positive response from some individuals and a negative response from others. A universal feature of the charismatic leader is his capacity to inspire hatred as well as loyalty and love; he arouses fanatical hatred on the part of those who remain devoted to the old order of things in the society. Thus the devotion to Martin Luther King, Jr. by many Americans was equalled by the hatred of others who did not want black Americans to receive equal rights.

In a personal communication to Tucker, Erik H. Erikson suggested that there are certain historical conditions, such as the waning of religion, in which people in large numbers become "charisma-hungry." He distinguished three forms of distress to which a charismatic leader may minister: "fear," as the subliminal fear of nuclear destruction, "anxiety," especially that experienced by persons in an "identity-vacuum" or the condition of not knowing just who or what they are, and "existential dread," or the distress that people experience when the rituals of their existence have broken down. A charismatic leader, then, is one who offers people salvation in the form of safety, identity, rituals, or some combination of these, saying in effect, "I will make you safe," "I will give you identity," or "I will establish rituals."

We are living in a period of rapid social change in which many individuals may be afraid, have no identity, or are losing the rituals on which they have previously based their lives. A large number of people in distress, however, does not mean that a movement for change led by a charismatic leader will arise. To be a charismatic leader a person must have an extraordinary power of "vision" and be able to communicate it to others, or he must have unusual powers of practical leadership to achieve the goals which will alleviate his followers' distress. Above all, the charismatic leader must have a sense of mission, a belief both in the social-change movement he leads, and in himself as the chosen instrument to lead the movement to its destination. He must appear extremely self-confident to inspire others with confidence that the movement he leads will, without fail, prevail and will ultimately reduce the distress of his followers.

Leadership, Power, and Machiavellianism

If charismatic leaders found social movements and bring them into power, it is the machiavellian leaders who consolidate and wield the power they obtained. The current leadership theories in social psychology for the most part ignore (1) the fairly primitive, prerational aspects of leadership and followership discussed in the previous section on charismatic leadership and (2) the realities of how power is often handled. Throughout man's history there have been theorists who conceive of leadership essentially in terms of possession and exercise of power for self-enhancement. Early in the 1950's Richard Christie began a program of research on individuals who manipulate others for political and personal reasons. His research originated from an interest in organizationally-oriented leaders who take over and run social movements once the movement obtains power, that is, leaders who wield political power.

Christie (Christie and Geis, 1970) began reading the historical literature on how political leaders should govern. Two common themes seem to implicitly run through much of what he read. The first is the assumption that man is basically weak, fallible, and gullible. The second is that if people are so weak, a rational man should take advantage of the situation to maximize his own gains or, alternatively, if others cannot be trusted because of their weakness, one should take steps to protect oneself from their follies. On the basis of his reading, he made the following assumptions about political leaders who manipulate followers for political and personal reasons. First, there will be a relative absence of effect in the interpersonal relationships of the leaders, since it is easier for them to manipulate other people if they view them as objects rather than as fellow humans. Second, since manipulative leaders take a utilitarian rather than a moral view of their interactions with others, they will not be concerned with conventional morality.

Third, since successful manipulation of followers depends upon an accurate perception of their needs and of "reality" in general, the leaders will not be grossly psychopathological. That is, neurotic and psychotic tendencies would distort perceptions and communications in ways which would undermine one's ability to manipulate. Finally, since the essence of successful manipulation is a focus upon getting things done rather than a focus upon long range ideological goals, the leaders will have low degrees of ideological commitment.

Christie and Geis (1970) note that throughout history individuals have felt that those who acquire positions of social power do so by the use of guile, duplicity, and other opportunistic strategies. Such a "manipulator" is usually seen as exploiting the weaknesses, failings, and foibles of other persons for his own purposes. Traditionally, the "machiavellian" is someone who evaluates others impersonally in terms of their usefulness for his own purposes. In an investigation of the possible effects of a medical education on values and attitudes of students, Christie and Merton (1958) found that over the years medical students came to see others as impersonal objects, not particularly trustworthy, and open to manipulation should this be necessary to achieve one's ends. They used the term machiavellianism to describe this syndrome. Christie and Geis subsequently set out to construct a measure that would reflect this dimension more directly. They developed a scale of 20 value statements, to which respondents indicated their degree of agreement or disagreement. Many of the statements were directly taken from sentiments expressed by Machiavelli in *The Prince*. Respondents, for example, were asked the extent to which they agreed with the following:

1. The best way to handle people is to tell them what they want to hear.
2. Anyone who completely trusts anyone else is asking for trouble.
3. One should take action only when sure it is morally right.
4. All in all, it is better to be humble and honest than to be important and dishonest.

Individuals who tended to agree with the first two statements and to disagree with the second two would be given a high score in Machiavellian propensities. Scores on the test were found to be highly reliable over time, and if an individual tended to agree strongly with one Machiavellian statement, he would also tend to agree with the others. The next important question was whether scores on the measure were indicative of how the person would treat other human beings.

Perhaps the most convincing evidence for the validity of the test came from a study conducted by Geis, Christie, and Nelson (1963). They asked subjects to perform the role of an experimenter whose task was to give an important personality test to another subject. Each subject was told that for experimental purposes it would be desirable if he could distract the test taker from his work, and that he could use any method to confuse or distract the test taker. This placed the subjects in a position in which they were at complete liberty to manipulate another person. The question was whether high scorers on the Machiavellian scale would be more manipulative than would low scorers. The behavior of the subjects was observed and recorded and the results were striking. High scorers on the Machiavellian scale found twice as many ways to manipulate the test taker as did the low scorers, and manipulated him more than twice as often. Other research has demonstrated that high scorers on the scale of Machiavellianism, in comparison with low scorers, tend to be more aggressive in game behavior, better at "conning" others to gain outcomes for themselves, and more likely to achieve better grades in large lecture courses (intelligence held constant). To their embarrassment, social psychologists tend to have high scores on the measure.

Authoritarian leaders

Most leaders throughout history have been authoritarian. Whether they led by virtue of an inherited title, their ability to persuade, or their power to coerce, they stood *above* their followers. They made the decisions and their followers, with more or less good will, accepted them.

Authoritarian leadership implies interaction. If we see strong leader dominance in groups from nursery school (Parten, 1932) to the modern corporation (Argyris, 1957) there must be corresponding readiness to accede to such control. Bass (1960, p. 226) quotes a National Research Council book: "No amount of legal authority over the grizzly bears of British Columbia would enable you to get yourself obeyed by them out in the woods." Authority becomes power only when subordinates accept it.

All human beings begin life in total physical dependence. As babies we were once wholly dependent on parents who were bigger, wiser, more competent and powerful. Most human beings go through life with some tendency to respond to parent substitutes who seem bigger, wiser, more competent and powerful. We bring out of childhood a built-in readiness to follow authority figures. We invent supermen to fit the pattern of our needs. The real problem for social psychology is not the authoritarian leader, but the emergence in some situations of other forms of leadership. From the earliest days of prehistoric and even prehuman existence, the herd has had its strong and dominant leader. When any situation becomes extremely frustrating, even competent and normally self-reliant adults search for someone on whom they can depend to set things right in what Erich Fromm has called "escape from freedom."

In discussing, in the preceding chapter, how groups proceed to work together, we noted that they usually have to deal first with the power question. They want to know who is going to lead. If the official status leader abdicates, as in some t-groups and therapy groups (Bradford *et al.*, 1964; Bion, 1949, 1951), members struggle to replace him. They feel frustrated by the lack of direction. Discouragement turns to apathy and a desire to withdraw. A "strong leader" seems to be the way out. A general sense of frustration and despair in Italy and Germany preceded the rise of Mussolini and Hitler. After study of 35 dictatorships, Hertzler concluded that usually disillusion, resulting from problems too great for the old regime, led to the demand for a strong leader (1940). Hook (1943) has reported that, historically, the more acute the social crisis, the greater the demand for a hero-savior.

In very large groups, members commonly expect the good leader to make decisions for them without consulting them (Hemphill, 1950). They accept direction as a matter of course or of preference. The average member invests relatively less of himself in his large group affiliations. To surrender decision making for this little segment of his life, is no great sacrifice of autonomy. Indeed, to try to participate effectively in the affairs of a large college, church, trade union, or political party would be very time-consuming. It is simpler to let the responsible officials run the organization.

Sometimes the authoritarian leader, with the wholehearted support of his numerous followers inaugurates important social changes. William James (1880) was one of the many (Jennings, 1960) who espoused the "great man" theory of history. Carlyle's *Heroes and Hero Worship* minimizes the contribution of other social forces and exalts the divine revelation which comes into the world through prophets like Mahomet, poets like Shakespeare and Dante, priests like Luther and Knox, and rulers like Cromwell or Frederick the Great.

Arnold Toynbee in his extensive *Study of History* (1934) distinguishes between the creative leaders, who arouse *mimesis,* or spontaneous loyalty, and those creative leaders who dominate by coercion. In its most vital period of development, a civilization generates creative leaders. Later, when the social aim diminishes to consolidating the prestige and position the state has already won, the leadership becomes merely dominant. A related distinction has been made by Pareto, an Italian political theorist (1916). He has introduced the conception of a "circulation of the elite"; the "lions" do the pioneering; then the "foxes" follow and shrewdly gather in benefits for themselves. Eventually new lions arise to challenge the corruption and drive out the foxes.

The craving to be dependent contends with another strong human drive for autonomy and independence. Authoritarian leaders usually combat this unwelcome resistance by reliance upon tradition, threat or personal gifts. They lead by custom, by coercion, and *by charisma.* It should be recognized that in life most leaders use a combination of assets. The commanding general on a post leads partly by virtue of his abilities, partly by virtue of the respect given his position, and partly by his power to punish any who disobey. The professor in a class also combines in his leadership some admiration for his talent, some deference due his position, and some conformity because otherwise the student might suffer.

THE AUTHORITARIAN PERSONALITY

Some people like to dominate or be dominated. They see the world as a continuous struggle in which the stronger come out ahead and the weak submit. This personality pattern, called the "authoritarian" or "antidemocratic" has been extensively investigated by social psychologists. It is measured by an instrument called the "F- (for fascist) scale." Interest has been stimulated especially by the fact that this concept links the dynamics of individual personality with positions on vital social issues.

Abstract 13

TITLE   The Authoritarian Personality

AUTHORS   T. W. Adorno, E. Frenkel-Brunswick, D. J. Levinson, and R. N. Sanford.

PROBLEM   Is there a type of personality which is particularly susceptible to antidemocratic propaganda and hence potentially fascistic?

SUBJECTS   Some 1,500 men and women in colleges, professional groups, labor groups, service clubs, middle-class groups, church groups, psychiatric clinic, state prisons.

PROCEDURES Tests were developed for Anti-Semitism (AS-scale), Ethnocentrism (E-scale), Political-Economic-Conservatism (PEC-scale) and Implicit Anti-democratic Attitudes. The last named has become widely known as the F-scale, because it is concerned with susceptibility to fascism. Many subjects were also interviewed, given TAT and other projective tests.

SOME FINDINGS Intercorrelations of the several scales suggest a common factor:

	F-Scale	A-Scale	E-Scale
AS	.53	—	—
E	.73	.68	—
PEC	.52	.43	.57

The type of personality associated with the term "authoritarian" has components of: (1) conventional values; (2) authoritarian submission, as shown for example in not questioning family or religious standards; (3) authoritarian aggression; (4) anti-intraception, which is expressed in opposing introspection, paying attention only to the objective and external rather than to inner thoughts and feelings; (5) superstition-stereotypy; (6) pseudo-toughness; (7) concern with power; (8) cynicism about human nature; (9) projectivity, meaning a tendency to imagine strange, evil, destructive forces at work in much of life; and (10) preoccupation with sex as dangerous and immoral. TAT pictures are often interpreted by those with high F scores as involving an act of impulsive aggression (man-slaughter, rape, murder) which is condemned and for which the offender must suffer severe punishments. Parents are seen as dominating and children as submissive. Men are domineering toward women. Sex is seen as an instrument of power for achieving conquest and status.

Subjects scoring low on the F-scale show more self-acceptance, more matter-of-fact attitudes toward parents and other relatives. For low scorers sex is more apt to imply warmth, companionship, and mutual affection. Low-scoring persons are more tolerant and understanding; high scorers are more repressed, rigid, and inclined to project disturbing feelings onto suspected threats from outside themselves.

SOURCE: Published by Harper and Brothers, 1950.

The history of the research illustrates its connection with political viewpoints. Before Hitler came to power in Germany a group of German social scientists was already apprehensive. They asked themselves what force might possibly hold back the rising Nazi tide. They could not trust the Prussian army or the aristocracy which were closely allied. They saw little strength in the wavering middle classes who never fought for anything or in the unorganized peasants. Only the working class might have the necessary power, but research indicated that children of workers were as firmly bound by autocratic paternal authority as any others. Democracy had no real strength in German family life; hence, the social scientists concluded, it could have no solid foundation in the political affairs of the nation. These social scientists decided to leave Germany even before the Nazis came to power.

After emigrating to the United States, this group asked themselves, "Might fascist movements succeed also in the United States? Can it happen here?" Their hypothesis was that a certain type of personality is especially susceptible to the appeal of authoritarianism. They argued that, in a democracy, the bent toward being a dictator or submitting to a dictator is a constant peril. By test, interviews and case histories, they tried to discover what sort of person seeks to dominate others or to be dominated by others. The general outline of their study is in Abstract 13 and below is a case study of a high scorer.

Case 1: Mack—A Student High in Authoritarian Ideology

Mack, a 24-year-old undergraduate, plans to study law. He is of Irish extraction. Mack's mother died when he was six and his sister ten. Their father worked in a lumber mill. Mack finished high school, had a year in business college, then a wartime Civil Service job as a clerk in Washington for a while, and was in the Army but given a medical discharge because of "stomach trouble." His upbringing was strict. His mother and the aunt who took over after the mother's death insisted on regular church attendance, but since high school Mack has been busy with other things. He was a sickly child. His father was stern, shy, disliked meeting people, and had a quick temper.

On the test of "Anti-democratic Trends" (the F-scale) Mack scored higher than

177

the mean of any group tested except the men in the San Quentin prison. Among the items which contributed to his relatively high score were the following, to which he agreed:

	Mack's response
(Conventionalism) "What a man does is not so important so long as he does it well."	+2
(Authoritarian submission) "It is essential for learning or effective work that our teachers or bosses outline in detail what is to be done and exactly how to go about it."	+3
(Authoritarian aggression) "Homosexuality is a particularly rotten form of delinquency and ought to be severely punished."	+2
(Anti-intraception) "Novels or stories which contain mainly action, romance and adventure are more interesting than those that tell about what people think and feel."	+2
(Power and toughness) "To a greater extent than most people realize our lives are governed by plots hatched in secret by politicians."	+3
(Destructiveness and cynicism) "When you come right down to it, it's human nature never to do anything without an eye to one's own profit."	+3
(Projectivity) "The sexual orgies of the old Greeks and Romans are nursery school stuff compared to some of the goings-on in this country today, even in circles where people might least expect it."	+1
(Sex) "Sex crimes, such as rape and attacks on children, deserve more than mere imprisonment; such criminals ought to be publicly whipped."	+2

Following are some direct quotations from the interview with Mack. *Politics:*

> I worked there in Washington and saw things I would put a stop to. There is a concentration of power in the bureaus . . . I was the right-hand man of the General there when the OWI was introduced . . . It was fun knowing about the background, knowing about the secret committees . . . Eventually the President will have to appoint a strong Cabinet to run things for him. There is no doubt that the system is becoming more centralized . . . Dewey's honesty and straightforwardness appeal to me greatly but a man has to use some underhandedness to get across the highest ideals.

Minorities: Mack agreed with the statement: "Negroes have their rights, but it is best to keep them in their own school districts and schools and to prevent too much contact with whites." He asserts: "It would be a mistake to have Negroes for foremen and leaders over whites." He also would agree that: "Citizens or not, no Jap should be allowed to return to California."

Crime: Interpreting a TAT picture of an older and younger man together

Mack said: "The young fellow indicates the type of person who might do violence if pushed too far . . . I think he could easily murder somebody on being oppressed."

Searching for some questions which would predict anti-Semitism without specifically referring to Jews, the Anti-Defamation League found that agreement with the following five propositions correlated highly with the score on both the F-scale and the scale of Anti-Semitism.

1. The most important thing to teach children is absolute obedience to their parents.

2. Any good leader should be strict with people under him in order to gain their respect.

3. Prison is too good for sex criminals. They should be publicly whipped or worse.

4. There are two kinds of people in the world: the weak and the strong.

5. No decent man can respect a woman who has had sex relations before marriage.

Among the many correlations with the F-scale, the following are typical. High authoritarians have been found to be significantly:

1. more prejudiced against unpopular minorities (Campbell, McCandless, 1951).

2. committed to traditional views of the proper roles for husbands and wives (Levinson, Huffman, 1955; Nadler, Morrow, 1959).

3. more conservative or reactionary in political attitudes (Gump, 1953).

4. less able to participate effectively in democratic or leaderless groups (Bass et al., 1953).

5. unable to make accurate estimates of attitudes of others (Christie, Cook, 1958).

6. more frequently Catholic; less frequently Unitarian, Congregationalist, Jewish or nonreligious (Levinson, Schermerhorn, 1951).

7. more frequently studying engineering than psychology or other social sciences (Davidson, Kruglov, 1953).

8. more suspicious and exploitive in human relations (Deutsch, 1960).

9. more apt to come from culturally underprivileged backgrounds and to be low on education. The correlation of F-scale with intelligence or with years of education in samples of adults runs $-.50$ to $-.60$ (Christie, Cook, 1958).

In the course of the research on the F-scale, several improvements have been made on the original technique. For example, the items were all stated in such a form that acquiescence gave high F scores. Christie et al., (1958) worked out a balanced version which made it possible to correct for response-set and to measure authoritarianism and acquiescence as separate variables. A second criticism has called attention to the bias of the F-scale toward identifying rightwing authoritarianism of the pro-fascist variety. Hence communists usually score very low. But there is obviously a left wing or procommunist kind of dogmatism, intolerance, tendency to domineer, and to exploit others. Rokeach (1956) has developed a Dogmatism Scale which focuses on rigid, stereotyped thinking, whether tending left or right politically. This updates a scale measuring "Fair Mindedness" developed by one of the authors (Watson, 1925).

Authoritarian dictatorships are not simply strange, subversive foreign systems of government. There are numerous parents, teachers, supervisors, employers, and officials in every community whose bent is toward command and whose interest is power. The struggle for democracy is not primarily a matter of foreign relations. Discomfort in egalitarian situations and distrust for democratic procedures are deeply rooted in almost every institution of American society.

FUNCTIONAL THEORY
OF LEADERSHIP

Dissatisfaction with the trait approach to leadership resulted in research studies focusing more upon the leader's skills, or what he does, than upon the nature of his deeper personality. This approach to leadership seeks to discover what actions are necessary for a group to achieve its goals under various conditions, and how different group members take part in these group actions. *The performance of acts which help* the group achieve its goals is termed leadership. The functional approach to leadership stresses the performance of these acts, termed *group functions*. Leadership functions include setting goals, helping the group proceed toward these goals, and providing necessary resources. Other functions not directly related to goal achievement, such as improving the group's stability and insuring the satisfaction of individual members are also part of the leadership role. According to this approach, leadership is seen as function-centered rather than position-centered, and therefore, groups should be flexible in assigning leadership functions to various members as conditions change. Only group members who are sensitive to changing conditions, and who can adapt to changes can be effective leaders for any period of time. In principle, leadership may be performed by one or many members of the group.

The concept of functional leadership includes two basic ideas (Cartwright and Zander, 1968); (1) any member of a group may become a leader by taking actions that serve group functions and (2) any leadership function may be served by various members performing a variety of behaviors. Leadership, therefore, is specific to a particular group in a particular situation. It can depend on the background of the group members, the nature of the goals or the organization of the group. It can also depend upon outside expectations or pressure exerted on the group to behave in certain ways. All of these influence the nature of leadership behavior and the choice of which members will perform these behaviors.

The functional approach to leadership assumes that under specific circumstances, any given behavior may or may not serve a group function. Under one set of conditions, a particular behavior may be beneficial; under another set of conditions that same act may be dysfunctional. For example, when a group is trying to define a problem, suggesting a possible solution may not be helpful, but when a group is specifying alternative solutions to a defined problem, suggesting a possible solution may be quite helpful.

The skills of a designated leader or the holder of an office may, furthermore, make him well qualified to perform important group functions under certain conditions and poorly qualified under others. A bomber pilot, for example, may be an excellent leader for the new crew while the plane is in the air, but may be totally inadequate for survival leadership if the plane crashes (Cartwright and Zander, 1968). A change in the task of the group often calls for a new set of leadership skills, and the same person may not be able to alter his own actions to meet the demands of the new situation.

It is useful to distinguish among various group functions according to the type of group objective to which the function contributes. *Goal achievement* and *group maintenance* are generally considered to be the two basic categories of group objectives (Cartwright and Zander, 1968). Examples of member behaviors which help in the achievement of the goals of the group are: "initiates action," "keeps members' attention on the goal," "clarifies the issue," "develops a procedural plan," "evaluates the quality of the work done," and "makes expert information available to the group." Acts which contribute to maintenance or improvement of the group are exemplified by the following: "keeps interpersonal relations pleasant," "arbitrates or mediates disputes," "provides encouragement," "gives the minority a chance to be heard," "stimulates self-direction," and "increases the interdependence among members."

Any given behavior in a group may affect both goal achievement and group maintenance. Both may be served simultaneously by the actions of a member, or one may be served at the expense of the other. Thus, a member who helps the group work cooperatively on a task may simultaneously help the group reach its goal and increase group solidarity. On the other hand, a member who pushes exclusively for task accomplishment may help the group accomplish its task, but in a way which creates friction among members so that the future existence of the group is endangered.

Finally, the functional approach to leadership assumes that leadership is a learned set of skills which anyone with certain minimal requirements can acquire. Effective group membership and leadership depend upon flexible behavior, the ability to diagnose what behaviors are needed at a particular time for the group to function most efficiently, and the ability to fulfill these behaviors or to get other members to fulfill them (Johnson, 1970). A skilled member or leader, therefore, has to have diagnostic skills in order to be aware that a given function is needed in the group, and he must be flexible enough to provide diverse types of behaviors as required under different conditions. In addition, he must be able to utilize other group members and obtain their cooperation in providing needed group functions.

The functional approach to leadership is at this time the most concrete and direct approach available for improving the leadership skills of an individual and the effectiveness of a group working on a task. Individuals can be taught the diagnostic skills and behaviors which facilitate group task accomplishment and maintenance of good working relationships (See Abstract 14). For this reason it is frequently used by consultants to work groups and by directors of leadership-training programs to improve the effectiveness of group members.

CONTINGENCY THEORY OF LEADERSHIP

Perhaps the most well-developed theory of leadership is the result of the research and theoretical work of Fiedler (1964, 1967, 1969). He studied leadership in a variety of situations, including high school basketball teams, surveyor teams, Belgian naval personnel, Navy ROTC cadets, and B-29 crews. Although he recognizes that leadership functions are shared, he was concerned only with the person performing the traditional leadership role of directing and coordinating task-relevant group activities. To be considered a leader, the individual must either be appointed by an agent of a larger organization of which the group is a part, or be elected by the group, or be identified as the most influential member on task-relevant questions on a sociometric questionnaire. The leader's effectiveness was defined in terms of his group's performance in achieving group goals. Implicit in this statement is the assumption that the more nearly the group achieves its goal, the more effective is the leader. It is assumed that task-relevant abilities and skills of members of different groups are similar.

From his studies on leadership Fiedler concluded that what most frequently distinguishes the leader from his coworkers is that he knows more about the group task, or that he can do it better; a tennis team is likely to choose its captain from excellent rather than poor players, the foreman of a machine shop is more likely to be an excellent machinist than a poor one.

Fiedler distinguished leaders on a continuum extending from high person-orientation (that is, permissive, accepting, democratic, group-oriented leadership which provides general rather than close supervision and is concerned with the effective use of human resources through participation) to high task-orientation (that is, directive, controlling, autocratic leadership which takes responsibility for making decisions and directing group members). In many types of groups, Fiedler found no consistent correlation between scores on this dimension and group effectiveness. The person-oriented leader was more effective in some situations and in other situations the task-oriented leader was more effective. To reconcile these findings, Fiedler provides a theoretical analysis of the various group situations he studied in terms of their: (1) leader-member personal relationships—the extent to which the leader is admired, loved, and trusted; (2) task structure—the degree to which the group's assignment can be programmed and specified in a step-by-step fashion; and (3) position power of the leader—the authority vested in the leader's position. These three dimensions relate to the kind of power and influence the group gives its leader. Based on several studies, he found leader-member relations the most important factor in determining the leader's influence over the group; task structure as next most important, and position power as third. Under most circumstances, the leader who is liked by his group and has a clear-cut task and high position power will be highly influential; the leader who has poor relationships with his group members, an unstructured task and weak position power will be unable to exert much influence over the group.

By re-examining the results of his earlier studies and by conducting new research, Fiedler is able to show that a task-oriented leader performs best in situations at both extremes—those in which he has a great deal of influence and power, and those in which he has no influence and power over the group members. Relationship-oriented leaders tend to perform best in mixed situations where they have only moderate influence over the group. Thus when the leader is on very good terms with the group members, when the task is clearly structured, and when there is high position-power, the group is ready to be directed and is willing to be told what to do. Similarly when the situation is highly unfavorable, permissive leadership may lead to disintegration of the group. Only moderately favorable or moderately unfavorable situations call for considerate, relation-oriented leadership; in this case the members are free to offer new ideas and suggestions, and the leader typically cannot force group members to comply with his wishes.

The major strength of Fiedler's theory is that it specifies the conditions under which different leadership behaviors may be expected to be effective. It is a clearly defined theory yielding testable hypotheses which have been confirmed by a variety of research studies. It is currently the most promising theory of leadership and will undoubtedly be strengthened by modifications derived from future research studies.

Abstract 14

TITLE   Morale and Leadership Training

AUTHOR   A. Bavelas

PROBLEM   Can poor leaders be quickly transformed into good leaders?

SUBJECTS   Six Works Progress Administration recreation leaders in a community center; three were retrained, the other three served as controls. Ages varied from 35–45; experience in recreational leadership averaged three years. All had been rated as poor or unsatisfactory group leaders.

PROCEDURES   All six leaders were observed on the job and their behavior with children was recorded in frequency of each category. Training consisted of a kind of "clinic on the job." Leaders observed one another at work. They observed the trainer working with their group. They role-played possible ways of handling incidents. They studied and criticized motion picture films of the way in which they had actually responded to situation on the job. They noted improvements from session to session in the records of their work. Theory was given incidentally in relation to actual behavior. Training occupied two hours a day, four days a week for three weeks. Then all six leaders were again observed and their behavior with children recorded.

SOME FINDINGS   Trained leaders gave fewer directions after training and vested more responsibility in the children. Untrained controls did not change. The success of the trained leaders was further evident in the fact that the number of children voluntarily attending their group doubled, pupil enthusiasm rose and remained high; the quality of the work produced improved.

SOURCE: G. Watson (ed.), *Civilian Morale*. Boston: Houghton Mifflin, 1942, pp. 143–65.

LEADERSHIP WITHIN ORGANIZATIONS

Most leadership behaviors in our society take place within organizations, such as businesses, industries, schools, and churches. Most of the social psychological literature on leadership, however, has overlooked the operation of leadership processes in social organizations. In this section leadership within organizations will be discussed.

The social psychological bases of organizations are comprised by the role behaviors of members, the norms prescribing and sanctioning these role behaviors, and the values in which the norms are embedded (Katz and Kahn, 1966). Leadership within organizations begins with the formal role system which, among other things, defines the authority hierarchy. Authority is legitimate power, power which is vested in a particular person or position, which is recognized as so vested, and which is accepted as appropriate not only by the wielder of power but by those over whom it is wielded and by

other members of the organization (Katz and Kahn, 1966). The most pervasive law of organizations is that the occupants of certain roles respond
to and obey certain kinds of requests from occupants of certain other roles
and, therefore, compliance with authoritative requests becomes a generalized role expectation in organizations.

The logic of the authority system is as follows (Katz and Kahn, 1966). In
every organization, certain activities must be performed if the organization
is going to survive and function effectively. The primary means the organization has to insure the performance of these activities is to stipulate them as
role requirements. An initial condition for membership becomes the acceptance of the role. Next, a set of supervisory roles are created to see that the
requirements of the basic organizational roles are fulfilled. With the creation
of supervisory roles on several levels, the conventional pyramid of authority
in organizations appears. To insure that the admonitions of the supervisors
are obeyed, an organizational law is established: subordinates shall obey
their designated supervisors with respect to matters of role performance. Finally, to insure effectiveness of the organizational law, a system of rewards
and punishments is established under control of the authority structure. To
insure that authority is not misused, organizations usually stipulate that authority is role relevant and can be used only in role relationships.

Throughout an organization, the leadership behaviors of the supervisors
affect the functioning of their subordinates. A classic study on group leadership conducted by Lewin, Lippitt, and White (1939), although it has some
shortcomings, demonstrated dramatically that the same group of individuals
will behave in markedly different ways when operating under leaders who
behave differently. In this study, clubs of 11-year-old children were supervised by leaders who adopted each of three styles for a specified period of
time: autocratic (the leaders planning for and directing the children), democratic (joint planning with group decisions), or laissez-faire (no leader intervention). When the clubs were under an autocratic leader, they were
more dependent upon him and more egocentric in their peer relationships.
When rotated to a democratic style of leadership, the same children evidenced more initiative, friendliness, and responsibility. These children continued to work even when the leader was out of the room. Their interest in
the work and in the quality of their product was higher. The number of aggressive acts decreased, furthermore, under democratic leaders as compared
to either the autocratic or the laissez-faire leaders.

Since the leadership style of a supervisor affects the group's functioning, it
is important that he adopts a style which contributes to both task effectiveness and the maintenance of the group in good working order. Supervisory
effectiveness has been studied by many different behavioral scientists.
Deutsch and Hornstein (in press) state that work group effectiveness is positively correlated with the degree to which the supervisor is perceived by his

subordinates as (1) defining roles and organizing functional structures; (2) allowing sufficient individual autonomy; and (3) being considerate of their welfare. Kahn and Katz (1960) summarized the findings of several studies and concluded that the supervisors of more effective groups: (1) played a differentiated role better and spent more time in planning what was to be done, in providing necessary materials, and in initiating next steps; (2) delegated authority to others more often; (3) checked up on the subordinates less often and were more supportive in their manner; and (4) developed cohesiveness among their associates more than did the supervisors of poorer functioning groups. In Likert's (1961, 1963) work on supervision, five characteristics of good supervisors have appeared with considerable consistency: (1) they spend their time in supervisory rather than in production work; (2) they are more person-centered and more considerate; (3) they encourage subordinates to speak their minds freely; (4) they usually react supportively rather than punitively to mistakes of subordinates; and (5) they supervise less closely, that is, they enlarge the area of responsibility to subordinates. One important exception to the effectiveness of this kind of supervision is encountered when top management does not support supervisors and foremen in a person-centered approach. Pelz (1952) found that a supervisor's influence on subordinates depended greatly on his status with his superiors: If his friendliness toward employees runs counter to what the top administrators believe and practice, he loses their respect and also that of his own subordinates, and his effectiveness is diminished.

Likert (1961) has summarized many of these findings into what he calls the principle of supportive relationship: "The leadership and other processes of the organization must be such as to ensure a maximum probability that in all interactions and all relationships within the organization each member will, in the light of his background, values, and expectations, view the experience as supportive and one which builds and maintains his sense of worth and importance" (p. 103).

The factor analytic studies of Halpin and Winer (1952) and Fleishmann, Harris, and Burtt (1955) resulted in two factors which account for most behavior of leaders in large organizations: *consideration* and *initiating structure*. Consideration involves human qualities such as warmth, respect, empathy, and approachability. Initiating structure defines leader behaviors such as subordinate role definition, establishment of channels of communication both up and down, and development of organizational patterns for goal achievement. Every supervisor combines these two factors in some way; the optimal balance between the two is largely determined by the nature of the goals and the membership of the group. Fleishmann, Harris and Burtt (1955) found that the employees of a large industrial organization liked working under foremen who were high in consideration and disliked working under those who were high in initiating structure. Proficiency ratings of the foremen based solely on the output of their subordinates revealed, however, that in production divisions the foremen with higher proficiency ratings were those who showed more initiation of structure while in the nonproduction divisions those with the higher proficiency ratings manifested more consideration. In the production divisions, however, employee absenteeism was found to be positively related to foremen's initiating structure and negatively related to consideration. Thus, the most effective leader is not necessarily the one preferred by his subordinates.

In summarizing the total available evidence, Shartle (1956) concludes that a pattern of leader behavior high in both consideration and initiation of structure tends to increase group effectiveness. In a recent study in Japan, Misumi and Tasaki (1965) confirmed this hypothesis. It is a difficult task to be high in both consideration and in initiating structure and, therefore, in many groups the two areas of leadership are informally divided between two different individuals.

Since the vast majority of the research done on supervision and group effectiveness is correlational, and no cause and effect relationship has been demonstrated, any application of the findings must be tentative. It should be remembered, furthermore, that under some conditions the relationship between the supervisor's style and group effectiveness should be quite high, and under other conditions it may be low. Merei (1949) demonstrated that when a leader is placed in a group which has well established norms and traditions, he has to adapt his style of leadership to conform to the norms and traditions of the group in order to gain influence. Finally, having a considerate supervisor who initiates structure may increase group effectiveness under some conditions but not under others. Fiedler (1958) presents evidence that an over-considerate, nondiscriminating supervisor is less effective than one who differentiates between competent and incompetent workers and who is critical of incompetent workers. In a 1968 article he also presents evidence that the leaders of more effective groups tend to be those who are concerned with successful completion of the task if the situation is either very easy or very difficult. When the situation is of intermediate difficulty, the most effective leader is one who devotes his attention primarily to friendly interpersonal relations.

TEACHERS

Each classroom traditionally is a separate subsystem within the school (Johnson, 1970). The classroom basically has two positions, teacher and student. These positions are complementary in that they are interrelated, and one cannot function without the other. The teacher is a person who teaches students; students are persons who learn with the aid of a teacher. It is within the role interdependence relationship of the teacher and students that students learn.

Amidon and Hunter (1966) define teaching as an interactive process, primarily involving classroom talk, which takes place between the teacher and the students, and occurs during certain definable activities. The role behaviors of the teacher which they identify as teaching activities are: motivating the students, planning for classroom activities, informing students, leading discussions with students, disciplining students, counseling students, and evaluating students. This conception of teaching is based upon the research on Flander's Interaction Analysis for observing the direct and indirect use of teacher influence in the classroom (Amidon and Flanders, 1966; Amidon and Hough, 1967). Direct influence consists of stating the teacher's own opinions or ideas, directing the pupil's action, criticizing his behavior, or justifying the teacher's authority or use of that authority. Indirect influence consists of soliciting the opinions or ideas of the pupils, applying or enlarging on those opinions or ideas, praising or encouraging the participation of pupils, or clarifying and accepting their feelings. Research basically suppports the notion that teacher flexibility in the use of direct and indirect methods of influence in the classroom correlates highly with teacher success in terms of student achievement.

In the classroom, as in any group, the teacher, as the role vested with the greatest authority, has to be concerned with accomplishing the assigned tasks, and with maintaining good student-teacher and student-student relationship. From the functional leadership viewpoint, the teacher provides effective leadership when he diagnoses what role behaviors are needed to facilitate task accomplishment and improve relationships, and either provides these behaviors or gets the students to provide them. For example, the teacher may diagnose that in order for the group to learn from a classroom discussion, more students must volunteer information about the discussion topic and must disclose their reactions to the topic. The teacher would then ask students for information and reactions, and would legitimize students asking each other for their reactions and any information about the topic they might have. In this way, the needed behaviors will occur.

Another way the teacher may provide leadership within the classroom is in structuring the learning situations in which students are placed. Two elements are important in structuring learning in the classroom. One is the extent to which cooperative or competitive interdependence among students is formed, and the second is the extent to which students are allowed to determine what happens within the classroom.

Deutsch's (1949, 1962) research on cooperation and competition and other studies extending his work indicate that cooperative interdependence among students will result in more satisfaction with classroom work and in better relationships among students. There is also evidence that more learning will take place in cooperatively structured classrooms than in competitively structured classrooms. Cooperative interdependence can be structured in a classroom in two ways. The first is by setting goals (such as giving all members of a subgroup the same grade, determined by how well they do as a whole in mastering a set of materials) which can be accomplished only through cooperative effort. The second is to divide a learning task so that there is a division of labor, that is, the individuals involved can accomplish the learning goals only if other individuals all do their part of the project. In addition to other advantages of cooperative interdependence, the teacher may wish to minimize the interpersonal competition characteristic of classroom life. Many behavioral scientists have noted the destructive aspects of interpersonal competition within the classroom. Sexton (196-) states:

> The present, highly competitive, system of marks, exams, and comparisons of sorts should be replaced by other types of incentives to learning. If there is to be competition, emphasis should be on group, rather than on individual competition. Marks and grades hurt more than they help; they discourage students from studying "hard" subjects or taking good but thorough teachers; they discourage really independent and critical thinking.

Perhaps the most effective way to obtain strong commitment to learning on the part of students is to involve them in the decision making about what takes place within the classroom. Research on group decision making indicates that students will probably be more committed to learning goals developed through group discussion than to learning goals imposed upon them by a teacher or school. Kostick (1957), for example, found that group discussion could be used to induce a college class to set higher achievement goals. A number of studies, which will be discussed in other chapters, have demonstrated that group discussion and involvement in decision making will increase one's commitment to accomplishing the group's goals.

Another way teachers can provide leadership in the classroom is by modeling ideal behavior. Providing an example of how one wants others to behave is probably one of the oldest influence techniques. There is a tendency to seek out admirable people as models for imitation; this tendency is probably strongest during childhood and adolescence, but continues throughout adult life. There is evidence that individuals in cooperative relationships will imitate others more than individuals in competitive relationships (O'Connell, 1965). A teacher, therefore, who models desirable behaviors and who has developed a cooperative relationship with his students will often influence students to imitate his behavior.

Finally, the teacher's supervisory style affects classroom work. A supervisory style which builds and maintains the student's sense of worth and importance, which is focused on both the consideration and initiating structure aspects of the classroom work, will be most likely to facilitate student learning.

THERAPISTS

The leader of a psychotherapeutic group has a role similar to that of the democratic leader of a youth group or the student-centered teacher in a classroom. All three confront individual differences and abilities and are responsible for developing a group climate that will lead members to engage in productive work.

A therapist usually deals with more disturbed personalities than are found in clubs of the community center or classes in the high school. There are exceptions, of course. It is easy for the layman to exaggerate the differences between the average personality and the neurotic. Almost everyone at some time during his life could benefit from psychotherapy. But because the psychotherapist's patients are generally more deeply disturbed, he has to discipline himself more carefully. Most effective leaders for therapy groups have experienced the self-revealing processes of some kind of psychoanalysis and have been trained by supervisors with insight. Unlike most teachers and group workers, the psychotherapist is equipped to recognize the pathological patterns that appear and reappear in disturbed persons. Some believe that medical training provides the best foundation for work with these cases. The psychotherapist who has had medical training is called a psychiatrist. Others advocate basic training in psychology, clinical psychology, and social psychology for the psychotherapist. Increasingly, social workers are also entering the field, treating groups of parents, groups of adolescents, or groups of other clients formerly seen individually.

Analysis of their procedures shows that good psychotherapists share certain similarities, regardless of the discipline under which they were trained. One study (Fiedler, 1950) of individual psychotherapists adhering to several different schools (Freud, Adler, Rogers) showed that the successful and experienced practitioners resembled one another more than they resembled the novices in their own school. The practitioners agreed that the ideal therapeutic relationship is one in which the therapist stays close to the patient's problems, helps the patient feel free to say what he likes, keeps the patient active, accepts all the patient's feelings as understandable, and gives the patient the freedom to make his own decisions. The therapist, according to this consensus among therapeutic schools "is able to participate completely in the patient's communication," and he "sees the patient as a co-worker on a common problem." The distinguishing feature of the successful therapist was that he seemed to be fully aware of what the patient was communicating.

This awareness is as true of a leader in group psychotherapy as of therapy with a single patient. The therapist in charge of a group must keep constantly in rapport with the feelings of those who are not speaking as well as of the one who, at any moment, holds the floor.

The categories devised by Bales (Chapter 4) to record participation in a group have been used also to report what a therapist does (Fiedler, 1950). The following table summarizes the type of response made to 27 typical statements of supposed patients, by 25 psychiatrists, 7 psychologists, and 9 social workers. Some had been trained as psychoanalysts, others had worked with Rogers on client-centered therapy. Bales' categories 2 (Shows tension release), 9 (Asks for suggestions), and 11 (Shows tension) appeared so rarely that these have been omitted from the table. Differences among the three professions (medicine, psychology, and social work) proved negligible. Leaders with a psychoanalytic approach did more exploration of feelings and more interpretation. Those trained in client-centered counseling were more apt to restate, clarify, and reflect feelings. These differences were especially marked among the less experienced therapists. With greater experience, the therapeutic leaders became less doctrinaire and were able to utilize more of the procedures which the other school found helpful.

TABLE 5–2

Frequency of Each Type of Response by Therapist

Categories		Responses			
		Psychoanalytic		Rogerian	
No. Bales	Psychotherapeutic Form	Less Experienced	More Experienced	Less Experienced	More Experienced
1. Shows solidarity	Reassures	5%	6%	2%	4%
2. Agrees	Permissive acceptance	16%	16%	4%	6%
3. Gives suggestion	Defines, proposes	4%	8%	1%	3%
4. Gives opinion	Interprets	12%	8%	2%	6%
5. Gives orientation	Restates, reflects	11%	17%	90%	59%
6. Asks orientation	Asks factual questions	8%	6%	0	0
7. Asks opinion	Explores feelings	38%	33%	1%	18%
8. Disagrees	Ignores requests, complaints; thwarts	6%	4%	0	2%
9. Shows antagonism	Aggressive remark	1%	1%	1%	2%
	Totals	100%	100%	100%	100%

The investigators found that over a period of time, the propositions of patients and therapists became more and more similar in theme. The pairs developed harmonious roles. The amount of reference by patient and by therapist to the immediate, current relationship of the two persons concerned correlated .72 in the first two sessions, but rose to .88 during the third and fourth month. Frequency of reference to feeling and emotion (again between patient and therapist correlated only .23 for the early sessions, but .70 during later months. Regardless of theory, the evolving realities in the dyad led to congruent therapist behavior. When patients were pouring forth their stories, all therapists listened. When patients were blocked, hesitant, and confused, most therapists naturally asked more questions or offered more specific suggestions to get the process going again. There was some evidence in these studies that when therapists were too quiet and noncommittal, patients felt it harder to communicate and were more apt to withdraw from therapy. While good leaders, teachers, and therapists learn to listen and to wait, it is possible to become too unresponsive. All leadership calls for two-way communication. The best leaders are seen as authentic persons (Rogers, 1963). An attempted integration of the findings from scientific study of "group dynamics" and those from clinical experience with group psychotherapy is offered by Durkin (1964). Her interpretation of reactions of the group to its leader may be helpful:

> At the beginning the members . . . tend to perceive the therapist in the image of the good, all-giving, omnipotent mother. They expect final answers and formulae for cure from him and seem willing to accept whatever he says. During that period they are likely to be very much afraid of the group as a whole. As they gradually become disappointed in the therapist's magical power, they become angry that he will not wave his wand in their behalf and begin to cast him in the role of the "bad mother" . . . Eventually . . . they begin to see the therapist much more realistically and become more able to treat him as a peer.

In the past few years, several reviews of the research on psychotherapy have tried to specify which therapist behaviors "cause" individuals to improve their ability to function effectively in life situations. A brief summary of the conclusions of those reviews will be given here. Bierman (1969) contrasts the findings on therapist behaviors on two dimensions, activity and affection. The activity dimension is a continuum stretching from therapist behaviors which are active, concrete, confronting, expressive, and structuring to therapist behaviors which are passive, ambiguous, abstract, evading, and guarded. The affection dimension reaches from therapist behaviors which are loving, warm, accepting, and prizing to those which are rejecting, hostile. and cold. On the basis of his review, he concludes that optimal effects occur under conditions of active therapist engagement plus positive therapist regard for his patient.

Reviews of the literature by Bergin (1966), Traux and Wargo (1966), and Traux and Carkhuff, (1967) conclude that there is a positive correlation between therapist behaviors demonstrating therapist warmth, authenticity, accurate understanding of the patient's statements and feelings, and both patient self-exploration and independent criteria of patient change. These findings support Rogers's (1951) theory that effective psychotherapy depends upon the therapist communicating to the patient (1) accurate understanding of the patient's "inner world;" (2) a feeling of nonpossessive warmth for and acceptance of the patient as a person; and (3) authenticity and genuineness on the part of the therapist. Much of the research cited in the reviews, however, is of dubious quality. It is almost entirely correlational evidence, furthermore, which (as was discussed in Chapter 1) does not prove that the therapist behaviors cause the patient's improvement. It is possible, for example, that as the patient becomes better, the therapist likes the patient more, which results in the expression of therapist positive regard towards the patient. Or, some third variable, such as the mere fact that the therapist and the patient spend time in a cooperative relationship may be causing both the patient's improvement and the therapist's expression of positive regard for the patient. There is a need for experimental research which demonstrates causal relationships between therapist behaviors and patient improvement. Some experimental evidence supporting Rogers' theory comes from studies of interpersonal negotiation. They indicate that when one person communicates his understanding of another's attitudes, the other becomes convinced that he has been heard and understood clearly, and so becomes more willing to reach an agreement; one's expression of warmth towards another produces favorable attitudes toward one (Johnson, 1969a).

In the future, psychotherapy will consist of a set of specific techniques that can be differently applied under specifiable conditions to specific problems (Strupp and Bergin, 1969). Practitioners, however, wait upon controlled research studies to better conceptualize the psychotherapy process and the conditions under which different techniques will be beneficial to patients.

SUMMARY

Any time two or more individuals join together to attain a mutually desired goal, a group structure develops. Leadership constitutes a particular influence relationship between two or more persons who depend on one another for the attainment of mutual goals within a group situation. The leaders influence the followers, and the followers, in turn, influence the leaders by reciprocating with such reinforcements as status, recognition, and esteem. A series of studies demonstrate that symbolic manifestations of esteem activate a person to take a leader role.

The effort to find some key trait, common to the personality of all leaders, which will always result in successful leadership has been unrewarding. It seems that leadership is not so much inherent in some individual, but rather describes a form of social interaction. The interrelationship between the leaders and the led is clearly evident in the case of authoritarian leaders.

All human beings begin life in total physical dependence. This dependency need remains with us to some degree, and it is on this need that the authoritarian leader depends. He leads by custom, by coercion and by charisma. Some people like to dominate or be dominated. This personality pattern, called "authoritarian" or "antidemocratic" has been extensively investigated by social psychologists. Democracy cannot survive in a society dominated by authoritarian personalities.

Trying to define leadership by traits has been ineffective. Current research focuses more on a leader's skills than on the nature of his deeper personality. The performance of acts which help the group achieve its goals is termed leadership. Leadership, then, is seen as function centered rather than position centered. Leadership functions change as conditions in the group change. It is sometimes necessary, therefore, to change leaders. According to the functional definition, (1) any member of a group may become a leader by taking actions that serve group functions and (2) any leader function may be served by various members providing a variety of behaviors.

According to Fiedler there are two types of leaders: the person-oriented and the task-oriented. In some situations the person-oriented leader is more effective and in some situations a task-oriented leader is more effective. The determining variables are (1) leader-member personal relations, (2) task structure, and (3) position power of the leader.

One type of leader is the charismatic leader. He inspires followers to accept his leadership out of love and passionate devotion to him. The more acute the distress of an individual, the more he is susceptible to a charismatic leader. Charismatic leaders often instigate social revolution.

If charismatic leaders found social movements and bring them into power, it is the machiavellian leaders who consolidate and wield power obtained. The machiavellian leader is a manipulator. Christie has make three assumptions about the manipulative leader: (1) He sees others as objects rather than individuals, (2) Since the manipulators are utilitarian there appears to be a lack of concern with conventional morality, and (3) There is little gross psychopathology as manipulators need to perceive accurately and not through a veil of psychosis or neurosis.

Most leadership behaviors in our society take place within organizations. Leadership within organizations begins with the formal role system which, among other things, defines the authority hierarchy. Organizations are concerned with accomplishing tasks and to effect this, roles are defined for individuals to play and thereby help in accomplishing the task. To be sure the supervisors are obeyed an organizational law is established: subordinates shall obey their designated superiors with respect to matters of role performance.

In an organization, attitude of the leader affects the performance of the individual. Groups do better with a democratic leader rather than with an autocratic or laissez faire leader. A pattern of leader behavior high in both consideration and initiation of structure tend to increase group effectiveness.

Teaching is an interactive process between teachers and students. There are many ways in which a teacher may influence a student. One way is through direct influence, a teacher stating his own opinion or ideas and imposing them on the class. Then there is indirect influence where the teacher solicits the opinions and ideas of students. The indirect approach seems to be more effective. As a leader, a teacher may diagnose what student role behaviors are needed in order to facilitate task accomplishment and better relationships. The teacher structures learning experiences for the student. He determines whether the classroom relationships will be on a competitive or cooperative basis. There is evidence that a cooperative interdependence is much more healthy than a competitive interdependence. The teacher also determines how active students can be in the setting of learning goals. Another way teachers provide leadership in the classroom is by modeling ideal behavior. Finally the teachers supervisory style affects classroom work. A style which builds the student's sense of worth will facilitate student learning.

Another kind of leader is the therapist. The psychotherapist has a role similar to that of the democratic leader of a youth group or the student-centered teacher in a classroom. All three confront individual differences and abilities and are responsible for developing a group climate that will lead members to engage in productive work. It appears that optimal effects occur when the therapist is active and transmits warmth to the client. However, the cause-effect relationship between therapist and client is not yet clearly understood.

CHAPTER 6

Structure, Process, Attitude

THE S-P-A THEORY

Here we will present a conceptual system within which to integrate many of the experimental findings of social psychology. Specific findings become part of the science as they fit into general theories and larger systems. The concepts which emerge in this chapter will be applied throughout the remainder of the book. Social conflict, race relations, and other phenomena of our culture will be interpreted largely in terms of the approach developed in this chapter. The specific influences which mold and change attitudes will be explored systematically in the next chapter. Here we shall be concerned with a basic way of thinking about how attitudes and behaviors relate to the objective pattern, or *Gestalt*, of situations.

BASIC CONCEPTS

Response to situation

Much psychological literature explains why different persons, if placed in much the same situation, behave differently. These differences in response among individuals may be attributed to heredity, to native intelligence, to age or stage of development, to previous learning, to conditioning, or to the persisting influence of powerful emotional experiences. Differential psychology, genetic (or developmental) psychology, psychometrics, psychology of personality, abnormal psychology, and clinical psychology are concerned mainly with accounting for *differences* in the response of different persons to situations essentially similar in structure.

Social psychology, like anthropology, is also concerned with the other half of the human picture—with *similarities* of response among various personalities. Despite all differences of personality, most people in a given culture show generally similar patterns as they satisfy needs for food, clothing, shelter, companionship, sex, and security. In our own society, most of us are accustomed to sleeping at night, rising in the morning, and having an American-type breakfast, going off to school or to work, eating again at noon, and perhaps resting during evenings and holidays. We have common understandings about birthdays, weddings, child care, schools, jobs, money, newspapers, automobiles, elections, laws, government, life insurance, and funerals. Later we shall explore some of the differences between one culture or subculture and another. In this chapter the emphasis is upon consistent meaning, feelings, and behavior among different individuals in response to a common and recurring situation.

Whatever brings about the typical response to a certain situation continues to operate so long as the situation remains constant. When the situation changes, behavior and feelings change correspondingly. When storm clouds suddenly appear on a hot summer afternoon, thousands of persons on a crowded beach simultaneously begin hastily to gather up their robes, blankets, umbrellas, radios, and lunch baskets and to move toward shelter and transportation home. Another illustration is graduation from school. Student life, for college seniors, has its well established characteristic schedules, responsibilities, and privileges. After commencement, with college days over, typical changes occur in schedules, responsibilities, and privileges. The diploma marks a transition to a different set of behaviors and feelings.

Field theory

The view to be presented in this chapter derives from what is sometimes called "Field Theory" (Deutsch, 1954). The essential idea is that objects in a field take on their dynamic character as a result of their position in the field. The movement of a bit of iron toward a magnetic pole is not due simply to innate traits of the moving part, but to the pull exerted by the field at the point where the particle is placed. The course of a stream is not inherent in the water, but follows the topography of the bed and banks. Likewise, most human behavior is responsive to its setting. In one group we lead; in another we participate equally with others; in a third, we are silent and apprehensive.

To account for these differences in behavior, we must look to the situation or field in which the action takes place. Except during conflicts, we seldom focus on *ourselves* as we respond. Like an experienced cyclist, we follow the course of the road, avoid stones and puddles quite automatically as we move toward our goal.

Social system-position-role

Social scientists have developed a set of concepts for describing and understanding similarities of behavior in a culture. Every society includes a num-

197

ber of subunits of organized interaction which may be called *social systems* (Linton, 1936). A family, a college, a business, a baseball team, or a hospital is a social system. The social system may be as small as a newlywed couple or as large as an army, the Roman Catholic church, or the United Nations.

Each social system is composed of interrelated *positions.* Some sociologists, anthropologists, and social psychologists prefer the term "status" rather than position. Since, in popular usage, status often implies differential prestige in a hierarchy, we prefer the more neutral term, position. People may occupy different positions in a social system—on a baseball team, for example —and yet be equal in prestige status. In a family, the positions are indicated by the words father, mother, son, daughter, grandmother, aunt, and so forth. In a college there are positions such as those of freshman, senior, faculty, janitor, librarian, dean, or president.

For every position there are expected behaviors which may be called *roles.* In baseball, the role of the pitcher differs from that of the catcher, batter, short stop or left fielder. Each position calls for appropriate role behavior. The several positions in the social system of the family imply distinctive roles with certain obligations and privileges for a father, mother, oldest son or daughter or baby. Each position in the social system of the Army has a well defined role associated with it. The role behavior appropriate to any position in a social system is largely independent of the unique personality characteristics of the particular individual who may occupy it at a given time. However different in personality make-up the teachers in a school, the priests in a church, or the clerks in a store may be, there are fairly well understood ways in which any teacher as teacher, any priest as priest, or any clerk as clerk is supposed to behave. Some things are required by the job. Whoever becomes the new mayor of the town is expected to perform the official duties associated with that position. Individuals, with all their special traits and private lives, may come and go, but positions continue to make fairly stable demands. In a hospital, an administrator, a doctor, an X-ray technician or a nurse may leave and be replaced by a very different individual but the role behaviors appropriate to these positions remain fairly fixed. There are certain things that a doctor, nurse, technician or administrator must do, willingly or unwillingly, and other things he may not do, whatever his inclinations.

Norms

Since there needs to be, and usually is, a fair degree of agreement within the social system on the role-behavior which is thought appropriate for a given position, this consensus may be called a *norm.* The term norm was introduced in Chapter 3 to describe the understanding, attitudes, codes of behavior and frames of reference which are shared by members of a group. Among the most vital norms for any group are those which define role expectations for the main positions. In a family, for example, the expectations of behavior appropriate to father, to mother, to son, to daughter, and to other relatives, are of very great importance. Where the role-expectations and role-behavior agree and the norm is firmly established, the members take it all for granted. Discussion and controversy arise when behavior does not accord with expectations, or when expectations differ.

Current campus controversies have arisen in part because of changing roles for teachers, students, and administrators. Once it seemed quite clear, and in many small conservative colleges it still is, that administrators decide on policy, teachers decide what and how to teach, students docilely submit. Students now demand a voice in determining what is to be studied, how it is to be taught, and everyone now wants to influence policy making. This redefinition of roles, while sometimes abrasive, makes college much more exciting today.

Varying conceptions of a role

Although role, as the dynamic aspect of any position, seems to be a simple concept, we have already begun to notice a distinction between the expected role and the enacted role. We also note possible differences in the role various persons associate with a given position. One of the problems of a modern teacher is that some supervisors, colleagues, pupils, and parents think a teacher should behave in one way while others have a different opinion. The result is role-conflict. Role-conflict may be related to differences among the following:

(a) self-definition of the role
(b) role expectation by others
(c) actual role-behavior
(d) role-behavior as perceived by self
(e) role-behavior as perceived by others

As an example, we may note a wholly imaginary college professor bicycling from the campus into town wearing a beret. The corresponding views might be:

(a) I am continuing an activity I found enjoyable as a student in Europe (self-definition).
(b) A professor should dress conservatively and behave with gravity (definition by others).
(c) Riding the bicycle, wearing the beret, nodding at acquaintances (actual role).

(d) I guess I look gay, relaxed, calm, youthful, attractive—not as stodgy and conventional as those others (self-perception).

(e) How nutty some professors are (perception by some others).

Role and feeling

How we feel varies with what we do. The same person will experience different feelings in the various roles of roommate, unsatisfactory student of French, top student in chemistry laboratory, ordinary second trumpet in the band, good tennis player, reader of a letter from lonely parents, borrower of money from a friend, an escort for a girlfriend on a date, although all of these and other roles may have arisen during one day.

Princes and princesses who are to inherit a throne are trained from infancy to the behaviors appropriate to their role. Their feelings are also adapted to the requirements. At levels of less prestige, there are similar prescriptions. In French Canada (Miner, 1939) the eldest son, to whom the farm property passes has a different set of experiences from those of his brothers who may expect to be priests or go into teaching or business. The eldest comes to think of himself as the farm proprietor long before he officially assumes the role; during boyhood he sees changes in agriculture, markets or taxes as they will one day affect him.

From structure to attitude

In our culture tradition has emphasized the dependence of behavior on attitudes. Evangelical Christians have been brought up to believe that "out of the heart are the issues of life." Proposals for social improvement have typically taken the form of changing people's feelings first, and then finding appropriate expression in changed laws and institutions. The central figure in reform movements has been the missionary, reformer, orator, or pleader who could move men's hearts. Once the inner changes had been brought about, it was rather taken for granted that the objective arrangements would be correspondingly altered. The movement toward American independence has been seen as beginning with impassioned speeches like those of Patrick Henry; opposition to slavery with the appeal of *Uncle Tom's Cabin*, William Lloyd Garrison's *Liberator*, and the superb oratory of Wendell Phillips.

In the behavioral sciences today, the flow of causation is more often viewed in the reverse direction. A social system having a certain pattern or structure establishes positions with prescribed roles. In the process of carrying out these roles, individuals develop corresponding outlooks, attitudes, and feelings. A change in the system brings changes in positions and roles, and the changed interaction alters the way participants are feeling. The general formula runs S→P→A: from Structure to Processes to Attitudes.

Abstract 15

TITLE The Chinese Indoctrination Program for Prisoners of War: A Study of Attempted Brainwashing

AUTHOR Edgar H. Schein

PROBLEM How did the Chinese (and North Korean) Communists succeed in influencing so many American prisoners to collaborate to some extent?

SUBJECTS Twenty repatriated Americans who had been prisoners of war in North Korea.

PROCEDURE Interviews (two to four hours) with each man at Inchon, Korea, and on a transport returning to the United States.

SOME FINDINGS 1. Social relationships were manipulated to break down reliance on customary patterns. Both commissioned and noncommissioned officers were separated from the other men. If any effective organization emerged among the prisoners, the key figures were removed. Sometimes young, inept or malcontent men were appointed to squad command, a procedure that was often gratifying to the nominated leader but actually disorganizing in its effects on the group. Religious services were forbidden. Mail from home was held up to create an impression of domestic unconcern and neglect. Spies and rumors of informers led to suspicion among the men, who became afraid to trust anyone. Continuous reports of collaboration by other prisoners suggested a new acceptable norm.

2. Rewards were distributed in accordance with sound learning theory. Men who signed communist petitions, served on peace committees, talked on the radio, etc., were given better food or living conditions or more status and freedom of movement.

3. Direct propaganda was used in daily lectures, discussions off and on through the day, news broadcasts, and reading material. Repetition was characteristic. The Americans were usually confused about just why they were fighting and hence more open to communist logic. Their understanding of communism was often small and clouded.

4. Personal persuasion was also employed. Each individual case history was studied; the class status of the man's family was interpreted to him as guilty exploitation of the workers or as justifying his siding with the working class. Injustices were emphasized, and the atmosphere was one of friendliness, fairness, and warmth.

5. Minor infractions of the many camp regulations were used to threaten men with severe punishment unless they publicly confessed their wrong-doing. Then the error was analyzed to bring home to the offender his mistaken perception or motivation. The effect on self-confidence was humiliating. Promises to try to improve were elicited. Many men found subtle ways of complying with the letter of the demands while evading the intent.

6. No mysterious drugs or hypnotic techniques were employed in brainwashing. The psychological pattern of physical deprivation, weakened social support, reduced self-assurance, accompanied by logical arguments and rewards for cooperation, represents only the rational application of psychological principles familiar to the West.

SOURCE: *Psychiatry*, 1956, XIX:149–172.

Some social interactions which proceed from the attitudes of individuals do affect the procedures and the structure of social systems, but these are fewer and less influential than those which flow in the S→P→A direction.

In practice, both religious and secular institutions have often followed the S→P→A sequence. Retreats, monasteries, and nunneries set up situations designed to restrict interaction and so to intensify the desired attitudes. In military training, camp life is an essential factor in separating the recruit from the habits, comforts, and attitudes of his home. An impressive example of the manipulation of a situation to affect attitudes is found in reports of so-called brainwashing of captured Americans in North Korea. Abstract 15 indicates that while efforts to influence attitudes directly by argument and persuasion were employed, the unusual effectiveness of these techniques was probably due to the structure of a situation which cut men off from earlier ties and rewarded them for new kinds of interaction.

Another social scientist (Biderman, 1963) has challenged a popular view that American POWs behaved weakly or shamefully under the stresses described in the Schein report. Despite the pressures, few gave in.

DIMENSIONS

What variables in the structure of the situation, S, are particularly potent in affecting behavior processes and psychological characteristics? The earliest and most influential are the relationships determined by the structure of the primary group the family. As the child matures, he associates with neighborhood groups; their make-up modifies his way of looking at life.

In larger social systems, we shall examine the way in which such factors as (a) size; (b) spatial arrangements; (c) the structure of productive work; (d) the prestige hierarchy; (e) sanctions; (f) power, and (g) conflict operate to shape the processes of interaction which, in turn, form the mentality of individuals. Each of these parameters of the social system will be examined in the sequence just named.

Primary group structures

It is not just the particular personalities in the family, but their roles and relationships which establish the matrix for the psychological development of the individual. A sociologist, Talcott Parsons, has expressed the idea cogently.

The *goals* of the human individual, in the human personality sense, are not primarily given in his biological constitution, but must be learned in the process of socialization. . . . Not only are other human beings, as discrete objects, individually and severally the most important objects in the child's and indeed any human being's, situation of action, but the *system of relationships* in which these objects stand to each other, and which includes the child himself, constitutes the most fundamental *structure* of the situation or environment in which his action takes place. A child, throughout his life cycle, is never exposed to just one person or "social object" but always to structured *systems* of social objects.

The only child, at an early stage, learns relationships mainly to adults who are deeply interested in him. The only child's expectations do not fit his first encounters with other children or with indifferent or hostile adults. Children born into large families may become skillful mainly in relating to slightly older or slightly younger peers. An informed report (Beaglehole, Ritchie, 1961) on Maoris living in Rakau, New Zealand, attributed the warmth and social spontaneity of adults to a sequence of experiences in the family: (a) absorbed attention of parents during the first year of life; (b) displacement then by the next child; and (c) diversion of the affiliation needs from the parents to a peer group.

The size of a family or kinship unit housed together varies in different cultures, and these variations in size have been found to be related to ensuing attitudes. Children in the larger units are less involved in intense emotional relationship with their particular father or mother. Uncles and aunts (or equivalents) are at hand to serve some of the children's needs. When grandparents live in the same house, they are in a position to supervise their married children. This tends to perpetuate some family traditions ("for the sake of the old folks") and to prolong some resentment in the parents who would like to outgrow the pattern of childhood dependence. Whiting and Child (1953) note that sororal polygony (one husband marrying two or more sisters) has the advantage that the several wives have been interacting since babyhood and are quite accustomed to living together. Their personalities are much less changed by marriage than if each had gone off with her husband to a new and distant home. There are other personality differences related to size of family. A humorist commented that one of the important things learned in a large family is that it is futile to expect justice.

When the large family—the tribe or clan—lives together, a child feels related to many aunts, uncles, and cousins as well as to his own parents and siblings. His security and status are less precarious; they cannot be altered because he happens at some moment to displease his particular father or mother. He belongs in a larger system. The wife may feel the continuing support of her brother and her clan because they can be relied upon to support her if her husband does not prove compatible.

In modern American marriage, the couple usually leaves their family of origin. The bride is uprooted from the home she has known and becomes almost wholly dependent on her husband. "Going home to mother" is seldom practicable. Children usually have only a weak relationship with relatives outside the immediate family. The new family is more autonomous and independent, but the members are very dependent on one another.

The order in which children are born gives each a differentiated role within the social structure. Oldest children, for example, are inevitably displaced as others come along. They are expected to help more in the home and to set a model for younger siblings. They are likely to develop a greater sense of responsibility and more hostility, guilt and anxiety. Schachter (1959) found the older childen more in need of reassurance from companions, more conformist, more likely to become alcoholics, more prone to seek psychotherapy, and more likely to join organizations.

Most family systems assign to girls a different status from that of the boys. Some of the effects of sex-stereotypes will be discussed later, in Chapter 11.

A particularly interesting deviation from our system of family life is found in the child-rearing institutions on communal farms (*kibbutzim*) in Israel (Bettelheim, 1969). Children grow up with their age group and are cared for by professionally trained persons. They may be with their own parents only for play periods after work and on holidays. Available studies seem to indicate no serious emotional deprivation. The two most frequent noted characteristics of *kibbutz* children are: (1) easy, warm, friendly, trusting relationships to adults, extending even to visiting strangers, and (2) lack of drive to mate sexually with young people of the opposite sex with whom they have grown up. Some explain this second attitude as a consequence of the relaxed, family-like, intimacy of children who have bathed and slept together since infancy; others suppose that at adolescence such intimacy arouses unusually powerful repressive forces (incest taboo), leaving the individual free to respond emotionally only to strange lovers.

An interesting observation by anthropologists (Whiting *et al.*, 1956) is that societies in which family patterns encourage exclusive and intense emotional relations of a boy to his mother are likely to develop initiation rites for adolescent boys, involving painful hazing, periods of isolation, trials of endurance, and sometimes genital mutilation. After passing these trials, the boy is presumed to have outgrown the emotional ties of childhood, and is permitted into the secrets, lodges, and councils of the adult males.

It is sometimes argued (Maslow, Diaz-Guerrero, 1960) that the problem of delinquency in contemporary American life is caused largely by the weak role assigned to fathers. The authors point out that in Mexico, although "broken homes" are frequent and fathers may spend very little time at home with their children, the delinquency rate is low. This is attributed to the strong position of the father in the traditional Mexican community. Although physically the father may be absent, he is psychologically very much in the picture. The father in the United States, these writers maintain, has no such assured status. Even if he is physically present, he may be psychologically a nonentity. The hypothesis is interesting because it postulates another connection between the structure of the primary group and ensuing attitudes. The evidence, however, for the proposed connection between ineffective fathers and delinquent children is not yet persuasive. There are such cases, but there are also numerous cases of delinquents whose fathers brutally dominate the home.

The term "primary group" applies to all very influential face-to-face relations, and so extends beyond the family. The gangs described in Chapter 3 define patterns of interaction among boys in many city neighborhoods. Social cliques may be exclusive and define certain other ethnic or national or religious or occupational groups as unacceptable.

On the point of social acceptance, certain animal studies, while having only qualified relevance to human social behavior, offer interesting hypotheses about connections between S and P and A. An alley cat has traits that are different from the cat raised on cushions and cream. Rats that are given too easy a life turn out to be less effective at problem-solving (Hebb, 1949). Puppies reared in cages may be quite healthy and noticeably less timid than those which run about normally (Thompson and Heron, 1954). The ducklings (described in Chapter 2) which were placed in the unusual situation of depending on a Greylag goose for maternal care interacted and formed a sexual preference different from what is regarded as instinctively normal for the species (Lorenz, 1952). Kittens brought up with puppies or with mice show friendly rather than hostile attitudes (Haldane, 1947). Bass which grew up alone in secluded spots, sheltered by vegetation, ate any little fish which strayed into their territory. When the ponds were cleared before they were stocked, all the fish grew up together, visually aware of one another. They shared food and "nobody tried to eat anybody" (Montague, 1950). Such attitude studies in animals do not prove that racially integrated neighborhoods, schools, work groups or playgrounds will reduce prejudice in children. We shall examine the evidence on this point in Chapter 9. What they do show is that the organization of the social environment can even modify behavior usually regarded as instinctive in animals. We noted earlier (Chapters 2 and 3), the general rule that increased interaction fosters friendlier feeling. Thus we would expect that changes in a school, business or community which remove some people from one social setting and place them in another, will cause some previous friendships to fade while new ones develop. Children are sent off to camps and to boarding schools to permit a break from home-bound attitudes and to encourage the acquisition of a different outlook.

We shall look next at several characteristics of larger social systems which affect interaction patterns and intrapsychic preferences. The first of these parameters is size.

Size of social system

We have noted that size of family has an effect on members; the same is true of other groups. When a group is too large (as reported in Chapter 3), several do not speak, and the group cares less for them. When the leadership activity of each individual is measured, recording his initiative and his ability to influence others in a leaderless group discussion, the scores vary inversely with the size of the group. In one study, when only two members participated, each was found to rate a leadership score of 23; when there were six members each averaged 17; with 12 members the rating went down to 12 (Bass, 1959). An experienced T-Group trainer (Luft, 1966) reports a typical structural intervention as follows.

One group became bogged down as every effort to work was trumped and blocked by its members. Instead of calling attention to this process, a perfectly acceptable intervention, I proposed that the group split into two subgroups on a self-selective basis. The shift took place quickly; chairs and other furniture were moved, and the subgroups became immersed in a flood of new interactions and new talk. When they returned to the group as a whole, one could observe at once the infusion of new data and feelings. They talked about the basis of self-selections, the new freedom they felt, and looked more boldly at the reasons for their stalemate.

The size of an audience affects both the speaker and the members. It is inspiring to speak to thousands, dismaying to address a scattering of listeners in a large auditorium. In a small room, the field would not seem so empty.

Size has been found to be an important factor affecting processes of supervision. If a supervisor has only a small number of subordinates, he can keep very close watch over their work. Although this might seem desirable, studies by the Institute of Human Relations at the University of Michigan have led to the opposite conclusion. People do not like to work with a supervisor hovering over them. Their morale is better when they feel that they are trusted with freedom to do their work in their own way. Hence, some companies have changed their pattern of organization toward giving a supervisor much larger numbers of workers to control. With a large group of subordinates, it becomes impossible to oversee every move of every individual. Obviously, more independence and autonomy must be granted. A change in the size of the supervised unit (S) thus leads to a change in the closeness of supervision (P) and affects morale (A).

Quite an opposite conclusion influences a well-known managerial precept concerning "span of control." Since the number of possible interactions increases geometrically when the number of persons increases arithmetically, the principle has been laid down that a working team with its manager should not be larger than five or six (Urwick, 1956). As size increases beyond this, most members cease to deal with other members as differentiated individuals and begin to see pairs or cliques. Intimacy decreases; there are too many strangers to warrant full trust. Decisions are made by power politics; coercion replaces consensus.

In Chapter 4 we noted advantages in group thinking over individual problem-solving efforts; some of these advantages increase with size of the working group, e.g. range of resources; probability of an unusually able individual; and canceling of chance errors. These are offset however, by time-constraints limiting participation; increased competitiveness and aggressiveness of those who do speak; withdrawal of the more passive; clique formation; increased leader domination; and repressive decision-making.

When a group of workers is large, each tends to concentrate more on his own task and to pay less attention to associates. In one study of a large bank with 350 tellers, one seldom offered to help another; in a branch which carried on the same functions with only 14 tellers, there was a greater sense of working together. Each more often volunteered help to another.

The size of units in which racial integration is practiced has been shown to be an important variable. The study in Abstract 16 indicates that white soldiers whose immediate associates were white were less favorable to the black companies or battalions than were white troops who interacted with blacks in their own companies. The larger the unit which was racially homogeneous, the less interracial interaction took place and the less favorable were attitudes of each race toward the other. When blacks and whites in the same company shared the daily routines of the barracks, mess hall, drill, and other duties, the effect on attitudes was to create the highest level of mutual acceptance.

The size of a community affects the processes of interaction, and the consequent attitudes of its citizens. A sparsely settled area fosters individual self-sufficiency. In a village, everyone knows his neighbors and knows that they keep an eye on him. In a large city, the individual feels the freedom of anonymity. In the small town, one must adapt, without choice, to old and young, rich and poor, bright and dull, moral and immoral (Hicks, 1947). In a large city, one can more freely choose one's associates from a wide assortment of types and interests. In cities, primary group attachments are weakened and traditions are forgotten. Radical movements, in politics, art, fashions, and morals, usually start in cities.

Changes in American character have come with the transition from the small settlements of pioneer days to the modern metropolis. Where human contacts are superficial and transient, surface effects are sought more than depth and lasting qualities. The role of the anonymous "they" who own the city houses, provide urban transportation and water, bring goods to the supermarket, and schedule the movies and television leaves the individual free from many responsibilities which he would normally assume if living in the country. *Stadtluft macht frei* (City air makes one free) says an old German proverb quoted by the urban sociologist Park (1916). Free, and irresponsible, "wheeling and dealing," "speed it up," "here today and gone tomorrow" —these are common attitudes of the highly mobile city life. The loose social organization of the city permits development of a wide variety of occupations, personality types, attitudes, and interests. These observations on size of community involve spatial proximity as well as numbers, and we proceed next to a review of spatial structures.

Abstract 16

TITLE   Opinions about Negro Infantry Platoons in White Companies.

AUTHORS   Information and Education Division, U.S. War Department

PROBLEM   What did white soldiers think (in 1945) of integration with Negro troops? Were those who had had such experience more or less favorable?

SUBJECTS   250 officers and 1,710 white enlisted men in European Theatre of Operations field forces.

PROCEDURE   Survey by trained interviewers.

SOME FINDINGS   Question: Has your feeling changed since serving in the same unit with colored soldiers?

ANSWER: 77 percent of officers with such experience reported more respect and more favorable opinions; 19 percent no change; 4 percent no answer. None reported less favorable attitudes.

QUESTION: Some Army divisions have companies which include Negro and white platoons. How would you feel about it if your outfit was set up something like that?

	Would dislike it
Answer:	
1,450 men with no experience with Negro troops	62 percent
180 men in same regiment or division but not in a company which includes Negro platoons	22 percent
80 men in company with Negro platoons	7 percent

SOURCE: *Report No. B-157*, Information and Education Division, Army Service Forces, Washington, D.C., U.S. War Department, 1945.

Space and arrangement

Closely related to the size of a social system are its spatial characteristics. Interest in location as determiner of behavior has been intensified by the concept of "territoriality" popularized by Ardrey (1966). Birds, quadrupeds and men clearly recognize their home territories and behave differently there than on spaces belonging to others. "Where are you from?" we commonly ask as one way of identifying a stranger.

Hall (1959, 1966) has undertaken precise measurement of how close individuals wish to be to intimate friends (6-18 inches), acquaintances (2-4 feet), or to others in public settings (12 feet or more).

The seating arrangement in a room modifies the interaction patterns and the consequent attitudes. A lecture hall is laid out to suggest focus on the speaker. Members of the audience are most likely to converse, if at all, only with their near neighbors. The same determining forces lead passengers on a train, bus, or plane to limit their remarks, as a rule, to their seatmates. If a room is designed to facilitate discussion, the seats are arranged in a circle so that each participant can see every other. Sometimes they sit around a table. Steinzor (1950) observed that when groups were seated in a circle, members interacted most with those who sat opposite them; least with their neighbors on each side who were out of the direct line of vision.

Another observer, Sommer (1961), recorded the spontaneous geographic arrangement of visitors (to a mental hospital) who were asked to sit down around a table for a few moments of discussion. One was arbitrarily appointed to lead the discussion. The designated "leader" almost always chose the seat at one end of the table, and the other members chose the seats at the "foot" of the table opposite the leader. When the visitors were sent by two's to wait in a room with two parallel couches, their choice of seats depended on the distance between the couches. If the couches were 2 feet to 3 feet apart, dyads usually sat facing one another (ratio 3:1). With 4 feet or more between couches, members almost always sat alongside each other (ratio 9:1). A later study of students in a college library (Felipe, Sommer, 1966) found that they moved away when an experimenter came too close, and if he again moved close, they fled. Elderly women in a hospital ward increased their social interaction when chairs were re-arranged to form small groups (Sommers, Ross, 1958). Ward (1958) separated two members of a five-man group, seated in a circle, by empty chairs on either side of this pair. Leadership more often emerged from one of the two, than from any of the other three persons.

Spatial arrangements at work are even more potent because they operate for something like 40 hours a week. A sociometric study of 494 factory workers (James, 1951) showed that those who worked near one another, or who worked on a joint project were especially well acquainted and likely to be friends. In the Western Electric plant at Hawthorn the inspection group who worked together at the front of the room formed one clique, and the soldering group located at the back of the room, another (Roethlisberger, Dickson, 1939). A study of 70 bomber crews (Kipnis, 1957) showed that choice of a partner for a work task or a social companion was strongly influenced by physical arrangements facilitating interaction.

One corporation found its efficiency reduced by poor communication among departments. Sometimes two or more departments duplicated work; both collected the same statistics; jurisdictional disputes arose over who should be doing what. Departmental empire building and rivalry intensified tendencies to claim credit and put blame elsewhere. The solution was to move the vice presidential offices. Formerly each vice-president had been close to the department he directed; some occupied whole floors; others were in separate buildings. The change brought all these departments heads onto one floor where they would see one another several times each day. Interaction brought better communication and improved cooperative attitudes. The good of the corporation as a whole took precedence over the concern for only the VP's own distinct area. Psychological change proceeded from spatial change.

Recent psychiatric studies (Kinzel, 1969) have found that prisoners with a history of violent behavior feel more threatened by the close approach of another person. Their "circle of privacy" is larger than average. They more quickly resent the intrusion of an outsider, however gentle he may be.

As overpopulation continues and living space becomes scarcer, the social psychology of crowding becomes more evident. Millions of families endure chronic discomfort from lack of space. A letter from a doctoral candidate reports her move from an apartment to a large old house:

Our family is entirely different without the peeves of overcrowding. My husband couldn't stand the children before; now he is gloriously happy with an upstairs sitting-room which is quiet. I feel suddenly joyous to have a place where I can hear good music, away from the blare of the TV. Such a difference house geography makes!

Historians recognize that the exploration of a new country follows routes laid out by Nature. Rivers become highways to the interior; high mountain ranges are barriers. Colonies form first along the coast and develop their own traditions and norms. Out on the frontier the isolation fosters different styles of life and different attitudes.

An ecological study of attitudes as shown by the vote in South Carolina for "Dixiecrat" Thurmond in the 1948 presidential election showed that districts with a larger percentage of Negro population cast more votes for this segregationist candidate ($r = .39$) and that largely rural districts also cast more such votes ($r = .41$). These are partial correlations, with other factors statistically held constant (Heer, 1959).

People who live near one another interact more often and are more likely, consequently, to develop similar attitudes. One study (Caplow, Forman, 1958) reported a correlation of .48 between frequency of interaction and geographic nearness for families living along a single lane. The correlation may reflect the decision of families that see each other frequently to live near one another. But in other instances, strangers brought into proximity become good neighbors.

Studies of the shopping habits of farm dwellers who lived between two towns showed that the proportion of the shopping done by a family in one town rather than the other varied with the size of the town and inversely with the square of the distance between the farm home and the town (Reilly, 1929). Frequency of telephone calls between cities likewise varies with the size of the city and inversely with the distance between them (Zipf, 1947). Dodd (1953) found that the spread of a slogan among housewives in a community depended largely (72 percent) on the interactions between women whose homes were not more than 100 yards apart. Only 37 percent heard about the slogan from an informant living more than a block away.

These studies—largely sociological—are significant for social psychology because psychological variables in perception, feelings and behavior seem to
be predictable from parameters of the social field.

A study in Arkansas (Loomis, Davidson, 1939) found that geographic location within a community was a major factor in determining which families
associated with which others. Families that associated with one another also
belonged to or made use of many of the same organizations. The relationship
here is probably circular: Proximity, friendship, and participation in community agencies all affect one another. Further evidence of similarity in attitudes among associated families appeared when those who migrated out of
the community tended to visit mainly with other families who had also left
town; those who remained associated mainly with others who remained.

A study of attitudes of residents toward a tenant council (Festinger, *et al.*,
1950) showed that those living around the same court, and hence interacting
more often, tended to be in general agreement. Some court groups favored
the council; others were opposed. Those who deviated within groups were
typically less than 30 percent. The more cohesive the court (measured by
sociometric choice), the fewer the deviates. Even so minor a spatial factor as
having apartment doors opening onto the same inner court increased both
cohesion and similarity of attitude.

Experience in interracial housing projects adds evidence for our hypothesis. When certain buildings were reserved exclusively for black or for white
families, cohesion developed among residents within each of those buildings,
but families in a separate building or of a different race were regarded with
suspicion (Deutsch, Collins, 1951). When race was disregarded and families
located in order of application—the so-called pepper and salt mixture—many
families found their immediate neighbors to be of a different race. Through
the normal processes of interaction, acquaintances and friendships soon
developed across the barrier of race. Another study (Wilner, Walkley, Cook,
1951) indicates that eventual feeling about fellow tenants of the other race
could be predicted more accurately from proximity in the building than
from the attitude (favorable or prejudiced) the tenants had when they moved
in.

Interesting evidence of homogeneity of attitudes among those who live in
close proximity appears in surveys of different types of city neighborhoods.
Studies of delinquency (Shaw, 1942) reveal that certain areas within cities
have especially high rates of crime among youth; others are relatively low.
In Chicago, a region just outside the business district of the "Loop" had been
high in delinquency rate for decades. The actual population of the area had
changed: Irish, Italian, Polish, and black people had each predominated for
a time. But, regardless of race, nationality, or religious affiliation, the youth
in this area were a problem for the police. Deteriorated housing, lack of
community facilities, and other structural factors in the region kept young

people on the streets and in gangs. Gangs in a given area developed delinquent norms which lived on in the group even though particular individuals came and went. In several run-down areas of New York City, the only method which broke up the antisocial traditions and action patterns was physical relocation. When the old Hell's Kitchen tenement houses were torn down, and the residents were forced to live in other sections, the new apartment houses which replaced the slums brought new standards of conduct into the neighborhood.

Structure of productive work

People who do different work develop different attitudes. The farmer in all lands is bound to manual labor, rooted in the soil, and moves with the cycle of seasons. A changed agricultural technology produced a new type of modern American farmer who works with machines and the applied sciences, who uses the commercial and cultural resources of cities, who may participate in county, state or national politics, and whose outlook is no longer narrow and provincial. Yet, all farmers have some concerns in common which differentiate them from factory workers, magazine writers or movie stars. Professor Robert E. Park, one of the earliest students of the sociology of city life, observed: "The effects of the division of labor as a discipline, i.e., as a means of molding character, may (therefore) be best studied in the vocational types it has produced. Among the types which it would be interesting to study are: the shopgirl, the policeman, the peddler, the cabman, the nightwatchman, the clairvoyant, the vaudeville performer, the quack doctor, the bartender, the ward boss, the strikebreaker, the labor agitator, the school teacher, the reporter, the stockbroker, the pawnbroker; all of these are characteristic products of the conditions of city life; each, with its special experience, insight, and point of view determines for each vocational group and for the city as a whole its individuality" (1916).

Adam Smith, in one of the classics of economics, noted that "The difference of natural talents in different men is in reality much less than we are aware of; and the different genius which appears to distinguish men of different professions when grown up to maturity, is not upon many occasions so much the cause as the effect of the division of labour" (1776). Here he supports the sequence of our thesis: form of work (S-P) leads to distinct psychological attributes (A).

Millar (1793) writing at about the same period, related regional and national characteristics to the prevalent occupations: "In searching for the causes of those peculiar systems of law and government which have appeared in the world, we must undoubtedly resort, first of all, to the differences of situation, which have suggested different views and motives of action to the inhabitants of particular countries. Of this kind are the fertility or barrenness of the soil, the nature of its productions, the species of labor requisite for procuring subsistence, the number of individuals collected together in one community. . . . The variety that frequently occurs in these and such other particulars must have a prodigious influence upon the great body of the people; as, by giving a peculiar direction to their inclinations and pursuits, it must be productive of corresponding habits, dispositions and ways of thinking."

A study (Stogdell et al., 1956) of naval officers who had moved from one assignment to another indicated that more than half of the variance in what men did was determined by the job rather than by the personality of the man. While there were noticeable traits of behavior carried by the particular individual as he moved from one job to another, there were even more characteristics necessarily required by the position and evidenced by one man after another as he assumed the particular role.

Organizational structure has been studied in the laboratory by varying channels of communication. Leavitt's (1951) findings, presented in Chapter 3, show satisfaction varying with centrality in the structure. Key men are high in interaction and obtain the most psychic reward. Replications (Guetzkow, 1954; Shaw, et al., 1957) also found that the all-channel network, in which each is free to communicate with every other, leads to greater satisfaction among participants, partly because they experience less sense of restraint.

One dimension of a task which has a powerful influence upon interaction processes and hence upon attitudes is its specificity. If a worker has been given a very limited job, with instructions, he interacts very little with his fellow workers on job-related matters. If several workers who have previously had such narrow assignments are brought together as a team and allowed to cooperate in a larger, more meaningful project, they usually interact frequently, help one another, turn out better products and enjoy the work more.

A study (Kornhauser, 1962) of the mental health of factory workers led to the conclusion that the kind of the work men were doing affected their emotional adjustment. Each worker was rated for tension, anxiety, hostility, social withdrawal, alienation, and dissatisfaction with himself and with life. Kornhauser classified 57 percent of skilled workers as having good mental health; 37 percent of semiskilled workers as good; but only 12 percent of those doing repetitive work as having good mental health. He investigated the possible effect of differences in education, but found that this was not a significant factor. The emotional state of the men was most closely and clearly correlated with what they had to do to earn their wages and with "associated life conditions."

In another study, several ministers took jobs on assembly lines in Detroit factories and kept diaries of their experiences. One of their observations was that, to their surprise, they found themselves adopting many practices they had condemned from the pulpit. They swore, cheated, lied, hated, loafed on the job, and behaved in ways closely resembling the actions of other workers in similar situations.

An unusually clear demonstration of the effect of a changed situation on attitudes is found in Lieberman's report (1956) on workers who became foremen or shop stewards. An attitude inventory was given to 2,500 workers. During the ensuing year, 23 of these men became foremen and 35 became shop stewards. In their new jobs, foremen were more promanagement and shop stewards were prounion. Inspection of their earlier responses showed no significant differences between the attitudes of the men who later became company officials and those who later became union officials. After they stepped into the new role, they each took on the attitudes of the related reference-group. Foremen became more like other managers; shop stewards became more like other trade union leaders.

Most people are capable of both competitive and cooperative behavior; which pattern they adopt may depend on the work situation. Mintz (1951) showed that when subjects were stimulated to compete at drawing cones up through a narrow-necked bottle, frustrating jams ensued. When they were instructed to cooperate, the subjects perceived their tasks differently, were successful in permitting every member to draw out his cone within the time limit, and felt pride in their achievement. Some games, like tennis, stress courtesy and minimize taking any unfair advantage of an opponent. The same player may behave differently on the tennis court than he would in a football contest. Workers also respond to the overall climate of their enterprise. We described earlier the change in children when bricklaying was undertaken as a team enterprise rather than individual competition (Tseng, 1952). Parallel changes have been observed in engineering students, working cooperatively or competitively at problem solving (Deutsch, 1949). The conforming traits of the "organization man" (Whyte, 1956) may well have arisen as a consequence of the change from small competitive enterprises to immense corporations which now encourage a high degree of cooperation within the company, and agreements to prevent price wars among the leading companies.

Technological changes, such as the introduction of automation in industry, alter the work structures, the positions and roles, and the attitudes of workers. One pertinent study (Mann, Hoffman, 1956) compares a new electric power plant with the older plant which continued to operate nearby. Many jobs, such as the regulation of supply of coal and air and water to the boiler, which are manually operated by a fireman watching gauges in the old plant, are controlled by automatic devices in the new plant. Fewer employees are needed in the new plant and jobs have been redefined. Operators in the new plant have had to master parts of the production process which were quite outside their former specialized function. As a consequence they have been rotated through several working situations and report a higher level of job-satisfaction with their expanded knowledge and responsibilities. Mainte-nance workers who were formerly skilled in a single craft—mechanics, elec-tricians, welders, pipefitters, and others—have been replaced by multiple-skill members of a team. The latter are less identified with a particular trade. The large capital investment in the plant has led to continuous operation which has created dissatisfied workers who do not like rotating shifts. Changes in equipment have thus brought a variety of changes in operating procedures and have caused corresponding changes in the attitudes of the employees.

Prestige hierarchy

In most social systems some positions are regarded as "higher" and as bring-ing more prestige to the occupants. Persons who move up in the hierarchy obtain ego-satisfaction and show increased self-regard. Those who move "down" in such a structure are likely to become frustrated, disappointed, hostile, alienated or self-rejecting.

Security of status has an important influence on attitudes. In older so-cieties where differences of caste or class have been thought of as divinely prearranged and sanctioned, each level takes its rights, privileges, and duties for granted. The secure upper class members are relatively free from pres-sure to conform. They may go about as they please. Secure lower-class mem-bers experience little craving to rise. American society does not ordain fixed status for most of its members. The business executives who head depart-ments in dynamic companies would like to be promoted to vice-president; they fear replacement or demotion. They are under constant strain which sometimes produces ulcers. Those lower in the scale, having been taught that everyone has a fair chance to rise, and being under constant appeal from advertising to aspire to higher standards of living, struggle to get a foothold on the next rung of the ladder. Some eventually resign themselves to permanent ceilings and find ways to take life as easy as possible without losing their jobs.

Some insight into the attitudes generated by status levels can be obtained from simple laboratory exercises. A study (Kelley, 1951) of college students assigned to high status ("the best and most important job in the group") or low status ("menial and routine, a poorer job") jobs in an experimental task brought out a connection between lower status and the introduction of more communication irrelevant to the task. Low-status members more often failed to understand directions.

Another difference in communication was that the high-status students more freely criticized their subordinates but said little about any problems they themselves found in their work. They seldom criticized any other high-status persons. They apparently fell into an upper-class defensive pattern of admitting no defects in themselves or their own jobs, while directing their accusations at the lower status workers. A control group, doing the same work without any definition of high- or low-status jobs, expressed significantly more criticism toward fellow workers, whatever their job. The experimenter concluded that the introduction of a sense of hierarchy operates as a general restraint on the free expression of criticism. An interesting angle is the difference in expression of criticism between low-status workers who were frozen in their type of job, and those who were told they might win promotion to a higher level task. Those who viewed themselves as potentially mobile were less free in their criticism of the higher-up's.

Factors which impede interaction within a work group also influence the resulting attitudes. In Chapter 2, Bavelas' experiment was described. When the situation (S) permitted free two-way communication (P) the outcome was a friendly attitude (A). When telephone communication from one party was arbitrarily restricted to "yes" or "no," as it often is in the reaction of a boss to a request, the ensuing attitudes became hostile.

Within an organization, communication is best between persons of approximately equal status. Many a man, popular with his co-workers, has suffered a puzzling sense of rejection after he has been promoted to a supervisory role. In one firm this process was reversed. When Mr. B., a budget man, was seen by foremen as a "higher-up," they told him only what they wanted him to know and concealed vital facts. When Mr. B.'s job was redefined as a consultant and assistant to the foremen, their behavior and attitudes became much more open toward him.

In Chapter 9, we shall see that members of socioeconomic classes who have little direct communication with other classes develop distorted stereotypes. In "Middletown" (Lynd, 1929) two generations ago the boss and workers called one another by first names; they sat beside each other in church and sent their children to the one public school. In a large modern corporation, size, structure, and geographic separation of the absentee directorate mean that workers usually have little if any contact with top management, and none at all with the board of directors. This social structure perpetuates stereotypes of the boss as a bloated "Moneybags" and of the "lower class" as irresponsible, ungrateful, and lacking in sensible thrift. Each class can readily become a scapegoat onto which the other projects its distress.

A study of changes in attitude related to high-prestige Greek-letter residences on a college campus (Siegel, 1957) showed that those freshmen who wished to join such groups scored higher on the antidemocratic (F-scale) test; those who had a year of residence there remained high in F-scale scores; but those who had lived a year in lower-prestige residences became more democratic in their attitudes.

A study of race prejudice among white college students found that an important factor was "equal status contacts" (Allport, 1954). If contacts were limited to a situation in which one race had prestige and dominance, while the other was subservient, communication processes were impeded. Each said to the other only certain "appropriate" things. Prejudice could easily remain undiminished. Contacts based on equality, between co-workers or fellow students, led to freer communication and more genuine mutual appreciation of one another as fellow human beings. A study (MacKenzie, 1948) was made of attitudes among Civil Service employees. The study indicated that employees who had known blacks only in subordinate positions, such as cleaning women or porters, had more illusions about white superiority than those who had known blacks as coequal fellow workers or as supervisors.

This principle of equal-status interaction as an antidote for prejudice will be very useful in Chapter 9, when relations among ethnic groups will be more fully considered. Without noting differences in the prestige structure, it would be difficult to account for the fact that resistance to desegregation is strongest in those areas in which black-white ratio is 50 percent or more (Tumin, 1957). Obviously there are numerous interracial contacts in such a situation, but they operate within a pattern of white supremacy and black subordination. Under these conditions, interactions reinforce the existing norms. The basic issue in the Supreme Court decision of 1954 on public school desegregation was whether schools could be racially separate and yet equal. In a society of equal status, separation would not necessarily be derogatory for either race. Given the prestige structure of most American communities, North or South, residential and school segregation implies separation because of inequality. It reinforces attitudes of prejudice.

Sanction structure

The S-P-A formulation applies to all attempts to influence behavior and attitudes by manipulating the sanctions, i.e., the rewards and punishments. A prime example is legislation. When the laws provide premiums for certain kinds of behavior and penalties for not conforming, most people follow the legally prescribed path. Moreover, they come to feel that this is quite right and proper; they internalize the traffic lights (laws).

Psychologically, the sanctions operate mainly through reinforcement or positive rewards of satisfaction when certain acts are performed. The restraining influence of fear of punishment leads to avoidance of the situation, the agent of control, the punishment, or perhaps to avoidance of the prescribed act. In any case, actual effects are more potent than promises.

Every successful parent and teacher has learned that children respond to what one does rather than to what one preaches. Empty threats and enticements do not have a lasting effect. A parent may say, and believe, that he wants his child to be helpful in the home. If, however, the child finds that nothing happens when he fails to fulfill a request for some work, and that when he does do so, no one expresses any special appreciation, such actions build tendencies to evade home tasks. A teacher may claim that he is interested in stimulating an attitude of inquiry in his students. If, however, he brushes aside student questions and grants high semester grades on the basis of correct answers to his factual questions, his students will tend to stress mastery of facts over throughtful exploration of the unknown. A manager may say that he values initiative and enterprise in his subordinates; if, however, he rejects their proposals and rewards the yes-man, his organization will breed conformists. Colonial powers, asserting that they want to develop the capacity of the natives for self-government, have often suppressed every emerging leader who exercised initiative and won a following.

In Mintz's experiment it would not have been very effective to urge subjects to be "cooperative" as long as the rewards and punishments were based wholly on individual achievement. In Deutsch's experiment some groups worked cooperatively because they shared a common fate. They all had to survive or perish together. The control groups allowed one individual to win his reward at the expense of others.

In a similar experiment (Katz et al., 1958) subjects were asked to build designs with erector units, to solve puzzles, to discuss human relations problems, and to roll a ball along a large spiral, a task which required manual skill. Some subjects knew they were being rated and given bonuses for individual performance; others were given bonuses only for the performance of their whole group. Group rewards inspired more helping of others, more giving of suggestions, and less rejection of others' ideas.

Power structure

In earlier chapters we have seen that groups under autocratic leaders develop behavior and outlook different from the patterns fostered by democratic leadership. In the famous Lewin, Lippitt (1939) experiments, one variant was to exchange a single member. Bob had been in a group with an autocratic leader and had shown the behavior characteristic of his fellow members—outwardly docile with repressed hostility. Bill had been in a democratic group characterized by friendly talk, cooperative planning, and interest in the work. When the two changed places, each took over the patterns which had previously marked the other. Apparently neither heredity nor early childhood experiences made the boys egocentric or cooperative, social or hostile. When they moved into a new S, the processes of interaction, P, changed, producing distinctly different attitudes, A.

Another report (McCandless, 1942) describes what happened in a state training school when one of two comparable cottages shifted from the autocratic leadership which had been traditional in both to a more democratic style of control. In both cottages, before the change, the more dominant and aggressive boys had been most popular. After the change, this relationship fell to zero in the cottage that became democratic; the other did not change.

System norms

Behavior and attitude in a given position are strongly influenced by the norms of the larger system. In Chapter 3 we observed that it is hard to induce a gang member to change his individual behavior against the expectations of his social group. It is easier to change individual behavior by changing the direction of activities in the whole gang. The group norm carries the individual with it. Sometimes a group with delinquent norms has to be broken up in order to free its members to enter new groups with other norms. This has happened in many congested urban areas (e.g. "Hell's Kitchen") where public housing has replaced slum tenements.

The failure of group therapy to bring much change in attitudes of boys who have been behavior problems at school may be related to the fact that the school system has not changed. Sarri and Vinter (1969) found that they could influence unruly pupils while in the therapeutic group setting but that once back in the classroom with its unwelcome pressures, expectations and relationships, life again became intolerable for these boys.

Studies of pupil performances show that students from educationally-deprived lower-class background make much more academic progress if they enter a school in which the other children came from better homes with more advantages. Their level of aspiration adjusts to the norms of their school.

Forcing institutional change

Institutions are systems which define processes of interaction, and hence mold the attitudes of participants. Usually they are so potent that needed changes cannot be brought above by individual members working from within. Institutions, like individuals, do not change so long as established patterns produce expected results. They change only when forced to do so because the customary procedures no longer work. Hence if change is needed and overdue, the tactic has to be disruptive. The campus riots—1967 on—have speeded up change in colleges. The boycott of table grapes—1967-70—forced the growers to recognize a union.

The strategy of disconfirming expectations about institutional operation will be discussed further in Chapter 13. The point to be stressed here is that the S→P→A sequence operates so powerfully on most members that their attitudes tend to conform to what the institution expects of them. Change has first to be thrust upon the system; then individual attitudes change.

Total milieu

In this chapter we have looked at one dimension of the structural situation after another: position, roles, size, spatial arrangements, organization of production, prestige, hierarchy, sanctions, power patterns, and so on. Changes along any of these dimensions of S require corresponding changes in P and in A. Our final proposition is that situations are integral, and the total milieu has a combined influence.

Abstract 17

TITLE	Individual and Mass Behavior in Extreme Situations.
AUTHOR	Bruno Bettelheim
PROBLEM	What happens to human beings in such an atmosphere of terror and torment as a Nazi concentration camp?
PROCEDURE	The author was confined in Dachau and Buchenwald during 1938–39. He observed his fellow prisoners who, despite their malnutrition, had to perform hard labor and were tortured. Differences in reaction between new prisoners (less than one year in the camp) and old prisoners (three years or more) were noted.
SOME FINDINGS	1. New prisoners thought of return to the outer world; old prisoners of how to adjust to camp conditions.

2. The group, in the interests of its own security, imposed on all members regression to infantile behavior, living in childlike dependence on the guards, unable to plan beyond the present moment, indulging in fantasies and groundless boasts.

3. Old prisoners eventually accepted the values of the Gestapo guards. They took over verbal expressions and copied acts of physical aggression toward newcomers and the weak. Torture of suspects by the prisoners themselves imitated Nazi models. With bits of material old prisoners tried to make their costumes resemble uniforms of Nazi guards. They prided themselves on exhibitions of toughness. A game of seeing who could take the most blows without complaining was played by guards and copied by prisoners. Nazi racial discrimination was also adopted by some of the old timers.

SOURCE: *J. abnorm. soc. Psychol.,* 1943, XXXVIII:417–452.

At the worst extreme of the scale is a horrible milieu like a Nazi concentration camp. In Abstract 17, Bruno Bettelheim's observations are summarized. Long-term prisoners in a concentration camp became as free of conscience and as brutal as their depraved guards. It is a moving and frightening demonstration of the power of the S-P-A line of control. It is also significant that the rehabilitation of men who had been war prisoners in camps less cruel than Buchenwald also seemed to require special therapeutic treatment. The

British developed for this purpose "Civilian Resettlement Units," which were transitional settings, part way between camp conditions and civilian life. At the positive end of the scale are utopias, designed to bring about behavior and attitudes which bring most satisfaction. In *Walden Two* a psychologist, B. F. Skinner (1955), describes a total milieu which he believes would foster the best human relations.

In this chapter we have seen how changes in the structure of a situation lead to adaptations in social interaction and bring consequent changes in attitude. Within this broad framework, we will examine more closely, in Chapter 7, the psychological processes by which attitudes arise and are modified.

SUMMARY

Social psychology is concerned with explaining the differences and similarities found among and between individuals and groups. Generally, people in similar positions or situations respond alike. It is when the structures or the processes of interaction within a social system change, that individuals change their attitudes and ways of responding. Each social system has designated positions, such as principal, teacher, librarian, father, mother, son, general, major, private. Each designated position calls for the display of appropriate behavior. This appropriate behavior is broadly defined as a role which exists independently of the personal characteristics of the person fulfilling the role. The role is independent because there is usually high agreement within the society concerning the expected behaviors for a particular role. This consensus of society is called a norm. As norms change, roles are redefined, and conflict may result. Role conflicts arise when differences occur between an individual's own definition of his role, and the role expectations of a variety of others, the actual carrying out of the role, or the perception of the role behavior of oneself and others.

Historically Western Society has looked at reform as the necessity of changing attitudes first and changing behaviors and structures second. The theoretical position of this chapter is that a change in a social system creates positions with prescribed roles. In carrying out roles the participants' feelings and attitudes are changed. This process we term, structure—process—attitude, S-P-A. This theory is closely related to field theory, which looks for causes of behavior in the environment rather than inside the individual.

The S-P-A theory calls for us to look at such factors as size, spatial arrangements, structure of work, hierarchy of prestige, social sanctions, power, and conflict to grasp the dimensions of structures in societies. Changes in any one or all of these factors lead to changes in the processes of the system and the interactions of the members, which subsequently change the attitudes, opinions, and behavior of the individuals involved.

CHAPTER 7

Attitudes

PRACTICAL PROBLEMS FOR YOU TO SOLVE

In the near future we are faced with the possibility of the destruction of our natural environment and of air and water pollution so extensive that it will endanger the physical and mental development of the future and present generations of the United States. Dubos, for example, states:

Man is not on his way to extinction. We can adapt to almost anything. I am sure that we can adapt to the dirt, pollution, and noise of New York City or Chicago. That is the real tragedy—we can adapt to it. As we become adapted we accept worse and worse conditions without realizing that a child born and raised in this environment has no chance of developing his total physical and mental potential. It is essential that we commit ourselves to such problems as a society and as a nation, not because we are threatened with extinction, but because, if we do not understand what the environment is doing to us, something perhaps worse than extinction will take place—a progressive degradation of the quality of human life.

With pollution increasingly becoming a serious threat to the health of most of the population of the United States and the physical and mental development of future generations, which would you do if you were requested to plan a project aimed at changing the attitudes of the United States citizens toward pollution and the destruction of our natural environment? What would you do to induce attitude change so that the degradation of the quality of human life due to pollution is halted? What techniques of attitude change would you use?

In the next 35 years or so the world population will be twice as large as it is now. At that rate of growth, in 900 years there will be 6,000,000,000,000,000 people on our planet. Obviously there is not enough space or food to support the numbers of people who may result if our population growth is not curbed. If it is not, there is a high probability that widescale famines and massive breakdowns in social order will result. What if you, the reader, were employed to change people's attitudes about issues concerning overpopulation such as birth control and the legalization of abortion? What would you do to induce attitude change so that famine and unnecessary human deaths were prevented? What techniques of attitude change would you use?

Changing racial attitudes on a wide scale basis is one of the most impor-tant and pressing social psychological questions facing the United States to-day. We are faced with the possibility of a civil war between blacks and whites due primarily to the prejudiced attitudes whites hold toward blacks. Changing prejudiced attitudes toward other ethnic groups such as Indians and Mexican-Americans, toward the lower class, and toward women may be just as important as changing antiblack attitudes. What would you, the reader, do if you were requested to devise a program by which prejudiced attitudes were eliminated and equalitarian attitudes were developed? What techniques of attitude change would you use?

The solution to these social problems is crucial for the future of our coun-try, friends, family, and ourselves. Yet they are not the only issues involved in attitude development and change. Attempts to influence our attitudes happen many times a day; advertisements try to influence us to buy consum-er products, your professors attempt to influence you to study this book more carefully, your friends may try to influence your attitudes toward the use of drugs, and so on. Everyday each of us tries to change someone's atti-tudes and each of us is influenced by someone who is trying to change our attitudes. This is what makes the area of attitude formation and change one of the most fascinating topics in social psychology. The material presented in this chapter will attempt to answer the questions, "What can be done to in-crease the likelihood that persons whose attitudes you are trying to change will actually be influenced?" and "How can you recognize attempts to change your attitudes and understand the strategy being used on you by other people?"

DEFINITIONS

In Chapter 2 an *attitude* was defined as a predisposition to respond toward a particular person or group of persons, a particular object or group of objects, in a favorable or unfavorable manner. Attitudes are relatively enduring pre-dispositions which give continuity to behavior over time, but they are learned rather than innate. Thus, even though attitudes are *not* momentarily transient, they are susceptible to change. Predispositions, such as attitudes, are *hypothetical constructs*, that is, they cannot be observed directly and, therefore, are assumed to exist on the basis of how a person behaves.

In daily living a person is constantly confronted with a variety of regularly repeated situations. There probably is not a day in a college man's life when he doesn't see an attractive girl. What he considers to be attractive, what he considers an appropriate way to meet a girl, are attitudes which affect how he behaves. Predispositions, such as attitudes and values, develop to help the person anticipate and thus cope with recurrent events. Reliance upon attitudes is part of a fundamental psychological economy which can be described as a "least-effort" principle: whenever possible, apply past solutions to present problems. A person imposes as much psychological organization upon the events in his daily life as possible in order to free his attention and energy for coping with surprises.

Attitudes give a person a simplified and practical guide for appropriate behavior. Because all experiences cannot be grasped in their uniqueness, a person tends to group them into convenient categories and synthesize useful generalities about relationships among these abstract categories. Like any other generalization, an attitude involves an over-simplification of the complexity of an individual's life.

In defining what is meant by an attitude, it may be helpful to differentiate among opinions, beliefs, values, and attitudes. An *opinion* is a verbal expression of an underlying belief, value, or attitude. A *belief* expresses the relations between two cognitive categories when neither defines the other; most commonly held beliefs concern the associated characteristics of an object. Thus, a statement that lions are dangerous is a belief associating the characteristic "dangerous" to the object "lion." Or, a statement that God is alive associates the characteristic "alive" with the object "God" and, therefore, is a belief. A *value* exists whenever an emotion implying liking or disliking attaches to a cognition; values express a relationship between a person's emotional feelings and particular cognitive categories. When a person states, "stealing is wrong," he is expressing a value as he is attaching feelings (wrongness) to the category "stealing." Anything that a person approaches, desires, or espouses reflects a positive value, anything that he avoids, dislikes, or deplores reflects a negative value.

Both attitudes and values have properties which define what behavior is expected and desired; they can both, therefore, be thought of as motivational-perceptual states which direct action. That is, both attitudes and values serve as perceptual sets which motivate an individual to take certain actions when confronted with certain situations. Despite these common qualities, traditionally attitudes and values have been differentiated. For one thing, individuals hold many more attitudes than values. Rokeach (1966) states that a grown person probably has tens of thousands of beliefs, hundreds of attitudes, but only dozens of values. A cluster of attitudes surround a value; that is, for any given value, a cluster of attitudes express the value.

When you observe a person's behavior, consistent patterns can be seen. A person, for example, may always go to church on Sunday morning and always read the newspaper every day. When you ask the person why he does these things he may say he likes being well informed concerning the news and that he likes being in church. From such statements you may conclude that the person has some underlying predisposition (i.e., attitudes and values) which determine his behavior. You may then hypothesize that by changing the person's attitudes it would be possible to produce long-lasting changes in his behavior. Thus, if you wanted to change his behavior concerning pollution, birth control, or ethnic prejudice you might approach these problems by attempting to change his attitudes in order to change his behavior. Since a person often teaches his children and friends his attitudes, beliefs, opinions, and values, you might hypothesize that more enduring changes in behavior in more people will result if you change a person's attitudes than if you just attempt to change directly only the behavior in question. In addition, a change in attitudes may result in a wide variety of changes in behavior while a direct attempt to change a specific behavior may not generalize to other behaviors. Changing a person's attitudes about ecology, for example, may result in his convincing his family and friends to change their behavior which affects air and water pollution or the destruction of our natural environment and may result in his changing a wide variety of behaviors, such as buying only certain types of consumer products which do not contribute to pollution and changing the practices of his business in order to reduce pollution. Modifying only the amount of littering he engages in, on the other hand, may not generalize to other behaviors affecting the ecology and he may not attempt to influence other people to stop littering. This line of reasoning has led to a great deal of emphasis upon attitude change in our society.

Merely defining attitudes as enduring, general, and learned tells us little about how to measure or change them. In fact, defining attitudes in this way only implies that they are states which exist inside the person and which exert some control over his overt behavior. How they exert control is left ambiguous. Therefore, to solve these problems, social psychologists have come up with more precise definitions of the components of attitudes. Jones and Gerard (1967) define attitudes as the implication of combining a belief with a relevant value and propose that attitudes may be changed by changing either the underlying belief or the underlying value. Traditionally, attitudes have been divided into three components: affect, cognition, and behavior. The affective component consists of a person's evaluation of, liking of, or emotional response to some object or person. The cognitive component is conceptualized as a person's beliefs about, or factual knowledge of, the object or person. The behavioral component involves the person's overt behavior directed toward the object or person. Defining attitudes in this way leads to strategies of changing any of the affective, cognitive, or behavioral components of the attitude in order to produce attitudinal change. This conceptualization of attitudes also gives more precise guidelines concerning how attitudes may be measured; physiological response or verbal statements may be used to measure the affective component, the cognitive component may be measured by self-ratings of beliefs or by the amount of knowledge a person has about a topic, and the behavioral component could be measured by direct observation of how the person behaves in specific stimulus situations.

Before we proceed to discuss how attitudes may be created, reversed, or intensified, it should be noted that there are serious ethical issues involved in deliberately attempting to develop certain attitudes in other people or to change another person's attitudes. Before such an attempt is made, the value and necessity of such attitude development and change must be weighed against the possible charges of manipulating and brainwashing individuals. There are social issues and problems so compelling that attitude change must take place in order for a solution to be found. Yet attempting to change another person's attitudes carries with it a responsibility not to work against the person's best interests and needs.

ATTITUDE ACQUISITION AND CHANGE

There are a variety of ways of approaching attitude development and change. For one thing, attitudes are learned and, therefore, it is possible to approach attitude acquisition and change from a learning theory approach. Yet attitudes are largely composed of meanings; how two attitudes relate to each other depends upon their meaningful content, not just upon their both being learned. Thus there is a cognitive approach to attitude acquisition and change. Third, attitudes are developed only if they serve a function for the individual; that is, a person develops attitudes to cope with his world by forming relatively stable orientations toward common objects of his experience. Thus, attitude acquisition and change may be approached from a functional point of view. Finally, most attitudes are influenced by other people with whom a person interacts and values. Thus, social influence theories are relevant to the issues of attitude development and change. In the next four sections of this chapter these four approaches to attitude acquisition and change will be discussed.

LEARNING THEORY APPROACHES

Part of the definition of attitudes indicates that attitudes are learned. This suggests that all techniques known to increase or decrease learning should be applicable to the acquisition or changing of attitudes. Since attitudes are learned, attitude change may be simply a matter of new learning. In this section the learning theory approaches to attitude acquisition and change will be discussed. Two basic principles of conditioning will be applied to attitude acquisition and change. The first, *stimulus generalization,* refers to the fact that when a particular response habitually follows a particular stimulus, elements similar to, or closely associated with, this stimulus also show a tendency to elicit a similar response. Stimulus generalization is involved in classical conditioning. The second, *response reinforcement,* refers to the fact that responses are more clearly fixed the more they are associated with rewards. Response reinforcement is involved in operant conditioning. Finally, the research on attitude formation and change by Carl Hovland and his colleagues will be discussed.

Classical conditioning

Staats (1967, 1968) argues that the acquisition of attitudes takes place through classical conditioning. Many stimulus events in our environment elicit emotional responses in a particular individual. New stimuli (conditioned stimuli or CS) attain the power to elicit these same emotional responses if the new stimulus is consistently paired with the old stimulus (i.e., the unconditional stimulus, or UCS). For example, if electric shocks and loud, harsh sounds (UCS) evoke negative emotional responses, then words (CS) consistently paired with shocks and loud, harsh sounds will also evoke negative emotional responses (Staats, Staats, and Crawford, 1962). The same classical conditioning process will be effective in conditioning the positive emotional responses attached to rewarding activities such as eating to words consistently paired with the rewarding activities.

Staats goes on to argue that the principle of "higher-order conditioning" further extends the generality of his theory. If a word has attained the ability to produce a certain emotional response because it has been paired with some significant event in the environment, then still a third word or event can come to produce the emotional responses if it is paired with the conditioned stimulus. In other words, once a stimulus has come through classical conditioning to elicit an emotional response, it can transfer the response to a new stimulus with which it is paired. If, for example, through classical conditioning the word "dangerous" has been paired with painful stimuli to evoke negative emotional responses; and another word "noxious" is paired with "dangerous," the negative emotional responses conditioned to the word "dangerous" will transfer to the word "noxious" and in the future "noxious" will also elicit a negative emotional response.

Coming back to the question posed in the first section in this chapter, if you were hired to create an attitude change project aimed at changing prejudiced attitudes whites have toward blacks in our society, how would you use the conditioning theories in learning to do so? How would you condition whites to have positive attitudes toward blacks? How would you explain white prejudice towards blacks on the basis of conditioning theory?

A classical conditioning explanation for the learning of prejudiced attitudes would be that the conditioned stimulus "black person" is consistently paired with the unconditioned stimulus of social rejection by whites. The negative emotional responses to social rejection are then conditioned to the stimulus "black person." Prejudiced attitudes then become a predisposition to respond unfavorably to the stimulus "black person."

If prejudiced attitudes are learned through classical conditioning procedures, then it stands to reason that they may be changed through counter-conditioning procedures. *Counter-conditioning* (Bandura, 1969) involves repeatedly pairing a stimulus which evokes a negative emotional response with a stimulus which evokes a positive emotional response; such a procedure will condition the positive emotional response to the negative stimulus if the positive stimulus elicits more powerful responses than the negative stimulus. If, for example, the stimulus "black person," (which elicits a negative emotional response in whites) is paired with the stimulus "middle-class characteristics and values," (which elicits a positive emotional response in most whites), in the future the stimulus "black person" will elicit a positive emotional response if the emotional responses elicited by "middle-class characteristics and values" are more powerful than the emotional responses elicited by "black person."

To see if in fact counter-conditioning procedures could be used to reduce the prejudiced attitudes of white elementary school children, Litcher and Johnson (1968) conducted a study in the public schools with 68 white second-graders. The experimental groups used a multiethnic reader which included characters from several different ethnic groups for four months while the control groups used the regular readers which included only whites. In both readers all the characters were portrayed as being well dressed, living in well-kept homes, clean, friendly, hardworking, and middle class. In order to ensure that the emotional response to "middle class characteristics and values" was more powerful than the emotional response to "black person," the study was conducted in a Midwestern city where blacks made up less than .2 percent of the population; the probability was very high that the children participating in the study had no direct experience with blacks and that the black community did not represent an economic or social threat to the white community. The attitudes toward blacks of the children in the study, therefore, were probably not firmly rooted in direct experiences.

In conducting an experiment in a setting such as the public schools it is necessary to control for several variables. The researchers, for example, would want to be able to demonstrate that any differences found between the experimental and control groups were due to the type of reader used, not due to the teachers, the classrooms, the schools used in the study, or the ability level of the students. Some teachers, for example, might be motivated to influence the findings of the study; to control for this factor Litcher and Johnson randomly selected four teachers from volunteers within the school system. The volunteering teachers' interest in the study was prompted by the opportunity it offered them to participate in research; their volunteering was not based upon an interest in prejudice. In order to demonstrate that any differences found between the experimental and control groups were not due to the actual teachers involved with each group, each teacher in the study taught both an experimental group and a control group as similarly as possible. In order to ensure that the results of the study would generalize across classrooms, schools, and teachers, four teachers were used in two different schools. Finally, to control for the reading level of the students, through random assignment two classrooms (one in each school) used the multiethnic reader in their upper reading group and the regular reader in their middle reading group; the other two classrooms (one in each school) used the regular reader in their upper reading group and the multiethnic reader in their middle reading group.

Litcher and Johnson's findings were quite clear. Initially all the children in the study had negative attitudes toward blacks. On the pretest there were no significant differences between the experimental and the control groups. On the posttests, however, the children in the experimental groups responded significantly more favorably toward blacks than did the children in the control groups. Thus it may be concluded that curriculum materials may be used to counter-condition more favorable attitudes towards blacks in white children. The implications of this finding hardly need elaboration. While it is not possible, due to lack of material resources and the distribution of the black population in the United States, for every white child to have direct experiences with blacks (although Litcher and Johnson recommend such direct contact), it is possible to increase the visibility of blacks in the curriculum materials of the schools. According to the findings of Litcher and Johnson's study, such an action should, through the reduction of prejudiced attitudes, increase racial harmony in our country.

STATISTICAL AND PRACTICAL SIGNIFICANCE

Statistical significance refers to the probability that a given research finding may not be attributed to "chance" but rather to the treatment in the study. In the Litcher and Johnson study, for example, statistical significance tells the reader what the likelihood is that the reduction of prejudice found in the experimental groups was due to chance fluctuations on the tests rather than to the type of reader used. In that study the statistical significance was very high; that is, the probability that the findings are due to chance fluctuations in the responses of the children are far less than one in a hundred. In most social psychological studies, however, the minimum standard of acceptability of the significance of the findings is arbitrarily set at $p < .05$. This means that the difference found would occur only five times in 100 by chance alone. Therefore, we may infer that this occasion is one of the other 95 times when the difference is not attributable to chance.

When large numbers of subjects are used in a study (e.g., 100 subjects or more), it becomes increasingly easier to obtain statistically significant results. Because of this, statistical significance cannot be discussed separately from practical significance. The practical significance of the findings of a research study depend upon how powerful the treatment effects will be in real life situations. It may be possible, for example, for a very small difference between the experimental and control groups to be statistically significance when 500 or 1000 subjects are used in the study; but such a small difference will not be very powerful when it is applied in "the real world." In the Litcher and Johnson study the practical significance of the results is quite high due to the fact that a small number of subjects was used and due to the fact that the experiment was conducted in a "real life" setting. Many of the laboratory experiments conducted by social psychologists, however, should be carefully scrutinized to ensure that the statistical significance found in the experiment is also of practical significance.

Operant conditioning

To apply the basic idea of operant conditioning to attitude change, it only needs to be noted that attitudes which are rewarded are more likely to be developed and maintained. If a favorable attitude toward a particular church is more apt to bring us rewards from people important to us then we will tend to develop the attitudes associated with such reinforcement. There is a great deal of research in learning concerning the effectiveness of reinforcement in influencing behavior. Yet the evidence concerning the effects of reinforcement upon the acquisition of attitudes is mixed. Scott (1957, 1959) conducted experiments testing the notion that if opinions expressed initially, in the absence of a supporting attitude, are reinforced, a supporting attitude is developed. He utilized a debate setting in which subjects were required to uphold a particular viewpoint in a debate. They either won or lost the debate. The winning may be seen as reinforcing the verbal behavior. His results indicate that the winners changed their attitude in the direction they advocated in their speech while losers did not. Subsequent studies by Dahlke (1963) and Kiesler (1965), however, have not replicated Scott's results. Whether or not reinforcement affects the development of attitudes, there are clear results that the expression of opinions which reflect attitudes is increased by the reinforcement one receives for doing so (Verplanck, 1955).

REPLICATION OF RESEARCH

In reading social psychological materials, the reader is often confronted with reports of dozens of studies which all have the same findings. Such replications may appear to be unnecessarily repetitious, but in actuality they are not. Replication of previous studies is a very important aspect of scientific endeavor. In the section on the acquisition of attitudes through operant conditioning, for example, it was noted that Scott's research has not been fully replicated. This points up the need for replication of research studies in social psychology.

Social psychological research is based upon *induction*, the collecting of evidence about the relationship among variables in order to establish a generalization (i.e., a theory) from which one is able to predict what the relationship among the variables studied will be in the future. Hypotheses are tested in a research study in order to establish and verify theories. The results of the study either verify or refute the hypothesis. Even if the results verify the hypothesis, however, the researcher cannot predict with total certainty that the same results will be found in the future, because even though all past observations have been identical, the next instance may still be the exception to the rule. The fact that all elephants so far observed have been some color other than orange does not mean that the next elephant seen will not be orange. It does mean that the probability is very low that the next elephant seen will be orange. The greater the number of times an event or a relationship among variables has been observed, the higher the probability that the event or the relationship will also be observed in the future, given similar conditions.

Good research is performed so carefully and described so completely by those reporting it that others can repeat or *replicate* the same investigation with different subjects under nearly identical conditions. Replication of specific research with the same results (or the "same results" within the expectations of chance variation) is generally taken by the scientific community as further verification or *justification* of the hypothesis. The greater the number of studies which have all verified the hypothesis, the higher the probability that the relationship among variables specified by the hypothesis will be observed in the future, given similar conditions. Near replications, furthermore, may be performed with only slight variations in order to demonstrate the precise conditions under which the relationship exists among the variables. If, however, the replications find different results, the hypothesis needs further explanation and if there are contradictory results over several replications, the scientific community may interpret the whole lot as refutation of the hypothesis.

The relationships among variables which social psychologists study are usually complex. This means that the theories and hypotheses advanced to explain the relationships need a long series of replications and near replications in order to be verified. For this reason research should not be read or performed in isolation, but in maximum relation to as many other pertinent research studies as possible. In fact, it is only in relation to the other pertinent studies that the significance of any single research study is likely to be apparent.

THE YALE COMMUNICATION AND ATTITUDE CHANGE PROGRAM

Carl Hovland and his associates at Yale developed a program of empirical research organized around the theme sentence, "Who says what to whom with what effect?" The Yale approach is derived from learning theory and assumes that man is a rational, information-processing organism who can be motivated to attend to a communication, to learn its contents, and to incorporate it into his verbal repertoire of responses when this learning is rewarded. The instrument of change is a formal, structured communication. The agent of change is either the actual or anticipated reward for agreeing with the communicator, or else the awareness of the logical and rational necessity for accepting the information and position advanced. The Yale group conducted a considerable amount of research on the conditions under which attitudes are influenced by information. Much of their work tests the theory of attitude change Aristotle advanced in his *Rhetoric*. Aristotle identified three elements of an attitude change situation: the personal characteristics of the communicator; the frame of mind into which the audience is put; and the apparent proof provided by the words of the message. Aristotle developed a well-formulated theory concerning how these three factors influence attitude change. His work is an example of how modern social psychological research is used to confirm the validity of ancient theories of human behavior. The theme sentence of the Yale group ("Who says what to whom with what effect?") leads to the same organization of knowledge about attitude change under the headings of: communicator or source, communication or message, and audience. Not included in this paradigm, but clearly relevant, are the media of transmission of the message and the situation in which the message is received.

The characteristics of the communicator

Aristotle noted that an effective communicator must be a man of good sense, good will, and good moral character. It is not surprising, therefore, that much of the research on which personal characteristics of the communicator influence the attitude of his audience has focused on the trait of credibility. In discussing the credibility of the communicator, it is necessary to assume that the audience consists of rational, problem-solving individuals motivated to adjust their belief systems as closely as possible to external reality. The *credibility* of the communicator has been analyzed into his apparent expertise, trustworthiness, and objectivity; that is, his perceived ability to know the correct stand on the issue, and his motivation to communicate this knowledge without bias. One of the earliest studies on credibility demonstrated that the more credible the source of information, the more the attitude change immediately after an influence attempt (Hovland & Weiss, 1951). Over a four-week period, however, there was a tendency for the audience to dissociate the source from the message, and no attitude differences attributable to credibility of source could be determined. Later studies (Bergin, 1962; Aronson, Turner, and Carlsmith, 1963) found that the greater the discrepancy between the position of the communicator and that of his audience, the more effective he will be in changing their attitudes, provided he is highly credible. If the communicator has low credibility, a large discrepancy of attitudes will greatly diminish the influence he has upon the audience.

In their discussion of communicator characteristics, Jones and Gerard (1967) define attitudes as the implication of combining a belief with a relevant value. From their point of view, strategies for changing attitudes focus on changing either the underlying belief or the underlying value. They differentiate between the communicator's perceived expertise and the extent to which he is a desirable peer holding the same values as the audience. Jones and Gerard theorize that if a communicator is attempting to undermine a particular belief by an appeal to facts, his success will be determined by how much of an expert he is perceived to be. If, on the other hand, he has chosen to attack the value premise underlying the attitude, he will be effective to the extent that he is perceived as a valued peer holding the same values. When his values do not coincide with those of his audience, the force of his message is reduced. Their theory receives some indirect support from a study conducted by Weiss (1957) which demonstrated that a communicator was more effective when he had established prior attitude congruence with the audience. This result suggests that values on one issue can be used to establish assumed coorientation for purposes of influencing an audience on another issue. A more recent study by Aronson and Golden (1962) also provides some support for the position of Jones and Gerard, but a direct test of their hypotheses has yet to be conducted. At this point they have an interesting, but unsubstantiated theory.

The intent of the communicator may affect the response of the audience. There is some evidence that when an audience believes the communicator is not trying to influence their attitudes, his effectiveness is greater than when his communication is seen as an influence attempt (Walster and Festinger, 1962).

There is also evidence (see Zimbardo and Ebbesen, 1969) that what an audience thinks of a communicator may be directly influenced by what they think of his message, and communicator characteristics irrelevant to the topic of his message can influence acceptance of its conclusion.

The nature of the communication

Without a communication of some kind there can be no persuasion. The ability of the communicator to organize and phrase his message skillfully determines much of his effectiveness in changing the attitudes of his audience. Aristotle was deeply concerned with the nature of arguments, their logical coherence and emotional appeal, and the language used by the communicator to get these various aspects of the message across. In addition, social psychologists have focused on some of the more obvious questions of practical importance concerning the presentation of information.

The first practical question which researchers in attitude change studied was whether the communicator should tell his audience the arguments supporting opposing viewpoints. One of the earliest experiments directed explicitly at this issue was conducted during World War II (Hovland, Lumsdaine, and Sheffield, 1949). The researchers found that whether a one-sided or a two-sided communication was more effective in changing attitudes depended upon certain characteristics of the audience. For those individuals who opposed the communicator's position, the two-sided argument had a greater impact than the one-sided argument; the one-sided argument was more effective for those who favored the communicator's position. When the audience was divided on the basis of their educational level, furthermore, it was found that for the more educated men, the two-sided argument was more effective irrespective of their initial position. The one-sided argument was overwhelmingly more effective for the less educated men with an initially favorable attitude.

It is obvious that attempting to influence an audience which is favorably disposed to one's viewpoint is a very different situation from talking to an unfavorably disposed audience. When the audience is initially unfavorable to the communicator's position, he must: (1) unfreeze the initial decision and put his audience in a choice situation; (2) convince the audience that his view is the one it should prefer; and (3) establish a firm attitude which resists future attempts by other communicators to change it. When the audience is favorably disposed to the communicator's position, his task is to give as much support to their attitudes as possible. An experiment by Lumsdaine and Janis (1953) indicates that an audience which is exposed to a two-sided argument has more ability to resist counterpropaganda than does an audience which is exposed to a one-sided argument.

The second question of practical importance investigated by social psychologists dealt with the order of presenting arguments. In presenting a two-sided argument, does the material presented first interfere with the assimilation of material presented second (primacy effect) or does material presented second retroactively interfere with material presented first (recency effect)? Aristotle argued in favor of a primacy effect. An early study by

Lund (1925) demonstrated that when positive and negative communications were presented on an issue, the communication presented first had more effect on the audience's attitudes, thus supporting Aristotle's position. Cromwell (1950), however, found strong support for a recency effect, thus calling into question the previous research and theory. One attempt to reconcile the discrepancy between the two studies was made by Hovland, Campbell, and Brock (1957); they found that when a person commits himself to the communication he receives first, the second communication does not have much effect. Thus it may be that in Lund's study, the audience became committed to the position presented first, while in Cromwell's study they did not.

Probably the classic study in the area was conducted by Miller and Campbell (1959). Their hypotheses on whether a primacy effect or recency effect would dominate were based on classical knowledge concerning rates of forgetting over time. From the work of Ebbinghaus (1885), and from subsequent work on forgetting, it is known that a person's memory for newly learned material decays rapidly, but at a decelerating rate. A great deal of forgetting occurs immediately after something new is learned, but the *relative* rate of forgetting decreases over time. On the basis of the forgetting curves alone only a recency effect would be expected. The recency effect would be more dominant if there were a time lapse between the presentation of the first and second messages, and the attitude measurement were taken immediately after the presentation of the second communication. With a time interval both between the messages, and between the second message and the measurement of the audience's attitude, the recency effect would tend to be reduced because forgetting occurs more rapidly immediately after learning.

To test these predictions, Miller and Campbell compared four experimental treatments for both recall of content and attitude change. In the first condition, the second message was presented immediately after the first, with recall and attitude measurement immediately after the second message. On the basis of forgetting alone, a small recency effect would be expected here. In the second condition, the two messages were presented one right after the other but the subject's recall and attitude were measued a week later. Here any recency effect would be expected to have disappeared, because the two messages had occurred close together in time relative to the delay between their presentation and measurement of the audience's attitudes and recall. Miller and Campbell assumed, furthermore, that the first message would have an initial advantage, a prior-entry effect in this condition, which would result in a primacy effect. In the third condition, the second message was presented a week after the first message, and the subject's recall and attitude were measured immediately thereafter. Here a strong recency effect would be expected, because the memory of the first message would have considerable time to decay. In the last condition, there was a delay of one week between the messages *and* between the second message and the measurement of the audience's recall and attitude. Here a slight recency effect would be expected. The attitiude change results of the experiment appear in Table 7-1; they support the predictions. In terms of recall, strong recency effects were found in conditions three and four, and in no condition was a primacy effect found. Thus there is some support for the conclusion that coming first gives a statement no greater probability of being remembered, but does give it greater probability of being believed.

TABLE 7-1

Mean Attitude Scores from the Miller and Campbell Study, 1959

Condition	Pro-con Presentation	Con-pro- Presentation	Difference	Direction
$1(X_1X_2O)$[a]	5.94	5.88	0.06	
$2(X_1X_2-O)$	4.50	6.61	−2.11	Primacy
$3(X_1-X_2O)$	6.00	4.33	1.67	Recency
$4(X_1-X_2-O)$	5.47	5.58	−0.11	

[a] The shorthand characterization of the conditions employs a standardized symbolization of experimental treatments (Campbell, 1957), in which X_1 and X_2 represent the experimental stimuli, O represents the process of observation and measurement, and spacing from left to right represents the time dimension.

Subsequent studies which have replicated aspects of the Miller and Campbell study (Thomas, Webb, and Tweedie, 1961; Insko, 1964) have found support for the recency effects but not for the primacy effects. A primacy effect seems to be a consequence of a series of factors, such as awareness of intent to influence, complexity of the message, and the attempt to measure the communicator's effect (Cohen, 1964).

The third question dealt with the impact of emotional appeals on the changing of attitudes. Hovland, Janis, and Kelley (1953) hypothesized that emotional appeals would increase an audience's motivation to accept the communicator's conclusions. In a study using fear appeals Janis and Feshbach (1953) demonstrated that if an emotional appeal stimulates too much fear, its message will be rejected and little attitude change will take place. Although the literature on emotional appeals has mixed findings (Kiesler, Collins, and Miller, 1969), there is evidence that the greater the fear aroused by the communication the greater the attitude change, provided that the communicator recommends explicit and possible actions which will reduce the fear. If the communicator just arouses fear without specifying how it may be reduced, attitude change will not be likely to take place. In addition, practical experience in advertising does indicate that moderate levels of emotional arousal will facilitate the changing of an audience's attitudes.

Finally, there will probably be more attitude change in the direction the communicator wants if he explicitly states his conclusions than if he lets the audience draw their own, except when they are rather intelligent; then implicit conclusion drawing is more effective (McGuire, 1969).

The present attitudes of the audience

The effectiveness of any communication is obviously determined by how successfully it is tailored for its intended audience. A communication intended to induce better health habits in young children will probably not have much impact upon adults. Factors such as the audience's pre-exposure to the communication, their present attitudes, their education and cultural background, and their commitment to their present position all affect the extent to which they are susceptible to a given communication.

The present attitude of the audience will have at least two major effects upon the communication of information concerning an issue. First, if the audience disagrees with the position of the communicator, it may avoid hearing or attending to the message he is presenting. That is, individuals probably expose themselves selectively and with a particular orientation to different kinds of information. If they expect a communication which supports their own convictions, they will probably assume an open and receptive orientation towards it. If they expect the communicator to hold opposing views to their own, they will either avoid the message or will be prepared to take what he says with a grain of salt. Second, if the audience is not able to avoid exposure to a discrepant message, they can use a variety of psychological mechanisms, such as misinterpretation, for coming to terms with the discrepancies introduced by the information.

A series of studies indicate that forewarning an audience of the communicator's intention of converting them to his point of view creates resistance to his message (Ewing, 1942, Allyn and Festinger, 1961; McGuire and Papageorgis, 1962; McGuire, 1964; McGuire and Millman, 1965; Freedman and Sears, 1965). There is also evidence that an audience initially unfavorable to the communicator's point of view which is distracted during the communicator's presentation will be more influenced by the communicator's message than will an audience which has not been distracted (Festinger and Maccoby, 1964; Freedman and Sears, 1965). It seems that when listening to a communication to which the audience is opposed, they engage in some sort of silent dialogue and counterargue with the communicator, thus reducing the effectiveness of the communication. When the audience is distracted, their counterarguing is less effective.

There is evidence that the individual's personality traits affect his susceptibility to persuasion; in general, individuals with low self-esteem are more easily influenced than are individuals with high self-esteem (Mausner, 1953; Janis, 1954, 1955). Individuals who are highly persuasible are equally susceptible to the arguments of the communicator and of any person who presents counterarguments in the future.

A number of studies have demonstrated that actively role-playing a previously unacceptable position increases its acceptability to the audience (Janis and King, 1954; King and Janis, 1956; Culbertson, 1957; Greenwald and Albert, 1968). These studies have basically compared the effects of role playing on the audience's attitudes with the passive exposure to the same materials. Several explanations have been hypothesized to explain such findings. King and Janis (1956) have postulated that improvised arguments originating with oneself may be less apt to evoke implicit interfering responses than externally-imposed persuasion and may be hand-tailored to suit the individual's own motivations. Janis and Gilmore (1965) have stressed the role of positive incentives in motivating a "biased scanning" that increases the salience of arguments which would support the enacted position. Shifting one's attitudes to conform to role-performance has alternatively been interpreted by dissonance theory as a means of reducing cognitive dissonance arising from the knowledge that one's public behavior is discrepant from one's private beliefs. Other explanations include having a generally enhanced regard for one's own productions relative to others' (Greenwald and Albert, 1968) and the effort spent in improvising arguments may be a source of enhanced regard for one's own arguments (Zimbardo, 1965). Whatever the mediating process, the evidence is clear that attitudes are modified by active role-playing.

One of the most interesting lines of research on the characteristics of an audience which affects its vulnerability to attitude change appeals is whether they have been inoculated against the arguments of the communicator (McGuire, 1964). McGuire's initial assumption was that the characteristic mode of belief defense is avoidance of exposure to opposition arguments, so that the person's ideological state tends to be analogous to the health of an individual raised in a germ-free environment. His inoculation theory is based upon an analogy with physical medicine; just as it is possible to stimulate the body's defenses against germs by the inoculation of small doses of the germ in a weakened form, it may be possible to stimulate a person's attitudinal defenses by inoculating him with a weak form of the counterattitudinal arguments he is likely to encounter. This inoculation should be strong enough to stimulate his defenses, but not to overcome them. The format of McGuire's experiments was essentially the same; there was a defense-building session followed by an attack. He chose cultural truisms, such as "mental illness is not contagious" and "it's a good idea to brush your teeth after every meal if at all possible" for his attitude change issues.

A person's defenses against a disease may be built up by supportive procedures, such as plenty of sleep and an adequate diet, but in the long run this proves to be less effective than immunization by inoculation of a weakened form of the disease. Similarly, McGuire argued that it is possible to build resistance to opposing arguments by providing a person with arguments that support his belief (supportive defense); however, it would be less effective than providing him with small doses of arguments he would have to encounter in order to maintain his belief intact (refutational defense). In several experiments (one of which is reported in Abstract 18) McGuire and his associates compared the effectiveness of a refutational defense with a supportive defense. The refutational defense is clearly superior to the supportive defense in producing resistance to attitude change. It is interesting to note that in a measure administered immediately after the defense-building session, the supportive defense proved superior to the refutational defense, but the

---

Abstract 18

TITLE The Relative Efficacy of Various Types of Prior Belief-Defense in Producing Immunity against Persuasion.

AUTHORS William J. McGuire and D. Papageorgis

PROBLEM Will exposure to possible counter-arguments (with refutation or support for present beliefs) strengthen the ability to defend present beliefs? Which is more effective—mobilizing arguments to bolster present beliefs or refuting possible counter-arguments?

SUBJECTS 130 freshmen at a university.

PROCEDURE Subjects indicate strength of their agreement (on a 15-interval scale from definitely false to definitely true) with each of four propositions concerning health:
a. Chest X-rays should be taken once a year.
b. Penicillin benefits mankind.
c. Mental illness is not contagious.
d. Teeth should be brushed after every meal.
The first immunizing session required writing a 20-minute essay defending a belief. Half of the subjects wrote supporting arguments; the other half developed refutations for possible counter-arguments.
A second immunizing session presented supporting arguments or refutations of counter-arguments.
There followed exposure to strong arguments against (a) beliefs which had been treated in the immunizing sessions and (b) beliefs which had not been so treated.

SOME FINDINGS Untreated beliefs, subjected to strong counter-arguments, dropped from 12.6 to 6.6 on a 15-point scale.
Immunized beliefs rose during the immunizing sessions from 13.3 to 14.1; the counter-arguments reduced this acceptance to 8.0; the final level remained significantly higher than for non-immunized.
Refuting imagined counter-arguments was significantly more effective than cumulating supportive arguments ($p = .001$).

SOURCE: *J. abnorm. soc. Psychol.*, 1961, 62:338-345.

---

supportive defense did not sustain the truism against attack as well as did the refutational defense. Not only did the refutational defense produce resistance to the same counterarguments used in the inoculation session, but it generalized this resistance to novel counterarguments which the audience had not been previously exposed to.

McGuire's theory assumes that the ineffectiveness of the supportive defense rests on the lack of stimulation of a defensive stance. If the audience were mildly threatened before receiving the supportive arguments, it would presumably be more receptive to those arguments, and they would therefore confer resistance. In his experiments he found that the resistance effect of the combination of defenses, first refutational and then supportive, was greater than the sum of the effects of each type of defense administered separately. In a related experiment he substantiated the medical analogy further. Just as physical immunization gradually builds up to a maximum as antibodies are formed following inoculation, and then gradually decays, making periodic booster shots necessary, the supportive defense shows a decay with time in its resistance-creating potential. The refutational defense shows an increase after two days, and then a decrease by the seventh day. McGuire hypothesized that the refutational defense is threatening to the individual's belief system. Consequently, he will be vigilant toward arguments that might be used to bolster his beliefs, and will seek out information which supports his position. After the individual obtains enough supportive evidence to assuage the anxiety he felt concerning the correctness of his attitudes, he will decrease his vigilance, and, therefore, his resistance will gradually be lowered. The supportive defense, however, does not threaten the subject and therefore does not induce vigilance for further supporting information. Consequently, it will decay much faster than will the refutational defense situation.

APPLICATIONS AND CRITICISMS

All the methods and techniques of social psychology are designed to provide data to evaluate theories. The purpose of building and testing theories is to improve the generalization of verified knowledge to practical situations. This is only possible to the extent that one employs methods that provide a good test of one's theories and good theories for guiding one's pursuit of new data. There are two basic points which can be made about the work of Carl Hovland and his associates involved in the Yale Communication Research Program. The first is that the quality of the research is very high. In terms of methodology and procedures, many of the studies are among the best conducted. The second is that Hovland and his associates have not developed any systematic theory of the attitude change process. Their research is homogeneous enough to be classified as an "approach" to the study of attitude change, but it lacks something in terms of significance because the results do not fall into any compelling pattern and there is no integrating theory to facilitate the application of the findings of the studies. In fact, although the Yale researchers have been guided by the central notion of learning theory, they have not consistently organized their hypotheses and findings in a learning framework.

Because of the lack of an overall theoretical framework, the application of the findings of the above research to such applied problems as racism, over-population, and ecology is difficult. Procedures for presenting the source of the message, the way the message is organized, and possible ways of select-ing an audience most receptive to the message are, however, suggested by the research discussed. The reader may wish to take the major findings of the Yale researchers and plan a program by which the ecological attitudes of the rest of the students in the class may be changed.

COGNITIVE THEORY APPROACHES

The learning theorists approach the field of attitude acquisition and change primarily through the notions that attitudes are learned associations devel-oped through reinforcement. Yet such a "conditioning" approach to attitude analysis may neglect other key points about attitudes. One of these is that attitudes are largely composed of meanings. How some attitudes relate to others depends on their meaningful content, which is a matter of the organi-zation of meanings within systems of symbols. The elements within these symbolic systems must be seen in their combination and not simply as dis-crete responses. All of this suggests that principles of cognitive organization as well as principles of conditioning need to be considered for understanding the learning of attitudes. Specifically, two principles of cognitive organiza-tion will be discussed: the priciple of simplicity and the principle of evalu-ative consistency.

In order to use an idea or an impression a person must simplify the infor-mation available to him. Processes of cognitive simplification in order to or-ganize one's perceptions were discussed in Chapter 2. The principle of sim-plicity is that our cognitive world tends to become organized into a good "gestalt"; that is, people tend to organize their cognitions into a framework of maximum uniformity and regularity. All of the gestalt principles relating to the organization of perceptions discussed in Chapter 2 may also be ap-plied to the organization of cognitions. Attitudes, as one type of cognition, are organized, therefore, into systems which are characterized by simplifica-tion in order to get a good "gestalt."

Closely related to the tendency to simplify our cognitions is a tendency toward an evaluative consistency. Attitudes possess an evaluative quality. The principle of evaluative consistency holds that we tend to have similar evaluations of cognitive elements which are associated together. That is, if we closely associate two attitudes in our thinking, we shall tend to have similar evaluations, pro or con, in regard to them. And, conversely, if we have similar evaluations of two objects, we shall be more apt to organize them together.

There are several consistency theories of attitude change. Each theory postulates a basic "need" for consistency among attitudes or between attitudes and behavior. Most of the theories further assume that the presence of inconsistency produces "psychological tension," or at least is uncomfortable, and in order to reduce this tension, a person "rearranges" his psychological world to produce consistency. Examples of this consistency are innumerable: a person who will not work in the same room with a member of a different ethnic group will not invite such a person home for dinner; a political liberal does not support politically conservative organizations; if we make a new friend we will tend to like his family. In this respect the concept of attitudinal consistency presumes human rationality. It holds that behavior and attitudes are not only consistent to objective observers, but that individuals try to appear consistent to themselves.

McGuire (1966) lists several ways in which inconsistency may be created within an individual who has a basic striving toward consistency. First, there may be logical inconsistencies among attitudes. Second, inconsistency may arise as a result of the person occupying simultaneously two conflicting social roles. Third, a person's environment may change, leaving him with a variety of attitudes which no longer have any usefulness. Fourth, a person may be pressured into behaving in a way which is inconsistent with his attitudes. Finally, a person may change one of his attitudes only to have his new attitude be inconsistent with other attitudes he also holds. This list of sources of inconsistency, which is not exhaustive, suggests that inconsistency occurs regularly and often in a person's life.

The social psychologist who first systematically developed the concept of attitudinal consistency was Heider (1958). His theory is mainly concerned with the relationships among three things: the perceiver P; another person O; and some object X. There are two types of relations that may exist between each pair of these three things: the liking relation and the unit relation. Within each type of relation there are two subtypes, positive and negative. In the liking relation either P likes O or P does not like O. In the unit relation separate entities comprise a unit when they are perceived as belonging together; for example, members of a family may be perceived as a unit, a person and his actions may be perceived as a unit. Within each type of relation, there are eight possible configurations among the three things. They are presented in Figure 7-1. Each of these configurations may be regarded as a particular psychological state existing among the two people and an object, as perceived by one of the people. In defining his central theoretical concept,

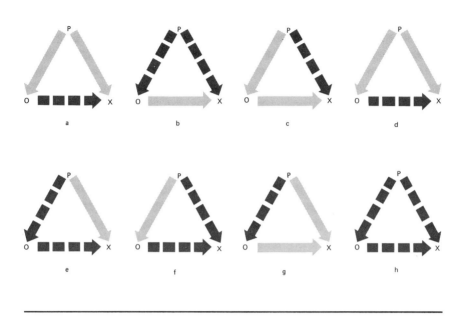

FIGURE 7-1
A positive relationship is indicated by an unbroken line; a negative
relationship is indicated by a broken line. The direction of the
relationship is indicated by the arrow. States a, b, e, and f are
balanced states; states c, d, g, and h represent unbalanced states.

balance, Heider states that the balanced state exists when the perceived
units and experienced liking co-exist without stress. Specifically, this means
that if all three relationships are positive (P likes O, P likes X, O likes X), or
if two of them are negative and one positive (P likes O, P dislikes X, O dislikes X), the state is referred to as balanced; all other combinations are unbalanced. The balanced state is assumed to be a stable state, which resists
influence from outside sources. The unbalanced state is assumed to be unstable and in addition to produce psychological tension within the individual
that becomes relieved only when change within the situation takes place in
such a way that a state of balance is achieved. Thus, balanced states are stable states and resist change; unbalanced states are unstable states and should
change so that they produce balance.

There are a variety of experiments which generally support Heider's theory (Jordan, 1953; Burdick and Burnes, 1958; Prince, Harburg, and Newcomb, 1966). They indicate that while it is easy to explain individuals' behavior in balance theory terms, it is not easy to predict what individuals will

do from balance theory. Heider's theory is historically important because it has stimulated the development of several other balance theories, yet in and of itself it does not have high predictive power and has not stimulated a great deal of research. In terms of practical application, it does lead to the helpful notion that in order to change a person's attitudes you must create a state of imbalance among his present attitudes or between his attitudes and his behavior and then offer him a way to reduce this imbalance by changing his attitudes in the direction desired by the communicator.

The derivative of Heider's balance theory which has led to the greatest amount of experimental research and most certainly the most ingenious experimental designs is dissonance theory. Dissonance theory (Festinger, 1957; Brehm and Cohen, 1962; Aronson, 1968) is concerned with the relations among "cognitive elements" and the consequences when elements are inconsistent with one another. Cognitive elements are defined as bits of knowledge, or opinions and beliefs about oneself, about one's behavior, and about one's environment. Two cognitive elements may be: "The knowledge that most serious accidents are caused by drunken drivers," and "The knowledge that I often drive after I have been drinking heavily." In dissonance theory three possible relationships are posited: (1) they may be irrelevant to one another (the knowledge that I drink heavily and that the sun is shining in Hong Kong); (2) they may be consistent with one another (the knowledge that I drink heavily and the belief that heavy drinkers are considered to be more masculine), referred to by Festinger as a *consonant* relationship; and (3) they may be inconsistent with one another (the knowledge that I sometimes drink heavily before I drive and that heavy drinkers often cause automobile accidents), referred to by Festinger as a *dissonant* relationship. More formally, dissonance is defined as, considering two elements alone, the opposite of one element would follow from the other. The two basic postulates of the theory are: (1) the existence of dissonance creates psychological tension or discomfort and will *motivate* the person to reduce the dissonance and achieve consonance, and (2) when dissonance exists, not only will the person attempt to reduce it, but he will actively attempt to avoid situations and information which would increase the dissonance. It is important to emphasize that the relationship between elements need not be logically consonant or dissonant; it could be psychologically consonant or dissonant as well.

Festinger emphasized that dissonance is a post-decision phenomenon. That is, if a person chooses among several possible alternatives, after his decision is made he may feel some dissonance concerning the attractiveness of the other alternatives to the one he chose. Once a student has chosen to go to one college, for example, he may feel some dissonance concerning the possibilities of attending other colleges. Such dissonance is reduced by increasing one's attraction to the chosen alternative and downgrading the unchosen alternatives. Thus, the student will find reason to increase his attraction to the college he chose to attend and to decrease the appeal of the other colleges he did not choose to attend. In such a situation, the commitment of the person to his decision affects the occurrence of dissonance. Dissonance theory hypothesizes, therefore, that there may be less objectivity and more bias in the way a person views and evaluates the alternatives *after* he makes his decision than *before* he makes it. A variety of studies support these predictions of dissonance theory (Brehm, 1956; Walter, 1964; Festinger, 1964; Brehm and Cohen, 1959).

Deutsch, Krauss, and Rosenau (1962) feel it is useful to think of post-decisional dissonance as a form of "defensiveness" and to think of "dissonance reduction" as a defense mechanism used to defend oneself against anxiety. They conducted an experiment which supports the notion that when a person experiences dissonance after making a choice, he is attempting to defend himself against a perceived implication of his choice which is contrary to his self-conception. They feel it is the inconsistency between the cognitions of self and of the choice, rather than the inconsistency in selecting one alternative rather than another that is critical to the occurrence of postdecisional dissonance. Aronson (1968) also feels that the major source of dissonance is the relation between cognitions and self-attitudes. Since a person expects himself to make correct decisions and to act in a sensible, moral way, any cognitions that he chose incompetently or that he acted immorally creates anxiety about himself which must be defended against by dissonance reduction. Such dissonance reduction will lead a person to justify his choice and behavior.

In focusing dissonance theory upon attitude change, research has been conducted in the area of "forced compliance." Suppose a person is induced to behave in a manner that is contrary to his attitudes. The induction ordinarily takes place as a result of either promised reward for complying or threatened punishment for noncompliance. The person will experience some dissonance between his attitudes concerning appropriate behavior and the knowledge that he has behaved in an opposite way. Research in the area of conformity (e.g., Secord and Backman, 1964) reveals that very subtle group pressure induces people to behave in ways vastly inconsistent with their attitudes; thus forced compliance situations are not uncommon. In a forced compliant situation the magnitude of the dissonance experienced is a function of the importance of the private attitudes and the magnitude of the punishment or reward which induced the person to engage in the behavior. The more important the attitudes and the *smaller* the motivating punishment or reward, the greater will be the dissonance. The dissonance will be reduced by changing the cognitive element which is easier to modify; in most cases this is the attitude. If the person cannot take back, deny, or justify his behavior, changing his attitudes so that they are consistent with his behavior is the only way to reduce dissonance, given that the attitude change will not introduce large amounts of new dissonance with other attitudes the person holds.

The classical study testing the forced compliance derivations of dissonance theory was conducted by Festinger and Carlsmith (1959). In their experiment subjects were given an extremely boring task to do and then asked by the experimenter, as a favor, to tell other subjects how enjoyable and interesting the experiment had been. One group of subjects was hired to tell the deception at a rate of $1; a second group of subjects was hired at the rate of $20; a third group which served as a control were not asked to engage in the deception. Afterwards, the subjects' attitudes toward the task were measured and the results indicate that those subjects who received only $1 rated the task significantly more enjoyable than did the subjects in the other two conditions. There have been a variety of other studies testing the same hypothesis; some have supported the Festinger and Carlsmith findings, some have not. Taken as a group, the studies have led to some controversy concerning the validity of many of the studies testing dissonance theory.

Dissonance theory, along with most other attitude change theories, is based upon the assumption that attitude change comes out of conflict, discrepancy, inconsistency, or discontent with the status quo. The "paradise" of dissonance theory is a state of lack of tension. Yet it is apparent that the production of dissonance can stimulate interest and arouse curiosity. People seek out dissonance as well as avoid it. The same observation may be made about balance theory; under certain conditions individuals may seek out imbalanced states. Seeking out new experiences, fantasizing, going to scary movies, engaging in competitive activities, creating a new work of art, all may be instances where a person does not seek maximum consistency in his thoughts. In our everyday adjustment the demands to simplify and make our experience more consistent may be far more dominant than our demands for elaboration, complexity, and novelty. But this is not to say that the principles of simplicity and evaluative consistency apply absolutely. In the future a theory needs to be developed which can specify the conditions under which a person organizes his cognitive world into a good gestalt and the conditions under which he explores, complexifies, and elaborates.

The application of cognitive theories to the practical issues which need attitude change programs in order to influence people's behavior relies upon the procedure of creating states of imbalance or dissonance and influencing the way in which the audience reduces the tension aroused by such states. Presenting new information about the attitudes of other individuals whose opinions the audience values may induce a state of imbalance when the audience's attitudes are discrepant with those presented. For example, if the audience likes the President of the United States and does not believe in birth control, they may feel tension when they learn that the President does believe in birth control and wants them to support it. Such a state of imbalance may be resolved by either disliking the president or changing their attitudes about birth control. With a little planning, the situation probably could be structured so that the audience will change its attitudes, not its liking for the president. Or, following dissonance theory, if an audience can subtly be influenced to engage in birth control, they will be in a state of dissonance which may be resolved by either denying or justifying their behavior or by changing their attitudes. Again, the situation could be structured so that it is their birth-control attitudes which are changed, not their perceptions of their behavior.

FUNCTIONAL APPROACH

Of what use to a person are his attitudes? This question epitomizes the central focus of the functional approach to attitude development and change. The learning and cognitive approaches indicated some of the specific psychological principles that guide the learning of attitudes. But there is also a need to indicate the broader functions of attitudes. The functional approach to attitudes construes man as an organism striving after certain goals and analyzes attitudes in terms of the extent to which they facilitate obtaining these goals. It is an attempt to understand the reasons people hold the attitudes they do, to specify the psychological needs which are met by having an attitude. The most prominent exponent of the study of the different kinds of functions served by attitudes is Daniel Katz (Sarnoff and Katz, 1954; Katz and Stotland, 1959; Katz, 1960). Katz states that there are four functions of attitudes: (1) instrumental, adjustive, or utilitarian; (2) ego defensive; (3) knowledge; and (4) value-expressive.

The *adjustive function* of attitudes recognizes that people strive to maximize the rewards in their external environment and to minimize the penalties. Thus a person develops favorable attitudes towards the objects which are associated with the satisfaction of his needs and unfavorable attitudes toward objects which thwart him or punish him. The *ego-defensive function* revolves around the notion that a person protects himself from anxiety by obliterating threatening external and internal stimuli. Thus attitudes can function like defense mechanisms to protect a person from acknowledging his conflicts and deficiencies to himself and other people. To a considerable degree, for example, prejudiced attitudes help to sustain the individual's self-concept by maintaining a sense of superiority over others. The *knowledge function* refers to the fact that people seek knowledge to give meaning to what otherwise would be an unorganized chaotic world. People need standards or frames of reference for understanding their world and attitudes help to supply such standards. Attitudes help people establish a degree of predictability, consistency, and stability in their perception of the world. Finally, the *value-expression function* of attitudes involves the notion that attitudes give positive expression to an individual's central values and his self-concept. Satisfactions are derived from the expression of attitudes which reflect one's cherished beliefs and his self-image.

Relatively few experiments have been conducted to test the validity of Katz's functional theory of attitude change. Most of the research which has been conducted has centered around explorations of the ego-defensive function, and rather confusing results have been found. There are difficulties, furthermore, in applying the functional approach to attitude change to applied problems such as the three mentioned in the introduction to this chapter. The functional theories state that one cannot proceed to change attitudes until one knows what function the particular attitudes serve for the individuals one wants to change. Since the same attitude serves different functions for different persons, it is difficult to arrive at an attitude change program aimed at changing the racial, ecological, or birth control attitudes of large numbers of people. One would not know what kind of persuasive appeal or what kind of procedure to use unless he knew the functions the attitudes served for each of the individuals in his audience. At present there is no technology for assessing the function of attitudes and, therefore, this approach does not seem helpful to a person interested in changing attitudes. Despite this, however, much of the advertising approach to attitude development is based upon the functional theories of attitude change. An entire industry, called motivational research, has developed from the assumption that consumers respond to appeals which tap the irrational, emotional, and unconscious aspect of their needs.

SOCIAL INFLUENCE APPROACH

The correctness of most of our attitudes cannot be checked against physical reality. In the area of ecology, for example, most people do not experience the degree of air and water pollution which surrounds them or fully realize the impact of littering and using nonreturnable cans and bottles on the environment. Where the dependence upon physical reality is low, the dependence upon social reality to assess the extent to which one's attitudes are valid is correspondingly high. An attitude is valid to the extent that it is anchored in a group of people with similar attitudes. It is, of course, not necessary that all people you associate with agree with your attitudes, but it is important that some relevant reference group share your attitudes. Festinger (1950, 1954) developed social comparison theory to focus upon the importance of having other people share one's attitudes. He emphasizes that individuals are dependent upon other people for information to establish the validity of their attitudes. The experiments conducted by Asch (1956) and the literature on conformity, furthermore, indicate that the attitudes one's reference groups hold are very powerful influences upon the development of a person's attitudes and how well the attitudes are sustained over time.

We have previously discussed the theory and research on conformity, reference groups, group norms, group decision making, and social comparison processes—all of which is relevant to the issue of the social influences upon attitude acquisition and change. Only the implications of this literature, therefore, will be summarized here. They are:

1. The attitudes of an individual are strongly influenced by the groups to which he belongs and those to which he wants to belong;

2. A person is reinforced for conforming to the group standards and norms and punished for deviating from them;

3. Those individuals who are most attached to the group are probably least influenced by communications which conflict with group norms;

4. Attitudes which persons make known publicly are harder to change than private attitudes;

5. Audience participation in group discussions and group decision making helps to overcome resistance to developing the new attitudes the communicator is presenting;

6. The support of even one person weakens the powerful effect upon an individual of a majority opinion;

7. A minority of two people who are consistent in their deviant responses can influence the majority of a group;

8. One's resistance to a communication which presents attitudes counter to group norms increases with salience of one's group identification.

It is evident that (1) when individuals are subject to the stabilizing effects of a group's attitudes, the influence of external persuasive communications will be diminished and (2) any successful attempt to develop or change attitudes must provide continuing social support for individuals to hold the attitudes. An attempt to change ecological attitudes, for example, would either have to seek out groups which held the appropriate attitudes and try to integrate the audience into those groups or to change the audience's reference group norms so that they would support the desired attitudes. Both of these approaches should be effective. There is considerable evidence that as one's reference group changes, so do one's attitudes. There is also considerable evidence that if a group decides to adopt new attitudes its members will also adopt the new attitudes. The importance of the social influence approach to attitude acquisition and change is in focusing attention upon how powerful social influences are in acquiring, changing, and sustaining over time the attitudes contained in persuasive messages.

NEED FOR AN INTEGRATED THEORY

The four major approaches to attitude acquisition and change have been reviewed. Learning theories, cognitive organization theories, functional theories, and social influence theories all have something important to offer the area of attitude acquisition and change. A person interested in changing the racial attitudes of members of our society should be concerned with the way in which attitudes are conditioned and reinforced, the way in which the meaning of the concepts involved are organized, the motivation for individuals to hold racial attitudes, and the social pressures upon the individuals to have certain racial attitudes. Yet there is a need for a broader theory which could include all of these approaches to attitude acquisition and change and relate the research conducted on each approach in a meaningful way. Unfortunately, at present there is little work being conducted on relating the different theories to each other. Such research and the reformulation of the theories to include the phenomena dealt with by the other theories is vitally needed.

In addition, there is a need to establish more precisely the ways in which attitudes affect behavior. In the beginning of this chapter it was noted that attitudes are motivational-perceptual states which are underlying predispositions to behavior. Fishbein (1967), however, notes that after more than seventy-five years of attitude research, there is little consistent evidence supporting the hypothesis that knowledge of an individual's attitudes will allow one to predict the way he will behave. A strict learning theorist would argue that the learning of attitudes and the learning of behavior occurs independently and, therefore, there may be little relation between a person's attitudes and behavior. A person, for example, may learn to have a positive attitude towards a professor but whether he engages in friendly behavior towards the professor depends upon the reinforcement he receives for doing so. Another problem in trying to predict a person's behavior by a knowledge of his attitudes is that most situations are sufficiently complex that several attitudes may be relevant to any action taken. Predicting whether a student who has favorable attitudes toward a professor will engage in friendly behavior, for example, may depend upon knowing such things as how the student feels physically (he may be sick and want to avoid other people) and what behaviors are competing with the predicted behavior (he may want to study for an exam which he has later on in the day or he may want to meet his girl-friend more than he wants to be friendly with the professor). A more specific theoretical formulation of the way in which one may predict behavior from knowing a person's attitudes needs to be formulated and researched.

THEORY, RESEARCH, AND GENERALIZATION OF RESULTS TO APPLIED SITUATIONS

All the methods and techniques of social psychology are designed to provide data to evaluate theories. The essence of the dialogue between theories and findings is to broaden one's understanding of "reality" and increase the range of applicability of one's conclusions. That is, the purpose of building and testing theories is to improve the generalization of verified knowledge to practical situations. This is only possible to the extent that one employs methods that provide a good test of one's theories and good theories for guiding one's pursuit of new data.

For the practitioner reading behavioral science theory and research it should be kept in mind that research results are never absolutely certain and, therefore, theories are never forever fixed. No finding is sacrosanct and any theory is potentially subject to alterations when new data comes in. When theories and research findings are generalized to applied situations, furthermore, the practitioner must remember that it is not an absolute truth being generalized, it is a probability statement that given certain conditions, a relationship between two variables may hold.

There are two major problems in generalizing research findings to practical situations. First, since applied situations are usually much more complex than research situations, there is no way to tell for certain whether the necessary conditions for the desired relationship between two variables are present or whether or not they are confounded by other variables present in the complex applied situation which were absent or controlled in the experimental situation. The second problem comes from the characteristics of the subjects used in the research. The important question here is how similar they are to the persons one wants to generalize the findings to. What is found to be highly probable behavior under certain conditions for white, middle class sophomores may or may not be highly probable under the same conditions for lower class, nonwhite elementary school students; only further research can tell.

It is very difficult, therefore, to make specific generalizations from social psychological research and theory to applied situations. The implications of social psychological research are hypotheses for action which increase the practitioner's ability to deal with the interpersonal aspects of any situation he faces.

RESPONSIBLE SOCIAL PSYCHOLOGY

There are at least two meanings of the concept of responsibility in science (Hilgard, 1971). The first meaning relates to the integrity of the scientific findings; they must be objective, reported fully and accurately, and be the result of sound methodology. The first demand is that a responsible science be a good science. In relation to this meaning of responsibility, the research and theory on attitude change and other areas of social psychology must be beyond question. There should be a wide level of agreement among social psychologists upon both the facts resulting from research and the theory to which the facts apply. There must be conclusive evidence that the theory and research is valid in order for the knowledge to be applied to problems which people, groups, and our society face.

The second meaning relates to how the knowledge generated by social psychologists is used. A responsible science must be one in which the applications of scientific findings are considered. Just as a biologist employed by the Government to work on germ-warfare projects must consider how his findings are to be applied, the social psychologist working in the area of human behavior must consider how the knowledge generated by his research and theory will be used. The way in which advertising companies and politicians apply the knowledge on attitude formation and change has to be a vital concern of social psychologists who conduct research in the area. As the literature reviewed in this chapter indicates, we have the technology to affect attitudes in the direction a communicator desires. This technology can be put to use constructively in changing racial attitudes to reduce the conflicts in our society, in changing ecological attitudes to stop the destruction of our natural environment, in changing attitudes related to the crisis the world now faces concerning overpopulation. The attitude change technology, however, has been also put to use in areas of advertising such as cigarette smoking and in manipulating political attitudes of the public in ways which may be injurious to individuals' health and to the health of our democracy. Many social commentators feel that deception and manipulation are deeply ingrained in our present society. "Adam Smith" (1967), for example, states:

The world is not the way they tell you it is.

Unconsciously we know this because we have all been immunized by growing up in the United States. The little girl watching television asks will she really get the part in the spring play if she uses Listerine, and her good mother says no, darling, that is just the commercial. It is not long before the moppets figure out that parents have commercials of their own—commercials to keep one quiet, commercials to get one to eat, and so on. But parents—indeed all of us—are in turn being given a whole variety of commercials that do not seem to be commercials. Silver is in short supply and the (U.S.) Treasury is running out and begins to fear a run. So the Treasury tells the *New York Times* that, what with one thing and another, there is enough silver for twenty years. Those who listened to the commercial sat quietly, expecting to get the part in the spring play, and the cynics went and ran all the silver out of the Treasury and the price went through the roof.

How may the public protect themselves against the misuse of social psychological knowledge? One common way suggested is to educate the public in the use of the techniques of attitude change so that they may recognize when the persuasion techniques are being applied and be on guard against the message. How may social psychologists influence how the knowledge they generate is applied? This question has not received an adequate answer.

SUMMARY

An attitude is a predisposition to respond toward a particular person or group of persons, a particular object or group of objects, in a favorable or unfavorable manner. Attitudes are relatively enduring, learned predispositions which give continuity to behavior over time. They help a person deal with repetitive situations and give a simplified and practical guide for appropriate behavior.

There are four major ways of approaching the area of attitude acquisition and change. Attitudes are learned and, therefore, it is possible to apply learning theory to attitude development and modification. Two basic principles of conditioning can be applied. The first, stimulus generalization, refers to the fact that when a particular response habitually follows a particular stimulus, elements similar to, or closely associated with, this stimulus also show a tendency to elicit a similar response. The second, response reinforcement, refers to the fact that responses are more clearly fixed the more they are associated with rewards. In addition, Carl Hovland and his associates at Yale have conducted numerous studies from a learning theory approach upon the theme sentence, "Who says what to whom with what effect?" Their research emphasizes the credibility and other characteristics of the communicator, the number of sides, order, and emotional appeal of the message, and the characteristics of the audience which may affect their persuasibility, such as their present attitudes, whether they have been forewarned about the influence attempt, their personality, their involvement in the message through role playing and whether they have been inoculated against the communicator's message.

The second way of approaching the field of attitude acquisition and change is through how different attitudes relate to each other in terms of meaning. This approach emphasizes that principles of cognitive organization as well as principles of conditioning need to be considered for understanding the learning of attitudes. Two such principles are the principle of simplicity which states that our cognitive world tends to become organized into a framework of maximum uniformity and regularity and the principle of evaluative consistency which states that persons tend to have similar evaluations of cognitive elements which are associated together. The consistency theories which have been developed upon these principles postulates a basic "need" for consistency among attitudes or between attitudes and behavior and that the presence of inconsistency produces "psychological tension" which motivates the person to rearrange his psychological world to produce consistency. Heider's balance theory and Festinger's theory of cognitive dissonance are among the more important consistency theories.

The third approach to the study of attitudes deals with the question, "Of what use to a person are his attitudes?" This functional approach assumes that man is an organism striving after certain goals and it analyzes attitudes in terms of the extent to which they facilitate obtaining these goals. Katz has hypothesized four possible functions of attitudes: (1) instrumental, adjustive, or utilitarian; (2) ego defensive, (3) knowledge; and (4) value-expressive.

Finally, the last major approach to the study of attitudes discussed in this chapter is the social influence approach. This approach focuses upon the influences other people's attitudes and expectations have upon a person's attitudes.

From these approaches a fairly effective technology for developing and changing attitudes has been developed. The way in which this technology is applied is of concern to many social psychologists.

CHAPTER 8

Culture and Personality

Our central thesis—set forth in Chapter 6—is that structures lead to processes which result in certain attitudes (S-P-A). The most comprehensive and influential of these structures is what anthropologists call the *culture*. From cultural systems arise regular processes of interaction which form corresponding patterns of personality.

In his *Psychological Anthropology*, F. L. K. Hsu has proposed, more specifically, that "maintenance systems" lead to certain correlative child training practices and these to personality variables (1961, p. 356). He adds that the personality variables may then be regarded as causal for "projective systems," such as magic, myths, and rituals. Personality is thus viewed as depending on the child-rearing practices, which, in turn, are greatly influenced by the maintenance systems, that is, "the basic customs surrounding the nourishment, sheltering, and protection" of the members of the society.

CULTURAL RELATIVITY

Culture

Culture is the matrix that molds the main characteristics of most or all the members of a society. "Every baby," said John Dewey, "is laid in a cradle of custom." How he will view the world; how he will speak and think; how he will eat, play, work, and enjoy himself; his ethical ideals and how he will worship—all these patterns are largely predetermined by the cultural setting into which he is born. "The individual," says Linton, "is only an incident in the life history of his society" (p. 12).

"Culture" as used in the social sciences refers to the total way of life characteristic of a somewhat homogeneous society of human beings. This meaning of the term should be distinguished from the popular use of "culture" to refer to refinement in intellectual and aesthetic realms. Linton (1945) defines culture as "the configuration of learned behavior whose component elements are shared and transmitted by the members of a particular society."

The culture of a tribe, region, nation or larger society or civilization includes all its man-made objects, its customs, art, science or myths, other organized knowledge, traditions, ceremonies, economic practices, child-rearing practices, political institutions, its values, and religion. All the influences discussed in preceding chapters—the structure-process-attitude sequence and the flow of propaganda through the media of mass communication are parts of the larger complex called the *culture*.

Challenge to instinct theory

The major impact of anthropological studies upon psychology began in the late 1920s. In 1928 Margaret Mead, in a widely discussed study, reported that emotional upheavals during adolescence which had been attributed to innate glandular changes were not apparent under the different conditions of Samoan culture. In 1924, William Graham Sumner's observations on the wide variety of practices—often irrational—reported earlier in his *Folkways* (1906)—was systematized (in collaboration with A. G. Keller) in a four-volume science of society; and in 1927 Malinowski published his criticism of Freud's view of the Oedipus Complex as universal.

During the first quarter of the twentieth century, most psychology had been founded upon instinct theories. E. L. Thorndike devoted the first and largest part of his three-volume educational psychology (1913) to an inventory of hundreds of what he regarded as inborn connections in the human make-up. McDougall (1908) preferred to relate human behavior to seven basic instincts with corresponding emotions: flight, repulsion, curiosity, pugnacity, self-abasement, self-assertion, and the parental instinct.

Backed by prevailing instinct theories, defenders of the *status quo* mocked all reformers with the argument, "you can't change human nature!" Why do we have wars? "Man is driven by unalterable instincts of hostility, aggression, pugnacity." Why do we operate a capitalistic profit-seeking economy? "It rests soundly upon man's acquisitive instinct." Social institutions such as families, clubs or churches were simply accounted for as expressions of instincts of mating, gregariousness, and religion. Class and ethnic group discrimination were barricaded behind alleged instincts of "consciousness of kind," of "dominance and submission." A provocative study (Pastore, 1949) of the broader social attitudes of 12 prominent defenders of instinct theories showed 11 of them conservative or reactionary. The converse also held. Among 12 scientists who emphasized human plasticity and the potency of the environment, 11 could properly be called "liberal" or even "radical" in their social theories.

Quite possibly the economic depression of the 1930s, moving many intellectuals toward left-wing political views, hastened the reaction against the older instinct theories. Social change seemed required, and evidence that men could change was welcome. A pertinent example is the English biologist, J. B. S. Haldane, who served for some years as an official member of the Communist Party. His discussion of human nature (1947) emphasizes experiments like that of Kuo, who worked with kittens. Eighteen kittens which were raised in cages along with mice or white rats as playmates never, at maturity, killed the kind of rodent they had associated with in their early months. Among 20 reared in isolation from other rats and from mice, only nine showed the traditionally "instinctive" response of springing upon and killing a running mouse. In a third group of 21, which were allowed to see their cat mother kill mice, all but three later demonstrated the same kind of behavior—an impressive S-P-A sequence.

As doubt about the inevitability of instinctive behavior increased, older studies were recalled. One was Conradi's demonstration (1905) that English sparrows, brought up in a cage with canaries, did not develop their usual harsh chirp but a softer note and, after three months, actual trills. The behaviorism of John B. Watson (1919) hypothesized that proper conditioning could make any baby of adequate intelligence into "rich man, poor man, beggar man, thief; doctor, lawyer, merchant, chief."

The flood of evidence which overwhelmed traditional instinct theory came from the anthropologists. Few human actions could seem more "natural" than nodding approval, shaking one's head in negation or smiling when pleased. Yet LaBarre (1947) reports: "Among the Ainu of northern Japan, for example, our particular head noddings are unknown":

. . . the right hand is usually used in negation, passing from right to left and back in front of the chest; and both hands are gracefully brought up to the chest and gracefully waved downwards—palms upwards—in sign of affirmation. . . .

The Semang, pygmy Negroes of interior Malaya, thrust the head sharply forward for "yes" and cast the eyes down for "no." The Abyssinians say "no" by jerking the head to the right shoulder, and "yes" by throwing the head back and raising the eyebrows. The Dyaks of Borneo raise their eyebrows to mean "yes," and contract them slightly to mean "no."

A Bengali servant in Calcutta rocks his head rapidly in an arc from shoulder to shoulder, usually four times, in assent; in Delhi a Moslem boy throws his head diagonally backward with a slight turning of the neck for the same purpose; and the Kandyan Singhalese bends the head diagonally forward toward the right, with an indescribably graceful turning in of the chin, often accompanying this with a cross-legged curtsey, arms partly crossed, palms upward—the whole performance extraordinarily beautiful and ingratiating. Indeed, did my own cultural difference not tell me it already, I would know that the Singhalese manner of receiving an object (with the right hand, the left palm supporting the right elbow) is not instinctive, for I have seen a Singhalese mother *teaching* her little boy to do this when I gave him a chunk of palm tree sugar. I only regretted, later, that my own manners must have seemed boorish and subhuman, since I handed it to him with my right hand, instead of with both, as would any courteous Singhalese.

Smiling, indeed, I have found may also be mapped after the fashion of any other culture trait; and laughter is in some senses a geographic variable. On a map of the Southwest Pacific one could perhaps even draw lines between areas of Papual hilarity and others where a Dobuan, Melanesian dourness reigned. In Africa, Gorer noted that laughter is used by the Negro to express surprise, wonder, embarrassment and even discomfiture; it is not necessarily or even often a sign of amusement; the significance given to "black laughter" is due to a mistake of supporting the idea that similar symbols have identical meanings. (La Barre, W., 1947; Reprinted by permission)

Hissing in Japan is a sign of courtesy and polite deference to social superiors; the Basuto applaud by hissing; but in England hissing is rude and public disapprobation of an actor or a speaker. Spitting in many parts of the world is a sign of utmost contempt; and yet among the Masai of Africa it is a sign of affection and benediction, while the spitting of an American Indian medicine man upon a patient is one of the kindly offices of the healer. Urination upon another person is a grave insult in most parts of the world, but it is part of the transfer of power from an African medicine man in initiations and curing rituals. As for other opposite meanings. Western man stands up in the presence of a superior; the Fijians and the Tongans sit down. In some contexts we put on more clothes as a sign of respect; the Friendly Islanders take them off. The Toda of South India raise the open right hand to the face, with the thumb on the bridge of the nose, to express respect; a gesture almost identical among Europeans is an expression of extreme disrespect.

Patterns of sexual behavior certainly meet the criteria of "instinct" because they have a biological and physiological basis and are so nearly universal. Yet, as Ford and Beach (1951) have shown, different cultures foster widely different attitudes and behaviors. There is no agreement among human societies on the age when sex activity may begin, on the kind of partner who may be chosen, on monogamy, on the preferred time, place or positions of intercourse, or on the moral or religious significance of various forms of sexual expression. Among 18 cultures in which males have a distinct preference, five prefer the slender female, while thirteen prefer plumpness. Our culture expects male initiative, and psychoanalysts have generally assumed that this is innate and healthy. Yet Yerkes (1936, 1943) found that among our chimpanzee cousins the female was more apt to initiate intercourse. Ford and Beach tell us that among the Kwoma, the Maori, and the Mataeo, women are considered to be more highly sexed and properly signal to men by pinching them or scratching their hands. In the ceremonial dances of the Gaojiro, girls may try to trip the men, and if they succeed, the man must make love to a woman who has thus captured him. Among the Lepcha, women must not take the initiative except that aunts may seduce their nephews and most boys begin their sex life in this way.

Children were regarded, in Victorian morality, as innocent of sex interests.

One of the surprising revelations associated with Freud arose from his conclusion that children's pleasure seeking normally includes stimulation of their sexual organs. Freud recognized that the "latency period" in which children are not sexually active, is not physiological but is found only in cultures which repress the sex impulses of children (Hartmann *et al.*, 1951). Malinowski (1929) reported that, in the Trobriand Islands, children play at intercourse, under observation by adults, as acceptably as American children might play dolls a party.

It seems right and natural to most members of our society that men should prize chastity in a wife, but this is by no means universal. "Among certain peoples of India, a man may compel his wife to bear him a child by another man. In some West African tribes, a girl is not considered for marriage until she has successfully borne a child" (Britt, 1949, p. 80). Wife-lending is an approved form of hospitality among the Eskimos.

Homosexual behavior is so repugnant to many in our society that it has often been severely punished by law. Yet in a majority (49 of 76) of the societies on which information is available. Ford and Beach have found that homosexual activity is considered normal and acceptable for some of the members. Special roles of considerable prestige may be assigned the homosexuals, as among the Chuckchee, or the Koniaq. It was a highly esteemed relationship in Ancient Greece. Aristotle, in his *Politics*, proposed homosexual attachments as a preferred way of limiting excessive population increase. Among the Siwans and Keraki all boys are reported to enjoy some homosexual activities. In other societies (Truk; Carolinians) no boys or men were known to engage in them (Kluckhohn, 1954, p. 928).

Taboos against incest seem to be almost universal today; yet among the highly honored royalty of Egypt, Peru, and Hawaii the mating of brothers and sisters was approved (Lowie, 1940, p. 332). Brother-and-sister twins might marry in Bali and the ancient Persians seem also to have accepted incestuous unions (Masters, 1963).

The stimuli for shame depend likewise upon the culture. Herodotus speaks with disgust of Egyptians who perform excretory processes in the privacy of their houses rather than on the public street as was done in Athens. There are numerous cultures in which neither nakedness nor excretion is a source of shame. It thus, turns out that the universal "sex instinct" can tell us little or nothing about whether given individuals will be prudish or salacious; celibate or profligate; homosexual or heterosexual, monogamous, polygamous or polyandrous; whether their sentiments of shame will be connected with excretion, sex, eating, dress, or the persons with whom they converse.

Other so-called instincts have fared no better.

"Pugnacity" as a human universal does not tell us why wars are unknown to Eskimos but flourish in modern industrial nations. Neither does it explain the reluctance of many men, even in our war-oriented world, to being drafted into a wartime army. No modern nation relies for military defense on the desire of its males to engage in combat. Cultures vary in the premium they place on aggressiveness. Among the Ojibwa Indians, insults were repaid by knife wounds and trespassing on hunting grounds by murder. "War parties" arose because some man had visions of successful conquest. Yet other Indians—notably the Zuni of Southwestern North America—seem to have almost no instances of violent attack. Among the South Sea island cultures, the Mundugumor have been reported (Mead, 1928) to be aggressively violent and vengeful, while the Arapesh, on the same island, are mild and gentle.

A particularly instructive example of situational influences (S-P-A) in development of aggression may be found in the Comanche Indian culture (Kardiner, 1945). Early records describe them as humble, harmless, and placid with tolerance even for trespassing. Then came new technical instruments—horses for riding and guns for shooting. At the same time the white settlers—English, French, and Spanish—placed a premium on plunder. In this altered situation, the Comanches became fierce brigands. Later the military forces of the United States confined the Comanches to their reservation. The patterns of predatory raiding and war could no longer be enacted. These Indians under the new social structure became docile, inert, and apathetic.

Many futile arguments have been held over whether human nature is basically competitive, violent, and destructive, or cooperative, peace-loving, and constructive. The answer is that no instinct places man in either category. In some cultures, many situations call forth hostile responses; in other cultures, hostility is rare. Among the Arapesh, helpfulness and generosity are highly valued. The ideal man is not a boss but a servant of the community. Personal security is found in warm, accepting group relationships. The Kwakiutl (British Columbia) are much more competitive. Hierarchy of rank is prominent. Individuals strive competitively for noble titles which can be won by ceremonial feasts ("potlatches") during which numerous possessions are destroyed to humiliate rivals. The Ifugao (Philippines) landowners seek prestige through property. Cooperation is practiced within the kinship group, but rivalry against other families is the rule. Eskimos operate much more individually, with only a minimum of either cooperation or competition.

So we might continue to explore other traditional "instincts," which may be little more than rationalizations of our present culture. In our economy, the existence of an "acquisitive instinct" seems obvious. In the Arapesh culture, however, a man may work harder cultivating a neighbor's garden than his own. The Lesu have no scheme of ownership for land or other property. Among the Dakota Indians, property was valued only in order to win prestige by giving it away. Trade and bargaining were not practiced and hoarding possessions was despised. These and other examples are cited by

Mead (1937). Even in America, few can be induced to work for money as hard as some will voluntarily work at recreational activities like mountain climbing or playing football or domestic duties or caring for a two-year-old child.

The alleged "parental instinct" is found in some form in most animals but there are others which attempt to destroy or consume their offspring. Some cultures have induced parents to expose babies to die unattended or to sacrifice their first born. Even with all the pressure toward child welfare in our American culture, the Society for Prevention of Cruelty to Children keeps busy—and most of the offenders are parents.

If a religious instinct is posited to account for those who worship, then there should be a nonreligious instinct to account for the millions who ignore or reject the religious institutions of their society.

The conclusion toward which the evidence points is that human beings are biologically highly adaptable, and the uniformities we observe are usually produced by cultural influences rather than predetermined in the organism.

Cultural relativity: a revolution in thought

Awareness of the diversity of human mores and behavior came as as a blow to the ego and as a revolutionary movement in the world of ideas. Copernicus had made men realize that our earth was not the center of the universe. A second shock came when Darwin surmised that men have evolved as a natural part of the animal kingdom. Freud struck a third great blow when his findings implied that reason had a relatively weak and subordinate voice in the control of human behavior. Yet none of these developments seem quite as disquieting as the raising of the question whether "our way of life" is necessarily the one right, wise, natural, and divinely ordained order of existence. Do others have as much right as we to claim certainty or superiority for their patriotism, their religion, their economic order, their political system, their sex attitudes, their kind of art, music or dance? It must be expected that men will react vigorously against so "subversive" a question.

One reaction, which characterized an early stage in anthropology, was the attempt to arrange a ladder of evolution with our own system at the top. Thus savages could be thought to have the lowest grade of customs; barbarians would come a little later and higher; civilization is seen moving through history to our present peak. There is an ounce of truth and a ton of appeal in this doctrine. It is satisfying to put the outsiders, the deviants, and the heretics in their inferior place. There is truth in the contention that over the millennia, since the days of the first manlike anthropoids, but particularly in recent centuries, men have increased their speed of movement, the distance over which their voices can be heard, the weights they can lift, the precision of their tools, the power of their weapons, and (since writing began) the store of accumulated knowledge. Average life expectancy has probably increased fairly steadily. It is tempting to think, by analogy, that we who have the biggest machines must also have evolved the finest families and a superior spiritual life. Lewis Henry Morgan (*Ancient Society,* published in 1877) was one of the chief exponents, among ethnologists, of the idea of a unilinear evolution. His view that men have progressed from savagery to barbarism and on to civilization fits certain lines of historical development, but does not accord with more recent extensive and critical studies. We have come to respect more values in preindustrial cultures and to recognize many important differences among them. No simple ladder of development is widely applicable.

Herskovitz (1948) for example, has called attention to some of the remarkable achievements of men in nonliterate societies. Despite lack of the assistance which our technology would provide, pygmies in the Congo have built excellent suspension bridges from vines; Mayans in their culture had achieved a calendar of extraordinary accuracy; the pre-Spanish Peruvians constructed remarkable buildings; and the Polynesians accomplished marvels of navigation. Arts flourished in cultures which preceded Ancient Greece, and there is no evidence to prove modern man superior to many primitive peoples in the quality of his human relationships.

Another defensive reaction has been the quest for universals. Are there not some actions which all decent men approve and others which are invariably condemned? The uniformities discovered in anthropology are mainly categorical rather than substantive. Every society has some kind of language, some numerical counting, some preferred foods, some magic, some pressure toward conformity, some sort of deference paid to parents. But this does not tell us anything about the merits of the many kinds of language, arithmetic, food, magic, conformity, and deference which different cultures develop. All cultures rate some behaviors as better than others, but they do not agree to a great extent on the specific values.

There are some attitudes which are common to most cultures. Lying to members of one's in-group is almost universally condemned. Asch writes with cogency: "We do not know of societies in which bravery is despised and cowardice held up to honor, in which generosity is considered a vice and ingratitude a virtue" (1952, p. 378). But universality is not necessary to establish ethical values. Would bravery or generosity become less desirable to any of us, if, in some corner of the globe or at some period of history, ingratitude and cowardice had been more admired?

Cultural relativity also makes it hard to define in absolute terms the normal and abnormal in mental health. Whether one who sees ghosts and treats dreams as evidence of reality is sane or sick seems to depend on his culture. In some societies not to believe in ghosts and omens would be a serious symptom of deviation. A self-effacement that would be normal for a Zuni Indian in New Mexico would seem pathological in a Kwakiutl of Vancouver Island. It was normal in many American Indian cultures to induce hallucinations by fasting and self-torture. A non-Indian American living in the same geographical region today would be sent to a mental hospital for much less. One's belief that his associates are persecuting him by black magic and the Evil Eye would be psychotic on a contemporary college campus but would have seemed sensible enough on Dobu Island near New Guinea. Not only health norms but also sickness patterns vary with the culture. Some seem to be characterized by the development of certain psychopathic syndromes; in Malaysia the insane run amuck (*amok*); only among the Ojibway and Cree Indians of Canada are men seized with the Windigo psychosis which makes them compulsive cannibals.

Later in this chapter we shall return to the difficult problem of evaluating whole cultures. First, however, we must explore the way in which the various elements of a culture affect psychological processes. We may begin with language and its relation to the way minds work.

CULTURAL INTEGRATION

Culture, language, and thought

The Marxist argues, and the anthropologist generally agrees, that in different societies "men who live differently think differently." Some anthropologists and students of language have argued also that "men who speak differently think differently." One cannot be sure whether observed differences in vocabulary are cause or effect. If Eskimos have numerous words for different kinds of snow while we have only the one inclusive term, that difference in speech arises from other experiences which have led to the distinctions. The different words, once developed, may well sharpen the subsequent perception of snow. In every field the specialist knows many terms that emphasize distinctions important for him but not for the layman. Technical words support but do not, in themselves, create the thought-habits. The lakuti language has only one word for a color range which includes both blue and green; are those who speak it less likely to be aware of the change of color on a lake when the clouds give way to a bright blue sky? One hypothesis, proposed by Roger Brown (1958), is that the more readily codable a category is in language symbols (short, definite name) the more available it will be for general psychological use.

A more significant difference may be the categories which require different forms or endings. Are sex differences more vital to a child who has learned that every noun must be masculine, feminine or neuter? If, as a Chinese writer (Chang) has argued, Western languages lead one to ask first what an object is and later what one should do about it, while Chinese imply the "what" by giving priority to the "how," does this represent a basic difference in approach to life?

The hypothesis of linguistic determinism was suggested by Boas and then formulated by Sapir many years ago (1929). "Human beings are very much at the mercy of the particular language which has become the medium of expression for their society. The 'real' world is to a large extent unconsciously built upon the language habits of the group. The worlds in which different societies live are distinct worlds, not merely the same world with different labels attached."

Whorf (1950), after years of study of the Hopi language which differs from the "Standard Average European" languages far more than these tongues differ from one another, has noted that the Hopi do not employ our categories of past, present, and future. They distinguish rather between a realm of objective, manifested reality and a realm of subjective, to-be-manifested reality which exists in the mind or heart of men, animals, plants, rocks, and all nature. What is to come is thought of by the Hopi not as proceeding along a time dimension but as unfolding from the inner potential of things. The child learning such a language is prepared to experience a world which seems markedly different from our three-dimensional space, our three tenses, and our emphasis on distinction between the animate and inanimate. In the Hopi super-classification, a kinship is implied within a system which includes certain men, certain animals, certain birds, plants, and supernatural beings. Other men, animals, plants, and so forth, belong together in another and different category. This kind of language system results from a way of thinking but in turn the language tends to instill and to the essentials of that system.

Another illustration may be found in Lee's analysis (1938) of the Wintu language, which emphasizes the kind of evidence for an event. If it is directly experienced, one verb form is used. If it is hearsay, another form is required. If it occurs regularly, still another form is used. A study of Navajo speech (Kluckhohn, Leighton, 1946) reports that their verbs indicate whether an act is about to start, is in progress, is about to stop, and whether the act occurs repeatedly. Verbs of manipulation, in the Navajo tongue, differ in form depending on the shape (long and rigid; long and flexible; flat; etc.) of the object handled. This suggested to Carroll and Casagrande (1958) that Navajo-speaking children might be more likely to classify objects by form than would English-speaking children of the same tribe. About 64 percent of 48 children (age 3-7) whose speech was predominantly Navajo chose on the basis of form, while only 35 percent of 30 children whose speech was predominantly English chose by form rather than by color or size. It is interesting to note, however, that the choices made by a sample of 40 children living in and around Boston resembled the Navajo-speaking children's responses more than they did those of the English-speaking Indians. The authors surmise that this may have been due to play, by the Massachusetts children, with toys of the form-board type. This observation reminds us that while language plays some part in shaping thought, other cultural experiences should also be considered.

Adults, who spoke both French and English fluently, brought up in middle-class families in France but now living in the United States, were given Thematic Apperception Test pictures to respond to in one language and (six weeks later) to tell a different story in the other language. When speaking French, the subjects told stories in which characters more frequently responded to conflict situations by withdrawal and then doing as they pleased. Verbal aggression against peers was also more common when the language reinstated attitudes of French culture. In English, the women subjects told stories which included significantly more achievement motivation. The results confirmed predictions that middle-class French culture fosters more private autonomy and pride in verbal prowess, while American culture emphasizes more need to achieve (Ervin, 1964).

Several studies have dealt with the Japanese language and its personality correlates. For example, in Japanese there are many synonyms for unhappiness but few for happiness. Many songs, poems, and maxims represent ways of coping with melancholy (Minami, 1954). An analysis of the 61 most popular songs in postwar Japan (Kato, 1959) showed the prevailing themes to be pessimism, loneliness, and resignation. The language reflects the culture of course, but also sensitizes the child to certain values rather than others. Distinctions of hierarchical position influence pronouns in Japanese. There are several ways of saying "you" and "I," depending on relative prestige.

Arguments against the potency of language for giving structure to basic mental processes are found in the similarity of groups related in culture but different in language (the Hopi and the Hopi-Tewan; the Finns and the Swedes) or groups alike in language but quite different in culture. Holy Rollers, share-croppers, hippies, and bankers may all speak English!

The cultural gestalt

While language, games, occupations and other parts of a culture may each exert some influence on the psychological processes and attitudes of members, a greater effect stems from the culture as a whole. Underlying each culture is a climate of feeling, a pattern of relationships, and a system of values. Personality emerges from the matrix of the whole culture, not from a particular feature.

A school of anthropology today asserts that these factors are related. There is a consistency within a culture very much as there is in personality. A basic Gestalt principle has been carried over from general psychology to the description of a culture: Every part is what is and where it is because of its relation to the whole. Various bases for unity have been emphasized—the child-rearing practices, the economy, and the type of life are perhaps the most important.

Kardiner and Linton have contributed the unifying concept of "basic personality." Their postulates are:

1. That the individual's early experiences exert a lasting effect upon his personality, especially upon the development of his projective systems.
2. That similar experiences will tend to produce similar personality configurations in the individuals who are subjected to them.
3. That the techniques which the members of any society employ in the care and rearing of children are culturally patterned and will tend to be similar, although never identical, for various families within the society.
4. That the culturally patterned techniques for the care and rearing of children differ from one society to another.

If these postulates are correct, and they seem to be supported by a wealth of evidence, it follows:

1. That the members of any given society will have many elements of early experience in common.
2. That as a result of this they will have many elements of personality in common.
3. That since the early experience of individuals differs from one society to another, the personality norms for various societies will also differ.

The basic personality type for any society is thus that which follows from the early experiences the members have in common. It is not the whole, unique personality of any single member—it is the value-attitude system shared by all members.

Numerous specific studies bring out correlations between the child-rearing practices of a society and the adult personality. Presumably the causation is circular. If children are taught unquestioning obedience and adult religion also emphasizes strict obedience to the laws of God (or the gods) each tends to reinforce the other. Societies in which adults permit children great freedom to indulge sex impulses turn out to be societies which also encourage sex enjoyment by adults and in which impotence or frigidity is rare. It seems plausible that the adult attitudes are partly responsible for the child-rearing practice and that the child-rearing practice makes its contribution to the adult attitude.

Abstract 19 presents the result of testing several hypotheses concerning the association of adult personality traits with the child-rearing practices normal for the culture. It seems quite clear that those societies which leave their young children with a memory of shocks and disappointments in connection with early nursing and weaning, tend to be also societies which believe adult illness most likely to be caused by something the patient *ate*. It is likewise impressive that where sex acts in childhood arouse considerable anxiety, there are (in 11 of 14 such societies) prolonged taboos on parental intercourse after the birth of a child. Some other plausible correlations do not stand up so well.

A study (Whiting *et al.*, 1958) of 56 societies with adequate data, showed that it was usual (48 of 56) for babies to sleep with the mother until weaned, which was after they were one year old. In half of these societies both parents shared the bed with the child, but in the other 24, the father was pushed out by the infant and had to sleep in another bed, sometimes in another hut. About half of the societies permit resumption of intercourse as soon as the mother has recovered from childbirth, but half set a taboo on sex

---

Abstract 19

TITLE   Child Training and Personality

AUTHORS   J. W. M. Whiting and I. L. Child

PROBLEM   In what ways do cultures which train children differently, vary in the adult personality patterns?

SUBJECTS   Reports in Human Relations Area files covering about 75 different primitive societies. Data are reported only for those cultures about which the files contain enough information to permit confident judgments. This sometimes meant only 20 or 25 societies.

PROCEDURE   Judges read the material available and rated each culture on:
1. initial satisfaction potential (oral, anal, sexual, dependence, and aggression) and
2. anxiety generated by socialization (oral, anal, sexual, dependence and expression.)
The age at which weaning, toilet training, modesty training, training to inhibit heterosexual play, and independence training normally take place was estimated for each culture. Adult personality was studied for each culture only as expressed in customs and interpretations related to illness: oral explanations and therapy; anal explanations and therapy; dependence explanations and therapy; sexual explanations and therapy; aggression explanations and aggression-avoidance therapy.

SOME FINDINGS   1. Most societies have been more initially indulgent than were the Midwestern, American, white, middle-class mothers reported by Davis and Havighurst. The Americans weaned children earlier than any of 52 primitive societies except the Marquesans; they were less indulgent in giving babies oral nursing satisfaction than any of 51 societies again excepting the Marquesans; in severity of weaning, societies ranged from 6 (mild) to 15 (severe) with the Americans rating 13. Toilet training by American mothers began earlier than for any of 25 primitive societies, except the Tanala. Severity of toilet training in 20 societies ranged from a mild 6 to a severe 18, with Americans tied with Tanala at 18. Indulgence of masturbation ranged, in 17 societies, from a highly restrictive 10—the American score—to a very permissive attitude of 19 among the Alorese of Indonesia. Heterosexual play ratings ranged from 4, the most severe, to 20 the most indulgent, with the American attitude near the restrictive end of the scale. Age at beginning independence demands ranged from 2 to 6, with the U.S. group judged to begin at 2½. Tolerance for aggression in children ranged from 5 to 17 with the Americans a little below the median of 11.

2. Relations to adult interpretation of illness

	Oral explanation of illness	
	Absent	*Present*
High anxiety in childhood socialization of oral impulses	3	17
Low anxiety	13	6

3. In 20 societies which generated high anxiety in children about eating, most (17) attributed adult illness to something eaten. This view of the cause of sickness was less common (6 of 19) in societies which did not generate childhood anxiety about eating. In societies which forbade aggression in children, illness was usually explained by adults as due to someone's hostility (12 of 16 societies). The relationships to adult interpretations were less clear in the case of childhood anxieties about sex, excretion, and dependent behavior. Recommendation of therapeutic sex gratification was more common in societies which permitted sexual play among children.

SOURCE: New Haven: Yale University Press, 1953.

---

for the entire nursing period, averaging more than two years. Anthropologists hypothesized that "Societies which have sleeping arrangements in which the mother and baby share the same bed for at least a year and those which have a taboo on resumption of intercourse for more than a year after childbirth are more likely than others to have a ceremony of transition from boyhood to manhood." The initiation ceremonies—emphasizing separation of the son from his mother and his identification with the society of adult males, usually includes painful hazing, isolation from females, and operations on the genitals. Among the 25 societies which do not exclude the father from the marital bed for a prolonged period, 23 have no such initiation ceremonies. Among the 20 which do practice the exclusion, 14 have the puberty transition ceremonies. Of the six exceptions, four societies have a kind of substitute for such initiation—a requirement that the adolescent move out of his parental house and go to a special male residence to live until married.

The McClelland and Friedman study (1952) brings out another line of consistency within cultures. Those, like the Navajos, which expect children at an early age to act independently turn out to be also cultures which cherish folk-tales emphasizing heroic achievements. Those which, like the Flathead Indians, are least concerned with getting children to assume responsibility at an early age, have folk tales which do not stress achievement.

The child-rearing pattern itself is contained within the larger context of family relations. Hsu (1961) has defined several major patterns.

The *father-son* axis is characteristic of cultures which stress the patrilineal connections. Ancient China is a prime example. Boys are brought up to honor their fathers, grandfathers, and more remote male ancestors. Sons must be, above all, obedient; they are supported and protected by their fathers; they become heirs and patriarchs. Marriage is arranged, not for love, but to produce sons and so continue the family name. A man whose wife fails to produce sons is obligated to take a concubine. A wife or concubine must please her husband's parents. These are conservative societies. Places and obligations are traditionally defined. Government is autocratic with subjects willingly submissive. Religion is ancestor worship or a derived polytheism.

The *mother-son* axis is exemplified by the Hindus. Passive dependence on maternal care persists as a world view. Although the adult culture is male-centered, children are left largely to the care of the women's side of the household. The father is a minor and often remote figure in the child's world. In religion, there are numerous female deities: Kali, Durga, Radha, Sita, Parvati, and others. Ramakrishna noted that the "God lover finds pleasure in addressing the Deity as Mother" (Hsu, 1961, p. 430). Dependence on the supernatural is like that of a baby on its mother. Rituals are forms of ingratiation to win favors. The ultimate bliss is felt to be reunion with the One.

The *husband-wife* axis is especially evident in Europe, where the husband dominates, and in the United States, where there is a closer approximation to equality. Boys and girls seek their mates largely on their own responsibility, and in the climate of romantic love. The young couple may not meet their in-law parents until after the engagement or sometimes until the marriage. Each individual man is on his own; he does not expect his family to make his way for him. Freedom and self-reliance are very important. Conflict between generations is frequent. Social change is readily advanced. Religious denominations multiply as each person asserts his right to make or adopt his own creed.

The *brother-brother* axis Hsu finds mainly in Africa, but it might well characterize also such American Indians as the Comanche. Boys at an early age leave the parental home to live with peers of about their own age. Blood-brother rites bind pairs and initiation ceremonies induct into more mature stages. Secret societies are common. Whereas the main links in the father-son pattern stretch across the generations, those of the brother-brother pattern reach out to include contemporaries. Sibling rivalry becomes competition for prestige or leadership in the gang. With less need to emphasize ties to the past or future, these cultures have been less likely to develop written languages.

It is not necessary to regard the four proposed types as "pure" or even as the best possible classification. What is evident is another application of the S-P-A formula: The structure of family obligations develops corresponding processes of interaction and consequent personality patterns.

So simple a variable as the size of the family unit has implications for attitude development. The large extended family does not put so heavy a bur-
den of work on the one mother; more adults share in child-care; it can consequently be more indulgent (Hsu, 1961, p. 359). Children who are given this
more attentive and happier childhood grow into adults who regard the universe as more benevolent. Whiting (1959) finds that societies which raise
children more permissively are not afraid of ghosts at funerals. But the extended family tends also to preserve tradition. Grandparents, aunts, and uncles keep the immediate parents from radical innovation in dealing with children. Free expression of children's aggressive impulses is less tolerable in the
crowded setting of the extended family. One study (Whiting, 1961) shows
that in two-parent households only 25 percent were "severe" in restricting
aggression by children, while 92 percent of extended families were above the
median in this kind of control. Children who are inhibited in expression of
aggression in childhood become adults who are unlikely to approve aggressive action within the in-group. Wright (1954) showed that this attitude is
reflected in folk tales. Societies which are strict in repressing children's aggression are more apt to tell tales in which an aggressive actor is a stranger
or in which the in-group hero is aggressive only toward out-group enemies.

Another reaction to over-strict control is a sense, in children, that they
have been unjustly treated. They resent the punishments and feel justified in
some acts of compensation or retaliation. Societies which are severe in weaning and in punishment of children have been found to be high in frequency
of theft (Hsu, 1961, p. 373). This is probably related to the fact, important
particularly in understanding delinquency, that offenders often come from
homes where punishment has been severe.

The extended family—as in the old Chinese culture—seems to reduce the
likelihood of intense emotional relationships with any one member. The boy
can pattern himself in part after several male models. The girl's frustrations
within the household do not all stem from her mother. In the old Samoan
society (Mead, 1928) children felt they "belonged" in the homes of aunts
and uncles as well as with their own parents; hence when relationships at
home became uncomfortable, they had well-accepted places of refuge. Oedipus and Electra complexes seem less likely to arise in cultures which enable children to have warm dependent relationships with a number of adults
of opposite sex.

Other determinants of culture

Psychologists and psychiatrists have explored especially the child-rearing
practices and their connection with cultural patterns, but other factors also
exert strong influence. Geographic location affects the way men make a living

and this, in turn, is intimately related to their customs, recreation, worship, and the traits they try to develop in children.

A settled population, living by cultivation of plants and animal husbandry, is likely to develop different character ideals and social relationships. Here, children must work in the fields or tend herds. They must be obedient, reliable, and industrious. Presumably these societies will develop standards of child behavior different from those of the nomadic hunters.

A test of this hypothesis is summarized in Abstract 20.

Another indication of the way its economy influences a culture is found in the use of dreams. Hsu (1961, p. 326) has shown that hunting and fishing societies, in which men are very dependent on luck, usually (80 percent) regard dreams as communication with supernatural powers while among more settled and secure agricultural communities, only 20 percent did so.

As societies find or develop techniques of food production which raise them above a subsistence level, other activities emerge. Arts and crafts progress to a higher level than is possible when all efforts are devoted to the struggle for survival. Political relationships likewise become more elaborate when food production can sustain a larger superstructure.

The conditions of life of Bushmen on the Kalahari desert of Southwest Africa are almost unbelievably difficult (Thomas, 1959). They are always hungry, and, during most of the year, also thirsty. They get moisture only by eating plants that survive the hot drought. When nights grow cold, lacking warm clothes and having little fuel, they huddle together for comfort. They have no spare energy for fighting among themselves. They share possessions freely to avoid envy of one by others. Theft is unknown. Danger is met by escape rather than aggressive attack. Thus, moral values reflect the economic necessities.

The system of distributing whatever goods are produced also has ethical implications. In some cultures when one person kills a large animal or raises a large crop, he shares freely with other members, expecting them to do likewise when they have good fortune. Generosity is thus a virtue. In other cultures, whatever is produced goes to a chief or council, and is redistributed in some way to the consumers. Here a premium is placed on obedience by the producers and on *noblesse oblige* for the distributors. In economies where individuals bargain in a market, those persons who are most successful and admired are shrewd and crafty. The skills of salesmanship rate high in the marketing orientation (Fromm, 1955).

Abstract 20

TITLE   Relation of Child Training to Subsistence Economy

AUTHORS   Herbert Barry III, Irvin L. Child, and Margaret K. Bacon

PROBLEM   To explore the relationship of a culture's type of subsistence economy to its emphases in child training.

SUBJECTS   The 104 societies studied were selected from categorizations by Murdock and by Bacon and Barry. Those societies categorized as *high* in accumulation of food were the predominantly pastoral, or predominantly agricultural combined with much animal husbandry; those classified as *low* were predominantly hunting and fishing; two intermediate types were mixed and tending toward either high or low.

PROCEDURE   Two judges rated the societies on strength of socialization as expressed in rewards and punishments, and the sum of the two judgments was used. They rated:
1. Obedience training
2. Responsibility training
3. Nurturance training—training child to be helpful toward siblings and other dependent people
4. Achievement training, usually on basis of competition or of standards of excellence
5. Self-reliance training—to be independent of others in supplying own needs
6. General independence training—broader than #5 to include all kinds of freedom from control.
The ratings were for childhood years from age 4 or 5 almost to puberty, and separate ratings were made for boys and girls. Ratings were ranked for each society so that relative emphasis would be shown within the society.

SOME FINDINGS   Responsibility and obedience were emphasized in the high accumulation economies, and achievement, self-reliance, and independence in the low. The relationships held true for both boys and girls. The following figures show the correlations of the six ratings with high accumulation of food:

	Boys	Girls
Responsibility	+.74	+.62
Obedience	+.50	+.59
Nurturance	−.01	+.10
Achievement	−.60	−.62
Self-reliance	−.21	−.46
Independence	−.41	−.11

Thirty-nine of the societies at the extremes showed scores in the expected direction; only seven showed high accumulation with individualistic assertion or low accumulation with compliance.

SOURCE: *American Anthropologist,* 1959, LX:51-63.

Change in the economic base of a culture brings corresponding changes in most other aspects and, of course, in the typical personality which the culture forms. History affords numerous illustrations—a British town before and after the industrial revolution; a New England community before, during, and after the dominance of whaling; a southern town during slavery and after its end; or the emergence of a California city from frontier days to its modern patterns of life. The historian, Frederick Jackson Turner (1921) developed a famous interpretation of American culture and character, based on the influence of our frontier. Individualism, independence, egalitarianism, enterprise, expansionism, neighborly cooperation, and international isolationism were all fostered by pioneer conditions.

Anthropologists have provided a case study (Linton, Kardiner, 1939) of two cousin-tribes. They were once much alike in their dry-rice economy, their communal sharing, their family life and religion. One community remained in this state and serves as a kind of control. The other turned to cultivation of rice in the rich flooded area. With the change in economic activity and the introduction of private property the tribal unity waned; a youth problem emerged; with new insecurities, even the gods became threatening. Indeed whenever cultures become more fragmented into special-interest groups, the disintegration seems to arouse increased terror of sorcery.

A more typical instance of cultural change has been reported from Nigeria by Margaret Mead (1955). In many parts of the modern world an advanced technology impinges upon a well-organized primitive culture. The coming of the British administrators and the building of a railroad upset the old prestige hierarchy and the marriage system, destroying the morale of a people. Disputes were no longer settled by the traditional rites, and the elders lost authority. Wives were no longer acquired by the sanctioned process; consequently some children were regarded as illegitimate. Ensuing epidemics, crop failures, and other misfortunes were viewed by many as the revenge of the powerful elders.

In the preceding example, economic change was accompanied by political change. Recognition that a changed form of government may result in changed attitudes is at least as old as Herodotus who wrote: "While they were under despotic rulers the Athenians were no better in war than any of their neighbors, yet once they got quit of despots they were far and away the first of all. . . . While they were oppressed they willed to be craven, as men working for a master, but when they were freed, each one was zealous to achieve for himself." In the newly liberated colonial peoples, we see a similar psychological change.

An interesting example of the effect of political structure on character has been described by Haring (1953). Japanese have been consistently described as formal, rigid, and almost compulsive. This has not so often been related to their three centuries of police tyranny. On one island—Amami Oshima—a population of Japanese descent has lived free from political dictatorship. Here one discovers the people to be more relaxed, more spontaneous, and freer in interpersonal relations.

The Gestalt of a culture is best expressed in its characteristic "style." Kardiner (1954) has described the Comanches as giving children a high degree of security which then led to little anxiety despite the actual dangers of adult life. The 'Comanche Indian babies were welcome; there were few taboos about birth (or disposal of the after-birth); the cradle-board kept the child so close to the mother, they were fed whenever hungry; fathers tended to "spoil" children; there was no anxiety about eating, defecating or sex play in childhood. The adolescent boys banded together in a close brotherhood. Spoils of hunting were fairly divided. There was little prestige hierarchy and that for only a limited time. The adult culture included much cooperation, extending even to wife-sharing. The Comanche religion included no malevolent magic and no ingratiating procedures. There was no concept of misfortune as punishment because this was not the pattern of childhood relation to parents.

Contrast this with the culture of Alors (DuBois, 1944). Here the mother cares for her infant for only a fortnight; then returns to work in the fields. Most babies are brought up by older siblings who freely tease them. They arouse maternal solicitude only when they are sick. What does this mean for the adult culture? The basic mood of interpersonal relations is one of distrust and suspicion. Even sex relations are distorted by selfishness and disputes. Folk tales show hatred of parents. Sorcery is an important element of religion. Illness is very prominent.

Sometimes the integration and style of a culture enables it to resist the impact of the customs of their neighbors. The long survival of enclaves of Shakers and Mennonites within the American social scene has been due to the powerful cohesive influence of their way of life, with their religion as the most integrative force. In her *Patterns of Culture* (1934); Ruth Benedict has described the culture of the Pueblo Indians as "Apollonian," with the implication of sanity, balance, reason and moderation. All around them were neighboring tribes whose lifestyle was "Dionysian," built of famine and feast, hardship and orgies, dull routines and ecstatic rites. Usually, ways of living tend to spread to neighboring cultures, a process called diffusion. The Dionysian ceremonies, however, were rejected by the Pueblos. Exposure to the activities of another culture does not automatically mean incorporation of what that culture offers. Artifacts and institutions and beliefs diffuse only if they are compatible with and acceptable to the older culture. The Pueblos were insulated from influence because of the cohesive power of their different style which integrated much of their lives. Rorschach tests given to Hopi Indians (Thompson, 1950) confirmed the Benedict hypothesis of Apollonian character. The young people tested were found to be restrained, disciplined, and cautious, but still reasonably imaginative and able to enjoy pleasure in moderation.

Some cultures are generally relaxed and easy-going, with little anxiety in practical affairs or in religion. Others are tense, apprehensive, and worried over both daily troubles and the dangers of witchcraft and evil spirits. Some, like the industrialized West, are energetically innovative; others still see "nothing new under the sun."

NATIONAL CHARACTER

Observers who have lived for a time in England, France, Germany, and Italy have little doubt about typical differences in outlook and response among the people in those countries and see them as different again from Japanese or Americans.

A concept of "national character" is vulnerable to grave misinterpretations. One is racist. The Nazis represented this error at its worst. They taught that Germans were biologically gifted with desirable traits which other nationalities lacked. Hence they saw themselves as a "Master Race." The racist connotation of nationality can be found also in such writers as Count de Gobineau (1855), Madison Grant (1916), Houston Stewart Chamberlain (1925), and Lothrop Stoddard (1920), all of whom saw the Nordics, and especially the Teutons, as innately superior to all the races of darker complexion. They attributed most of the ills of social change to failure to keep the chosen racial stock pure and dominant.

Anthropology has shown many instances of peoples alike in race but different in culture. Benedict's (1934) description of southwestern Indians is one example. The South Sea Islanders (Mead, 1928) furnish another. Biesheuvel (1950) describes two Bantu groups in Africa: the Pedi who are punitive, conformist, and warlike; the Lovendu who reject corporal punishment, love peace, and cultivate individuality. LeVine (1960) reports the Gusii as authoritarian and the Nuer as egalitarian. We noted earlier that there has been noticeable change in attitudes from the warrior Vikings to the rather complacent life of modern Scandinavia.

The concept of national character does make sense when we recognize many forms of personality-shaping activity which do correspond to national boundaries. Insofar as members of one nation differ from members of other nations in the language they speak, the newspapers they read and trust, the literature they value, the stories they tell children, the films they see, the heroes they celebrate, their understanding of history, the goods they make and consume, the arts they cultivate, the government which they obey, and the religion they follow, they will become different kinds of persons. Not all will be alike, but their modal (most common) personality pattern will have some features arising from these shared interactions. Their generally accepted practices and ideals will show the influence of communications which affect them inside the national boundaries. The kind of person who rises to prominence and is accorded general admiration may be sharply different in two tribes or nations which otherwise have much in common.

Many Americans believe that the big differences between life in this country and life in communist nations result in basic personality contrasts.

Gorer's analysis of Russian character (1949) connects the tight swaddling of infants with the submissiveness of the Russian people to dictatorship by czars or commissars. A much more enlightening, although more complex, analysis is one derived from intensive examination of life histories of individual Russians, as conducted by the Harvard Project in the Soviet Social System. Adult refugees of varying social position have been studied, and it is apparent that individual Russian personalities vary widely. One published account (Bauer, 1953) presents Colonel Kamen of the Red Army, an authoritarian elitist, cherishing his own independence, with very little ideological commitment, and the quite different humanitarian Chestny, who joined the Komsomols, strove for Soviet ideals, and became a member of the Communist party. He refers to "love for mankind and some sort of an invisible, undeveloped Christianity," which, he adds, may be "invisible under the cloak of Marxism." Of course, the fact that the individuals studied have all been defectors limits the usefulness of any generalizations for understanding the more typical Soviet citizens who remain loyal.

Watson, in a study not previously published, analyzed the characters and themes in six novels widely read in the Soviet Union around 1960. The heroes and heroines were predominantly innovators in science and technology. They were devoted to the popular welfare. The villains were frequently officious bureaucrats, selfish schemers, or persons like the professor who had done all his creative work many years before but who tended, by virtue of his prestige, to hamper the creative work of youth. Love interest was much less evident than it is in American novels or would have been in Russian literature of the nineteenth century. The dramatic conflicts were generally related to social change, with the reactionaries eventually vanquished and the innovators victorious. Education was seen as a major factor in changing the lives of people, and the Communist party was usually portrayed as on the side of the angels. It is apparent that if Soviet youth are internalizing the values expressed in these novels, their national character will be quite different from that of the Russians portrayed by Chekhov and Tolstoy.

A thoughtful attempt to compare values in several cultures has been made by Morris (1956). Considering Canada, China, India, Japan, Norway, and the United States, he finds differences along five significant dimensions of value:

1. responsible moral outlook
2. vigorous action
3. rich inner life
4. response to Nature
5. senuous self-enjoyment

He concludes: "It is as if persons in various cultures have in common five major tones in the musical scales on which they compose different melodies" (p. 185).

Cultures change

The national character of one era cannot safely be projected into the future. We referred earlier in this chapter to the transformation of the Betsileo when a new pattern of growing rice was adopted, and to the effects of British conquest on the Tiv culture.

In a broader sense, the contemporary Greeks exemplify little of either the classic Athenian or Spartan character. The Portuguese, once intrepid explorers, have almost ceased to venture forth. Modern Italy is not organized by Roman patterns. The peaceful Scandinavians were once the militant Vikings. One must view national character as changing along the dimension of time. In the last chapter we shall discuss in more detail the processes by which cultures change and some of the resulting stresses on personality.

EVALUATION OF CULTURES

Is it possible to describe some cultures—certain ways of life—as clearly superior to others? We may have our personal preferences, usually choosing the culture in which we have spent most of our lives, but is there any objective basis for describing some cultures as "better" or "higher" than others? Do some cultures more fully develop the potential of personality?

In the last analysis, it is impossible to make any completely objective judgment about the goodness of a culture. As an extreme example, if some society should adopt universal infanticide and thus exterminate itself, would that be "bad"? Only on our assumption—not shared by the other society—that survival is valuable. Whatever we may admire in a strange culture is approved because *we* value it on the basis of *our* upbringing. The other culture may or may not agree. Whatever we condemn necessarily reflects *our* values.

Given even a slight measure of agreement on a few rather obvious values, fairly objective comparisons become possible. For example, if it is granted as desirable that human life should continue, we can then criticize policies that we believe to be mass-suicidal, like those involved in tendencies toward the spread of lethal radiation. If it is agreed that it is good to survive and better to live in harmony than to suffer conflict, a number of cross-cultural principles emerge. They are quite formal—not dependent on any particular form of economy, family life, language, education, art, government or religion. They are very nearly transcultural axioms.

1. *A culture is better than others if it meets more effectively the basic organic needs of most members on at least a minimum level.*

If the human organism is not given enough food, water, and oxygen it cannot survive. Deprived of sleep or subjected to intense cold or poisoned by drugs, humans being suffer and die. Needs for some self-respect, some sexual relations, for some kind of communication and companionship, and for new and zestful experiences may be less acute than the obvious physical necessities, but a culture denies them at its peril.

2. *A culture is better if it does not foster in childhood strong behavior patterns which later have to be abruptly denied and broken down.*

All cultures, to some extent, differentiate the roles of children from those of adults. Children are necessarily dependent and it would seem sensible gradually to foster the independence demanded of adults. A sharp break— fully dependent this year and completely on his own next year—severely strains human adaptability. The expectation that a child who is overindulged should suddenly become a parent capable of subordinating his own gratifications is likely to be disappointed.

3. *A culture is better if it provides most members with means to realize the ambitions it instills.*

If a culture encourages most people to believe they need and must have things which only a few can obtain, then it fosters discontent. It encourages delinquent detours to cbtain what cannot be acquired legitimately. It fosters anomie and the rejection of its norms and way of life.

4. *A culture is better if it fosters compatible general attitudes in its various sectors.*

If some institutions of a culture encourage scientific ways of thinking and recommend these methods as generally valid, while other institutions urge reliance upon unquestioning acceptance of dogma, some conflict can be predicted. A culture that teaches love of fellow men but gives its major rewards to those who exploit their fellows, will find itself in trouble. If one sector is taught not to tolerate behavior which other sectors are taught to believe desirable—for example, the hostility of many communities toward certain deviate religious minorities—conflict seems inevitable. Many youngsters are attracted by gang activities which are sanctioned by their own neighborhood but punished by the representatives of the larger community.

A particularly important contradiction exists between rigidity and progress. A static society may glorify its traditional institutions, but if one sector of a culture is dedicated to research, innovation, and rapid obsolescence, while other sectors try to hold fast to the old ways, some values will have to suffer.

5. *A culture is better if it minimizes conflicts between roles.*

If a culture tells mothers they should stay at home and care for young children but makes it necessary for them to work away from the children eight hours a day, it is creating dissatisfaction. A graduate student who is "expected" to spend full time at study and likewise "expected" to earn enough to support his wife and child, feels the incompatibility of his roles. A senator who is supposed to act on the principles of his own conscience and judgment, but who must keep the support of his constituency in order to be reelected runs into another role-conflict. Another role-conflict is that facing sincere Christians asked to support destructive armaments.

6. *A culture is better if its members can correctly predict much of their own behavior and that of other members.*

In a strong culture, the parts must be articulated. Members must have the reassurance of knowing approximately what to expect in common situations. The quite unpredictable members are regarded as "insane," are segregated, and given special care. To the extent that collective actions bring the expected results, the culture is healthy; if action is initiated to satisfy certain desires and it does not do so, the result is frustration and resentment. Superstitions that lead members to expect that which does not happen are not very viable.

7. *A culture is better if it makes possible communication among those who must collaborate.*

The Tower of Babel remains an impressive parable of the consequences of trying to work together without a common language. Institutions which keep interdependent people from interacting—"Iron Curtains" or "Golden Curtains"—bring about actions which may disintegrate the culture and perhaps all the world around. In our world of many diverse cultures, recently brought into close proximity, that culture which can best initiate and sustain genuine communication with others, has the best chance for world leadership.

SUMMARY

Culture—the composite of all the man-made objects, economic practices, child-rearing activities, political forms, customs, values, art, science, myths, literature, knowledge, and religion characteristic of a society—profoundly influences personality development.

The findings from different cultures challenge the view of original nature and the instinct theories popular half-a-century ago. "You can't change human nature" has been the axiom of conservatives, but personality and attitudes differ in different cultures and change as the cultures change.

The various features of a culture are not wholly independent; they are integrated in a characteristic Gestalt. The language men speak affects their way of perceiving the world; the way men earn their living results in a common outlook for those in similar occupations. A central determining factor in any cultural Gestalt is the child-rearing practices. They determine, and are in turn, reinforced by the adult attitudes.

Similarities among the citizens of a particular nation are not racially determined but flow from the influence of the common language, newspapers, television programs, stories told to children, heroic figures, goods consumed, government, and religion.

Cultures are better if they: meet the organic needs of members; have similar value patterns for youth and adults; provide means for all members to meet the goals they inculcate; foster compatible attitudes in various parts of the culture; minimize role-conflict; and facilitate communication and predictable behaviors among members.

CHAPTER 9

Socioeconomic Class

Within any broad, inclusive "culture" there are subcultures which also exert a distinctive influence on their members. The most powerful of these are socioeconomic classes.

The idea of class differences is as old as recorded history. "Now in all states there are three elements: one class is very rich, another very poor, and a third in the mean." So observed Aristotle, in his *Politics*, many centuries before capitalism or socialism had taken form. Aristotle noted also that each class develops a characteristic social outlook. "Those who have too much of the goods of fortune, strength, wealth, friends, and the like are neither willing nor able to submit to authority. The evil begins at home; for when they are boys, by reason of the luxury in which they are brought up, they never learn, even at school, the habit of obedience. On the other hand, the very poor, who are in the opposite extreme, are too degraded. So that the one class cannot obey, and can only rule despotically; the other knows not how to command and must be ruled like slaves. Thus arises a city, not of free men, but of masters and slaves; the one despising, the other envying." Aristotle saw most hope for a rational outlook in the middle class.

When the Declaration of Independence was proclaimed, Adam Smith, an English economist who is sometimes regarded as the father of capitalist theory, was writing an analysis which sounds much like that made by Karl Marx some generations later. "The whole annual produce of the land and labour of every country, or what comes to the same thing, the whole price of that annual produce, naturally divides itself, it has already been observed, into three parts: the rent of the land, the wages of labour, and the profits of stock; and constitutes a revenue to three different orders of people; to those who live by rent, to those who live by wages, and to those who live by profit. There are the three great, original and constituent orders of every civilized society, from whose revenue that of every other order is ultimately derived" (1776). Adam Smith, like Aristotle, had doubts about the wisdom and virtue of the ruling class. Merchants and manufacturers, he observed, usually concentrate more on making profits for themselves than on the general welfare.

In the first section of the *Communist Manifesto*, issued in 1847, Marx and

Engels gave the doctrine of class conflict its classic statement:

The history of all hitherto existing society is the history of class struggles. Free-man and slave, patrician and plebeian, lord and serf, guild-master and journey-man—in a word, oppressor and oppressed—stood in constant opposition to one another, carried on an uninterrupted, now hidden, now open fight, a fight that each time ended, either in a revolutionary reconstitution of society at large, or in the common ruin of the contending classes. . . .

The modern bourgeois society that has sprouted from the ruins of feudal society has not done away with class antagonisms. It has but established new classes, new conditions of oppression, new forms of struggle in place of the old ones.

Our epoch, the epoch of the bourgeoisie, has simplified the class antagonism. Society as a whole is more and more splitting up into two great hostile camps, into two great classes directly facing each other—bourgeoisie and proletariat. . . . The executive of the modern State is but a committee for managing the common affairs of the whole bourgeoisie.

Marx defined "class" by relation to the processes of production. Owners derive their income from what they have; workers derive theirs from the work they do. A more common idea is to think of class in terms of amount of income: rich, average or poor. Yet people distinguish between economic class and social class. The graph of self-designated social class is symmetrical (Figure 9-1) that of self-named economic class is skewed toward more in low-income categories (Wallace, Williams, Cantril, 1944).

If, instead of asking people to classify themselves, we ask them to tell us about the classes of people who live in their community, another set of results is found. This prestige criterion has been the one most widely used by social psychologists. It was used by Davis and his associates to study a Southern town (1941), by Warner to study "Yankee City" (1941-1945) and "Jones-ville" (1949), and by Hollingshead to study "Elmtown" (1949).

People seem to agree on their identification of fellow citizens who belong in upper, middle, or lower strata. In "Jonesville," ten informants mentioned 340 different persons as they talked with the interviewer. There were 426 instances in which two or more informants mentioned the same individual. The informants agreed on the "class" in 95 percent of the cases. "Class" is obviously apparent to the typical citizen. The status of a family probably depends partly on their income, partly on the house and neighborhood where they live, partly on their family history in the community, partly on their dress, moral conduct, social participation, speech, and education.

Six prestige classes have been commonly discerned:

About 1% Upper-upper (wealth and distinguished lineage)
About 2% Lower-upper (wealth and prestige)
About 11% Upper-middle (important business and professional)
About 28% Lower-middle (white collar, small business, skilled workmen)
About 33% Upper-lower (semi-skilled and service employees)

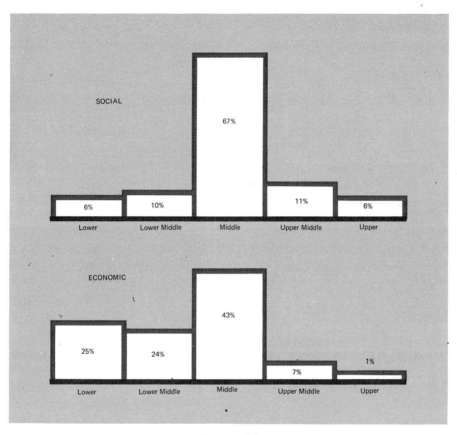

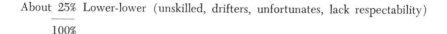

FIGURE 9-1

About 25% Lower-lower (unskilled, drifters, unfortunates, lack respectability)

100%

The perspective in which these classes are viewed depends on the status of the viewer. A typical member of the upper-lower class will be conscious of a sharp gulf between himself and the destitute, shiftless lower-lowers, but will tend to telescope the more remote upper-middle, lower-upper and upper-upper, regarding them all as rich and snobbish. A typical member of the lower-upper class may not differentiate the upper-lower from the lower-lower—they are all "poor people living in run-down neighborhoods."

Still another approach to the definition of classes is the use of attitudes as the determining factor. People whose opinions, interests, and tastes are similar are regarded as belonging to a given class.

A cross section of American male adults was asked by Centers (1949), "In deciding whether a person belongs to your class or not, which of these things do you think it most important to know: What his family is; how much money he has; what sort of education he has; or how he believes and feels about certain things?" The most frequent response (47 percent) referred to beliefs and feelings. Education (29 percent), family (29 percent), and money (17 percent) were seen as less vital (p. 91).

Lazarsfeld (cited by Lipset, Bendix, 1951) found that in 1948 one's attitude toward the controversial Taft-Hartley Act, designed to restrict trade unions, was a better index of objective class position than was a direct question about the class in which an individual believed he should be placed.

Other indices of class have included residential section, type of home, automobile owned, speech (as illustrated in England by Shaw's *Pygmalion*), and dress (blue-collar used to indicate manual labor). A major consideration in upper class families is that children should marry at or above their present class level.

All of these ways of stratifying an industrial society have a large measure of overlap. The large stockholder in one or more corporations would rate as "upper" by his income level, his self-ascription, his reputation, his ownership, his attitudes and interests. The wage earner in a small factory would be at working-class level in his actual earnings, his way of making his living, his status as seen by others, his views of himself, and his core of attitudes, opinions, and tastes. Correlations among five factors—prestige of occupation, average I.Q. of members of an occupation, years of schooling of those in the occupation, average income of the occupation, and restriction of size of family—range from .81 to .95, indicating that all five measure very much the same thing (Cattell, 1942). When a list of 26 occupations was rated for prestige by graduate students and by skilled and unskilled laborers, the agreement was high (correlation coefficient of .94). For both groups, physicians and bankers were high; farmers and policemen were near the middle; unskilled, casual laborers and unemployed men were at the bottom.

Using this core of agreement on what is meant by upper, middle or lower classes, we turn to exploration of ways in which the class structure affects processes of interaction and so molds distinctive attitudes.

Differences among classes in patterns of parent-child relationships have been reported in many studies, but there is always overlap and the patterns change over time. In general, corporal punishment is more frequent in lower-class homes; reliance on pride and shame (Super-ego controls) more frequently is found in middle and upper classes (Davis, 1944, 1950). Kohn (1959) found more emphasis on obedience and neatness in lower-class homes; more concern for the child's happiness and intellectual growth at higher class levels. Nye (1951) reported generation conflict between parents and adolescents causing trouble in 42 percent of lower class homes but in only 15 percent of upper class families.

Several studies have shown that the conditions of lower-class life may impede normal intellectual development. A report to the American Orthopsychiatric Association (Knoblock, Pasamanick, 1960) indicated that of 300 Baltimore babies, all normal at birth, those living in lower-class homes would, on the average, be noticeably retarded by the age of three. The retarding homes had more illness; the mother was more likely to be working, and there was less stimulus to intellectual growth. A comparison of two nursery schools (Gesell, Lord, 1929) showed that the children in a lower-class neighborhood whose mothers had to go to work each day were less well developed in speech and in play initiative. Nutritional differences play some part, but cultural deprivation seems to be the major factor. Welfare and educational projects such as "Headstart" (inaugurated in some cities in 1965) help to make up for early handicaps, but age 4 may be too late.

School experience and social class

The public school is a curious class hybrid. The School Board members who control its policies come largely from the upper-middle (72 percent in three cities) or lower-upper (16 percent) class. They are men (and a few energetic women) of considerable influence in the community. The principal school administrator—the superintendent—is usually a member of the Rotary Club and associates with the leading business and professional families. The school teachers are regarded as middle class (96 percent), although some of them have risen from farm or city working-class homes. Two-thirds of the elementary school pupils come from working class or lower-lower-class homes. The school is thus controlled by the uppers, taught by the middles, and attended mainly by the lowers. Attitudes characteristic of each group may well be in conflict with the other two. According to Allison Davis, "Our public schools for the lowest third of our population, the schools in slums, are almost a complete failure. The staffs of these schools generally are aware of their basic failure and are demoralized" (Davis, 1950). This is true of the shabby rural schools for children of tenant farmers as well as of the "blackboard jungles" of the big cities.

The most impressive study of how social class operates in the public schools of a typical American community is "Elmtown's Youth." Upper-class pupils are more apt to take the college preparatory course, to get good grades, to obtain personal counsel from teachers on school work, to join music organizations, to attend athletic and social events, and to be chosen for the Student Council. The lowest group—Class 5—commonly take a trade or domestic science course; have the highest proportion of failures; get counsel mainly as discipline problems; seldom participate in athletic, musical, or social affairs or student government; are much more likely to drop out before graduation. Some 60 percent of Class 1 and 2 (Highest) belong to the Boy Scouts or Camp Fire girls; only 1 percent of Class 5. In the higher classes, 74 percent went to church; only 19 percent of Class 5 attended church. Each class chose about 75 percent of friends from the same socioeconomic class.

More of Class 1 and 2 went bowling; more of Class 4 and 5 went roller skating or to public dance halls.

Some of the stories make the class distinctions in Elmtown more vivid. When the principal of the high school started a campaign against tardiness by detaining late pupils after school, he was obstructed in enforcing this regulation against the upper-class pupils: they usually had excuses which would get them out of detention—Kathy getting her hair done; Frank driving up late in his father's Cadillac. "The idea is all right," said the Superintendent, "but it won't work in every case." When "Boney" Johnson, a boy of lower status (Class 4), tried to evade detention, however, the principal's anger was unrestrained. He ridiculed Boney's neat appearance ("Pretty boy!") and later engaged in a fight in which he pulled the pupil's cap over his eyes and struck the boy three times with the heel of his hand against the base of the skull. "Nothing came of it, except—Boney quit school," a report of the incident concluded.

Studies have demonstrated further that the most important single factor affecting the child's reading level in elementary school is the socioeconomic class of parents (Barton, Wilder, 1964). Thirty-three percent of the teachers who taught classes in which the majority of the pupils come from lower working-class homes reported average reading retardation of one year or more. The corresponding percentages of retardation were 10 percent for upper working-class areas, 6 percent for middle-class groups, and only 3 percent in upper-class regions. Retardation in reading was found to increase over time in schools serving children from the working class. The proportion of teachers who taught pupils from lower working-class areas who reported retardation in reading of a year or more was 4 percent in first grade, 16 percent in second grade, 32 percent in third grade, 50 percent in fourth grade, and 60 percent in fifth grade. Reading advancement of a year or more was reported by 10 percent of teachers whose pupils were largely lower working class as contrasted with 41 percent of middle-class pupils and 66 percent of upper-class pupils. The differences lies not so much in what is done in the classroom as in the activities, possessions, and values of the home.

The fact that intelligence test scores are generally lower in the poorer neighborhoods is often used to explain the school failures. Davis contends (1950, p. 45) that at least part of the variation in test performance is due to selection of items which upper-class pupils have more chance to learn; e.g., what a "sonata" is. Conceivably, a vocabulary test might be developed which contained the argot of a slum neighborhood and which would handicap the upper-class children. Is it not arbitrary to call either examination a measure of "native intelligence"? Since what children feel important differs in different subcultures, what they know and can do, will also vary with the subcultures of socioeconomic class. There can be no culture-free test which will measure innate ability apart from the influence of up-bringing.

The most important fact, however, is that despite all the handicaps, many children from lower-class homes do attain high levels of achievement. One of the authors, in a preface to Frank Riessman's *The Culturally Deprived Child* wrote: "The great reservoir of undiscovered and undeveloped intellectual talent in America is not in upper-class or middle-class neighborhoods." Because there are so many more children in working-class homes than in the homes of professional men or business leaders (about 15 or 20 to 1), even if the *proportion* of intellectually gifted youngsters is lower in the less advantaged group, the actual numbers are greater. In a study (Byrns, Henmon, 1936) of seniors in Wisconsin high schools, the proportion with IQ's over 120 was 25 percent of pupils whose parents were in the professions, and 12 percent of those whose parents were unskilled laborers. Another study (Eels, 1951) shows IQ's over 120 in 40 percent of the "high status" homes and in 11 percent of the "low status" homes. If we applied this ratio to "Yankee City" (Warner *et al.*), where 3 percent of the population were "upper class" and 58 percent "lower class," we would find 12 percent of all "gifted" children coming from upper-class homes and 64 percent from lower-class homes.

With increased opportunities and attention, the proportion might be much higher. The principle of "compensatory spending" (Conant, 1964) is being gradually accepted, helping to reverse the still common situation in which children from the best homes and neighborhood are provided also with the best schools and teachers.

As we go up from elementary school to college, each year shows a larger proportion of children from homes of professional, proprietor, and managerial groups (Mulligan, 1951). School performance of children from what are now called "disadvantaged" homes is affected by many handicaps. Motivation is often weak; more school seems unnecessary to many parents in need of the dollars a working teenager might earn. Parents who have been able to earn an adequate livelihood despite limited schooling may see little use in study. Homes are not equipped with encyclopedias or dictionaries. School curricula are often remote from the urgent concerns of modern life. Neighbors and friends reinforce values which are antiacademic. Rogoff's (1960) study showed that the achievement of pupils is strongly affected by the socioeconomic class of their schoolmates. "No matter how privileged or underprivileged the kind of family from which they come, high school seniors at least double their chances of scoring in the top fourth in aptitude if they attend a school where most of their classmates are from the upper strata."

Attendance at college has become increasingly important as a prerequisite for all professional and high managerial positions. A study (Warner *et al.*, 1944, p. 52) of high school students with IQ's of 110 or over showed that if socioeconomic status were above average, 93 percent finished high school and 57 percent went on to college. If the homes were below average, only 72 percent finished high school and only 13 percent went on to college. One study (Sibley, 1942) indicated that college attendance could be much better predicted from the occupational status of the father than from the high IQ of the pupil. In Milwaukee, Helen Goetsch found among 1,023 high school graduates with IQ's over 117, if the family income was more than $8,000 (in the 1930s) *all* the graduates went on to college. Among the equally bright graduates from low income homes, only about 25 percent were able to go to college full time (Goetsch, 1939).

Acceptance in college, success in academic pursuits and in campus social life are generally higher for the students from homes of higher socioeconomic class. A study at the University of Indiana (Mueller, 1940) of 1,600 women students showed that if father was in a large business, 90 percent were in sororities; if father was a farmer or a semiskilled worker, only 17 percent were in sororities. Social honors (Prom Queen, Homecoming Queen, etc.) were five times as likely to go to the daughter of a prominent businessman as to the daughter of a farmer or worker. The index of academic honors was 144 for students from homes of the professional class, 128 for those from the big business category, but only 94 for those from homes of farmers or semiskilled workmen.

The school and college system is for some students a ladder by which they climb to a status above that of their parents. For many more, however, the trip through high school and college is on a ticket providing first-class, second-class, or third-class accommodations, depending on the socioeconomic class status of the home.

Participation in other organizations

We have examined the important influence of social class upon the kind of experience boys and girls have in school. The same kind of differences emerge in other organizations outside the school. The summary of *Elmtown's Youth* presented earlier in this chapter shows that youth organizations fail to reach the lower-class adolescents.

A study (Bonney, 1942) of sociometric choices of second grade children in several Texas schools showed that peer preference correlated .52 with parental occupational status. A measure of how much parents participated in community life (this is a fair index of class status except for the small number of upper-uppers who may hold aloof) correlated .62 with the popularity of their second grade children. The tendency of all children to admire and approve children from higher status homes is supported by another study (Warner *et al.*, 1949). Fifth and sixth grade children in midwestern "Hometown" were asked to guess who was meant by the statement: "Here is someone who is thought to be very goodlooking" or, at another point in the questionnaire, "Here is someone whom most people think not goodlooking at all." A child from the top social class group (upper-middle) was chosen as "goodlooking" about 20 times as often, on the average, as was a child from the lowest (lower-lower) class. The "not goodlooking" child was most often from the lower-lowers; least often from the upper-middles.

Most studies show children choosing their best friends on the basis of propinquity (Chapter 2). Although a school class may include children from different neighborhoods, the out-of-school contacts usually have more influence. One investigator (Cook, 1945) found that in a junior high school about 75 percent of the seventh grade students chose friends from their own social class—upper, middle or lower. In this school the teachers tried deliberately to democratize the friendship relations. Pupils were selected across class lines to work together on committees and projects. The students were tested again when they left junior high school: About 65 percent of the choices fell within the class of the chooser. Thus a school integration policy, carried on over several years, could make only a slight impression on the social attitudes formed by out-of-school associations.

Maas (1951) has called attention to differential *styles* of participation related to socioeconomic class. He finds lower-class boys and girls in clubs relating, with dependence or counter-dependence, mainly to the adult leader. Middle-class youngsters are more likely to ignore the appointed leader and to pay attention mainly to their peers.

Adult participation in community organizations is also differentiated by socioeconomic class. Some organizations are intended for a specific class: trade unions are for workers; exclusive country clubs are for the select. Participation in these organizations leads to interaction with others of similar outlook, intensifies in-group solidarity, and deepens the psychological cleavages which separate social classes.

SOCIAL AND POLITICAL ATTITUDES

Few generalizations in social psychology are so well supported by many kinds of evidence as the truth that "men who live differently think differently."

Attitudes of classes on social issues derive from an historic heritage. Immediate, realistic "interests" are sometimes obscured by loyalty to honored traditions. The frightful conditions under which men, women, and children worked in the early stage of the Industrial Revolution are familiar to students of English history. It helps to understand some working-class attitudes, today, to recall that in the needle trades in New England, in the early days, women working full time could earn only about $60 in an entire year. In the shoe industry in Massachusetts, 15,000 women were employed at wages from 8 cents to 50 cents a day. Debtors were still being sent to prison. In 1832, 40 percent of the workers employed in Massachusetts factories were children under 16 years of age. In those days it was a "criminal conspiracy" to organize a trade union. After the organizers had been convicted in Pittsburgh in 1814, the local newspaper triumphantly announced: "It puts an end to those associations which have been so prejudicial to the successful enterprise of the capitalists." When the Master Carpenters in Boston began their struggle to win a ten-hour day, the employers published a statement declaring: "We cannot believe this project to have originated with any of the faithful and industrious sons of New England, but are compelled to consider it an evil of foreign growth and one which we hope and trust will not take root in the favoured soil of Massachusetts." To cut the working week to 60 hours, the employers believed, would encourage idleness, dissipation and vice.

A generation later when labor organization was gaining momentum, it was met with wage cuts, blacklisting of leaders, riots, and court injunctions. The labor movement has had its heroes, some glorified in song, like Joe Hill, many more unsung: Terence Powderly, "Mother Jones," George Henry Evans, or Eugene Debs. They seldom appear in our school history texts.

The particular issues which divide the opinions of the employing class and those of the working class have changed with time, but there are underlying attitudes which persist. The right of workers to organize, maintain, and develop unions is one such issue. On the question: "Would you agree that everybody would be happier, more secure, and more prosperous if the working people were given more power and influence in government?" 31 percent of the middle-class business, professional, and white collar workers said "yes," while 64 percent of the working-class manual workers said "yes." The view that factory workers do not get enough pay was found twice as often (37 percent) among the urban workers as among the urban middle class (18 percent) (Centers, 1949). In another poll (Kornhauser, 1939) the highest of four income groups included 28 percent who "favor strong labor unions." As income went down, this proportion rose to 84 percent in the lowest income group.

In general, organizations of the working class are in favor of public support for better housing, better schools, better health, and community recreational facilities. In 1829, the establishment of public schools headed the list of reforms urged by the Workingmen's party of Philadelphia. Five years later, the unions of The United States of America in their convention demanded an "equal, universal, republican system of education." The following year they urged free public libraries and infant schools. Social security legislation was strongly supported by labor organizations.

Opposition to taxation is greater at upper income levels. A public opinion poll (American Institute of Public Opinion, January 9, 1940) asked a sample of citizens: "Do you consider the amount of income tax which you have to pay as too high or about right?" The complaint that the tax was too high was made by 48 percent of those paying less than $50 per year; the proportion of objection increased steadily as the tax grew larger, reaching 71 percent for those paying $500 or more. Because of sales taxes, the poor may actually pay a larger proportion of their income in taxes than do most rich families (Miller, Rien, 1964).

The main target of disfavor in American society is the lower-lower class. These chronic economic failures are seen as shiftless, dirty, lazy, irresponsible, and immoral. Sensational stories about relief recipients who wear mink coats or live in comfortable hotels arouse widespread indignation; subsequent correction of misleading stories is rarely reported. Proposals that men on relief should be forced to take any kind of job, however distressing the conditions, if it pays a minimum wage, have had almost unanimous public support (American Institute of Public Opinion, January 24, 1965). A majority of the people have supported the view that unwed mothers who continue to have children should be punished by withdrawal of their relief payments (A.I.P.O., January 27, 1965).

Questioned on the "major cause of poverty," most Americans with incomes of $7,000 a year or more answer: "lack of effort." The poor, however (those with incomes under $3,000 a year), reply: "circumstances beyond our control" (A.I.P.O., December 16, 1964).

A particularly interesting study (Jones, 1941) examined attitudes of citizens in a midwestern manufacturing city shortly after the Congress of Industrial Organizations (CIO) had been organized during the 1930s. A series of situations—foreclosure on the mortgage of a poor farmer, eviction of impoverished unemployed tenants—was followed by a choice of whether to uphold traditional property rights or whether to disregard these in favor of humanitarian principles (Table 9–1).

TABLE 9–1—ATTITUDES TOWARD PROPERTY RIGHTS

Score Interval	Percent of Responses	
	C. of C.	CIO Leaders
24–32 (Strongest for property rights)	94%	5%
16–23 (More weight for property rights)	6%	11%
8–15 (More weight to humanitarian sympathy)	0	29%
0— 7 (Strongest for humanitarian sympathy)	0	55%
	100%	100%

The median position of several occupational groups was:

Chamber of Commerce	29
Farmers	20
Chemists	18
Teachers	16
Small merchants	12
Ministers	12
AFL leaders	8
CIO leaders	6

It is interesting to note that labor leaders were less uniform in outlook than were the business leaders. One reason may be that the press and radio quite consistently supported the business viewpoint. Businessmen thus experienced total support; labor representatives were exposed to counter pressures from the mass media.

Because working-class groups are strong on human sympathy and inherit a long tradition of fighting injustice, they are more prone to support drastic social reforms. Centers (1949) combined replies from questions on government ownership of industry, social security, satisfaction (or rather, dissatisfaction) with America as it is, more power for workers, and identification with workers in strikes to give an index of general "radicalism," the proportion of "radicals" among big business officials was 2 percent; among white collar workers 5 percent; among farmers 7 percent; among skilled manual workers 10 percent, and among the semiskilled or unskilled 19 percent. On issues which might admit outgroups to share in their privileges, trade unions have been divided. While some pioneered in outlawing racial discrimination, others have strongly resisted opening their ranks to blacks. Few labor organizations have been active on behalf of women's rights, and some craft unions have restricted apprenticeships to relatives of present members.

More lower-class than upper-class citizens in almost every underprivileged nation lean toward Communism. Lipset (1959) argues that higher authoritarianism in lower-class citizens arises because the lower-class child typically gets more punishment, less love and indulgence, is exposed to more quarreling at home, and so starts with a chip on his shoulder. The hostility is intensified by frustration in school and living under conditions clearly worse than those he sees others enjoying. "All of these characteristics combine to produce a tendency to view politics, as well as personal relationships, in black-and-white terms, a desire for immediate action without critical reflection, impatience with talk and discussion, lack of interest in organizations which have a long-range gradualistic political perspective, and a readiness to follow leaders who offer a demonological interpretation of the presumably conspiratorial forces." (pp. 495-6)

The most privileged classes, used to the exercising of power to work their own will, are also inclined to be impatient with democratic processes. In the early nineteenth century, de Tocqueville saw the more affluent classes with "a hearty dislike of democratic institutions," but a need to conceal their real feelings. It was the evil genius of Hitler in the 1930s that he could mobilize the secret support of the wealthy elements and the overt impatience of the frustrated to overthrow democratic institutions. Similar patterns can be observed in rightwing authoritarianism in Latin America and Asia exploiting, as Hitler did, "anticommunism" as a rallying cry for establishing military and financial dictatorships.

Whenever a society is stratified, members come to think of themselves as having characteristics attributed to their class. This internalizing of the norms of the culture, however prejudicial, gives kings a royal air and slaves a servile mentality. The shaping of self-concepts by the class system is one of its most serious consequences. The ruling group feel that their virtue and ability correspond to their position of power. The lower classes are often low also in self-esteem. Psychologists sometimes refer to this kind of stereotype as a "halo effect." The point we are making now is that the upper-class children come to believe that they deserve these halos; the lower-class children also accept a view of themselves as dull, dirty, and disorderly. An experiment (Harvey, 1953) in which adolescents estimated how well they would perform in throwing darts at a target showed that those who had high status with their peers were expected to do better than average; they also overestimated their own performance. The correlation was even more marked in groups of lower socioeconomic status. The boys with low standing were not expected to perform well, and they thought they were doing less well than they objectively did. We shall meet this phenomenon of internalization of inferiority feelings again in the chapters that examine race prejudice and sex prejudice.

Class differences in values

David Riesman has characterized the working class as oriented to present needs and satisfactions; the middle class as centering its attention on the future and sacrificing present satisfactions for the hope of things to come; the upper class as trying to preserve its prestige and traditions out of the past. In another sense, however, the lack of contact between lower-class adults and the currents of thought expressed in colleges, serious magazines, and lectures and discussions of ideas means that these disadvantaged citizens are apt to hold fast to the views and values passed on by word of mouth from earlier generations. Thus a study in Michigan (Lehmann, 1960) showed that college students whose parents had only elementary schooling were more rigid, dogmatic, traditional, and authoritarian in attitude than were students whose parents had gone to college.

In empirical study of statements differentiating junior high school pupils by social class (Phillips, 1950) the following opinions were reported:

Differentiating upper-class youngsters

"Really nice people don't associate with just anybody."
"Marrying a person of your own social rank is very important."
"It makes a difference to your parents whether your friends come from good families or not."
"You can try a lot of things to make people respectable but you can't make up for poor family background and training."

"Some of the most popular people at school are my close friends."

Differentiating middle-class youngsters

"You should finish college because graduation from high school isn't much of a start."

"The world is all mixed up today because people are not religious enough."

"Those young people who are most popular with the opposite sex frequently are not such nice persons."

"Families need to stay in one place; moving often from one city to another is bad."

"People should take an interest in magazines which deal with community government and social problems."

Differentiating lower-class youngsters

"Almost any boy swipes a few things now and then."

"The boys and girls who like school most are usually sissies or teacher's pets."

"If you always live as you are supposed to, you lay yourself open for others to take advantage of you."

"Most people will learn more by working four years than by going to school for four years."

"Everybody should get married and have a family as soon as possible."

It is clear that the upper-class attitudes reflect exclusiveness; the middle-class values traditional Puritanism and upward-striving; the lower class places little value on school or property rights.

Most studies of delinquency show high rates in the lower-class sections. Here, as Merton (1949) has observed, people accept as desirable our material goals but see themselves as handicapped in ever attaining their ends by fair means. Yet, as Sutherland (1940) has made clear, financial losses due to white collar (upper-class) crimes (embezzlement, tax evasion, collusive bidding, stock manipulation) far exceed the costs of holdups and burglaries.

One of the sentiments which seems more evident in the working class is solidarity. Poor families help their neighbors because they remember their own need and realize that misfortune may strike them next. One report (Davis et al., 1941) tells how lower-class brothers and sisters expect to turn to one another for help. Another (Useem, 1942) finds in "Prairietown" that "mutual aid is far more common among the low-status people." An interesting illustration of the same tendency is found in W. F. Whyte's (1943) comparison of two street-corner gangs in an eastern city. Chick led a group of ambitious boys who looked forward to college. They participated in the uplifting activities of the local settlement house. Doc's "corner boys" had no use for the social agency. "Everybody that goes there thinks they're a little better than the next fellow."

Doc said: "Chick would step on the neck of his best friend if he could get a better job by doing it. . . . I would never do that. Bill, I would never step on Danny even if I could get myself a $50-a-week job by doing it. None of my boys would do that."

Another time he said: "I suppose my boys have kept me from getting ahead. . . . But if I were to start over again—if God said to me, 'Look here, Doc, you can pick out your friends in advance,' still I would make sure my boys were among them—even if I could pick Rockefeller and Carnegie!"

Studies of job choices show that "a chance to rise" is very important for middle-class applicants, but congenial relations with fellow workers rate higher with factory and clerical operatives.

A study (Stephenson, 1957) of the jobs to which ninth graders aspire distinguished between their actual plans and their wishes "if things were different." For pupils from upper-class homes this distinction was not too important. About 80 percent wanted to go into Class I (highest) or Class II occupations and about 80 percent really planned to do so. Lower-class students (whose fathers worked at jobs in Class V or Class VI (lowest) did not usually aspire to continue in the same level. Less than 10 percent would choose such jobs; but about 20 percent were making plans to enter work in the Class V or Class VI category. More (about 60 percent) aspired to Class I or Class II occupations, but when they were asked to be realistic less than 20 percent felt they could make plans to do so. The results indicate that nearly half the youths from lower levels were already aware that their work would not correspond to their desires; others will be disillusioned later.

For the ordinary worker, a secure job is valued more than one with risk but chance for advancement. In Centers' study (1949) twice as many workers as middle-class adults expressed preference for "a job which you were absolutely sure of keeping"; almost twice as many middle-class as working-class adults voted for "a job where you could express your feelings, ideas, talent or skill."

Another investigation (Chant, 1932) showed that the primary reason given by white collar workers for preferring a job is "opportunity for advancement;" among factory workers this ranked in sixth place. The top demands for blue-collar workers were: (1) security; (2) comfortable working conditions; and (3) pleasant working companions.

The emphasis upon security is natural and almost inevitable in the many millions of American families who live close to the borderline of subsistence and who have no savings. Maslow (1954) has argued that in the hierarchy of needs physiological demands (food, water, sex, sleep) must first be met. Next, comes the need for security and safety. When these are fairly assured, men seek social acceptance and approval. Given all these, people become concerned for esteem by others and by self. Beyond all motives lower in the scale is the need for self-actualization through creative expression. Uncertainty about satisfaction of more basic needs keeps most members of the working class from feeling strongly motivated toward the last named goals.

Life-chances vary with class

While Americans like to believe that everyone in this country is given approximately equal opportunity, this belief may not fit the facts. Consider, as an extreme example, the migratory agricultural workers whom *Time* magazine (Aug. 8, 1960, p. 66) described as a "national disgrace." Their income (1958) averaged about $960 a year. They have no unions, no minimum-wage protection; they do not vote. A child of eight or nine may spend all day working in the fields; school attendance is sporadic and desultory. The probability is that the children will be malnourished and virtually illiterate.

Opportunity to be born into a family which welcomes the baby is greater in middle and upper classes which are more likely to practice family planning. The kind of house, furnishings, and neighborhood are all factors clearly related to social class. Success and popularity in school depend to a surprising extent upon social class. The vocabulary children acquire and the topics on which they are informed vary, as a rule, with the class position.

Health problems are more prevalent at lower socioeconomic levels. In the United States, a child born into a white family of the upper class had (in 1940) a life-expectancy of 68 years as compared with only 60 years in a white family of the lower class (Mayer, Hauser, 1953). Infant survival depends, in part, upon class factors linked with housing, health facilities, and the parents' education. Even within the working class, those lower in status are more likely to suffer from ulcers (Vertin, 1954). Arteriosclerosis and coronary disease were most prevalent among rank-and-file workers in industrial organizations; frequency of such illness decreased as status in the hierarchy rose (Lee, Schneider, 1958; Pell, D'Alonzo, 1961). Frequency of illness in a large public utility was consistently related to status in the organization (Kasl, French, 1962). Men who received promotions achieved better health records; those demoted had increased sickness (French, 1963).

An assessment of mental health of automobile factory workers (Kornhauser, 1962), based on intensive interviews with the men and their wives, showed large differences *within* this working-class sample. Skilled workmen were found usually (57 percent) to be in a healthy emotional condition, but among the men with repetitive, assembly-line jobs only 10-15 percent were rated as in good mental health. Problems in adjustment increased as one moved down the scale from more responsible jobs to those with low pay, little security, low status, repetitive tasks, and little chance for promotion.

The educational handicaps of lower-class children have been described earlier. The best schools have been in the best neighborhoods. Within the school the class structure of the community may be extended, with upper-class children headed for Ivy League colleges; middle-class children going to state colleges; lower-class children taking commercial or trade training or dropping out. When children leave school, the lower-class dropouts are likely to remain unemployed or to find only dead-end jobs.

Small wonder then, if strains, tensions, discouragement, and resentment become chronic in lower-class populations! The results in terms of unhappiness and personality maladjustment are apparent in the following two abstracts. Bradburn's study (Abstract 21) shows less happiness and more anxiety in the low-income group and in the economically depressed community. The Hollingshead and Redlich book is particularly striking because it reveals that the prevalence of insanity (psychoses) increases with each step down the class scale and that psychoanalytic therapy is seldom available for the lower-class patients (Abstract 22).

Lower-class members are particularly likely to show what social psychologists call *anomie* (Durkheim, 1897; Srole, 1951), meaning a sense that they do not share in the norms of society. The mean level of anomie in a small city in New York State rose from 0.5 in the highest socioeconomic class to 2.4 in the lowest (Mizruchi, 1960). A poll on "satisfaction with income, housing, work, and education of their children showed 78 percent of whites satisfied, but only 38 percent of Negroes (American Instititute of Public Opinion, 1965).

As sociological and psychological studies have focused increasing attention on the handicaps faced by youth from lower-class homes and surroundings, conditions have begun to change. Cloward (1965) has challenged what he terms the social agencies "disengagement from the poor." Harrington (1963) has written of *The Other America,* poverty off the beaten track and often invisible to the public:

I discovered this personally in a curious way. After I wrote my first article on poverty in America, I had all the statistics down on paper. I had proved to my satisfaction that there were around 50 million poor in this country. Yet, I realized I did not believe my own figures. The poor existed in the Government reports . . . but they were not part of my experience. I could prove that the other America existed, but I had never been there.

The Federally supported Anti-Poverty program, launched in 1964, has initiated projects of research and service in the interests of lower-class groups which have been long ignored.

It is probably overoptimistic to expect much change in life-chances for lower-class youth in this generation. The "War on Poverty" will be won only

Abstract 21

TITLE   In Pursuit of Happiness

AUTHOR   Norman M. Bradburn

PROBLEMS   How happy and well adjusted are typical Americans? Is this dependent on the economic status of the individual?

SUBJECTS   About 100 men, age 25 to 49, in each of four towns in Illinois. Two towns are badly depressed economically, another has shown recent improvement, and the fourth has been consistently prosperous. A short form was administered to 516 more men and to 1,097 women.

PROCEDURE   Interviews, guided by a schedule.

SOME FINDINGS   1. Of the 2,006 respondents, 24 percent reported that they were "very happy"; 59 percent said "pretty happy" and only 17 percent said "not too happy.

2. The percent of "not too happy" replies increased with age, reaching 27 percent for those over 60.

3. The percent of "not too happy" was greatest in those with least education; 25 percent for those with eighth grade or less.

4. The percent of "not too happy" was greatest in the lowest income group (31 percent for those with less than $3,000 a year) and decreased steadily as income rose (only 7 percent, for those over $8,000).

5. The percent of "not too happy" was highest for the widowed (about 40 percent); next highest for the divorced or separated (about 30 percent); lower for the single (about 25 percent) and lowest among the married (about 12 percent).

6. Among those men presently unemployed, 33 percent were "not too happy" as against 12 percent for the currently employed and 9 percent for the self-employed.

7. On an anxiety index (referring to such symptoms as nervousness, aches and pains, dizziness, headaches, twitching, and rapid heart beat), 51 percent of the low-income group (under $3,000) scored high, whereas only 34 percent of the high-income group ($10,000 or over) had similarly high anxiety scores.

8. Overall satisfaction with their job was correlated (employed men only) .80 with wage-satisfaction, .77 with liking the employer; and .70 with liking the kind of work. Those low on job satisfaction were particularly likely to wish they had chosen another line of work (32 percent of the lows; 8 percent of the others) and to feel (79 percent) that the job did not use all their abilities. Job satisfaction was more closely related to general happiness among married, employed men, than was absence of marital tension.

9. In the community which was most prosperous and in the one where conditions were improving. 13 percent rated themselves as "not too happy"; 20 percent did so in the depressed areas. Men who said they "worry a lot," made up 19 percent of those from the prosperous region and 29 percent of those from depressed areas. The relationship of happiness to community prosperity was *not* found in persons of higher socioeconomic status. In the prosperous town, 14 percent of upper class ($5,000 or more, high school grad or more, white-collar job) people were unhappy, as compared with 11 percent of upper-class people rating themselves as unhappy in the depressed area.

10. Marital tension was reportedly high for 54 percent of the married men under 50 years of age in the prosperous community as compared with 41 percent of the same group in the depressed areas.

SOURCE: Chicago: University of Chicago, National Opinion Research Center, 1963

slowly, if ever. Attempts to give power to representatives of the poor in Community Action Programs have faltered (Moynihan, 1969). The dynamics resemble those of colonial peoples. The rulers reluctantly concede a bit of self-government, watching closely with suspicion. At the first evidence of error or corruption the old rulers take over again, saying: "We tried to give more responsibility, but the [repressed] people were unable to use it wisely!" The same pattern can be seen in elementary schools and colleges, where teachers have cautiously granted students some freedom only to withdraw it because students rather inexperienced in self-direction disappointed the faculty.

New programs to provide the poor with better housing, health care, food, or recreation are advanced with impressive publicity but then allowed to dwindle as the upper-class and middle-class controllers feel a pinch of taxation or resentment at contributing to the "unworthy."

Abstract 22

TITLE   Social Class and Mental Illness: A Community Study

AUTHORS   August B. Hollingshead and Fredrick C. Redlich

PROBLEM   Is mental illness related to class in our society? Does a patient's position in the status system affect how he is treated for his illness?

SUBJECTS   The community of New Haven, Connecticut.

PROCEDURE   New Haven residents under psychiatric care were located and sociological and psychiatric data about them were obtained. A community census (5 percent sample) was taken for comparison. Subjects were stratified according to Hollingshead's Index of Social Position (ecological area of residence, occupation and education).

SOME FINDINGS   1. Psychiatric illness increased from 553 per 100,000 in upper classes (I, II) to 1668 per 100,000 in Class V.

2. Most problems in upper-class circles were called neurotic (65 percent) rather than psychotic; in Class V they were 90 percent psychotic.

3. Psychotherapy had been given to 98 percent of the upper-class neurotic patients but to only 67 percent of those in Class V. Custodial care was the principal treatment for 23 percent of the Class V neurotics, but for none from Classes I-II.

4. Schizophrenics from the upper class received psychotherapy in 52 percent of the cases; among the lowest class only 9 percent were treated.

5. Mean expenditure per patient was $1,450 per year for patients from Class V; $3,487 for patients from Classes I-II.

SOURCE: New York: John Wiley and Sons, 1958.

Vertical mobility

An important question remains: How fixed is class position? Can individuals not rise or fall in socioeconomic status? Many Americans have been brought up on the "Log-cabin to White House" or "Office boy to President of the Company" theme. Such cases occur but rarely affect the life-chances of most people.

A poll of a national sample (National Opinion Research Center, 1947) showed that about 40 percent of the business and professional men were sons of business or professional men. Only about 13 percent came from occupations ranking below skilled labor. A similar proportion had moved down in one generation from business or professional fathers to semiskilled, service, and labor occupations. Another study (Centers, 1948) concluded that 71 percent of fathers had sons not more than one step removed on his seven-step scale of occupations. In "Jonesville" (McGuire, 1950) three of the four upper-class adults came from upper-class families and the other from an upper middle-class level. No one moved from lower-lower class to upper middle or upper class. No one moved down from upper-middle or upper class to the lower-lower.

The route by which men rise to high positions has been altered during the twentieth century. In earlier days, a factory workman might become foreman, then supervisor, and rise eventually to a high management position. Lynd, in his studies of Middletown (1937), noted that the step up from foreman to an executive position had become harder, even by 1935. More and more often, the supervisors of production, sales, accounting, and personnel were brought in from colleges and technical schools, not from the workbench.

A study of the "Establishment" in England included cabinet ministers, directors of the big banks, prelates of the Church of England, and other elite. "Between one-quarter and one-third of the persons in the Establishment went to Eton; about two-thirds attended one of the six high ranking private boarding schools. More than 70 percent went to either Oxford or Cambridge" (New York Times, February 1, 1959, p. 8). Family relationships in the Establishment were evident in the old aristocratic names. One family linked the Prime Minister and the Duke of Devonshire. Another linked two cabinet members and the Director of the Bank of England.

Is mobility in America increasing? Has the great increase in high school and college attendance improved the chances of youth to rise to upper classes? A study (Taussig, Joslyn, 1932) of 15,000 business leaders (in the late 1920s) showed that among the older men (60 and over) 28 percent had fathers who had been laborers or farmers; among the younger men (under 40) only 17 percent had fathers from the manual labor category.

Data from Indianapolis (Rogoff, 1953) showed that 30 percent of upper- and upper-middle-class groups (professional, proprietors, managers, and officials) had sons who in 1910 had reached the same category. In 1940, the proportion was 29 percent. No increase in mobility into this favored group could be seen over a generation. At the working-class end of the scale, the proportion of skilled, semiskilled, and unskilled workers whose sons remained in one of these same categories was 75 percent in 1910 and 67 percent in 1940. The proportion of sons of workers who achieved some professional or managerial status was 16 percent in 1910 and 19 percent in 1940. Another comparison based on over 8,000 business leaders (Warner, Abegglen, 1955) showed that, in 1928, 71 percent had had fathers who were executives, owners of business, or professional men; in 1952, the comparable figure was 68 percent.

Barber (1957) after reviewing these and other comparative studies concludes: "There seems to have been no fundamental change in the amount of mobility in the United States over the last hundred years" (p. 431). Even if most young people continue schooling beyond high school, class status of the family may well determine whether the better educated youth becomes a vice president or a truck driver. The upper-class young man may well find a spot in his father's business; if not, he is well accepted by the scions of other important families, and his father knows their fathers. He may start "at the bottom of the ladder" as a token concession, but he is no ordinary workman. He usually moves quickly to top positions.

The upper-class girl has her debut at which she is introduced socially to the young men (and their families) who can offer the most in the way of social prestige and wealth. There may be an occasional elopement with a family chauffeur and a serving maid may marry the son of her millionaire employer. The Cinderella theme, however, while romantically appealing represents less than one case in a thousand. Young people from families of high privilege usually set up homes of high privilege; the sons and daughters of working-class families usually establish the kind of homes in which they themselves grew up.

Class prejudice

We turn, in the next chapter, to the dramatic changes taking place in ethnic group relations. Before concluding the discussion of socioeconomic class, we need to recognize that much of what is regarded as ethnic group prejudice may actually be prejudice against a lower class. Middle-class people may object to black neighbors or to black children in their formerly all-white school, not primarily because of skin color, but because they fear that these "intruders" will bring what they envisage as lower-class habits of cleanliness, lower-class health problems, and lower-class standards of conduct. The class barrier in such cases is the real problem. Integration across class lines within one ethnic group is sometimes more difficult than is integration of different ethnic groups within the same socioeconomic class. The hostility—overt or hidden—of lower classes toward upper classes of the same ethnic group can be quite as virulent as that of blacks toward whites.

SUMMARY

Throughout history societies have consisted of stratified subcultures based upon socioeconomic class differences. In some societies these differences have been very rigid; that is, being born into a certain socioeconomic class meant that one would always remain a member of that class. In other societies, such as the United States, class membership is more flexible in that it is psssible to move from one class to another. In the studies of socioeconomic class differences in the United States, membership in a socioeconomic class has been operationally defined in several different ways. One is to simply ask individuals what socioeconomic class they belong to; quite commonly individuals accurately describe themselves in terms of belonging to the upper, middle, working, or lower class. Since there are high positive correlations between prestige of an occupation, average IQ of individuals within an occupation, years of schooling members of an occupation have, average occupational income, size of family, and a person's attitudes, interests, and tastes, the definition of socioeconomic class membership is often operationally considered as one or more of these factors.

Child rearing practices tend to be related to the socioeconomic class to which the parents belong. Past research, for example, has found that the working class emphasizes traditional behaviors such as neatness and obedience while the middle class emphasizes happiness, consideration, self-control, and curiosity. Since child-rearing practices are constantly changing, however, these findings may not always be accurate. One of the consequences of child-rearing practices is whether children know the basic skills required by schools when they begin first grade. Some studies indicate that upper class children come to school with many of the basic skills and tend to remain in school through graduation from college. Lower class children, on the other hand, tend to come to school lacking some of the basic skills, tend to present teachers with problem behaviors, and either drop out of school or fail to go on to college because of financial difficulties. Explanations other than child-rearing practices for these differences have included hypothesizing that lower class children have less intelligence, that teachers treat children from certain socioeconomic classes differently (that is, they reward and encourage upper-class children for achievement while they ignore the achievement of lower-class children), that lower-class children tend to go to school with lower-class peers which increases the conflict between the skills they are taught at home and the skills needed in a school setting, and that there is a lack of congruence between the life style of the lower class child and the life of the school. In terms of the explanation hypothesizing lower intelligence in lower class children, it should be noted that a variety of studies have demonstrated that lower-class children participating in special projects do improve on IQ and achievement test scores to a level equal with upper-class children.

There are a variety of other characteristics which seem to differentiate between socioeconomic classes in the United States. Class membership is related to the organizations in which individuals participate including churches, social clubs, political parties, and volunteer agencies. The poverty class is distinguished by holding few, if any, memberships outside the family. Membership in political parties and voting practices are patterned along socioeconomic class lines. The lower classes support legislation for better housing, better schools, better health programs and recreational facilities. The upper classes oppose greater taxation for these programs and are prone to view others as lazy. The values of the upper class, furthermore, emphasize the preservation of prestige and past traditions. The lower class values the present and the middle class seems to sacrifice the present in hopes of a brighter future. Lower-class boys have job aspirations which are higher than their father's while middle class boys are more likely to aspire to jobs which are similar to their father's. Finally, the lower class tends to have less access to health services and has more prevalent health problems than do the other classes. The lower class reports less happiness and greater anxiety than do the higher classes. The poverty class especially seems to experience anomie and reports feelings of not sharing in the norms and values of our society; this leads sometimes to cynical and fatalistic views of health and life problems.

Americans have traditionally maintained that it is possible to move upward in socioeconomic class membership in our society. The research over the past 100 years indicates that vertical mobility is possible, but no more so today than it has been in the past.

Socioeconomic classes do exist in America. Children, beginning in the fourth grade or so, categorize classmates as rich or poor and use this classification to explain behavior such as cheating and being popular. Class membership seems to result in differences in beliefs, values, attitudes, opinions, and behaviors. Class membership is based upon such factors as education, occupation, income, and race. All socioeconomic classes tend to disfavor the lower-lower class. Prejudices against ethnic groups in many cases, furthermore, may be more accurately identified as prejudices against other social classes.

CHAPTER **10**

Race and ethnic barriers in psychological relationships

DEFINITIONS

We all inherit physical differences that distinguish some groups of people from others. Hair color, eye color, dimensions of the skull, shape of nose or lips, stature, skin color, blood type, and weight are just a few of the bodily characteristics by which individuals can be classified into groups. In actuality, there are innumerable differences which can be identified and used for categorizing individuals. The western world has historically used a small cluster of the many differences among individuals as a basis for classifying them into "races." Although a satisfactory definition of *race* is difficult to find, there is general agreement that it is correctly applied to a subdivision of mankind distinguished by the possession of common characteristics, usually physical, determined by genetic or hereditary factors (Klineberg, 1965). Anthropologists, concerned with the scientific study of man, have reached no agreement on the significant dimensions of race or the number of human races. Some anthropologists recognize only three or four races, others categorize 30 or 40. Racial classification at the present stage of our knowledge is largely an arbitrary and subjective process. The notion of race, however, has played and continues to play a vital role in relations among men. Popular views of races and racial differences are largely mythological folklore which are often used to justify exploitation or discrimination.

Because of the difficulties in defining what a race is, social psychologists have generally replace the term with the concept of ethnic group. An *ethnic group* is a collection of individuals considered both by themselves and by others to have in common one or more of the following characteristics: (1) national origin; (2) language and cultural traditions; (3) religion; or (4) readily identifiable physical features (Harding *et al.*, 1969). The concept of ethnic groups is useful, since most humans typically identify with some ingroup, and correspondingly reject certain outgroups. Children quickly learn the difference between "our family," "our neighborhood," "our school," "our religion," "our kind of people," and others. National patriotism is one of the most intense manifestations of ingroup loyalty; many people grow up to believe categorically that it would be better to die than to live under a rival government. The technical term for the feeling that the group in which one is a member and with which one identifies is right and admirable while outsiders are wrong and despicable is *ethnocentrism*. In this chapter we shall be concerned with the social psychology of ethnocentrism. In various parts of the United States, blacks, Jews, Mexicans, Orientals, Indians, and French-speaking groups have been targets of discrimination and prejudice. In the history of various American communities, older and better established groups have looked down upon the Irish, Swedish, German (Dutsch), Polish, Hungarians, Puerto Ricans, or other recent immigrants. Quakers, Catholics, Jews, Mennonites, Mormons, and other religious groups have been attacked by hostile neighbors. In other parts of the world as well as in the United States, majority groups have limited the opportunities of minorities, because of differences in physical characteristics, religion, language, or ancestry. Ethnocentrism is the principal barrier to the practice of the brotherhood of man.

RACIAL DIFFERENCES

Whenever significant economic, political or cultural differences exist between two ethnic groups living together, differences in the standard of living, and in the intellectual and personality characteristics of the dominant and subordinate groups become apparent. The observed differences are often attributed to ethnic group. Innate superiority is attributed to the dominant ethnic group; the subordinate group is considered inferior. Thus British officials who governed colonial peoples easily assumed that their superior status was justified by their God-given virtues as Englishmen. With intelligence tests based on school achievement, one can readily determine that typical Hindu Brahmins (the highest caste) score higher than outcast Hindus; that colonialists surpass the New Guinea natives; that Mexicans who are heirs of the Spanish conquest outclass the Indian peons. Such comparisons do not show, however, what the outcasts, the New Guinea natives, or the Indian peons would have achieved if they had been transferred at birth to a culturally privileged home. In the United States, for example, several studies have demonstrated that the longer Negro children have lived in an educationally more favorable environment, the greater was their superiority to peers of their own age. Intelligence score differences of this kind must be regarded as cultural rather than ethnic group in origin (Klineberg, 1935; Pettigrew, 1964; Deutsch and Brown, 1964).

One of the most marked characteristics of ethnocentrism is the conviction that one's own group is superior to other groups, that the characteristics of one's own group are superior to the characteristics of other groups. The exploitation of other groups can be justified on the basis of such feelings of superiority. It has been a sad blow to highly ethnocentric individuals to find that geneticists and physical anthropologists generally conclude that the actual differences in physical characteristics among ethnic groups give no support to popular notions of "superiority" or "inferiority" of one ethnic group (Klineberg, 1965). At this point the "political" use of behavioral science research and theory becomes highly evident. Researchers who are personally ethnocentric-oriented have conducted a few studies which found various differences among ethnic groups; other researchers who are equalitarian-oriented have conducted numerous studies which demonstrate no inherent differences. On the one side are individuals who are attempting to use research findings to promote segregation and discrimination, on the other side are individuals who are attempting to promote integration and equality. Both sides claim scientific objectivity. Such claims are, of course, an illusion; the way in which the researcher phrases his questions, the nature of the theory he is attempting to validate, how he defines his independent and dependent variables, what criterion he uses to confirm his hypotheses, the inferences he draws from his data, are all influenced by his political orientation. Scientific research inevitably loses some of its objectivity when it is used to promote social policy.

A recent article by Arthur R. Jensen (1969) has reopened the controversy over whether there are hereditary differences between blacks and whites in intelligence. He argues that the heritability of intelligence is quite high; that is, that genetic factors are far more important than environmental forces in producing IQ differences among individuals as well as between populations. He reports that blacks test about 11 IQ points below the average for the white population when socioeconomic class is held constant. On the basis of his hypothesized relationship between genetic inheritance and intelligence, he implies that such differences in measured IQ are based upon hereditary differences between blacks and whites, that is, blacks are inherently inferior to whites with regard to problem-solving and conceptual-learning ability. His paper was immediately used to justify segregated schools and other discriminatory practices against blacks in the United States.

The reaction to Jensen's paper has been immediate and intense. Although Jensen presents an impressive review of the research, most behavior scientists have concluded that his arguments have little validity. In most of the studies on which he based his arguments, race was defined solely by skin color, as judged by the researcher. To assume that socially defined classifications of skin color represent genetically quite different populations is absurd. Jensen ignores the cultural biases in the IQ tests used in much of the research he cites. Although it was once naively believed that culture-free IQ tests could be developed, all attempts to do so have been unsatisfactory.

Most of the tests commonly used to assess IQ have been demonstrated to be culturally biased. Black Americans, Indians and Mexican Americans do not have the same cultural heritage that white Americans do. It is obvious that if most white Americans were given tests measuring their ability to function effectively in the cultures of a different ethnic group, they would seem grossly inferior to members of that group. What IQ would you have if you were tested on the following questions?

1. Which word is out of place here? (a) Splib, (b) Blood, (c) Grey, (d) Spock, (e) Black.
2. A "Handkerchief Head" is: (a) a cool cat, (b) a porter, (c) an "Uncle Tom," (d) a hoddi, (e) a preacher.
3. Cheap "chitlings" will taste rubbery unless they are cooked long enough. How soon can you quit cooking them to eat and enjoy them? (a) 15 minutes, (b) 2 hours, (c) 24 hours, (d) 1 week (on a low flame), (e) 1 hour.
4. "Hully Gully" came from: (a) East Oakland, (b) Fillmore, (c) Watts, (d) Harlem, (e) Motor City.
5. Who did "Stagger Lee" kill (in the famous blues legend)? (a) his mother, (b) Frankie, (c) Billy, (d) his girlfriend, (e) Johnny.

These questions were taken from a test developed by Watts social worker, Adrian Dove, to measure intelligence as the term applies in lower-class black Americans during the mid-1960s. The answer to all the questions is (c). If you missed more than three it would have to be concluded that you have an unusually low IQ in comparison with lower-class blacks.

Jensen ignores the evidence that indicates that the social psychological factors of the testing situation affect performance in ways which are detrimental to minority group students. The competitiveness of testing situations, relished throughout white society, is atypical of many minority group communities. Largely due to the discrimination minority group members are subjected to, cooperation rather than competition is the norm. Another complicating factor is the attitude of minority group students toward being examined by a white person. Many feel more hostility than they are able to express. Even two-year-old Negro children were less responsive to a white psychologist than to a Negro (Pasamanick and Knobloch, 1955). Negro college students expressed more anger over racially derogatory stereotypes when interviewed by a Negro than when the questioner was white (Whittaker et al., 1952). Negro adults queried in public opinion polls expressed more hostility and gave more informed answers when the interviewer was Negro (Cantril, 1944; Price and Searles, 1961; Katz et al., 1964; Pettigrew, 1964). Is there a relationship between repressed anger and poor test performance? Apparently there is. When white students were subjected to treatment which aroused hostility, those who did not express it freely suffered greater decrements in performing cognitive tasks (Goldman *et al.*, 1954; Rosenwalk, 1961).

Finally, the finding that *even when* socioeconomic class is controlled, blacks tend to score lower on IQ tests than whites is crucial to Jensen's argument. But to assume that socioeconomic class is the only variable which needs to be controlled in order for the groups to be equated for test performance is an oversimplification bordering upon gross misrepresentation. Numerous other factors influence the test performance of minority group members; one of the most important is that the minority group member has grown up in a society in which he or she has been subjected to discrimination and derogation which a white individual of the same socioeconomic class has never experienced.

As long as ethnic group relations are a social and political issue, controversy over what measured differences between the white majority and various other ethnic groups really mean will continue. At present the weight of the evidence indicates: (1) that there is no scientific proof of innate ethnic group differences in intelligence; (2) that the obtained differences in test results are best explained in terms of factors in the social and educational environment; (3) that as the environmental opportunities of different ethnic groups become more similar, the observed differences in test results will also tend to disappear (Klineberg, 1965).

THE PROBLEM OF PREJUDICE

It is one thing to establish that there is no scientific basis for attributing superiority in intelligence, physique, or personality to one ethnic group or inferiority to another. It is quite another matter to understand and to cope with the *feelings* of superiority and inferiority which are attributed to ethnic group membership. Barriers have traditionally been erected against the free participation of certain races in voting, property ownership, place of residence, restaurants, schooling, use of public facilities, and in access to positions of prestige. Some of these obstacles are vestiges of a time when one ethnic group was enslaved by another. The same kind of barriers, however, are found against minority groups that have never been enslaved. Next to the way in which black Americans and Indians have been treated in the United States, one of the most severe persecutions ever suffered by one ethnic group at the hands of another was the cruel mistreatment and genocide of millions of Jews by the Nazis. Clashes between Hindus and Moslems in India and Pakistan and between Israelis and Arabs in the Middle East threaten world peace. It has become urgently important today to find ways to reduce tension across the lines of ethnic group membership.

In defining "prejudice," a starting point is that the term has a bad connotation. This implies that a prejudiced attitude departs in some way from some kind of norm (Harding *et al.*, 1969). The norms involved are standards of conduct that everyone feels some obligation to follow, but that are not actually followed by everyone. Harding and his associates specify three different norms from which a prejudiced attitude may be said to depart: the norm of rationality, the norm of justice, and the norm of human-heartedness. The *norm of rationality* enjoins persistent attempts to secure accurate information, to correct misinformation, to make appropriate differentiations and qualifications, to be logical in deduction and cautious in inference. Prejudice deviates from the norm of rationality because it is characterized by hasty judgment or prejudgment, overgeneralization, stereotyped thinking, refusal to modify an opinion in the face of new evidence, and refusal to admit or take account of individual differences. The *norm of justice* prescribes a standard of equal treatment; unequal treatment on the basis of membership in a minority group is called *discrimination,* and the norm of justice enjoins an individual to avoid discrimination himself and to recognize and oppose it when he sees it directed by others against a third party. The *norm of human-heartedness* enjoins the acceptance of others in terms of their common humanity, no matter how different they may be from oneself. Prejudiced treatment of others, that ranges from indifference through rejection to active hostility, is a deviation from this norm and is often called *intolerance.*

The relationship between the white majority in the United States and the ethnic minorities can be characterized by three major qualities (Carmichael and Hamilton, 1967): indirect rule, economic deprivation, and social inferiority. Taking blacks as an example, whites make practically all the decisions for blacks in our society. Whether neighborhoods are integrated or segregated, whether slum clearance projects include or exclude black neighborhoods, how schools attended by black children are operated and what their curriculum consists of, and the type of employment opened to blacks are all decided by whites. Because of discrimination in education and employment, blacks are often relegated to the lower socioeconomic class by the white majority. If the money that blacks do receive were invested to improve their communities, some improvement could be hoped for, but the vast majority of businesses, houses, stores, bars, concessions, and theaters in black neighborhoods are owned by whites. Carmichael and Hamilton (1967) state that literally billions of dollars have been made by whites in the black ghettos, and all of it has been spent in the white suburbs with practically none spent to improve life in the ghettos. Finally, to be black is to be inferior in our society. Historically, the white majority has communicated to blacks that if they adopt the values and habits of whites they can gain partial acceptance, but if blacks have different values and act in different ways, they will be considered "culturally deprived," inferior, and undesirable.

In the past fifteen years or so there has been much political debate concerning the improvement of the opportunities and life of black Americans.

One outcome of all this rhetoric seems to be a feeling on the part of many whites that numerous opportunities are now available for blacks in our society. While it is probably true that there is less discrimination toward middle-class blacks, discrimination against lower-class blacks has increased. The June 1966 report of the Bureau of Labor Statistics noted that the jobless rate of nonwhite males between the ages of 14 and 19 rose from 7.6 percent in 1948 to 22.6 percent in 1965. Corresponding figures for unemployed white male teenagers were 8.3 percent in 1949 and 11.8 percent in 1965. Price (1966) notes that in the ten-year period from 1955 to 1965, 970,000 new jobs were opened to teenagers, but only 36,000 of those jobs were given to nonwhite teenagers. For adults, the ratio of nonwhite to white adult unemployment has remained double (in June, 1966, 4.1 percent for whites and 8.3 percent for nonwhites). Nor does education seem to ease the effects of discrimination. The unemployment rates in 1965 were higher for nonwhite high school graduates than for white high school dropouts. A nonwhite man must have between one and three years of college before he can expect to earn as much over his lifetime as a white man with less than eight years of education; even after completing college and spending at least one year in graduate school, a nonwhite man can only expect to earn as much during his working life as a white high school graduate (Brimmer, 1966). The hopelessness of the situation is increased by the fact that in many black neighborhoods food, housing, and other necessities are more expensive than they are in white middle class neighborhoods. The conclusion seems to be that while many whites believe that life has been significantly improved by all the political rhetoric about equal opportunities and poverty programs, in actuality the condition of black Americans has been deteriorating, and the blacks know it. Thus, in 1965 (American Institute of Public Opinion, May 5) while two-thirds of white Americans believed that Negroes are treated as well as whites in their communities, only one-fourth of the Negroes agreed.

Not only does education fail to alleviate the effects of discrimination, it is one of the institutions that perpetuates it. Education, along with residential segregation and employment discrimination are social structures perpetuating racial prejudice. These are closed cycles of prejudice, and can operate without conscious malice by many of the whites involved. To oversimplify in order to illustrate our point, let us examine a cycle of discrimination involving education and employment which operates to perpetuate the low economic status of Black Americans (Parsons, 1959; Miller, 1966). First, obtaining a "good" job in our society has become increasingly dependent upon getting a college education. In order to "qualify" for many employment opportunities blacks have to have been graduated from college in order to "certify" their ability to perform the work adequately. Entrance into college, however, is usually dependent upon being placed in a college preparatory course in high school. Being placed in a college preparatory curriculum in high school is dependent upon achievement in elementary and junior high school, with achievement in elementary school being the most important criterion. In elementary school, achievement is evaluated on the basis of the child's cognitive learning and "responsible citizenship," and in most elementary schools the two factors are not clearly differentiated. The child's preschool experiences influence both his academic performance and his social behavior in the elementary school, with independence training being a major factor in preparing a child for school. Because of their socialization into a different value and behavior structure, lower class black children are much more likely to receive lower grades in elementary school than comparable middle class white children and, consequently, they do not get into a college, and are then limited to a certain level of occupation. In short, a lower class black background results in poor grades in a school geared to middle class white children, which means that college opportunities are not available, which ensures that the individuals involved will stay lower class. Cycles of discrimination such as this one can operate with individuals at every level feeling that they are not personally prejudiced. The elementary school teacher who evaluates a lower-class black child on the basis of criteria based upon white, middle class behaviors, can feel that she is treating everyone equally. The high school counselor who guides the lower class black student into a noncollege preparatory curriculum can feel that he is basing his decisions entirely upon academic records in elementary school, not upon ethnic group membership. The college entrance committee can feel secure that they are not discriminating against any ethnic group by allowing only students who achieved good grades in college preparatory classes to enter their college. Finally, the employer can feel that he is not prejudiced when he hires only college graduates. But the end result of the whole process is to exclude lower class ethnic group members (along with many lower class whites) from an equal opportunity to obtain a good job and a good education in our society. This whole cycle is complicated further by the fact that when housing is segregated along ethnic group lines, even black children from middle class homes grow up in neighborhoods which are basically lower class oriented and which, therefore, do not prepare them to function well in white middle class schools. Perhaps one of the greatest ironies of ethnic group relations is that after an ethnic group is segregated, relegated to low income employment and poor schools, the product of this social system is often blamed for being its victim. Thus instead of blaming the white racism which structures the child's environment, the child is blamed for being from a lower class home, or for being unable to perform well in a situation dominated by white, middle class culture.

Another social structure in which prejudice is evident is the legal structure. One of the most tragic consequences of prejudice is the miscarriage of justice. For nearly a century, "lynch law" was used "to keep the Negro in his place." The sad history has been well related by Raper (1933). Lynchings have been repudiated in every section of the United States today, but in 1965 it was still impossible to obtain a conviction in the murder of civil rights leaders in some Southern states. The problem of justice exists in the North as well as in the South. On January 9, 1924, James Montgomery, a Negro mechanic of Waukegan, Illinois, was sentenced to life imprisonment for rape. Prior to this, the prosecuting attorney, a white man named Ashbel V. Smith, had illegally raided Montgomery's home to seek evidence of bootlegging. There was no such evidence. Mr. Montgomery, believing in our American code of justice, sued for damages and won $125 in a civil suit. The affronted prosecutor swore: "I'll get you!" He did. The police chief in Waukegan threatened Mr. Montgomery with Ku Klux Klan retaliation if he attempted any legal defense to the rape charge. The alleged victim of the rape was a demented woman of 62; the doctors who examined her found she had never been assaulted, but all this evidence was suppressed. Owing to the interest of another white Illinois attorney, Luis Kutner, the case was re-opened in 1946 and Mr. Montgomery was set free after spending much of his life—from the ages of 31 to 54—in prison.

One of the evidences of prejudice, and a factor in its perpetuation, has been the use of stereotypes in magazine stories, films, and television programs. A study in 1946 (Berelson and Salter, 1946) of 185 short stories in eight well known magazines showed that heroes and heroines were almost always Anglo-Saxon, but that unsavory characters, crooks, and villains tended to be foreigners. In 100 movies with Negro characters, 75 were disparaging and stereotyped. Awareness of such prejudices has probably improved conditions since the 1940s. Much of the classical literature to which children are exposed, however, reflects the history of racism and white supremacy that has extended in our culture for centuries. In Shakespeare's play, *The Tempest,* for example, a black slave named Caliban appears. He is represented as a pagan, anti-Christ, and being of the devil. The feeling of that time towards blacks is expressed in Caliban's name; if you transpose the "l" and the "n," his name becomes Canibal. This play reflects the position of England toward blacks and slavery. In 1550 Captain John Hawkins entered the slave trade on the basis that slavery was justified because Africans were heathens. In the play the white slave owner, Prospero, describes his slave in the following terms, "We'll visit Caliban my slave, who never yields us kind answer," "Thou poisonous slave, got by the devil himself . . . ," "Thou most lying slave, whom stripes may move, not kindness," "Abhorred slave, which any print of goodness wilt not take, being capable of all ill." In a somewhat later novel, *Robinson Crusoe* by Daniel Defoe, the Christianizing of the slave was satirized. The double motivation of white Christian countries toward the non-Christian world, both to enslave and to convert, had raised the question of what to do with a slave who was converted—do you set him free, or do you keep him in slavery? For a time all Christian slaves were freed, but when slaves became valuable property, the slave holders began to rebel against this loss of investment. Prior to the writing of *Robinson Crusoe*, the King of England had resolved much of the controversy by declaring that a slave could be converted and still not be freed. In his book Defoe portrays the black, personified in a character named Friday, as (1) a grateful servant who loves his white master for saving him from cannibalism of his heathen past; (2) an unusually handsome black because his features were those of a white man and (3) a person who felt that being a slave to a white man was much preferable to being a free black man. Such satire, which was aimed at highlighting the more ridiculous aspects of current social thought, may be lost upon children and teenagers who now read *Robinson Crusoe;* instead it may reinforce the blatantly false picture that enslaving other ethnic groups was justified and that many slaves liked slavery better than their previous life as free men.

Thus the norms concerning ethnic group relations in one's society are communicated through social structures and economic and political traditions, and are reflected in the mass media and literature. It should be noted, however, that for many people society communicates conflicting norms. Thus in the United States there is a commitment expressed by the Bill of Rights and the Constitution that all men shall be treated equally and be given an equal opportunity to succeed and at the same time the superiority of whites over other ethnic groups is communicated. How individuals handle such conflicts depends upon personal characteristics, such as the need to conform to pressures from one's peers and from authorities, and situational factors, such as the liberalism or conservatism of one's community.

EFFECTS OF PREJUDICE ON NEGRO SELF-EVALUATION

The basic prejudices of white Americans which limit the opportunities of ethnic groups have a profound impact upon the self-evaluation of minority group members. A large volume of research indicates that blacks have negative self and racial attitudes (Ausubel and Ausubel, 1963; Bernard, 1958; Clark, 1955; Clark and Clark, 1958; Deutsch, 1963; Jefferson, 1957; Kardiner, 1951; Myrdal, 1944; Bayton, 1942; Kershovits, 1928; Johnson, 1943; Frazier, 1940, 1957a, 1957b; Katz and Braly, 1933; Meenes, 1943). Clark (1955), for example, states that as children develop an awareness of racial differences and of their racial identity, they also develop an awareness and acceptance of the prevailing social attitudes and values attached to race and skin color. Self-rejection (and rejection of other blacks), therefore, begins at an early age and becomes embedded in the personality as a part of the total pattern of ideas and attitudes that American black children learn from the larger society. For (as Clark so aptly says), if society says it is better to be white, not only white people but blacks will come to believe it.

More specific research indicates that the negative self and racial attitudes of blacks affect their (1) attitudes toward society (Bernard, 1958; Clark, 1955; Harris, 1963), (2) maturation processes (Ausubel, Passow, 1958; Carlson, 1963; Engel, 1959), (3) motivations and aspirations (Carlson, 1963; Clark, 1955; Jefferson, 1958), and (4) academic and vocational performance (Harvey, 1953; Katz and Braly, 1958; Katz and Benjamin, 1960; Katz and Cohen, 1962; Katz and Greenbaum, 1963; Klineberg, 1963; Pettigrew, 1964; Whyte, 1943).

James Baldwin (1963) wrote that his father was "defeated" because in his heart he really believed what white people said about him. Convincing non-white ethnic groups that they are inherently inferior to whites has been one of the bastions of white ethnocentrism. For those individuals who want to eliminate discrimination against nonwhite ethnic groups in our society, increasing the self-respect of the victims of discrimination is of prime importance. As long as individuals believe they are inferior, they will not seriously attempt to achieve equality.

Lewin (1948) states that the groups to which a person belongs are the ground upon which he stands. They give or deny him social status, security, and help. In discussing how to raise a minority group child, Lewin stresses that instilling a clear and positive feeling of belongingness to the minority group is one of the few effective things minority group parents can do for the later happiness of their children. A strong feeling of being part of the group and having a positive attitude toward one's group membership is, for children and adults alike, the sufficient condition for avoiding self-hatred.

Lewin recommend that black children be taught to be proud of their black heritage. One of the few attempts to do so has been the teaching of black history, since the distorted and disparaging views many blacks have of themselves can be ameliorated by a positive presentation of black history and culture. To obliterate negative racial self-images among blacks, however, one must also change white racial attributes. In this respect, teaching black history to whites may be more important than teaching it to blacks. When whites evaluate blacks positively, self-rejection due to racial identity will end among blacks.

The way blacks are treated in the curriculum materials of most schools may be a major cause of the negative attitude toward blacks shared by black and white children. In 1949 the American Council on Education conducted a study to evaluate prejudice in textbooks. They found that the average text, or curriculum guide, tended to ignore blacks, particularly in regard to their position in present day America. It was not until after 1960, however, that the treatment of the black in the curriculum materials of the school became a serious issue in American education. Studies in New York

(Brooklyn Association for the Study of Negro Life and History, 1961), California (Stammpp, 1964), and Michigan (Michigan Curriculum Committee for Better Human Relations, 1963) concluded that (1) the majority of the textbooks were misleading and offensive, especially in the treatment of black history; (2) the problem was not necessarily one of poor selection, but rather lack of suitable books; (3) a final solution to the problem must wait until the attitude and approach of the textbook industry changes; and (4) the harmful effects of the present books demand an immediate counteraction through the use of supplementary materials and resources. Marcus (1961), furthermore, reports two studies, one done in 1949 and one conducted in 1960 on the treatment of blacks in textbooks. He concludes (1) present day textbooks ignore the black; (2) the black, if referred to, is associated with the slavery period; and (3) illustrations of the blacks in textbooks are completely inadequate. No improvement in the situation was found to have taken place between 1949 and 1960; in 1960 the evidence still indicated the existence of black stereotypes, inferior illustrations, and inadequate reference to the present day black American within textbooks.

Johnson (1966, 1967) conducted two studies on the effects of teaching black history to black children. Both studies were conducted in cooperation with a voluntary civil organization which was dedicated to improving the self- and racial attitudes of black children by teaching black history. The results of the first study indicate that participation in a Freedom School in which they were taught black history did significantly raise the self and racial attitudes of the participating boys. In addition, it leads to a significantly stronger conviction on the part of both girls and boys that blacks and whites are equal, as illustrated by the following remarks: "When I was younger I thought whites were better than blacks, but since I've been attending Freedom School I've learned that there is no superior race," "The white man isn't any better than the Negro." "I found out that whites are not better than Negroes and that all men are the same." The second study compared the racial attitudes of (1) a group of black children and teenagers who were participating in a Freedom School where they were being taught black history and (2) a militant interracial civil rights group of teenagers. The results indicate that both groups had positive attitudes toward Negroes, despite the fact that they perceived "most whites" as having negative attitudes. In addition, the participants in the Freedom School evaluated blacks higher than did the black members of the civil rights group.

DETERMINANTS OF ETHNIC ATTITUDES

Ethnic attitudes, like any other attitude or set of attitudes, are learned. During socialization into our culture, individuals learn the culturally approved attitudes toward various ethnic groups. On the basis of a review of research,

Goodman (1964) recognizes three overlapping stages in the development of ethnic attitudes: (1) ethnic awareness, (2) ethnic orientation or "incipient" ethnic attitudes, and (3) adult-like ethnic attitudes. During the nursery school years (age three or four) ethnic attitudes begin to take shape in the form of emerging ethnic awareness; the child becomes aware that ethnic group distinctions are made, and that he and others are clustered into such groups. Awareness does not depend upon being in racially mixed neighborhoods or integrated situations; both Clark and Clark (1939) and Goodman (1952) found that there were no differences in ethnic group awareness between children who attended racially mixed or segregated nursery school. Not only are young children aware of ethnic group differences, they are also aware of the value judgments society places upon those differences. Thus Clark and Clark (1939) found that children as young as three identify a white doll as "good," and a Negro doll as "bad;" this finding has been replicated by many different studies (Blake and Dennis, 1943; Radke, Frazer, and Hadassah, 1949; Goodman, 1952; Radke and Trager, 1950; Landreth and Johnson, 1953; Gregor and McPherson, 1966). Between the ages of four and eight, children seem to learn a general orientation to ethnic relations and use many words and concepts embodying stereotypes of other ethnic groups without full awareness of their meaning or their potentially derogatory implications. As the child grows older the behavior and attitudes defined as appropriate by society become more consistent until the teenagers' behavior and attitudes are indistinguishable from those of adults.

Given the great deal of evidence that ethnic group prejudice is evident in very young children, even in children who have never seen a member of the ethnic groups they are prejudiced against, the question of how these attitudes develop can be raised? What influences young children to learn society's attitudes toward ethnic groups almost as soon as they learn to talk? There is no simple answer to this question. Many factors influence the ethnic attitudes of individuals in our society. One factor may be the English language itself. The words children are taught structure their conceptualization of the world in which they live, and serve as guideposts to the attitudes and values of their society. In a real sense, those who define the words of the English language define the ethnic group attitudes of the individuals who speak the English language. Four ethnic groups commonly recognized in the United States, for example, are described by the colors of their skin, red for Indians, yellow for Asians, black for Negroes, and white for Caucasians. When one looks at the various meanings and synonyms for the four words, red, yellow, black, and white, it becomes clear just who wrote the dictionaries. Some of the meanings for the word "red" are: to be or become angry; to have a noisy good time by visiting bars and so on (in "paint the town red"); to lose money or be in debt, and to be politically radical or revolutionary. Some of the meanings for the word "yellow" are jealous or melancholy, cowardly or untrustworthy, cheaply sensational to an offensive degree, and choleric. Some of the meanings for the word "black" are: soiled, dirty, evil, wicked, harmful, disgraceful, sad, dismal, gloomy, sullen, angered. Yet when one comes to the word "white" the picture changes; some of its meanings are: morally or spiritually pure, spotless, innocent, free from evil intent, happy, fortunate, auspicious, honest, honorable, fair, dependable, purity, silvery. Just by learning the emotional associations with the words for colors a child can learn the basic attitudes toward ethnic groups in our society. It is by no accident that the above words carry the associations they do. Although there are other explanations for the associations made with the colors representing ethnic groups, the relationship among the whites who defined the English language, the history of white racism in the world, and the meanings of the words cannot be ignored. The history of ethnic group prejudice goes far back into the history of civilization in Europe and has continued for thousands of years. It may be hypothesized that this heritage has resulted in basic archtypes or at least norms in our culture which individuals learn and support with little awareness of their effect on attitudes and values. Certainly, with ethnic group prejudice so deeply embedded in our language, thought, and culture it is probably impossible not to be prejudiced.

Thus, prejudiced attitudes toward minority ethnic groups reflect broad cultural norms in our society which indicate that members of our society should be prejudiced; these norms are taught through our language, our social structures, and by our parents and peers. The more deeply discrimination and prejudice against an ethnic group are embedded in the broad cultural norms of our society, the more resistant to change and the more permanent prejudiced attitudes will be. There is, unfortunately, no satisfactory theory concerning why ethnic prejudice exists, how these attitudes are determined, and why certain attitudes are maintained over centuries while others change rapidly in a few years. There are several limited theories which may account for the determination of some ethnic attitudes under limited conditions.

There is evidence that in general the more education a person has, the less likely he is to have ethnic prejudices (Allport, 1954; Williams, 1964). There is also some indication that upper-class white gentiles are most likely to feel threatened by competition with Jews while lower-class individuals are most likely to feel threatened by competition with blacks (Williams, 1964). Thus both one's education and one's socioeconomic background may affect the socialization of prejudice towards ethnic groups.

One line of research in ethnic group relations has focused upon the amount and types of contact between ethnic groups. Frequent contacts with members of other groups increase the salience of attitudes toward these groups. If contact takes place under conditions of genuine cooperation or serious competition or conflict, personal contact between members of different ethnic groups may play a decisive role in the formation of intergroup attitudes.

A fairly well-established finding is that prejudiced individuals are more susceptible to frustration than are tolerant individuals. A common theory concerning hostility between ethnic groups is that under certain conditions hostility resulting from frustration is displaced upon minority groups. Williams (1947) describes the conditions necessary for the displacement of hostility in the following terms: (1) Frustrations or deprivations are imposed by sources which are either difficult to define or locate, or are persons or organizations in a position of power or authority over the individual, or are persons to whom the individual is closely tied by affectional bonds. (2) Aroused hostilities are blocked from direct expression against the sources of frustration. (3) Substitute objectives of aggression are available and are highly visible and vulnerable, that is, they are not in a position to retaliate (page 52.).

Rokeach and his associates have argued vigorously for the importance of "belief congruence" as a determinant of ethnic attitudes (Rokeach, 1960; Rokeach and Rothman, 1965); a claim which has been challenged by Triandis (1961). Certainly countless religious wars have been started by differences in belief, and belief in different political ideologies may result in conflict among nations. Rokeach asserts that for certain types of individuals, perceived similarity or dissimilarity of beliefs is more important than ethnic differences in willingness to associate with other individuals on friendly terms. For white American college and high school students in the 1960s, Rokeach's assertion has been validated (Smith, Williams, and Willis, 1967).

Changes in prejudice

One of the authors for several years collected case studies of persons who had undergone marked changes in prejudice. Some acquired at a certain point prejudices they believed they had never had before. Others experienced the discarding of a prejudice they had carried with them from earlier years. Study of the factors responsible for a definite change in prejudice shed light on the probable causes and the possible procedures for overcoming prejudice.

Four types emerged. The most common was *Conforming*. When a person moved out of one environment into a new one in which the norms differed, in time he became aware of a change in himself. If brought up in a community where black inferiority was taken for granted, he held that view without questioning it; when going away to college or into the military, or to a job in another section of the country, he encountered admirable people who rejected the prejudices he had always accepted. Before long, persons in the *conforming* category accepted the norms of their new reference groups. In some cases conformity went in the other direction; a New England boy, for example, marrying into an old Southern family and moving to the South to live, took over the accepted prejudices of his wife and in-laws.

Another type of change in prejudice stressed some dramatic incident. This we have called *Generalizing*. Because. someone was cheated by a merchant he believed to be Armenian (or black, or Jewish, or Scandinavian) he concluded that all persons of that ethnic group should be regarded with suspicion. An instance of change in the opposite direction was a young woman who brought with her to New York strong anti-Jewish attitudes. One day her cat fell from the window of her apartment and was killed. A kindly elderly woman living in a ground-floor apartment tried to comfort the young woman. The latter was given tea and cakes and sympathy by a lady she then discovered to be Jewish. After this incident the young woman reported a wholly new attitude toward Jews—now she believed them to be warm-hearted rather than selfish.

A third type of change, called *Profiting*, was related to gains or losses of money or prestige.

"Personally, I have no prejudice. Why some of my best friends are ——— and ———. But in consideration of my customers ———." So speaks the hotel owner, the restaurant keeper, the private school trustee, the real estate operator, and many others who believe that a policy of discrimination has a direct bearing on their income or property values. These business people are not conforming because of mere imitation and habit. Their interests are affected by exclusion of certain groups.

Historically, prejudice-for-profit may well be the oldest form. Slaves have been kept in many societies by owning classes which raised their own standard of living through exploitation of the labor of those regarded as inferior. It was not until the decline in cotton prices undermined the plantation economy (which employed three-fourths of all American slaves in 1850) that abolition became politically feasible. The lingering traditions of the slave era account for many of the problems faced by the Deep South in providing full citizenship and equal status for Negroes. It is still true, however, that educational and job discrimination helps to keep a supply of cheap Negro labor for household work and relatively unskilled tasks. In western states, general acceptance of low standards of living and of community services for Mexican agricultural workers is conducive to their profitable exploitation. On the Pacific coast, Oriental immigrants were welcomed without much difficulty until they became sufficiently numerous and successful to compete with the white men economically. (Shrieke, 1936). Japanese-American personalities had not changed noticeably, but their changed economic role made them targets of hostility. Earlier, in various Midwestern communities other immigrant groups aroused similar prejudices because they accepted low wages in their desperation for work. They may have been Irish or Swedish or Italian. Dollard (1938) has described the derogatory attitudes of a community toward German immigrants who were competing for jobs in the local woodenware plants. A student from Iran told one of the writers that in a Kurdestan village where he taught, the Moslem's hostility toward the Baha'i waxed and waned with the season, reaching its peak in the spring when competition for land and irrigation water was at its height. Later, after the harvest, when both groups had to work together in dealing with government officials, amity prevailed! The cycle is repeated year after year.

The *Profiting Hypothesis* states simply that individuals develop, maintain, and rationalize attitudes which they find expedient and profitable in some way. Change occurs when the formerly rewarding activity ceases to bring the expected gains or when it brings penalties greater than the rewards. This is a derivative of the concept of economic man.

The fourth type of change may be called *Projecting*. This more psychodynamic theory of prejudice attributes negative attitudes toward ethnic groups to projection. In order to relieve anxieties, repressed personalities attribute to others the dangerous impulses they refuse to recognize in themselves; they project these forbidden traits especially onto certain outgroups which it is "proper" to despise and to reject. There is evidence that prejudiced students tend to view the whole world as hazardous and its inhabitants as untrustworthy (Allport and Kramer, 1964). The most impressive evidence on the psychology of creating scapegoats comes from studies on the authoritarian personality conducted in California by a group of social scientists exiled from Germany and Austria prior to World War II. As was discussed previously, individuals with authoritarian personalities tend to be especially prone to hostility toward outgroups. In the study summarized in Abstract 23, the typical anti-Semite was narrowly conservative, quite conventional and proper, and apparently quite content with herself and her upbringing. Exploration of less conscious reactions brought out great turmoil beneath this placid mask. Concern with sex and violence fostered anxiety and almost paranoid trends. All of the evil was projected onto acceptable targets. Denying their own sexuality, the women students projected it to Negroes or Jews or to the dangerous lower-classes. Blind to their own aggressive impulses, the conventional young women became fearful of the threatening "others." Several studies have demonstrated that a person who is prejudiced against one ethnic group is likely to be prejudiced against many different ethnic groups. The common element seems to be the need on the part of the prejudiced person to find scapegoats, and he sees that "outsiders" are acceptable targets.

Abstract 23

TITLE   Some Personality Factors in Anti-Semitism

AUTHORS   E. Frenkel-Brunswik and R. N. Sanford

PROBLEM   What personality characteristics are found in those who are most prejudiced against Jews?

SUBJECTS   216 students, mainly women, at the University of California. Analysis is based on 8 who were "high" vs. 8 who were "low" in anti-Semitism.

PROCEDURES   All students were given a test of agreement with statements that Jews are offensive, clannish, apt to cheat, corrupt or threatening and that they should be avoided, excluded or suppressed. Other questionnaires described opinions on general political issues and group memberships. The 8 high and 8 low on anti-Semitism were given TAT, Rorschach, and other projective tests.

SOME FINDINGS   "Subjects with high scores on anti-Semitism were found to be characterized by two major trends. First, they exhibited a kind of conservative attitude; although they showed few signs of having developed an organized social-political outlook, they tended automatically to support the *status quo*. Secondly, the approach of these subjects to social issues was found to be characterized generally by ethnocentrism, that is, a tendency to hold in high esteem one's own ethnic or social group, to keep it narrow, unmixed and pure, and to reject everything that is different. The typical anti-Semitic girl differs in her appearance very markedly from those who are against anti-Semitism. Most girls in our limited sample of high extremes were very well groomed, their appearance being in the best middle-class tradition. The surface of most of these anti-Semitic girls appeared to be composed and untroubled. They seemed to be satisfied with themselves and with their situation generally. Their behavior was conventionally decorous. There are, however, indications that there is at the same time much doubt and feeling of insecurity beneath the surface. It was difficult in the interviews to get much material from them. They were sensitive to this encroachment from the outside, resistant to any 'prying into their affairs.' Our selected anti-Semitic girls declared without exception that they liked their parents. More of them subscribed to the statement, "No sane, normal, decent person could ever think of hurting a close friend or relative." Likewise, they tend to agree that 'He is indeed contemptible who does not feel an undying love, gratitude, and respect for his parents.' Our anti-Semitic subjects subscribe more readily to the statement "Obedience and respect for authority are the most important virtues children should learn" (Critical Ratio 4.4; n = 140).

"In the thematic apperceptions of these subjects, *aggressive* themes stand out. Not only is the preoccupation with *destruction* markedly more pronounced than in the productions of the low extremes, but it appears to be relatively extreme. In story No. 1, of Case 6, a murder is being committed; in story No. 3, the husband has lost both legs, and the father is mentioned only to tell us that he has been killed; in story No. 4, a man is being foiled and captured; in No. 5, a man has been killed; in story No. 6, the hero is being convicted and severely punished. Very similar are the stories of Case 4: In story No. 3, the father and son are both killed; in story No. 4, the man is a traitor; in story No. 5, he is sent to a concentration camp; in story No. 6, the hero is electrocuted; in story No. 10, the hero is burned to death and the father killed in battle. Likewise, for Case 7, in story No. 5, the 'boyfriend' is killed in an accident; in story No. 9, a man is electrocuted; and in story No. 10, the boy 'has some kind of physical handicap.'

"Thus for the group of 140 women, there is a Critical Ratio of 4.4 between the upper and lower quartile (in terms of the explicit anti-Semitism scale) on the item, 'Although many people may scoff, it may yet be shown that astrology can explain a lot of things.' Similarly, there is a significantly greater readiness to react in the affirmative to such an item as 'It is more than a remarkable coincidence that Japan had an earthquake on Pearl Harbor Day, December 7, 1941,' or to statements about the essential limitations of the natural sciences 'in understanding many important things.'

"In the stories we hear about the 'voice of suspicion' and about haunted houses, there is frequent reference to exceptional mental states like insanity, trance, being under a spell, communicating with the dead, etc. This can be seen throughout the stories but especially in the story about the picture of a hypnotist. Anti-Semites generally emphasize the complete subjugation of the hypnotized person shown in the picture, the hypnotist's misuse of his 'superhuman' powers in inducing evil or 'queer' deeds, getting vital information, etc.

"In the picture-stories of these subjects, a sharp differentiation is made between those people who are nice and have money, possessions, and power and who possess the right attitudes and standards, on the one hand, and those who are bad, sinister, morally depraved, and live in slums, on the other. Asked to list the great people they admire the most, the upper quartile name patriots and people with power and control; whereas the lower quartile list humanitarians, artists, and scientists. (The critical ratio is again 3.) It seems generally true, on the basis of the interview material, that those scoring high on the anti-Semitism scale are primarily attracted by the strong man rather than by the political program as such. Aggression in these cases is not manifested by the heroine, but is projected into the environment, or destiny, or 'lower' people such as proletarians, Jews, Mexicans, etc."

SOURCE: *Journal of Psychology*, 1945, XX:271-291. Reprinted by permission.

The following case illustrates how some aspects of prejudice toward ethnic groups originates from repressed feelings and projection. The case of Margery is interesting because it illustrates how psychotherapy, bringing a release of the repressed feeling about her mother, permitted friendliness to replace prejudice.

Case 3: Margery and Her Mother

Margery was 20—one of the prettiest and most often dated girls in college. Several times she had been on the verge of getting engaged to one or another of her persistent and very eligible suitors, but each time she backed away from marriage. "I'm just so happy at home," she said, "and my mother is so wonderful to me, that I can't bring myself to leave her."

Margery joined a Child Care Training course and found several Negro girls in her class. Rather than sit in the only vacant chair which was next to one of the Negroes, Margery asked another white student to move over. Margery suggested to her friends that they all avoid sitting beside a Negro girl in class, in the library, or in the lunchroom. Several teachers talked to Margery. One explained that race prejudice had no scientific basis. Margery was unmoved. Another teacher laid down the law: "We can't have any discrimination on our campus." This had no effect on Margery.

When Margery came to the psychological counselor it was not because of her prejudices but because her papers always came in late. The psychologist listened quietly. "I don't know why I can't get my work in on time," said Margery, "except that I'm so mad at the teachers. They're so bossy! So different from my mother who has always been so sweet!"

When Margery's father died, she had become the center of her mother's life. Mother did everything for her. Always wonderful and unselfish. But gradually across many hours of talk, Margery's story changed. It was hard to live up to mother's image of a model girl. Mother did expect so much. Also, it was true, mother wanted Margery always near. She had threatened suicide one time when Margery talked of marriage. Maybe it wasn't so nice that mother always bought every article of Margery's clothing. "I don't like her *owning* me!" said Margery one day. Later she was able to say, "I hate her dominating me with all that sweetness and devotion!"

With this recognition, Margery no longer felt obligated to idealize her mother. She no longer projected her resentment onto women teachers.

Before long Margery became engaged. No one said anything more about race relations, but Margery worked successfully on a committee project with a Negro classmate. "I can't understand," she said one day, "how I could ever have treated those girls the way I did. They're as nice as any of my other friends."

After a period of open rebellion against her mother, Margery married and gradually was able to admit that, despite some resentment, she really loved her mother.

ACTION AGAINST PREJUDICE

Education and persuasion

Changing attitudes through the use of information and persuasion techniques was discussed in Chapter 7. Ethnic attitudes may be changed in the same ways as any other attitude, although when ethnic attitudes are supported by the culture into which one is socialized, the forces opposing attitude change may be formidable.

Attempts to change race attitudes often begin with reasoned arguments or moral suasion. In his great pioneering study of race relations in the United States, the Swedish sociologist, Gunnar Mydral (1944, 1962) contrasts the American creed of democratic and Christian ideals with the social, economic, and political arrangements which foster discrimination. He believes that in this *American Dilemma* the ethical ideals will eventually triumph over the practical institutional operations of segregation. What Festinger (1957) calls the effort to "reduce cognitive dissonance," certainly works toward bringing theory and practice into more consistency.

In Chapter 7 we reviewed the sources of attitudes and the effectiveness of several ways of influencing them. Most people are inclined to agree with what they believe to be the majority viewpoint, or the one upheld by persons of high prestige. One of the problems in changing attitudes on race is that prejudice is strongest in regions where both the majority and the prestige figures sustain it.

The study by Green (1952), showed that pupils who received more information about Negro achievements adopted more favorable attitudes. In reviewing cases of changed attitudes, we discovered no instance in which scientific texts, factual pamphlets, or informative lectures initiated a significant reduction of prejudice. We did find, however, that many people, after they had had interpersonal experiences which opened their minds to a new outlook, made use of information to justify, to stabilize, and to reinforce their new outlook. A study (Mainer, 1963) revealed that high school pupils who reported a program of intergroup education in their school changed more in the direction of less prejudice than did the controls.

Harding and his associates (1969) note that most correlational studies have reported that persons with considerable information about a specific group tend to have more favorable attitudes toward that group. There is no way of learning, however, whether changes in attitude resulted from increased information, or increased information resulted from favorable attitudes, or to what extent both resulted from other personality or situational factors. Harding and his associates feel that school courses may produce favorable changes in the ethnic attitudes of students if (1) a favorable balance of information about an ethnic group is presented; (2) the instructor communicates to the students that his own attitude toward the ethnic group is more favorable than theirs; and (3) a positive relationship between instructor and students exists to the point that they will accept his feelings and action orientations toward the group as well as the information he presents.

Defining an attitude as a combination of a belief and a relevant value, attitudes may be changed most easily by changing beliefs; Jones and Gerard suggest that beliefs about various ethnic groups are perceived relationships between members of the ethnic group and certain characteristics evaluated as "bad" (laziness, dirtiness, untrustworthiness, and so on). Information may change such beliefs by changing the perceived relationship between the characteristics and the ethnic group or by associating the ethnic group with positive characteristics. Research in learning indicates that repeatedly pairing the ethnic group with positive characteristics will result in the ethnic group eliciting the positive response associated with the positive characteristics, if the positive characteristics elicit more powerful responses than the original negative responses to the ethnic group. The less prejudiced a person is, in other words, the easier it is to change his attitudes toward an ethnic group through presenting positive information about the ethnic group. Johnson (1966, 1967) demonstrated that pairing blacks with positive information about black history resulted in more favorable evaluation of blacks on the part of black children. Perhaps the classic study in the area, however, was conducted by Litcher and Johnson (1969). Controlling for the effects of the teacher, the classroom, the school, and the reading ability of the children, they compared the ethnic group attitudes of second grade children who used a multiethnic reader which included characters from several different ethnic groups (all pictured in ways which would make them seem very clean, industrious, middle-class individuals) with the ethnic group attitudes of similar children who used a reader which included only whites. Use of the multiethnic readers resulted in marked positive changes in the children's attitudes towards black Americans.

Intergroup contact

Contact between ethnic groups may lead to either an increase or a decrease in intergroup prejudice. Contact and interaction do not necessarily lead to acceptance of others as equals. For favorable ethnic attitudes to develop, at least one of five major conditions must be present. The different ethnic groups must have common goals, whose accomplishment does not involve intergroup competition. Cooperative interdependence must exist between the groups, that is, they must cooperate in order to achieve their goals. Status of both groups must be equal. Furthermore, either custom, law or authority must support the reduction of intergroup prejudice. Finally, the members of neither ethnic group must be perceived as acting in ways which confirm existing negative stereotypes.

Sherif (1966) found that intense conflict between two groups was most successfully reduced when they were confronted with a compelling problem which could be solved only by cooperative action. Deutsch (1962) demonstrated that cooperative interdependence resulted in positive attitudes among individuals. Master and slave, however, can be cooperatively engaged in the pursuit of common objectives; only interaction as *equals* can reduce the tendency toward discrimination. MacKenzie (1948), in a study reviewed in Abstract 24 found that persons who had known individuals of another ethnic group at a level of work and education equal to their own generally had favorable concepts of that ethnic group, and were quite ready to associate with its members. Those who had known only inferior-status representatives were less favorable and less ready to associate with the other group's members. One of the first and most effective attempts to influence attitudes of white students toward black Americans employed the principle of interaction with blacks of equal or superior status (Smith, 1943). Forty-six white graduate students visited Harlem, where they met black lawyers, actors, writers, teachers, psychologists, businessmen, and others on a level at least equal to that of the visitors at teas, dinners, and other social events. Before-and-after tests showed a marked rise in favorable attitudes toward Negroes in forty of the participants, and a follow-up a year later indicated that the attitudes of acceptance persisted. In a series of case studies conducted by Watson on individuals who had changed their attitudes toward ethnic groups, 90 percent of those who changed prejudices because of the influence of some other person or persons did so in response to someone of equal or higher status. Research reported in Chapter 3 indicated that most individuals will conform to group norms and to the demands of authority.

From this it follows that social custom and authority could be used to resolve prejudices between ethnic groups. Finally, Deutsch and Collins (1951) indicate that contact between ethnic groups will resolve prejudice only to the extent that members of the different groups are not perceived as acting in ways which confirm negative stereotypes.

Most of the studies on intergroup contact between ethnic groups unfortunately, do not specify very precisely the conditions under which the contact took place. In terms of contact within the schools, Singer (1967) found that white fifth grade children in integrated schools, compared with white children in segregated schools, are more accepting of black Americans and more familiar with black celebrities. The more intelligent the white child in the integrated school, the more favorable are his attitudes toward blacks. Harding and his associates (1969) review a number of studies on interethnic group contact in educational settings, recreational settings, residential settings, and occupational settings; the bulk of the evidence indicates that contact among individuals from different ethnic groups often does result in more favorable attitudes. We would strongly hypothesize that the extent to which contact does resolve prejudices depends upon how many of the five major conditions discussed above are present.

Legislative and political approaches

In the latter part of the nineteenth century, state legislatures in the American South enacted a series of laws to control the behavior of Negroes toward whites and vice versa. The laws were vigorously enforced and the behavior they advocated became established folkways. Recently a series of decisions by the United States Supreme Court and some legislation of the U.S. Congress were aimed at changing the established customs of black-white relations. The classic Supreme Court decision involved integration of the schools. Pettigrew and Cramer (1959), in a study of demographic factors affecting the speed of desegregation, concluded that the smaller the proportion of Negroes in the population, the quicker the school district was likely to desegregate. Dwyer (1958) found that opposition to school integration is minimized when administrative policies and actions are clear, definite, and firm. Vacillation leads to opposition and possible conflict. Favorable administrator attitudes lead to greater intergroup contact within the schools. Clark (1953) felt that immediate rather than gradual desegregation reduced obstacles to peaceful transition and decreased the likelihood of resistance; resistance he found to be associated with ambiguous or inconsistent policies, ineffective action and conflict between competing authorities. Efficient desegregation is dependent on the unequivocal support of prestige leaders, the firm enforcement of changed policy, the willingness to deal with violations, the refusal of those in authority to tolerate subterfuges, and the readiness to appeal to morality and justice. Harding and his associates (1969) note that the process of changing ethnic attitudes only begins with passage of the legislation; whether or not change occurs and how fast it occurs, depends on (1) the skill and energy of the enforcing body; (2) the strength of opposition; and (3) the strength of supporting groups opposed to discrimination.

It is possible to legislate contact among members of different ethnic groups in schools, neighborhoods, businesses and so on. Whether or not this enforced contact will change attitudes and behavior, however, seems to depend upon such factors as the firmness and consistency of the enforcing agency and the unanimity of authority figures in supporting the change. It is primarily through legislation and decisions made by courts on the constitutionality of discriminatory practices that the social structures which so obviously reflect prejudiced attitudes will be changed. In the following section we will discuss the elimination of barriers to interethnic group contact.

Eliminating barriers

If most prejudice arises from conformity to the prevailing mores, surely strong preference must be given to any action program which has the effect of eliminating barriers based on race, creed, ethnic group, or nationality.

Abstract 24

TITLE	The Importance of Contact in Determining Attitudes toward Negroes
AUTHOR	Barbara K. MacKenzie
PROBLEM	Do stereotypes break down when members of formerly segregated groups interact?
SUBJECTS	234 employees of a government agency in Washington; 1,700 college students.
PROCEDURE	Questionnaires; one part reporting "willing to associate with Negroes" (work, club, ride next to, eat with, live near); another reporting adjectives thought appropriate to Negroes; a third part reporting kinds of jobs held by Negroes the respondent had known.
SOME FINDINGS	"Willingness to associate" was expressed by 49 percent of the students who had personally known blacks only in positions of white-collar, skilled worker or unskilled worker, but by 83 percent of students who had known black students or blacks in professions.

Among Civil Service employees, where contact was more independent of preference, the corresponding proportions were 41 percent for those who knew personally only lower-status blacks and 85 percent for those who knew equal or higher-status blacks.

Those who considered blacks equal or superior to whites in intelligence, ambition, carefulness, regularity of attendance and steadiness at work represented 42 percent of those who knew personally only lower-status blacks and 74 percent of those who had known equal or higher-status blacks.

SOURCE: *Journal of Abnormal Social Psychology,* 1948, XLIII:417-441.

The Fourteenth and Fifteenth amendments tried, in a sweeping fashion, to eliminate political barriers and to give every citizen "equal protection of the laws." The clear intent of these amendments was nullified by the folkways of the South. Not until about a century later was substantial progress evident. The progress resulted from action in limited areas to remove specific barriers in housing, education, employment, community services, voting, and life in the armed forces.

We live in an era of struggle to eliminate the barriers which have unfairly handicapped millions of our fellow human beings. There are those who counsel caution and patience. Change of custom is always resisted. Proposals for change are turned aside with the rejoinder, "The time is not yet ripe." A rising militancy is evident in the struggle for civil rights, housing, and employment opportunities. People—particularly, but not exclusively, those who have suffered long—are determined to wait no longer. Yet a public opinion poll (April 11, 1965) showed that two-thirds of white adults in the South believed that integration was being pushed too rapidly.

There is no longer any doubt about the eventual outcome. A Gallup poll in 1957 asked a sample of Southerners: "Do you think the day will ever come in the South when whites and Negroes will be going to the same schools, eating in the same restaurants, and generally sharing the same public accommodations?" At that time, 45 percent said "Yes." The figure climbed steadily to 53 percent in 1958, 76 percent in 1961, and reached 83 percent in 1963 (American Institute of Public Opinon, July 19, 1963). The significant truth is that much of the hope and heart had gone out of the resistance, and those who were fighting for integration had achieved the fresh confidence evident in the sit-in's and other mass demonstrations of the late 1950's and early 1960's. The same poll showed that by the summer of 1963, 75 percent of Southerners expected the end of segregation within ten years.

In the following sections we shall illustrate from the fields of housing, education, work, community services, and the armed forces how the elimination of barriers and the encouragement of equal-status contacts have increased acceptance of minoritry groups.

a. *Housing*. In Chapter 6 we referred to a study of Wilner, Walkley, and Cook showing that attitudes of white housewives toward black families living in the same building could be predicted more accurately from their proximity to black neighbors than from their initial attitudes. Living near a black family and making friends with them led to favorable attitudes toward blacks in general. Note that families had no choice in this matter. They had to take whatever space was available. The arrangement was set up first and, in accord with the S-P-A sequence, the attitudes were changed.

Similar factors operated in the two kinds of housing projects compared by Deutsch and Collins (1951). Living in integrated apartment houses had far more favorable impact on attitudes than did living in neighboring but racially homogeneous buildings.

Abstract 25

TITLE   Desegregation: Resistance and Readiness

AUTHOR   Melvin M. Tumin

PROBLEM   What kind of person is ready for desegregation? What kind is resisting?

SUBJECTS   187 white male adults rural and urban in Guilford County, North Carolina.

PROCEDURE   Interviews by graduate students with a sample representative of households with at least one employed male.

SOME FINDINGS   1. The prevailing view is that blacks are inferior to whites in: (a) responsibility (73 percent); (b) morality (69 percent); (c) ambition (67 percent); and (d) intelligence (59 percent).

2. Persons most resistant to desegregation had the most unfavorable image of the black, those most amenable to desegregation held, on the average, the most favorable image.

3. The higher the socioeconomic class (property, power, prestige) the more favorable is the image of the black and the greater is readiness for desegregation.

4. The higher the level of education—even with occupational level constant—the greater the readiness for desegregation.

5. Church attendance is not clearly correlated with attitude on desegregation.

6. Greater exposure to mass media news (frequency of listening to *news* on radio, TV, or reading newspapers or news magazines) is associated with more favorable image scores and more readiness for desegregation.

7. The group most ready for desegregation contains "respondents who have had some college education; earn upwards of $6,000 a year; are exposed to three or more mass media; have a relatively large percentage of professionals among them; and have significantly more white-collar than blue-collar workers" (p. 198). "The principal advocacy of social change, as is implied in the term desegregation, comes from those who have the widest perspective on themselves and their communities, and the deepest sense of stake in the community-in-process" (p. 199).

SOURCE: Princeton, N.J.: Princeton University Press, 1958.

---

b. *Education.* Racial integration in the schools increases equal-status contacts. Twelve years before the Supreme Court decision of 1954, the proportion of white Southerners who believed black intelligence to be as high as that of whites was only 20 percent (Hyman, Sheatsley, 1964). School desegregation was approved by only 2 percent in 1942; 14 percent in 1956; 30 percent in 1963. Although in 1963, 61 percent of white parents in the South said they would object to sending their children to schools where a few of the children were black, by 1965 the objectors had dropped to 37 percent. Some characteristics differentiating those who are most ready to support desegregation are brought out in Abstract 25.

Other research confirms the impression that the core of resistance is in the less educated, lower socioeconomic levels. It is more rural than urban and more likely to be the older rather than the younger citizens. Centers (1938) had already noted that while 33 percent of people in professional occupations favored giving blacks the same privileges and opportunities given to whites, only 15 percent of manual workers and 8 percent of farm tenants agreed. Tumin (1958) has noted the remarkable fact that in North Carolina persons with no children were more resistant to school desegregation than were parents of one, two, or three children. Their resistance found full sway because they did not mind closing down the schools entirely. Parents had to think more responsibly about the oncoming generation. The greater opposition in families with four or more children was interpreted as due to the fact that the average level of education was much lower for this group of parents.

The point may well be made again that resistance is not confined to the South or to the impoverished classes. A poll (American Institute of Public Opinion, June 1963) of Northern views showed that 75 percent of whites would consider moving from their present neighborhood if large numbers of blacks moved in. Another poll (May 23, 1965) showed that in northern communities about one white parent in seven would object to his children's attending a school with even a few black children. As far as economic status is concerned, the John Birch Society, whose leaders and support have come from upper-class levels, in its March 1964 Bulletin, urged members to fight the Civil Rights Bill (in its official position, opposing the sections on public accommodations and attacking the bill as Federal encroachment on private property rights) with "the most massive protest—by mail, telegram, by advertising, by the distribution of literature, by personal conversations . . . that we have ever undertaken with regard to any legislation." The headline they suggested for three-column advertisements was: "Every vote for the Civil Rights Act of 1963 is a Nail for the Coffin of the American Republic."

Education has an even greater task than that of bringing black and white children together into the same classrooms. Some ways must be found to make up for the deficits produced by pre-school deprivation and poor instruction in former years in black schools. The New York City Commission on Human Rights on October 23, 1963, adopted the policy of being "color conscious" rather than "color blind." "The Commission," they said, "urges preferential treatment to deal with the historic and existing exclusion pattern of our society. For a limited period, until the gap is closed, we urge aggressive action in every area to accelerate the minority group's full participation in the benefits of American freedom. Society must work affirmatively for integration rather than negatively for desegregation. Color-consciousness as a concomitant of such an effort is necessary and appropriate." For schools, this means a policy like that discussed in Chapter 9 to offset the handicaps of children from homes of lower socioeconomic status. It means more nursery schools, smaller classes, more exciting curricula, cultural enrichment activities, better guidance services, more scholarships, and other aids to bring deprived pupils up to the levels of which they are potentially capable. A program in Junior High School 43 in New York City, providing many such features, resulted (according to their Third Annual Progress Report) in an increase in IQ for 75 percent of the pupils after three years and an increase in the proportion failing no tenth-grade subjects from 5 percent in 1953 to about 30 percent in 1957 and 1958.

c. *Work.* During World War II, Fair Employment legislation was enacted. A poll (September 24, 1945) showed that national opinion immediately after the war was almost equally divided between those who favored and those who opposed such laws. Manual workers were more ready to support such a law (52 percent) than were business groups (43 percent). Youth (under 30) were more favorable (55 percent); people over 50 less ready to reduce barriers (only 38 percent favored a Fair Employment Practices Commission.

There is evidence to support the contention that prejudices diminish when employers or unions undertake to give equal employment opportunities. A study (Brophy, 1946) of the National Maritime Union's fight for racial equality on the job showed that their pioneering insistence that members must work with competent seamen of any race had resulted in the elimination of much of the prejudice found in other union groups. In the average American craft union, 71 percent were "prejudiced" by Brophy's index; in British unions 40 percent were in the prejudiced category; in the National Maritime Union only 4 percent made the prejudiced responses during the interviews. Another significant finding was that members of any union who had never worked with blacks were much more likely to be prejudiced against them (54 percent); those who had five or more experiences with blacks as fellow crew members were less likely to be prejudiced (only 10 percent).

A report by the Winchester Repeating Arms Company in New Haven states that as a result of their wartime employment and upgrading of black workers, "some of the chief objectors to working with blacks became strong supporters of the new policy" (New York State War Council).

An instructive comparison has been made (Watson, 1947, pp. 71-2) between two different techniques for opening positions on public transit buses to blacks. In Washington, D.C., a poll was taken with questions loaded against integration: "Will present operators walk out if Negro operators are employed?" "Will present operators resort to acts of violence if Negro operators are employed?" The answers indicated that it would be dangerous to attempt integration. In Philadelphia, likewise, the white drivers and conductors were asked whether they would accept black coworkers. They, too, answered "No" and a strike was called. In Cleveland, the integrative action was taken without fanfare. One morning a driver was introduced to his new conductor who happened to be black. The procedure was exactly the same as it would have been with a new white employee. Very few difficulties were encountered. The change was accepted by almost everyone as routine. Apprehension is often raised in the contemplation of change, although the actual difficulties may prove to be minor. In Philadelphia, six months after the protest strike, black drivers were taken for granted by customers and by other employees, and one black had already been elected to an important union office.

Experience in introducing black employees in offices brought out a similar pattern. Raising issues for debate created many anxieties—about lunchrooms, washrooms, public reaction, and so forth. If the usual routines were followed, a few employees might raise their eyebrows over the skin color of their new coworkers, but no real difficulty arose. We have called this the *fait accompli* technique.

The introduction of black sales clerks in a New York department store (Saenger, Gilbert, 1950) was studied by psychologists. As long as the new employees simply sold goods over the counter, in the usual way, customers were not disturbed. But when customers were polled to discover their verbal attitudes, a substantial number of those who had not actually objected to being served by a Negro clerk reported that they thought this would be objectionable. Again, integration proceeded more effectively when it was simply a *fait accompli.*

The theories and facts presented in Chapter 6—the S-P-A sequence—fully confirm the observation that changes in practice may well precede changes in attitudes. It is more effective to attack discriminatory barriers than to try to change the prejudices while the segregated institutions remain. Living and working under segregated conditions generates prejudice faster than it can be eliminated by exhortation or education. Reliance on methods of persuasion, while life runs in segregated patterns is like bailing out a leaky boat which refills faster than the dipper can take the water out. If discrimination is institutionalized in separate facilities and buildings—in residential areas, schools, churches, eating places, playgrounds, movie houses, seats for travel, drinking fountains, waiting rooms, and lavatories—these restrictions inculcate prejudice far more effectively than the best preachers of brotherhood can eliminate it.

Acceptance of a person of another ethnic group as a coworker does not always lead to acceptance in other relationships. As we reported earlier in this chapter, men might work congenially in the mines but separate into different social communities in the evening. A study in a New York department store produced similar evidence. Clerks of different ethnic groups worked well together and were quite willing to work in interracial settings on another job, but after working hours, a "five o'clock shadow" descended and there was little social contact (Harding, Hogrefe, 1952).

d. *Community services.* Court decisions have opened to all ethnic groups such public facilities, as trains, buses, waiting rooms, and parks. Occasional protests have arisen, but most of the desegregation has been maintained. Consistent with the S-P-A sequence, once the new structure has been laid down, behavior and attitude changes follow.

Experience in desegregating recreational groups is reflected in a study (Yarrow, Campbell, 1958) of attitudes and behavior of children in interracial camps. At the end of camp, white and black friends were about equally desired by white children. If separate cabins for blacks and whites were maintained, few cross-racial friendships developed.

Churches vary in their readiness to provide interracial facilities, but often they have been in advance of other community agencies. This accords with Myrdal's thesis on the importance of conscience (1944). In St. Louis and New Orleans, the Catholic parochial schools were integrated before the public schools took this step. One study (Campbell, Pettigrew, 1959) is based on interviews with 29 white clergymen in Little Rock, Arkansas, which encountered problems with school desegregation in the fall of 1957. Only five supported the segregationist view, although all 29 thought their congregations were predominantly (about 75 percent) segregationist. Sixteen were "inactive integrationists." They acknowledged that desegregation is a Christian obligation, but they avoided controversy and conflict as far as possible. Most of them were seriously threatened by opposition within their churches: Several resigned, or were transferred, within a year after the incidents at the high school. Eight clergymen were really active on behalf of integration. All of them were ministers of small churches in working-class districts, and most were affiliated with sects more fanatical in their views than are the large denominations.

Churches have had no struggle with the obvious contradiction between Christian ideals and the practices of most white members. One study (Friedrichs, 1959) showed that in a small New Jersey city where 90 percent of those polled were church members, 68 percent said: "I would not consider it fair for any white, myself included, to sell or rent a house in this neighborhood to a Negro family." Respondents seemed baffled when asked what they would do to end de facto segregation in the public schools. Less than 10 percent could think of a single step or act to implement their beliefs. It is not clear whether they did not feel any obligation, as Christians, to facilitate integration or whether they approved the policy but lacked any corresponding action program.

An historic event was the Inter-religious Convocation on Civil Rights which on April 28, 1964, brought together in Washington the largest assemblage of Catholic priests, Protestant ministers, and rabbis ever congregated for a common cause. Equally notable were parades led by clergymen of several faiths in Selma, Alabama, in the spring of 1965. It is no small service to define clearly the united concern of religious conscience. We saw earlier that by 1963 most segregationists had, for the most part, lost hope of preserving racial barriers. It is even more significant that they could no longer count on the support of the spokesmen of moral and religious institutions. Good conscience was also abandoning the old order.

The direct challenge to discrimination

Since World War II civil rights leaders have undertaken a widespread program of direct challenges to discrimination in the United States. Cases 4 and 5 illustrate the early stages of what is now known as the civil rights movement.

Case 4: Persuasion Is Not Enough

Prior to 1930, black teachers were generally willing to accept the salaries offered in their largest white-collar occupation, although these were below what was paid to white teachers. By 1933, the Virginia Society for Research (Negro) had appointed a committee (to try) to implement the school laws of Virginia which required "separate but equal" facilities. Two methods of attack were considered by the research society. The first was the cooperative method. The facts were to be presented in an objective and friendly manner. White school officials were to be given an opportunity voluntarily to improve the situation. It was argued that "Blacks can never expect to force the majority to take any action it doesn't want to take. The best way is to make white friends who are interested in improving conditions." The second strategy considered was that of coercion. Some maintained that the best thing was to try to secure court action against school boards. They argued "No amount of persuasion would induce white school officials to risk their positions and social status to equalize black teachers' salaries, no matter how friendly these white officials may be."

For two and a half years the cooperative attack was tried. In no instance were we able to get even a promise from white officials that they would work toward equalization. One black principal who, in accord with the research society's decision, tried to publicize the facts taken from the state school report, was summarily discharged for "disturbing the good relations that had existed between the races for many years." Some white officials evaded by saying "The time is not ripe." Others were more pugnacious and announced that they would take action when they were good and ready and never in response to pressure from the blacks.

Recognizing that the cooperative approach had got them nowhere in Virginia's cities, counties, or with the state legislature, funds were raised for a legal staff. The Virginia branch of the NAACP cooperated. A woman science teacher volunteered as a test case. She was promptly discharged by the school board and other teachers were warned that if they attempted court action they, too, would lose their jobs. Nevertheless there were other volunteers. In June 1940, the Federal Circuit Court of Appeals ruled that a citizen could not be forced to sign away his Constitutional rights and that the single salary scale must be applied. The school board attorneys accepted this ruling and drew up what they thought might be a satisfactory compromise. They got the consent of a leading black principal to accept this, although it was not what the black teachers had asked. This principal was promptly repudiated by his group as a traitor. The black group, through their own attorneys, eventually won a much better settlement, one which brought the 250 black teachers of Norfolk an additional $150,000 a year. The school board worked amiably with the committee representing the black teachers, showing none of the evasiveness or hostility which they had shown earlier to the cooperative approach. Their attitude was "The court has settled this, so now let's get together and make it work."

The new black militants in the South can be better understood through the following case.

Case 5: John—Youth Militant

John is a Negro, one of six children of a carpenter in North Carolina. He recalls that as a boy he wondered what was wrong with him, mentally, that he had to go to a segregated school. He was 13 when his father, deeply thrilled, told him of the Supreme Court decision, with the implication that it meant a better chance for an education. He entered a newly integrated junior high school that autumn and worked hard for good grades. His father gave a dollar to the child with the best report card each term.

At the age of 15, John read the life of Gandhi and was greatly impressed. "He was an amazing guy. He goes to prison, then gets out and he does the same thing again immediately . . . I began to wonder why couldn't I be a Gandhi myself, doing something for the race." He became interested in the bus boycott in Montgomery, Ala., and Martin Luther King, Jr. became another hero of his adolescence. "I began to wonder," said John, "why my father had never done something to change conditions." John recalls that his grandmother said of segregation, "You'll never change it, it's been going on for years!"

He enrolled in A. & T. College in Greensboro in the fall of 1959. He and three friends had bull-sessions far into the night. All had been members of the NAACP but none had heard of CORE. "There were many words and few deeds; we did a good job of making each other feel bad."

On the night of January 31, 1960, one of the boys proposed that they try to buy a lunch in downtown Greensboro the next day. John agreed and dared the hesitant boys: "Are you or aren't you a man?"

They dressed carefully in coats and ties. They were determined to be gentlemanly and dignified. They expected to be arrested and feared physical violence. They sat at the counter and read school books until the store closed. A black woman cook came out of the kitchen and scolded them: "It is because of people like you that our race can't get ahead!" she shouted. A white woman came and sat on the stool beside John and said in a low tone: "You're doing a good job. It should have been done 100 years ago!" Outside a crowd of whites gathered and shouted epithets at them.

The first of the non-violent sit-in's, leading to freedom rides and other demonstrations had begun. John did not know at the time how big a movement he and his friends had begun. He did know that he felt great. "I used to feel kinda lousy, like I was really useless." At last he had *done* something more than talk.

SOURCE: F. Solomon, J. R. Fishman, "Youth and Social Action." *Journal of Social Issues,* 1964, 20:36–46.

With the beginnings of the sit-ins in 1960, direct action against overt manifestations of discrimination became widespread. Believing that if most white Americans knew the facts concerning the extent and the injustice of the discrimination against black Americans they would support equality, the basic strategy of the civil rights movement was to make discrimination overt and marshall public support for its elimination. There were two basic assumptions made by advocates of this approach. The first was that self-insight promotes change; that is, when white America sees itself as it really is, then it will change in order to eliminate the discrepancy between the ideology of a pluralistic democracy in which all men are treated equally and the reality of discrimination against minority groups. Carmichael and Hamilton (1967), for example, stated that the assumption of the civil rights movement was that only when one's true self—white or black—is exposed, can American society proceed to deal with the problems from a position of clarity and not from one of misunderstanding. The second assumption was the white Americans were motivated by a sense of moral justice; that is, blacks felt that whites would do the "right" thing when they learned the truth about how blacks are treated in the United States. The 1964 Freedom Summer during which hundreds of white civil rights workers worked in Mississippi was such an attempt to focus national attention on ethnic prejudice in the South in a naive belief that if the country knew what Mississippi was like they would take steps to change the interracial situation in that state.

The results of the civil rights movement of the early 1960s for many young people was bitter disillusionment with white America. Believing strongly in democracy, in equality for all men, in the Constitution of the United States and the Bill of Rights, the young civil rights workers could not understand why ethnic group discrimination was allowed to continue. As more and more individuals willingly went to jail, suffered beatings from antagonistic whites and policemen, and were even killed, all with little apparent impact upon the barriers of prejudice they were trying to eliminate, the disillusionment increased and the extremeness of the actions taken by the civil rights workers increased. Carmichael and Hamilton (1967) emphasized that blacks must stop deluding themselves that the basic intentions of *most* white people are good. Bob Dylan summed up the disillusionment of the youth with the too often empty rhetoric espoused by white leaders with the line, "I got nothing to live up to." The whole process was beautifully summarized by Jack New-field (1966):

Perhaps these desperate pioneers, who created the sit-ins, the freedom rides, the freedom parties, the summer projects, the whole superstructure of myth that illuminated the freedom movement for one historical moment, perhaps they now believe that only their own final destruction can somehow prove [to] the non-white majority on this planet the utter wretchedness of the nation they tried so long to reform and redeem. (p. 82)

With the failure of the civil rights movement of the early 1960's came an increasing interest in political power. Increasingly black militants felt that instead of attempting to be similar to whites, they should be developing their own culture. Instead of integration, attention became focused upon control over their own lives and the development of black political power. Thus the slogan, Black Power, became popular. Carmichael and Hamilton (1967) define *Black Power* as (1) black self-determination, that is, the full participation by black people in the decision making processes affecting the lives of black people and (2) black self-identity, that is, the recognition of the virtues in themselves as black people. A statement made by Frederick Douglass in his West India Emancipation Speech in August, 1857 became a general orientation:

Those who profess to favor freedom yet deprecate agitation, are men who want crops without plowing up the ground; they want rain without thunder and lightning. They want the ocean without the awful roar of its many waters. . . . Power concedes nothing without demand. It never did and it never will. Find out just what any people will quietly submit to and you have found out the exact measure of injustice and wrong which will be imposed upon them, and these will continue till they are resisted with either words or blow, or with both. The limits of tyrants are prescribed by the endurance of those whom they oppress.

Changing a more powerful adversary

The civil rights movement represents an example in which a low power group attempts to change a group with high power. There has been some recent theoretical interest in the issue of how in a conflict situation, one can change a more powerful adversary. How, for example, may blacks change the way whites treat them? Deutsch (1969) assumes that the goal of such a change attempt is to establish authentic cooperative relationships in which the two groups are equals. He states that the ability to offer and engage in authentic cooperation presupposes an awareness that one is neither helpless nor powerless, even though one is at a relative disadvantage. Cooperative action requires a recognition that one has the capacity to "go it alone" if necessary unless one has the freedom to choose *not* to cooperate, there can be no free choice to cooperate. Thus if blacks want to change the white majority group, they have to have the group cohesiveness and group strength to function independently of the white community if necessary. As long as blacks cannot operate without the white community, there is no real opportunity for authentic cooperation with whites. In addition, the high power group must also be motivated to cooperate with the low power group; the low power group has to find goals which are important to the high power group, and which they cannot accomplish without the cooperation of the low power group.

Deutsch (1969) notes that a low power group can use a variety of strategies to influence a high power group. By building its own organizations and developing its own resources, a low power group can make itself less vulnerable to exploitation by providing with alternatives to forced dependence upon the high power group. A low power group can augment its power by allying itself with third parties. A low power group can attempt to use existing legal procedures to bring pressures for change. A low power group can search for other kinds of attachments with the high power group which, if made more salient, can increase its affective or instrumental dependence upon the low power group. A low power group can attempt to change the attitudes of those in high power through education or moral persuasion. Finally, the low power group can use harassment techniques to increase the high power group's costs of adhering to the status quo.

There are at least two strategies which the high power group will use to insure the continuance of power differentials between the two groups (Jones and Gerard, 1967). The first is to instill norms in the society legitimizing the high-power group's power and making illegitimate any attempt on the part of the low power group to change the status quo. The first action of most individuals or groups who obtain power is to create these norms. Thus most communities have traditionally strong norms stating where minority group members may live, what occupations they may be employed in and where they must to go school. They also have procedures to make both whites and nonwhites believe that the status quo is "legitimate" and "right."

The second strategy available to a high power group is to make the consequences of attempts to change the status so disastrous that the low power group will be deterred from attempting them. This can be done either by heavily punishing any attempt on the part of the low power group to change the status quo or by giving the low power group a variety of benefits or rewards which can be withdrawn at the first sign of rebelliousness. Of the two, the second seems to be more effective; the threat of punishment has never worked effectively as a deterrent to behavior, but paternalistic leadership which attempts to keep everyone happy has been applied successfully in combating unions and racial change in many parts of the country.

Cultural pluralism

The removal of barriers is not identical with forced homogeneity and amalgamation. Many members of minority groups, while concerned about having equal opportunities for employment, housing, education, political office, and recreation, are also eager to preserve their own culture and identity. The democratic objective is not to make all alike, but to give each the opportunity to realize his own goals. The elimination of enforced segregation does not imply that Protestants, Catholics, Jews, blacks, Puerto Ricans, French-Americans, Spanish-Americans, Japanese-Americans, Italian-Americans, Polish-Americans, and other ethnic minorities may not develop their own institutions and culture patterns whenever and insofar as they wish to do. American life will be richer *for its varied colors and forms.*

In the following chapter another kind of barrier—perhaps the most widespread and serious of all—will be examined.

SUMMARY

In this chapter we have considered barriers which lead to the breakdown of brotherhood between peoples. Western cultures have taken a few of the differences which exist between peoples and have used these differences to determine racial classifications. Race is defined as a subdivision of mankind possessing common genetic or hereditary characteristics. Social psychologists have adopted the concept of ethnic groups as more precise term than race. An ethnic group is a collection of individuals having in common any of the following (1) national origin; (2) language and cultural traditions; (3) religion; or (4) readily identifiable physical features. Members of an ethnic group may display ethnocentric behavior which is characterized by feelings of superiority, loyalty, and pride in their own group and feelings that the other group is inferior, despicable and immoral. It is obvious that within the definition of ethnic group, many people display feelings and actions which are ethnocentric.

Ethnocentrism has long been evident in discussions of the distribution, inheritance, and influences on intelligence. The accumulation of evidence indicates that (1) there is no scientific proof of innate ethnic group differences in intelligence, (2) the obtained differences in test results are best explained in terms of factors in the social and educational environment, and (3) as the differences in environmental opportunities disappear differences in test results will also tend to disappear.

Despite scientific evidence to the contrary, we find that deep prejudices exist between groups in areas far beyond the issue of the acquisition of intelligence. Harding has defined prejudice as departures from the norm of rationality, the norm of justice and the norm of human-heartedness. Therefore, we find prejudiced persons making little or no effort to secure accurate information, believing and supporting unequal justice for themselves and others and acting in ways which deny the common humanity for all men.

America has recently seen increased rhetoric and development of programs presumably intended to strike down some of the intolerance, injustice and lack of humanity towards minority ethnic groups. Most whites now believe that opportunities are more available to blacks as a consequence. Although this may be true for the middle-class black, unemployment for non-white males is double the rate for white males. In addition, the life-time earnings of college-educated black males are equal to that of white male high school dropouts.

How do these attitudes perpetuating intolerance and injustice against various ethnic groups develop? They are learned. The acquisition of attitudes is influenced by language, by social structures which propagate discrimination and segregation in housing, education, and justice, and through literature, and the heros and heroines which the culture selects.

Ethnic groups who have been subjected to the prejudice of the dominant groups tend to have negative attitudes towards themselves and their group, believe they are inferior and make few attempts to achieve equality. With these obstacles improving the self image of ethnic groups becomes difficult. One way is by teaching a more relevant and honest history of the participation of the ethnic group in the history of the nation. Other programs have focused on increasing the quality and frequency of contact between members of the dominant and minority ethnic group. Cooperative ventures on common problems have reduced conflict. Legislative programs have removed some barriers to opportunities. When these attempts have failed, we have seen direct challenges to the dominant group.

Part of the concern of social scientists has focused on understanding the determinants of prejudice. Increased education tends to decrease prejudice. Individuals who are susceptible to frustration tend to be more prejudiced. Rokeach asserts that for some people, perceived similarity of beliefs is a more important determinant than ethnic group differences. Studies of change in prejudice suggest four dynamic patterns: (1) Conforming, (2) Generalizing, (3) Profiting, and (4) Projecting.

How can prejudiced attitudes be changed? Techniques include increasing information about specific groups. Legislative and administrative actions have increased opportunities for equal opportunities while causing minimal upset in the dominant group. Many of these attempts to reduce prejudice have not been particularly successful, which has led to an interest in how a low status and power group can attempt to change a more powerful group. Deutsch asserts that the ability to offer and engage in authentic cooperation presupposes an awareness that one is neither helpless nor powerless. The low power group needs cohesion, third power allies, legal pressures, education, accent on similarities, ability to go it alone, and harassment to influence the more powerful group. As the low power group attempts to change the status quo the high power group will try to legitimize their power and punish attempts to make changes.

CHAPTER 11

Psychological aspects
of sex roles

Following the Structure-Process-Attitude sequence, we shall look first at the social situation which defines subordinate positions for women, then note the roles associated with these positions, allowing for biological differences, and then discuss the attitudes which are thus formed.

THE TRADITION

Male dominance

Older, deeper, and more widespread than discrimination based on socioeconomic class or ethnic group is inequality of sex roles. Hunt (1959) quotes some indignant feminist as saying that "Woman was the earliest domestic animal of man." In the mores acceptable when the early chapters of Genesis took form, woman was an after-thought, created from one of Adam's spare parts, as a companion for the man.

In primitive societies we find that such activities as fishing, handicraft, marketing, or cooking may be assigned primarily to men or primarily to women, but if the activity carries high prestige in any society, it is restricted to men. This is particularly true of religious ceremonies and the healing practiced by witchdoctors. Even in matrilineal societies political power was usually vested in a father, husband, brother, or uncle. Throughout the history of mankind, there has been a tradition of female subordination.

Older than the Ten Commandments, although expressed in them, was the tradition of Jewish tribes that a wife was a form of property like a house, an ox, ass, man-servant or maid-servant. Longer rites of purification were required if a mother gave birth to a daughter rather than a son. In synagogues women were excluded and men gave thanks that they were Jew not Gentile, free not bond, and male rather than female.

The ancient Chinese culture placed the highest value on male children. Girls might be sold as slaves or left to die. A Chinese maxim taught: "A woman married is like a pony bought—to be ridden or whipped at the master's pleasure."

Ancient Greece, according to Demosthenes, ordered matters to male convenience. "We have hetairae for the pleasures of the spirit, pallages (concubines) for sensual pleasure, and wives to bear our sons." Wives in Athens were confined to the gynaeceum, a limited area in the rear of the house; their persons and property controlled by their male guardians. Plato thanked the gods that he was free and not slave, man and not woman. Aristotle thought that femininity might be defined by "a certain lack of qualities; we should regard the female nature as afflicted with a natural defectiveness."

Christianity, despite the glorification of the Virgin, continued to symbolize the ordinary woman's lot as properly ruled by her husband even as the church is ruled by Christ. The Jewish values as expressed in Genesis were continued. "Neither was man created for the woman but the woman for the man," wrote St. Paul. St. John Chrysostom said: "Among all savage beasts none is found so harmful as woman." St. Thomas Aquinas saw man as far above woman as Christ is above man. Woman's testimony bore no weight in canon law. Hunt (1959) cites as typical a medieval statute of Villefranche in Gascony which granted husbands the right to beat their wives as they pleased, with only the limitation that it must not be so severe as to cause death.

Other major religions have been even less ready to give status and dignity to human females. Hinduism recognized goddesses, but woman's lot on earth is ruled by men. The Koran teaches that "Men are superior to women on account of the qualities in which God has given them pre-eminence." In the long lines of Buddhist masters and sages, stretching over twenty-five centuries, no woman is included. An old Russian proverb teaches that: "A dog is wiser than a woman; he does not bark at his master."

Virginia Woolf (1929) called attention to the handicaps which William Shakespeare's sister would have had if she had been born with his talents. A lady in seventeenth-century England lived "protected" but immured within households. She could have received but little education, and careers in the theatre, publication, and business would all have been barred to her.

Even the iconoclasts, whose thoughts had laid the foundations of our democratic society, replacing feudalism, continued to assume that woman's place was subordinate. Jean-Jacques Rousseau wrote: "Woman was made to yield to man and to put up with his injustice." John Adams was asked in 1776 by his talented wife, Abigail, to see to it that the new government should not "put such unlimited power into the hands of the husbands."

"I long to hear that you have declared an independency and, by the way, in the new code of laws . . . I desire that you should remember the ladies and be more generous and favorable to them than your ancestors," she wrote. "If

343

particular care and attention are not paid to the ladies we are determined to foment a rebellion and will not hold ourselves bound to obey laws in which we have no voice or representation." President Adams, in the usual male tradition, laughed at this and accused his wife of a subversive notion, probably generated by the British enemy. The women petitioned, paraded, and picketed, but the Continental Congress paid no attention.

Only about a century ago Schopenhauer (1851) expressed with vigor the prevailing view of his time as follows: "Women are big children all their life long."

We may well agree with Beauvoir (1953) that "woman has always been man's dependent if not his slave; the two sexes have never shared the world in equality."

Parallels in ethnic group and class prejudice

Statistically, women are seldom in the "minority," but when this term implies a subordinate status, it fits. The sociologist Louis Wirth defined a minority as "any group of people who because of their physical or cultural characteristics, are singled out from the others in the society in which they live, for differential and unequal treatment, and who therefore regard themselves as objects of collective discrimination." (In Linton, 1945, p. 347.)

At a press conference in 1957, a woman reporter, Mrs. May Craig, asked President Eisenhower: "Sir, you have been, and others have been, very active in trying to wipe out discriminations which are based on race, creed, religion, and color. Why have you not been as active in trying to wipe out discrimination based on sex . . . ?"

Mrs. Craig was not the first to see some parallel between ethnic group discrimination, which has now become front-page controversial news, and sex discrimination, which has rarely been publicized until quite recently. The woman's rights movement a century ago was closely associated with the anti-slavery movement. The first Woman's Rights Convention was held in 1848, during the heat of the Abolitionist movement. William Lloyd Garrison's *Liberator* was supporting woman's rights as well as emancipation of Negro slaves.

In 1937, the Carnegie Corporation invited a young Swedish economist and sociologist, Gunnar Myrdal, to make an objective study of black-white relations in the United States. One appendix to his two volume survey (Myrdal, 1944, 1962) is entitled: "A parallel to the Negro problem." Among the similarities between the historic plight of blacks in a white-dominated culture and that of women in a male-dominated culture, he reported the following:

1. Both have "high social visibility" owing to physical appearance or dress.

2. Originally both were forms of property, controlled by an absolute patriarch.

3. Women, minors and blacks might not vote. (The Fifteenth Amendment came a half century before the Nineteenth!)

4. Neither wives nor blacks, historically, had legal rights over property or guardianship of children.

5. Both were believed to have inferior mental endowment, and only limited educational opportunities were provided for them. Later a special type of education was deemed appropriate.

6. Each has been assigned to a "place" in the social system; as long as they stayed obediently in this subordinate status, they were approved; any effort to alter this scheme was abhorred.

7. "The myth of the 'contented woman' who did not want to have suffrage or other civil rights and equal opportunities had the same social function as the myth of the 'contented black.' "

8. It has been difficult for either to attain important public office.

9. There have been certain jobs allocated to women and others to blacks; they are usually low in salary and in prestige.

10. It has been thought to be "unnatural" for white men to work under black supervisors or for males to work under female direction. Women prefer not to have woman bosses; blacks often feel the same way about working under other blacks.

11. A kindly paternalism as of a guardian and a ward has been thought the ideal solution (Myrdal, 1944)

It is possible to add many more parallels. For example:

12. It has been argued in the case of both blacks and women that God made them different and that it is His will that there should not be real equality.

13. Both blacks and women are appreciated—even loved—in their nurturant role. The dominant group is delighted to be nursed, fed, clothed, and cared for by these servants.

14. Both women and blacks, in studying history, discover that white males occupy most of the heroic roles. Less than 1 percent of the statues erected to great historic figures in America honor either women or blacks. A typical school child's list of the important names in history will seldom include any woman or black. This probably limits aspiration for many children.

15. Women and blacks are said to be more emotional than rational.

16. The areas in which these two "minorities" are first allowed to win distinction are music and acting.

17. They are reported to be inclined toward superstition and magic; they are supporters of traditional religion.

18. It is considered proper to pay them less for the same work than

would be paid to white males; women and blacks are said not to have such heavy responsibilities.

19. It is traditional to speak of a "black problem" as though the blacks and not the whites were at the root of it; similarly the "woman problem" is really a problem created mainly by men.

20. It is convenient to ignore or deny any real problem in the relations of blacks and whites or masculine and feminine roles. If "agitators" would only keep out, everything could be worked out harmoniously.

21. A major technique for meeting the problems the dominant groups prefer to repress is humor. Almost every joke book contains anecdotes about dominating wives or stories in Irish, Jewish, or black dialect. In recent issues of a popular male-oriented magazine were cartoons lampooning the woman driver, the wife carrying a rolling pin, the harried husband pushing a baby-carriage, the mother and daughter in league to spend the bread-winner's money; a marriage license was defined as one which gives a woman the right to drive a man, and bridegrooms were advised to "Let your wife know right from the start who's boss; there's no use kidding yourself!"

President Eisenhower responded to Mrs. Craig's question with a typical joking parry: "Well," he replied. "it's hard for a mere man to believe that woman doesn't have equal rights!"

22. Students of race prejudice are familiar with the expression: "But you are an exception." The same pattern appears in connection with the woman boss. A study by Patrick (1944) found that the actual personality of women executives seldom corresponded to the stereotype, but the stereotype still persists. Both men and women are generally reluctant to work under a woman boss. When they do experience a woman administrator who is able and admirable, they regard her as an exception and preserve their prejudice.

23. There is a mystique behind the rational discussion of sex and race discrimination. The myths of Pandora and of Eve attribute to women the source of evil in life. The term "Black" applied to Arts or Magic also denotes evil and may be extended to race.

The lower-class parallel

Sex-role barriers resemble class restrictions as well as race discrimination. The factory worker, in a capitalist society, faces some of the same problems which confront blacks in a white society or women in a male-dominated culture. It is important to note the parallels because they give unity to a socio-psychological problem larger than that of any specific prejudice.

Using Myrdal's 11 points, there are at least nine parallels between the role assigned women and that of the low-paid industrial worker.

1. Overalls distinguish the worker from the boss; dresses the woman from the man.

2. The right to vote was once linked to property; neither women nor workers were eligible.

3. Women, like workers, were thought to have inferior mental endowment; when education was offered it was of a special kind, more concerned with hands than head.

4. Both women and workers were expected to accept their ordained place.

5. There has been a myth of the "big happy family" in the factory to parallel the myth of the contented woman.

6. It has been difficult for women or working men to attain high public office.

7. Jobs allocated to women and to working men are usually low in pay and prestige.

8. Upper-class men would find it incongruous to work under the direction of either a woman or a factory worker.

9. Kindly paternalism is commended.

The role of the worker resembles that of women also in being considered assigned a subordinate place by God, living in a history made by heroes coming almost entirely from other classes; being called emotional (susceptible to agitators) rather than rational; deserving less pay than the bosses; constituting a "labor problem." Both women and organized labor are sometimes said today to have tipped the balance of power in their own favor.

These parallels show that whenever a social system provides special privileges for some members and arbitrarily denies them to others, elaborate rationalizations will develop to defend the rightness and necessity of the discrimination.

As students of a science, it is our task to go beneath and beyond the stereotypes popularly accepted and to examine more carefully the facts. To what extent are the prevailing privileges for men the result of physical or mental superiority?

DIFFERENCES SCIENTIFICALLY ESTABLISHED

Biological

Biologically, it is evident that males are the weaker not the stronger sex. About 135 males are conceived for every 100 females, but miscarriages and still-births are more common among male babies, leaving a ratio of 106 to 100 at birth. One study of infant mortality in the first four months after birth showed 72 percent of the deaths to be males. Life expectancy at every age is greater for the female. Differences in mortality are especially large in baby-hood, before life-tasks have been differentiated, and hence cannot be correctly attributed to the strains of men's work. Census estimates for 1975 predict three million more women than men in the United States, and the disproportion increases with age. The biological handicaps of males arise from what has been called "that half-crippled" X-Y chromosome which appears in every male cell. Hemophilia is found only in males. Specific disorders like color-blindness, stuttering, epilepsy, ulcers, and gout are more common in males than in females. Probabilities of a heart attack in the age period between 30 and 62 are ten to one for men as compared with women. More women than men survive almost every serious ordeal: famine, plague, bombardment, or concentration camps. While the biological factors in behavior disorders can seldom be disentangled from learned reactions, it is noteworthy that males are more prone to school misbehavior, incorrigibility, juvenile delinquency, alcoholism, drug addiction, serious crime, and suicide.

Man's only clear advantage—the larger skeletal frame and stronger muscles—was very important in the struggle for survival under primitive conditions, when male domination probably began. A parallel development can be seen among the apes. The strong male is dominant because he can run faster, shove harder, and push others around. Under conditions of modern urban life, mere muscle-strength has become less important. Machines, easily controlled, can lift heavier weights and move things about more efficiently than can human strength.

In the reproductive process, the male role is dramatic but really minor and conceivably dispensable. In some laboratory experiments with lower animals, it has been possible to start the process of division and multiplication of the ovum by stimuli other than male sperm. There are frogs and rabbits hopping about whose only father has been a bit of chemical or the touch of an electric needle.

There are important differences between men and women related directly to their sexual functions. There is no male counterpart for menstruation, pregnancy, parturition, or lactation. Males can have intercourse only when aroused to erection; females can perform their role without desire. Men are usually more quickly ready for intercourse; in women the processes of physical stimulation take a little longer. Men commonly come to orgasm more quickly, and considerate husbands learn to time their reactions to the responses of their wives. The sex drive in human males can be easily conditioned to pictures or other stimuli. So-called perversions and fetishisms are much more commonly found in men (Ellis, 1900-1910). Exhibitionism and peeping are more frequently male activities. Ford and Beach (1951) report that in lower animals it is also true that the male sex urge can readily be conditioned to neutral signals; in female animals this is difficult.

Data on frequency of desire show great individual variation. On the average, the post-pubertal male feels the pressure of sexual desire two or three times a week. At every age from childhood to old age, average frequencies of sex outlet, reported by Kinsey, are greater for males than for females. Yet a small number—about 3 percent—of women report frequency of intercourse higher than that found in any men. More typical of physiological and psychological differences is that sex desire in the female is often related to the menstrual cycle; in men the hormones show no such pattern. About one-third of women can live comfortably with no sex activity; very few men can do so.

The Kinsey data have been criticized on several grounds which are pertinent to social psychology. One is that a statistical norm is not an ethical norm; what is now done does not govern what ought to be done. Another problem, left unsolved by the extensive record of present practice, is the relative contribution of physiological factors and of the effects of training. Apparent differences between men and women may be innate or they may be the consequences of differential upbringing, social standards, and controls. It is reasonable to suppose that periodicity related to the monthly cycle is innate; that the exploitation of lower-status females by males who hold higher economic and social positions arises in the social system. The concern of young women for a marriage which will guarantee economic security and emotional support may stem both from instinctive maternal impulses and from the arrangements, customs, and expectations of our culture.

A subtle psychological difference arises from the difference in readiness for intercourse. The male, often and quickly aroused, has a sense that his is the natural initiative. The female reaction is described by Beauvoir: "Her passive eroticism makes desire seem to her not will and agression but an attraction akin to that which causes the divining rod to dip; the mere presence of her flesh swells and erects the male's sex; why should not hidden water make the hazel rod quiver?" (1953, p. 599) So she would explain an alleged feminine credulity for astrology, telepathy, clairvoyance, faith-healing, and bizarre religious cults.

At one time, the problems of the menopause or "change of life" were supposed to afflict women but not men. More recent research indicates that women engaged in creative professional careers may suffer little, if at all, from the glandular readjustments in middle life (Davidoff, Markewich, 1961), while the male reaction to growing old has been given increasing attention. Differences once thought to be biological seem to be largely culturally conditioned reactions. Few persons of either sex experience without some dismay the waning of vital energies.

On general energy and vitality, evidence of sex differences is meager and contradictory. Boys are reported to be more active than girls, harder to toilet-train, and generally less corrigible. They enjoy, as every parent of boys knows, more rough-house, wrestling, tumbling, and fighting than the modern living room can absorb without damage.

On the other hand, there is a kind of life-force in the typical woman as she chooses a father for her children, builds a home to provide security, gives birth, and fights against any odds for the welfare of her children, which is at least as powerful as the male achievement drive. In some career women also, there is evidence of a remarkable animation. Ernest Jones, a leading psychoanalyst, concludes: "Whatever the average may be in the two sexes, that indefinable quality called 'vitality' reaches on occasion a higher pitch of intensity, amounting to true genius, in the female sex than it ever does in the male" (1959, p. 76). Jones and George Bernard Shaw were particularly impressed by the evident "vitality" in such prominent actresses of their day as Ellen Terry and Mrs. Patrick Campbell (B. Watson, 1964, p. 75). There have been relatively few ruling queens, but the records set by Elizabeth I, Catherine the Great, the Empress Maria Theresa, and Queen Victoria can be equalled by few, if any, kings.

Intelligence and temperament

One of the first applications of intelligence tests, after they had been devised early in the twentieth century, was to discover whether boys were better endowed than girls. Gradually results established the conviction that there is no real difference in intellectual level. At a given stage of development girls may talk or read a little better than boys, but the advantage does not last; by college age no difference is found between the sexes in aptitude for higher education. The larger proportion of males in most courses in mathematics and engineering is today attributed largely to cultural factors; it is believed that, given comparable incentives, females could do about as well as males in any kind of mental work. We are so well aware of this today it may be hard to realize that the finding met considerable resistance at first. Terman and Miles (1936) further showed that as one ascends the intelligence scale, the differences in interests and personality between the sexes become less and less marked.

Personality differences, like the biological, show fairly consistent superiority for the female. More boys than girls turn out to be behavior problems and truants at school. More boys than girls are referred to child-guidance clinics (Gilbert, 1957). Under-achievement is twice as characteristic of gifted boys as of gifted girls (Gowan, 1955).

At the adult level, four times as many men as women become chronic alcholics. The criminal population is largely male. Men automobile drivers are more likely to get into fatal road accidents than are women. Jahoda (1933) studied an Austrian village in which almost everyone had been unemployed for years. Morale broke down in the men more seriously than in the women. Durkheim (1897) found in several countries in Europe that male suicides were about four times as common as female suicides.

Perhaps the major factor in most of these personality differences is that girls are better able (by nature or training) to accommodate themselves to an unpleasant situation. A good illustration of the point is found in an experiment by Patchen (1958). Junior high school pupils were given a list of simple tasks and asked to rate "how well you think you would like doing them." Alphabetizing a list of names, for example, was rated unpleasant; modeling in clay was attractive. Later these youngsters were assigned certain tasks. Some pupils got the jobs they had chosen; others were given unattractive chores. The girls assigned unchosen tasks did more work than the boys; they did better quality work; and they expressed less resentment at the allegedly "impartial" scheme which led to their particular work assignment.

Definitive studies on sex differences in temperament in infants and young children are lacking, but parents and teachers commonly report that boys are more assertive, aggressive, and obstreperous. It may be argued that this masculine nonconformity will ultimately provide a dynamic force for progress (Lindner, 1952). Along the way, however, it seems to produce serious problems of adjustment.

Anthropological evidence

As noted in Chapter 8, many of our traditional Western stereotypes about the naturally masculine or feminine have had to be revised in the light of differences among cultures. Mead (1928) describes the "masculinity" of Tchambuli men as centered upon grace, sensitivity, and ceremony. "Every man is an artist and most men are skilled not in some art alone, but in many: dancing, carving, plaiting, painting, and so on. Each man is chiefly concerned with his role upon the stage of society, with the elaboration of his costume, the beauty of the masks that he owns, the skill of his own flute-playing, the finish and elan of his ceremonies, and upon other people's recognition of his performance."

"Feminity" in the Tchambuli culture, means productive work. Gardening and fishing are women's occupations. The manufacture of mosquito-bags is done by women, but the bargaining during their sale is an art left to men. Final decisions on most major matters, such as marriage arrangements, lie with the women. Men are believed to be timid, suspicious, and prone to gossip; women are self-reliant, competent, easygoing. Tchambuli females often take the initiative in sex relations.

Another pattern emerges among the Arapesh, different from both the Tchambuli and our own culture. It is masculine, in Arapesh culture, to be gentle and helpful and to take care of small children. It is feminine to carry very heavy loads on one's head; strong neck and shoulder muscles (a "bull neck") is a feminine characteristic.

Among the Todas, housework is sacred and reserved for men. Among the Manu it is believed that men particularly delight in playing with babies. In one Philippine tribe, tradition has it that no man can keep a secret.

It is difficult to find in biological, psychological, or anthropological science any solid justification for male dominance. Any differences in competence seem to be socially conditioned rather than inherent.

Emancipation

In Western Europe and the United States the movement for rights of women began about 1800. We quoted Abigail Adams' protest earlier in this chapter. In 1792, Mary Wollestonecraft first published her remarkable *Vindication of the Rights of Women*. Later, she married William Godwin, who shared her advanced outlook, and who described his beautiful image of her in his novel *St. Leon* (1799). Their daughter, Mary, at age 17, eloped to France with the already married poet, Shelley, putting too great a strain on her father's liberal views.

The first college for women, Mt. Holyoke, was opened in 1837.

By the middle of the nineteenth century more substantial thinkers were developing the doctrine of sex-role equality. John Stuart Mill (1869), while recognizing that women had "not yet produced any of those great and luminous new ideas which form an era in thought, nor those fundamentally new conceptions in art," attributed this not to any lack of native ability in females but to differences in the education given boys and girls. Women, he noted, have to be always ready to set aside any project of their own to minister to the needs of any members of their families. Mill suspected that many of the ideas for which men have received the credit had been suggested to them by women; he admitted that this was true in his own case. He saw with special clarity the restriction imposed on wives by the expectation that they must at all times please their husbands. "I am far from pretending," he wrote, "that wives in general are no better treated than slaves; but no slave is a slave to the same lengths and in so full a sense of the word, as a wife is." (1869, 1929 ed., p. 248)

The antislavery movement, as we have said, was closely linked with the woman's rights campaign. William Lloyd Garrrison was a leader in both. Lucy Stone lectured against slavery on weekends and for women's rights on weekdays. Lucretia Mott and Elizabeth Stanton, pioneer feminists, met at an antislavery convention in London. Julia Ward Howe—famous for the *Battle Hymn of the Republic*—was also active in asserting the need to emancipate women. In 1848, when the slavery issue was dividing opinions across the nation, the first Woman's Rights Convention met at Seneca Falls, New York. They saw "man" as the enslaver:

He has compelled her (woman) to submit to laws in the formation of which she has no voice. . . . He has taken from her all right to property, even to the wages she earns. . . . In the covenant of marriage . . . the law (gives) him power to deprive her of her liberty and to administer chastisement. . . . He closes against her all the avenues of wealth and distinction which he considers most honorable to himself. . . . He has denied her the facilities for obtaining a thorough education, all colleges being closed against her. . . . He has endeavored in every way that he could to destroy her confidence in her own powers, to lessen her self-respect, and to make her willing to lead a dependent and abject life.

In 1853, the Rev. Theodore Parker proclaimed in Boston: "The domestic function of woman does not exhaust her powers. To make one-half the human race consume its energies in the functions of housekeeper, wife and mother, is a monstrous waste of the most precious material God ever made."

Ibsen's *A Doll's House* shocked Europe in 1879. When Nora's husband, Torvald, tried to tell her to accept her sacred obligation to be a wife and mother she replies: "I believe that before all else I am a reasonable human being, just as you are—or at all events, that I must try and become one." Near the end of the nineteenth century, George Bernard Shaw wrote: "No change that has taken place in our century has been more obviously a change for the better than the change in the relations between men and women." (1895, p. 108).

During the twentieth century, opportunities for women have been extended in many directions. The first person to parachute successfully from an airplane was Tiny Broadwich (Georgia Brown) in 1913. Amelia Earhart flew across the Atlantic only a year after Lindbergh's pioneer flight. Women were granted suffrage by Constitutional Amendment—after more than 70 years of struggle—in 1920. The first woman to enter Congress, Jeanette Rankin, had been elected in 1916. During World War II, several branches of the armed forces enlisted women and gave them officer's ranks and privileges. The first woman to enter the cabinet of the President of the United States was Frances Perkins, appointed Secretary of Labor by President Franklin D. Roosevelt in 1932. Willingness to vote for a well-qualified woman for President is rising. In 1937 only 34 percent of a sample poll reported that they would support a woman, if nominated by their chosen party. The proportion of supporters rose to 57 percent in 1963 (American Institute of Public Opinion, November 15, 1963). This may be compared with willingness to support, under the same conditions, a Catholic (84 percent), a Jew (77 percent), or a black (47 percent). In the Soviet Union, about three-fourths of the physicians are women, as are nearly one-third of their professional engineers. In 1963, the first woman cosmonaut was launched by the Soviet Union.

Prejudices still persist

Is today's woman a second-class citizen? "Yes!" insist many of the women in our society. John F. Kennedy's Commission on the Status of Women reported in 1963 that women earn up to 40 percent less than men, on the same jobs. As of November, 1969, 9,000 of the 44,000 complaints filed with the

Equal Employment Opportunity Commission were charges of discrimination against women in business and industry. According to the Department of Labor statistics, women are disproportionately concentrated in the under-paid and menial jobs. Within the same occupations, the median income of women employees is estimated at 50 to 60 percent of that of men. Women in 1968 were reported to be holding only 1.5 percent of the top-grade non-appointive positions in government. Census studies for 1967 showed that 5.2 percent of white women were earning $7,000 or more that year in comparison with 41.5 percent for white males and 9.5 percent for all nonwhites. The U.S. Department of Commerce reported that for 1967 men's annual pay average for all jobs was $7,298; women's annual pay was $4,273 or 48.6 percent of men's.

Top prestige jobs are reserved primarily for men. It will be many decades before a woman becomes President of the United States or Chief Justice of the Supreme Court. There are fewer women college presidents today than there were a generation ago; most of the women's colleges are headed by men, but no men's colleges have yet dared to seek a woman president. In occupations primarily staffed by women, men still give the orders. The doctor directs the nurse; the school superintendent leads the teachers; men in the social work profession have a better chance for administrative positions.

THE BASIC PROBLEM

Primary roles differ

The root of the discrimination is the assumption that a man's vocation is primary; his role as husband and father is secondary. For women the reverse is true: reproductive and nurturant functions are primary while occupation is secondary. If children are ill and require attention, father still must go to his office; mother must stay home from her job. If father's company wants to transfer him, he goes despite inconveniences to his family. If mother can get a better job elsewhere, she is not free to accept the opportunity unless she can guarantee appropriate child care.

In our society, and in most others, the boys are brought up to achieve; the girls to conform. Among 110 cultures studied (Barry *et al.*, 1957) while there was little difference between the treatment of boys and of girls in early infancy, during childhood most cultures foster self-reliance and achievement in boys; obedience, nurturance, and responsibility in girls. About 80 percent of the known societies follow this pattern; in 10 percent there is little difference; about 10 percent cultivate the traits in reverse, with the females bent on mastery and the males submissive.

The difference in primary emphasis is built into boys and girls all through their lives. The toys of boyhood are building blocks, trains, guns and punching bags; those of girlhood are dolls, doll houses, doll clothes, and tea sets.

Hartley (1961) asked 90 girls and 40 boys (age 8 and age 11) who, in their view, performed each of 150 different acts related to daily life. For example, "Who mostly fixes this kind of thing (a lamp with a broken plug)?" or "Who usually uses this (a shovel)?"

She found about 99 percent agreement that sewing, scrubbing a floor, washing or ironing clothes, dusting, or using a vacuum cleaner were woman's duties. Men were seen as putting out fires, repairing cars, teaching a boy to ride a bicycle, cutting down trees, fixing plumbing, working in a mill, driving a truck, or piloting a plane. There can be little doubt about the greater interest and excitement in the male list. Sixty-eight percent of the items assigned mainly to women were in the area of household care; for men, only 26 percent were connected with the home. Boys and girls agreed on almost all the items, and the distinctions were as well established at age 8 as they were by age 11. Further data are in Abstract 26.

When Hartley (1959) asked boys of 8 and 11 what boys need to know and to be able to do, the answers were: "They have to be able to fight in case a bully comes along; they have to be athletic; they have to be able to run fast; they must be able to play rough games; they need to know how to play many games—curb-ball, baseball, basketball, football; they need to be smart; they need to be able to take care of themselves; they should know what girls don't know—how to climb, how to make a fire, how to carry things; they should have more ability than girls; they need to know how to stay out of trouble; they need to know arithmetic and spelling more than girls do."

Boys think men are very important and able to do what they like. They

---

Abstract 26

TITLE   Children's Concepts of Male and Female Roles.

AUTHOR   Ruth E. Hartley

PROBLEM   How do children see the male and female roles in our society today?

SUBJECTS   47 boys and 110 girls; 23 at age 5; 63 at age 8; 71 at age 11.

PROCEDURE   A battery of play, pictorial, and verbal tasks. Some data summarized here come from responses to the following questions:
1. "Suppose you met a person from Mars—or the moon—and he knew nothing about the way we live here, and he asked you to tell him about girls (your age) in this world—what would you tell him girls need to know or be able to do?
2. "What would you tell him boys need to know or be able to do?
3. "What would you tell him women need to know or be able to do?
4. "What would you tell him men need to know or be able to do?"
Other data come from analysis of responses to two in a series of pictures. One of these showed a woman with a briefcase walking away from a house, watched by a child within the house. The other showed

a man leaving a watching child. The interview question for the first picture was: "This little girl is at home and her mother is going to work—how does the little girl feel about that? What makes you think so?" Other questions followed up the responses.

SOME FINDINGS 1. Children see women as functioning mainly in the home; 65 percent of responses (to the person from Mars question) fell into this category; only 6 percent referred to a work role for women.

2. Children see men as functioning also in the home (32 percent, of which 6 percent referred to activities commonly regarded as women's part of housework) but 27 percent referred to the work role. Other important categories for men were recreation and community life.

3. In the response to the picture of a woman leaving home, 64 percent of the subjects fancied that the woman was uncomfortable or unhappy about leaving. The percentage perceiving this kind of feeling rose from 53 percent at age 5 to 73 percent at age 11. In response to the picture of a man leaving, 69 percent reported him uncomfortable about it and the age trend was the same (53 percent at age 5, 83 percent at age 11). As to whether the adult disliked the work, 45 percent of the children thought the woman did; 39 percent thought the man did. This negative attitude toward woman's work satisfaction was more common among children whose mothers did not work (54 percent compared with 37 percent).

4. The proportion of girls who said they planned to work after marriage was significantly ($p < .01$) larger than the proportion of boys who said they would consent to their future wife's working.

SOURCE: *Merrill-Palmer Quarterly*, 1960, VI:83–91.

---

are the boss; they have the most money; they get the most comfortable chair; but they get angry a lot. They are more fun than mothers and have better ideas."

Concerning women's traditional household activities, Hartley received the following reflections: "They are always at those crazy household duties and don't have time for anything else." "Their work is just regular drudging." "Women do things like cooking and washing and sewing because that's all they can do." "If women were to try to do men's jobs the whole thing would fall apart with the women doing it." "Women haven't enough strength in the head or in the body to do most jobs." "In going to adventurous places women are pests—just a lot of bother. They die easily and they are always worried about their petticoats." "I don't know how women would get along without men doing the work."

Although most women hold a job at some time in their lives, work is not viewed as fulfilling personality needs in women as it does for men. Indeed, it is sometimes maintained that men have erected the complicated structure of civilization—its farms, factories, mines, banks, governments, arts, and services—in a strenuous effort to compensate for their obvious inability to bear a child.

Psychological studies of work satisfaction show that for both men and women, one's vocation fulfills many important needs other than providing income. Yet, a public opinion poll in the United States (1946) asking: "Do you think married women whose husbands make enough to support them should or should not be allowed to hold jobs if they want to?" brought a majority of "should not" answers from both men and women!

A study (Hartley, 1961) of working mothers showed that most of them viewed their job "as an aspect of their nuturant function. It is another way in which they can serve their families. They do not substitute work for family obligations—they *add* it to the traditional roster of womanly duties and see it as another way to help their husbands and provide for the needs of their children. Their husbands are still seen as the major and responsible breadwinners—they consider themselves merely as *helping* persons in this area."

Mary Ellen Chase, for three decades a teacher at Smith College, asked in an article in *Life* magazine: "Why is it that with their vast new freedom of opportunity, with time, talents, and encouragement, our women, with rare and notable exceptions, are not becoming great scientists, doctors, musicians, artists and writers? The best of the girls in our colleges display remarkable mental grasp and ability, do a very high grade of work and are potentially brilliant scholars and thinkers. What becomes of these abilities after those degrees are taken?"

The answer seems to lie in the subordinate place of vocation for women. Their hearts are seldom wholly in their work—not because of their hormones but because of the mores. A bachelor, unlike a spinster, is assumed to have chosen his role. An elderly woman teacher once confided to her friends: "Being an old maid isn't half bad after you quit struggling!" But that struggle, diverting a good share of attention from age 15 to 45, can irreparably damage a career.

CONSEQUENCES

What are the consequences of the assumption that girls should seek their main fulfillment as wives and mothers while for men the husband-father roles are secondary to vocational achievement? We shall examine in following sections effects on the feminine ego, on male development, and the consequences for society generally.

Female role impairs her ego

Whether the growing girl accepts her prescribed role, or rejects it, or vaccilates in conflict, she is in trouble.

Suppose she embraces the "feminine mystique" as prescribed and succeeds in her efforts to attract boys, to get engaged by Christmas, to have a wonderful June wedding, to move to her own home, and to have babies soon. This was the predominant pattern among Vassar girls in 1956 (Sanford, 1956). "Strong commitment to an activity or career other than housewife is rare." "Vassar girls, by and large, do not expect to achieve fame, make an enduring contribution to society, pioneer any frontiers, or otherwise create ripples in the placid order of things. . . . Her future identity is largely encompassed by the projected role of wife-mother" (Bushnel, 1962). Another study—this one in a Midwestern university showed that the main goal of 70 percent of the freshmen women was to find a suitable husband.

For a few years, the teen-age girl, if she is attractive and popular, may have a princess role. She may live in a gratifying whirl of admiration, flattery, and servility. Meanwhile, of course, less attractive and unpopular girls may be miserable, suffering a quite unwarranted self-devaluation because they have few dates and those not with the boys of their choice. The campus queen herself, however, does not occupy her throne for more than a few years. Girls may be more eager than men for marriage as ceremony and status, but most studies show that the experience of being married proves more satisfying to husbands than to wives. Men continue their vocation; they see numerous friends of both sexes outside the home; they enjoy the comforts of home. For the wife the insistent, monotonous, confining routines of baby care, diapers, cleaning, sorting, chauffering, shopping, and money worries may be a painful contrast to her glamorous premarital visions. "Men," says one woman writer, a mother of three children, "are abashed . . . knowing that working is self-indulgent compared to keeping house and rearing children." The housewife grows inexorably older and, despite desperate efforts, less attractive to men. Her gay ascent was swift, her melancholy decline, prolonged.

Few boys, even in the exciting teen-age years, would gladly have been born girls. One study of fourth graders showed ten times as many girls wishing they could have been boys, as boys who would have chosen to be girls. A Gallup poll (July 15, 1965) showed that 16 percent of adult women wished at one time that they were men; only four percent of men had ever wished to be women.

Several studies have shown that girls do not usually find their life-role ego-gratifying. They do not identify with their mothers as readily as boys identify with their fathers (Emmerick, 1957). Both men and women see the male role as closer to what would be ideal for a human being (Eastman, 1956). A public opinion poll (*Fortune*, 1946) asked whether men or women had the more interesting life. A substantial majority of both men and women agreed that men's lives are more interesting. Distenfeld (1964) found that men generally rated themselves closer to their ideal of the masculine role than did women to the ideal feminine role. The masculine role was seen by both sexes as more socially desirable. Self-esteem was highest in women both married and employed.

The study in Abstract 27 explores whether women get more sense of worth from their roles at home or on the job.

A study of 614 wives living in or near Detroit (Wolfe, 1959), showed high satisfaction in 61 percent of the marriages in which authority was rather equally divided between husband and wife. In marriages where the husband dominated, 51 percent expressed high satisfaction. Wife domination was rare —only 19 cases—and only five of these reached high satisfaction.

Abstract 27

TITLE   Social Roles of American Women: Their Contribution to a Sense of Usefulness and Importance.

AUTHORS   R. S. Weiss and N. M. Samelson

PROBLEM   How do American women feel about family, housework, job, and community life outside the home? Where do they get most sense of feeling useful and important?

SUBJECTS   569 women over 21, selected to be a true probability sample of that population in the United States on the basis of age, marital status, education, and occupation.

PROCEDURE   Open-end interviews focused on the question: "What are some of the things you do which make you feel useful and important?"

SOME FINDINGS   1. The depressed response, "*nothing* makes me feel useful or important" was given by none of the younger women but by about 20 percent of the older unmarried women, employed or unemployed.

2. Job activities were more frequently mentioned as a source of self-esteem than were housework, family, or informal community relations for every category of employed women except the older unmarried, who were more apt to be generally dissatised, but spoke of housework and job and family about equally often. Among the 93 married and employed women, 59 percent referred to job satisfactions and only 39 percent to gratifications from their housework.

3. Among women who were college graduates, housework was less often a source of self-esteem (31 percent as compared with 46 percent for less educated) and job was more often recognized (66 percent as compared with 52 percent).

4. Interpersonal relations in the family were less frequently mentioned than job or housework as a source of self-esteem, by every category in the study except young mothers with pre-school children and unmarried, unemployed, middle-aged women.

5. Informal interaction outside home or job was prominent in the responses of only one group: young unmarried women, 42 percent of whom mentioned these satisfactions. For other categories, the outside contacts were mentioned by about 28 percent of the unemployed women and 15 percent of the employed.

SOURCE: *Marriage and Family Living*, 1958 XX:358–366.

Reaction to the subordinate status and less desirable role is the real root of what psychoanalysts have termed "penis envy." Alfred Adler saw more clearly than Freud that the deprivations which girls feel arise not primarily from their anatomy but from their social role. Even if mother rules the household, she commonly treats the father as a prestige figure. His property, his tastes and prejudices, his decisions, are all to be respected. Often, he is the point of contact with what the child thinks of as that strange and important world beyond the home. When the wife sees that her life-chances are dependent upon her husband's success, she makes a life-project of husband management—his health, his appearance, his social contacts, his speech, his attention to business, his public relations. The daughter's Electra complex may be less a desire to go to bed with her father than to shine in reflected glory. Girls covet the freedom men enjoy more than they do the phallus.

Girls who accept the idea of male superiority build the corollary view of their own inferiority. They conclude that it is right for men to get better jobs and more pay. They shun working under a woman executive. They are bored by social gatherings exclusively female.

In a study (McKee, Sheriffs, 1957) of several hundred college students it was found that 61 percent of the women, but only 29 percent of the men, reported being troubled by feelings of intellectual inferiority. Girls believe women generally less able than men. Data support the conclusion that men are not intellectually superior to women.

Women who accept second-class citizenship and identify with the prescribed sex-role do not try to keep up with political issues. They echo their husband's opinions. This accounts, in part, for the disappointment of the advocates of women's suffrage, who expected that it would bring a wave of social improvement. It is interesting to note that while 58 percent of men said they would vote for a well-qualified woman if their party nominated her for President; only 51 percent of the women would support such a candidate (American Institute of Public Opinion, Nov. 15, 1963).

In a study (Remmers, Radler, 1957) of teen-agers, the differences were even more marked. Opposition to women holding high office was expressed by 31 percent of teen-age boys, but by 61 percent of teen-age girls. The prejudice against their sex seems somewhat stronger in women themselves than in men.

The damaging consequences of accepting the wife-mother role as the overriding meaning of woman's life become particularly apparent after the child-raising years. The self-concept is an internalized version of the evaluation others have given to a person. Girls who find themselves born to a subordinate status—aware at an early age that their opportunities for self-realization are more limited than those open to boys, subject for 30 years to conflict between the reproductive and more generally productive roles, under pressure to conform to a less desired social pattern, excluded from almost all positions of top prestige—almost inevitably question, as mature women, their own worth. Some may protest the social discrimination—Margaret Mead estimates that about one woman in four is outspoken about her resentment—but the more usual result is self-derogation. Pauline Wilson (1950), interviewing woman college graduates 20 years after graduation, found 90 percent of them troubled by a sense of disappointment, frustration, and futility in their lives.

The internalization of blame may result, as it does sometimes with ethnic minorities, in rejection of one's own group. Women sometimes complain that conversation with other women is superficial and silly. Men are also bored occasionally by other men, but they blame it on the individual, not the whole sex. Women are likely to prefer male doctors, dentists, lawyers, ministers, and psychotherapists. Dissatisfied with their own mothers and with themselves, they admire few women and set a discouraging model for their daughters.

Discontent usually increases in the age group of women just beyond 40. If single, they have to face the fact that they have not fulfilled woman's traditional role—marriage and motherhood. If married, their children are ready to leave the home. The average woman today marries at about 20 and has had her last child before she is 25. At 45 or 50 years of age, her period of reproductive functioning—supposed to be her primary source of self-esteem—is over. The woman, who has been taught and pressured to put her love-life and children ahead of any other interests, finds herself no longer glamorous to men, and no longer needed by her children. At about 50 years of age, when men of comparable ability are stepping into their posts of highest responsibility, women find themselves with no meaningful occupation. Restlessly, they turn increasingly to beauty parlors, community organizations, alcohol, churches, and psychotherapists, but in this society there is no really satisfying answer. George Bernard Shaw has pointed out that if most men were as cut off from intellectual and public interests as are most women, the father-in-law jokes might be as common as those that caricature mothers-in-law (B. Watson, 1964, p. 158).

Often when women try to adapt themselves to their disadvantaged status, they add to their rejection. If they show that they are sorry for themselves and seek pity, they are likely to be scorned. If they transfer their distress to somatic symptoms, they may make many visits to the doctor complaining of disorders that have no organic basis. Their pains are real enough, and the lack of diagnostic confirmation increases the woman's sense of her own worthlessness.

Often a woman puts the blame for her dissatisfaction on the decisions of her career. "I should not have dropped out of college!" "If only I hadn't been such a fool as to get married at that time!" "What a bill-of-goods that man sold me! If only I'd had enough sense to choose so-and-so instead!" "I could have made something of myself if it hadn't been for having to care for that relative." Thus the sad refrains of self-accusation continue.

Some women rebel vigorously and develop careers. As the Weiss and Samelson study, summarized earlier, has shown, such women find increased self-esteem from their success at work. But they find the path harder as they achieve more success. A woman can easily become an office manager; she is like to encounter more prejudice against her as a vice president.

The rebellion of the active woman may lead to conscious or unconscious revenge on the dominant males in this man's world. Some women enjoy any opportunity to cut down male egoes. They are sometimes called "castrating females." Any self-assertion or self-satisfaction in boys or men, stirs up their rancor. As mothers and teachers they can inflict serious damage on young males.

The woman who tries to combine homemaking with a career not only has many practical complications, but may suffer also from a sense of guilt. Herzog (1960) reports that although children are not often really deprived by a mother who holds a job, working mothers nevertheless feel guilty when they leave house and children for their careers. They also feel they are lacking something when they are not working or earning. In suburban communities where most mothers spend the day at home, the mother who commutes daily to a job in the city is looked at with some envy and some criticism. She responds to both; she feels fortunate in not being immured in kitchen and laundry chores; she also wonders whether she is doing the right thing for her family. Sometimes she vaccilates—stays home and becomes bored; takes a job and feels "driven" and guilty; gives it up for home and restless boredom —and on through the cycle.

Small wonder that Betty Friedan can quote mothers as saying: "I feel empty somehow—incomplete;" "I feel as if I don't exist;" "I feel like crying without any reason." She quotes from *Newsweek:* The American housewife "is dissatisfied with a lot that women of other lands can only dream of. Her discontent is deep, pervasive, and impervious to the superficial remedies which are offered at every hand" (1963, p. 20; 24). A study (Davidoff, Markewich, 1961) of 50 college-educated women confirmed Wilson's observation, ten year's earlier, of a discrepancy between the values cultivated in college and the actual opportunities open to the women for achievement, success, and recognition. The volunteer jobs open to them seemed beneath the self-respect of the abler women.

Males suffer too

While women are under pressure to emulate a stereotype which stresses family life and neglects other important aspirations, males are pressed into striving for achievement which may not give full play to the potential of boys and men for tenderness, intimacy, and love. Any display of affection among males is highly suspect in our culture, although in ancient Greece and many other lands it has reached high levels. Boys are disciplined to repress tender feelings. They may not cry. They must not do anything that may label them as a "sissy." They must fight when they would rather run away, compete destructively when they might prefer cooperative friendship. A study of kindergarten boys (Hartley, 1959) showed that more distinctive and appropriate sex-role behavior was demanded from them than it was from girls their age. Boys had more anxiety about their ability to perform the required roles.

The commuter father may see very little of his family. During much of the year he is up before dawn, gulps his breakfast, departs before his family are out of bed, returns after dark for a late dinner, and may have evening meetings or a briefcase of homework before bed. Since other men take this heavy work load for granted, he, too, seldom wonders whether this prescribed occupational role really fulfills his whole self and destiny. Men are also expected to take strong initiative in courtship and sex relations; to support wives who may, if they choose, be self-indulgent and idle; to keep up with community, national, and world affairs; to serve in the armed forces; and generally to show forebearance and strength, come what may. This is no easy assignment if we recognize that, by nature, the male is no more equipped for such roles than is the female. Many men enjoy cooking; most fathers would appreciate more time with their children. A fairly typical misfortune is that of the man who intends to make friends with his sons and daughters but puts it off until it is no longer possible to achieve close understanding.

Boys, seeing less of their fathers than girls of their mothers, find it harder to identify with them. If the father is seen as a remote and *punishing* agent (Hartley, 1959), it is difficult for the son to choose him as a life model. The demand that one become a strong, decisive, courageous, bearer-of-burdens and protector of the weak, able to cope with all difficulties from broken equipment to world affairs, is heavy indeed when there is seldom anyone around to set such an example.

Hacker, in an article with the meaningful title, *"New Burdens of Masculinity"* (1957), lists such role prescriptions as: (1) being patient, gentle, understanding yet sturdy as an oak; (2) being a person on whom a wife can rely to make decisions but who leaves her free to make her own; (3) compulsion to succeed in gainful employment; and (4) a virility which can be demonstrated only by evoking orgasm in his mate. To these are added the recent threat of competition from women in the professions, business, and industry. Some men, should women become their colleagues and share their daily routines, may find it impossible to sustain the image of the male's remarkable achievements at work.

As with every other form of discrimination, it is not only the direct victims who are injured. Boys and men suffer indirect consequences of sex discrimination against females which are almost as bad as the effects upon girls and women. Most boys today are brought up in early life surrounded by women and girls. Baby nurses in the hospital, mothers and mother-helpers at home, nursery school, kindergarten, and elementary school teachers are almost all women. In varying degrees they all suffer from their subordinate status. To some extent, they express their resentment—usually unconsciously—on the boys in their care. Or, in compensation, they become "smothering mothers," spoiling boys by overprotection.

In adult life, the man's closest and most continuous companion is his wife. Her limitations and her emotional frustrations inevitably impinge upon the man's own life. An interesting illustration is the "child wife" type, described by Greenacre (1947). The ideal wife in certain upper-class circles in Europe and in our own South was a pampered, infantile, pretty, frivolous, light-headed, extravagant, flirtatious creature who needed the protection of a big strong man.

Some men prefer women who are silly, frilly, and dependent. Charlotte Brontë wrote of one fictional character: "At heart he could not abide sense in women: he liked to see them as silly, as light-headed, as vain, as open to ridicule as possible . . . inferior toys to play with, to amuse a vacant hour and to be thrown away" (Vol. I, p. 166) . However gratifying this may be to the ego of a young male, the time is likely to come when he would be happier with a helpmate who equals him in good sense, good conversation, and responsibility.

Intelligent girls who learn to act dumb on dates may flatter male vanity, but they deprive their companion of the stimulation and challenge which their ideas and viewpoints might have contributed. Without true reciprocity both partners lose the opportunity for growth in the dimensions of mature personality. Many men suffer in adolescence, in maturity, and in old age from the limited horizons our culture has imposed upon their most intimate partners. As George Bernard Shaw has said: "Men are waking up to the perception that in killing women's souls they have killed their own" (1932, p. 8).

Talents lost to society

The unused potential of women represents a loss to our civilization. "All geniuses who are born women," said Stendahl, "are lost to the public good." If we are concerned about a shortage of scientists in the United States, it may be salutary to recall that 40 percent of the members of the Academy of Sciences in the Soviet Union are women. The lives of men, too, may have been endangered and impoverished by the absence of discoveries that women might have made, the music they might have composed, the books they might have written, and the philosophic insights they might have generated.

ACHIEVEMENT MOTIVATION IN WOMEN

Psychologists assume that the motive to achieve is one of the major determinants of anyone's attempts to succeed. There is a great deal of research conducted on the achievement motivation theories of McClelland and Atkinson. From that research social psychologists are able to predict the achievement behavior of males as a function of the strength of their achievement motivation. The sparse data available about the achievement motivation of women is contradictory and inconsistent with the achievement theory for men. Yet it may be the failure of society to socialize achievement motivation in females which accounts for the general lack of achievement oriented behavior in many of the females in our society. For instance, Bardwick (1971) notes that academically talented girls are less likely to enter college and complete the undergraduate degree than are equally bright young men; academically talented girls are less likely to take advanced degrees; they are less likely to use the PhD's they do complete; they are less productive than men even if they do take the PhD, remain unmarried, and continue to work full time; and in general girls underestimate their academic abilities and choose academic majors and jobs that are not challenging. An explanation of this data may have to include more than just a statement about the discrimination against women in the marketplace (although that is a serious problem for our society); it has to include also a statement about how females are socialized in our society and how this socialization affects their achievement motivation.

A current review of the research and theory in achievement motivation as it applies to men can be found in Johnson (1970). Briefly, the motive to achieve may be described as a motive to be competent in a situation in which there are standards of excellence (Atkinson, 1964; McClelland, 1958). The person who is high in achievement motivation takes pride in his work when he is held responsible for his actions, when he is informed of his level of performance, when there are criteria of performance, and when he is not certain of success. The amount of effort that will be expended in the pursuit of achievement depends upon the person's stable level of achievement motivation, his expectancy of success in the specific task or area, and the value he places on success in that area. The person with a high achievement motive has developed an internal standard of excellence, is independent, persistent, undertakes realistic tasks, performs well academically, and has clearly understood goals. This model predicts the direction, magnitude, and persistence of achievement behaviors in males, but not in females.

Bardwick (1971), in summarizing much of the psychological research on women, states that girls are generally more dependent, more conformist, more persuasible, and more vulnerable to interpersonal rejection than are boys. She concludes that females are usually socialized in such a way that social approval dominates their motive structure while boys are usually social-ized in ways which make them more independent of social approval and more reliant upon internal standards of excellence in achievement situations. Similarly, Veroff (1969) states that the literature on achievement motivation suggests that for boys the achievement motive is easily cued by internal stan-dards of excellence, but for girls external support is critically important. Sev-eral studies have found that young girls use achievement as a primary means of securing love and approval from others. This is congruent with the re-search which indicates that during adolescence, when excelling in academics gets to be threatening to the social prestige of the majority of girls, many girls will strive to succeed only as long as most of their friends do not know how well they are doing. Unfortunately, in our society academic-vocational achievement is usually perceived as a threat to the more important social success of a female.

It seems that the development of achievement motivation in females in our society is more complicated than is the development of achievement motiva-tion in males. Veroff (1969) feels that the development of achievement mo-tives in girls requires a somewhat rejecting attitude by the mother when the girl is young, an appropriate timing of stress and mastery when she is in mid-dle childhood, her acceptance of the appropriateness of female achievement, and a female role-model who is not too strong and domineering. She should also not have experienced too strong an emphasis on interpersonal gratifica-tion during early childhood.

Matina Horner (1968, 1969) has focused attention on an additional vari-able involved in the achievement behavior of females, the fear of success. She states that (1) the achievement situation is competitive, (2) competi-tion may be viewed as a "sublimated" form of agressive behavior, (3) any type of agressive behavior is negatively sanctioned by society as unfeminine, (4) therefore, a female who is successful in achievement situations outside the home, especially against male competitors, finds herself in a position con-sidered unfeminine (and masculine), (5) this creates conflict for the female, evidenced by her higher anxiety level which is in turn reflected in her behav-ior, and (6) rather than fearing failure, as is common for males in achieve-ment situations, females are motivated by the fear of success. Being success-ful in achievement oriented situations, in other words, may create, in addi-tion to the obvious and overt social rejection that a competitively achieving girl may experience, an internal anxiety about one's femininity.

Horner thinks that females are threatened by success because outstanding academic or other competitive achievement behaviors are consciously or un-consciously equated with a loss of femininity as well as leading to real social rejection. Maccoby (1963) has written that "the girl who maintains qualities of independence and active striving necessary for intellectual mastery de-fies the conventions of sex-appropriate behavior and must pay a price in anxiety." Horner (1968) has reported a study in which she hypothesized that the motive to avoid success is more characteristic of women than of men and is more characteristic of women who have high motives to achieve along with the ability to succeed in competitive achievement. Using 90 female and 88 male freshman and sophomore college students as subjects, Horner asked the females to write a story to the cue, "After first-term finals, Anne finds herself at the top of her medical-school class"; the men were given the cue, "After first-term finals, John finds himself at the top of his medical-school class." Three main responses emerged from the women's stories. The most frequent types of response reflected fears of being socially rejected, of losing friends, of losing dating or marriageable qualities, the fear of isolation as the result of success, and a desire to keep the success a secret by pretending that it had nothing to do with intelligence. The second most frequent type of response reflected guilt, doubts about one's femininity, despair about the success, and anxiety about one's normality. The third group of stories used denial of different kinds such as denying any effort or responsibility for the success or changing the content of the cue. As Horner had predicted, the response of the fear of success was significantly more common for the women than for the men. Of the 90 women in the study, 59 wrote stories which reflected this fear while only 8 of the 88 men did so. In another part of the study Horner had her subjects engage in tasks in competitive and noncompetitive situations in order to see whether fear of success was aroused by the aggressive overtones of competition, especially when men and women competed. More than two-thirds of the men did best under competition, as against less than one-third of the women. Of the women who were high in the motive to avoid success, 77 percent did significantly better in the noncompetitive situation; of the women who were low in the motive to avoid success, 93 percent behaved similar to the men, performing at a significantly higher level in the competitive situation. Thus, when predicting the achievement behavior of women, in addition to the level of their achievement motivation and their fear of failure, we also have to determine their fear of success.

THE FUTURE

Women's liberation

The historic association between movements for women's rights and for black emancipation continues today as the new black militancy has become the fore-runner of an aggressive demand for liberation of women.

There are many different groups involved and their demands vary. Some, like Women's Strike for Peace, belong with general left-wing radicalism. Others, such as National Organization for Women (NOW) are concerned almost exclusively with liberating women from male chauvinism. Some struggle for an Equal Rights amendment to the Constitution; others demonstrate at city hall for more day-care centers. Many are concerned to end specific economic discrimination (the average male worker in 1968-69 had a 70 percent higher salary than the average employed female; in departments of sociology and political science only 4 percent of the full-professors are women). A small number regard heterosexual intercourse as violation of the female body. Kate Millet in her brilliant, scholarly and impassioned book *Sexual Politics* (1970) argues that exploitation of women by men is worse than that of blacks by whites or workers by owners.

At the same time, relatively few women are actively involved with any of the crusading groups. Most want a husband and children; many would like an interesting job which is compatible with their family responsibilities. They do not see "Women's Lib" as a necessary aid: Feminine separatism has had even less appeal than black separatism.

Resistance

Goals, in sex role as in race relations, now lie in the direction indicated by words like democracy, equality, mutuality, reciprocity, collaboration, comradeship, freedom, liberty, and self-actualization. The obstacles are now not so much economic or political as psychological.

The first obstacle is the pretense that there is no problem. We are further along in dealing with ethnic group or religious prejudice than we are in coping with sex prejudice because it is the fashion among men to complain, seriously or in jest, that women have everything their own way. Little research has yet been done on sex prejudice, in comparison with the great accumulation of data on racial prejudice. The first step is to affirm the problem.

A second difficulty lies in freeing men from the sense that their worth and security would be threatened by increased freedom and recognition for women. It is always hard for a dominant group to see that elimination of their special advantages would be a long-term benefit. It will be some time before the traditional-minded whites in the South recognize that blacks as well educated, well paid, and well housed as themselves will be a positive asset to the whole society. Employers have found it difficult to accept the idea that rising wages will benefit the entire economy. As long as men feel that their masculine dignity and privilege depend upon being able to look down on women, they will resist change.

While the old-fashioned dominating male can still be found in every social class, it is particularly in the less-educated lower classes that the old stereotypes are asserted and defended. The "war between the sexes" is fought most relentlessly in lower-class circles. As noted earlier, the higher one goes on the scale of intelligence and education, the fewer distinctions there are in dignity, freedom, interests, and values between men and women. Here again is a noteworthy parallel with the civil rights movement for blacks. It is predominantly the lower-class white who is most ardent and bitter in his opposition to increasing opportunities for other ethnic groups.

Satisfaction with male dominance is highest in men who score high on the F-scale which is an indicator of authoritarian personality. One study (Nadler, Morrow, 1959) showed a correlation of .66 between the F-scale and a questionnaire devised to measure approval of "open subordination of women." The questions referred to women's inferiority, lack of judgment, narrow-mindedness, superficiality, and need for male direction. Another scale in the same study was called "chivalry." This stressed the helplessness of women, their purity, delicacy, and the demands of courtly etiquette in relations of men with women. The chivalry scale correlated .35—only a fair measure of agreement—with the open-subordination scale. Chivalry also was closely related (r = .60) to authoritarianism. Both chivalry (r = .73) and open-subordination of women (r = .45) were associated with ethnocentrism in attitudes toward other races and ethnic groups. Put more positively, men who have a less prejudiced, more accepting and more egalitarian attitude toward other human beings are likely to show it in their relations with minority races, unpopular religions or nationalities, and also in their relations with women.

A third difficulty connected with improvement in the opportunities given women for self-fulfillment lies in the uncertain effect upon the emotional relations of the sexes.

Will the elimination of barriers of prejudice damage in some way the masculine-feminine polarities? Does equality imply in any degree the mannish woman and the effeminate man?

When we go beyond anatomical differences to try to understand masculine and feminine temperament, we move at once into a realm structured by culture. It may be true, as psychoanalytic theory maintains, that in the sexual act men are naturally more aggressive and women naturally more receptive. Yet this is surely an oversimplification of a complicated human relationship in which both partners may feel tenderness, thoughtfulness, erotic pleasure, intense passion, vigorous activity, and quiet relaxation. In any case we cannot assume that attitudes toward all other persons, things, and ideas derive from the relationship of sexual intercourse. Neither general biology nor human physiology can tell us what it means to have a masculine or a feminine outlook on life.

If we follow Jung, we explore the unconscious archetypes of the *Animus* and the *Anima*. It is true that adolescent girls *fantasy* masculine figures like a knight or, in modern times, a James Bond or an astronaut. Any hard-working husband, however, whose meals must be cooked, his socks washed, and who worries over the household bills must be sadly disillusioning to a wife enamored of the *Animus* figures.

Men, too, have in their psyche symbolic *Anima* figures of ineluctable woman. Woman is the morning star, the unfolding rose, the precious jewel, the cyclic moon, the tides of ocean, the fertile earth, the chattering brook, the graceful cat, the singing bird, the changeable wind. Woman is nymph, siren, the Sphinx, the alluring Venus, the enchanting Circe. This aura of *Anima* femininity seems to be expressed mainly in contemplating actual or potential sweethearts; one seldom associates it with the women that one may encounter as middle-aged scrub-women, sales clerks, bookkeepers, high school teachers, or the club ladies of the cartoonist, Helen Hokinson. Men may note very little *Anima*-enchantment in some of the finest and most wholesome mothers, aunts, and grandmothers. But the magic is in the male lover's unconscious needs and will be cast over the object of his romantic affection, however silly or sensible she may be.

We do not know what the authentic sex-differentiation in personality would be in a genuinely equalitarian society, for neither boys nor girls have ever grown up in such a world. It seems probable that to view masculine and feminine in dichotomies like aggressive-receptive, active-passive, dominant-submissive, decisive-responsive, leading-following, commanding-yielding, is a culturally-induced error. Men and women are first of all human. Both must meet the basic needs of life as other animals do, but both have the higher needs to make their lives meaningful and spiritually satisfying. Both enjoy, want, and appreciate the same things—adventure, security, responsibility, being cared for, creativity, artistic achievement. Both have a practical bent and a streak of idealism; both are often rational, sometimes irrational.

Again we may quote Shaw as a prophet of the New Day for women. "What women had to do was not to repudiate their femininity but to assert its social value; not to ape masculinity but to demonstrate its insufficiency." (1920, p. 443) Or, Simone de Beauvoir in the same spirit: "To recognize in woman a human being is not to impoverish man's experience; this would lose none of its diversity, its richness, or its intensity if it were to occur between two subjectivities." (1953, p. 261)

New roles

While some other countries—notably Sweden and the Soviet Union—have moved further than has the United States toward giving women freedom and equal opportunity to order their own lives, there is no pattern in other societies that can provide the answers we seek. Changes are needed in many aspects of life, and progress cannot be measured along a single linear scale. A better quality of life for men and for women cannot be guaranteed by equal rights legislation.

An essential first step is to recognize that both men and women are human beings entitled to develop their potentialities in their own chosen way. When someone asked Shaw the secret of his remarkable understanding of women—as demonstrated in the creation of characters like Lady Cecily, Major Barbara, Ann Whitefield, Candida, and Lina Szcaepanowska—he replied: "I always assumed that a woman was a person exactly like myself, and that is how the trick is done" (B. Watson, 1964, p. 21).

If it is true, as Existentialists maintain, that self-fulfillment requires projects subjectively proposed and pursued in freedom, this self-determination is as important for women as for men. Whether life will center primarily upon love, marriage, and children, or primarily upon achievement in science, business, engineering, or the fine arts is a choice which every individual—man or woman—should feel free to make for himself or herself. For some men and women family life will come first; for others, it will not. Some men and some women may choose to keep a fairly even balance of interests in the home and outside. What is important is to keep all choices free and open, for women as well as for men.

For historic-social reasons and because of biologically connected factors, women will probably complement the masculine patterns in modifying our civilization. Because women have not been deeply involved in the world's exploitation, competition, chauvinism, and militarism, they may have remained free from some of the usual masculine assumptions and illusions.

Again, because of physiological differences and a long history of limited opportunities, we need today a policy that goes beyond simple equality. "Equal consideration," writes one wise woman, "will always dictate special privileges for women." This is analagous to the principle of compensatory expenditures on education for lower classes and for minority ethnic groups, as proposed in the preceding chapter.

Increasingly, psychologists think of social change not in terms of exact design and rigid prescription but in terms of evolution, emergence, becoming, and the fuller realization of human potentialities (Allport, 1955; Murphy, 1958). Our civilization is embarked upon such a process as we give new opportunities to children from lower classes, minority ethnic groups, and to women. Masculine and feminine potentialities may emerge more distinctively and more attractively in the new freedom than they have ever seemed in any historic culture. If the old barriers go down and each sex is genuinely free to affirm its own nature and to define its own goals, we may expect greater self-realization and more valuable forms of interrelationship. The essential conditions are freedom, self-discovery, and growth.

Margaret Mead has happily described the emergence of new role patterns as "a ballet in which each couple must make up their steps as they go along. When he is insistent, should she yield, and how much? When she is demanding, should he resist and how firmly? Who takes the next step forward or the next step back?" (1955, p. 14)

Transition

Here and in the preceding two chapters, we have used the resources of social psychology to aid in efforts to reduce such barriers to human development as are set up by class disadvantage, ethnic group prejudice, and sex discrimination. In the chapters which follow, we shall show how social psychology can contribute to the reduction of international tensions and conscious direction of social change.

SUMMARY

The subordination of women is an integral part of the history of the world. Restrictions against women are parallel to those against different races and socioeconomic classes. Social systems which do discriminate against females often develop elaborate rationalizations to defend the rightness and necessity of these discriminations. Who among the readers of this book has not heard the saying, "A woman's place is in the home?"

There do appear to be differences between males and females. Biologically women may be stronger than men, and may have a greater life expectancy. Intellectually men and women appear to be similarly endowed. Women in our society are less likely to become alcoholics, criminals, or school problems than men. The alleged differences between the sexes, however, appear to be a product of social training rather than genetic inheritance. Women in our society, for example, are raised to see their role as a mother and wife. An occupational interest is secondary to this role. Whether women accept this prescribed role or not, they tend to find marriage less satisfying than do their husbands. Women are troubled by feelings of intellectual inferiority and to retrieve their personal dissatisfactions may internalize the blame and reject other women or project the blame and enjoy cutting down male egos.

In a society with sex roles so specifically prescribed, the expectations men have for female behavioral patterns increase the difficulties women have in obtaining equal rights. Married persons spend a great portion of their life with their spouse and each can deprive the other of the stimulation, challenge, and growth necessary for satisfying lives. Not only do men's stereotypes of appropriate female behavioral patterns help convince women that they should be a wife and a mother at the expense of a personal career, but the expectations females have towards males uphold the male role definitions of being the provider and protector of females. The role expectations for both males and females help keep females in an inferior position in our society.

In the United States, occupational prejudices still persist against women. Women hold inferior jobs and receive less pay than men. Following a period of dormancy, women's rights has recently become a major social issue. Women's liberation groups are springing up all over the country and are having an increasing impact upon the socialization of females. Obtaining equal rights for females in our society is, however, far from easy. Obstacles to changing the status of women are primarily psychological. Some of the obstacles are: (1) the pretense that there is no problem; (2) the feeling held by many men that their worth and security would be threatened by increased freedom and recognition of women; (3) the unknown effect of greater opportunities for women upon emotional relations between men and women; and (4) the absence of the ability to accept that all people are human beings and are entitled, therefore, to develop their potentialities in their own way.

Given genuine freedom and support, both men and women are likely to create new roles more satisfying to themselves and more valuable to society.

CHAPTER 12

Social psychology of interpersonal, intergroup, and international conflict

MANKIND'S PROBLEM

Matthew Arnold, in his poem "Dover Beach," said

> . . . the world which seems
> To lie before us like a land of dreams,
> So various, so beautiful, so new,
> Hath really neither joy, nor love, nor light . . .
> We are here, as on a darkling plain
> Swept with confused alarms of struggle and flight,
> Where ignorant armies clash by night.

In this century wars have become more and more disastrous. World War I killed 12 million in battle. World War II cost 21 million lives in battle and 15 million more in air raids. One B-52 bomber now carries in a normal payload more explosive power than all the shells and bombs of World War II (Hoagland, 1964). A third World War might kill all life over large areas and conceivably make the whole planet uninhabitable. Even during the past 25 years of relative peace, experiments with nuclear weapons have already distributed in the atmosphere, in plants, and in the bodies of animals, radioactive iodine, strontium 90, and plutonium, imperiling present and future generations. President John F. Kennedy warned:

> Today every inhabitant of this planet must contemplate the day when this planet may no longer be habitable. Every man, woman, and child lives under a nuclear sword of Damocles, hanging by the slenderest of threads, capable of being cut at any moment by accident, or miscalculation, or madness.

In his Inaugural address he spoke of two powerful groups of nations, "both racing to alter that uncertain balance of terror that stays the hand of mankind's final war." A similar theme was expressed by Harvard psychologist Henry A. Murray (1960, p. 12):

A war that no one wants, an utterly disgraceful end to man's long experiment on earth is a possibility we are facing every day. Events are hanging by a thread, depending on an accident, or some finger on a trigger, on a game of wits and tricks, or pride and saving faces.

As a species man stands in a maze of conflicts between nations, religions, ethnic groups, and generations, any one of which could start World War III. For the last 20 years or so man has had the technology and raw materials to obliterate every living thing upon the earth. This massive stockpile of destructive technology has made war and other forms of violence unthinkable as a means of resolving conflicts. Yet the basic answer to conflict situations seems to be "kill" or "repress by force." If man as a species is to survive, he must learn how to handle conflicts constructively. Perhaps the most important question facing the world today is whether man can learn to do so.

Imagine yourself to be a visitor from another planet, engaged in a field study of man. You are to make a prediction about how successful man will be in handling future conflicts. You survey his technological capacities for self-destruction, his stockpiles of weapons, you look at his past and present behavior in conflict situations, then you make a prediction about his survival. What would your prediction be? Lorenz (1963) says the following:

An unprejudiced observer from another planet, looking upon man as he is today, in his hand the atom bomb, the product of his intelligence, in his heart the aggressive drive inherited from his anthropoid ancestors, which this same intelligence cannot control, would not prophesy long life for the species.

We approach a crossroad at which we either educate ourselves, allies and enemies alike, in the nature of human behavior, using this knowledge to promote future behavior, or we continue along a road leading to the extinction of our species. And this, in the evolutionary view, will be about as significant as the extinction of the icthyosaur. (p. 49)

THE NATURE OF CONFLICT

To understand the nature of conflicts we must define what a conflict is, specify its source, and evaluate its potential functional and dysfunctional consequences. A *conflict* exists whenever incompatible activities occur (Deutsch, 1969); an action which is incompatible with another action prevents, obstructs, interferes with, injures, or in some way makes that action less likely or less effective. The incompatible actions may originate in one person (intrapersonal), one group (intragroup), two or more persons (interpersonal), or two or more groups (intergroup). A conflict may arise from several different sources, some of which are (1) differences in information, beliefs, values, interests, or desires, (2) a scarcity of some resource such as money, power, time, space, or position, and (3) rivalries in which one person or group competes with another (Deutsch, 1969).

There is often a basic confusion between the terms "conflict" and "competition." Although competition often does produce conflict, not all instances of conflict reflect competition (Deutsch, 1969). In conflict derived from competition, the incompatible actions of the individuals involved reflect incompatible goals. Conflict, however, may occur even when there is no perceived or actual incompatibility of goals. Two individuals, for example, could be in conflict over the means they will use to accomplish a single goal which they both desire and can jointly share; such controversy is a common part of cooperation. Conflict of this type is not competitive so long as the cooperators are motivated to select the best means to their mutual goal, rather than insisting on the ones which they initially advocated. This distinction between conflict and competition is an important one for Deutsch, as it is his contention that conflict can occur in both cooperative and competitive contexts. Which processes of conflict resolution are employed will be strongly influenced by the context within which the conflict occurs.

A superficial reading of many social psychological theories which emphasize tension reduction, dissonance reduction, good balance, and good form would seem to imply that the psychological utopia would be a conflict-free existence (Deutsch, 1969). Many discussions of conflict cast it in the role of causing psychopathology, war, and social disorder. Yet it is apparent that most individuals seek out conflict through such activities as competitive sports and games, plays, television, and books, and through interpersonal activities such as teasing. Deutsch (1965) notes that conflict is often of personal and social value, and is certainly a pervasive and inevitable aspect of life. It can also have many useful functions: (1) it prevents stagnation, (2) it stimulates curiosity and interest, (3) it is the medium through which problems can be solved, (4) it is the root of personal organizational, and social change, and (5) it is often part of the process of testing and assessing oneself and, as such, it may be highly enjoyable as one experiences the pleasure of the full and active use of one's resources.

The question, therefore, is not how to eliminate or prevent conflict, but rather how to make it productive, or at the very least, how to prevent it from being destructive. A social psychologist would phrase the question as, "What are the conditions under which the participants in a conflict will resolve it in productive rather than destructive ways?"

AGGRESSION IN HUMANS

Definition of aggression

Aggression in humans has been studied by all the behavioral sciences. In addition, in an attempt to explain the origin of human aggression and to put it in its proper biological perspective, studies of aggression in many different species have been made. Although it may seem obvious to a layman what aggression is, social scientists have difficulty agreeing what behavior should be considered aggressive. The simplest definition, which is favored by those with a learning approach to the subject, is that aggression is any behavior which inflicts harm or could harm others. Thus, the person's behavior itself determines whether or not a particular act is aggressive.

Other social scientists who are not strict learning theorists feel that this definition is inadequate because it ignores the intention of the actor; they feel that the motive is crucial in deciding whether or not an act is aggressive. If, for example, an angry person picks up a gun and fires it at another person, but the gun happens to be unloaded, he would not be considered to be engaging in an aggressive act by the learning theorist as his behavior did not result in harm to another person. Yet he intended to harm the other person. Similarly, if a surgeon operated upon a patient in order to save his life, according to the strict learning definition this would be an aggressive act, as it causes harm to the patient; yet the surgeon did not intend to harm the patient, he intended to help him. Or if a person accidently knocked a flowerpot off a windowsill and it hit a passerby below, the strict learning theorists would label this behavior as aggressive. If intention was included in the definition of aggression, this behavior would not be considered aggressive, since no harm was intended. This alternative definition is more difficult to apply in research and theory, as it does not depend solely upon observable behavior. It is often difficult to diagnose what another person's intentions actually are and, therefore, it is difficult to determine whether or not he is being aggressive. But this limitation must be accepted, for only by including the intention of the actor can aggression be meaningfully defined.

Finally, it may be helpful to differentiate between hostility, anger, and strategic aggression. A person is *hostile* who, through personality characteristics, response style, or habit, has a propensity to react to situations with aggression. Individuals differ in the number of aggressive acts they perform in proportion to the degree of hostility they have. *Anger* is a physiological arousal state coexisting with fantasied or intended acts culminating in harmful effects for another person. Aggression is frequently accompanied by anger. Finally, there are instances in which others may be unintentionally hurt in the process of attempting to achieve certain goals; this is called *strategic* or *instrumental* aggression.

Two views of the nature of human aggression

When one examines the behavior of a variety of animals, man's aggressive behavior is astonishingly unusual. Aggressive encounters occur frequently between members of the same species in most vertebrates and in many invertebrates. But overt fighting to the death very rarely occurs in vertebrates, and it is doubtful whether it ever occurs in mammals under natural conditions. *Man appears to be the exception.* Freeman (1964), quoting Richardson (1960), states that, "the unimagined strata of malignity in the human heart" has resulted in the death of 59,000,000 human beings from wars and other murderous quarrels between the years of 1820 and 1945. No group of animals is more aggressive or ruthless in their aggression than the adult members of the human race. The extreme nature of human destructiveness and cruelty is one of the principal characteristics which separates man, behaviorally, from other animals.

If it is true, as the evidence seems to indicate, that man is unique in the animal world as a killer, what makes him so? Why did man become saddled with the "curse of Cain?" Aggression seems to be a deep-seated, universal drive in all vertebrates, but the murderous way in which man's aggressive drives are expressed seems to be uniquely human.

In accounting for aggression in human relations, traditional theorizing falls into two main camps, the instinctivist camp and the environmentalist camp. Disagreement centers on what is apparently a dead issue in other areas of social psychology: Is aggression an instinct, and do animals and humans alike tend to share it involuntarily? The instinctivist camp states that aggression is a primordial disposition inhering in human nature. According to Holloway (1968), an *instinct* is generally understood to be a quite specific response pattern, invariant in its development, maturation, and expression, which occurs in the presence of a quite specific cluster of stimuli from the environment; it is regarded as an innate, genetically determined pattern which comes about without a reference to, or in the absence of, learning. Lorenz (1964, 1963) represents the instinctivists when he states: "There cannot be any doubt, in the opinion of any biologically-minded scientist, that intraspecific aggression is, in Man, just as much of a spontaneous instinctive drive as in most other higher vertebrates" (1964, p. 49). The environmentalist camp, on the other hand, states that aggression is a learned pattern of behavior which depends entirely on the cultural, social, political, and economic conditions surrounding men.

Two of the more provocative, but controversial, treatments of aggression as an instinct are those of Lorenz (1963) and Dart (Audrey, 1961).

Lorenz's view of human aggression

On the basis of a variety of studies with several different species of animals, fish, and birds, Lorenz analyzes the natural history of aggression in terms of its survival value for the species. In his opinion, the most important survival value of intra-specific aggression deals with territoriality. Territoriality refers to the tendency of members of the same species to have a well-defined territory which they defend against the intrusion of other members of their species. Each animal defines his own sphere, from which other members of his species are repulsed; this has ecological benefits, such as spacing out the animals so that overcrowding and depletion of resources is prevented. Territorial aggression gives an ideal solution to the problem of the distribution of members of any one species over the available environment so that the overall chances for the survival of the species are optimized. Even the weaker members of the species are able to obtain territories in which they can survive, even if they are small and undesirable territories.

The second benefit of aggression for the survival of a species Lorenz sees as sexual selection, that is, the selection of the best and strongest members of the species for reproduction. This is accomplished by the fighting of rival members of the species, particularly males. For example, when two males fight over the opportunity to breed with a female, the stronger, more healthy male will win, thus improving the chances of future generations of the species to survive. Another function of rival fighting is the selection of an aggressive family defender, which ensures adequate protection of the young against dangers. Finally, in many species aggression leads to a social ranking among a group which ensures that the best suited are placed in leadership positions.

According to Lorenz's analysis, therefore, aggression is an essential part of the survival of a species. It helps divide up the environment so that, within the potentialities offered, everyone can exist. The best father, the best mother are chosen for the benefit of the progeny. The children are protected. The community is frequently organized so that a few wise males acquire the authority to make and carry out decisions for the good of the whole community.

In his study of aggression in a wide variety of species other than man, Lorenz *never* found that the aim of aggression was the extermination of fellow members of the species concerned. This of course does not negate the fact that under unnatural circumstances, aggressive behavior may have a destructive effect.

Lorenz then addresses himself to the question, "Why is it that in other species of vertebrates aggression does not end in murder?" "How do other species handle aggression in ways which settle differences without the death of some of the members involved?" One of the primary ways seems to be *ritualization*. Through a ritualized fight, two members of a species can determine which is stronger without hurting the weaker. A typical ritualized fight is two male deer who lock horns and engage in a shoving contest until one gives up. Such types of ritualized fights are quite common in many different species. It should be noted, however, that ritualized fighting which achieves a decision by the mere exhaustion of one of the combatants rather than by physical damage can be used effectively only if the vanquished accepts his defeat and is subdued.

Secondly, many animal species seem to have *instinctual mechanisms inhibiting killing* and injuring members of their own species. There are three features peculiar to these mechanisms: (1) The correlation between the deadliness of an animal's natural weapons and the inhibition preventing their use against other members of its species is quite high; the more dangerous the species, the greater the inhibition against injuring others of the same species. (2) There are special appeasing rites for releasing the inhibition against killing in aggressive animals. (3) There is no absolute reliance on this inhibition, which may occasionally fail.

A third way of handling aggression is the effective use of *threat behavior*. In many species other than man, threat behavior precedes actual fighting and functions to "size up" the opponent, to measure his fighting potential before combat is actually engaged in.

Finally, there seems to be a tendency in some species to *redirect* aggression when inhibitory factors prevent its discharge in the direction of the eliciting rival. While inhibited from expressing aggression toward a defeated rival, animals occasionally attack some neutral object, such as a tree.

On the basis of ritualization, inhibition, threat behavior, and redirection of aggressive behavior Lorenz attempts to formulate some ideas concerning the control of aggressive behavior in man. While his research with species other than man is quite sound, his extrapolation to human aggression is of doubtful validity. Deutsch (1969) explains why mechanisms such as Lorenz discusses are not viable with humans. Paradoxically, it is man's superior intellect that makes these mechanisms ineffectual. With so many intellectual and physical resources available for waging battles, it is difficult to determine beforehand who will be the victor when one man (or nation) attempts to impose his wishes upon another. Most animal species can forecast the outcome of conflict accurately through threat behavior and ritualized demonstrations, and so physical conflict to settle disagreements is normally avoided. The versatility of man's techniques for achieving domination over other men makes it highly likely that combat will arise, because the combatants will have discordant judgments of the potential outcome. Misjudgment of the opponent's willingness and capability of fighting has sometimes turned controversy into combat as increased tension has narrowed the perceived outcomes of conflict to victory or defeat.

Other hypotheses about the uniqueness of man's murderous behavior have been derived from the assumed lack of instinctual inhibition against harming another human and the results of studies conducted on aggressive behavior in animals in "unnatural" environments. It has been hypothesized that with the rapid development of weapons, man's potential for destructiveness has far outstripped any inhibitions against killing members of his species and in addition use of weapons at a distance could possibly vitiate any inhibitions he does have. Other scientists have hypothesized that perhaps man is a prisoner within an unnatural environment he has created for himself. Research on a variety of animal species indicates that when they become overcrowded in an environment, mechanisms for controlling aggressive behaviors break down and they do kill each other. It has also been noted that animals placed in unnatural conditions such as zoos engage in pathological aggression, that is, they aggress in ways uncharacteristic of the same species in the natural environment. Perhaps in gaining dominance over nature, man has placed himself in an unnatural environment where his inherent mechanisms for handling aggression have broken down.

Lorenz's position, however is clear. He feels that intraspecific aggression normally fulfills a species-preserving function and the fantastic aggression we see in humans today is aggression gone wrong. It is a behavioral breakdown, a biological malfunction which we need to correct if our species is going to survive.

Dart's view of human aggression

With the exception of man, every modern primate is inoffensive, nonaggressive, and primarily a vegetarian. When one looks at the modern primates it is difficult to understand how man could have descended from such nonaggressive species. The question becomes: Why is man, the killer, so different from the other primates on the earth?

Raymond Dart, on the basis of discoveries which have been confirmed by Robert Bloom and L. S. B. Leakey, provides an answer (see Audrey, 1961). He states that some 800,000 years ago there lived around the edge of Africa's Lake Victoria, a small, advanced, man-like ape (*Australopithecus africanus*) who used tools for hunting and probably for killing his own species. Dart concludes that man is immediately descendent from this branch of carnivorous predatory apes, who used lethal weapons. The evidence for their carnivorous nature seems to be the remains of many chewed animal bones (including those of their own species) around their cooking fires. It is Dart's position that man emerged from his anthropoid background for one reason only, because he is a killer. Dart also theorizes that the use of weapons was the primary impetus to man's development. He states that weapons put new and multiplying demands on the nervous system for the coordination of muscle and touch and sight, which resulted in man's enlarged brain. The conclusion of his line of reasoning is that the continual development of better weapons is based upon the genetic necessity to outfight rival species, that man designs and competes with his weapons as birds build distinctive nests.

In summary, Dart explains man's unique murderous qualities as being genetically inherited from our hypothesized ancestors, a carnivorous killer ape in central Africa. He states that it is because we are Cains' children; because man is a predator whose natural instinct is to kill with a weapon, he survived while environmental upheavals were extinguishing many other species.

Dart's theory is highly controversial, and Lorenz's view of aggression in man is not shared by many behavioral scientists. Both theories are, however, provocative and interesting hypotheses concerning the uniqueness of man's aggression. As we pointed out in Chapter 8, using the concept of "instinct" to account for social institutions such as war and organized aggression has proven to be unsatisfactory in the past. Holloway (1968) notes that there appear to be precious few (if any) examples of instincts in man, and no evidence for an aggressive instinct. Scott (1965) concludes that aggressive behaviors even in animals are modifiable through learning. Certainly the concept of "instinct" is not helpful in predicting human behavior in any specific instance for, while man is aggressive in many situations, there are also many other situations in which he is not. The concept of an "aggressive instinct" does not lead to reliable predictions concerning how individuals will respond to different situations. Aggression in humans, furthermore, is a complex activity which can be expressed in many different ways. The hardships mankind has nearly always faced, poverty, starvation, substandard health, overpopulation, exploitation, disease, provide ample motivation for aggressive behavior without having to posit an instinctual need to aggress. Yet there is no refuting the uniquely murderous ways in which human aggression is expressed.

Environmentalist view of human aggression

The environmentalist viewpoint of the nature of human aggression is represented by individuals who believe that aggression is learned behavior. Anything which teaches a child that aggression is acceptable and effective in facilitating the accomplishment of his goals will increase his overall level of aggressiveness; anything that teaches him that aggression is wrong and will decrease the likelihood of accomplishing his goals will have the opposite effect. In general, frustration, annoyance, and attack all tend to make people behave aggressively. The major area in which research on aggression has focused, however, is upon the relationship between frustration and aggression.

Since its formulation thirty years ago, the frustration-aggression hypothesis has been a popular explanation for aggressive behavior (Dollard *et al.*, 1939). Originally the hypothesis was stated that, "occurrence of aggressive behavior always presupposes the existence of frustration and, contrariwise, the existence of frustration always leads to some form of aggression" (p. 1). In other words, frustration always leads to aggression and aggression is always a consequence of frustration. When frustrations are strong and numerous, we would expect persons to show more aggression. But aggression may be inhibited, and the very inhibition itself adds to the frustration. What happens then is the nurturing of an aggressive tendency, increasing the general predisposition of a person to respond aggressively even though the original object of frustration may not elicit aggression.

Many qualifications have been added to the original frustration-aggression hypothesis. Miller (1941) noted other possible consequences of frustration besides aggression. Berkowitz (1962) emphasized the concept of anger in mediating between frustration and aggression, and the role of interpretation in perceiving frustration and in selecting targets for aggression. Buss (1961) suggested that frustration is typically less important than other causes of aggression. Generally, however, the idea that frustration tends to give rise to aggression remains a key hypothesis in contemporary social psychology.

Frustration can be loosely defined as the interference with or blocking of the attainment of some goal. If a person wants to perform some act, obtain some objective, or go somewhere and is prevented, we say he is frustrated. There are several studies which demonstrate that being frustrated does result in aggressive feelings and behavior. Funkenstein and his associates (1954), for example, gave subjects a difficult digit-span test and then repeatedly criticized the subjects' efforts by making sarcastic comments and generally annoyed the subjects while they were trying to perform. In a second task, the subjects were required to speak as rapidly as possible but were given acoustical feedback that confused their speech, caused stuttering, and made rapid speech practically impossible; in addition, electric shocks were administered whenever the subjects spoke slowly. Although subjects were quite calm and relaxed before the tasks, afterward they were highly aroused and reported feelings of anger and aggression.

Perhaps the classic study in the area was conducted by Barker, Dembo, and Lewin (1941). They showed children a room full of attractive toys but did not allow them to enter it. The children stood outside looking at the toys, wanting to play with them, but unable to reach them. Finally, after they had waited for some time, the children were allowed to play with the toys. Other children were given the toys without first being prevented from playing with them. The children who had been frustrated smashed the toys on the floor, threw them against the wall, and generally behaved very destructively. The children who had not been frustrated were much quieter and less destructive.

Looking at broader aspects of society, Hovland and Sears (1940), in a study which was confirmed by Mintz (1946), presented evidence that economic depressions produce frustration because people cannot get jobs or buy things they need and are greatly restricted in all phases of their lives. The evidence revealed a striking relationship between the price of cotton and the number of lynchings in the South from the year 1882 to 1930. When cotton prices were high, there were few lynchings; when prices were low, the number of lynchings was relatively high. A drop in the price of cotton signified a depressed period economically, and this depression produced frustration, which, in turn, led to more aggression. An extreme manifestation of the increased aggression was the increase in lynchings.

Although frustration usually arouses aggression, there are circumstances when it does not, and factors other than frustration can also produce aggression. Whether or not frustration arouses aggression depends in part on how arbitrary is the frustration. The more arbitrary the frustration, the more aggression is aroused. Thus, if a person who is frustrating another person gives a good explanation of why it is necessary, aggressive feelings will be minimized. In other words, a person's understanding of a situation influences his reaction to frustrations. One's cognitive interpretation of the situation has a major effect on his motives and emotions.

Human aggression is a learned response to frustration. An individual will be likely to respond to frustration with aggression when the person responsible for the frustration is of low status, weak, and incapable of retaliation. The individual will be more fearless in expressing his aggression when he has the support of other individuals to do so. When the person has high expectations of success in accomplishing his goal, he will be more likely to react aggressively to frustration than will an individual who has low expectations for success. Finally, factors such as the perceived intent of the frustrator and his responsibility for producing the frustration seem to be basic determinants of the amount of aggressive feelings the frustration generates. To the extent that the frustrator intends to hurt us as an end in itself, rather than as a by-product of other pursuits, hostility and counterattack are the natural reactions.

The environmentalist views that aggression is a learned response to frustration or that it is a learned strategy for goal accomplishment are considered optimistic theories. This is because if aggression is learned, it can be unlearned. From this point of view, once individuals are taught that aggression is an unacceptable and unsuccessful way to obtain desired goals or to eliminate frustrations, human aggression will markedly decrease. While the optimistic simplicity of this theoretical approach to human aggression is appealing, it does not explain why aggression in humans so often results in murder.

Perhaps the major alternative explanation to the instinct and learning theories of aggression in humans is the theory based on intergroup identity and competition studies. It is to this body of theory and research to which we now turn.

INTERGROUP CONFLICT

Perhaps the most interesting and best known studies conducted on intergroup conflict were performed under the direction of Muzafer Sherif (1966). Conducted in the early 1950s, subjects in the series of field experiments were twelve-year-old boys who attended a summer camp run by the experimenters. All boys were strangers to one another prior to attending the camp so there were no established relationships among them. The camp setting, isolated from outside influences, afforded the experimenters a unique opportunity to manipulate the conditions and circumstances of interaction between the camp members. The investigators were interested in studying intergroup relations, and especially the effectiveness of various techniques for reducing hostility between groups. To create intergroup conflict, the experimenters divided up the campers into groups and instilled in each group an *esprit de corps* by such procedures as assigning names (e.g., "Bull Dogs," "Red Devils") to the groups and structuring their daily activities so that interdependent, coordinated activity among the group members was necessary in order to achieve desired goals (the food, for example, needed to be cooked and prepared over a camp fire and distributed to the group members—without coordinated planning such tasks could not be accomplished).

Following the successful development of two "ingroups" within the camp characterized by mutual good feeling among ingroup members, the experimenters attempted to induce conflict between the two groups by requiring them to participate in competitive activities in which the winning group was rewarded and the losing group was not. For a time the two groups displayed good sportsmanship, but after a series of competitive activities they were increasingly hostile towards the other group. The hostility mounted until the two groups were having "garbage fights," throwing mashed potatoes, leftovers, bottle caps, and the like in the dining hall.

Sherif's studies have been replicated by a variety of individuals in several different settings. Perhaps the most systematic replication of Sherif's work was conducted by Blake and Mouton (1962). Sherif and Blake and Mouton both found that competition between two or more groups has certain definite and very predictable effects on intragroup relations, intergroup relations, and negotiations between groups.

Within the group there is a strong upward shift in group cohesion as the group members join together to defend their group against defeat. There is a refinement and consolidation of the ingroup power structure as militant leaders take control. Values and norms governing ingroup behavior change. During the competition, personal reputations merge with the group reputation, and personal stakes become involved. There is high member satisfaction and identification with the group and the group's position on the issues involved in the conflict. At the same time, the opposing group and their position are belittled and devalued. Conformity is demanded from the group members. Finally, a task-oriented approach is adopted by the group.

Between the groups, an attitude of hostility and inaccurate and uncomplimentary stereotypes form. Interaction and communication decrease between the members of the competing groups. When given a chance to clarify the position of the other group, the situation is used to belittle the competitor's position, to cast doubt on its validity, and to demonstrate its inferiority in relation to the position of one's own group. This intensifies the conflict. High distrust exists between the groups. Finally, as the group elevates its own position, it downgrades the other group and their position.

In negotiations there are distortions of judgment concerning the quality of the competing solutions, with one's own solution as "good" and the other group's solution perceived as "bad." Negotiators are relatively blind to points of commonality between their own and contending proposals, and tend to emphasize the differences. The orientation of both negotiators is to win for their group, not to reach a mutually satisfying agreement. This results in the "hero-traitor" dynamic, in which a negotiator who "wins" for his group is seen as a hero and one who "loses" for his group is seen as a "traitor." When a neutral third party decides who is "right" and who is "wrong," the winner perceives the third party as being impartial and objective; the loser perceives the third party as being unfair, biased and thoughtless. Both sides see themselves as objective and rational and the other side as irrational—the only loyalty is to one's own group position; this excludes any questions of objectivity from negotiations. The common result of negotiations is deadlock. Finally, the representative is caught in a conflict between his own beliefs and perceptions and the mandates given to him by his group.

RESOLVING INTERGROUP CONFLICTS

Contact between groups

In his experiments on intergroup conflict Sherif (1966) tested several different methods for reducing the conflict between groups once it had developed. To find out the effects of social contact between groups on intergroup conflict, Sherif devised situations where members of the rival groups were given an opportunity to make social contact with each other in pleasant situations. There were several different contact situations, including eating together in the same dining room, watching a movie together, and shooting firecrackers in the same area. These contact situations had no effect in reducing intergroup conflict; if anything they were utilized by members of both groups as opportunities for further name-calling and conflict. Sherif then concluded that contact between groups in pleasant situations does not in itself decrease the existing intergroup tension. He concludes that contact between rival groups will resolve the conflict only when the groups come together to work cooperatively towards goals which are more important to the groups than the continuation of their conflict. We would hypothesize that the extent to which contact between competing groups reduced conflict depends upon: (1) common goals, the accomplishment of which does not call for any competition across group lines; (2) cooperative interdependence, that is, in order to accomplish their common goals the groups have to cooperate with each other; (3) equal status in the situation; (4) the sanctions of custom, law, or authority favoring the reduction of conflict; and (5) no misperceptions of the opponents as confirming negative stereotypes.

Common enemy

In his studies Sherif (1966) demonstrated that it is possible to reduce the hostility between two groups by presenting them with a common enemy against whom they are banded together. He arranged a softball game in which the two groups in conflict within the summer camp situation were combined to play against an outside group of boys from a nearby town. The common enemy approach was found to be effective in reducing the hostility between campers. This approach, however, has little promise for conflict resolution as it fails to resolve the conflict, and only transfers it from two small groups to two larger groups. Bringing some groups together against others means larger and more devastating conflicts in the long run.

Superordinate goals

Since cooperation toward common goals had been effective in forming the two ingroups in Sherif's study, he reasoned that it would be effective in reducing the conflict between groups. Sherif defined *superordinate goals* as goals which cannot be easily ignored by members of two antagonistic groups, but whose attainment is beyond the resources and efforts of either group alone; the two groups, therefore, must join in a cooperative effort in order to attain the goals. Sherif arranged a series of superordinate goal situations for the two antagonistic groups of campers to engage in. One such goal involved repairing the water-supply system which the experimenters had earlier sabotaged. Another was cooperating together to obtain money to rent a movie that both groups wanted to see. And still another involved getting a truck to move, which had suddenly broken down on its way to bring food for a camp-out. After the campers had participated in a series of such activities their attitudes toward members of the outgroup changed; several friendships among members of different groups were formed, members of the rival group were no longer disliked, and the friction between the groups disappeared.

   The characteristics of the superordinate goals introduced by Sherif in his studies are (1) they were introduced by a third party (the experimenters);

(2) they were perceived by the campers to be natural events in no way identified with the third party; (3) they were not perceived by the two groups of campers as being aimed at resolving the conflict; and (4) they transcended the conflict situation to restructure the competitive relationships between the groups into a cooperative one. It is apparent that in most conflict situations such superordinate goals are not feasible alternatives. A third party, for example, rarely has the power to initiate goals with the above characteristics. A participant in a conflict, furthermore, could not easily initiate such a superordinate goal in an attempt to resolve a conflict. Johnson and Lewicki (1969) compared the effectiveness of a superordinate goal having all of the characteristics of the superordinate goals used by Sherif with a superordinate goal which was initiated by one of the participants in the conflict, was identified with the initiator, and was perceived as being aimed at resolving the conflict. They used a group of 36 college students who were participating in a four day leadership training program in their experiment. An intergroup competition exercise similar to ones used in the experiments of Blake and Mouton (1962) was used. They found that while the Sherif-type superordinate goal was effective in reducing competition between groups, it tended to lead to a premature cooperation leaving the basic conflict between the groups unresolved. It may be hypothesized, for example, that once the superordinate goals are accomplished, the groups would still be faced with a basic conflict which may then become reactivated. The second type of superordinate goal, on the other hand, became caught up in the competitiveness of the situation and increased, rather than decreased the conflict. The group initiating the superordinate goal used it as a key argument in an attempt to reach an agreement with the opposing group. Feeling that they had the best interests of both groups at heart and that initiating the superordinate goal was an initial concession on their part, they felt that the opposing group should be quite accommodating to their wishes. The opposing group, however, tended to view the superordinate goal as part of a competitive strategy aimed at furthering the initiating group's vested interests, and refused to accept it. What resulted was an intensification of the conflict, increased misunderstanding, and a refusal by both groups to compromise.

Sherif's notion of resolving conflicts through the use of superordinate goals is a slight elaboration of the principle that groups which cooperate with one another towards the accomplishment of common goals will have harmonious and friendly relations. Deutsch's (1949, 1962) theory of cooperation and competition easily subsumes Sherif's work. As was discussed in previous chapters, Deutsch defines a cooperative social situation as one in which an individual or group can reach his goal only to the extent that all other individuals or groups in the situation also reach their goals. He states that the psychological consequences of joint cooperative behavior are (1) the actions of the groups are interchangeable; (2) actions which increase the likelihood of the two groups accomplishing their goals are favorably evaluated; and (3) the groups have high mutual influence. Deutsch (1965) states that cooperative or competitive relations are self-perpetuating; once cooperative relationships have been established between two groups, there are strong tendencies for the two groups to continue cooperating with each other. From Deutsch's theory, therefore, one would predict that even when there is intense hostility between two groups, joint cooperative action to accomplish goals which are of vital importance to both groups will result in mutual liking and continued cooperation. As will be discussed in more detail later, accurate perceptions of the other group, effective communication, positive attitudes, and definitions of potential conflicts as problems to be solved are all characteristic of cooperative relationships between groups.

Blake's intergroup conflict resolution procedure

Robert Blake and Jane Mouton (1962) pioneered a procedure by which two groups in conflict consult with a behavioral scientist to resolve their differences. Their procedure originated from a series of experiments they conducted on intergroup conflict. From their experiments they concluded that the primary characteristic of intergroup conflicts was the development of "win-lose" attitudes—both groups became committed to competitive approaches to settling their differences; that is, they wanted to "win" at their opponent's expense rather than attempting to find some mutually satisfying solution. Blake and Mouton then developed a procedure for changing "win-lose," competitive orientations to intergroup conflicts to a cooperative orientation. First, each group spends several hours developing their self-image as a group and the image they have of the opposing group. Then the two groups come together and share the results. With the help of a behavioral science consultant the two groups compare the way they perceive themselves with the way the other perceives them and vice versa. It is quite common that identical perceptions of the other group as unreasonable, unethical, unwilling to cooperate, are made by each group, while at the same time each group sees itself as being very reasonable, ethical, and willing to cooperate. These differences in perception are then clarified. The two groups next meet separately for several hours to diagnose the present relationship between themselves and the other group, what problems exist, why they aren't being constructively handled, what the other group contributes to their mutual conflicts, and so on. The groups then come together and share their diagnoses. They then attempt to consolidate the key issues causing conflicts between the groups and the main sources of friction. Finally the two groups plan the next stages for the cooperative solution of their conflicts.

During the above activities Blake emphasizes the avoidance of three basic traps which lead to increased, rather than decreased, conflict. The first is avoiding the "win-lose" dynamics where every action of the adversary is seen as one group dominating the other. He teaches the participants how to recognize "win-lose" attitudes and behaviors, and attempts to set norms proscribing them. Secondly, he emphasizes avoiding what he calls the "psychodynamic" fallacy where the motivation for the adversary's behavior is seen as personality factors rather than the dynamics of intergroup conflict. It is very easy to blame the conflict upon sick, vicious, power hungry individuals rather than viewing the adversary's behavior as a predictable result of intense intergroup conflict. Finally, Blake emphasized avoiding self-fulfilling prophecies where, for example, by presuming that one's adversary is belligerent, one engages in hostile behavior in an attempt to defend oneself through a good offense, thus provoking belligerent behavior on the part of the adversary, which confirms one's original expectations.

Blake and his associates have used this procedure quite successfully with a large number of intergroup conflict situations. As an industrial consultant with businesses which were having severe union-management or interdepartmental conflicts, he has successfully resolved their conflicts. The procedure he pioneered is now commonly used by a variety of behavioral science consultants in many different intergroup conflict situations, often with success.

Deterrence

In a conflict between two street gangs, one gang manages to obtain several guns; this, they feel, will resolve the conflict because their superior weapons will deter the other gang from any aggressive acts towards them. In his speeches a former president of Columbia University, Nicholas Murray Butler, reviewed the enormous financial cost of World War I. He argued in the 1930s that airplane bombing would be so destructive that a new war could not be begun or pursued. Yet he was speaking only eight years before the outbreak of the far more expensive and destructive World War II. The invention of gunpowder was thought to be sufficient to deter any future major conflicts. Each year many countries in this world spend large portions of their wealth on the development of new weapons and new ways to kill their fellow man; if they ever obtain clear military superiority, they believe, then no one will dare challenge them.

Throughout recorded history, strong nations have been prone to assume that their impressive power would succeed in preventing others from attacking their interests. A common strategy used in intergroup conflict is threatening one's opponent to deter him from engaging in undesirable behaviors. The concept of *deterrence* has come to stand for any of a series of strategies which would forestall possible aggression by making aggression "costly." Its use depends upon the communication of a threat that if the other group engages in aggressive behavior, one's own group will be forced to inflict harm on the aggressor. Thus deterrence rests upon the threat of punishment. As it is employed in modern international conflicts, it is a subtle notion that the deterred remains hostage for his own good behavior; hostage in the sense that the populace of a country will be destroyed if their leaders misbehave. In intergroup conflicts the use of deterrent strategies has repeatedly resulted in arms-races in which each group attempts to achieve military superiority through the stockpiling and the development of weapons. Such arms-races often reach absurd levels; The Federation of Atomic Scientists declared in its *Bulletin* several years ago: "With the stockpile . . . that now exists it is possible to cover the entire earth with a radiation level which for ten years would remain sufficiently intense to prove fatal to all living beings on land." Yet the efforts of the nuclear powers to stockpile more of the lethal weapons as a deterrent continue, as if having the potential to kill everyone twice is a greater deterrent than just being able to kill everyone once.

Deterrence is one of the major strategies being used in international conflicts and, therefore, the future of the world may depend upon its viability. Yet a close examination of its assumptions and the empirical support for their validity is frightening. One of the key assumptions is that one's opponent is rational; being rational means that each side has clear goals from which it expects to reap rewards and, therefore, it is willing to suffer certain costs in order to achieve its goals. A deterrent strategy is one which threatens to make the enemy's costs of attempting to achieve his goal greater than his potential rewards for achieving it. Unfortunately, most intergroup conflicts are sufficiently complex that one's goals are often hazy and constantly changing so that one is never sure just what rewards are to be gained if one achieves them. Consequently, there is no rational way to weigh costs against gains in many instances. Yet the use of deterrence presupposes that one's enemy is doing precisely that. There is evidence, furthermore, from research on interpersonal conflicts that individuals will intensify conflict even when the costs of continuing conflict are much greater than the potential gains (Deutsch and Krauss, 1962).

Another major assumption made by advocates of deterrent strategies is that a group can engage in various threatening and warring acts without losing control of its conduct or the ensuing interaction. Thus the group is assumed to be able to escalate or deescalate a conflict whenever it chooses to do so; a country, for example, may choose to escalate a conflict by committing a certain number of troops to attack another country but then at a future date decide to deescalate by reducing the number of troops. There are numerous behavioral scientists, however, who believe that once warlike activities are initiated, they have a propelling power and dynamic of their own which leads to a loss of self-control on the part of the parties involved. There is considerable evidence from research on interpersonal conflicts that as the conflict becomes more intense the likelihood of misunderstandings, biased perceptions, and breakdowns in communication increases, thus reducing the control participants have over their own behavior. Even if a group's leadership does remain in control of their behavior during an intense conflict, the members of the group may lose control and exert pressures upon them.

In order for deterrent strategies to work, threats must be believable. One way to increase the believability of threats is to make their execution inevitable and irreversible; an extreme example of such a commitment is a doomsday machine which will automatically exterminate the enemy if he attacks. In conflict situations misperceptions of the opponent's willingness to carry out his threats are common. Yet the stability of deterrence assumes that each side can quite accurately assess the opponent's capabilities to inflict damage and the seriousness of his intent to carry out his threats. Since deterrence is based upon the use of threat, we shall briefly examine the research on threat in more detail.

A *threat* is generally conceived of as the communication of an intention to do harm to another; the purpose of a threat is to establish, in the threatened party, the expectation that if he performs some undesired act, he will suffer some harm. A successful threat is one which does not have to be carried out. Deutsch (1960 and Deutsch and Krauss, 1962) demonstrated that in a conflict, if one party is able to threaten the other, he will tend to do so in an attempt to force the other to yield. The more irreconcilable the conflict is perceived to be, the stronger the tendency to use threat. If the party being threatened is of equal or superior status, however, he will feel hostility toward the threatener and tend to respond with counter-threat and/or increased resistance to yielding. Deutsch feels that the use of threat changes the parties' perception of the conflict situation. Their competitive orientation will be strengthened, and in order to "save face" the threatened party will refuse to yield and react with increased aggressiveness toward the other. Thus the use of threat often escalates the conflict and decreases the likelihood of a mutually beneficial settlement.

Deterrence is based upon the assumption that one is facing an enemy whose intent is primarily hostile. Most conflicts between groups are sufficiently complex so that each side has both hostile and friendly intentions towards the other. The use of deterrent strategies may lock the parties into strategies impelling the use of force for conflict resolution.

The preoccupation with force, power and military superiority that results from emphasizing deterrent policies may exclude the possibility of other strategies, such as cooperative development projects. One of the greatest dangers of assuming that one's opponent is predominately hostile is that such assumptions can easily become self-fulfilling prophecies, so that by increasing use of deterrence, conflicts are intensified rather than resolved.

Since the use of deterrence involves the threat of punishment, a brief review of the research on punishment may add to our examination of the effectiveness of deterrence as a strategy of conflict resolution. There is some disagreement in the literature on the effectiveness of punishment in influencing behavior. Bandura (1962) states that relatively severe punishment is ineffective in eliminating undesired behavior. In a more recent review of the literature, however, Walters and Parke (1966) conclude that punishment, if well-timed, consistent, and sufficiently intense, effectively suppresses undesired behavior. There is general agreement, however, that the suppressive effect of punishment is usually only of value if alternative, socially desired behaviors are elicited and strengthened while the undesirable behavior is held in check (Bandura and Walters, 1963; Walters and Parke, 1966). The effective use of deterrence rests upon the assumption that punishment will effectively suppress behavior and that the threat of punishment is sufficient to suppress undesired behavior. But according to learning theory, behavior can be modified better by rewarding desired behaviors than by punishing undesired behaviors. The use of deterrence in intergroup conflict rarely, if ever, places much emphasis upon rewarding the desired behaviors one's enemy displays.

There is little empirical support for the effectiveness of deterrence. In Sherif's studies of intergroup conflict, he observed several attempts by one group to deter behavior in the other; none of the attempts at deterrence were successful. Noting that deterrent strategies have frequently been used in intergroup conflicts throughout man's history, Naroll (1966) studied anthropological files on 48 different societies to determine the effectiveness of various strategies for avoiding war. He identified a series of warlike traits which indicated a military orientation, and correlated the presence of those traits in a society with its frequency of involvement in wars. If the deterrence theory is correct we would expect to find that the greater the military orientation of a society the less frequently it would actually be involved in a war. The results provide no support for the deterrence theory; very few of the measures of military orientation seem to have any impact, one way or the other, on the frequency of war.

Sherif (1966) notes that the use of deterrent strategies changes the groups which follow them. These strategies necessitate an early definition of what one wishes to accomplish in a conflict. This decision becomes "frozen" and blocks future attempts to redefine one's goals. Sherif's experiments demonstrated that waging a conflict through force and the threat of force changes the ordering of priorities within each group, the nature of the relationship among the members, the ideas of who is to be heeded and trusted, and the qualities needed in leadership.

If there are conditions under which deterrence can be effectively used to avoid the intensification of conflicts, they are yet to be clearly specified. As the future of the world rests in the hands of politicians and military personnel who believe that the use of deterrence is effective, we are presently in a frightening situation. Let us hope that in the future, the emphasis in handling intergroup conflicts will change from strategies which rely upon the threat of forcefully imposed punishment and harm to strategies which accentuate the cooperative development of all groups to improve the quality of their existence.

SUMMARY OF CAUSES OF AGGRESSION

Is man an evolutionary mistake? Is man an aberrant species? Is man's aggressiveness simply learned behavior taught to each new child by his parents? Or is man enslaved by his tendency to identify with certain groups and to impose the beliefs and practices of his group upon others? There is no doubt that one of the primary ways man is distinguished from other animals is that he kills his fellow man. There is great reason to be concerned whether man will not only destroy his own species but all the living things upon the earth out of his seemingly uncontrollable aggressiveness. The goals of science, as was discussed in Chapter 1, are to discover the conditions under which certain behaviors will be engaged in order to be able to predict human behavior, to understand its causes and to control it. Man's aggressive behavior is fairly predictable. But we must be able to diagnose its causes if man is to be able to control it. Neurophysiologists might point to the structure of our brains as the source of aggression. A social psychologist would focus on the dynamics of intergroup conflict, the evolution of man as a species, or on the way in which man learns aggressive behavior.

In the next section the dynamics of conflict situations will be explored further with an emphasis upon ways to maximize the constructive aspects of conflict while minimizing its destructive aspects.

DIMENSIONS OF CONFLICT SITUATIONS

The conflicts most individuals find themselves in involve only a few other persons. Wives and husbands commonly have conflicts to resolve; parents and children, a teacher and a student, two friends, all at times are in conflict with one another. The ability to fight constructively, to handle interpersonal conflicts constructively, is one of the most necessary skills in our society. Yet many people seem to lack this skill. George Bach, in a 1962 *Life* magazine article describing his work with married couples on the verge of divorce, expresses strong opinions concerning the ability of Americans to fight constructively. What dismays Bach is not bloodshed *per se* in fighting, it is the native cowardice and abysmal crudity of the American fighting style. Most husbands and wives, he has found, will avail themselves of any sneaky excuse to avoid a fight in the first place. But if cornered they begin clobbering away at one another like dull-witted Neanderthals. They are clumsy, weak-kneed, afflicted with poor aim, rotten timing, and no notion of counterpunching.

What is more they fight dirty; their favorite weapons are the low blow and the rock-filled glove.

Perhaps the leading theorist in the field of interpersonal conflict is Morton Deutsch; it is primarily his research and theory that is discussed in this section. Deutsch (1966) states that to resolve a conflict productively there must be a clear perception of the other's position and motivations, accurate communication, a trusting attitude toward the other, and a definition of the conflict as a mutual problem. Each of these four areas is discussed in the following sections. The implications of his theory for intergroup and international conflict will also be discussed.

Perception in Conflict Situations

In conflict situations the antagonists often distort or misperceive their opponent's position and motivations. These misperceptions are so common that they can be found in almost any competitive conflict situation; typical misperceptions include the mirror-image, the mote-beam mechanism, the double standard, and the oversimplified self- and enemy-image.

The *mirror-image* can be defined as the situation where two competing parties hold similar but directly opposite views of each other. The concept was formulated by Bronfenbrenner (1961), a social psychologist who was allowed to travel alone in Russia, without a guide, during the summer of 1960. He devoted much of his time to striking up conversations with Russians in public conveyances, parks, stores, restaurants, or just on the street, making sure that he talked with individuals who did not take the initiative as well as those who did. For example, he would decide before entering a restaurant to sit at the third table on the right and interview whoever was sitting there. During his conversations he would inquire about how the individuals felt about America and Americans. At first he was deeply disturbed by the distorted view the people he talked with had of America, but gradually he developed an even more disturbing awareness. The Russian's distorted picture of America was curiously similar to the American's view of Russia. Both Russians and Americans saw the other country as a dangerous aggressor and the government of the other as exploiting and deluding its people. Both thought that the mass of the people of the other country was not really sympathetic to the regime they lived under, that the other country could not be trusted, and that the policies of the other country verged on madness. Thus, both Russians and Americans felt threatened by the other country and both felt innocent—*they* want war, *we* want peace, *we* are right, *they* are wrong, *we* are good, *they* are evil. The perceptions of each country was the mirror-image of the other's.

In every important international conflict, the same myth tends to recur. The pattern is that of the knighthood legends and can be called the Sir Galahad Syndrome. A fair damsel is threatened by a dragon; a knight in shining armor rides to the rescue, slays the dragon, and carries off a happy maiden. Since the cold war began after World War II both the United States and the Soviet Union have tended to see themselves in the role of Sir Galahad whose "strength is as the strength of ten because his heart is pure." Each sees the other side in the role of the monstrous dragon. Humanity—or Korea or Vietnam or whatever land next emerges as the focus of conflict—has the role of the distressed damsel. The pattern is ancient but persistent.

The *mote-beam mechanism,* similar to projection, consists in perceiving certain characteristics in others which one does not perceive in himself (Ichheiser, 1949). These characteristics are perceived as though they were peculiar traits of the other and, hence, the differences between the other and oneself are accentuated. Since the traits we are unable or unwilling to recognize in ourselves are usually traits we consider to be undesirable, the mote-beam mechanism results in a view of the other as peculiarly shameful or evil. Since the mote-beam mechanism works on both sides, there is a tendency for each side to view the other as peculiarly immoral and for the views to mirror each other. This perceptual distortion, which is common in highly competitive conflicts, takes its name from a Bible verse, "Thou hypocrite, first cast out the beam (a large piece of timber) out of thine own eye; and then shalt thou see clearly to cast out the mote (a small particle of dust) out of thy brother's eye" (Matthew, 7:5).

The *double standard* is the process whereby ingroup or personal virtues become outgroup or opponent vices. It means simply the same action is evaluated good for oneself and bad for the opponent. A recent study by Oskamp (1965), for example, demonstrated that American students are likely to rate more favorably an action of the United States directed toward the Soviet Union than the identical action directly by the Soviet Union toward the United States; the placement of U.S. missile bases near Russia, for instance, was evaluated much more favorably than the placement of Russian missile bases near the United States.

Finally, there is commonly an *oversimplified view of oneself and the opponent* in competitive conflicts; one sees himself or his group striving for humanitarian goals, as being totally good, with "God on his side." The opponent, on the other hand, is perceived as striving for illegitimate goals, as being criminal, immoral, and the representative of the devil.

The above perceptual distortions can be found to varying degrees in almost any competitive conflict, whether it is between countries, generations, a wife and a husband, or between two students. Such distortions contribute toward misunderstanding between the patients involved in a conflict which in turn contributes to escalation and inhibits resolution. A few principles of perception explain many of the underlying roots of these perceptual distortions (Deutsch, 1962b).

First one's perception of an opponent's behavior is determined both by the perception of the behavior itself and by the perception of the context in which the behavior occurs. Behavioral contexts are often quite ambiguous in conflicts, so one tends to impose his own context upon the opponent's behavior. Thus the opponent's and one's own behavior may be interpreted quite differently depending upon from whose frame of reference one is viewing the behavior. When the two parties in conflict are from different cultures, the misunderstandings can be phenomenal. An example of such a misunderstanding is as follows:

The scene was a small square in the city of Hue, South Vietnam, on a summer day in 1965. The place was known as a rendezvous for American GIs and Vietnamese girls. A couple of military police were on duty to keep order. On this day, one of them had supplied himself with some candy for the children who played in the square and crowded around the Americans. As he started his distribution in a *friendly mood*, a swarm of youngsters jumping and reaching, pressed about him. With a laugh he tossed the candy out on the cobblestones. Immediately the children descended like locusts, each intent on grabbing a piece. A young Vietnamese school teacher happened by at this moment, and seeing the scrambling children, he spoke to them in stern and emphatic tones. He told them to pick up the candy and give it back to the American. After some hesitation, they sheepishly complied. Then, facing the soldier and speaking in measured English with a tone of suppressed anger and scorn, he said, "You Americans don't understand. You are making beggars of our children, prostitutes of our women, and Communists of our men!"

From *Peace in Vietnam* by the American Friends Service Committee. 1966, page 1.

In the above example the two parties were allies, but their interpretation of the American's behavior was astonishingly different. To the American he was being generous and helpful, to the Vietnamese he was reinforcing the children for begging and dependency. Such misunderstandings are the rule, not the exception, in conflicts when the parties use their own frame of reference to interpret their opponent's behavior and they contribute to the mirror-image effect.

Second, one's perceptions are influenced greatly by his expectations and preconceptions. Research in selective sensitization indicates that individuals given certain expectations will perceive some objects or events but not others (Postman and Brown, 1952; Dearborn and Simon, 1958); preconceptions also affect the understanding and recall of a message or an event (Allport and Postman, 1945; Pepitone, 1950). Both these lines of research support this principle. If one expects the opponent to act aggressively, then any action he takes may be judged as aggressively motivated.

Third, our perceptions of the external world are more often determined indirectly, by the information we receive from others, than by our direct experiences. Communication is selective, and it becomes increasingly simplified and distorted the more human links it passes through (Allport and Postman, 1945). Distortion in communication tends to take characteristic form: there is a tendency to accentuate the unusual, bizarre, controversial, deviant, violent, and unexpected; on the other hand, there is a tendency for people who are communicating to their superiors to transmit only information which fits in with the preconceptions of their superiors.

The tendency to distort information as it passes through a communication chain becomes cumulative and sometimes quite large when several of the human links have conscious or unconscious reasons to distort the information in the same direction. White (1966), for example, analyzed the way in which information made available to the American Public concerning the Vietnam War became disorted. First, the Vietnamese whom Americans in Vietnam met and used as information sources—army officers, educated people, officials, city people, and those who speak English—were precisely the ones most likely to support the government and oppose the Viet Cong. Second, many Vietnamese who were associated with the government have vested self-interests in maximum support from the United States, and this often led to deception; at the same time, Vietnamese with views disapproved by the government were not likely to speak up as freely as the orthodox supporters of the government do out of fear of imprisonment. Third, the hopes and fears of the Americans in Vietnam who were involved in the war often ran high. Quite understandably their wishful thinking tended to add to the distortion inherent in what they were told by their Vietnamese allies. Fourth, there was, and still is deliberate censorship, both official and unofficial, by Vietnamese and by Americans in Vietnam of what information was allowed to be published. This often took the form of "gentlemen's agreements" between reporters and official sources of news. Finally, there were pressures toward conformity and patriotism in the American media and among the American people which tended to distort what information was published and passed from person to person. Because of such tendencies toward distortion of information, all of which operated in the same direction, the information the American public received may have been of doubtful validity. This is characteristic of conflict situations, even small scale personal conflicts. What a distant relative hears about a marital conflict may be similarly biased by passing through a variety of human links, all of which tend to favor one of the persons in the marriage.

The fourth principle of perception is that our perceptions of the world are often very much influenced by the need to conform to and agree with the perceptions of other people. If all of one's associates and friends perceive an event a certain way, there are obviously strong pressures for one to perceive it the same way. The research on the strength of pressures for conformity has been reviewed elsewhere in this book.

Fifth, there is a considerable body of psychological research which indicates that an individual attempts to perceive his environment in such a way that it justifies his feelings, beliefs, and behavior. Thus, a person who is afraid will tend to perceive others as fearful and anxious and the world as being a frightening place (Feshback and Singer, 1957). Or if a person feels hostile, he is likely to perceive the world as frustrating and unjust, and so on.

Finally, intense fear, threat, or conflict tends to impair perceptual and cognitive processes. When tension increases beyond an optimal, moderate level, it reduces the range of perceived alternative actions, reduces the time-perspective in such a way as to focus on the immediate rather than the overall consequences of the perceived alternatives, and polarizes thought to a simplistic view of the conflict. In addition, it leads to stereotyped responses, increased defensiveness and conformity to group norms, and increased distortion of information and actions.

Perhaps the most tragic result of perceptual distortions is that they are so difficult to correct once the conflict becomes highly competitive. Deutsch (1962b) gives three reasons for the perpetuation of distortions. First, parties in conflict often make major psychological investments in the distortions and giving up the distorted view of the opponent is costly in such terms as loss of social face, guilt over past actions towards the opponent which no longer seem justified, ambiguity concerning how one should relate to the opponent, and personal instability. Certain distorted perceptions perpetuate themselves because they lead the individual to avoid contact or meaningful communication with the opponent. This will be discussed in more detail in the next section which deals with communication, but there are many examples of communication being cut off in conflict situations, such as the wife who goes home to mother after a quarrel with her husband, the severing of diplomatic channels between two countries involved in a dispute, or the segregating of blacks or Indians in areas of the United States which are dominated by white racists. Finally, distortions are often perpetuated because they evoke a self-fulfilling prophecy—because one views the opponent as being vindictive, one treats him in such a way as to evoke vindictiveness, which confirms the original misperception.

Communication in conflict situations

In order for a conflict to be handled constructively, there must be a means to communicate with the opponent, either overtly or tacitly. Effective and continued communication is of vital importance in resolving a conflict (Rapoport, 1960; Douglas, 1957). A considerable body of research indicates that when a situation is purely cooperative, the communication of relevant information is open and honest, with each party interested in informing as well as being informed by others; in a purely competitive situation, however, communication is either lacking or misleading, and conflict resolution is thereby inhibited (Sherif, 1966; Blake and Mouton, 1962; Newcomb, 1947; Deutsch, 1949, 1962, 1966). Competition gives rise to espionage or other techniques to obtain information about the other which the other is unwilling to communicate, and "diversionary tactics" to delude or mislead the opponent about oneself.

Conflict situations, however, are rarely purely cooperative or purely competitive. In most conflict situations, the participants have mixed motives toward one another; on the one hand each has an interest in cooperating to reach a settlement; on the other hand each has competitive interests with regard to the nature of the settlement. Two managers within a company, for example, may disagree on how to solve a problem, but they do want to find a solution to the problem. A husband and wife who disagree about how to raise their children need each other's cooperation in carrying out any type of child-rearing practice, but each may want the other to accept his ideas as the best way. In order for a mixed-motive conflict to be resolved productively, the cooperative interests of the participants must be strong enough to overcome their competitive interests.

The research on communication in conflict situations has adopted a rather limited definition of communication in order to control precisely what takes place in the experimental setting. *Communication* has most often been defined as the transmitting of a message to a recipient(s) with a conscious intent to affect the latter's behavior (Miller, 1966). The researchers have typically eliminated direct interaction between subjects and operationally defined communication as the passing of notes or of telephone linkages. In most research the nonverbal communication occurring in direct interaction has been excluded. In addition, the tacit communication involved in how a person behaves has often not been adequately controlled in the research studies or has been ignored; thus while a written message stating that one intends to behave cooperatively is considered a communication, the cooperative behavior which tacitly communicates cooperative intent is not.

Deutsch (1958) used this restricted definition of communication in his studies on the development of trust. He concluded that communication is likely to be effective in inducing trust if the following features are clearly expressed in the message: (1) one's intention; (2) one's expectancy concerning the receiver's behavior; (3) one's planned reaction to violations of one's expectancies ;and (4) the means for restoring cooperation after a violation of expectancies has occurred. Loomis (1959) conducted a modified replication of Deutsch's experiment by using the four basic features of expectation, intention, retaliation, and absolution. He concluded that one will be successful in inducing cooperation from another to the extent to which *all four* features are included in one's communications.

In a series of experiments, Deutsch and Krauss (1962, 1966) manipulated the communication of two subjects bargaining over a telephone line. Their results are surprising and interesting. They found that, given the opportunity to communicate, individuals participating in the bargaining game under competitive conditions refused to do so. Such a tendency to break off communication or refuse to communicate with one's opponent is a common characteristic of conflict situations (Newcomb, 1947), and usually leads to escalation of the conflict and increased destructive consequences. Deutsch and Krauss next required the subjects to communicate with each other; they found that the subjects then used the channels of communication to communicate lies and threats as well as promises and trustworthy statements. The more intense the conflict, the greater was the tendency to use the telephone linkage to lie, threaten, and call one's opponent names. In their next experiments they required that the compulsory communication be fair and aimed at increasing the possibilities of cooperation. They also varied the point at which the communication channels became available to the subjects. They concluded that communication which helps bargainers reach cooperative agreements is characterized by being compulsory, by reflecting a norm of fairness, and by being introduced after the bargainers have experienced the destructive effects of mutual competition.

Communication has many functions within conflict situations. It is through communication that participants in a conflict coordinate efforts at resolving their differences, provide information concerning their position and their motivations, reason together, bargain, exercise influence, and expedite the development of a settlement. One of the most crucial characteristics of communication in conflict situations is its credibility. Communicating one's intentions, expectations, and readiness to retaliate and absolve, for example, will have no effect upon the opponent unless it is credible. Berelson and Steiner (1964) pointed out that credibility has an effect on the acceptance of the conclusions reached by the recipient of the communication. Few studies, however, have been conducted on the effects of communication credibility on conflict resolution. Gahagan and Tedeschi (1968), defining *credibility* as the degree to which a communicator's behavior matches the content of his communication, found that trust was engendered by the communication of credible promises. They also found that when the opponent can predict one's behavior, he will be sensitive to it, but if he is unable to predict one's behavior, he will ignore it in deciding how to behave. Horai and Tedeschi (1969) varied the credibility of threats, the magnitude of punishment given for noncompliance to directives, and the sex of the target individual. They found that the more a threatener's verbal messages correspond to his subsequent behavior (that is, the more credible his threats are), the more compliance by the target individual. When punishment for noncompliance was low, however, even if the credibility of threats was high, the target individuals were prone to noncompliance.

The extent to which communication facilitates conflict resolution is also affected by the degree of understanding of the opponent's position and motivation. Many conflicts are based upon misunderstandings and misperceptions; this will be discussed in more detail in the next section. Accurate communication can facilitate mutual understanding, but mutual understanding of each other's position and motivations, however, does not mean that the conflict will be resolved. There are conflicts in which the participant's positions are incompatible or mutually exclusive. In such a case increased understanding only makes such incompatibilities more apparent and increases rather than decreases the conflict. Johnson (1967) demonstrated that increased understanding of each other's positions between two individuals involved in a negotiating situation increased cooperation when the negotiator's positions were compatible, but increased competition when their positions were incompatible.

Finally, it should be remembered that the receiver of communication is not passive, impartially admitting every bit of information that might happen to come his way. Selective perception and selective attention affect an individual's response to communications. People "prepare" themselves for information, especially in conflict situations where trust is apt to be low. Such preparatory states have strong selective and directive effects on what information is ultimately admitted or ignored, and how it is organized if received. The anticipation of entering into communication with a person who holds a contrary opinion or with whom one is in conflict leads to a tighter organization of the received information, to a marked tendency to overselect items supporting one's own position. Thus, Blake and Mouton (1962) found that even when participants in a conflict reported that they knew both their own and their opponent's positions equally well, when tested they did not know their opponent's position nearly as well as they knew their own; in addition, they tended to focus upon the differences between the opponent's position and their own, while ignoring the similarities. Under competitive conditions, individuals who hold almost identical positions often get into violent disagreements and refuse to agree on any point under discussion. What is needed in many conflict situations is a procedure by which such misunderstandings based upon selective perception and selective attention can be avoided. We turn to such a procedure next.

Role reversal

Given the tendency in competitive conflicts situations to distort one's perceptions of the opponent's behavior and motivations and the difficulties in communicating in ways which have low probabilities of being cut off or misunderstood, there is a need for procedures that reduce distortions in perception and insure effective communication. A procedure that has had marked success in various applied settings in eliminating misunderstandings, perceptual distortions, and defensive adherence to one's point of view is role reversal.

In *role reversal* one or both persons in a discussion presents the viewpoint of the other. That is, given that A and B are in a discussion, A takes B's role and presents B's point of view and/or B present's A's point of view. Although first proposed as a procedure to insure accurate communication in negotiations by Cohen (1950, 1951) and elaborated by Rapoport (1960) and Deutsch (1962), role reversal theory has centered around the work of Carl Rogers (1951, 1952, 1965). Rogers discusses role reversal as a means of facilitating communication between two individuals. He states that the major barrier to mutual interpersonal communication is the human tendency to judge, to approve to disapprove, to evaluate the statement of the other person from one's own point of view. If the situation is charged with strong feelings and emotions, one's own frame of reference tends to dominate, and there is little likelihood of real communication. If a person is able to achieve the frame of reference of the other, that is, if he can see the expressed ideas and attitudes from the opposite side, he can avoid this evaluation tendency. Role reversal is suggested as the primary means of understanding the other's ideas, attitudes, and behavior from the other's frame of reference. By role reversing, furthermore, one communicates that he is attempting to understand the other's frame of reference, which reduces the other's defensiveness by convincing him that he has been clearly heard and understood. According to Rogers' theory, however, it is not the routine reflection of what the other is saying which increases the cooperativeness and trust in the situation. Through role reversal one needs to communicate that he is: (1) accurately understanding the other's "inner world;" (2) feeling nonpossessive warmth for and acceptance of the other as a person; and (3) behaving authentically and genuinely in the situation (Rogers, 1951). Truax and Wargo (1966) and Bergin (1966) present considerable evidence that accurate understanding, nonpossessive warmth, and authenticity are essential for growth and development in the therapy relationship.

Despite the promise of role reversal as a communication technique for inducing cooperation in interpersonal and intergroup conflict situations, there has been no research on its use until very recently. Johnson (1966, 1967) examined the effects of role reversal and direct presentation of one's position upon the participants in a highly competitive intergroup negotiation situation. He found that role reversal resulted in more understanding of the opponent's position than did self-presentation without role reversal. Mutual understanding of the other's position, however, does not mean that agreement will be easier to reach by the two parties. Some misunderstandings cloud real differences between individuals, the clarification of which would increase the competitive forces in the situation by removing any possible benevolent misunderstandings. Other misunderstandings cloud similarities and

403

points of agreement between the parties; the clarification of these would lead to the resolution of the conflict. When role reversal was adequately performed Johnson found that when legitimate opposed differences were clarified, conflict increased; when misunderstandings and false expectations were clarified, conflict decreased.

In Johnson's (1967) initial study on role reversal, a powerful third party (the experimenter) required two competitive negotiators to engage in role reversal. There are, however, many negotiating situations where third parties are not able to intervene (Fisher, 1964). Johnson and Dustin (1970) investigated the use of role reversal by a cooperatively oriented individual to increase the willingness of an individualistically oriented or a competitively oriented opponent to agree to a mutually beneficial compromise. A negotiator is individualistically oriented when he is concerned with making as profitable an agreement for himself as possible, regardless of what his opponent makes, while a competitively oriented negotiator is concerned with making more profit than his opponent. Johnson and Dustin found that with the use of role reversal, more agreements were reached in a shorter period of time in the individualistic than in the competitive conditions. These results indicated that role reversal can be used productively by one participant to increase the willingness of his opponent to reach an agreement; the more competitively oriented the opponent, however, the less successful role reversal will be in encouraging cooperation.

Role reversal may be classified as one type of role playing. *Role playing* includes a wide variety of procedures in which a person enacts the behavior of another person or assumes and publicly espouses a set of opinions with which he disagrees. There is a critical difference between the theoretical work on role reversal and role playing. In the conflict literature, role reversal is hypothesized to influence primarily the listener, not the actor; in the attitude change literature, role playing is considered a self-persuasion technique aimed at influencing the actor, not the listener. In an experiment to determine the initial effects of the role reversal upon the listener and the actor, Johnson (1971a) compared three conditions, one where the subject listened to his opponent role reverse, one where the subject engaged in role reversal, and one where neither the subject nor his opponent engaged in role reversal. He found that the greatest attitude change occurred in the actor condition and the least occurred in the listener condition. These results support the attitude change explanation of the efficacy of role reversal, and indicate that the initial effect of listening to one's adversary role reverse is to reinforce one's attitudes about the issue being negotiated.

These three studies document the efficacy of role reversal for increasing understanding of the opponent's position and inducing cooperative behavior in negotiation situations, but they shed little light on the variables which mediate its effectiveness. It is clearly not the routine reflection of what the opponent is saying which increases the cooperativeness and understanding in a conflict situation. Johnson (1966) found that the emotional involvement in taking the role of the other and the adequacy (comprehensiveness, completeness) with which the other's position was presented both affect the efficacy of role reversal. To probe further, Johnson (1971b) conducted a study in which the warmth with which an individual role reversed and the accuracy of role reversal were varied. He found that accurate role reversal, compared to inaccurate role reversal, resulted in the conviction that one has been clearly heard and understood and in a willingness to reach an agreement in negotiations; warm role reversal, compared to cold role reversal, resulted in favorable attitudes toward the actor, but did not affect the listener's willingness to reach an agreement. The implication of these results is that one may create positive interpersonal attitudes by warm role reversal, but an opponent can be induced to compromise only by an accurate portrayal of his position.

Attitudes toward the opponent

The attitudes one has toward another in conflict situations may influence how one behaves. For example, when an individual distrusts his opponent, he will often hide information or communicate misleading information; when he trusts his opponent he will communicate openly and honestly. Deutsch (1966) states that cooperative relationships lead to a trusting, friendly attitude toward the opponent and increase one's willingness to response helpfully to the other's needs and requests; competition, on the other hand, leads to a suspicious, hostile attitude toward the other while increasing one's readiness to exploit the other's needs and refuse the other's requests.

Although considerable evidence indicates that cooperative interaction leads to positive attitudes among participants, positive attitudes between two parties does not necessarily lead to cooperation. Several investigators have found that individuals who are positively oriented will behave more cooperatively than will individuals who are negatively oriented (Borah, 1963; Ex, 1959; Rice and White, 1964). Krauss (1966), however, demonstrated that positive attitudes toward the opponent will affect one's cooperativeness only when the positive attitudes are strongly anchored in one's self-esteem system. He theorized that when an individual is in competition with another towards whom he has positive attitudes, a state of imbalance exists which generates tension. The individual may reduce this tension by moving towards a balanced state; balance may be achieved by either changing his attitudes toward the other or by reorienting his behavior towards cooperation. When his attitudes toward the other are strongly anchored, a person will reorient his behavior; when his attitudes are weakly anchored, he will change his attitudes.

In a more recent study Johnson (1971b), using an intergroup negotiation situation, found that the amount of warmth a negotiator expressed towards his opponent was related to the opponent's affection for the negotiator and his perception of the negotiator as a similar, accepting, and understanding individual. Nevertheless, the opponent still felt bound to his group's position, and was unwilling to reach an agreement. In this case positive attitudes did not facilitate agreement. Certainly many individuals may have quite positive attitudes towards each other (a husband and wife, for example) and still be unable to resolve conflicts. Thus the conditions under which one's attitudes toward the opponent will facilitate the resolution of a conflict have yet to be fully explored.

Task Orientation

Whether a situation is defined as cooperative or competitive will have several influences upon task orientation (Deutsch, 1966). In a predominantly cooperative situation, individuals tend to recognize the legitimacy of each other's interests and search for a solution accommodating the needs of both sides; when the situation is predominantly competitive, individuals tend to deny the legitimacy of the other's interests and consider only their own needs. In a predominantly cooperative situation, individuals attempt to influence each other through persuasion, striving to enhance mutual power; in a predominantly competitive situation, individuals try to coerce each other while attempting to increase their own power and decrease the power of others. Perhaps the most important aspect of task orientation in a conflict situation, however, is how the conflict is defined.

Those who define the causes, labels, and size of a conflict also appear to specify the way in which it should be handled. Many conflicts in schools, for example, are defined as being *caused* by maladjusted, deviant students; this implies that a reasonable solution would be to expel the "sick" students, send them to a special school, or get them into therapy. By attributing rebellious student behavior to personal pathology and labelling misbehaving students as sick, the school effectively denies its own shortcomings and responsibility for the conflict. This is often a clear organizational defense, for if the school's organizational pathologies became defined as the cause of student misbehavior and failure, the legitimacy and effectiveness of the school would be brought into question.

The way in which conflicts are *labelled* often influences the ease with which they are resolved. Deutsch (1966), for example, discusses a study conducted by one of his students where a bargaining game was presented as a game of "chicken" and as a problem solving situation. When the situation was described as being a test of who will "chicken out" first, the bargainers were highly competitive; when the game was described as a mutual problem the two bargainers had to solve, they were basically cooperative.

In terms of size, the smaller the conflict the more easily it is resolved (Deutsch, 1966). Participants often have a choice of defining a conflict as being large or small and usually the larger the definition, the harder it is to resolve. A conflict can be reduced by defining it as being between two individuals rather than between two groups, as being over the application of a principle rather than over the principle itself, as representing a small procedural precedent rather than a large one, and as representing a small substantive issue rather than a sizeable one. Any expansion of the definition of the size of a conflict increases its motivational significance to the participants and intensifies their emotional involvement, which makes a limited defeat less acceptable or more humiliating than mutual disaster. A reduction of the definition of the size of a conflict decreases its motivational significance to the participants and their emotional involvement. Thus they are more willing to compromise to reach an agreement.

In discussing the resolution of international conflicts, Fisher (1964) notes that while countries such as the United States do not seem willing to refer large issues to the International Court of Justice or let them be decided by any group of neutrals, small issues can be adjudicated. He recommends that any major conflict should be dealt with as a number of small issues rather than as one large one. He states that no country is likely to fight over what it perceives as a small issue; only when a country fears that it might lose a great deal, or hopes to gain a great deal, will it go to war. When issues are considered separately and in terms of their smallest size, the process of settling disputes should be peaceable. Thus one technique of lessening the risk of war and improving the process of international settlement is to separate and reduce the size of issues.

Conflicts will be easier to resolve if the legitimacy of each side is not questioned, if both sides rely primarily upon strategies of persuasion, if the conflict is not seen as being caused by the pathologies of the individuals on the other side, if it is labelled as a joint problem solving situation instead of a win-lose game of "chicken," and if it is defined as small. Such a problem solving orientation to a conflict is much more easily obtained when the situation is predominantly cooperative; if, however, a conflict becomes predominantly competitive, participants can facilitate its resolution by attempting to define it as a small, joint problem solving situation.

THE INITIATION OF COOPERATION

There are, in addition to the theory and research already discussed, other conclusions from the literature on conflict resolution on how to induce an opponent to cooperate. Deutsch (1964) theorizes that there are four critical tasks in changing an adversary's hostile orientation to a cooperative one. First, one must be able to show the adversary that his anxieties and difficulties with the present situation outweigh any possible gains he might have from being hostile; this provides some motivation for change. Second, one must show him that his anxieties and difficulties are causally connected with his competitive, hostile orientation. Third, one must insure that he provides the adversary new experiences to facilitate change, experiences that show a genuine interest in the adversary's well being rather than experiences that justify the defensive hostile orientation of the past. Finally, one must insure that the adversary perceives that he will gain rather than suffer, have less anxiety than more, if he adopts a new orientation to the relationship.

If one is truly interested in inducing cooperation he should avoid the use of threat; threats will only increase the competitive aspects of the situation, and will often provoke the events it is aimed at deterring, especially if the threatened party sees the threat as an illegitimate attempt to make him yield (Deutsch and Krauss, 1962). Threat is an aggressive behavior and the most probable response to aggressive acts is counter-aggression. Under most conditions, in order to induce cooperation in others, threats and other attempts at intimidation should be avoided.

A number of studies have dealt with the behavioral strategies for inducing cooperation in an adversary. Solomon (1960) studied the effects of three different strategies upon an opponent's behavior in a bargaining game. The three strategies he used were: (1) unconditional cooperation, where no matter what the opponent does one responds cooperatively; (2) unconditional competition, where no matter what the opponent does one responds competitively; and (3) conditional cooperation, where whatever the opponent does, one matches his behavior. The most effective strategy for inducing cooperation was the conditional cooperative one. The unconditional competition seemed to escalate conflict while the unconditional cooperation was exploited with very little guilt. A number of studies have corroborated Solomon's results.

One of the shortcomings of Solomon's study was that there was no way to signal the opponent when one was behaving cooperatively or altruistically in the unconditional cooperation condition or when one was behaving defensively or aggressively in the unconditional competition condition. Recently Deutsch and his students (Deutsch, Epstein and Canavan, 1967) extended Solomon's study by contrasting a number of different strategies: (1) turn the other cheek, in which a cooperative move was made on the first trial of a 60-trial bargaining game, an altrustic move on the second trial, and cooperative moves thereafter except that one responded to attacks or threats by altruistic moves; (2) reactive defensiveness in which one made cooperative moves on the first three trials and reciprocated the opponent's behavior thereafter except that one responded self-protectively when the opponent aggressed rather than with counter-aggression; (3) reactive hostility in which one made a cooperative move on the first trial and thereafter responded aggressively to any noncooperative move and cooperatively to any cooperative or altruistic moves; (4) reformed sinner, where one behaved aggressively for the first 15 trials and thereafter consistently followed a "turn the other cheek" or a "reactive defensiveness" strategy. The results indicate that the "reactive defensive" strategy is most effective in inducing cooperation in the opponent while the "reactive hostility" strategy induces the least cooperation. The "turn the other cheek" strategy did not produce cooperation, it produced exploitation of the opponent who was unwilling to defend himself. In the "reformed-sinner—turn-the-other-cheek" strategy, however, there was less exploitation of good will. The "reformed-sinner—reactive-defensive" strategy, on the other hand, was not as effective as following a "reactive-defensive" strategy all the way through.

Several conclusions can be drawn from this study. Under the conditions of the experiment, neither a punitive nor a rewarding response to noncooperative behavior is most effective in eliciting mutually rewarding cooperation. Rewarding noncooperative behavior leads to exploitation unless it has been preceded by a convincing display of aggressive potential. The effect of punishing noncooperative behavior may completely overshadow any attempts at cooperation. A strategy that does not reciprocate hostility, but nevertheless does not allow it to be rewarding, seems to be effective in eliciting cooperative behavior so long as it is also generously responsive to the other's cooperative behavior. Thus what seems to be most effective in inducing cooperation is a strategy that is generously responsive to the other's cooperative behavior, does not reciprocate hostility, but does not allow hostility to be rewarding.

CONSTRUCTIVE ACTION IN INTERNATIONAL CONFLICTS

It is not the obligation of a social psychologist to direct statesmen, but responsible officials and citizens may be able to use the facts and principles of this young science in planning wise courses of action. Earlier in this chapter we showed that psychological knowledge reveals fallacies in several naïve approaches toward achieving world peace. Are there action programs which rest upon sound psychological insight? At least six approaches have been proposed or endorsed by some social psychologists: (1) building a world government; (2) increasing transnational interaction; (3) setting superordinate international goals; (4) graduating reciprocation; (5) educating in conflict resolution; and (6) making life more satisfying. We shall describe each briefly and examine the supporting evidence.

World government

The social structure of sovereign national powers engaged in competitive struggle produces, as we have seen, the attitudes and behaviors which drive toward war. To change the attitudes we must change the structure. The idea of a world organization is at least as old as its proposal by Immanuel Kant in 1795. The paramount loyalties of men cannot be attached to the human race until most of the population of the world has been incorporated in a more effective union than the present United Nations.

We know that new nations and new supranational organizations can come into being only when certain basic psychological and social factors are present. Deutsch (1953) lists: common knowledge, common traditions, common values, communications, and the possibility of command. Each of these has become more evident as technology has given us more rapid travel and the possibility of worldwide newspapers, telephones, radio, and television programs.

Another prerequisite lies in public opinion. World leaders, differing on many policies, are nearly unanimous on the need to make the United Nations into what President Kennedy called "a genuine world security system."

Back in the 1920s, a study of the attitudes of 1,700 students in eight nations showed overwhelming support, even then, for the proposition: "Some form of international government is inevitable." The percentages of agreement were as follows: 68 in Austria, 84 in Czechoslovakia, 83 in Denmark, 79 in England, 80 in France, 83 in Germany, 71 in Switzerland, and 74 in the United States (Harper, 1931).

Since the founding of the United Nations, a majority of adults in the United States has favored a stronger international police force. In the fall of 1950, 80 percent favored our participation in a standing U.N. army—ready for action at all times. In May 1951, over 60 percent favored making the United Nations into a world government with power to control the armed forces of all nations, including those of the United States. Seventy percent of the Americans polled favored sending the U.N. Emergency Force into the Sinai peninsula in 1956. A proposal to build up the Emergency Force to a size great enough to deal with small wars anywhere in the world won support by a three to one ratio, in 1964 (American Institute of Public Opinion, May 28, 1964).

Once such action is taken, the probability is that support will further increase. Toynbee (1963) reminds us that when the Chinese and the Roman empires were established, the peoples united within them at first regretted the loss of their previous national sovereignty. Eventually, however, loyalty to the super-state came to take first place in the hearts of the citizens. The fears of the colonies in North America about the Articles of Confederation and later the Constitution which bound them into the United States are now recalled only by historians.

A comprehensive and technically sophisticated design for world government has been offered by Grenville Clark and Louis B. Sohn in their book *World Peace Through World Law* (1960). They propose complete and general disarmament, and an international police force, compulsory arbitration of international disputes, a reliable revenue system for the United Nations, and the development of the General Assembly into a genuine legislative body.

Several psychologists have suggested ways in which a supranational organization might be strengthened. E. L. Thorndike proposed that, in order to gain trust, it should issue money which would be valid in every country of the world and perhaps also passports and travel insurance. He also made the suggestion that the United Nations would become more glamorous if it staged world fairs with elaborate ceremonies in every part of the globe. E. C. Tolman suggested that the U.N.'s international police force should somehow combine the romantic appeal of the Canadian Mounted Police with the humanitarian aura of the Red Cross.

A commission of psychologists from six nations, meeting at the Accra Assembly in June 1962 recommended the establishment by a world organization of two institutes. A "World Institute for Research in Behavioral Science" would initiate and coordinate research on reducing international tensions and on building support for peace. A "World Communications Center" would develop a newspaper and broadcast programs free from the bias of all current, nationally oriented media. It would certify school textbooks in geography, history, and other social studies as factually accurate from an objective point of view, thus transcending national loyalties.

The present obstacle to implementing plans for world government is mistrust between the Communist and Western nations. Both sides agree in principle. The draft treaties submitted to the Disarmament Conference in Geneva in 1962 by Moscow and Washington were remarkably alike. Both aimed at total and permanent disarmament. Both sides accepted inspection and control by an international agency to enforce the agreement. The one key point of disagreement was that the United States wanted to set up inspection and enforcement procedures first; then to disarm. The Russians wanted disarmament first, then the operations of inspection. The United States was suspicious that false claims of disarmament would be made. The Russians suspected that the early stages of inspection would be merely espionage designed to learn Soviet military secrets and to take advantage of them. The Chinese communists were even more suspicious and unwilling to consider disarming.

The problem now seems to be how to create enough trust so that practical steps toward disarmament and world government can be taken. In his book *The Hard Way to Peace* (1962) sociologist Amitai Etzioni contends that in attempting to ban nuclear weapons—the ultimate destroyers—we have begun at the wrong end of the scale. He proposes that major powers agree first to scrap the relatively useless items—old battleships and bombers and outmoded fighters. Prearranged amounts of these weapons might be delivered to some checkpoint for destruction or modification to civilian uses. Compliance could be checked absolutely. Then more tanks or planes or ships or guns might be brought in. Gradually, armament would be reduced and if all principals fulfilled the agreements, some trust would be built. Eventually it might be possible to deal with the terrible weapons of last resort. Etzioni calls this the "working-toward" effect. In 1964, a similar proposal at the Disarmament Conference was referred to as the "bomber bonfire."

Transnational interaction

In Chapters 2 and 3 we introduced the theorem that liking usually increases with frequency of interaction. In Sherif's boys camp model, interaction increased friendship up to the point where the groups became competitive. Hence the general theorem must be qualified and limited to interactions under conditions which share satisfaction rather than win-lose struggles.

The term "transnational" was first used, so far as the authors know, by Laurin Zilliacus to differentiate between activities in which nations cooperate (international) and those in which people cooperate with no special reference to national identification and boundaries. His "Mail for the World" (1953) is an interesting account of the growth of one great transnational activity—the Universal Postal Union. Astronomers are transnational when they cooperate to advance their common knowledge regardless of country. For a scientist, the validity of an observation is all that matters; the nationality of the observer is irrelevant. The American philosopher, Josiah Royce, writing of "the Beloved Community" as a social ideal, used world ties of scientists as his model. Robert MacLeod reports that he was present with some American physicists when they heard the news of the first successful Sputnik: "Hurrah!" they said, "we've done it!" For the scientist in America it was "we," not "they."

There are many transnational communities of interest. Musicians are concerned mainly with the talents of the composer or performer, not with the legal body which collects his taxes. Athletes enjoy first-rate achievement and competition, which is not related to nationalities. Beauty in painting, sculpture, dance, drama, or poetry does not come in packages that bear the label of nationality. Health and education are served by contributions from many lands. The larger the role played by transnational concerns, the less people are likely to overemphasize nationalism. Religious organizations and youth-serving agencies like the Boy Scouts cross national boundaries in calling their members together for meetings. The international trade unions can serve a similar purpose.

The greatest transnational force is probably economic trade. A poll (American Institute of Public Opinion, October 25, 1963) inquired of Americans: "Should the United States and Russia work out a business arrangement to buy and sell more goods to each other? While 33 percent remained opposed to such transactions, 55 percent supported them. The proportion favoring doing business with the Soviet Union rose from 30 percent in 1948, to 40 percent in 1953, to 55 percent in 1955, 1959, and 1963. The products as well as the transactions help to build community.

In his presidential address to the Society for Psychological Study of Social Issues (1961) Morton Deutsch proposed development of international contests in many fields, following some of the procedures worked out for the Olympic Games.

Cherrington's (1934) report on sixteen American students attending a seminar on international relations in Geneva, Switzerland, in 1929 yielded mixed results. They were 90 percent international-minded before they left this country and did not appreciably change that position. They came to rate specific proposals "doubtful" or "uncertain" more often at the end of their summer study. The writer has observed similar changes in intelligent adults visiting the Soviet Union in "traveling seminars" under his leadership. The adults did not grow markedly more or less favorable in their attitudes; rather they came to appreciate the diversity and complexity of the people in the host country. They become less ready to make generalizations. Kelman (1965) found that participants in a two-month international seminar on broadcasting at Brandeis University, tested before and after the meetings and compared with back-home controls, became more favorable in attitudes toward Americans, but showed an even greater change in the complexity and differentiation of their images of this country.

Other data come from attitude studies of children in camps composed of participants from several countries (Twitchell-Allen, 1956). Bjerstedt (1958) introduced a "picture-story device" with stories written about four pictures which included children of different races; also the "four-nationality story" requiring a story that includes individuals from Russia, America, China, and France. When the picture stories were analyzed for references to cross-national friendships, it was found that 79 children of 11 years of age participating in Children's International Summer Village (C.I.S.V.) camps in Europe made 41 percent of such references at the beginning of their stay and 59 percent at the end. A reunion of children who had been in the C.I.S.V. camp two or three years earlier, scored 75 percent for cross-national friendship references. Bjerstedt found it easier to develop friendships in these camps across national lines than it was to build boy-girl friendships at this age.

Attitude changes as a result of the usual kind of tourist travel abroad have not yet been sufficiently appraised. The effects may be expected to be relatively slight since interaction is often limited to hotel clerks, railway porters, taxi drivers, waiters, and guides. Moreover, the "equal status" condition, emphasized in Chapter 10, is usually lacking. The shock-effect for travelers on their first trip, with little background and experience, may result in quite unwarranted generalizations about the foreign nation. For some travelers, there is a high correlation between the comfort of hotel rooms and their estimate of the culture and attractiveness of the people of a country.

Hayakawa (1960) has made an ingenious proposal that could be applied to increasing understanding between the United States and such countries as Communist China. Discussing the Soviet Union, he made the suggestion that we invite a large number of Russian spokesmen—perhaps thousands, of "teachers, journalists, parliamentarians, jurists and plant managers to come here and explain their way of life, their national purposes, their hopes for the future." His interest is not so much in what we might learn in such a process as in the influence that our listening would have upon the visiting spokesmen. "Whoever has the emotional strength and the courage to begin listening to the other fellow instead of shouting at him can become the psychotherapist for the other. . . . The funny thing about human beings, including you and me and the Russians, is that we tend to respect the intelligence of, and eventually to like, those who listen attentively to our ideas even if they continue to disagree with us."

As we conclude our review of the effects of available transnational experiences upon attitudes, we must recognize that the impact is usually slight. Evidence indicates that the rather superficial transnational friendships formed by athletes during Olympic games or by scientists during international conferences will not noticeably lessen inter-governmental tensions. The Nazis were able to use young Germans who had been friendly tourists in Scandinavia for their military occupation of those lands. Only if transnational interaction occurs in an atmosphere in which tensions have already become less threatening—possibly through effective world government—can the results be lasting. How can powerful tensions be reduced?

Graduated reciprocation: a virtuous circle

While mounting threats create a vicious circle, mounting acts of generosity may form a virtuous circle. This theme underlies a proposal made by Charles E. Osgood, then president of the American Psychological Association

(1962). The pattern of behavior in relationships where tension exists has been, in the past, to seek every possible little advantage and never to give a *quid* without first getting firm hold of the *quo*. Any concession has been taken as a sign of weakness. The Osgood idea of progressively reducing international tensions is to give a little something—not so much as really to weaken security—and see whether the act of good will may not be voluntarily reciprocated, even though there was no prior agreement that it would be, and no such demands made. Any nation can begin the experiment, unilaterally. The first gesture might be giving up a threatening but not too necessary base, or reducing some significant but not essential armament. It might be an offer of needed food, medicine, machines, or services. The psychological probability is that such an act of friendliness would arouse some gift in return. If it did not—and this is an important part of the plan—another concession would be given. It may be expected that the first step will be viewed with mistrust. So another, and another must be taken. If the acts of benevolence are genuine and are seen as desirable by the recipient nation, and if they persist long enough to demonstrate a new approach, it is likely that the former opponent will venture on some reciprocal act of his own choice. In interpersonal relations this procedure is sometimes called "heaping coals of fire" on the partner's head. In Christian doctrine, it is loving an enemy and doing good to those who have mistreated us.

A timely example might be the offer of some of our food surplus to the hungry people of mainland China—an offer with no strings attached. Peking might not reciprocate immediately but might find some way to ease some of the present tensions. In any case, the act of giving helps build a reputation for moral leadership.

Education in conflict resolution

Earlier we indicated that the attempts of educators to change attitudes of children while the adult social system remains unaltered will probably fail. Yet when modifications such as stronger world government, increased transnational experiences, cooperation toward super-ordinate goals, and graduated benevolent reciprocation have been introduced, there remain important supplementary educational tasks.

Knowledge of other nations is no guarantee of good will toward them, but ignorance is likely to be a distinct handicap.

There are great gaps to be filled in the average American's knowledge of our world. In one poll, half of the citizens proved unable, on the outline map of Europe, to identify the location of countries as geographically conspicuous as Spain or Greece. In a book about life in a small town Hicks (1947) reports that at the beginning of a game, a player offered the ground-rule which was accepted by all: "Anything across the pond is out!" Only American cities, persons or place names were acceptable. While school curricula are now giving more attention to world geography, world history, world art and literature, many college graduates know little of the new African states, the Inca empire, Bangkok dancers or the Hindu Vedas.

Students majoring in the area of social science—or especially well-informed—are more likely to emerge as world-minded (Manry, 1928; Wrightstone, 1934; Cherrington, 1934; Smith, 1947; Grace, Neuhaus, 1952). Belief in the possibility of peaceful resolution of conflicts between the Soviet Union and the United States increases with level of education from 42 percent for those who have not finished high school to 61 percent for college graduates (American Institute of Public Opinion, January 1, 1961). Willingness to recognize Communist China also increased with educational level.

Recent progress in applied behavioral science has increased our understanding of the distortions which are created by a "win-lose" orientation and of the possibility that genuinely integrative solutions can be achieved in conflict situations (Blake, Mouton, 1961; Horwitz, 1964; Walton, 1965). The first Training Laboratory in Conflict Management was held at Bethel, Maine, in 1964. Executives from many kinds of organizations are acquiring skill in the creative approach to the resolution of conflict. As this kind of education becomes more widespread and effective, it cannot but have an impact on the time-worn but fallacious assumption that the alternatives in international disputes are only dominance or submission.

Increasing life satisfaction

The greatest hostility toward others is shown by individuals suffering from conflicts and frustrations. In one of the earliest studies of attitudes toward foreign nations (1928) the author discovered that among scores of American groups tested, the ones who most despised Chinese and Japanese were farmers in drought-threatened North Dakota and prisoners in the Bridewell, Chicago's city jail. Helfant (1952) found that high school students who wanted drastic punitive action against the Soviet Union showed more symptoms of emotional difficulty than did the tolerant pupils. Earlier we noted, also, that sometimes a war seems to promise relief from tedium or chronic dissatisfaction with the conditions of peacetime living. It seems evident that whatever makes life more interesting, more challenging, and more satisfying will reduce the tendency to seek outlets in hatred and revenge. One of the handicaps of the peace movement is that the image of war is virile and dramatic; that of peace is pale and insipid. Emerson asked: "Who can blame men for seeking excitement? They are polar, and would you have them sleep in a dull eternity of equilibrium? Religion, love, ambition, money, war, brandy—

some fierce antagonism must break the round . . . or no spark, no joy, no event can be. . . ."

William James used this principle in developing his famous essay *The Moral Equivalent of War*. He believed that to be satisfying, life must be strenuous, intense, vivid, effortful, and heroic. He suggested enlisting youth in difficult and hazardous crusades against the causes of disaster and in conquest of Nature and disease.

Freud symbolized the forces of love, creation, and life in the mythological figure of Eros. He symbolized by Thanatos the opposite forces of hate, destruction, and death. He saw Eros and Thanatos "locked in an eternal duel." Those who seek peace are engaged against Thanatos. They should not neglect to strengthen their ally, his eternal adversary. In every land are too many hopeless, loveless, miserable, frustrated, embittered, and vengeful people. In top posts in enterprises of government, business, and science are too many impersonal, dehumanized, bureaucratic individuals operating only as institutional mechanisms, not as persons whose lives are finding rich satisfaction and fulfillment. If our quarrelsome world is ever saved, it will have to be done by those who love life freely. In earlier chapters we have written about dyadic love and friendship, enjoyment of group membership, psychotherapy, personal autonomy, and cultures which are healthy and free from race, class or sex prejudice. These developments are pertinent to the creation of conditions which enhance satisfaction in the here-and-now, thus diminishing the strength of destructive drives.

To rely mainly on increased personal happiness to stop war would be naive. The forces of economic and political rivalry among nations operate powerfully to condition hostile attitudes even in individuals whose personal emotional life is reasonably well-adjusted. And, in pacifist groups, there is no remarkable shortage of disturbed personalities. Yet Freud's basic insight remains true. Whatever enhances the human capacity to love, correspondingly decreases hatred and destructiveness. War is not a simple projection of personal hostility. Innumerable enterprises of worldwide cooperation are facilitated by persons easily capable of empathy, concern for others, and trustworthy friendships.

Toward an uncertain future

The half-dozen proposals just presented for reducing international tensions carry no guarantee of safe-conduct for mankind. The grave threat described at the beginning of the chapter persists. One thing we do learn from history, however, is that extrapolation from any present point is likely to be misleading. Consider, for example, the changing alliances between the United States and other nations over two centuries.

OUR NATIONAL LOVES AND HATES

1775	Loved British, hated French; French and Indian War
1776	Loved French, hated British; American Revolution
1799	Hated French; sea battles with France
1812	Loved French, hated British; War of 1812
1846	Loved Southerners, hated Mexicans; Mexican War over Texas
1861–64	North and South hated each other; North hated British; Civil War, British aiding South
1898	Hated Spanish; Spanish-American War
1899	Hated Chinese and Filipinos; conquest of the Philippines
1900	Loved Japanese, hated Chinese; Boxer uprising in China
1904	Loved Japanese, hated Russians; Russo-Japanese War
1914	Hated Mexicans; Marines land at Vera Cruz
1914	Loved Japanese and Russians; allies in World War I
1914	Loved British and French; hated Austrians and Germans, beginning of World War I
1915	Loved Italians; Italy joins Allies in World War I
1916	Hated Mexicans, Pershing invades Mexico
1917	Loved Japanese and Chinese; allies in World War I
1918	Loved Italians, hated Russians, our troops invade Russia
1927	Loved Japanese, hated Chinese; U.S. bombards Nanking
1935	Hated Italians; Italy invades Ethiopia
1936	Loved Chinese, hated Russians; Communists despoil China
1939	Loved British and French; hated Germans and Russians; beginning of World War II
1939	Loved Finns, hated Russians; Russia invades Finland
1941	Loved Russians, hated Finns; Russia fights Germany and Finland
1941	Loved Filipinos, hated Japanese, war with Japan
1941	Loved British, Chinese, Dutch, Russians; hated Germans, Italians and Japanese; World War II
1942	Loved some French, hated others; Vichy regime
1942	Loved Mexicans, most Latin-Americans; allies in World War II
1943	Loved Chinese; tried to love Russians, British
1947	Loved Chinese; hated Russians
1955	Loved West Germans, Japanese; hated Russians, Chinese, and East Germans

(Adapted from Mark R. Shaw)

Not only alliances but ideologies change with time. Christians and Moslems have learned to live in mutual tolerance in many parts of the world, despite the hostilities of the Crusades. Political and religious absolutists have asserted that they possessed infallible doctrine and dogma, but under changed conditions have found it possible to revise their doctrines expediently.

During the heat of the Reformation, Martin Luther proclaimed: "It is far better to be a hangman or a murderer than a priest or a monk." And on the other side, Pope Pius V wrote to Catherine de Medici: "It is only by the complete extermination of heretics that the King will be able to give back the ancient workshop of the Catholic religion to this noble kingdom. If Your Majesty continues to war openly and zealously until they are all massacred, Divine succor will not be wanting." The aroused citizens of that day would never have been able to forsee a time when Protestants and Catholics could live as good neighbors. They had to war intermittently for several centuries before admitting that neither could convert nor exterminate the other, that "peaceful coexistence" was not only a possibility but the only real possibility.

In controversy we are likely to overestimate the rigidity of our opponents. "*We* can change," we think, "but *they* will never learn!" One of the safest predictions is that the dogma of today will be revised by later generations. Most human beings learn and change. By the time we have opened our own minds to unrecognized truth, other nations will also have moved to new understanding. We shall have more to say about processes of change in the final chapter.

CONCLUSION

The future of mankind depends to a large extent upon the ability of individuals to deal with conflict constructively. In the beginning of this chapter we asked the reader to make a prediction concerning the future of our species based upon his technological capacity to destroy and his past behavior in conflict situations. There are many scientists who, along with Lorenz, feel that mankind is at a crossroads where we either develop the ability to handle conflicts constructively or destroy ourselves. The reader now has some basis to judge for himself or herself what mankind's future may be; the uniquely murderous way in which man has expressed his aggressiveness, the destructive cycles of intergroup conflict, the knowledge base we do have concerning how to handle conflicts constructively, all may influence the optimism or pessimism of the reader.

There are many different suggestions concerning how mankind might become more competent in conflict situations. Lorenz and others suggest increased self-understanding, along with mechanisms to control man's aggressive nature. Other's suggest the inhibition of aggression through emphasizing mankind's capacity for concern for other humans; such a suggestion is contained in the words of the following song:

> Lord, we don't need another mountain,
> There are mountains and hillsides enough to climb,
> There are oceans and rivers enough to cross,
> Enough to last until the end of time. . . .
> What the world needs now, is love, sweet love
> No, not just for some, but for everyone.

The position taken by many social psychologists and by the authors of this book is that individuals learn conflict behavior, and the ability to handle conflict constructively depends upon learning the relevant strategies and skills which will maximize the constructive aspects of conflicts while minimizing potential destructive aspects. Thus the hope for the survival of mankind depends upon finding constructive means of dealing with conflicts and encorporating these into the behavioral repertories of all men.

It is easy to be pessimistic about the future. There are so many critical problems affecting the survival of mankind. For those who are searching for a basis of hope, the words of R. D. Laing (1967, p. 30) may be helpful:

> It is quite certain that unless we can regulate our behavior much more satisfactorily than at present, then we are going to exterminate ourselves. . . . Yet if nothing else, each time a new baby is born there is a possibility of reprieve. Each child is a new being, a potential prophet, a new spiritual prince, a new spark of light precipitated into the outer darkness. Who are we to decide that it is hopeless?

SUMMARY

What accounts for man's aggressive behavior which has led to the death of almost 60 million people in a little more than 100 years? One group of scientists explains man's aggression as instinctual behavior which has its roots in the protection of territory and the assurance that the best members of the group propagate the species. Others explain man's uniqueness as a killer of his own as behavior which is learned and therefore which may be unlearned or redirected. Social psychologists have focused on the dynamics which exist in intergroup conflicts to understand man's aggression and to learn how conflicts may be resolved constructively.

Conflicts surround each of us daily in our relationships with friends, colleagues, parents, neighbors, loved ones, mates and passers-by. Additionally, conflict abounds in our cities, states, nation and the world. Conflict situations are characterized by perceptual distortions and misperceptions concerning the motives and positions of others. The distortions arise from looking at the other person's situation in terms of one's own perspective and expectations. Our view of the situation is biased and makes us liable to act in ways which produce confirmations of our expectations, rather than allowing the other to make his motives and expectations clear. Communication is vital to perceiving a conflict. We are often influenced heavily by how our friends see the situation. Our personal reaction to conflict is often intense fear and deep threat to our being—reactions which can impair our cognitive and perceptual processes.

Within the confines of the conflict situation, constructive solutions can be obtained and destructive aspects contained. Communication is necessary for constructive solutions. Resolution is easier to obtain if both sides accept the legitimacy of the others' concerns, if persuasion is the primary technique used, if reliance on personal pathologies is avoided, if the situation is a joint venture rather than a win-lose game, and if the conflict is defined as small in scope. Gaining the cooperation of the other party seems to be most effective when cooperative behavior and intentions of the other are generously responded to and when hostility is not reciprocated nor allowed to be rewarding.

In the area of international relations, particularly in the arms race and war skirmishes, nations use threat, deterrence, surveillance, and severing of communications. The research on interpersonal conflict indicates that these techniques have not been successful in resolving interpersonal conflicts—can they then be effective in the international arena?

A number of behavioral scientists have seen hope in such developments as: (1) world government, (2) transitional interaction, (3) graduated reciprocation, (4) education in conflict resolution, and (5) increasing life satisfaction. Perhaps the future of each reader will be decided by how well he learns to constructively deal with conflicts with friends, loved ones, governments, and nations.

CHAPTER 13

Psychology
of social change

SOCIAL CHANGE

To most of mankind, throughout history, change has come so slowly that it has passed unnoticed. "The thing that hath been, it is that which shall be, and that which is done is that which shall be done: and there is no new thing under the sun." So the world seemed in the Old Testament Book of Ecclesiastes. Food, clothing, housing, occupations, technology, rituals, illness, and hazards seemed to change as little as climate. What was, seemed always to have been. When men wanted to go somewhere they walked or rode a horse or sailed a boat. The distance of oral communication was limited to the natural range of shouts. Food was cooked over an open fire from the days of the caveman until about a century ago, and the only way of illuminating a room at night was with a flame. "The memory of man runneth not back to the contrary," said English law. Prayers and ceremonies, it was thought, would be effective only as long as every word and gesture remained unchanged. One generation passed, and another came, but ways of life continued to be constant, predictable, and dependable. Children sought to walk in parental footsteps and to live by ancient wisdom. Each child was placed in a well-worn cradle of established custom because the older generation knew best.

Accelerating change

The human organism, gifted as it is for adaptation, evolved under conditions which remained essentially stable for many centuries. *Homo sapiens* appeared only about 100,000 years ago, and what we know as civilization represents less than 10 percent of his time on earth. Julian Huxley (1942) estimates the tempo of human evolution during recorded history (the last 5,000 years) as "at least 100,000 times as rapid as that of pre-human evolution." During the past three centuries (less than one-third of 1 percent of the age of *homo sapiens*) the period allowable for assimilation of a major change has decreased from nearly a century to less than a decade.

At the beginning of this century, no one had seen a movie or an airplane, heard a radio or jazz music, shopped in supermarkets, lunched in a cafeteria, eaten an ice cream cone, paid income tax, or worried about Communist nations. At mid-century there were still no nuclear submarines. H-bombs, electronic computers, space rockets, or tranquilizers.

Technological change has risen exponentially as shown in Figure 13-1. Expenditures on research and development have doubled each decade since 1930. Speed of travel increased by a factor of 10 when man moved from

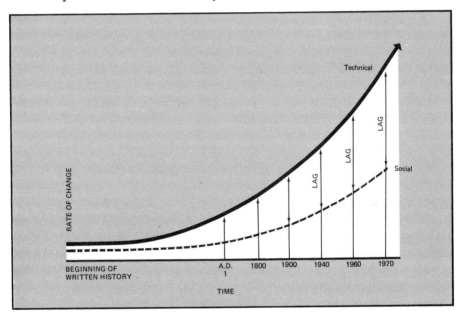

FIGURE 13-1

horses to trains and from trains to planes, but by a factor of 25 from planes to rockets. A similar curve would graph the distance over which one man's voice could be heard or the explosive power of weapons.

This unprecedented rate of technical change creates demands for individual and instutional adaptation which men in past ages have never had to meet. Youth can no longer follow the parental footsteps, nor can they be prepared by 12 or 16 years of schooling for a lifelong vocation or the understanding of the problems of their world 20 years later. Executives in government, business, education, and other fields are required to make more major decisions and to make them more quickly. Innovation is followed by obsolescence before it has been well assimilated.

The problem of adaptation is particularly severe in cultures long isolated, but now caught up in a wave of rapid industrialization. In some regions, transportation moved from primitive forms to airplanes within a decade. After World War II the average life-expectancy in the island of Mauritius in the Indian Ocean increased from 31 to 51 years during a period of only eight years, a gain which took nearly a century in Western Europe and the United States (Hoagland, 1964). Peoples with a long history of cultural stability are now thrust into processes of change for which they are psychologically and educationally unprepared.

McClelland has shown (1961) that a psychological emphasis on working hard to achieve excellence has historically appeared in cultures prior to the development of a high level of business enterprise. The contemporary cultures which are being industrialized by diffusion rather than by development from within their own institutions lack this psychological foundation. People in these cultures can drive automobiles today but they never went through a period similar to the years when Henry Ford worked at the horseless carriage.

McClelland's data support a view that the attitudes were inculcated first, and the society later came to embody the corresponding social systems—a reversal of the S-P-A sequence. Evidence that sometimes the level of energy in the culture affects individual motivation comes from a subsequent study (Veroff, 1963) of African students in the United States. Students coming from Kenya, where electric power output per capita had increased four-fold in the decade 1950-1960, were more likely to score high in drive for competitive excellence than were those coming from Ghana, where there had been only a 50 percent increase in kilowatt hours per capita during that same decade. Among 47 new arrivals in the United States, 40 percent were high on the need for achievement measure; among the 32 who had lived here for more than a year and a half, 60 percent scored high. Life in a more dynamic culture fosters achievement values, and the newly industrialized nations will probably acquire an enterprise psychology much faster than it developed in Western Europe or the United States.

Resistance to change

Men usually enjoy the excitement and challenge of new experience, but the strange and untried is also disquieting and often threatening. Ogburn long ago (1922) pointed to the phenomenon called "social lag"—the failure of institutional adaptation to keep pace with technological advance. The dotted line in Fig. 12-1 suggests that social systems are not changing as rapidly as the techniques of mechanical, electrical, and electronic innovation. It is easier, for example, to manufacture automobiles than to redesign cities so that these cars can easily be parked near homes, offices, shops, and places of recreation. During the period of horse-and-buggy travel a county unit of government was most practical; today there are few functions that are best carried on at the county level, but county officials persist.

Why is there reluctance to change social patterns? What psychological factors underly the lag? Some are personality characteristics—other traits of social systems.

Personality factors

A basic law of learning is that organisms repeat responses which in the past have brought satisfaction. Thus habits become drives, a process which Allport (1937) has called "functional autonomy." Responses persist for a time even when they no longer bring the satisfactions to which they once led. The earliest habits—those formed in childhood—have particular strength because they had primacy and so have had years of reenforcement. They have provided the frame for later experiences. Habits are extremely resistant to change. Selective attention, selective interpretation, and retention all operate to keep early views intact. The individual ignores facts which do not fit into his framework of expectations, distorts them so they do fit, or forgets all about them.

The old, familiar ways are not only encrusted in the core of personality; they also carry a halo of virtue. The customary seems right and best. The superego defends what parents inculcated. During our childhood dependence the grownups were bigger, stronger, and wiser. Who, then, are we to question the teachings of our elders?

Resistance to change is supported by a network of interpersonal ties to individuals who represent the old patterns. We do not usually want to be "the first by whom the new is tried." After the others around us have changed, then we can go along with it, too.

We discount our own dissatisfactions because this has been the pattern of our socialization. From the first toilet-training on through school and work, we have learned that our own impulses must be brought into conformity with external demands. Self-assertion brought punishment and/or guilt. We reject our authentic rebellious responses and cripple the mainspring of humanistic innovation (Lindner, 1952).

A special problem arises from the tendency of change to evoke feelings of insecurity and anxiety. In a laboratory study, Hamblin (1958) found that when the rules of a game were suddenly changed in unexpected ways, players became more "self-oriented" (defensive, dominating, status-seeking, or dependent) and less likely to help one another in cooperative team endeavor. Praise was replaced by criticism and group morale declined. When people are disturbed, they tend to regress to the remembered or fantasied

425

security of earlier times. It is paradoxical that just at the moment when the pressure for change is greatest, there is the strongest impulse to retreat to the comparative safety and security of the old ways.

It is interesting to note the hypothesis that the ways of childhood persist in the inner fantasy life, while adaptation to modern changes goes on at the more superficial, rational, and instrumental level. Lee (1958) found that Zulu dreams reflected the culture that existed 50 to 75 years earlier and seldom the realities of the changed current scene. A study in rural Japan (Wagatsuma, De Vos, 1962) reached a similar conclusion: While love-marriages are approved in direct interviews, fantasy responses to T.A.T. pictures reflected the traditional Japanese preference for arranged marriages.

Resistance is often unconscious, but rationalized. Freud found that his patients who suffered from painful symptoms nevertheless tried many pretexts to keep from accepting the changes required for recovery. Analysis of the unconscious resistance which impedes adaptation and growth is a major factor in psychoanalytic therapy. It is sometimes difficult to discover the real grounds for resistance when the emotional reasons are covered by a cloak of plausible rationalizations. For example, in the Presbyterian Church in the United States (southern), opponents of merger with the larger (northern) Presbyterian Church in the United States dealt only with doctrinal disputes and patterns of church law in all their published documents. Little or nothing was said of ethnic group questions, job security, status, and other issues which those familiar with the struggle believed to be the underlying concerns (Dornbusch, Irie, 1959).

Certain kinds of personalities are especially threatened by change. Individuals who have not achieved genuine, wholehearted integration of their drives and impulses, but have managed by repression, suppression, and pretense to maintain a socially-acceptable facade, are likely to expect that changes will disturb their precarious equilibrium. Thus persons high on the F-scale are suspicious of social innovation and hostile to its advocates. They are susceptible, as reported in Chapter 10, to the projective form of ethnic group prejudice (McClintock, 1958). They lean to the radical right in politics (Bell, 1963; Forster, Epstein, 1964). Persons rated low in ego-defensiveness, on the other hand, have been found better able to adapt to change (Peak, Morrison, 1958; Niel, Dunn, 1960).

Some kinds of change awaken deep, irrational resentment. They arouse a mystique of the sacred. Sexual mores, religion, and national patriotism have this special quality. One may evade one's income tax without arousing much condemnation, but to refuse to salute the flag is intolerable. The campaign against adding fluoride to drinking water supplies in some communities has included a scare-story that this measure for reducing dental cavities is really a Communist plot. It is asserted that the chemical will rob American men of their virility and so facilitate the Red triumph (Davis, 1959).

Systems Seek to Preserve Stability

By nature, social systems have evolved or been designed to operate in a fairly steady equilibrium. A change in any part disturbs the rest of the system. The interlocking functions and the feedback systems operate to continue the customary activities. Reforms such as simplified spelling or the adoption of a metric system of weights and measures or a calendar in which days and dates would correspond over the years have obvious rational advantages but are not adopted because of the many related changes which would ensue.

Sometimes after a temporary change, the old ways are resumed in a kind of social homeostasis (Cannon, 1932). The impact of World War II on the class system in England has been described as follows: "When the manor house was on fire we all lined up in the bucket brigade; when the fire was out, the servants went back to the servant's quarters!" Waves of municipal reform in most large cities have been followed by a slow drift "back to normalcy."

Another element of stability in most social systems is the correlation of power and privilege. Those who enjoy special benefits in the status quo are not hospitable to changes which would threaten their privileges. Their reluctance to read the portents of the times, even when change is well along, has become memorable in the proverb that "Bourbons never learn!"

Further resistance arises from the fact that most change is introduced from outside the system. Hence it bears the onus of the foreigner—the stranger—the outsider whose ways are not our ways. A typical reaction to imagined outside agents of change occurred in a Northern state where a community launched a project involving a cooperative nursery school and a softball league. Soon rumors that the whole service enterprise was really a Communist scheme began circulating in the town. The whole project was planned and financed by Moscow, it was reported (Festinger *et al.*, 1948).

Despite inertia, anxiety, unconscious resistance, vested interests, and suspicion of the strange, change is constantly occurring. While adaptation in social systems may not keep pace with mechanical inventions, it is proceeding at an unprecedented rate. Introducing his anthropological account of a typical midwestern town, Warner (1949) wrote: "A dominant theme in the life of all American communities is social change." Our next interest is to review briefly some of the major historic theories men have proposed to account for change in the past and to predict its future course. Many of these still influence attitudes toward change today.

Historic Theories

An ancient view, still operative in many parts of the world, is that change is unpredictable and due to the whims of the gods or of fate. Persons holding this opinion take no responsibility for planning, initiating or guiding change. They accept whatever comes. Plato offered the interesting idea that God's attention to the affairs of the universe is intermittent; He sets it in order and leaves it; if it sinks into serious disorder, then He again intervenes and corrects it.

Two rather naïve views of social change are linear. One is the familiar assumption of progress. Our society is presumed to be getting better and better. Spencer (1876) paralleled "social evolution" with biological evolution. This view seems to be supported by the curves of both technological and social advance, symbolized in Figure 13-1. Comte (1830) saw altruism increasing as science advances. An opposite view, espoused by the more pessimistic (Swift, Carlyle, Malthus, Ortega y Gasset), is that a Golden Age existed sometime in the past and that every passing year brings a decline in values and increased problems and frustration. Growing population and proliferating weapons of mass destruction lend support to this view.

Cyclic theories envisage history as repeating certain recognizable sequences. Spengler's *Decline of the West* (1918) likened a civilization to an organism with stages of growth, maturity, and decline. Toynbee's celebrated analysis of 26 civilizations (1947) abandons the organic analogy, but finds a recurrent sequence: (a) response of a creative minority to some challenge; (b) degeneration into control by a merely dominant minority based on force rather than voluntary allegiance; (c) rise of an internal proletariat which, often assisted by outside enemies, ends the epoch and launches a new cycle. Another cyclic theory, propounded by Sorokin (1937–1941; 1947), describes a sequence from a "sensate" super-system, which finds reality empirically through the senses, to an "ideational" super-system in which spiritual reality is dominant. Between the two comes an "idealistic" era which combines them. The concept "super-system" is introduced because each way of understanding the world permeates many systems and areas of civilization, manifesting itself in the emphasis given within science, literature, art, law, ethics, and religion. Sorokin sees us today nearing the end of a several-century phase of emphasis on material values, with an increasing stress on scientific and technical conquests; he expects a swing toward ideational, super-sensory, and super-rational concerns. Cairns (1962) has described the cyclic view of history found in Hinduism, Taoism, Zoroastrianism, and in contemporary social scientists like Sorokin.

Dialectic theories, involving the union of opposites, are as old as philosophy, but most clearly formulated by Hegel in the famous sequence: thesis, antithesis, synthesis. Karl Marx has been the classic exponent of this view of social change (Marx, Engels, 1847). Each ruling class he saw as engaged in struggle with a rising opposition: oppressor vs. oppressed. The bourgeoisie won out against the aristocracy and created the capitalist-imperialist world. The working-class mission is to end this rule and to create a "classless" society in which everyone is both owner and worker. Marx's basic analysis is generally accepted in socialist as well as Communist nations; it is seen in capitalist countries as obsolete and seriously misleading. The value of the dialectic approach to processes of progress is not limited to its use by Marx. Teggart (1918) has emphasized that the controversies among intellectuals are often more productive than their harmonious collaboration. Many scientific and philosophic theses have been formulated in order to refute an opponent. Conflict is frequently a fertile source of new ideas.

It is true, also, that the problems of one generation are often left unsolved but become transformed or transcended. Santayana remarked that "Americans seem never to solve their problems; they amiably bid them 'Good-bye!' " Koestler has said:

"We can discern in the past a succession of levels of social awareness, like an ascending staircase. The age of religious wars ended when secular politics began to dominate human consciousness; feudal politics ended when economic factors assumed over-riding importance; the struggles of Economic Man will end by the emergence of the new ethical values of the new age. The great disputes are never settled on their own level, but on the next higher one. . . . Seen from the perspective of the next-higher historical level, the old controversies lose interest, appear drained of their meaning; and conversely, the exact properties of each succeeding period cannot be formulated from the lower level." (1945, p. 104).

The grand theories—theocratic, linear, cyclic or dialectic—are, in Allport's (1954, p. 9) phrase, too "simple and sovereign." Thus hypotheses may be illustrated by many sequences in history, but it is difficult to test them against an adequate sample of unselected data.

CULTURAL DIFFUSION

The kind of social change most frequently observed in both personal experience and in social science is that which occurs when some individual or group picks up and adopts some idea or mechanism or operation which he has observed in some other person or situation. Indeed, Tarde, one of the first social psychologists (1890), made imitation his central concept. The rapid expansion in anthropology since 1920 has added a wealth of evidence on diffusion from one culture to another.

In Chapter 8, we reported the alteration of the lives of the Tiv in Nigeria with the coming of the British. In a more recent (1956) study of social change, Margaret Mead has described the changes in the Manus between her first visit in 1929 and a revisit in 1954. A major intervening variable had been occupation by the U.S. forces during World War II. The 14,000 Manus had had direct or indirect contact with about a million American soldiers. The Manus were fascinated by all the equipment, machines, and gadgets. They were impressed, in a different way, with the American respect for human values and democratic relationships. During this time, one of their own able leaders, Paliau, came back to them and his personal qualities played a part in the ensuing changes. Also a religious hope, expressed in a "Cargo Cult," had failed to arrive. By 1953, the old culture had been almost wholly repudiated. The former fishermen now tilled the soil. Cooperative enterprises such as a town council, a communal dock, and a bank had replaced the primitive barter between individuals. Many of the severe taboos of the old religion had been relaxed and Christianity was espoused. Adult quarreling had diminished. Coeducational schools had been introduced, and men no longer dominated their wives. These changes were not byproducts of the diffusion of any one particular item of culture, but rather a sweeping movement into a new, Westernized order.

Among all primitive peoples urbanization and industrialization have weakened old cultures. Biesheuvel (1959) found in South Africa that old ties which had held men in conformity to traditional norms had been discarded. This was followed by a sense of release that seemed to lead to impulsive and lawless acts. On another continent, Hallowell (1951) found that the more acculturated Ojibwa Indians of Lac du Flambeau, Wisconsin, who spoke English, sent their children to school, and listened to the radio, showed more signs (Rorschach) of personal maladjustment. Spindler (1955) also used Rorschach tests in his study of the acculturation of Menomini Indians. The traditionalists who maintained the old way of life were found to be unemotional; the Indians in transition showed more anxiety and aggression; those who were really integrated into the white civilization appeared to have also achieved a healthy emotional adjustment.

A fascinating study in cultural change is that of two adjacent villages of Pueblo Indians (Dozier, 1957). An ancient quarrel, with charges of broken promises, kept them separate, although their houses were alike and not far apart. Intermarriage was discouraged. The Hopi village, like many others around it, cultivated personalities who were passive, fatalistic, and mystical. The Tewa, descendants of rebels who had fought off the Spaniards, were proud and militant, more active than passive, more worldly than mystical. The Hopi thought they were superior to the Tewa, who were a small cultural island in the large Hopi area. The big change came with the advance of white civilization into the region. Because Tewa values were congruous with the achievement-oriented, self-reliant white man's world, they adapted easily to stock-raising, wage labor, and public schools. Suddenly the Hopi found that the despised Tewa were surpassing them. The old prejudices faded away. Hopi and Tewa learned to work together in pottery manufacture and cattle cooperatives. Intermarriage, formerly discouraged, became acceptable, and the two communities joined even in religious ceremonies. The case illustrates how diffusion from the dominant, powerful industrial civilization suppressed one set of values (Hopi) and gave support to another. Similar changes, described in Chapter 8, occurred when the diffusion of guns and horses to the Comanches developed militant raiders, but the imposed power of peaceful government later stifled that belligerency and depressed the related social vitality.

DEMONSTRATIONS AND UTOPIAS

Learning new ways from observation of others underlies many projects which offer demonstrations as a technique for encouraging innovation. Model farms, model schools, model factories, and model communities have been designed to persuade observers to do likewise.

The usual outcome is that the demonstration project is a great experience for those who design and develop it, but it seldom is adopted by others (Redefer, 1950; Watson, 1964). Teachers who visit superb experimental schools and wish that they had similar buildings, equipment, pupils, and support feel incapable of transforming their own schools. The "Hawthorne effect" (referring to the high level of morale and production helps to make the original project highly successful, but this does not diffuse to imitators. Sometimes, as in the experiences of the Latter Day Saints in Illinois or the Doukhabors in Canada, the surrounding world is more hostile than admiring. In Meiklejohn's experiment at the University of Wisconsin and New College at Columbia, the noninvolved professors were more likely to be suspicious than converted. When the Agricultural Experiment Stations set up nearly ideal farms, these had far less influence than was later achieved by projects in which more typical farmers were persuaded to try out limited innovations in fertilizer, plowing, seed or cultivation. For most farmers, what their neighbors could do fell within their "latitude of acceptance"; what the State farms could do was not appropriate to their own powers.

The process of innovation

Introduction of change within a social system whether it is as small as a family or as large as a nation or worldwide corporation, moves through a fairly standard sequence of stages, each of which presents distinctive problems for social psychological study.

Felt dissatisfaction

Necessity proverbially leads to invention. Not all needs that are felt foster innovations, but when changes are introduced it is because some dissatisfaction has been felt. The need, however, may exist for many years before a solution is proposed. So long as a social system runs smoothly and produces about what is expected, innovation is resisted.

Lewin's view was that the process of social change moves in three stages:

431

(1) unfreezing the old structure; (2) developing the new forms; and (3) re-freezing or stabilizing the change. It is as though the heat of necessity were required to break down the incrustations of custom so that it can be molded into some more appropriate pattern.

Lippitt, Watson and Westley (1958) suggest four forces for change: (1) dissatisfaction or pain in the present situation; (2) dissatisfaction with a perceived discrepancy between what is and what might be; (3) external pressures on a system to force its change; and (4) internal motivation to grow and to improve. Greening (1963) found all four factors operative behind the change of policy in a voluntary general hospital in California, when it decided to accept alcoholics as normally "sick" patients. The four motives can be seen also in the introduction of new programs of mathematics and science teaching (Miles, 1964). Schools responded to dissatisfaction with the present, to the challenge of much better achievement, to pressures of public opinion after Sputnik, and to a wholesome desire on the part of teachers and administrators to improve their services.

Mort (1941, 1960) found that, on the average, 50 years had elapsed between the first recognition of a need in education and the development of the first practical invention for meeting the need. That was prior to 1940. Later studies (Miles, 1964) have indicated that the movement from the need to a practical remedy is more rapid than it was previously.

Diagnosis

Because of urgency, there is a strong impulse to cut short any diagnostic study and to work directly for some plausible remedy. Efforts to prevent delinquency, for example, are often undertaken with very little awareness of the basic social causes. Proposals for preventing war frequently accept uncritically such fallacies as are exposed in Chapter 12. One of the major contributions of social psychologists as consultants on change programs is that they insist on testing the diagnosis before going on to action plans.

Among the pertinent questions may be: What is the history of the alleged difficulty, when was it first noticed, and what attempts have previously been made to deal with it? Does it appear only at certain times, in certain parts of the organization, or under certain circumstances? Is it found also in certain other social systems? What is the attitude of influential persons and of the persons most directly involved?

A special difficulty often arises because managers think differently from researchers. Operators ask questions in the form: "What should I do?" Scientists seek answers to questions of truth. The answers provided by experimental inquiry yield systematic generalizations, but seldom do they prescribe the applications. The parent, teacher, or executive must cope with the concrete situation, and he is likely to be impatient with analyses of underlying forces.

Merton has observed that, "Characteristically the problem is so stated (by the policy maker) as to result in the possibility of the researcher's being seriously misled as to the 'basic' aspects" (1949). Characteristically, the policy maker's complaint is that the research findings do not tell him what he ought to do.

Diagnosis is further complicated by defensiveness. The need for any change is likely to be considered a reflection on the persons who have been responsible in the past. Consciously or unconsciously, they formulate the problem to exempt themselves from possible blame. So the community leaders approach a high delinquency rate by asking what should be done to negligent parents. Each nation approaches the problem of peace in terms of how to get the other side to change. A diagnostic study which includes the change-agent as part of the problem is rarely requested.

Whole and part

Changes in any part of a social system have consequences for other parts. When a change is proposed within one subsystem of a larger organization, it is necessary to consider how other, more or less related subsystems, will react. Administrators turn down many proposals which would have favorable results in part of the system because they can see the cost of its wider application.

In a toy factory, a team of women sprayed paint on toys moving steadily along a carefully paced assembly line. A psychologist persuaded management to let the workers try regulating the speed of this moving belt to fit their preferred pace. The workers were paid on a piece-work basis. They liked the innovation because they could speed up when their energy was high and slow down when they tired. The engineers were appalled by the irregular rates, but increasing output silenced their objections. Before long, production on this worker-regulated assembly line rose to uncomfortable heights. Workers in this department were taking home more pay than were supervisors in other parts of the factory. To cut their piece-rate would, of course, have demoralized these workers. Finally, despite the less efficient production, the uniform flow of work had to be resumed. Too much efficiency in one subsystem proved too upsetting to the balance of factors in the larger system of the plant (Likert, 1961).

In their case studies of change in industrial organizations, Mann and Neff (1961) illustrated how changes in the technique of producing seamless pipe affected the social structure of work groups and the consequent satisfaction of workers with their jobs. The use of computers in billing customers of a large utility created problems in the relationships of the accounting and sales divisions which had previously operated in relative independence. Introduction of electronic data processing in handling insurance applications and claims modified the responsibilities, authority, and power of several departments, not always to the satisfaction of those concerned. A study of change in a community-service organization (Dimock, Sorenson, 1955) concluded:

No part of institutional change is an island in itself: changes in program call for changes in every other part of the institution . . . and advance in one sector cannot proceed far ahead of change in other sectors. For example, program groups cannot be changed without officer training . . . which in turn is contingent upon advisor training . . . which in turn depends upon staff re-education. Similarly, changes in staff goals and ways of working are dependent upon administrative procedures, policies and budgets which in turn require changes in Boards and Committees.

A control group in one kindergarten experiment unexpectedly made more gain than did the experimental group because after the experimental group had left the room, the teacher, who taught both groups, became less burdened and more innovative.

Pressures from the more inclusive social system may nullify the progress made by subunits. There is evidence which supports the view that unless attitudes of top management also change, subordinates are likely to resist new practices.

Timeliness is a special case of the relationship of parts to the whole. "An idea whose time has come" is an idea that is being recognized and utilized simultaneously in many different parts of a system. A case in point is the wave of demonstrations against racial segregation beginning in 1959. The proliferation of projects to help culturally disadvantaged youth, drop-outs, and to lift standards of living in pockets of poverty after 1963 is another example. Progress which would have taken many years, at an earlier period, could be made in months because of parallel movements in other parts of the larger social system.

Because the same need may be felt in different parts of the world at a given stage in history, simultaneous inventions have been common. Ogburn (1938, pp. 90-102) lists 150 instances of parallel discoveries by inventors working independently. Barnett (1953) contends that although separated, the simultaneous inventors are really part of a large cooperative effort. They share the knowledge of their time, including its stereotypes and implicit assumptions; they share a common concern; often they have read the same materials and sometimes have been in direct or indirect communication. Perhaps both have been stimulated by rivalry. E. L. Thorndike has said: "The mother of invention is not necessity; it is the knowledge of other people's inventions."

Creative design

From the diagnosis emerge suggestions for possible remedies. The better the diagnosis, the greater the likelihood that the proposed changes will be pertinent and effective. Creative proposals may come from particularly able individuals or from group thinking as described in Chapter 4. They may arise within the organization or be brought in from outside (diffusion). Griffiths, studying change in school systems, concluded "The major impetus for change in organizations is from the outside." (1964, p. 431). Superintendents who initiated more changes were those more in touch with other schools and with other community agencies (Hemphill *et al.*, 1962). Pressures and suggestions for innovation more commonly arose in the public and the school board, rather than coming from principals, supervisors or teachers (Brickell, 1964).

Stages in the generation of an important creative idea have been found to include:

(a) a period of preparation, immersion in the problem, time for ideas to incubate (Ghiselin, 1955);

(b) a mood of openness to associations, ideas and hunches; playing with fantasies, letting intuitions emerge from pre-conscious or unconscious levels (Kubie, 1958);

(c) sudden, spontaneous emergence of an idea or ideas; these may be, at first, only half-formed and need to be held onto and worked at until one or another become clear and illuminating; sometimes a series of inspirations flows and the problem is to discard the less appropriate ones;

(d) elaboration, rational testing, criticism, exploration of consequences, revision, and improvement.

Most studies of creativity have dealt with great inventors or artists, but the same phases—at many lower levels—can be found in everyday discoveries relating to more commonplace activities, such as an idea for a letter to a friend, a way of saving time during shopping, or of eliminating a rattle in the car. Spiller (1929) has estimated that about 95 percent of technological progress has been the result of the accumulation of little improvements, contributed by unknown persons, rather than of the great inventions which made someone famous.

Force field analysis

Once a target for change has been defined, the problems of strategy and persuasion become central. A significant aid in analyzing the dynamics of a change situation is the diagramming of the forces acting for and against the proposed innovation. Kurt Lewin (1951) has pointed out that what seems rigid, immobile, and unchanging in a social situation seems so only because the forces pressing upon it offset one another and result in a temporary balance. He describes this as "quasi-stationary equilibrium."

A diagram may illustrate the balance or counter-balance of forces in a system at rest. In Figure 13-2 below the social system is represented by the circle in the middle.

Forces A, B, and C, their relative strength indicated by the length of each arrow, are pushing toward the Right. Forces X, Y, and Z are pushing to the Left. At that moment the system does not move, for the two sets of forces are equal and opposite. Movement to the Right (toward the goal +) may be initiated either by augmenting A, B or C or by weakening X, Y or Z. In an actual situation, many more vectors operate.

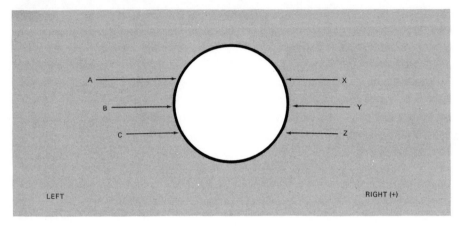

FIGURE 13-2

The value of the force analysis depends on the accuracy with which the main forces *pro* and *con* are identified and estimated. If the system represented by the circle is an individual and the goal (+) is to change his attitude on some issue, arrows like A, B, C, etc. might represent such forces as (A) his already considerable dissatisfaction with his earlier attitude, (B) his response to the intellectual challenge of a different approach; and (C) his desire to please some proponents of the change. Arrows like X, Y, and Z would, identify forces within him supporting the old attitude and opposing change. Thus X might represent his preference for taking the easy way of no-change; Y, his anxiety about possible inadequacy in the new role; Z, his desire to retain ties with old associates who might resent a different outlook.

If the circle represents a larger social system—say a city school system with the right hand goal an expansion of services for disadvantaged children—the vectors toward the right (goal, +) would designate the influential groups and individuals favoring such development; vectors in the reverse direction would stand for forces in the social system opposing the new program.

During the process of charting forces and counter-forces, a planning group may find it helpful to check out the direction, strength, and saliency of some of the presumed influences. Experience in the use of this device has shown that persons interested in a change are often mistaken about the amount of support or opposition which they attribute to other persons and groups. Exploration of the dynamics of the social equilibrium may lead to modifications of the proposed action which will increase support and lessen resistance.

Examination of the gains and losses may reveal that an innovation, despite its greater efficiency, is not adequate to overcome the inevitable confusion and waste of the change-over. Barnett (1953) speaks of the "marginal value" of certain inventions and improvements as insufficient to warrant the cost of their adoption. Morale in several industrial research departments was depressed by the fact that the company had failed to make use of some of their well-demonstrated improvements. It was hard for the creators of a new process to accept that fact that even though their proposal was superior to present practice, it would be too wasteful to change over. A parallel is the case of a teacher who has been reasonably successful with traditional methods. Perhaps some newer techniques are usually more effective, but their superiority may not be great enough to warrant discarding the accumulated materials, habits, and skills of the teacher's customary approach.

Reducing resistance

It is possible to increase the pressures in a quasi-stationary equilibrium without bringing about the desired change. Indeed, this often happens. Advocates of a reform try by argument, persuasion, inducements, threats, and coercion to effect movement in the direction of its adoption. But their activity alerts the opposition, who bring to bear their counter-arguments, counter-inducements, and counter-coercion. After a time, as shown in Figure 13-3 the pressures toward the goal (+) have mounted (longer arrows), but so have the counter-pressures, and the target has not moved.

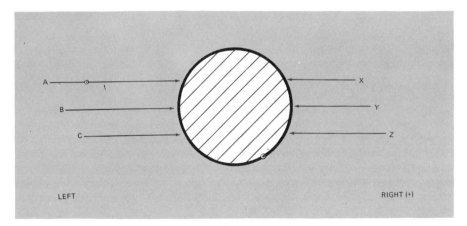

FIGURE 13-3

The diagnonal lines in the circle indicate high tension in the system as a result of pressures and counter-pressures.

The preferable strategy is to examine the resistance and to find ways to reduce it. If a child of 12 has not learned to read, despite normal ability and all the usual pressures from school, home, and other life situations, it will not help to exhort him harder and more often. This will only increase his conflict, frustration, and resentment. Wise psychotherapy examines the impedance which has thus far prevented him from making the customary progress. In a proposed social change—for example, purifying city air—the force analysis will probably show fairly strong pressures from health departments, housewives interested in reducing soot-fall, and citizens annoyed by smoke and smog. Why, then, has the change not been made? Who is afraid of what? What are the still unsolved problems of cost and enforcement? Finding ways around the real or imagined obstacles may be more efficient than a propaganda drive.

The dynamics may be illustrated by Figure 13-4. Arrows A, B, and C—the pressures for change toward the goal (+)—remain unchanged from their state in Figure 13-2, when the situation was stable. But the length of arrow X has been a little reduced, and arrow Y is much shorter. Now the resultant of the forces makes for movement to the right, toward the goal (+).

The principle that it is more rewarding to reduce resistance than to try to overcome it by greater pressure operates with almost all kinds of social change. Workers can be forced by management to accept a new pattern of production despite their feeling of insecurity, but this will increase tension and rebellious feelings. Or, as in the Coch and French experiment (1948), their insecurity about the change can be reduced by planning it themselves so they feel more confident of its success. Then the change can be made with less tension, aggression, and lowering of productivity.

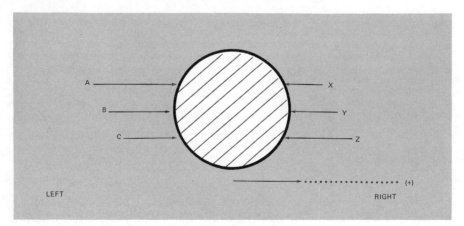

FIGURE 13-4

On racial integration, resistance can be defeated by superior force, resulting in reluctant acquiescence and continued tension, or, in other instances, some of the apprehension may be reduced because fears of lowered academic standards, violence, sexual immorality, dirt, and disease can be relieved. In the latter case, the process will be smoother and easier. In international relations, the arms race represents lengthening of the opposing force-vectors on both sides, with increased tension in the system. Osgood's "graduated reciprocation," described in Chapter 12, follows Lewin's admonition to reduce the resistance and thus to lower the tension levels. In those historic periods when opposing groups become more urgent, strenuous, and intense in pressing for their goals there is likely to be overt conflict but no real change in position. The centuries of religious wars (Moslem-Christian; Catholic-Protestant) did not end in the triumph of either side. When both sides relaxed the pressure and counter-pressure, the positions did not change but the dangerous tension gradually diminished.

Participation

One of the most successful strategies for increasing the pressure toward a social goal, and for simultaneously reducing resistance, is to involve the persons concerned in diagnosing the difficulty and designing the innovation.

Alfred Marrow, a social psychologist with a distinguished career as head of a business and in public service, has summarized the remarkable success of change-action based on participation and involvement:

> There was an increase of 42 percent in the number of housewives who served glandular meat cuts, an improvement of 56 percent in the number of persons answering bigoted remarks, an improvement in gang behavior that resulted in a reduction of 90 percent in the number of gang fights in Seaside, an improvement of 72 percent in the skills used by community leaders after their Workshop training, an increase of 24 percent in factory production, an improvement of 40 percent in the number of gainfully employed older workers, an improvement of as much as 52 percent in favorable attitudes toward Negroes among residents of interracial housing, an increase of 75 percent in the number of persons and organizations involved in intergroup activities in Northtown, etc.

The key words in successful introduction of innovations are *participation* and *involvement*. People enjoy and affirm the changes they make for themselves; they resist changes imposed on them by others. Even in research organizations, supposedly committed to the quest for new knowledge with no respect to source, there is a kind of provincial pride. In development and engineering shops, the "N.I.H. factor" ("not invented here") operates against proposals coming from "outsiders." It is even more important, however, that participants in the process of diagnosis and design have an apportunity to clear up misunderstandings and differences of interpretation before the changes are made. While proposals are still tentative and in flux, they can be modified so that potential opponents find some consideration given to their concerns. Participation in planning is too often limited to those already convinced and in favor of the change. This is one of the liabilities of reform movements. They set up the unproductive win-lose, dominance-submission relationship; they define their in-group as good and wise; the out-group as evil or stupid. The problem-solving orientation brings together all persons and groups concerned, so that what emerges from their thinking together is, as nearly as possible, a real integration. It is designed to incorporate the desires of all participants and to avoid or to minimize the consequences which any find undesirable. If the planning groups accept apparent resistance as justified doubts presenting still unresolved problems, a premature lineup of advocates vs. opponents can be avoided.

Temporary systems

Open exploration and creative integration are often encouraged by setting up conditions under which participants can interact with more freedom than they feel they have in their usual job and community roles. Miles (1964) refers to "temporary systems" devised to maximize opportunity for persons who are involved in working together to learn new ways of mutual understanding and collaboration. In a "training laboratory," a workshop, a conference, a religious retreat, or in group therapy changes are possible which would be very difficult in the customary social systems. People in families, schools, businesses, churches, and governments are very busy with their routine activities. They have relatively little time and energy to divert to the cultivation of the innovative life.

Miles has described three examples of temporary systems focused on promoting change in persons or organizations (1964, pp. 446-452). A human relations training laboratory for educators gave participants a chance to get away from the pressure of work and the patterns of personal relationship back on the job. In T-Groups, they became more aware of their own feelings and values and more sensitive to the experiences and needs of others. First, they had to "unlearn" their private conceptions of themselves, their associates, and their organization, which had become fixed with long experience. It is remarkable that after only two weeks in this special setting as many as 75 percent of the participants (as measured both by self-report and observations of associates on the job) showed noticeable improvement in ability to work with others.

A second case was an experimental summer school for children who were academically retarded. Teachers felt themselves to be part of a creative team, freed from the usual chores, to act simply as educators. More than 1,200 (of 1,500) children successfully "passed," and the participating teachers and principals gained a new confidence that they could, under suitable conditions, achieve far more than they had in the past.

Miles' third case involved a one-week conference of the managers of a British manufacturing company. Starting with the usual reserve, and defensiveness, participants learned to "open up" and "the emotional tone became one of eager involvement, extremely hard work, and a kind of equalitarian comaraderie which appeared to transcend preexisting relationships" (p. 451). A report recommending important structural changes was promptly accepted by the Board and implemented throughout the large industrial organization.

All of these experiments were characterized by: (1) time limits; (2) focus on a definite goal; (3) a defined and bounded group of participants; (4) physical and social isolation; (5) conditions facilitating better communications; (6) a norm of equalitarianism; (7) a norm of genuineness; authenticity, openness and frankness; (8) the norms of scientific thinking; and (9) an expectation of change in the persons and social systems. All of them successfully fostered such changes. Both individuals and organizations can learn to enjoy new experience and to take pride in change.

Leaders and consultants

Participation of the many does not preclude strong leadership by the most able. An important group skill, developed in training programs, is the ability to utilize the resources of all members. This includes, and with special emphasis, the resources of certain leaders. One of the most impressive demonstrations of change in a factory has been reported by Guest (1962). A new manager for Plant Y began by listening: he then set up regular meetings in which more men could participate more freely. Within three years, the plant changed from the poorest to the best in quality of output, low labor costs, safety record, freedom from grievances, and absenteeism. The changes—established by forceful leadership—were accepted by the workers and remained in effect after the original manager was promoted to a new position.

In their report on reorganizing a YMCA, Dimock and Sorenson described a procedure like that of Plant Y.

At the beginning the administrative leadership provides the initiative in planning and setting the steps in motion. Staff and constituency participate in and agree to the goals and plans. But such commitment is permissive rather than propulsive in the early stages. As the project proceeds, the involvement of staff, advisors and Boards become deeper; satisfaction and confidence in new skills develop; commitment is deeper and responsibility in the branches and groups increases. As operating responsibility is distributed and initiated at more points, internal motivation is strengthened.

The people who initiate and lead in experimental and demonstration projects within communities and business organizations are usually above the average in ability and in contacts with outside groups. The school superintendents whose systems first adopted modern mathematics were above their colleagues in education, status with their peers, and frequency of friendship interaction with them (Carlson, 1964). In a study of the rate at which doctors adopt new drugs (Menzel, Katz, 1956), it appeared that the leaders more frequently learned of the innovations from journal articles and professional meetings; the followers were more apt to rely on what salesmen brought to them. Men responsible for creative social inventions in another study (De Grazia, 1961) were high in drive for achievement, ability to see relationships, tendency to express ideas through action, and in "marginality," not feeling fully identified with the dominant culture.

Schools that are innovative have teachers who attend out-of-town meetings and who read widely to discover fresh ideas. Similar results were found with farmers. The more experimental-minded go more often to metropolitan cities. Eichholz and Rogers (1964) propose the generalization that "innovativeness varies directly with cosmopolitaness."

Consultants are important leaders in processes of change because they can bring into consideration a broader range of experience than that represented by the other participants. Their success frequently depends, however, on not being persuaded to do for the other persons involved what these individuals could do for themselves.

Consultation is the strategy of change which has made most use of the skills and insights of social psychology. Individuals suffering from neurosis, groups which reach an impasse, factories which have labor problems, organizations which want to be more effective, and communities seeking to overcome conflicts have frequently sought psychological help. In trying to help a society change, a consultant uses methods similar to those of a good therapist working with an individual patient. He helps the society only at the points where the society really wants help. His strategy for dealing with resistance is to bring it into consciousness and to examine and interpret it. He wishes to be seen as a welcome helper, not as one who imposes a change or even argues or persuades. Page (1959) has introduced the term "Socio-therapy of the enterprise."

Experience indicates that change in an organization is much more likely to be accepted if it has the support of top management (Watson, 1967). Whenever possible, consultants try to establish their contact with the president or other chief executive officer. Dimock and Sorenson (1955) caution that "because the whole agency is involved, in all of its policy making, administration, financial, building, personnel and program aspects, it is not possible for the executive officer to delegate modernization to some staff person." Griffiths (1964) states as one of his propositions: "When change in an organization does occur, it will tend to occur from the top down, not from the bottom up."

A sociologist interested in helping in a community action program found that he needed to work not only with the heads of formal organizations but also with persons who held key posts in the informal communication systems of the community. He mapped the ties of kinship and of "visiting" in the town and identified some who, although holding no office, were extremely influential. When five such persons viewed a farm demonstration, almost everyone in the community had heard about it the next day (Loomis, 1953).

Loomis experienced the initial suspicion and unwillingness to give information which we might anticipate in relationship to a stranger. One day, within a few hours, the community attitude changed to active cooperation. It developed that Mr. B., a figure of high prestige and a key man in the communications network, had gone to the county seat and talked with officials who had been informed about the Loomis project. With their approval, he could dispel the doubts of most farmers in Southtown.

Greening (1963) began his program of change in the hospital by winning the support of the President of the Board. Without this backing, the administration was reluctant to propose the program to the medical staff.

From the National Training Laboratory in 1947 came the term and concept of a "change agent," who operates usually as a consultant on a volunteer or professional basis. Lippitt, Watson, and Westley, in their book, *The Dynamics of Planned Change* (1958), pointed out the need to examine consultant-client relationships at every stage of the change action. How is the consultant seen by the various persons and groups concerned, before he enters the process? How does he see himself? What is his own motivation? If he is not successful in keeping responsibility for decisions clearly on the permanent members of the social system, he becomes the scapegoat for whatever goes wrong or proves disturbing. A good consultant helps the leadership within the organization to anticipate difficulties and to devise remedies. Yet, however well he operates, the consultant will be viewed with ambivalence by the clients. Psychotherapists are trained to expect some alternation in their patients between unwarranted rejection and equally unwarranted glorification and dependence. Experienced consultants to management are familiar with similar swings toward and against them.

In his *Helping People Change* (1963), Corey generalizes some of his experience from decades of consulting in the United States and in India. He doubts that technical competence in an area is sufficient to make an individual a good consultant. "Failures have seldom resulted, in my judgment, from a lack of knowledge about, and experience with, the specific area of activity in which change was undertaken." Corey notes that an All-American football player is not necessarily a good coach. He argues for continuing sensitivity to the subtlety of human relationships. It is not easy, particularly when working with other mature, sophisticated persons, to follow the undercurrents of feeling. "Most of us have developed many varieties of protective behavior that may keep a deterioration in human relations from coming to light. One of the characteristics of the best consultants I have worked with, however, is their ability to pick up cues of such deterioration and act to stop it" (p. 72).

The kind of empathy which enables the consultant to see the problem as the client does and to feel problems as the client feels them is closely akin to the demands on a psychotherapist. Corey notes in himself and in others a need to be vigilant against tendencies to translate the client's problems into terms more familiar to the consultant and to make an impression of brilliant competence. Corey's years of experience as an educator have left him with grave doubts about the effectiveness of most direct instruction. "I fell into the perennial trap," he reports, "of confusing an increase in knowledgeable talk about a problem with the capacity and drive to deal with it effectively." In contrast, he has found it rewarding and satisfying to become a genuine participant in a team project; to work closely with associates; and to let whatever teaching occurred be incidental to progress on the cooperative task.

The emphasis in the consultative approach tends to approve the kind of change where those who are affected are invited to participate in planning for, guiding, and evaluating what happens. This strategy enlists many different personalities, each contributing his special knowledge, his particular skills, and unique values. Group consensus is sought. The climate is one of cooperative problem-solving rather than of a win-lose struggle. As in McGregor's "Theory Y" it is assumed that people will rise to the challenge of such expectations, will reveal unexpected resources of ability, and will want to assume responsibility. One can say of the good consultant as Lao-tze said of the good leader: "When his work is done, his goal achieved, people will say, 'We did this ourselves!'"

There is another type of leadership, especially manifest in historic movements of reform and revolution. The heroic leader may take a stand for which there is not yet much support. He may slowly win adherents, or, perhaps, achieve recognition only after his death. Monuments have often been erected to prophets who were rejected by their contemporaries. Revolutionary movements have usually been led by intellectuals and persons of some prestige who have identified with the underprivileged. Jefferson and Washington came from a class which lived far more comfortably than most American colonists. Davis (1930) found that 60 percent of the leadership of the Bolshevik Revolution in 1917, came from upper classes which comprised only 7 percent of the population in Russia at that time.

Adaptation, evaluation, and revision

A change seldom, if ever, turns out to be exactly what its advocates expected. Unanticipated difficulties appear even in such carefully designed and tested bits of machinery as new models of motor cars. Social changes rarely lend themselves to pre-testing and control. Hence, what is required is commitment to a period of adaptation and improvement. The first consequences may be so disturbing as to lead to a demand to scrap the innovation and return to the old pattern. Many a promising development has been defeated because too much was expected too quickly. Mann and Neff (1962) caution: "It is essential to set realistic expectations about what a change will mean to those directly or indirectly affected." Over-optimistic expectations are forerunners of frustration.

Participation during the processes of diagnosis, design, and introduction of a change lays the foundation for continuing activity by these participants in whatever adjustments, adaptations, and revisions emerge as the process continues. Training workers in group problem solving and decision making may enable them to deal immediately with problems which might otherwise be referred to upper levels of management.

Evaluation of changes in a business can be made rather clearly through financial controls. It is more difficult to evaluate alleged improvements in the work of educational, recreational, community, government, and religious agencies.

Johnson's report on California schools (Miles, 1964, p. 169) reveals that only 68 of 1,507 schools reported any attempt to evaluate changes they had introduced and only ten had designed what he regarded as a respectable research procedure. A $3 million investment by a Foundation in a new program of teacher preparation in Arkansas actually turned out only 194 teachers and their success, relative to teachers trained in other ways, was never clearly evaluated. Few educational activities have been researched as extensively as has been the teaching of reading. Yet Barton and Wilder (Miles, 1964, p. 375) find that the results have not been incorporated in the readers published over a subsequent 30-year period. The "Hawthorne effect" and the "placebo effect" have seldom been separated from the other consequences of experiments in schools and other community agencies. The enthusiasm of the promoters and a fair amount of acceptance by the participants seem to suffice for the proclaimed success of a substantial proportion of new enterprises.

Spread of new ideas to others

We referred earlier, in discussing demonstration projects, to the fact that the success of a new approach in one setting, does not readily lead to its adoption by others. Mort (1941; 1960) found that after an innovation in education had first been demonstrated as practical, it typically took 15 years to reach the most progressive 3 percent of the school systems. Then followed 20 years of rapid spread and 15 more years to win over the slow adapters.

Hence, he found a 50-year period between first demonstration and its complete adoption.

Experience in New York State led Brickell (in Miles, 1964) to the conclusion that effective innovation requires three different kinds of people, each of which requires a different temperament and training: (1) the innovators, who design and promote the original idea; (2) the scientific evaluators, who test the effectiveness of the new operation, and (3) the successful disseminators. Brickell sees these personality types as incompatible and believes innovation as a whole suffers when the same people try to initiate, evaluate, and disseminate the idea or invention.

Brickell also notes the need to equip people with the skills required for operating in a changed way. Much of the resistance to an innovation arises from the insecurity of those who fear that they cannot succeed well with it. Trying to win acceptance of a new philosophy without developing the appropriate habits is likely to result merely in adoption of the new-fashioned phrases while continuing the old-fashioned behavior.

Studies of other social movements generally bear out Mort's concept of three phases in the spread of an innovation—first, a phase of slow recognition; second, rapid adoption, and finally a slow absorption of the remainder. The idea is graphically presented in Figure 13-5.

The growth cycle is made up of three phases with different psychological climates. The Pioneer phase extends from the first inception of the idea until the point of inflection (X) where the curve starts its rapid rise. The Expansion phase continues then until the second point of inflection (Y) where the curve becomes concave below and levels off in the Maturity phase.

Ideas for the improvement of an enterprise are usually adopted most read-

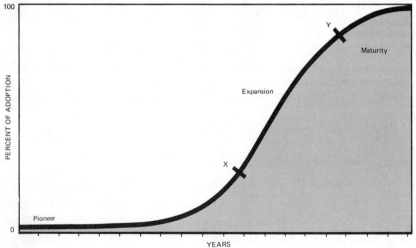

FIGURE 13-5

ily by the organizations which have previously been most progressive. It is generally easier to sell a new idea to the best farmers, the most successful businesses, the most progressive schools and communities. Mort (1941) found innovations more quickly adopted in schools with ample financial resources; the writer found most rapid acceptance of new ideas in YMCA's where community economic indices reflected high standards of living (Watson, 1946).

As any movement spreads, it assumes new forms and attracts new leadership. At this stage the pioneers are likely to be given haloes and set on pedestals to keep them from interfering with current operations. Often they do not submit without a struggle and the movement may divide between the orthodox purists and those who defer more to expediency.

A typical outcome of the Expansion phase is the acceptance of compromises and half measures. When a controversial movement begins to look as if it might reach its goal (G), opponents begin to try to salvage something by offering something less (G-n) in the hope that this will stop the advance. Thus a number of communities in the South, aware of the growth of the movement toward racial integration in the schools, built separate schools for blacks which were not only equal to but actually superior to the schools for white children. Similar efforts occurred with a few hospitals, housing projects, and recreation centers. The offer of (G-n) poses a problem for reform leadership. The offer represents a real advance but is less than the goal sought by the movement. The membership may divide between those who argue that half a loaf is better than none, and those who see that they would not have been offered half a loaf unless their movement had an excellent chance of winning much more.

Another issue concerns when to legislate. At what stage should advocates of a reform seek to embody their proposal in law? As William Graham Sumner (1906) expressed it, "Do stateways change folkways?" The failure and repeal of some laws—Prohibition is a noteworthy example—indicates that laws do not always prevail. Many people in the South doubted that the Supreme Court ruling on school integration could ever be enforced. On the other hand, the evidence reviewed shows that legislation has proven effective in bringing about integration in the Armed Forces, fair employment practices, and interracial housing projects. After a reform has passed the mid-point, where it has the support of a growing majority, a law or decree will greatly speed up the process of acceptance among the rest of the population.

While a movement for change remains controversial, much of the success of new legislation depends upon the commitment and firmness of responsible officials. Quick success of integration in the armed forces was produced by the unwavering stand taken by the President and the commanders.

In July 1954, while the Supreme Court was deliberating on its second order, designed to implement the May 17 statement of principles on racial integration in the schools, a conference of social psychologists was assembled to discuss whether a "forthwith" or a "gradual" compliance would work better. These psychologists rejected the gradualist proposal. They argued that it would lead to such undesirable results as: (a) evasion and postponement; (b) piecemeal efforts which might be regarded as discriminating against certain communities, schools or grades which become the "guinea pigs"; (c) seizing upon minor incidents to inflame resistance and bring the program to a halt. The gradualist approach was criticized as based upon some unwarranted psychological assumptions, for example, (a) that attitude changes must precede institutional change; or (b) that it is easier to change part of a school system than it is to change the whole system. The public opinion experts contended that a "go-slow" approach would be tantamount to encouraging reluctant local authorities to adopt weak, ambiguous, self-defeating measures. The social scientists made a case for:

1. "a clear and unequivocal statement of the policy of desegregation;
2. "firm enforcement . . . persistence in the face of initial resistance . . . willingness on the part of responsible authorities to deal with violations, attempted violations, and incitement to violation by legal action.
3. "refusal of authorities to tolerate subterfuges, gerrymandering, or other evasions.
4. "an appeal to the public in terms of religious principles of brotherhood and American democratic traditions of equal justice."

The conference recommended only the short delay required by educational administrators to work out the details of teacher and pupil reassignment. They endorsed the idea of a prestige agency—as free as possible from political ties—to bring together leading citizens of both races for the specific purpose of implementing quickly and fully the 1954 decision.

The Supreme Court did not accept this recommendation of the social scientists. In accord with public opinion, they deemed it wiser to give more time for communities to adjust to the prospective changes. A poll (American Institute of Public Opinion, May 9, 1956) at about that time showed 71 percent in favor of giving "a long period of years" for gradual integration, and only 18 percent who agreed with the social scientists that "the government should do everything it can to see that white and black children in all parts of the country go to the same public schools within the coming year." It is not possible now to know whether the more drastic demand for forthright and immediate and full desegregation would have provoked more or less resistance than has arisen.

Cities like St. Louis, Louisville, and Baltimore did move with decisive speed, and desegregation in these cities was rapidly accepted. Protest movements were quashed by the authorities, who remained firmly committed. A step of considerable importance was that those who had responsibility for the success of integration—all principals, supervisors, guidance personnel, and teachers, were explicitly prepared for their new roles. Pupils and their parents were brought into the processes of preparation. Attention was directed away from the question; "Are we going to comply?" to the question, "*How* can we best achieve the prescribed integration?" Trouble has arisen mainly in communities which regarded compliance as still open and debatable. The governors of Arkansas, Alabama, and Mississippi took a stand against enforcement of the court orders, leaving citizens confused on what the law required.

After a change has won general acceptance, the drive for its adoption abates. The late stages of a reform movement usually transform the crusade into a bureaucracy. With general acceptance, effort turns to "mopping up" a few areas in which the reform has not yet been fully accepted. The memory of the pioneers is ritualistically honored, but operations are carried on by men who like the prestige and power of the established enterprise. The change becomes part of the old order, and those who pioneered for it may be resistant to their successors who would introduce new and further changes. Is it possible to cultivate commitment not to some particular innovation but to a continuing process of improvement?

SELF-ACTUALIZATION

There is some indication that the values of our society are changing from a puritanical, achievement-oriented emphasis to a self-actualizing emphasis on the development of personal resources and the experiencing of joy and sense of fulfillment in one's life (Bennis, 1970). Slater (1970) discusses the collision currently occurring between the traditional culture based upon competition for scare resources in the United States and a new culture springing up among the youth based upon sharing plentiful resources to fulfill human needs and develop human potential. One indication of the changing emphasis in our society is the dramatic increase in the number of psychologists subscribing to a humanistic approach to the study of human behavior. Goldstein (1940) hypothesized that there is a drive for an organism to actualize its potentialities, that is, a drive towards self-actualization. Whether or not there is such a drive, it is apparent that self-actualization is an increasingly important concern for many people.

Two social scientists, Shostrom (1963) and Byrd (1970) have attempted a systematic analysis of the literature in self-actualization. Shostrom states that self-actualization can be considered as having two major dimensions, the use of time and the autonomy of the individual. Shostrom's views on the use of time are summarized in Figure 13-6. He defines *time-competence* as the ability to tie the past and the future to the present in meaningful continuity while fully living in the present. The self-actualized person appears to be less burdened by guilts, regrets, and resentments from the past than is the non-self-actualizing person, but instead uses the past for reflective thought. The future of the self-actualized person is tied to present goals; the non-self-actualizing person does not discriminate well between the past and the future. He is excessively concerned with the past or the future, or may be disoriented in the present because he is cut off from his past or his future. A person who is primarily past-oriented may be characterized by guilt, regret, blaming, and resentments. A person who is primarily future-oriented is an individual who lives with idealized goals, plans, expectations, and fears. A person who is exclusively present oriented is an individual whose past does not contribute to the present in a meaningful way and who has no future goals tied to present activity. Thus Shostrom describes the non-self-actualizing person as being time-incompetent.

In discussing the autonomy of the self-actualizing person, Shostrom follows Riesman (1950) in contrasting between an inner-directed and an other-directed person. The inner-directed person appears to have incorporated a psychic "gyroscope" which is initiated by parental influences and is further influenced by other authority figures. The source of inner-direction seems to be implanted early in life, and its direction is guided by a small number of principles which are rigidly adhered to. The *other-directed* person receives guidance from others and is directed by his contemporaries. Approval from others becomes his highest goal and he tends to invest all power in the actual or imaginary approving group. Manipulation in the form of pleasing others and insuring constant acceptance becomes his primary method of relating. An autonomous person is capable of conforming to the behavioral norms of society but is free to choose whether to conform or not; he is independent of both extreme inner- or other-directedness. He has liberated himself from rigid adherence to parental values or to social pressures and social expectancies. A self-actualizing person is autonomous. A non-self-actualizing person tends to be excessively inner- or other-directed, or he may be in a double-bind of not knowing whether to conform or to act autonomously and, therefore, may do neither well.

The time-competence and the autonomy of the self-actualizing person are related in the sense that a person who lives primarily in the present relies more upon his own support and expressiveness than does a person living primarily in the past or in the future. To live fully in the present means that one must be autonomous enough to reject both rigid inner values and excessive needs to conform to social prescriptions to obtain approval.

In addition to time-competence and autonomy, there are several other characteristics which differentiate self-actualizing individuals from non-self-actualizing persons. (Byrd, 1970; Shostrom, 1963). The self-actualizing person, for example, tends to hold humanistic values and applies them in a flexible manner. This flexibility leaves the individual open to new experiences

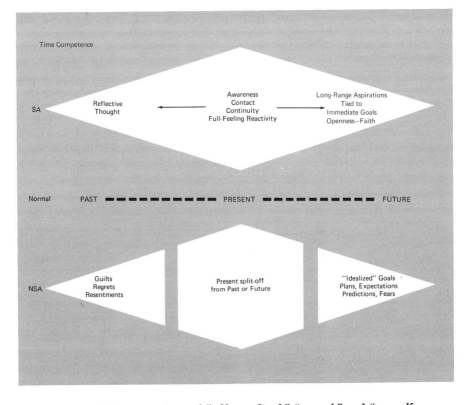

FIGURE 13-6. Comparison of "self-actualized," "normal," and "non-self-actualized" groups on the DDI time ration. (Adapted from E. L. Shostrom, *Manual for the Personal Orientation Inventory*. San Diego: Educational and Industrial Testing, 1963.)

without rigidly imposing his values upon each new event. The self-actualizing person is aware of himself, his motivations, his inner world, and expresses his feelings spontaneously. His sensitivity to his own needs and feelings inables him to obtain maximum appreciation of their fulfillment. His awareness of his needs enables him to satisfy them. The self-actualizing person appreciates his strengths and accepts his weaknesses and limitations. His love and trust for himself enables him to love and trust others, while at the same time he is realistic about his inadequacies. Such realism is based upon his perception of himself as a growing, changing individual, not as a finished product.

The self-actualizing person sees man as essentially good and life as basically a whole rather than a sum of many parts and polarities. A realization of the goodness of himself leads to a belief in the basic trustworthiness of human nature. He views himself and human nature positively. He recognizes, however, the basic conflicts that exist in living and is aware that many oppositions, such as good and evil, are intrinsically merged and coalesced to form unities. Finally, the self-actualizing person has interpersonal sensitivity and

451

deep, free relationships with others. He is not afraid to express his feelings, anger as well as love, but expresses them in ways which strengthen relationships, not fragment them.

The rapid technological change we have been experiencing for the past several years has resulted in a rapid cultural change within our society. Bennis (1970) states that our culture is changing from an emphasis on achievement to an emphasis upon self-actualization, from self-control to self-expression, from independence to interdependence, from endurance of stress to a capacity for joy, from full employment to full lives. The ability to handle such changes certainly is of upmost importance for life in our times.

CHANGE AS OUR WAY OF LIFE

The course of most civilizations, as traced by Toynbee (1933–39), has led from an initial period of enterprise to stabilization, control by a dominant minority, and the mistaken view that the prevailing institutions would endure forever. Growth and flexibility gave way to bondage to the traditions of the past and the power of rulers who were self-satisfied and blind to the need for change. Eventually the repressed energies broke through in revolution and transition to a new order.

It may be that we have now achieved emancipation from this age-old cycle of innovation, inertia, and insurrection. The United States has been described (in an issue of *Fortune* magazine) as pioneering with the new doctrine of "Continuous Revolution." If all our institutions remain open to the participation and creative contribution of their members, the steady flow of adaptive innovations will render revolutionary upheavals unnecessary.

The conditions which have brought accelerating change seem likely to continue, if they do not culminate in some all-destructive war. Education, science, invention, and wealth are cumulative. The higher the level they have reached, the more rapidly they can grow. Universal education once meant only the few years of schooling necessary for literacy. Now, in most parts of our country, it means high school education for all and college for an increasing proportion. More and more adults are involved in further education: in factories, stores, offices, and institutes, as well as on campuses (De Crow, Kolben, 1963; Clark, Sloan, 1958, 1962). Expenditures for research and development mount by billions of dollars. Communication and diffusion of knowledge increase as more and more people move about the globe. The norms of science—problem solving, search for new truth, holding hypotheses tentatively while testing them critically—increasingly pervade other areas of life.

The anchors of certainty in a world of flux are found in trustworthy and rational processes rather than in established institutions or doctrines. Faith that the answers of the past are infallible is replaced by confidence in procedures adaptable to changing conditions. In his *Human Nature and Conduct,* a social psychology written (1922) before most of the empirical data cited in this volume had become available, John Dewey wrote: (p. 323)

It sounds academic to say that substantial bettering of social relations waits upon the growth of a scientific social psychology. . . . It would have seemed absurd to say in the seventeenth century that in the end the alteration in methods of physical investigation which was then beginning would prove more important than the religious wars of that century. Yet the wars marked the end of one era; the dawn of physical science the beginning of a new one. And a trained imagination may discover that the nationalistic and economic wars which are the chief outward mark of the present are in the end to be less significant than the development of a science of human nature.

SUMMARY

In this chapter we noted that, historically, social groups have concerned themselves with social change. Before, children were raised and they in turn raised their children to follow in the footsteps of their ancestors. We have witnessed sweeping technological and social changes that have surpassed all previous changes combined in the past hundred years. As changes occurred, a time-lag set in between the introduction of a technology and its acceptance by the society. Also evident are the differences among individuals in resistance or adaptiveness to change. Various theories and practical skills have been developed to facilitate the process of change.

Individuals resist change for a variety of reasons. Old patterns of responses have brought satisfaction, and therefore persist whether they are adaptive or not. Change disrupts established interpersonal ties which can bring pain. Unexpected changes can make participants defensive and less cooperative. Organizations also resist change. A change in one part of the organizational structure brings change to all other parts of the system. Often those who have status and power resist change, because it might bring an undesirable change in their power position. Innovations that are suggested by those outside the system are usually resisted by those within the system.

The rapid changes in our culture indicate that the puritanical, achievement-oriented emphasis in our society is changing to an emphasis on experiencing joy and fulfillment with one's life. The new emphasis has been termed self-actualization. For the actualized person the past, present and future are tied together in a meaningful whole. In his relations to the world the self-actualized person is autonomous but capable of conforming to the norms of society, and free to choose whether to do so or not. Self-actualization represents an alternate goal to self-seeking, achievement-oriented existence.

Older theories of the change process have included: (1) theocratic theories which held that the future course of the world was in the hands of God and man should not interfere; (2) linear theories which held that society and man are becoming better or worse; (3) cyclic theories that envisioned societies as repeating recognizable patterns; and (4) dialectic theories which emphasized the union and competition between opposites.

A more recent theory that is used to account for change is the diffusion theory. This theory holds that mechanisms, ideas, and operations are adopted by individuals and groups from others. The emphasis is on how individuals and societies are made aware and receptive to new ideas, operations, and mechanisms. The diffusion process includes stages of dissatisfaction with the present, attempts to diagnose the difficulty, planning stages to develop effective changes, introductory phases, and final reevaluations of the situation.

In industries, resistance to the change process must be reduced, and it has been found that the support of the top management is necessary as well as that of as many persons who will be affected in the planning and diagnostic phases. With many participants the need for strong and effective leadership that can bring about the commitment of others is obvious. The leaders must also insure that methods for evaluating any innovations and changes are included, and that continual reevaluation in the future is possible.

Bibliography

A

ADORNO, T. W.; FRENKEL-BRUNSWIK, E.; LEVINSON, D. J.; and SANFORD, R. N. 1950. *The authoritarian personality.* New York: Harper.

ALLEE, W. C. 1938. *Social life of animals.* New York: Norton.

ALLEN, V. L. 1965. Situational factors in conformity. In *Advances in experimental social psychology,* ed. L. Berkowitz, vol. 2, pp. 133-175. New York: Academic Press.

ALLPORT, F. H. The influence of the group upon association and thought. *Journal of Experimental Psychology* 120: 159-182.

ALLPORT, G. W. 1937. *Personality: A psychological interpretation.* New York: Holt.

———. 1954. The historical background of modern social psychology. In *Handbook of social psychology,* ed. G. Lindzey, vol. 1, chap. 1. Cambridge, Mass.: Addison-Wesley.

———. 1955. *Becoming.* New Haven: Yale University Press.

ALLPORT, G. W., and POSTMAN, L. J. 1945. The basic psychology of rumor. *Transactions of the New York Academy of Sciences,* series II, 8: 61-81.

ALLYN, J., and FESTINGER, L. 1961. The effectiveness of unanticipated persuasive communications. *Journal of Abnormal and Social Psychology* 62: 35-40.

AMERICAN MANAGEMENT ASSOCIATION. 1948. *Executive personality and job success.* Personnel series 120. New York.

AMES, L. 1952. The sense of self of nursery school children as manifested by their verbal behavior. *Journal of Genetic Psychology* 81: 192-232.

AMIDON, E., and HUNTER, E. 1966. *Improving teaching: The analysis of classroom verbal interaction.* New York: Holt, Rinehart and Winston.

AMIDON, E. J., and FLANDERS, N. A. 1963. *The role of the teacher in the classroom.* Minneapolis: Paul Amidon and Associates.

AMIDON, E. J., and HOUGH, J. B., eds. 1967. *Interaction analysis: Theory, research, and application.* Reading, Mass.: Addison-Wesley.

ANDERSEN, W. A., and PLAMBECK, H. 1943. *Social participation of farm families.* Mimeo. bulletin no. 8. Ithaca, N.Y.: Cornell University Agricultural Experiment Station.

ANDERSON, N. H. 1961. Group performance in an anagram task. *Journal of Social Psychology* 55: 67-75.

ARDREY, R. 1961. *African genesis.* London: Collins.

———. 1966. *The territorial imperative.* New York: Atheneum.

ARGYRIS, C. 1957. *Personality and organization.* New York: Harper.

———. 1962. *Interpersonal competence and organizational effectiveness.* Homewood, Ill.: Dorsey.

———. 1964a. *Integrating the individual and the organization.* New York: Wiley.

———. 1964b. T-groups for organizational effectiveness. *Harvard Business Review* 42: 60-75.

———. 1968. Conditions for competence acquisition and therapy. *Journal of Applied Behavioral Science* 4: 147-179.

ARONSON, E. 1968. Dissonance theory: Progress and problems. In *Source book on cognitive consistency,* ed. R. P. Abelson, E. Aronson, T. M. Newcomb, W. J. McGuire, M. J. Rosenberg, and P. H. Tannenbaum, pp. 5-27. New York: Rand McNally.

ARONSON, E.; TURNER, J. A.; and CARLSMITH, J. M. 1963. Communicator credibility and communication discrepancy as determinants of opinion change. *Journal of Abnormal and Social Psychology* 67: 31-36.

ASCH, S. E. 1952. *Social psychology.* Englewood Cliffs, N.J.: Prentice-Hall.

———. 1956. Studies of independence and conformity: A minority of one against a unanimous majority. *Psychological Monographs* 70: 516.

ATKINSON, J. W. 1965. *An introduction to motivation.* Princeton, N.J.: Van Nostrand.

AUSUBEL, D. P. 1958. Ego development among segregated Negro children. *Mental Hygiene, New York* 42: 362-369.

AUSUBEL, D. P., and AUSUBEL, P. 1963. Ego development among segregated Negro children. In *Education in depressed areas,* ed. A. H. Passow, pp. 109-142. New York: Teachers College Press.

AVELING, F., and HARGREAVES, H. L. 1921. Suggestibility with and without prestige in children. *British Journal of Psychology* 18: 362-388.

B

BACHRACH, A. J.; CANDLAND, D. K.; and GIBSON, J. T. 1961. Group reinforcement of individual response experiments in verbal behavior. In *Conformity and deviation,* ed. I. A. Berg and B. M. Bass, pp. 258-285. New York: Harper.

BACKMAN, C. W. 1965. The compromise process and the affect structure of groups. *Human Relations* 17: 19-22.

BALDWIN, J. 1963. *The fire next time.* New York: Dial Press.

BALDWIN, J. M. 1897. *Social and ethical interpretations in mental development.* New York: Macmillan. Abridged and reprinted in C. F. Borgatta and H. J. Meyer, *Sociological theory* (New York: Knopf, 1956), p. 23.

BALES, R. F. 1950. *Interaction process analysis: A method for the study of small groups.* Cambridge, Mass.: Addison-Wesley.

———. 1952. Some uniformities of behavior in small social systems. In *Readings in social psychology,* ed. G. E. Swanson, T. M. Newcomb, and E. L. Hartley, pp. 146-159. New York: Holt.

BALES, R. F., and BORGATTA, E. F. 1955. Size of group as a factor in the interaction profile. In *Small groups,* ed. A. P. Hace, E. F. Borgatta, and R. F. Bales, pp. 396-413. New York: Knopf.

BALES, R. F.; STRODTBECK, F. L.; MILLS, T. M.; and ROSEBOROUGH, M. E. 1951. Channels of communication in small groups. *American Sociological Review* 16: 461-468.

BANDURA, A. 1962. Punishment revisited. *Journal of Consulting Psychology* 26: 298-301.

———. 1969. *Principles of behavioral modification.* New York: Holt, Rinehart and Winston.

BANDURA, A., and WALTERS, R. H. 1963. *Social learning and personality development.* New York: Holt, Rinehart and Winston.

BARBER, B. 1957. *Social stratification.* New York: Harcourt, Brace.

BARDWICK, J. M. 1971. *Psychology of women: A study in bio-cultural conflicts.* New York: Harper and Row.

BARKER, R. G.; DEMBO, T.; and LEWIN, K. 1941. Frustration and regression: An experiment with young children. *University of Iowa Study Child Welfare* 18, no. 1.

BARNETT, H. G. 1953. *Innovation: The basis of cultural change.* New York: McGraw-Hill.

BARNLUND, D. C. 1959. A comparative study of individual, majority, and group judgment. *Journal of Abnormal and Social Psychology* 58: 55-60.

BARRY, H.; BACON, M.; and CHILD, I. 1957. A cross-cultural survey of some differences in socialization. *Journal of Abnormal and Social Psychology* 55: 327-332.

BARRY, H.; CHILD, I. L.; and BACON, M. K. 1959. Relation of child training to subsistence economy. *American Anthropologist* 55: 51-63.

BARTLETT, F. C. 1932. *Remembering.* Cambridge, England: Cambridge University Press.

BARTON, A. H., and WILDER, D. E. 1964. Research and practice in the teaching of reading. In *Innovation in education*, ed. M. Miles, chap. 16. New York: Teachers College, Columbia University.

BASS, B. M. 1959. Effects of motivation on consistency of performance in groups. *Educational and Psychological Measurement* 19: 247-252.

———. 1960. *Leadership, psychology, and organizational behavior.* New York: Harper.

BASS, B. M., et al. 1953. Personality variables related to leaderless group discussion behavior. *Journal of Abnormal and Social Psychology* 48: 120-128.

BAUER, R. A. 1953. The psychology of the Soviet middle elite. In *Personality in nature, society, and culture*, ed. C. Kluckhohn, H. A. Murray, and D. A. Schneider, pp. 633-649. New York: Knopf.

BAUMRIND, D. 1964. Some thoughts on ethics of research: After reading Milgram's behavioral study of obedience. *American Psychologist* 19: 421-423.

BAVELAS, A. 1942. Morale and the training of leaders. In *Civilian morale*, ed. G. Watson, pp. 143-165. Boston: Houghton Mifflin.

———. 1957. Making leadership effective. *Nation's Business* 45, March, pp. 96f.

BAVELAS, A.; HASTORF, A. H.; GROSS, A. E.; and KITE, W. R. 1965. Experiments on the alteration of group structure. *Journal of Experimental Social Psychology* 1: 55-70.

BAYTON, J. H. 1942. The psychology of racial morale. *Journal of Negro Education* 11: 150-153.

BEAGLEHOLE, E., and RITCHIE, J. 1961. Basic personality in a New Zealand Maori community. In *Studying personality cross-culturally*, ed. B. Kaplan. Evanston, Ill.: Row, Peterson.

BEAUVOIR, S. de. 1953. *The second sex.* New York: Knopf.

BEKHTEREV, W. 1924. Die Ergebnisse des Experiments auf dem Gebiet der kollektiven Reflexologie. *Zeitschrift für angewandte Psychologie,* pp. 224-254.

BELL, DANIEL, ed. 1963. *The radical right.* New York: Anchor Books.

BENEDICT, R. 1934. *Patterns of culture.* Boston: Houghton Mifflin.

BENNIS, W. G. 1964. Patterns and vicissitudes in t-group development. In *T-group theory and laboratory method,* ed. L. P. Bradford, J. R. Gibb, and K. D. Benne, pp. 248-279. New York: Wiley.

———. 1970. A funny thing happened on the way to the future. *American Psychologist* 25: 595-609.

BERELSON, B., and SALTER, P. J. 1946. Majority and minority Americans: An analysis of magazine fiction. *Public Opinion Quarterly* 10: 168-190.

BERGIN, A. E. 1962. The effect of dissonant persuasive communications upon changes in self-referring attitudes. *Journal of Personality* 30: 423-438.

———. 1966. Some implications of psychotherapy research for therapeutic practice. *Journal of Abnormal Psychology* 71: 235-246.

BERKOWITZ, L. 1962. *Aggression:*

A social psychological analysis. New York: McGraw-Hill.

BERKOWITZ, L., and DANIELS, L. R. 1963. Responsibility and dependency. *Journal of Abnormal and Social Psychology* 66: 429-436.

BERNARD, V. W. 1958. School desegregation: Some psychiatric implications. *Psychiatry* 21: 149-158.

BERSCHEID, E.; BOYE, D.; and DARLEY, J. M. 1968. Effects of forced association upon voluntary choice to associate. *Journal of Personality and Social Psychology* 8: 13-19.

BERSCHEID, E.; BOYE, D.; and WALSTER, E. Retaliation as a means of restoring equit. *Journal of Personality and Social Psychology* (in press).

BERSCHEID, E.; WALSTER, B. W.; and WALSTER, E. Effects of accuracy and positivity of an evaluation on liking for the evaluator (in preparation). Mimeographed copy available from senior author.

BERSCHEID, E., and WALSTER, E. 1967. When does a harm-doer compensate a victim? *Journal of Personality and Social Psychology* 6: 435-441.

BERSCHEID, E.; WALSTER, E.; and BARSLAY, A. The effect of time on the tendency to compensate a victim (in preparation). Mimeographed copy available from senior author.

BERSCHEID, E., and WALSTER, E. H. 1969. *Interpersonal attraction.* Reading, Mass.: Addison-Wesley.

BETTELHEIM, B. 1943. Individual and mass behavior in extreme situations. *Journal of Abnormal and Social Psychology* 38: 417-452.

———. 1969. *Children of the dream.* New York: Macmillan.

BIDERMAN, A. D. 1963. *March to calumny: The story of American POW's in the Korean war.* New York: Macmillan.

BIERMAN, R. 1969. Dimension for interpersonal facilitation in

psychotherapy in child development. *Psychological Bulletin* 72: 338-352.

BIESHEUVEL, S., and LIDDICOST, R. 1959. The effects of cultural factors on intelligence test performance. *Journal of National Institute of Personnel Research, Johannesburg* 8: 3-14.

BION, W. R. 1948, 1949, 1950, 1951. Experiences in groups. *Human Relations* 1: 314-320, 487-496; 2: 13-22, 295-303; 3: 3-14; 4: 221-227.

BJERSTEDT, A. 1958. Ego-involved world-mindedness. Duplicated manuscript. University of Leind, Sweden. See also *Nordisk Psykologi* 10 (1958): 161-178.

BLAKE, R., and DENNIS, W. 1943. The development of stereotypes concerning the Negro. *Journal of Abnormal and Social Psychology* 38: 525-531.

BLAKE, R. R., and MOUTON, J. S. 1961. Comprehension of own and outgroup positions under intergroup competition. *Journal of Conflict Resolution* 5: 304-310.

———. 1962. The intergroup dynamics of win-lose conflict and problem-solving collaboration in union-management relations. In *Intergroup relations and leadership,* ed. M. Sherif, pp. 94-142. New York: Wiley.

BONNEY, M. E. 1942. A study of social status on the second-grade level. *Journal of Genetic Psychology* 15: 271-305.

BORAH, L. A., Jr. 1963. The effects of threat in bargaining: Critical and experimental analysis. *Journal of Abnormal and Social Psychology* 66: 37-44.

BORGATTA, E. F., and BALES, R. F. 1953. Interaction of individuals in reconstituted groups. *Sociometry* 16: 302-320.

BOVARD, E. W. 1959. The effects of social stimuli on the response to stress. *Psychological Review* 66: 267-277.

BOVARD, E. W., Jr. 1951. The

experimental production of inter-personal effect. *Journal of Abnormal and Social Psychology* 46: 521-528.

BOWLBY, J. 1951. Maternal care and mental health. *Bulletin World Health Organization* 3: 355-533.

———. 1961. Separation anxiety: A critical review of the literature. *Journal of Child Psychology and Psychiatry* 1: 251-269.

BOWLBY, J., and CANTAB, J. 1953. Maternal deprivation. *Journal of Mental Science* 99: 265-272.

BRADFORD, L. P.; GIBB, J. R.; and BENNE, K. D. 1964. *T-group theory and laboratory method.* New York: Wiley.

BREHM, J. W. 1956. Postdecision changes in the desirability of alternatives. *Journal of Abnormal and Social Psychology* 52: 384-389.

BREHM, J. W., and COHEN, A. R. 1959. *Explorations in cognitive dissonance.* New York: Wiley.

———. 1962. *Explorations in cognitive dissonance.* New York: Wiley.

BRICKELL, H. M. 1964. State organization for educational change. In *Innovation in education,* ed. M. Miles, chap. 20. New York: Teachers College, Columbia University.

BRIMMER, A. F. 1966. The Negro in the national economy. In *The American Negro reference book,* ed. J. P. Davis. Englewood Cliffs, N.J.: Prentice-Hall.

BRITT, S. H. 1949. *Social psychology of modern life.* New York: Rinehart.

BROCK, T. 1957. Commitment and persuasion. In *Order of presentation,* ed. C. I. Hovland, pp. 23-32. New Haven: Yale University Press.

BRONFENBRENNER, U. 1961. The mirror image in Soviet-American relations: A social psychologist's report. *Journal of Social Issues* 17: 45-47.

———. 1962. Soviet methods of

character education: Some implications for research. *Religious Education* 57 (4, res. suppl.): s45-s61.

BROOKLYN BRANCH OF THE ASSOCIATION FOR THE STUDY OF NEGRO LIFE AND HISTORY. 1961. The treatment of minorities in elementary school textbooks. *Negro Heritage* 1.

BROPHY, I. N. 1946. The luxury of anti-Negro prejudice. *Public Opinion Quarterly* 9: 456-466.

BROWN, R. L. 1958. Wrapper influence on the perception of freshness in bread. *Journal of Applied Psychology* 42: 257-260.

BRUNER, J. S.; SHAPIRO, D.; and TAGIURI, R. 1958. The meaning of traits in isolation and in combination. In *Person perception and interpersonal behavior,* ed. R. Tagiuri and L. Petrullo, pp. 277-288. Stanford, Calif.: Stanford University Press.

BUBER, M. 1955. *Between man and man.* Boston: Beacon Press. English translation first published by Macmillan, 1947. Pp. 19-20.

BUGENTAL, J. T. V., ed. 1967. *Challenges of humanistic psychology.* New York: McGraw-Hill.

BUHLER, C. 1935. *From birth to maturity.* London: Paul.

BUNKER, D. R. 1963. *The effect of laboratory training upon individual behavior.* Prepublication draft.

BURDICK, H. A., and BURNES, A. J. 1958. A test of "strain toward symmetry" theories. *Journal of Abnormal and Social Psychology* 57: 367-369.

BURGESS, E. W., and COTTRELL, L. S., Jr. 1939. *Predicting success or failure in marriage.* New York: Prentice-Hall.

BURNSTEIN, E., and WORCHEL, P. 1962. Arbitrariness of frustration and its consequences for aggression in a social situation. *Journal of Personality* 30: 528-540.

BUSHEE, F. A. 1945. Social

organization in a small city. *American Journal of Sociology* 41: 217-226.

BUSHNEL, J. 1962. Student culture at Vassar. In *The American college,* ed. N. Sanford. New York: Wiley.

BUSS, A. H. 1961. *The psychology of aggression.* New York: Wiley.

BYRD, R. E. 1970. Self-actualization through creative risk taking: A new laboratory model. Ph.D. dissertation, New York University.

BYRNE, D. 1961. Interpersonal attraction as a function of affiliation need and attitude similarity. *Human Relations* 14: 283-289.

———. 1969. Attitudes and attraction. In *Advances in experimental social psychology,* ed. L. Berkowitz, vol. 4, pp. 36-91. New York: Academic Press.

BYRNE, D., and BLAYLOCK, B. 1963. Similarity and assumed similarity of attitudes between husbands and wives. *Journal of Abnormal and Social Psychology* 67: 636-640.

BYRNE, D., and WONG, T. J. 1962. Racial prejudice, interpersonal attraction, and assumed dissimilarity of attitudes. *Journal of Abnormal and Social Psychology* 65: 246-252.

C

CAIRNS, R. B. 1966. Attachment behavior of mammals. *Psychological Review* 73: 409-426.

CAMPBELL, A., and COOPER, H. C. 1956. *Group differences in attitudes and votes.* Ann Arbor, Mich.: Michigan Survey Research Center.

CAMPBELL, D. T., and McCANDLESS, B. R. 1951. Ethnocentrism, xenophobia, and personality. *Human Relations* 4: 185-192.

CAMPBELL, E. Q., and PETTIGREW, T. F. 1959. Racial and moral crisis: The role of Little Rock ministers. *American Journal of Sociology* 64: 509-516.

CAMPBELL, J. 1949. *The hero with a thousand faces.* New York: Pantheon.

CAMPBELL, J. P., and DUNNETTE, M. D. 1968. Effectiveness of T-group experiences in managerial training and development. *Psychological Bulletin* 70: 73-105.

CANNON, W. B. 1932. *The wisdom of the body.* New York: Norton.

CANTRIL, H. 1940. *Invasion from Mars.* Princeton, N.J.: Princeton University Press.

———. 1944. *Gauging public opinion.* Princeton, N.J.: Princeton University Press.

CAPLOVITZ, D. 1963. *The poor pay more: Consumer practices of low income families.* New York: Free Press.

CAPLOW, T., and FORMAN, R. 1950. Neighborhood interaction in a homogeneous community. *American Sociological Review* 15: 357-366.

CAPLOW, T. A. 1956. A theory of coalitions in the triad. *American Sociological Review* 21: 489-493.

CARLSON, E. R. 1956. Attitude change through modification of attitude structure. *Journal of Abnormal and Social Psychology* 52: 256-261.

CARLSON, R. O. 1964. School superintendents and adoption of modern math. In *Innovation in education,* ed. M. Miles, chap. 14. New York: Teachers College, Columbia University.

CARMICHAEL, S., and HAMILTON, C. V. 1967. *Black power.* New York: Vintage.

CARROLL, J. B., and CASAGRANDE, J. B. 1958. The function of language classifications in behavior. In *Readings in social psychology,* ed. E. E. Maccoby, T. M. Newcomb, and E. L. Hartley, 3d ed., pp. 18-31. New York: Holt, Rinehart and Winston.

CARTWRIGHT, D. 1968. The nature of group cohesiveness. In *Group dynamics: Research and theory,* ed. D. Cartwright and A. Zander, pp. 91-109. New York: Harper and Row.

CATTELL, R. B. 1942. The concept of social status. *Journal of Social Psychiatry* 15: 293-308.

CATTELL, R. B., and NESSELROADE, J. R. 1967. Likeness and completeness theories examined by 16 personality factor measures on stably and unstably married couples. *Journal of Personality and Social Psychology* 7: 351-361.

CENTERS, R. 1938. Attitude and belief in relation to occupational stratification. *Journal of Social Psychology* 27: 159-185.

———. 1948. Occupational mobility of urban occupational strata. *American Sociological Review* 13: 197-203.

———. 1949. *The psychology of social classes.* Princeton, N.J.: Princeton University Press. P. 244.

CHAMBERLAIN, H. S. 1925. *Rasse und Personlichkeit.* Munich: F. Bruckmann.

CHANT, S. 1932. Measuring factors that make a job interesting. *Personnel Journal* 11: 1-4.

CHARTERS, W. W., Jr., and NEWCOMB, T. M. 1952. Some attitudinal effects of experimentally increased patience of a membership group. In *Readings in social psychology,* ed. G. E. Swanson, T. M. Newcomb, and E. L. Hartley, 2d ed., pp. 415-419. New York: Holt.

CHASE, S. 1951. *Roads to agreement.* New York: Harper.

CHERRINGTON, B. M. 1934. *Methods of education in international attitudes.* New York: Teachers College, Columbia University.

CHRISTIE, R., and COOK, P. 1958. A guide to published literature relating to the authoritarian personality through 1956. *Journal of Psychology* 45: 171-200.

CHRISTIE, R., and GEIS, F. 1970. *Studies in Machiavellianism.* New York: Academic Press.

CHRISTIE, R.; HANEL, J.; SEIDENBERG, B. 1958. Is the F-scale irreversible? *Journal of Abnormal and Social Psychology* 56: 143-159.

CHRISTIE, R., and MERTON, R. K. 1958. Procedures for sociological study of the values climate of medical schools. *Journal of Medical Education* 33: 125-153.

CLARK, H. B., and CLARK, M. K. 1940. Skin color as a factor in racial identification of Negro preschool children. *Journal of Social Psychology* 160.

CLARK, H. F., and SLOAN, H. S. 1958. *Classrooms in the factories.* Rutherford, N.J.: Fairleigh Dickinson University.

———. 1962. *Classrooms in the stores.* Sweet Springs, Mo.: Roxbury Press.

CLARK, K. B. 1953. Desegregation: An appraisal of the evidence. *Journal of Social Issues* 9, no. 4.

CLARK, K. B., and CLARK, M. K. 1958. Racial identification and preference in Negro children. In *Readings in social psychology,* 3d ed., ed. E. E. Maccoby, T. M. Newcomb, and E. L. Hartley. New York: Holt, Rinehart and Winston.

CLARK, R. A., et al. 1955. *Leadership in rifle squads on the Korean front line.* HRRO Technical Report 21. September. Reproduced by Document Service Center, Dayton, Ohio.

CLOWARD, R. A. 1965. War on poverty: Are the poor left out? *Nation* 201: 55-60.

CLOWARD, R. A., and OHLIN, L. E. 1960. *Delinquency and opportunity.* Glencoe, Ill.: Free Press.

COHEN, A. K. 1955. *Delinquent boys: The culture of the gang.* Glencoe, Ill.: Free Press.

COHEN, A. R. 1964. *Attitude change and social influence.* New York: Basic Books.

COHEN, J. 1950. Technique of role-reversal. The study of international conferences, World Federation for Mental Health, Paris meeting, August-September.

———. 1951. The technique of role-reversal: A preliminary note. *Occupational Psychology* 25: 64-66.

CONANT, J. B. 1964. *Shaping educational policy.* New York: McGraw-Hill.

CONNOLLY, C. 1945. *The unquiet grave: A word cycle by Palinurus.* New York: Harper. Compass Books edition, 1957, p. 54.

CONRADI, E. 1905. Song and call notes of English sparrows when reared by canaries. *American Journal of Psychology* 16: 190-199.

COOK, L. A. 1945. An experimental sociographic study of a stratified 10th-grade class. *American Sociological Review* 10: 250-261.

COOLEY, C. H. 1902. *Human nature and the social order.* New York: Scribner.

———. 1912. *Social organization.* New York: Scribner.

COREY, S. M. 1963. *Helping other people change.* Columbus: Ohio State University Press.

COX, C. M. 1926. *The early mental traits of three hundred geniuses.* Stanford, Calif.: Stanford University Press.

———. 1926. *Genetic studies of genius.* Vol. 2. *The early mental traits of three hundred geniuses.* Stanford, Calif.: Stanford University Press.

CROMWELL, H. 1950. The relative effect on audience attitude of the first versus the second argumentative speech of a series. *Speech Monographs* 17: 105-122.

CROMWELL, R. L.; ROSENTHAL, D.; SHAKOW, D.; and JOHNS, T. P. 1961. Reaction time, locus of control, choice behavior, and descriptions of parental behavior in schizophrenic and normal subjects. *Journal of Personality* 29: 363-380.

CROWNE, D. P., and MARLOWE, D. 1964. *The approval motive.* New York: Wiley.

CROWNE, D. P., and STRICKLAND, B. R. 1961. The conditioning of verbal behavior as a function of the need for social approval. *Journal of Abnormal and Social Psychology* 63: 395-401.

CULBERTSON, F. M. 1957. Modification of an emotionally held attitude through role-playing. *Journal of Abnormal and Social Psychology* 54: 230-233.

D

DAHLKE, A. E. 1963. The effects of reward and punishment on attitude change. Ph.D. dissertation, University of Minnesota.

DARLEY, J. M., and ARONSON, E. 1966. Self-evaluation vs. direct anxiety reduction as determinants of the fear-affiliation relationship. *Journal of Experimental Social Psychology,* supplement 1, pp. 66-79.

DARLEY, J. M., and BERSCHEID, E. 1967. Increased liking as a result of the anticipation of personal contact. *Human Relations* 20: 29-40.

DASHIELL, J. F. 1930. An experimental analysis of some group effects. *Journal of Abnormal and Social Psychology* 25: 190-199.

DAVIDOFF, I. F., and MARKEWICH, M. E. 1961. *The post-parental phase in the life-cycle of fifty college-educated women.* Ph.D. thesis, Teachers College, Columbia University.

DAVIDSON, H., and KRUGLOU, L. 1953. Some background correlates of personality and social attitudes. *Journal of Social Psychology* 38: 233-240.

DAVIS, A. 1944. Adolescence. In 43d yearbook, National Society of Education. Chicago. Chap. 11.

———. 1950. *Social class influences upon learning.* Cambridge, Mass.: Harvard University Press. Pp. 23, 34, 45.

DAVIS, A.; GARDNER, B. B.; and GARDNER, M. R. 1941. *Deep South.* Chicago: University of Chicago Press.

DAVIS, J. 1930. Study of 163 outstanding Communist leaders.

Proceedings of the American Sociological Society 24: 42-55.

DAVIS, K. E., and JONES, E. E. 1960. Changes in interpersonal perception as a means of reducing cognitive dissonance. *Journal of Abnormal and Social Psychology* 61: 402-410.

DAVIS, M. 1959. Community attitudes toward fluoridation. *Public Opinion Quarterly* 23: 474-482.

DAVITZ, J. R., and DAVITZ, L. J. 1959. The communication of feelings by content-free speech. *Journal of Communications* 9, March, pp. 6-13.

DEARBORN, D. C., and SIMON, H. A. 1958. Selective perception: A note on the departmental identification of executives. *Sociometry* 23: 667-673.

DeCROW, R., and KOLBEN, K., eds. 1963. *Continuing education for adults*. Chicago: Center for the Study of Liberal Education for Adults.

deGRAZIA, A. 1961. Elements of social invention. *American Behavioral Scientist* 5: 6-9.

DENNIS, W. 1960. Causes of retardation among institutional children: Iran. *Journal of Genetic Psychology* 96: 47-59.

DEUTSCH, M. 1949. An experimental study of the effects of cooperation and competition upon group process. *Human Relations* 2: 199-231.

———. 1953. Problems and progress of research in housing in its bearing upon race relations. *Racial Cultural Relations* 5: 65-95.

———. 1958. Trust and suspicion. *Journal of Conflict Resolution* 2: 265-279.

———. 1960. Trust, trustworthiness, and the F. scale. *Journal of American Social Psychology* 61: 138-140.

———. 1960a. The effect of motivational orientation upon trust and suspicion. *Human Relations* 13: 123-139.

———. 1961. The face of bargaining. *Operations Research* 9: 886-897.

———. 1962. Cooperation and trust:

Some theoretical notes. In *Nebraska symposium on motivation*, ed. M. R. Jones, pp. 275-320. Lincoln, Nebr.: University of Nebraska Press.

———.1962. Psychological alternatives to war. *Journal of Social Issues* 18: 97-119.

———. 1963. Bargaining, threat, and communication: Some experimental studies. Paper prepared for conference on "Conceptual and Experimental Analysis of Strategic Interaction and Conflict," Institute of International Studies, University of California, Berkeley, February 15.

———. 1966. Conflict and its resolution. Presidential address, Division of Personality and Social Psychology, American Psychological Association.

———. 1969. Conflicts: Productive and destructive. *Journal of Social Issues* 25: 7-43.

DEUTSCH, M., and BROWN, B. 1964. Social influences in Negro-white intelligence differences. *Journal of Social Issues* 20: 24-35.

DEUTSCH, M., and COLLINS, M. E. 1951. *Interracial housing: A psychological evaluation of a social experiment*. Minneapolis: University of Minnesota Press.

DEUTSCH, M.; EPSTEIN, Y.; CANAVAN, D.; and GUMPERT, P. 1967. Strategies of inducing cooperation: An experimental study. *Journal of Conflict Resolution* 11: 345-361.

DEUTSCH, M., and KRAUSS, R. 1962. Studies of interpersonal bargaining. *Journal of Conflict Resolution* 6: 52-76.

DEUTSCH, M.; KRAUSS, R.; and ROSENAU, N. 1962. Dissonance or defensiveness? *Journal of Personality* 30: 16-28.

DEUTSCH, M., and KRAUSS, R. M. 1960. The effect of threat upon interpersonal bargaining. *Journal of Abnormal and Social Psychology* 61: 181-190.

———. 1965. *Theories in social psychology.* New York: Basic Books.

DEUTSCH, M., and SOLOMON, L. 1959. Reactions to evaluations by others as influenced by self-evaluation. *Sociometry* 22: 93-112.

DEWEY, J. 1910. *How we think.* Boston: Heath.

———. 1922. *Human nature and conduct.* New York: Holt. P. 293.

DICKOFF, H. 1961. Reactions to evaluating by another person as a function of self-evaluation and the interaction context. Ph.D. dissertation, Duke University. Also reported in Jones, E. E. 1964. *Ingratiation.* New York: Appleton-Century-Crofts.

DIMOCK, H. S., and SORENSON, R. 1955. *Designing education in values: A case study in institutional change.* New York: Association Press.

DISTENFELD, J. 1964. *Perceived sex-role differences in men and women.* Ph.D. thesis.

DODD, S. C. 1953. Testing message diffusion in controlled experiments. *American Sociological Review* 18: 410-416.

DOLLARD, J. 1938. Hostility and fear in social life. *Social Forces* 17: 15-26.

DOLLARD, J.; DOOB, L. W.; MILLER, N. E.; MOWRER, O. H.; and SEARS, R. R. 1939. *Frustration and aggression.* New Haven: Yale University Press.

DORNBUSCH, S. M., and IRIE, R. D. 1959. The failure of Presbyterian union. *American Journal of Sociology* 64: 352-355.

DOUGLAS, A. 1957. Peaceful settlement of industrial and intergroup disputes. *Journal of Conflict Resolution* 1: 69-81.

DOUGLASS, J. H. 1939. The funeral of 'Sister President.' *Journal of Abnormal and Social Psychology* 44: 217-223.

DOZIER, E. P. 1957. The Hopi and the Tewa. *Scientific American* 196: 126-136.

DuBOIS, C. 1944. *Peoples of Alors.* Minneapolis: University of Minnesota Press.

DUBOS, R. 1970. We can't buy our way out. *Psychology Today* 3, March, pp. 20-22, 86-87.

DUNNETTE, M. D.; CAMPBELL, J.; JAASTAD, K. 1963. The effect of group participation on brainstorming effectiveness of two industrial samples. *Journal of Applied Psychology* 47: 30-37.

DURKHEIM, E. L. 1897. *Suicide.* Paris: Alcan. English edition by Free Press of Glencoe, 1951.

DURKIN, E. 1964. *The group in depth.* New York: International Universities Press.

DWYER, R. J. 1958. A report on patterns of interaction in desegregated schools. *Journal of Educational Sociology* 31: 253-256.

DYMOND, R. 1954. Interpersonal perception and marital happiness. *Canadian Journal of Psychology* 8: 164-171.

E
___

EASTMAN, D. 1956. *Self-acceptance and marital happiness.* Ph.D. dissertation, Teachers College, Columbia University.

EBBINGHAUS, H. 1885. *Memory.* Leipzig, Germany: Duncker.

EELLS, K., et al. 1951. *Intelligence and cultural differences.* Chicago: University of Chicago Press.

EICHHOLZ, G., and ROGERS, E. M. 1964. Resistance to the adoption of audio-visual aids by elementary school teachers. In *Innovation in education,* ed. M. Miles, chap. 12. New York: Teachers College, Columbia University.

ELKIN, D. G. 1926. *Influence of collective on children's ability to reproduce parts of their school work.* Detski Kollective i Rebenok. Pp. 221-226.

ELLIOTT, H. S. 1928. *The process of*

group thinking. New York: Association Press.

ELLIS, HAVELOCK. 1900-1910. *The psychology of sex.* Vols. 1-6. Philadelphia: F. A. Davis Company.

EMERSON, R. 1954. Deviation and rejection: An experimental replication. *American Sociological Review* 19: 688-693.

EMERSON, R. M. 1963. Power-dependence relations. *American Sociological Review* 27: 31-40.

ENGEL, M. 1959. The stability of the self-concept in adolescence. *Journal of Abnormal and Social Psychology* 58: 211-215.

ERICKSON, M. H., and ERICKSON, E. M. 1941. Concerning the nature and character of post-hypnotic behavior. *Journal of Genetic Psychology* 24: 95-133.

ERIKSON, E. H. 1963. *Childhood and society.* 2d ed. New York: Norton.

ERVIN, S. 1964. Language and T. A. T. content in bilinguals. *Journal of Abnormal and Social Psychology* 60: 500-507.

ESCALONA, S. K. 1945. Feeding disturbances in very young children. *American Journal of Orthopedic Psychiatry* 15: 76-80.

EWING, T. N. 1942. A study of certain factors involved in changes of opinion. *Journal of Social Psychology* 16: 63-88.

EX, J. 1959. The nature of contact between cooperating partners and their expectation concerning the level of their common achievement. *Acta Psychol. Amsterdam* 16: 99-107.

F

FAUNCE, D., and BEIGLE, J. A. 1948. Cleavages in a relatively homogeneous group of rural youths: An experiment in the use of sociometry in attaining and measuring integration. *Sociometry* 11: 201-216.

FAY, B. 1929. *Benjamin Franklin: The apostle of modern times.* Boston: Little, Brown.

FECHNER, G. T. 1876. *Vorschule der Aesthetik.* Leipzig: Breitkopf and Hartel.

FELIPE, N. J., and SOMMER, R. 1966. Invasion of personal space. *Social Problems* 14: 206-214.

FESHBACK, S., and SINGER, R. 1957. The effects of personal and shared threat upon social prejudice. *Journal of Abnormal and Social Psychology* 54: 411-416.

FESTINGER, L. 1954. A theory of social comparison processes. *Human Relations* 7: 117-140.

———. 1957. *A theory of cognitive dissonance.* Evanston, Ill.: Row, Peterson.

FESTINGER, L., and CARLSMITH, J. M. 1959. Cognitive consequences of forced compliance. *Journal of Abnormal and Social Psychology* 58: 302.

FESTINGER, L., and CARTWRIGHT, D., et al. 1948. A study of a rumor. *Human Relations* 1: 464-486.

FESTINGER, L., and MACCOBY, N. 1964. On resistance to persuasive communications. *Journal of Abnormal and Social Psychology* 68: 359-366.

FESTINGER, L.; SHACHTER, S; and BACH, K. 1950. *Social pressures in informal groups: A study of human factors in housing.* New York: Harper.

FESTINGER, L., and THIBAUT, J. 1951. Interpersonal communication in groups. *Journal of Abnormal and Social Psychology* 46: 92-99.

FIEDLER, F. E. 1950. A comparison of therapeutic relationships in psychoanalytic, non-directive, and Adlerian therapy. *Journal of Consulting Psychology* 14: 436-445.

———. 1958. *Leader attitudes and group effectiveness.* Urbana, Ill.: University of Illinois Press.

———. 1964. A contingency model of leadership effectiveness. In *Advances in experimental social psychology,* ed.

L. Berkowitz, vol. 1, pp. 149-190. New York: Academic Press.

———. 1967. A theory of leadership effectiveness. New York: McGraw-Hill.

———. 1969. Style or circumstance: The leadership enigma. *Psychology Today* 2, no. 10, 38-46.

FISCHER, P. H. 1953. An analysis of the primary group. *Sociometry* 16: 272-276.

FISHBEIN, M. 1967. Attitude and the prediction of behavior. In *Readings in attitude theory and measurement*, ed. M. Fishbein, pp. 477-492. New York: Wiley.

FISHER, R. 1964. Factionating conflict. In *International conflict and behavioral science*, ed. R. Fisher. New York: Basic Books.

FLEISHMAN, E. A.; HARRIS, E. F.; and BURTT, H. E. 1955. *Leadership and supervision in industry*. Columbus: Ohio State University Bureau of Education and Research.

FORD, C. S., and BEACH, F. A. 1951. *Patterns of sexual behavior*. New York: Harper.

FORSTER, A., and EPSTEIN, B. R. 1964. *Danger on the right*. New York: Random House.

FOSHAY, A. W. 1951. The teacher and children's social attitudes. *Teachers College Record* 52: 287-296.

FOURIEZOS, N. T.; HUTT, M. L.; and GUETZKOW, H. 1950. Measurement of self-oriented needs in discussion groups. *Journal of Abnormal and Social Psychology* 45: 682-690.

FOX, D. J., and LORGE, I. 1962. The relative quality of decisions written by individuals and by groups as the available time for problem solving is increased. *Journal of Social Psychology* 57: 227-242.

FRAZIER, E. F. 1940. *Negro youth at the crossways: Their personality development in the middle states*. Washington, D.C.: American Youth Commission.

———. 1957a. *Black bourgeoisie*. Glencoe, Ill.: Free Press.

———. 1957b. *The Negro in the United States*. New York: Macmillan.

FREEDMAN, J. L., and SEARS, D. O. 1965. Warning, distraction, and resistance. *Journal of personality and social psychology* 1: 262-266.

FREEMAN, D. 1964. Human aggression in anthropological perspective. In *The national history of aggression*, ed. J. D. Carthy and F. J. Ebling, pp. 109-121. New York: Academic Press.

FRENCH, J. R. P. 1941. The disruption and cohesion of groups. *Journal of Abnormal and Social Psychology* 36: 361-377.

FRENCH, J. R. P., Jr. 1963. The social environment and mental health. *Journal of Social Issues* 19: 39-56.

FRENKEL-BRUNSWIK, E., and SANFORD, R. N. 1945. Some personality correlates of anti-Semitism. *Journal of Psychology* 20: 271-291.

FREUD, S. 1951. *Group psychology and the analysis of the ego*. New York: Liveright. Originally published 1922. Quotations from pp. 14-25, 40.

FRIEDAN, B. 1963. *The feminine mystique*. New York: Norton.

FRIEDRICHS, R. W. 1959. Christians and residential exclusion. *Journal of Social Issues* 15: 14-23.

FROMM, E. 1955. *The sane society*. New York: Rinehart.

———. 1956. *The art of loving*. New York: Harper and Row.

FUNKENSTEIN, D. H. 1951. *Mastery of stress*. Cambridge, Mass.: Harvard University Press.

G

GAHAGAN, J. P., and TEDESCHI, J. T. 1968. Strategy and the credibility of promises in the prisoner's dilemma game. *Journal of Conflict Resolution* 12: 224-234.

GARDNER, B. B. 1948. What makes successful and unsuccessful executives? *Advancement of Management* 13: 116-125.

GEIS, F. 1965. Machiavellianism and the manipulation of one's fellow man. Paper presented at the 1965 meeting of the American Psychological Association.

GERARD, E. O. 1966. Medieval psychology: Dogmatic aristotelianism of observational empiricism? *Journal of the History of the Behavioral Sciences* 2: 315-329.

GERARD, H. 1953. The effects of different dimensions of disagreement on the communication process in small groups. *Human Relations* 6: 249-272.

GESELL, A., and LORD, E. E. 1929. Psychological comparison of nursery school children from homes of low and high economic status. *Journal of Genetic Psychology* 24: 554-557.

GEWIRTZ, J. L., and BAER, D. M. 1958. Deprivation and satiation of social reinforcers as drive conditions. *Journal of Abnormal and Social Psychology* 57: 165-172.

GHISELIN, B., ed. 1955. *The creative process.* New York: New American Library, Mentor Books.

GIBB, C. A. 1950. The sociometry of leadership in temporary groups. *Sociometry* 13: 226-243.

GILBERT, G. M. 1957. A survey of referral problems in metropolitan child guidance centers. *Journal of Clinical Psychology* 13: 37-40.

GILBERT, G. M., ed. 1956. *Psychological approaches to intergroup and international understanding.* Austin, Tex.: University of Texas. Pp. 19-23.

GOBINEAU, COMTE de. 1855. *Essay on the inequality of human races.*

GOETSCH, H. B. 1939. Inequality of college opportunity. *Journal of the National Education Association* 28: 271.

GOLDMAN, M.; HOROWITZ, M.; and LEE, F. J. 1954. Alternative classroom standards concerning management of hostility and effects on student learning. *O. N. R. Technical Report.* Reference in Pettigrew, T. F., ed. 1964. *Journal of Social Issues* 20, 55.

GOLDSTEIN, K. 1963. *The organism.* Boston: Beacon. Originally published 1939.

GOODACRE, D. M., III. 1951. The use of a sociometric test as a predictor of combat unit effectiveness. *Sociometry* 14: 148-152.

GOODMAN, M. E. 1952. *Race awareness in young children.* Cambridge, Mass.: Addison-Wesley.

———. 1964. *Race awareness in children.* 2d ed. New York: Crowell-Collier.

GORANSON, R. E., and BERKOWITZ, L. 1966. Reciprocity and responsibility reactions to prior help. *Journal of Personality and Social Psychology* 3: 227-232.

GORDON, B. F. 1966. Influence and social comparison as motives for affiliation. *Journal of Experimental Social Psychology,* supplement, 1: 55-65.

GORDON, K. 1924. Group judgments in the field of lifted weights. *Journal of Experimental Psychology* 7: 398-400.

GORER, G., and RICHMAN, J. 1949. *The people of great Russia.* London: Grosset.

GOWAN, J. C. 1955. The underachieving gifted child. *Exceptional Child* 21: 247-249.

GRACE, HARRY A., and NEUHAUS, J. O. 1952. Information and social distance as predictors of hostility toward nations. *Journal of Abnormal and Social Psychology* 47: 540-545.

GRANT, MADISON. 1916. *The passing of the great race.* New York: Scribner.

GREEN, M. W. 1952. *Interrelationships of attitude and information.* Ph.D. dissertation, Teachers College, Columbia University.

GREENACRE, P. 1947. Child wife as ideal. *American Journal of Orthopsychiatry* 17: 167-171.

GREENING, T. C. 1963. Planning for change. *Journal of the American Hospital Association* 37: 26-30.

GREENWALD, A. G., and ALBERT, R. D. 1968. Acceptance and recall of improvised arguments. *Journal of Personality and Social Psychology* 8: 31-35.

GREGOR, A. J., and McPHERSON, D. A. 1966. Racial attitudes among white and Negro children in the deep-South standard metropolitan area. *Journal of Social Psychology* 68: 95-106.

GRIFFITHS, D. E. 1964. Administrative theory and change in organizations. In *Innovation in education,* ed. M. Miles, chap. 18. New York: Teachers College, Columbia University.

GROSSER, D.; POLARISKY, N.; and LIPPITT, R. 1951. A laboratory study of behavioral contagion. *Human Relations* 4: 115-142.

GUEST, R. H. 1962. *Organizational change: The effect of successful leadership.* Homewood, Ill.: Dorsey.

GUETZKOW, H. 1954. *Organizational development and restrictions in communication.* Pittsburgh: Carnegie Institute of Technology.

GUMP, P. V. 1953. Anti-democratic trends and student reaction to President Truman's dismissal of Gen. MacArthur. *Journal of Social Psychology* 38: 131-135.

H

HACKER, H. M. 1957. The new burdens of masculinity. *Marriage and Family Living* 19: 227-233.

HAINES, D. B., and McKEACHIE, W. J. 1967. Cooperative versus competitive discussion methods in teaching introductory psychology. *Journal of Educational Psychology* 58: 386-390.

HAKMILLER, K. L. 1966*a*. Threat as a determinant of downward comparison. *Journal of Experimental Social Psychology,* supplement 1, pp. 32-39.

———. 1966*b*. Need for self-evaluation, perceived similarity, and comparison choice. *Journal of Experimental Social Psychology,* supplement 1, pp. 49-54.

HALDANE, J. B. S. 1947. *What is life?* New York: Boni and Gaer.

HALL, E. T. 1959. *The silent language.* Garden City, N.Y.: Doubleday.

———. 1966. *The hidden dimension.* Garden City, N.Y.: Doubleday.

HALLECK, S. L., and HERSKO, M. 1962. Homosexual behavior in a correctional institution for adolescent girls. *American Journal of Orthopsychiatry* 32: 911-917.

HALLOWELL, A. I. 1951. The use of projective techniques in the study of the socio-psychological aspects of acculturation. *Journal of Protective Techniques* 15: 27-44.

HALPIN, A., and WINER, B. 1952. *The leadership behavior of the airplane commander.* Columbus: Ohio State University Research Foundation.

HAMBLIN, ROBERT L. 1958. Group integration during a crisis. *Human Relations* 11: 67-76.

HAMILTON, G. V. 1929. *A research in marriage.* New York: Albert and Charles Boni.

HARDING, J., and HOGREFE, R. 1952. Attitudes of white department store employees toward Negro co-workers. *Journal of Social Issues* 8: 18-28.

HARDING, J.; PROSHANSKY, H.; KUTNER, B.; and CHEIN, I. 1969. Prejudice and ethnic relations. In *The handbook of social psychology,* ed. G. Lindzey and E. Aronson, vol. 5, pp. 1-77. Reading, Mass.: Addison-Wesley.

HARE, A. P. 1952. Interaction and consensus in different sized groups. *American Sociological Review* 17: 261-267.

HARING, D. G. 1953. Japanese national character: Cultural anthropology, psychoanalysis, and history. *Yale Review* 42: 375-392.

HARLOW, H. F. 1958. The nature of love. *American Psychologist* 13: 673-685.

HARPER, H. R. 1931. *What European and American students think on international problems.* New York: Teachers College, Columbia University.

HARRINGTON, M. 1963. *The other America.* New York: Macmillan.

HARRIS, L. 1963. The Negro in America. *Newsweek,* July 29, pp. 15-36.

HARTLEY, R. E. 1959. Sex-role pressures and the socialization of the male child. *Psychological Reports* 5: 457-468.

———. 1960. Children's concepts of male and female roles. *Merrill-Palmer Quarterly* 6: 83-91.

———. 1961. Sex roles and urban youth: Some developmental perspectives. *Bulletin on Family Development* 2: 1-12.

———. 1960. Some implications of current changes in sex role patterns. *Merrill-Palmer Quarterly* 6: 153-164.

HARTMANN, H.; KRIS, E.; and LOEWENSTEIN, R. M. 1951. Some psychoanalytic comments on culture and personality. In *Psychoanalysis and culture,* ed. G. W. Wilbur and W. Muensterberger, pp. 3-31. New York: International Universities Press.

HARVEY, O. J. 1953. An experimental approach to the study of status relations in informal groups. *American Sociological Review* 18: 357-367.

HAYAKAWA, S. I. 1960. On communication with the Soviet Union. *New York Times Magazine,* July 31.

HAYTHORN, W. 1953. The influence of individual members on the characteristics of small groups. *Journal of Abnormal and Social Psychology* 48: 276-284.

HEBB, D. D. 1949. *The organization of behavior.* New York: Wiley. P. 114.

HEER, D. M. 1951. Sentiment of white supremacy. *American Journal of Sociology* 64: 592-598.

HEIDER, F. 1958. *The psychology of interpersonal relations.* New York: Wiley. Chap. 7.

HEISE, G. A., and MILLER, C. A. 1951. Problem-solving by small groups using various communication nets. *Journal of Abnormal and Social Psychology* 46: 327-336.

HELFANT, K. 1952. Parents' attitudes vs. adolescent hostility in the determination of adolescents' socio-political attitudes. *Psychology Monographs* 67, no. 345.

HEMPHILL, J.; GRIFFITHS, D. E.; and FREDERIKSEN, N. 1962. *Administrative performance and personality.* New York: Teachers College, Columbia University.

HERSKOVITZ, M. I. 1948. *Man and his works.* New York: Knopf.

HERSKOVITZ, M. J. 1927. *Negro and the intelligence tests.* Hanover, N.H.: Sociology Press.

HERTZLER, J. O. 1940. Crises and dictatorships. *American Sociological Review* 5: 157-169.

HERZOG, F. 1960. *Children of working mothers.* Washington, D.C.: Children's Bureau. Publication 382.

HEYNS, R. W. 1948. *Functional analysis of group problems-solving behavior.* Mimeographed. Ann Arbor, Mich.: Psychology Department, University of Michigan.

HICKS, G. 1947. *Small town.* New York: Macmillan.

HILGARD, E. R. 1971. Toward a responsible social science. *Journal of Applied Social Psychology* 1: 1-7.

HOFFMAN, L. R. 1959. Homogeneity of member personality and its effects on group problem solving. *Journal of Abnormal and Social Psychology* 58: 27-32.

HOLLANDER, E. P. 1958. Conformity, status, and idiosyncrasy credit. *Psychological Review* 65: 117-127.

———. 1967. *Principles and methods of social psychology.* New York: Oxford University Press.

HOLLANDER, E. P., and JULIAN, J. W. 1969. Contemporary trends in the analysis of leadership processes. *Psychological Bulletin* 71: 387-397.

HOLLANDER, E. P., and WILLIS, R. H. 1967. Some current issues in the psychology of conformity and nonconformity. *Psychological Bulletin* 68: 62-76.

HOLLINGSHEAD, A. B. 1949. *Elmtown's youth.* New York: Wiley.

HOLLINGSHEAD, A. B., and REDLICH, F. C. 1958. *Social class and mental illness: A community study.* New York: Wiley.

HOLLINGSWORTH, L. M. 1942. *Children above 180 I.Q.* New York: World Book.

HOLLOWAY, R. J., Jr. 1968. Human aggression: The need for a species-specific framework. In *War: The anthropology of armed conflict and aggression,* ed. M. Fried, M. Harris, and R. Murphy, pp. 29-49. Garden City, N.Y.: Natural History Press.

HOMANS, G. C. 1950. *The human group.* New York: Harcourt, Brace.

———. 1961. *Social behavior.* New York: Harcourt, Brace and World.

HOOK, S. 1943. *The hero in history.* New York: John Day.

HOOVER, J. E. 1966. Crime in the United States. *Uniform Crime Reports,* August. Washington, D.C.: U.S. Department of Justice.

HORAI, J., and TEDESCHI, J. T. 1969. The effects of credibility and magnitude of punishment upon compliance to threats. *Journal of Personality and Social Psychology* 12: 164-169.

HORNER, M. S. 1968. A psychological barrier to achievement in women—the motive to avoid success. Symposium presentation at the Midwestern Psychological Association, Chicago, May.

———. 1969. Fail: Bright women. *Psychology Today* 3, no. 6.

HORWITZ, M. 1964. Training in conflict resolution. In *T-group theory and laboratory method,* ed. L. P. Bradford, J. R. Gibb, and K. D. Benne, pp. 365-379. New York: Wiley.

HOULT, T. F. 1958. *The sociology of religion.* New York: Dryden.

HOUSE, R. J. 1967. T-group education and leadership effectiveness: A review of the empiric literature and a critical evaluation. *Personnel Psychology* 20: 1-32.

HOVLAND, C. I.; CAMPBELL, E. H.; and BROCK, T. 1957. The effects of "commitment" on opinion change following communication. In *The order of presentation in persuasion,* ed. C. I. Hovland, pp. 23-32. New Haven: Yale University Press.

HOVLAND, C. I.; LUMSDAINE, A. A.; and SHEFFIELD, F. D. 1949. *Studies in social psychology in World War II.* Vol. III: *Experiments in mass communication.* Princeton, N.J.; Princeton University Press.

HOVLAND, C. I., and SEARS, R. R. 1940. Minor studies of aggression: VI. Correlation of lynchings with economic indices. *Journal of Psychology* 9: 301-310.

HOVLAND, C. I., and WEISS, W. 1951. The influence of source credibility in communication effectiveness. *Public Opinion Quarterly* 15: 635-650.

HSU, F. L. K. 1961. *Psychological anthropology.* Homewood, Ill.: Dorsey.

HULL, C. L. 1933. *Hypnosis and suggestibility.* New York: Appleton-Century-Crofts.

HUNT, M. M. 1959. *The natural history of love.* New York: Knopf.

HUXLEY, J. 1942. *On living in a revolution.* New York: Harper.

HYMAN, H. H., and SHEATSLEY, P. B. 1947. Some reasons why information campaigns fail. *Public Opinion Quarterly* 11: 413-423.

I

INDIK, B. 1963. Some effects of organization size on member attitudes and behavior. *Human Relations* 16: 369-384.

INDIK, B. P. 1965. Organization size and membership participation. *Human Relations* 18: 339-350.

INSKO, C. A. 1964. Primacy and recency in persuasion as a function of the timing of arguments and measures. *Journal of Abnormal and Social Psychology* 69: 381-391.

J

JAHODA, M. 1933. *Die arbeitslosen von Marienthal.* Vienna: Psychological Institute, University of Vienna.

JAKSBOVITS, L. A. 1968. Effects of mere exposure. *Journal of Personality and Social Psychology* 9: 30-32.

JAMES, J. 1951. Clique organization in a small industrial plant. *Re. Stud.,* State College of Washington, Pullman, Wash., vol. 125, pp. 125-130.

JAMES, W. 1880. Great men, great thoughts, and their environment. *Atlantic Monthly* 46: 441-459.

———. 1890. *Principles of psychology.* 2 vols. New York: Holt.

JANIS, I. L. 1954. Personality correlates of susceptibility to persuasion. *Journal of Personality* 22: 504-518.

———. 1955. Anxiety indices related to susceptibility to persuasion. *Journal of Abnormal and Social Psychology* 51: 663-667.

JANIS, I. L., and FESHBACH, S. 1953. Effects of fear-arousing communications. *Journal of Abnormal and Social Psychology* 48: 78-92.

JANIS, I. L., and GILMORE. 1965. The influence of incentive conditions on the success of role-playing in modifying attitudes. *Journal of Personality and Social Psychology* 1: 17-27.

JECKER, J., and LANDY, D. Liking a person as a function of doing him a favor. *Human Relations* (in press).

JEFFERSON, R. B. 1957. Some obstacles to racial integration. *Journal of Negro Education* 26: 145-154.

JENNINGS, E. E. 1960. *The anatomy of leadership: Princes, heroes, and supermen.* New York: Harper.

JENISON, A. R. 1969. How much can we boost I.Q. and scholastic achievement? *Harvard Educational Review* 39, no. 1, 1-123.

JOHNSON, C. S. 1943. *Patterns of Negro segregation.* New York: Harper.

JOHNSON, D. W. 1966. Freedom school effectiveness: Changes in attitudes of Negro children. *Journal of Applied Behavioral Science* 2: 325-331.

———. 1966. Racial attitudes of Negro freedom school participants and of Negro and white children active in civil rights. *Social Forces* 45: 266-274.

———. 1966. The use of role reversal in intergroup competition. Ph.D. dissertation, Columbia University.

———. 1967. The effects of a freedom school on its students. In *The urban r's: Race relations as the problem in urban education,* ed. R. Dentler, B. Mackler, and E. Warshauer, pp. 226-245. New York: Praeger.

———. 1967. The use of role reversal in intergroup competition. *Journal of Personality and Social Psychology* 7: 135-141.

———. 1968. The effects upon cooperation of commitment to one's position and engaging in or listening to role reversal. Unpublished research report, University of Minnesota.

———. 1970. The efficacy of role reversal: Warmth of interaction, accuracy of understanding and proposal of compromises. Paper presented at the annual convention of the American Psychological Association, September. Published in *APA Proceedings,* 1970.

———. 1970. *The social psychology of*

education. New York: Holt, Rinehart and Winston.

————. 1971a. The effectiveness of role reversal: The actor or the listener. *Psychological Reports* 28: 275-282.

————. 1971b. The effects of warmth of interaction, accuracy of understanding, and the proposal of compromises on the listener's behavior. *Journal of Counseling Psychology* 18: 207-216.

————. 1971c. The effects of expressing warmth and anger upon the actor and the listener. *Journal of Counseling Psychology* 18.

————. 1972. *Reaching out: Interpersonal effectiveness and self-actualization through increased interpersonal skills.* Englewood Cliffs, N.J.: Prentice-Hall.

————. 1972. *Readings in humanistic social psychology.* Philadelphia: Lippincott.

————. Role reversal: A review and summary of the research. *International Journal of Group Tensions* (in press).

JOHNSON, D. W., and DUSTIN, R. 1970. The initiation of cooperation through role reversal. *Journal of Social Psychology* 82: 193-203.

JOHNSON, D. W., and LEWICKI, R. J. 1969. The initiation of superordinate goals. *Journal of Applied Behavioral Science* 5: 9-24.

JOHNSON, R. C.; THOMSON, C. W.; and FRINCHE, G. 1960. Word values, word frequency, visual duration thresholds. *Psychological Review* 67: 332-342.

JOHNSON, S., and JOHNSON, D. W. 1971. The effects of other's actions, attitude similarity, and race on attraction towards the other. *Human Relations* 24.

JONES, E. E., and DAVIS, K. E. 1965. From acts to dispositions: The attribution process in person perception. In *Advances in experimental social psychology,* ed. L. Berkowitz, vol. 2, pp. 219-266. New York: Academic Press.

JONES, E. E., and GERARD, H. B.

1967. *Foundations of social psychology.* New York: Wiley.

JORDON, N. 1953. Behavioral forces that are a function of attitudes and of cognitive organization. *Human Relations* 6: 273-287.

K

KAHN, R., and KATZ, D. 1960. Leadership practices in relation to productivity and morale. In *Group dynamics: Research and theory,* ed. D. Cartwright and A. Zander. New York: Harper.

KARDINER, A. 1939. *The individual and his society.* New York: Columbia University Press.

KARDINER, A., and OVESEY, L. 1951. *The mark of oppression.* New York: World.

KASL, S. V., and FRENCH, J. R. P., Jr. 1962. Occupational status and health. *Journal of Social Issues* 18: 67-89.

KATZ, D. 1937. *Animals and men.* London: Longmans Green.

KATZ, D., and BRALY, K. 1958. Verbal stereotypes and racial prejudice. In *Readings in social psychology,* 3d ed., ed. E. E. Maccoby, T. M. Newcomb, and E. L. Hartley. New York: Holt, Rinehart and Winston.

KATZ, D., and KAHN, R. L. 1966. *The social psychology of organizations.* New York: Wiley.

KATZ, D., and STOTLAND, E. A. 1959. A preliminary statement to a theory of attitude structure and change. In *Psychology: A study of a science,* ed. S. Koch, vol. 3, pp. 423-475. New York: McGraw-Hill.

KATZ, I., and BENJAMIN, I. 1960. Effects of white authoritarianism in biracial work groups. *Journal of Abnormal and Social Psychology* 61: 448-456.

KATZ, I., and COHEN, M. 1962. The effects of training Negroes upon cooperative problem solving in biracial teams. *Journal of Abnormal and Social Psychology* 64: 319-325.

KATZ, I.; GOLDSTON, J.; and BENJAMIN, L. 1958. Behavior and productivity in biracial work groups. *Human Relations* 11: 123-142.

KATZ, I., and GREENBAUM, C. 1963. Effects of anxiety, threat, and racial environment on task performance of Negro college students. *Journal of Abnormal and Social Psychology* 66: 562, 568.

KATZ, I.; ROBINSON, J. M.; EPPS, E. G.; and WALY, P. 1964. Effects of race of experimenter and test vs. neutral instructions on expression of hostility in Negro boys. *Journal of Social Issues* 20: 54-59.

KELLER, H. 1903. *The story of my life.* New York: Doubleday. Pp. 253, 353-354.

KELLEY, H. H. 1951. Communication in experimentally created hierarchies. *Human Relations* 4: 39-56.

KELLY, G. A. 1963. *A theory of personality: The psychology of personal constructs.* New York: Norton.

KELMAN, H. C. 1965. Manipulation of human behavior: An ethical dilemma for the social scientist. *Journal of Social Issues* 21: 31-46.

KERCKHOFF, A. E., and DAVIS, K. E. 1962. Value consensus and need complementarity in mate selection. *American Sociological Review* 27: 295-303.

KERSTETTER, L. M., and SARGENT, J. 1940. Reassignment therapy in the classroom. *Sociometry* 6: 292-306.

KIESLER, C. A. 1965. Choice, reward, and attitude change. Unpublished manuscript.

KIESLER, C. A.; COLLINS, B. E.; and MILLER, N. 1969. *Attitude change.* New York: Wiley.

KIESLER, C. A., and KIESLER, S. B. 1969. *Conformity.* Reading, Mass.: Addison-Wesley.

KING, B. T., and JANIS, I. L. 1956. Comparison of the effectiveness of improvised vs. nonimprovised role-playing in producing opinion changes. *Human Relations* 9: 177-185.

KINSEY, A. C.; POMEROY, W. B.; and MARTIN, C. E. 1948. *Sexual behavior in the human male.* Philadelphia: Saunders. Chap. 10.

KINZEL, A. T. 1970. Body-buffer zone in violent prisoners. *American Journal of Psychiatry* 127: 59-64.

KIPNIS, D. U. 1957. Interaction between members of bomber crews as a determinant of sociometric choice. *Human Relations* 10: 263-269.

KLEIN, J. 1956. *The study of groups.* London: Routledge and Kegan Paul. P. 173.

KLINEBERG, O. 1935. *Race differences.* New York: Harper.

―――. 1963. Negro-white differences in intelligence test performance. *American Psychologist* 18: 198-203.

―――. 1964. *The human dimension in international relations.* New York: Holt, Rinehart and Winston.

KLUCKHOHN, C. 1954. Culture and behavior. In *Handbook of social psychology,* ed. G. Lindsey, chap. 25. Cambridge, Mass.: Addison-Wesley.

KLUCKHOHN, C., and LEIGHTON, D. 1946. *The Navajo.* Cambridge, Mass.: Harvard University Press.

KNIGHT, H. C. 1921. *A comparison of the reliability of group and individual judgments.* Master's essay, Columbia University.

KNOBLOCK, H., and PASAMANICK, B. 1960. Report, *New York Times,* February 27.

KOCH, S. 1969. Psychology cannot be a coherent science. *Psychology Today* 3, no. 4, pp. 14, 64-68.

KOGAN, N., and WALLACH, M. A. 1964. *Risk taking.* New York: Holt, Rinehart and Winston.

KOHLER, W. 1922. Zur psychologie des Shempansen. *Psychol. Forsch.* 1: 1-45.

KOHN, M. L. 1959. Social class and parental values. *American Journal of Sociology* 64: 337-351.

KORNHAUSER, A. W. 1939. Psychological basis of class divisions. In *Industrial conflict*, ed. G. W. Hartmann and T. Newcomb, p. 236. New York: Cordon.

———. 1962. Toward an assessment of the mental health of factory workers. *Human Organization* 21: 43-46.

KOSOFSKY, S., and ELLIS, A. 1958. Illegal communications among institutionalized female delinquents. *Journal of Social Psychology* 48: 155-160.

KOSTICK, M. M. 1957. An experiment in group decision. *Journal of Teacher Education* 8: 67-72.

KRAMER, E. 1964. Elimination of verbal cues in judgments of emotion from voice. *Journal of Abnormal and Social Psychology* 68: 39-396.

KRAUSS, R. M., and DEUTSCH, M. 1966. Communication in interpersonal bargaining. *Journal of Personality and Social Psychology* 4: 572-577.

KUBIE, L. S. 1958. *Neurotic distortion of the creative process*. Lawrence, Kansas: University of Kansas Press.

KUHLEN, R. G., and BRETSCH, H. S. 1947. Sociometric status and personal problems of adolescents. *Sociometry* 10: 122-130.

KVARACEUS, W.; GEBSON, J. S.; PATTERSON, F.; SEASHOLES, B.; and GRAMBS, J. P. 1965. *Negro self-concept*. New York: McGraw-Hill.

L

LaBARRE, W. 1947. The cultural basis of emotions and gestures. *Journal of Personality* 16: 49-56.

LAING, R. D. 1967. *The politics of experience*. New York: Ballantine.

LANDRETH, C., and JOHNSON, B. C. 1953. Young children's responses to a picture and insert test designed to reveal reactions to persons of different skin color. *Child Development* 24, June, pp. 63-80.

LASKI, H. J. 1929. The danger of obedience. *Harper's Monthly Magazine* 159: 1-10.

LAZARSFELD, P. F.; BERELSON, B.; and GANDET, H. 1944. *The people's choice*. New York: Duell, Sloan and Pearce.

LEAVITT, H. J. 1951. Some effects of certain communication patterns on group performance. *Journal of Abnormal and Social Psychology* 46: 38-50.

LEAVITT, H. J., and MUELLER, R. A. H. 1951. Some effects of feedback on communication. *Human Relations* 4: 401-405.

LeBON, G. 1895. *La foule* (The crowd).

LEE, D. D. 1938. Conceptual implications of an Indian language. *Philosophy of Science* 5: 89-102.

LEE, S. G. 1958. Social influences on Aulu dreaming. *Journal of Social Psychology* 47: 265-283.

LEHMANN, I. J. 1960. *Some socio-cultural differences in attitudes and values*. Report to the American Psychological Association.

LEVINE, R. A. 1960. The internalization of political values in stateless societies. *Human Organization* 19: 51-58.

LEVINGER, G. 1964. Note on need complementarity in marriage. *Psychological Bulletin* 61: 153-157.

LEVINGER, G., and BREEDLOVE, J. 1966. Interpersonal attraction and agreement: A study of marriage partners. *Journal of Personality and Social Psychology* 3: 367-372.

LEVINSON, D. J., and HUFFMAN, P. E. 1955. Traditional family ideology and its relation to personality. *Journal of Personality* 23: 251-273.

LEVINSON, D. J., and SCHERMERHORN, R. A. 1951. Emotional-attitudinal effects of an inter-group workshop. *Journal of Psychology* 31: 243-256.

LEWIN, K. 1948. *Resolving social conflicts.* New York: Harper.

———. 1951. *Field theory in social science.* New York: Harper.

LEWIN, K.; DEMBO, T.; FESTINGER, L.; and SEARS, P. 1944. Level of aspiration. In *Personality and the behavior disorders,* ed. J. M. V. Hunt, pp. 333-378. New York: Ronald.

LEWIN, L.; LIPPITT, R.; and WHITE, R. K. 1939. Patterns of aggressive behavior in experimentally created social climates. *Journal of Social Psychology* 10: 271-299.

LIEBERMAN, S. 1956. The effects of changes in roles on the attitudes of role occupants. *Human Relations* 9: 385-402.

LIKERT, R. 1961. *New patterns in management.* New York: McGraw-Hill.

———. 1963. Trends toward a worldwide theory of management. *Newsletter of Institute for Social Research,* October. Ann Arbor, Mich.

LINDER, R. 1952. *Prescription for rebellion.* New York: Grove.

LINTON, R. 1945. *The cultural background of personality.* New York: Appleton-Century.

———. *The study of man.* New York: Appleton-Century-Crofts.

LINTON, R., ed. 1945. *The science of man in the world crisis.* New York: Columbia University Press.

LIPPITT, R.; WATSON, J.; and WESTLEY, B. 1958. *The dynamics of planned change.* New York: Harcourt, Brace.

LIPSET, S. M. 1959. What religious revival? *Columbia University Forum.*

LIPSET, S. M., and BENDIX, R. 1951. Social status and social structure. *British Journal of Sociology* 2: 150-168, 230-254.

LITCHER, J., and JOHNSON, D. W. 1969. Changes in attitudes toward Negroes of white elementary school students after use of multi-ethnic readers. *Journal of Educational Psychology* 60: 148-152.

LOOMIS, C. P. 1953. Tapping human power lines. *Adult Leadership* 1: 12-14.

LOOMIS, C. P., and DAVIDSON, D. M., Jr. 1939. Measurement of the dissolution of groups in the integration of a rural resettlement project. *Sociometry* 2, no. 2, pp. 84-94.

LOOMIS, J. L. 1959. Communication, the development of trust and cooperative behavior. *Human Relations* 12: 305-315.

LORENZ, K. 1952. *King Solomon's ring.* London: Methuen.

———. 1963. *On aggression.* New York: Harcourt, Brace and World.

———. 1964. Ritualized fighting. In *The natural history of aggression,* ed. J. D. Carthy and F. J. Ebling, pp. 39-51. New York: Academic Press.

LORGE, I. 1953. *Evaluation of instruction in staff-action and decision-making.* Technical Res. Rept. No. 16. Maxwell Air Force Base, Alabama.

LOWIE, R. H. 1940. *An introduction to cultural anthropology.* New York: Rinehart.

LUFT, J. Structural intervention. *Human Relations Training News* 10, no. 2, pp. 1-2. National Training Laboratories.

LUMSDAINE, A. A., and JANIS, I. L. 1953. Resistance to counterpropaganda produced by one-sided and two-sided propaganda presentations. *Public Opinion Quarterly* 17: 311-318.

LUND, F. H. 1925. The psychology of belief: IV. The law of primacy in persuasion. *Journal of Abnormal and Social Psychology* 20: 183-191.

LUNDBERG, G. A., and STULE, M. 1938. Social attraction patterns in a village. *Sociometry* 1: 375-419.

LYLE, J. G. 1964. Environmentally produced retardation: Institution and preinstitution influences. *Journal of Abnormal and Social Psychology* 49: 329-332.

LYND, R. S., and LYND, H. M. 1929. *Middletown*. New York: Harcourt, Brace.

———. 1937. *Middletown in transition*. New York: Harcourt, Brace.

M

MAAS, H. S. 1951. Some social class differences in the family systems and group relations of pre and early adolescents. *Child Development* 22: 145-152.

McCANDLESS, B. R. 1942. Changing relationships between dominance and social acceptability during group democratization. *American Journal of Orthopsychiatry* 12: 529-535.

McCLELLAND, D. C. 1958. The importance of early learning in the formation of motives. In *Motives in fantasy, action, and society*, ed. J. W. Atkinson, pp. 437-452. Princeton: N.J.: Van Nostrand.

———. 1961. *The achieving society*. Princeton, N.J.: Van Nostrand.

McCLELLAND, D. C., et al. 1952. *The achievement motive*. New York: Appleton-Century-Crofts.

McCLELLAND, D. C., and FRIEDMAN, G. A. 1952. A cross-cultural study of the relationship between child-training practices and achievement motivation appearing in folktales. In *Readings in social psychology*, ed. G. E. Swanson, T. M. Newcomb, and E. L. Hartley. New York: Holt.

McCLINTOCK, C. G. 1958. Personality syndromes and attitude change. *Journal of Personality* 26: 479-493.

MACCOBY, E. E. 1963. Women's intellect. In *The potential of women*, ed. S. M. Faber and R. L. Wilson, pp. 24-39. New York: McGraw-Hill.

McDOUGALL, W. 1908. *Introduction to social psychology*. London: Methuen.

McGUIRE, C. 1950. Social stratification and mobility patterns. *American Sociological Review* 15: 195-204.

McGUIRE, W. 1966. The current status of cognitive consistency theories. In *Cognitive consistency: Motivational antecedents and behavioral consequents*, ed. S. Feldman, pp. 1-46. New York: Academic Press.

McGUIRE, W. J. 1964. Inducing resistance to persuasion. In *Advances in experimental social psychology*, ed. L. Berkowitz, vol. 1, pp. 191-229. New York: Academic Press.

———. 1969. The nature of attitudes and attitude change. In *The handbook of social psychology*, 2d ed., pp. 136-315. Reading, Mass.: Addison-Wesley.

McGUIRE, W. J. and MILLMAN, S. 1965. Anticipatory belief lowering following forewarning of a persuasive attack. *Journal of Personality and Social Psychology* 2: 471-479.

McGUIRE, W. J., and PAPAGEORGIS, D. 1961. The relative efficacy of various types of prior belief-defense in producing immunity against persuasion. *Journal of Abnormal and Social Psychology* 62: 338-345.

———. 1962. Effectiveness of forewarning in developing resistance to persuasion. *Public Opinion Quarterly* 26: 24-34.

McKEE, J. P., and SHERIFFS, A. C. 1957. The differential evaluation of males and females. *Journal of Personality* 25: 356-371.

MacKENZIE, B. K. 1948. The importance of contact in determining attitude toward Negroes. *Journal of Abnormal and Social Psychology* 43: 417-441.

MAIER, N. R. F., and SOLEM, A. R. 1952. The contribution of a discussion leader to the quality of group thinking: The effective use of minority opinions. *Human Relations* 5: 277-288.

———. 1962. Improving solutions by turning situations into problems. *Personnel Psychology* 15: 151-157.

MAINER, R. E. 1954. *Attitude change in intergroup education programs.* Lafayette, Ind.: Purdue University.

MAISEL, R. 1960. A study of small groups in basic training. Ph.D. thesis, Columbia University.

MALINOWSKY, B. 1927. *Sex and repression in savage society.* New York: Harcourt, Brace.

MANDLEBAUM, D. G. 1952. *Soldier groups and Negro soldiers.* Berkeley: University of California. Pp. 45-48.

MANN, F. L., and HEFF, F. W. 1961. *Managing major change in organizations.* Ann Arbor, Mich.: Foundation for Research on Human Behavior.

MANN, F. S., and HOFFMAN, L. R. 1956. Individual and organizational correlates of automation. *Journal of Social Issues* 12: 7-17.

MANN, R. D. 1959. A review of the relationship between personality and performance in small groups. *Psychological Bulletin* 56: 241-270.

MANRY, J. C. 1928. *World citizenship.* Iowa City, Iowa: University of Iowa.

MARCUS, L. 1961. *The treatment of American Negroes and minorities in secondary school textbooks.* New York: Anti-Defamation League of B'nai B'rith.

MARQUIS, D. G. 1962. Individual responsibility and group decision involving risk. *Industrial Management Review* 3: 8-23.

MASLOW, A., and DIAZ-GUERRERO, R. 1960. Delinquency as a value disturbance. In *Festschrift for Gardner Murphy,* ed. J. Peatman and E. L. Hartley, pp. 228-240. New York: Harper.

MASLOW, A. H. 1954. *Motivation and personality.* New York: Harper.

MASTERS, R. E. L. 1963. *Patterns of incest.* New York: Julian.

MATARAZZO, J. D.; SASLOW, G.; WIENS, A. N.; WEITMAN, N.; and ALLEN, B. V. 1964. Interviewer head-nodding and interviewee speech deviations. *Psychotherapy* 1: 54-63.

MAUSNER, B. 1953. Studies in social interaction, III. Effect of variation in one partner's prestige on the interaction of observer pairs. *Journal of Applied Psychology* 37: 391-394.

MAYER, A. J., and HAUSER, P. 1953. Class differentials in expectation of life at birth. In *Class, status, and power,* ed. R. Bendix and S. M. Lipset, pp. 281-284. Glencoe, Ill.: Free Press.

MAZUR, A. The littlest science. *American Sociologist* 3: 195-200.

MEAD, G. H. 1934. *Mind, self, and society,* pp. 42f. Chicago: University of Chicago Press.

MEAD, M. 1928. *Coming of age in Samoa.* New York: Morrow.

———. 1928. *Sex and temperament.* New York: Morrow.

———. 1946. Research on primitive children. In *Manual of child psychology,* ed. L. Carmichael, p. 678. New York: Wiley.

———. 1956. *New lives for old.* New York: Morrow.

MEAD, M., ed. 1937. *Cooperation and competition among primitive peoples.* New York: McGraw-Hill.

———. 1955. *Cultural patterns and technical change.* Prepared for UNESCO. A Mentor Book. Pp. 134-135.

MEAD, M., and WOLFENSTEIN, M., eds. 1955. *Childhood in contemporary cultures.* Chicago: University of Chicago Press.

MEADOW, A.; PARNES, S. J.; and REESE, H. 1959. Influences of brainstorming instructions and problem sequence on a creative problem-solving test. *Journal of Applied Psychology* 43: 413-416.

MEENES, M. A. 1943. A comparison of racial stereotypes of 1930 and 1942. *Journal of Social Psychology* 17: 327-336.

MEHRABIAN, A. 1968. Communication without words. *Psychology Today,* September, pp. 53-55.

MENZEL, H., and KATZ, E. 1956. Social relations and innovation in the medical profession. *Public Opinion Quarterly* 19: 337-352.

MEREI, F. 1949. Group leadership and institutionalization. *Human Relations* 2: 23-39.

MERTON, R. K. 1949. Applied social science in formulation of policy. *Philosophy of Science*, vol. 16, no. 3.

———. 1950. Contributions to the theory of reference group behavior. In *Continuities in social research: Studies in the scope and method of the American soldier*, ed. R. K. Merton and P. F. Lazarsfeld, pp. 40-105. Glencoe, Ill.: Free Press.

MEYER, M. 1903. Experimental studies in the psychology of music. *American Journal of Psychology* 14: 456-476.

MICHIGAN CURRICULUM COMMITTEE FOR BETTER HUMAN RELATIONS. 1963. *The treatment of minority groups in textbooks.* Lansing, Mich.: Michigan Department of Public Instruction.

MILES, M., ed. 1964. *Innovation in education.* New York: Teachers College, Columbia University.

MILGRAM, S. 1963. Behavioral study of obedience. *Journal of Abnormal and Social Psychology* 67: 371-378.

———. 1964a. Group pressure and action against a person. *Journal of Abnormal and Social Psychology* 69: 137-143.

———. 1964b. Issues in the study of obedience: A reply to Baumrind. *American Psychologist* 19: 848-852.

———. 1956a. Liberating effects of group pressure. *Journal of Personality and Social Psychology* 1: 127-134.

———. 1965b. Some conditions of obedience and disobedience to authority. *Human Relations* 18: 57-76.

MILL, J. S. 1929. *On the subjection of women.* London: Dent. Originally published 1869.

MILLAR, J. 1793. *The origin and distinction of banks.* Basel, Switzerland.

MILLER, N. 1941. The frustration-aggression hypothesis. *Psychological Review* 48: 337-342.

MILLER, S. M. 1966. The credentials trap. Speech to national meeting of Neighborhood Youth Corps, St. Louis.

MILLER, S. M., and REIN, M. 1964. Poverty and social change. *The American child.* New York: National Committee on Employment of Youth.

MILLET, K. 1969. *Sexual politics.* New York: Avon.

MILLS, C. W. 1951. *White collar.* New York: Oxford University Press.

MINAMI, H. 1954. *Nihonjin no Shinoi* (Psychology of the Japanese). Tokyo: Mainichi Shimbunsha.

MINER, H. M. 1939. *St. Denis.* Chicago: University of Chicago Press.

MINTZ, A. 1946. A re-examination of correlations between lynchings and economic indices. *Journal of Abnormal and Social Psychology* 41: 154-160.

———. 1951. Nonadaptive group behavior. *Journal of Abnormal and Social Psychology* 46: 150-159.

MISUMI, J., and TASAKI, T. 1965. A study on the effectiveness of supervisory patterns in a Japanese hierarchical organization. *Japanese Psychological Research* 7: 151-162.

MIZRUCHI, E. H. 1960. Social structure and anomia in a small city. *American Sociological Review* 25: 645-654.

MOEDE, W. 1920. *Experimentelle Massenpsychologie.* Leipzig: S. Hirzel.

MONTAGUE, M. F. A. 1950. Social instincts. *Scientific American,* April.

MORENO, J. L. 1934. *Who shall survive.* Washington, D.C.: Nervous and Mental Disease Publishing Company.

MORGAN, L. H. 1964. *Ancient society.* Edited by Leslie A. White.

Cambridge: Belknap Press of Harvard University. Originally published 1877.

MORRIS, C. W. 1956. *Varieties of human values.* Chicago: University of Chicago Press.

MORRIS, D. 1967. *The naked ape.* New York: McGraw-Hill.

MORT, P. R., and CORNELL, F. G. 1941. *American schools in transition.* New York: Teachers College, Columbia University.

MORT, P. R., and FURNO, O. F. 1960. *Theory and synthesis of a sequential complex.* New York: Teachers College, Columbia University, Institute of Administrative Research.

MOYNIHAN, P. D. 1969. *Maximum feasible misunderstanding.* New York: Free Press.

MUELLER, J. H., and MUELLER, K. H. 1940. Social-economic background and campus success. *Educational and Psychological Measurement* 3: 143-150.

MUKERJI, N. P. 1940. Work in groups and in isolation. *British Journal of Psychology* 30: 352-356.

MULLIGAN, R. A. 1951. Socio-economic background and college enrollment. *American Sociological Review* 16: 188-196.

MURPHY, G. 1958. *Human potentialities.* New York: Basic Books.

———. 1961. *Challenge of psychical research.* New York: Harper.

MURPHY, G., and MURPHY, L. B. 1931. *Experimental social psychology.* New York: Harper. Pp. 174-177.

MURRAY, H. A. 1938. *Explorations in personality.* New York: Oxford University Press.

———. 1960. A mythology for grownups. *Saturday Review,* June 23, pp. 10-12.

MURRAY, H. A., et al. 1948. *The assessment of men.* New York: Holt, Rinehart and Winston.

MYRDAL, G. 1944. *An American dilemma: The Negro problem and modern democracy.* New York: Harper. Revised 1962.

N

NADLER, E. B., and MORROW, W. R. 1959. Authoritarian attitudes toward women and their correlates. *Journal of Social Psychology* 49: 113-123.

NAROLL, R. 1966. Does military deterrence deter? *Trans-action* 3: 14-21.

NATIONAL OPINION RESEARCH CENTER. 1947. Jobs and occupations: A popular evaluation. *Opinion News* 9: 3-13.

NEWCOMB, T. M. 1943. *Personality and social change.* New York: Dryden.

———. 1947. Autistic hostility and social reality. *Human Relations* 1: 69-86.

———. 1961. *The acquaintance process.* New York: Holt, Rinehart and Winston.

———. 1963. Stabilities underlying changes in interpersonal attraction. *Journal of Abnormal and Social Psychology* 66: 376-386.

NEWFIELD, J. 1966. *A prophetic minority.* New York: Signet.

NIEL, R. G., and DUNN, R. E. 1960. Predicting success in supervisory training programs by use of psychological tests. *Journal of Applied Psychology* 44: 358-360.

NYE, F. 1951. Adolescent-parent adjustment—Socio-economic level as a variable. *American Sociological Review* 16: 341-349.

O

O'CONNELL, E. J. 1965. Effect of cooperative and competitive set on the learning of imitation. *Journal of Experimental and Social Psychology* 1: 172-183.

OGBURN, W. F. 1922. *Social change with respect to culture and original nature.* New York: Huebsch.

———. 1938. *Machines and tomorrow's world.* New York: Public Affairs Commission.

ORNE, M. T. 1962. On the social psychological experiment: With particular reference to the demand characteristics and their implications. *American Psychologist* 17: 776-783.

OSGOOD, C. E. 1962. *An alternative to war or surrender.* Urbana, Ill.: University of Illinois Press.

OSKAMP, S. 1965. Attitudes toward U.S. and Russian actions—a double standard. *Psychological Reports* 16: 43-46.

OSSORIO, P. G., and DAVIS, K. E. 1966. The self, intentionality, and reactions to evaluations of the self. In *Self in society,* ed. C. Gordon and D. J. Gergen. New York: Wiley.

P
──────

PAGE, M. 1959. The sociotherapy of the enterprise. *Human Relations* 12: 317-334.

PARETO, V. 1916. *Trattato di sociologia generale.* Florence.

PARK, R. E. 1916. The city: Suggestions for the investigation of human behavior in the urban environment. *American Journal of Sociology* 20: 577-612.

PARSONS, T. 1959. The school class as a social system: Some of its functions in American society. *Harvard Educational Review* 29: 297-318.

PARTEN, M. B. 1932. Social participation among pre-school children. *Journal of Abnormal and Social Psychology* 27: 243-269.

PASAMANICK, B., and KNOBLOCH, H. 1955. Early language behavior in Negro children and the testing of intelligence. *Journal of Abnormal and Social Psychology* 50: 401-402.

PASTORE, N. 1949. *The nature-nurture controversy.* New York: King's Crown Press.

PATCHEN, M. 1958. The effect of reference group standards on job satisfaction. *Human Relations* 11: 303-314.

PATRICK, C. 1944. Attitudes about women executives in government positions. *Journal of Social Psychology* 19: 3-34.

PEAK, H., and MORRISON, R. W. 1958. The acceptance of information into attitude structure. *Journal of Abnormal and Social Psychology* 58: 127-135.

PELL, S., and D'ALONZO, G. A. 1961. A three-year study of myocardial infarction in a large employed population. *Journal of the American Medical Association* 175: 463-470.

PELZ, D. 1952. Influence: A key to effective leadership in the first-line supervisor. *Personnel* 29: 3-11.

PEPINSKY, P. N.; HEMPHILL, J. K.; and SHEVITZ, R. N. 1958. Attempts to lead, group productivity, and morale under conditions of acceptance and rejection. *Journal of Abnormal and Social Psychology* 57: 47-54.

PEPITONE, A. 1950. Motivational effects in social perception. *Human Relations* 3: 57-76.

PERLS, F. S. 1969. *Ego hunger and aggression.* New York: Random House.

———. 1969. *Gestalt therapy verbatim.* Lafayette, Calif.: Real People's Press.

———. 1969. *In and out of the garbage pail.* Lafayette, Calif.: Real People's Press.

PETTIGREW, T. F. 1958. Personality and sociocultural factors in intergroup attitudes: A cross-national comparison. *Journal of Conflict Resolution* 2: 29-42.

———. 1964. *A profile of the Negro American.* Princeton, N.J.: Van Nostrand.

PETTIGREW, T. F., and CRAMER, M. R. 1959. The demography of desegregation. *Journal of Social Issues* 15: 61-71.

PHILLIPS, E. L. 1950. Intellectual and personality factors associated with social class attitudes among junior high school children. *Journal of Genetic Psychology* 78: 61-72.

POINCINS, G. de M., and GALANTIERE, L. 1943. *Kabloona.*

New York: Garden City Publishing Company.

PORTER, L., and LAWLER, E. E. 1956. Properties of organization structure in relation to job attitudes and job behavior. *Psychological Bulletin* 64: 23-51.

POSTMAN, L., and BROWN, D. R. 1952. The perceptual consequences of success and failure. *Journal of Abnormal and Social Psychology* 47: 213-221.

PRICE, D. O., and SEARLES, R. 1961. Some effects of interviewer-respondent interaction on responses in a survey. Report to American Statistical Association, New York, December 30.

PRICE, W. A. 1966. Economics of the Negro ghetto. *National Guardian,* September 3, p. 4.

PROVENCE, S., and LIPTON, R. C. 1962. *Infants in institutions.* New York: International Universities Press.

R
—————

RABBIE, J. M. 1963. Differential preference for companionship under threat. *Journal of Abnormal and Social Psychology* 67: 643-647.

RADKE, M. J., and HELEN, G. T. 1950. Children's perception of the social roles of Negroes and whites. *Journal of Psychology* 29: 3-33.

RADKE, M. J.; HELEN, G. T.; and HADASSAH, D. 1949. Social perceptions and attitudes of children. *Genetic Psychology Monograph* 40: 327-447.

RADLOFF, R. 1961. Opinion evaluation and affiliation. *Journal of Abnormal and Social Psychology* 62: 578-585.

———. 1966. Social comparison and ability evaluation. *Journal of Experimental Social Psychology,* supplement 1, pp. 6-26.

RAPER, A. 1933. *The tragedy of lynching.* Chapel Hill, N.C.: University of North Carolina Press.

RAPOPORT, A. 1960. *Fights, games, and debates.* Ann Arbor, Mich.: University of Michigan Press.

RAVEN, B. H., and RIETSEMA, J. 1957. The effect of varied clarity of group goal and group path upon the individual and his relation to his group. *Human Relations* 10: 29-44.

REDEFER, F. L. 1950. The eight-year study after eight years. *Progressive Education* 28: 33-36.

REICHENBACH, H. 1938. *Experience and prediction.* Chicago: University of Chicago Press.

REIK, T. 1945. *Psychology of sex relations.* New York: Farrar and Rinehart.

REILLY, W. J. 1929. *Method for the study of retail relationships.* Bulletin no. 2944. Austin, Tex.: University of Texas.

REMMERS, H. H., and RADLER, D. H. 1957. *The American teen-ager.* Indianapolis: Bobbs-Merrill.

RHEINGOLD, H. L. 1956. The modification of social responsiveness in institutional babies. *Monograph of Society for Research in Child Development* 21, no. 2.

RHINE, J. B. 1937. *New frontiers of the mind.* New York: Farrar, Rinehart.

———. 1940. *Extra-sensory perception after sixty years.* New York: Holt.

———. 1947. *Reach of the mind.* New York: William Sloane Associates.

RICE, G. E., and WHITE, K. R. 1964. The effect of education on prejudice as revealed by a game situation. *Psychological Record* 14: 341-348.

RICHARDSON, L. F. 1960. *Statistics of deadly quarrels.* London: Stevens.

RICHTER, H. E. 1963. *Eltern, kind, und neurose.* Stuttgart, Germany: Ernst Klett Verlag.

RIESS, B. F. 1937. A case of high scores in card guessing at a distance. *Journal of Parapsychology* 1: 260-263.

———. 1939. Changes in the attitudes of student political groups towards

481

methods of preventing war as a result of the Czechoslovakian crisis. Report to Eastern Psychological Association, March 31.

ROETHLISBERGER, F. J., and DICKSON, W. J. 1939. *Management and the worker.* Cambridge, Mass.: Harvard University Press.

ROGERS, C. 1952. Communication: Its blocking and its facilitation. *ETC.: A Review of General Semantics* 9: 83-88.

ROGERS, C. R. 1951. *Client-centered psychotherapy.* Boston: Houghton Mifflin. P. 521.

————. 1965. Dealing with psychological tensions. *Journal of Applied Behavioral Science* 1: 6-25.

ROGERS, E. M. 1962. *Diffusion of innovations.* Glencoe, Ill.: Free Press.

ROGOFF, N. 1953. Recent trends in urban occupational mobility. In *Class, status, and power,* ed. R. Bendix and S. M. Lipset, p. 445. Glencoe, Ill.: Free Press.

————. 1960. American high schools at mid-century. *Journal of Educational Sociology* 23: 252-259.

ROKEACH, M. 1960. *The open and closed mind.* New York: Basic Books.

————. 1966. The nature of attitudes. *The International Encyclopedia of the Social Sciences.* Mimeographed. East Lansing, Mich.: Michigan State University.

ROKEACH, M., and ROTHMAN, G. 1965. The principle of belief congruence and the congruity principle as models of cognitive interaction. *Psychological Review* 72: 128-142.

ROSEN, B. C. 1955. Conflicting group membership: A study of parent-peer group cross pressures. *American Sociological Review* 20: 155-161.

ROSENTHAL, R. 1966. *Experimenter effects in behavioral research.* New York: Appleton-Century-Crofts.

ROSENWALD, G. 1961. The assessment of anxiety in psychological

experiments. *Journal of Abnormal and Social Psychology* 63: 666-673.

ROUGEMENT, D. de. 1948. Romantic route to divorce. *Saturday Review of Literature* 31, November 13, pp. 9-10.

ROWLAND, L. W. 1939. Will hypnotized persons try to harm themselves or others? *Journal of Abnormal and Social Psychology* 34: 114-117.

S

SAENGER, G., and GILBERT, E. 1950. Customer reactions to the integration of Negro sales personnel. *International Journal of Opinion and Attitude Research* 4: 57-76.

SANCHEZ-HIDALGO, E. S. 1951. A study of the symbiotic relationships between friends. Manuscript in library of Teachers College, Columbia University.

SANFORD, N., ed. 1956. Personality development during the college years. *Journal of Social Issues* 12: 1-71.

SAPIR, E. 1929. The status of linguistics as a science. *Language* 5: 207-214.

SARNOFF, I., and KATZ, D. 1954. The motivational basis of attitude change. *Journal of Abnormal and Social Psychology* 49: 115-124.

SARRI, R. C., and VINTER, R. D. 1969. Group work for the control of behavior problems in secondary schools. In *Innovation in mass education,* ed. D. Street, pp. 91-119. New York: Wiley-Interscience.

SCHACHTER, S. 1951. Deviation, rejection, and communication. *Journal of Abnormal and Social Psychology* 46: 190-207.

SCHACHTER, S.; ELLERTSON, N.; McBRIDE, D.; and GREGORY, D. 1951. An experimental study of cohesiveness and productivity. *Human Relations* 4: 229-238.

SCHACHTER, S., and SINGER, J. E. 1962. Cognitive, social, and physiological determinants of emotional state. *Psychological Review* 69: 379-399.

SCHACHTER, S. 1959. *The psychology of affiliation: Experimental studies of the sources of gregariousness.* Stanford, Calif.: Stanford University Press.

SCHACHTER, S., et al. 1954. Cross-cultural experiments on threat and rejection. *Human Relations* 7: 403-439.

SCHEIN, E. H. 1956. The Chinese indoctrination program of prisoners of war. *Psychiatry* 19: 149-172.

SCHOPENHAUER, A. 1855. *Parerga und paralipomena.* Berlin.

SCHUTZ, W. 1959. *Firo: A three-dimensional theory of interpersonal behavior.* New York: Rinehart.

SCOTT, J. P., and FULLER, J. L. 1965. *Genetics and the social behavior of the dog.* Chicago: University of Chicago Press.

SCOTT, W. A. 1957. Attitude change through reward of verbal behavior. *Journal of Abnormal and Social Psychology* 55: 72-75.

———. 1959. Attitude change by response reinforcement: Replication and extension. *Sociometry* 22: 328-335.

SEARS, R. R. 1951. A theoretical framework for personality and social behavior. *American Psychologist* 6: 476-482.

———. 1963. Dependency motivation. In *Nebraska symposium on motivation.* Lincoln, Nebr.: University of Nebraska Press.

SEASHORE, S. 1954. *Group cohesiveness in the industrial work group.* Ann Arbor, Mich.: Institute for Social Research.

SEAY, B.; ALEXANDER, B. K.; and HARLOW, H. F. 1964. Maternal behavior of socially deprived rhesus monkeys. *Journal of Abnormal and Social Psychology* 69: 345-354.

SECORD, P. F. 1959. Stereotyping and favorableness in the perception of Negro faces. *Journal of Abnormal and Social Psychology* 59: 309-315.

SECORD, P. F., and BACKMAN, C. W. 1961. Personality theory and the problem of stability and change in individual behavior: An interpersonal approach. *Psychological Review* 68: 21-33.

———. 1964. *Social psychology.* New York: McGraw-Hill.

SHAPIRO, J. G. 1968. Responsivity to facial and linguistic cues. *Journal of Communication* 18: 11-17.

SHARTLE, C. 1956. *Executive performance and leadership.* Englewood Cliffs, N.J.: Prentice-Hall.

SHAW, C. 1938. *Brothers in crime.* Chicago: University of Chicago Press. P. 96.

SHAW, G. B. 1895. *Our theatre in the nineties.* Vol. 1, p. 108.

———. 1920. Woman since 1860. *Time and Tide,* October 8, pp. 442-445.

———. 1932. *Major critical essays: The quintessence of Ibsenism.* London: Constable.

SHAW, M. C. 1961. Definition and identification of academic under-achievers. *Guidance for the underachiever with superior ability.* Pp. 15-30.

SHAW, M. E.; ROTHSCHILD, S. H.; and STRICKLAND, J. F. 1957. Decision processes in communication nets. *Journal of Abnormal and Social Psychology* 54: 323-330.

SHEERER, E. T. 1949. An analysis of the relationship between acceptance of and respect for self and acceptance of and respect for others in ten counseling cases. *Journal of Consulting Psychology* 13: 169-175.

SHERIF, M. 1936. *The psychology of social norms.* New York: Harper.

———. 1966. *In common predicament.* Boston: Houghton Mifflin.

SHOSTROM, E. L. 1963. *Manual for the personal orientation inventory.* San Diego: Educational and Industrial Testing.

SHRIEKE, B. 1936. *Alien Americans.* New York: Viking.

SIBLEY, E. 1942. Some demographic clues to stratification. *American Sociological Review* 7: 322-330.

SIEGEL, A. E., and SIEGEL, S. 1957. Reference groups, membership groups, and attitude change. *Journal of Abnormal and Social Psychology* 55: 360-364.

SINCLAIR, U. 1930. *Mental radio.* New York: Albert and Charles Boni.

SINGER, D. 1967. The influence of intelligence and an interracial classroom on social attitudes. In *The urban r's: Race relations as the problem in urban education,* ed. R. A. Dentler, B. Mackler, and M. E. Warshauer. New York: Praeger.

SKINNER, B. F. 1955. *Walden two.* New York: Macmillan.

SLATER, P. E. 1955. Role differentiation in small groups. *American Sociological Review* 20: 300-310.

———. 1970. Cultures in collision. *Psychology Today* 4, no. 2, pp. 31-33, 66-68.

SMITH, A. 1937. *An inquiry into the nature and causes of the wealth of nations.* New York: Modern Library. Pp. 28-29, 248. Originally published 1776.

———. 1967. *The money game.* New York: Random House.

SMITH, C. R.; WILLIAMS, L.; and WILLIS, R. H. 1967. Race, sex, and belief as determinants of friendship acceptance. *Journal of Personality and Social Psychology* 5: 127-137.

SMITH, F. 1943. *An experiment in modifying attitude toward the Negro.* New York: Teachers College, Columbia University.

SMITH, M. B. 1947. The personal

setting of public opinions. *Public Opinion Quarterly* 11: 507-523.

SOLOMON, F., and FISHMAN, J. R. 1964. Youth and social action. *Journal of Social Issues* 20: 36-46.

SOLOMON, L. 1960. The influence of some types of power relationships and game strategies upon the development of interpersonal trust. *Journal of Abnormal and Social Psychology* 61: 223-230.

SOMMER, R. 1961. Leadership and group geography. *Sociometry* 24: 99-110.

SOMMER, R., and ROSS, H. 1958. Social interaction in a geriatrics ward. *International Journal of Social Psychiatry* 4: 128-133.

SOROKIN, P. A. 1950. *Explorations in altruistic love and behavior.* Boston: Beacon.

SOUTH, E. B. 1927. Some psychological aspects of committee work. *Journal of Applied Psychology* 11: 348-368, 437-464.

SPILLER, G. 1929. The dynamics of greatness. *Social Review* 21: 218-232.

SPINDLER, G. D. 1955. *Sociocultural and psychological processes in Menomini acculturation.* Berkeley: University of California Publications in Culture and Society.

SPITZ, R. A. 1945. Hospitalism: An inquiry into the genesis of psychiatric conditions in early chlidhood. *Psychoanalytic Study of the Child* 1: 53-74.

SPITZ, R. A., and WOLF, K. M. 1946. Anaclitic depression. *Psychoanalytic Study of the Child* 2: 313-342.

SROLE, L. 1951. *Social dysfunction, personality, and social distance.* Paper read before American Sociological Society.

STAATS, A. W. 1967. An outline of an integrated learning theory of attitude formation and function. In *Readings in attitude theory and measurement,* ed. M. Fishbein, pp. 373-377. New York: Wiley.

————. 1968. *Learning, language, and cognition.* New York: Holt, Rinehart and Winston.

STAATS, A. W.; STAATS, C. K.; and CRAWFORD, H. L. 1962. First-order conditioning of meaning and the parallel conditioning of a GSR. *Journal of General Psychology* 67: 159-167.

STAMPP, K. M. 1964. *The Negro in American history textbooks.* A report of Sacramento, California, Department of Education.

STEIN, D. D.; HARDYCK, J. A.; and SMITH, M. B. 1965. Race and belief: An open and shut case. *Journal of Personality and Social Psychology* 1: 281-290.

STEINZOR, B. 1950. The spatial factor in face-to-face discussion groups. *Journal of Abnormal and Social Psychology* 45: 552-555.

STENDLER, C. B. 1952. Critical periods in socialization and over-dependency. *Child Development* 23: 3-12.

STEPHEN, F. F., and MISHLER, E. G. 1952. The distribution of participation in small groups. *American Sociological Review* 17: 598-608.

STEPHENSON, R. M. 1957. Mobility orientation and stratification of 1,000 ninth graders. *American Sociological Review* 22: 204-212.

STOCK, D. 1964. A survey of research on T groups. In *T-group theory and laboratory method,* ed. L. P. Bradford, J. R. Gibb, and K. D. Benne, pp. 395-442. New York: Wiley.

STODDARD, T. 1920. *The rising tide of color against white world supremacy.* New York: Scribner.

STOGDILL, R. M.; SHARTLE, C. L.; COONS, A. E.; and JAYNES, W. E. 1956. A predictive study of administrative work patterns. Ohio State University Bureau of Business Research Monograph R-85. Columbus.

STONE, L. J. 1954. Critique of studies of infant isolation. *Child Development* 25: 9-20.

STONER, J. A. F. 1961. Comparison of individual and group decisions involving risk. M.A. thesis, M.I.T. School of Industrial Management.

STOUFFER, S. A. 1949. *Combat and its aftermath.* Vol. 2 of *The American soldier.* Princeton, N.J.: Princeton University Press. P. 136.

STOUFFER, S. A., et al. 1949. *The American soldier.* Princeton, N.J.: Princeton University Press. Vol. 1, p. 414.

STRUPP, H. H., and BERGIN, A. E. 1969. Some empirical and conceptual bases for coordinated research in psychotherapy: A critical review of issues, trends, and evidence. *International Journal of Psychiatry* 7: 18-90.

SULLIVAN, H. S. 1947. *Conceptions of modern psychiatry.* Washington, D.C.: William Alanson White Foundation. P. 8.

SUMNER, W. G. 1906. *Folk ways.* New York: Ginn.

SUTHERLAND, E. H. 1940. White-collar criminality. *American Sociological Review* 5: 1-12.

————. 1945. Is white-collar crime crime? *American Sociological Review* 132-139.

T

TANNENBAUM, R., et al. 1961. The process of understanding people. *Leadership and organization.* New York: McGraw-Hill.

TARDE, G. 1903. *Laws of imitation.* New York: Holt. Originally published 1890.

TAUSSIG, F. W., and JOSLYN, C. S. 1932. *American business leaders.* New York: Macmillan. P. 103.

TAYLOR, D. W.; BERRY, P. C.; and BLOCK, C. H. 1958. Does group participation when using brainstorming facilitate or inhibit creative thinking? *Administrative Science Quarterly* 3: 23-47.

TERMAN, L. M., and MILES, C. C. 1936. *Sex and personality: Studies in masculinity and femininity.* New York: McGraw-Hill.

TERMAN, L. M., and ODOR, M. H. 1947. *The gifted child grows up.* Stanford, Calif.: Stanford University Press.

TERMAN, L. M., et al. 1938. *Psychological factors in marital happiness.* New York: McGraw-Hill.

THIBAUT, J. W., and KELLEY, H. H. 1959. *The social psychology of groups.* New York: Wiley.

THOMAS, E. J., and FINK, C. 1963. Effect of group size. *Psychological Bulletin* 60: 371-384.

THOMAS, E. J.; WEBB, S.; and TWEEDIE, J. 1961. Effects of familiarity with a controversial issue on acceptance of successive communications. *Journal of Abnormal and Social Psychology* 63: 656-659.

THOMAS, E. M. 1959. *The harmless people.* New York: Knopf.

THOMPSON, L. 1950. *Culture in crisis.* New York: Harper.

THOMPSON, N. R., and HERON, W. 1954. The effects of restricting early experience on the problem solving of dogs. *Canadian Journal of Psychology* 8: 17-31.

THORNDIKE, E. L. 1913. *The original nature of man.* New York: Teachers College, Columbia University.

THORNDIKE, R. L. 1938*b*. What type of task do groups do well? *Journal of Abnormal and Social Psychology* 33: 409-413.

THORNTON, D. A., and ARROWOOD, A. 1966. Self-evaluation, self-enhancement, and the locus of social comparison. *Journal of Experimental Social Psychology*, supplement 1, 40-48.

THRASHER, F. M. 1927. *The gang.* Chicago: University of Chicago Press.

TIMMONS, W. M. 1939. *Decisions and attitudes as outcomes of the discussion of a social problem.* New York: Teachers College, Columbia University.

TORRANCE, E. P. 1954. *Some consequences of power differences in decision-making in permanent and temporary three-man groups.* Research Studies, State College of Washington, 22: 130-140.

TOYNBEE, A. J. 1934. *A study of history.* 6 vols. New York: Oxford University Press. Abridgment by D. C. Somervell, 1947.

———. 1963. Again nationalism threatens. *New York Times Magazine,* November 5, p. 23.

TRAVIS, E. L. 1925. The effect of a small audience upon eye-hand coordination. *Journal of Abnormal and Social Psychology* 20: 142-146.

TRIANDIS, H. C. 1961. A note on Rokeach's theory of prejudice. *Journal of Abnormal and Social Psychology* 62: 184-186.

TRUAX, C. B., and CARKHUFF, R. R. 1967. *Toward effective counseling and psychotherapy: Training and practice.* Chicago: Aldine.

TRUAX, C. B., and WARGO, D. G. 1966. Psychotherapeutic encounters that change behavior: For better or for worse. *American Journal of Psychotherapy* 22: 499-520.

TSENG, S. 1952. An experimental study of the effect of three types of distribution of reward upon work efficiency and group dynamics. Manuscript. New York: Teachers College, Columbia University.

TUCKER, R. C. 1968. The theory of charismatic leadership. *Daedalus* 97: 731-757.

TUMIN, M. M. 1957. *Segregation and desegregation.* New York: Anti-Defamation League, B'nai B'rith.

———. 1958. *Desegregation: Resistance and readiness.* Princeton, N.J.: Princeton University Press.

TURNER, F. J. 1920. *The frontier in American history.* New York: Holt.

U

U.S. WAR DEPARTMENT. 1945.
Opinions about Negro infantry platoons in white companies of seven divisions. Report no. B-157, Info. and Educ. Div. Army Service Forces.

URWICK, L. F. 1956. The manager's span of control. *Harvard Business Review* 34, May-June, p. 34.

USEEM, J., et al. 1942. Stratification in a prairie town. *American Sociological Review* 8: 331-342.

V

VEROFF, J. 1963. African students in the United States. *Journal of Social Issues* 19: 48-60.

———. 1969. Social comparison and the development of achievement motivation. In *Achievement related motives in children*, ed. C. Smith. New York: Russell Sage Foundation.

VERPLANCK, W. S. 1955. The control of the content of conversation. *Journal of Abnormal and Social Psychology* 51: 668-676.

VERTIN, P. G. 1954. Occupational health aspects of peptic ulcer. (In Dutch.) Groningen University. Cited in French, J. R. P., 1963.

VINACKE, W. E. 1959. Sex role in a three-person game. *Sociometry* 22: 343-360.

VINACKE, W. E., and ARKOFF, A. 1957. An experimental study of coalitions in the triad. *American Sociological Review* 22: 406-414.

W

WAGATSUMA, H., and DeVOS, G. 1962. Attitudes toward arranged marriage in rural Japan. *Human Organization* 21: 187-200.

WALLACE, J. M.; WILLIAMS, F. W.; and CANTRIL, H. 1944. Identification of occupational groups with economic and social class. *Journal of Abnormal and Social Psychology* 39: 482-485.

WALLACH, M. A.; KOGAN, N.; and BEM, D. J. 1962. Group influence on individual risk taking. *Journal of Abnormal and Social Psychology* 65: 75-86.

WALSTER, E. 1965. The effect of self-esteem on romantic liking. *Journal of Experimental Social Psychology* 1: 184-197.

———. 1966. The assignment of responsibility for an accident. *Journal of Personality and Social Psychology* 3: 73-79.

WALSTER, E.; ARONSON, V.; ABRAHAMS, D.; and ROTTMANN, L. 1966. Importance of physical attractiveness in dating behavior. *Journal of Personality and Social Psychology* 5: 508-516.

WALSTER, E.; BERSCHEID, E.; and BARCLAY, A. N. 1967. A determinative of preference for modes of dissonance reduction. *Journal of Personality and Social Psychology* 7: 211-215.

WALSTER, E., and FESTINGER, L. 1962. The effectiveness of "overheard" persuasive communications. *Journal of Abnormal and Social Psychology* 65: 395-402.

WALSTER, E., and PRESTHOLDT, P. 1966. The effects of misjudging another: Overcompensation of dissonance reduction? *Journal of Experimental Social Psychology* 2: 85-97.

WALSTER, E., and WALSTER, G. W. 1963. Effect of expecting to be liked on choice of associates. *Journal of Abnormal and Social Psychology* 67: 402-404.

WALSTER, R. H., and PARKE, R. D. 1964. Social motivation, dependency, and susceptibility to social influence. In *Advances in experimental social psychology*, ed. L. Berkowitz, pp. 232-278. New York: Academic Press.

WALTER, E. V. 1964. Violence and the process of terror. *American Sociological Review* 29: 248-257.

WALTON, R. E., and McKERSIE, R. B. 1965. *A behavioral theory of labor negotiations.* New York: McGraw-Hill.

WARD, C. D. 1968. Seating arrangement and leadership emergence in small discussion groups. *Journal of Social Psychology* 74: 83-90.

WARNER, W. L. 1949. *Democracy in Jonesville.* New York: Harper.

WARNER, W. L., and ABEGGLEN, J. C. 1955. *Occupational mobility in business and industry, 1928-1952.* Minneapolis: University of Minnesota Press.

WARNER, W. L.; HAVIGHURST, R. J.; and LOEB, M. B. 1944. *Who shall be educated?* New York: Harper. P. 85.

WARNER, W. L., et al. 1941, 1942, 1945. *Yankee city series: 1. The social life of a modern community; 2. The status system of a modern community; 3. The social systems of American ethnic groups.* New Haven: Yale University Press.

WATKINS, J. G. 1947. Antisocial compulsions induced under hypnotic trance. *Journal of Abnormal and Social Psychology* 42: 256-259.

WATSON, B. B. 1964. *A Shavian guide to the intelligent woman.* New York: Norton.

WATSON, G. 1946. *A comparison of adaptable vs. laggard Y.M.C.A.'s.* Int. Comm. of Y.M.C.A.

———. 1947. *Action for unity.* New York: Harper.

WATSON, J.; BREED, W.; and POSMAN, H. 1948. A study in urban conversation: Sample of 100 remarks overheard in Manhattan. *Journal of Social Psychology* 28: 121-133.

WATSON, J., and RIESMAN, D. 1964. The sociability project. In *Sociologists at work,* ed. P. E. Hammond. New York: Basic Books.

WATSON, J. B. 1919. Psychology from the standpoint of a behaviorist. Philadelphia: Lippincott.

WEBER, M. 1947. *Theory of social and economic organization.* New York: Free Press.

WEISS, R. S., and SAMELSON, N. M. 1958. Social roles of American women: Their contribution to a sense of usefulness and importance. *Marriage and Family Living* 20: 358-366.

WEISS, W. 1957. Opinion congruence with a negative source on one issue as a factor influencing agreement on another issue. *Journal of Abnormal and Social Psychology* 54: 180-186.

WHEELER, L. 1966. Toward a theory of behavioral contagion. *Psychological Review* 73: 179-192.

WHEELER, R. H. 1940. *The science of psychology.* 2d ed. New York: Crowell.

WHERRY, R. J., and FRYER, D. 1949. Buddy ratings: Popularity contest or leadership criteria? *Sociometry* 12: 179-190.

WHITE, R. K. 1966. Misperception and the Vietnam War. *Journal of Social Issues* 22, no. 3, pp. 1-164.

WHITE, R. W. 1959. Motivation reconsidered: The concept of competence. *Psychological Review* 66: 297-333.

———. 1963. Sense of interpersonal competence: Two case studies and some reflections on origins. In *The study of lives,* ed. R. W. White, pp. 72-94. New York: Atherton.

WHITING, J. W. M. 1959. Sorcery, sin, and the superego. In *Symposium on motivation.* Lincoln, Nebr.: University of Nebraska Press.

———. 1961. Cultural and sociological influences on development. In Maryland growth and development institute. Cited in F. L. K. Hsu, *Psychological anthropology.* Homewood, Ill.: Dorsey. P. 368.

WHITING, J. W. M., and CHILD, I. L. 1953. *Child training and personality.* New Haven: Yale University Press.

WHITING, J. W. M.; KLUCKHOHN, R.; and ANTHONY, A. 1958. The function of male initiation ceremonies at puberty. In *Readings in social psychology*, 3d ed., ed. E. E. Maccoby, T. M. Newcomb, and E. L. Hartley, pp. 359-370. New York: Holt, Rinehart and Winston.

WHITTAKER, E. M., et al. 1952. Perceptual defense or response suppression. *Journal of Abnormal and Social Psychology* 47: 732-733.

WHORF, B. L. 1950. An American Indian model of the universe. *International Journal of American Linguistics* 16: 67-72.

WHYTE, W. F. 1943. *Street corner society.* Chicago: University of Chicago Press.

WHYTE, W. H., Jr. 1956. *The organization man.* New York: Simon and Schuster.

WILLEMS, E. P. 1964. Review of research. In *Big school, small school,* ed. R. Barker and P. V. Gump. Stanford, Calif.: Stanford University Press.

WILLIAMS, R. M., Jr. 1947. *The reduction of intergroup tension: A survey of research on problems of ethnic, racial, and religious group relations.* Bulletin 57. New York: Social Science Research Council.

———. 1964. *Strangers next door.* Englewood Cliffs, N.J.: Prentice-Hall.

WILLIAMS, S. B., and LEAVITT, H. J. 1947. Group opinion as a predictor of military leadership. *Journal of Consulting Psychology* 11: 283-291.

WILLIS, R. H. 1963. Two dimensions of conformity-nonconformity. *Sociometry* 26: 499-513.

WILNER, D. M.; WALKLEY, R. B.; and COOK, S. W. 1951. *Residential proximity and intergroup relations in public housing projects.* New York: New York University, Research Center for Human Relations.

WILSON, P. 1950. *College women who express futility.* New York: Teachers College, Columbia University.

WINCH, R. F. 1952. *The modern family.* New York: Holt.

———. 1958. *Mate selection.* New York: Harper.

WISHNER, J. 1960. Reanalysis of "impressions of personality." *Psychological Review* 67: 96-112.

WOLFE, D. M. 1959. Power and authority in the family. In *Studies in social power,* ed. D. Cartwright, pp. 99-117. Ann Arbor, Mich.: Institute of Social Research, University of Michigan.

WOLLSTONECRAFT, M. 1929. *A vindication of the rights of woman, with strictures on political and moral subjects.* London: Dent, Everyman's Library. Originally published 1792.

WOOLF, V. 1929. *A room of one's own.* New York: Harcourt, Brace.

WORLD HEALTH ORGANIZATION. 1962. *Deprivation of maternal care.* Geneva, Switzerland.

WORLING, R. V. 1966. Maternal deprivation—a reexamination. *Canada's Mental Health* 14, no. 4, pp. 3-11.

WRIGHT, G. O. 1954. Projection and displacement: A cross-cultural study of folktale aggression. *Journal of Abnormal and Social Psychology* 49: 523-528.

WRIGHT, M. E. 1943. The influence of frustration upon social relations of young children. *Character and Personality* 12: 111-122.

WRIGHTSMAN, L. S., Jr. 1960. Effects of waiting with others on changes in level of felt anxiety. *Journal of Abnormal and Social Psychology* 61: 216-222.

WRIGHTSTONE, J. W. 1934. Civic beliefs and correlated intellectual and social factors. *School Review* 42: 53-58.

Y

YARROW, M. R.; CAMPBELL, J. D.; and YARROW, L. J. 1958. Interpersonal dynamics in racial integration. In *Readings in social psychology,* 3d ed., ed. E. E. Maccoby, T. M. Newcomb, and E. L. Hartley, pp. 623-636. New York: Holt, Rinehart and Winston.

YERKES, R. M. 1943. *Chimpanzees: A laboratory colony.* New Haven: Yale University Press.

YERKES, R. M., and ELDER, J. H. 1936. Oestrus, receptivity and mating in chimpanzee. *Comparative Psychology Monograph* 13, no. 65, pp. 1-39.

Z

ZAJONC, R. B. 1965. Social facilitation. *Science* 149: 269-274.

———. 1966. *Social psychology: An experimental approach.* Belmont, Calif.: Wadsworth.

———. 1968. Attitudinal effects of mere exposure. *Journal of Personality and Social Psychology* 9: 1-29.

———. 1970. Brainwash: Familiarity breeds comfort. *Psychology Today,* February, p. 32.

ZAJONC, R. B., and BURNSTEIN, E. 1965. The learning of balanced and unbalanced social structures. *Journal of Personality* 33: 153-163.

ZDEP, S. M., and OAKES, W. I. 1967. Reinforcement of leadership behavior in group discussion. *Journal of Experimental Social Psychology* 3: 310-320.

ZELENY, L. D. 1939. Sociometry of morale. *American Sociological Review* 41: 799-808.

ZILLER, R. C. 1957. Group size: A determinant of the quality and stability of group decisions. *Sociometry* 20: 165-173.

ZIMBARDO, P. G. 1965. The effect of effort and improvisation on self-persuasion produced by role-playing. *Journal of Experimental Social Psychology* 1: 103-120.

ZIMBARDO, P. G., and EBBSEN, E. B. 1969. *Influencing attitude in changing behaviors.* Reading, Mass.: Addison-Wesley.

ZIPF, G. K. 1947. The hypothesis of the "minimum equation" as a unifying social principle. *American Sociological Review* 12: 627-650.

Index of names

Index of subjects